*Wir achten und ehren Deutschland wie
unsere Eltern, Großeltern und Ahnen,
und wir lieben Amerika wie unsere Frauen,
Kinder und Enkelkinder.*

    Peter K. Schneider, Fairbanks, Alaska

*We respect and honor Germany like our
parents, grandparents and forefathers,
and we love America like our wives
children and grandchildren.*

AMERICA THE BEAUTIFUL

WORDS BY
KATHARINE LEE BATES
MUSIC BY
SAMUEL A. WARD

In 1893 an English teacher at Wellesley College wrote a poem that was to become the lyrics for one of the most beautiful of American patriotic songs. Katharine Lee Bates had been asked to lecture during the summer at Colorado College in Colorado Springs (the young Woodrow Wilson had also been invited), and it was during that summer that she conceived "America the Beautiful." Miss Bates later said that the chief inspiration for her poem had been the magnificent view from the top of Pikes Peak. Soon after the poem was printed in 1895—in *The Congregationalist*, a church magazine—it was set to various tunes and printed in hymnals. But by the 1920's it had become permanently associated with the tune "Materna," which Samuel Augustus Ward had composed in 1882 for the hymn "O Mother Dear, Jerusalem." Many modern-day Americans feel that the lyrical hymn written by Miss Bates and set to Ward's fine, singable tune should have been chosen as the national anthem of the United States.

2. O beautiful for pilgrim feet,
Whose stern, impassioned stress
A thoroughfare for freedom beat
Across the wilderness!
America! America!
God mend thine every flaw,
Confirm thy soul in self-control,
Thy liberty in law!

3. O beautiful for heroes proved
In liberating strife,
Who more than self their country loved,
And mercy more than life!
America! America!
May God thy gold refine,
Till all success be nobleness,
And every gain divine!

4. O beautiful for patriot dream
That sees beyond the years;
Thine alabaster cities gleam,
Undimmed by human tears!
America! America!
God shed his grace on thee,
And crown thy good with brotherhood,
From sea to shining sea!

North America, Home to 60 Million Germanic People

Nordamerika, Heimat von 60 Millionen Menschen deutscher Abstammung

Courtesy Hammond, Inc., Maplewood, NJ

The Team

Author and Publisher	Bert Lachner	Autor und Herausgeber
Co-Author	Ernst Ott	Co-Autor
Assistance	Arlene Lachner	Assistentin
Editor	Edward A. Michals	Redakteur

Editorial Contributions: Beiträge

Clarence Baumann
Maria Brand
Dr. Jürgen Eichhoff
Dr. Hartmut Fröschle
Heinz Giese
Anne-Rose Görge
Rose-Mary Kemper
Kenn Knoop
Bert Lachner
Father Gerold Langsch
Jill Metzler
Ernst Ott
Profs. E. and R. Reichmann
Prof. LaVern J. Rippley
Elsbeth M. Seewald
Dr. Karin Spiess
Dr. D. Heinrich Tolzmann
Katie Wald
Heidi Whitesell
Jack Williams

Regional Captains: Regionale Vertreter

Leo Berg
Maria Brand
Wally Bronner
Fritz Eggerts
Ernst Friedel
Joe Geiser
Josef Hammes
Sepp Holzer
Kathryn Jolowicz
Rose-Mary Kemper
Helga Kessel
Kenn Knoop
Rodney König
Hedy Lachmann
Eva Nanni
Heinz Paletzki
Prof. Eberhard Reichmann
Prof. Ruth Reichmann
Erwin Simon
Horst W. Stabenow
Helgard Suhr
Michael Wendl
Jack Williams
Ingeborg Wilm
Jack Wiebel
Horst Wolf

*My sincere gratitude extends to all of the above
who gave so generously of their time, talent,
and energy to make this book possible.*

Photography: Fotografie

Clubs and Societies
Departments of Tourism
Bert Lachner
Ernst Ott
Many others, see credits

Maps: Landkarten

Hammond Inc.,
Maplewood, New Jersey 07040
Rand McNally & Company
Chicago, Illinois

Translations: Übersetzungen

Bruni Johnson, et al.
Bert Lachner
Ernst Ott
Profs. E. and R. Reichmann

Graphics and Type: Gestaltung und Satz

Cover: Thomas W. Ryter Design
Park Ridge, Illinois
Embossing Die
E.C. Schultz & Co.
Elk Grove Village, IL 60007

Book: Art Department, TIP
Karen Frahm
Tim Gaber
Patricia Tirado

Film and Printing: Filmbereitung und Druck

The Irving Press (TIP)
Elk Grove Village, Illinois 60007
Kurt Blumenthal, President
Carolyn Ricciotti, Project Manager

Bindery: Buchbinderei

Reindl Bindery
Elm Grove, Wisconsin 53122

Distribution Vertrieb

Interpac, Inc.
Schaumburg, Illinois 60193

*Meinen herzlichsten Dank allen oben erwähnten
Freunden und Firmen, die so großzügig von ihrer
Zeit, ihrer Erfahrung und Energie gaben, um dieses
Buch zu verwirklichen.*

Bert Lachner

An epic document of all Germanic people on the North American continent.

HEIMAT *North* AMERICA
English and German

by Bert Lachner, Landmark Books Unlimited

HEIMAT *North* AMERICA
English and German

Published by Landmark Books Unlimited
Copyright © 1997, Bert Lachner & Associates, Inc.
389 Duane Street, Glen Ellyn, Illinois 60137-4389, USA

Phone: 630 / 858-3085 • Fax: 630 / 858-3087
E-mail: lachner@heimatland.com
Internet: www.heimatland.com

ISBN: 0-9640659-3-2

Library of Congress Catalog Card Number: 97-073455

Manufactured in the United States

Print Key: 7890126543

First, Limited Edition

August 1997

―――――――――――――

Verlegt von Landmark Books Unlimited
Copyright © 1997, Bert Lachner & Associates, Inc.
389 Duane Street, Glen Ellyn, Illinois 60137-4389, USA

Phone: 630 / 858-3085 • Fax: 630 / 858-3087
E-mail: lachner@heimatland.com
Internet: www.heimatland.com

ISBN: 0-9640659-3-2

Katalogisierungsnumber der Library of Congress: 97-073455

Hergestellt in den United States

Print Key: 7890126543

Erste, begrenzte Auflage

August 1997

Contents

Deutsch-Amerikanischer Tag 1995

Vom Präsidenten der Vereinigten Staaten von Amerika

Proklamation

Schon seit den Anfängen der Besiedlung Nordamerikas haben deutsche Immigranten unser Land durch ihre Industrie, ihre Kultur und ihre Teilnahme am öffentlichen Leben bereichert. Mehr als ein Viertel aller Amerikaner können auf deutsche Vorfahren verweisen. Viel wichtiger aber als Zahlen sind die Motive, aufgrund derer so viele Deutsche einen neuen Anfang auf dieser Seite des Atlantiks gemacht haben. Die ersten deutschen Immigranten wurden von Amerikas unvergleichlicher Freiheit und den in anderen Ländern nicht vorhandenen Möglichkeiten angezogen, und sie wurden dadurch zu dem enormen Beitrag inspiriert, den Deutsche zum amerikanischen Erbe geleistet haben.

Im Jahre 1681 lud William Penn deutsche Pietisten aus dem Rheintal ein, sich in der von ihm gegründeten Quäker-Kolonie anzusiedeln, und diese Deutschen gehörten zu den ersten von vielen, die auf der Suche nach Religionsfreiheit nach Amerika ausgewandert sind. Dieses Land hat die nach bürgerlicher Freiheit suchenden Deutschen willkommen geheißen, deren Idealismus das Beste, das ihre neue Heimat besaß, gestärkt hat. Johann Peter Zenger wurde im 18. Jhdt. als Herausgeber des New York Weekly Journal einer der Mitbegründer der Pressefreiheit. Carl Schurz, ein politischer Dissident und enger Verbündeter von Abraham Lincoln, war während des Bürgerkriegs Union-General, der für die Beendigung des Elends der Sklaverei kämpfte. Und deutsche Namen haben in den sozialen und arbeitsrechtlichen Reformbewegungen des 19. und frühen 20. Jhdts. einen bedeutenden Rang eingenommen.

Im den 300 Jahren deutscher Einwanderung in dieses großartige Land haben Deutsch-Amerikaner Bedeutung in allen Bereichen des öffentlichen Lebens erlangt. Wie Baron von Steuben zu Zeiten der Revolution und General Eisenhower im 2. Weltkrieg haben viele Amerikaner deutscher Abstammung in unseren Streitkräften ehrenvoll und mit Würde Dienst getan. Im Bereich der Wissenschaften haben Albert Michelson und Hans Bethe in unschätzbarem Maße zu unserem Verständnis des Universums beigetragen. Die Maler Albert Bierstadt und der Modernist Josef Albers haben unsere künstlerische Tradition verstärkt, und Komponisten wie Oscar Hammerstein haben die amerikanische Musik wesentlich beeinflußt.

Nicht einmal diese große Anzahl an herausragenden Namen kann all die Beiträge versinnbildlichen, die Deutsch-Amerikaner zur Geschichte unseres Landes geleistet haben. Während Teile des Mittleren Westens, sowie Pennsylvania und Texas, nach wie vor mit Stolz das Siegel der umfangreichen deutschen Bevölkerung des vergangenen Jahrhundert tragen, so haben Deutsch-Amerikaner ihren besonderen Ruf in allen Teilen der Vereinigten Staaten und in allen Bereichen des Lebens durch ihre weitreichende Anpassung und ihre umfassenden Aktivitäten erlangt.

IN ANBETRACHT DESSEN erkläre ich, WILLIAM J. CLINTON, Präsident der Vereinigten Staaten von Amerika, kraft meines mir von der Verfassung verliehenen Amtes und den Gesetzen der Vereinigten Staaten, hiermit den 6. Oktober 1995 zum Deutsch-Amerikanischen Tag. Ich fordere Amerikaner überall auf, die von Millionen Menschen deutscher Abstammung gemachten Beiträge zur Freiheit, zur Demokratie und zum Wohlstand unseres Landes anzuerkennen und zu feiern.

ZUM ZEUGNIS DESSEN habe ich nachstehend an diesem sechsten Tag des Monats Oktober Anno Domini neunzehnhundertfünfundneunzig und im zweihundertzwanzigsten Jahr der Unabhängigkeit der Vereinigten Staaten von Amerika meine Unterschrift geleistet.

Unterschrift

William J. Clinton

German Chancellor Helmut Kohl and U.S. President Bill Clinton in Milwaukee, May 1996.

German-American Day, 1996

By the President of the United States of America

A Proclamation

Germans were among the first settlers of the United States. They, like other immigrants to our country, came to America seeking a better life for themselves and their families. In building this better life, they have immeasurably enriched the lives of their fellow Americans.

From the beginning of the colonial period and throughout the history of our republic, German Americans have contributed their intellect, wealth, and culture to building, defending, and improving American life. Organized settlement in America by Germans began as early as 1683, with the arrival of German Mennonites in Pennsylvania at the invitation of William Penn. Pennsylvania soon became the center and stronghold of German settlement throughout colonial times as small, vigorous communities spread to Maryland and the other colonies. Today, robust German-American communities can be found throughout the United States.

The strength of character and personal honor so important in the German cultural tradition have also found their way into the core values of American society. More U.S. citizens can claim German heritage than that of any other national group. And every successive generation of German Americans seems to produce new heroes and heroines who earn the admiration of a grateful world.

For example, Carl Schurz served as a Union General in the Civil War and later rose to become a distinguished American statesman, both as Senator from Missouri and as Secretary of the Interior. Johann Peter Zenger, the publisher of *New York Weekly Journal* in the early 18th century, was an early and vigorous champion of the free press in America. And German-born Albert Einstein made monumental and historic contributions to our understanding of the universe.

Our culture has also benefited abundantly from German-American women. Anna Ottendorfer was a talented newspaper publisher and philanthropist. The four Klumpke sisters enriched American life with their contributions to art, medicine, music, and astronomy, while Lillian Blauvelt and Fannie Bloomfield Zeisler enhanced American music.

America has welcomed Germans in search of civic freedoms, and their idealism has reinforced what was best in their new country. German-American men and women have contributed immensely to the fabric of our Nation, and it is appropriate that we pause to honor their important role in building our country.

NOW, THEREFORE, I, WILLIAM J. CLINTON, President of the United States of America, by virtue of the authority vested in me by the Constitution and laws of the United States, do hereby proclaim Sunday, October 6, 1996, as German-American Day. I encourage Americans everywhere to recognize and celebrate the contributions that millions of people of German ancestry have made to our Nation's liberty, democracy, and prosperity.

IN WITNESS WHEREOF, I have hereunto set my hand this fifth day of October, in the year of our Lord nineteen hundred and ninety-six, and of the Independence of the United States of America the two hundred and twenty-first.

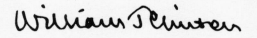

DEUTSCH-AMERIKANISCHER TAG 1987

VOM PRÄSIDENTEN DER VEREINIGTEN STAATEN VON AMERIKA

PROKLAMATION

Mehr Amerikaner können ihre Abstammung auf deutsche Vorfahren zurückverfolgen als auf irgend welche anderen Nationalitäten. Insgesamt sind mehr als sieben Millionen Deutsche in die Vereinigten Staaten eingewandert, und heute sind ungefähr 60 Millionen Amerikaner, also ein Viertel, deutscher Abstammung. Nur weniger Völker haben sich in die multikulturelle Vielfalt der amerikanischen Gesellschaft besser eingefügt und dennoch solche bedeutenden wirtschaftlichen, politischen, sozialen, wissenschaftlichen und kulturellen Beiträge zum Wachstum und Erfolg der Vereinigten Staaten geleistet, wie dies bei den Amerikanern deutscher Abstammung der Fall ist.

Die Vereinigten Staaten haben eine ganze Bandbreite deutscher Traditionen, Institutionen und Einflüsse angenommen. Vieles ist als Teil unseres Lebens so sehr verankert, daß die ethnischen Ursprünge nicht mehr deutlich sind. So sind z.B. Weihnachtsbäume und Broadway Musicals bekannte Merkmale der amerikanischen Gesellschaft. Unsere Kindergärten, Hochschulen, das Sozialversicherungssystem und die Gewerkschaften basieren alle auf deutsche Vorbilder.

Deutsche Lehrer, Musiker und begeisterte Amateure haben der klassischen Musik, Hymnen, Chorälen und Marschkapellen in unserem Lande unauslöschlich ihren Stempel aufgedrückt. Auf dem Gebiet von Architektur und Design zählen die Hängebrücke, das Bauhaus und der Jugendstil zu den deutschen Beiträgen. Deutsch-amerikanische Wissenschaftler haben dazu beigetragen, daß die Vereinigten Staaten weltweit zum Vorreiter in Forschung und Technik wurden. Die amerikanische Arbeitsmoral, ein wesentlicher Faktor beim schnellen Erreichen von Überlegenheit in Landwirtschaft und

Industrie der Vereinigten Staaten, basiert grundlegend auf dem Engagement der Deutsch-Amerikaner für hervorragende Leistungen.

Mehr als drei Jahrhunderte lang haben Deutsche zum Aufbau und zur Stärkung dieses Landes beigetragen. Die Vereinigten Staaten haben genommen und gegeben. Es liegt nur eine Generation zurück, als Amerika den Marshall-Plan vorgestellt und schnell in die Tat umgesetzt hat, wodurch der neuen deutschen Demokratie beim Aufstieg aus den Trümmern des

First signing of the Proclamation, Washington 1987.

Participants of the Signing Ceremony included: Ronald Reagan, Präsident der USA; Günther van Well, deutscher Botschafter in Washington; Dr. Lutz-Georg Stavenhagen, Staatsminister im Bundeskanzleramt; Dr. Don Heinrich Tolzmann, Präsident SGAS; Elsbeth M. Seewald, Nationalpräsidentin, DANK; Dr. Phillip Jenninger, Präsident des deutschen Bundestages; Senator Lugar, Indiana; Charles Wick, Director , U.S.I.A.; Mr. Weisshaupt, Deputy Secretary of State; Howard Baker, Chief of Staff to the President

Krieges zum Symbol der Demokratie in Mitteleuropa geholfen wurde. Durch die Berliner Luftbrücke brachte Amerika sein Engagement für die Verteidigung der Freiheit zu einem Zeitpunkt zum Ausdruck, als Berlin, das sich noch von den Auswirkungen des Krieges

erholte, sich der sowjetischen Bedrohung gegenüber sah, buchstäblich erwürgt zu werden.

Heute stellt die Bundesrepublik Deutschland ein Bollwerk der Demokratie im Herzen eines geteilten Europas dar. Deutsche und Amerikaner sind mit Recht auf ihre gemeinsamen Werte sowie auf ihr gemeinsames Erbe stolz. Mehr als drei Jahrzehnte lang war die deutsch-amerikanische Partnerschaft eine Stütze des westlichen Bündnisses, wodurch eine ganze Generation von Amerikanern und Europäern selbstbestimmt

aufgewachsen ist, um sich der Früchte der Freiheit zu erfreuen.

Somit ist die Geschichte unserer Länder miteinander verwoben. Nunmehr leisten wir gegenseitig Beiträge zum Handel, erfreuen uns der jeweiligen Kultur und lernen

gegenseitig aus unseren Erfahrungen. Der German-American Friendship Garden (Deutsch-Amerikanischer Freundschaftsgarten), der im District of Columbia in Kürze feierlich eröffnet wird, stellt ein Symbol dieser engen und freundschaftlichen Beziehungen zwischen Westdeutschland und den Vereinigten Staaten dar.

Der Kongress hat aufgrund des Public Law 100-104 (öffentl. Recht) den 6. Oktober 1987, dem 304. Jahrestag der Ankunft erster deutscher Immigranten in Philadelphia zum „Deutsch-Amerikanischen Tag" erklärt und hat dem Präsidenten den Auftrag erteilt, zur Begehung dieses Tages eine Proklamation abzugeben.

IN ANBETRACHT DESSEN erkläre ich, RONALD REAGAN, Präsident der Vereinigten Staaten von Amerika, kraft meines mir von der Verfassung verliehenen Amtes und den Gesetzen der Vereinigten Staaten, hiermit den 6. Oktober 1987 zum Deutsch-Amerikanischen Tag. Ich fordere alle Amerikaner auf, mehr über die Beiträge deutscher Immigranten zu Leben und Kultur der Vereinigten Staaten zu lernen und diesen Tag mit den ihm angemessenen Feierlichkeiten und Aktivitäten zu begehen.

ZUM ZEUGNIS DESSEN habe ich nachstehend an diesem zweiten Tag des Monats Oktober Anno Domini neunzehnhundertsiebenundachtzig und im zweihundertzwölften Jahr der Unabhängigkeit der Vereinigten Staaten von Amerika meine Unterschrift geleistet.

RONALD REAGAN

German-American Day, 1987

By the President of the United States of America

A Proclamation

More Americans trace their heritage back to German ancestry than to any other nationality. More than seven million Germans have come to our shores through the years, and today some 60 million Americans—one in four—are of German descent. Few people have blended so completely into the multicultural tapestry of American society and yet have made such singular economic, political, social, scientific, and cultural contributions to the growth and success of these United States as have Americans of German extraction.

The United States has embraced a vast array of German traditions, institutions, and influences. Many of these have become so accepted as parts of our way of life that their ethnic origin has been obscured. For instance, Christmas trees and Broadway musicals are familiar features of American society. Our kindergartens, graduate schools, the social security system, and labor unions are all based on models derived from Germany.

German teachers, musicians, and enthusiastic amateurs have left an indelible imprint on classical music, hymns, choral singing, and marching bands in our country. In architecture and design, German contributions include the modern suspension bridge, Bauhaus, and Jugendstil. German-American scientists have helped make the United States the world's pioneer in research and technology. The American work ethic, a major factor in the rapid rise of the United States to preeminence in agriculture and industry, owes much to German-Americans' commitment to excellence.

For more than 3 centuries, Germans have helped build, invigorate, and strengthen this country. But the United States has given as well as received. Just a generation ago, America conceived of and swiftly implemented the Marshall Plan, which helped the new German democracy rise from the rubble of war to become a beacon of democracy in Central Europe. The Berlin Airlift demonstrated the American commitment to the defense of freedom when, still recovering from war, Berlin was threatened by strangulation from the Soviets.

Today, the Federal Republic of Germany is a bulwark of democracy in the heart of a divided Europe. Germans and Americans are rightfully proud of our common values as well as our shared heritage. For more than 3 decades the German-American partnership has been a linchpin in the Western Alliance. Thanks to it, a whole generation of Americans and Europeans has grown up free to enjoy the fruits of liberty.

Our histories are thus intertwined. We now contribute to each other's trade, enjoy each other's cultures, and learn from each other's experiences. The German-American Friendship Garden, which will be dedicated in the District of Columbia in the near future, is symbolic of the close and amicable relations between West Germany and the United States.

The Congress, by Public Law 100–104, has designated October 6, 1987, the 304th anniversary of the arrival of the first German immigrants in Philadelphia, as "German-American Day" and has authorized and requested the President to issue a proclamation in observance of that day.

NOW, THEREFORE, I, RONALD REAGAN, President of the United States of America, do hereby proclaim Tuesday, October 6, 1987, as German-American Day. I urge all Americans to learn more about the contributions of German immigrants to the life and culture of the United States and to observe this day with appropriate ceremonies and activities.

IN WITNESS WHEREOF, I have hereunto set my hand this 2nd day of Oct., in the year of our Lord nineteen hundred and eighty-seven, and of the Independence of the United States of America the two hundred and twelfth.

Ronald Reagan

JOHN F. KENNEDY:
Die Deutschen

John F. Kennedy (1917 - 1963) war Präsident der Vereinigten Staaten vom Jahre 1961 bis zu seiner Ermordung im Jahre 1963. Er stammte aus einer irisch-amerikanischen Familie, und er selbst glaubte entschieden daran, daß die Stärke Amerikas in seiner ethnischen Vielfalt liege. Dieses Motto zieht sich wie ein roter Faden durch sein Buch, *A Nation of Immigrants* (Ein Einwandererland), aus dem dieser Abschnitt entnommen wurde.

Zwischen 1830 und 1930, der Zeit der größten Einwanderungswelle von Europa in die Vereinigten Staaten, kamen sechs Millionen Menschen aus Deutschland - mehr als aus jedem anderen Land…

Unter den verschiedenen Einwanderergruppen nahmen die Deutschen aufgrund ihrer großen geographischen wie beruflichen Streuung eine Sonderstellung ein. Dies war - zumindest teilweise - darauf zurückzuführen, daß die meisten nicht mittellos hier ankamen und daher nicht auf die Ostküste beschränkt waren. Das kostengünstige öffentliche sowie den Eisenbahngesellschaften gehörende Land und später die kostenlosen Familiensitze machten die Vereinigten Staaten für den deutschen Bauern, der dabei half, den Boden im neuen Westen zu bestellen und das Tal des Mississippi zu kultivieren, attraktiv. Die aufgrund ihrer Fertigkeiten gesuchten deutschen Kunsthandwerker wurden zu einem bedeutenden Faktor industrieller Expansion.

Fast jeder zur Union gehörende Staat hat von ihren intellektuellen und materiellen Beiträgen profitiert. Hart arbeitend und mit einem hervorragenden Wissen über landwirtschaftliche Methoden ausgestattet, verbreiteten die Deutschen den Ackerbau unter wissenschaftlichem Aspekt, sowie den Fruchtwechsel und die Erhaltung des Bodens. Ihnen wird zusammen mit den Skandinaviern der Verdienst zuteil, Millionen Hektar an Wildnis in ertragreiches Bauernland verwandelt zu haben.

Die urbanen Siedler gaben unseren Städten ein unverkennbar deutsches Flair. Cincinnati, damals als „Queen City" des Westens bekannt, Baltimore, St. Louis, Minneapolis und Milwaukee hatten alle einen großen Anteil deutscher Bevölkerung. Milwaukee, das einmal das „Deutsche Athen" genannt wurde, hat vielleicht den ausgeprägten deutschen Charakter länger als jede der anderen Städte erhalten.

In den urbanen Zentren wurden die Deutschen im Bildungswesen, der Wissenschaft, der Technik und den Künsten tätig. Deutsche Einwanderer gründeten und entwickelten Industrieunternehmen auf so unterschiedlichen Gebieten wie der Holzwirtschaft, der Lebensmittelverarbeitung, dem Brauwesen, der Stahlherstellung, der Elektrotechnik, der Herstellung von Pianos, der Eisenbahn und dem Druckwesen.

Ein kleiner, aber bedeutender Teil der deutschen Einwanderer bestand aus politischen Flüchtlingen. Die Reaktion in Deutschland gegen die Reformideen der Französischen Revolution hatte eine starke Unterdrückung des liberalen Gedankengutes zur Folge. Die Pressefreiheit war erheblich eingeschränkt, öffentliche Versammlungen wurden strengstens überwacht, und die Freiheit der Schulen und Universitäten war ebenfalls stark beschnitten.

Trotzdem hatte sich, genährt von jungen Intellektuellen an den Universitäten, eine liberale Bewegung gebildet, die dann in den Jahren 1830 und 1848 zu erfolglosen Revolutionen führte. Die Vereinigten Staaten hießen eine große Anzahl von Teilnehmern an der Revolution von 1848 willkommen - Männer, die einen hohen Bildungsstand, Substanz und sozialen Status besaßen, wie Carl Schurz, der Staatsmann und Reformer, und General Franz Sigel. Darüber hinaus gründeten einige der deutschen Religionsgruppen in Teilen Pennsylvanias, Ohios, Indianas, Texas' und Oregons utopische Gemeinden.

Durch die deutsche Einwanderungswelle kamen die chaotischen Zustände in Mitteleuropa nach Napoleon zum Ausdruck: das Bevölkerungswachstum, die weit verbreitete Hungersnot, der religiöse Zwist und die religiöse Unterdrückung. Unter den Deutschen befanden sich Lutheraner, Juden und Katholiken sowie Freidenker. Ihr Talent, ihre Ausbildung und ihr Fundament haben diese keimende Nation wesentlich bereichert…

Die Tatsache, daß heute fast jede amerikanische Großstadt ein Symphonie-Orchester besitzt, ist auf den Einfluß der deutschen Migration zurückzuführen. Leopold Damrosch und sein Sohn Walter halfen beim Aufbau der New Yorker Philharmonie, die hauptsächlich aus deutschen Immigranten zusammengesetzt war und das „Germania Orchestra" genannt wurde und zur Wiege ähnlicher Organisationen im ganzen Land wurde…

Gemeinsames Singen und Gesangsvereine gehen auf deutsche Einwanderer zurück, die sich ihrer Gesangsgruppen erinnerten. Der erste Männerchor wurde im Jahre 1835 in Philadelphia gegründet, der erste Liederkranz wurde im Jahre 1836 in Baltimore ins Leben gerufen. Überall wurden ihre Gegenstücke zu einem Charakteristikum deutsch-amerikanischer Gemeinden.

Die Ideen deutscher Einwanderer halfen bei der Gestaltung unseres Bildungssystems. Sie führten den Kindergarten oder die „Kinder-Spielschule" ein. Sie haben auch das Konzept der staatlichen Universitäten, den deutschen Universitäten nachgebildet, gefördert. Die im Jahre 1837 gegründete University of Michigan hat als erste Bildungsstätte die Philosophie, einer generellen Ausbildung in den freien Künsten eine handwerkliche Ausbildung hinzuzufügen, eingeführt. Das koloniale Konzept einer Universität als Vorbereitungsstätte feiner Herren auf ein Leben des Müßiggangs wurde durch die Einführung der Ausbildung in besonderen Fertigkeiten abgewandelt.

Die körperliche Ertüchtigung in den Schulen ist auf den Turnverein zurückführen, dessen Konzept von der amerikanischen Öffentlichkeit in Form des YMCA (Young Men's Christian Association; Christlicher Verein junger Männer) übernommen wurde.

Der Einfluß deutscher Immigranten hat unsere Sprache, unsere Sitten und Gebräuche und unsere grundlegende Lebensphilosophie durchdrungen … So wurden im Jahre 1688 die ersten Proteste gegen die Sklaverei von deutschen Siedlern, angeführt von Franz Pastorius, laut.

- John F. Kennedy, *A Nation of Immigrants,* New York, Harper Collins, 2. Auflage, 1964.

Lernen über unsere Welt: Deutschland Kultusministerium von Ohio

JOHN F. KENNEDY: The Germans

John F. Kennedy (1917-1963) was President of the United States from 1961 until his assassination in 1963. His family was Irish-American, and he himself was dedicated to the belief that the strength of America lies in her ethnic diversity. This theme runs through his book, *A Nation of Immigrants,* from which this selection is taken.

Between 1830 and 1930, the period of the greatest migration from Europe to the United States, Germany sent six million people to the United States - more than any other nation...

The Germans were unique among immigrant groups in their wide dispersal, both geographically and occupationally. This was due, at least in part, to the fact that most of them came with some resources, and were not forced to cluster along the Eastern seaboard. Attracted to the United States by cheap public and railroad lands, and later by free homesteads, the German farmer helped to farm the New West and to cultivate the Mississippi Valley. German artisans, much sought after because of their skills, became an important factor in industrial expansion.

Almost every state in the Union profited from their intellectual and material contributions. Hard-working and knowledgeable about agricultural methods, the Germans became propagators of scientific farming, crop rotation, soil conservation. They share with the Scandinavians the credit for turning millions of acres of wilderness into productive farmland.

The urban settlers lent a distinctive German flavor to many of our cities. Cincinnati, then known as "Queen City" of the West, Baltimore, St. Louis, Minneapolis and Milwaukee, all had substantial German populations. Milwaukee once called the "German Athens", has perhaps retained its distinctive German character longer than any of the others.

In the urban centers Germans entered the fields of education, science, engineering and the arts. German immigrants founded and developed industrial enterprises in the fields of lumbering, food-processing, brewing, steel-making, electrical engineering, piano-construction, railroading and printing.

A small but significant part of the German immigration consisted of political refugees. Reaction in Germany against the reform ideas of the French Revolution had caused heavy suppression of liberal thought. There was strict censorship of the press, of public meetings and of the schools and universities.

Nevertheless, a liberal movement had emerged, nurtured in the universities by young intellectuals. This movement led to

On the way to his famous "Ich bin ein Berliner" speech, then U.S. President John F. Kennedy, Berlin Mayor Willy Brandt, and German Chancellor Konrad Adenauer at the Brandenburg Gate. Photo by Will McBride, June 26, 1963. DHM (Berlin)

unsuccessful revolutions in 1830 and 1848. The United States welcomed a large number of veterans of 1848 - men of education, substance and social standing like Carl Schurz, the statesman and reformer, and General Franz Sigel. In addition, some of the German religious groups established utopian communities in parts of Pennsylvania, Ohio, Indiana, Texas and Oregon.

German immigration reflected all the chaotic conditions of Central Europe after Napoleon: the population growth, the widespread hunger, the religious dissension and oppression. The Germans included Lutherans, Jews and Catholics, as well as freethinkers. Their talent, training and background greatly enriched this burgeoning nation...

The fact that today almost every large American city has its symphony orchestra can be traced to the influence of the German migration. Leopold Damrosch and his son, Walter, helped build the famous New York Philharmonic. Originally composed mainly of German immigrant musicians and called the Germania Orchestra, it became the seed bed of similar organizations all over the country...

Community singing and glee clubs owe much to the German immigrant, who remembered his singing societies. The first Männerchor was founded in Philadelphia in 1835; the first Liederkranz was organized in Baltimore in 1836. Their counterparts have been a feature of the German-American community everywhere.

The ideas of German immigrants helped to shape our educational system. They introduced the kindergarten, or "children's play school". They also promoted the concept of the state-endowed university, patterned after the German university. The University of Michigan, founded in 1837, was the first such school to add to the philosophy of general liberal arts education an emphasis upon vocational training. The colonial concept of a university as a place to prepare gentlemen for a life of leisured culture was modified to include training in specialized skills.

The program of physical education in the schools had its roots in the Turnverein, or German gymnastic society. It was adopted and introduced to the American public by the YMCA.

German immigrant influence has been pervasive, in our language, in our mores, in our customs and in our basic philosophy....indeed, the first protest against Negro slavery came from Germantown settlers, led by Franz Pastorius, in 1688.

-John F. Kennedy, *A Nation of Immigrants.* New York: Harper Collins, 2nd Edition, 1964.

From: Learning About Our World: Germany Ohio Department of Education

Germans as Fellow Americans for 300 Years

Hail to Posterity!
Hail, future men of German-America!
Let the young generation yet to be
look kindly upon this.
Think how your fathers left their native land,
In Patience planned
New forest homes beyond the mighty sea,
There undisturbed and free
To live as brothers in one family.
What pains and cares befell,
What trials and what fears,
Remember! And wherein we have done well
Follow our footsteps, men of coming years!
Where we have failed to do
Aright, or wisely live,
Be warned by us, the better way pursue,
And knowing we were human, even as you,
Pity us and forgive!
Farewell, Posterity! Farewell, Germany!
Forevermore farewell!

Franz Daniel Pastorius
Father of German-America

CONCORD

1683 — 1983

America's First Germans • Die ersten Deutschen in Amerika

The nationwide observation of the "Tricentennial of German Immigration" in 1983 led to the belief that the 13 Krefelder Mennonite families, who arrived on October 6th, 1683 at Philadelphia on the Concord, were the first Germans in America. Not so, but their arrival marks the beginning of German group immigration.

German involvement with America goes back to the times of its discovery. Columbus' achievement in 1492 was aided by German cartographers, whose globes and maps showed the world as round. Cosmographer Martin Waldseemüller in 1507 suggested the name for the New World: "America"—assuming that the explorer Amerigo Vespucci had been its discoverer.

German encampment began in 1608 at Jamestown, Virginia, when German craftsmen arrived with the first English colonists. But Jamestown fell victim to starvation and disease.

Hundreds of Germans followed during the next decades, among them the Rhinelander Peter Minnewit (Minuit) who in 1626 purchased Manhattan from the Indians—not for Germany but for the Netherlands. He called the fort and settlement he built "New Amsterdam", later named New York.

Minnewit's role is a reminder of the fact that while the maritime powers—England, France, Spain and the Netherlands—carved up North America, Germany suffered the Thirty Years War (1618-48), resulting in the loss of some 20% of its population, destruction, and political disintegration into hundreds of independent principalities. And by 1688, the army of French King Louis XIV laid waste to the Palatinate. These dire circumstances ruled out participation in the race for colonies. Thus Germans coming to America were never colonists but always immigrants.

Like Minnewit, Jacob Leisler is remembered. Elected to replace the colonial governor of New York in 1689, he became a civil rights martyr in 1691 for his pursuit of greater independence from England.

Franz Daniel Pastorius führte 13 Krefelder Mennoniten Familien auf der Concord über den Atlantik nach Philadelphia. Sie landeten am 6. Oktober, 1683.

1626, Minnewit kauft Manhattan den Indianern ab.

Die zu beiden Seiten des Atlantik veranstalteten Festlichkeiten zum 300. Jubiläum deutscher Einwanderung (1983) haben zu der Annahme geführt, dass die 13 Mennonitenfamilien aus Krefeld, die am 6. Oktober 1683 von der "Concord" in Philadelphia an Land gingen, die ersten Deutschen in Amerika gewesen seien. Worauf der 6. Oktober - der Deutsch-Amerikanische Tag - wirklich hinweist, ist auf den Anfang deutscher Gruppeneinwanderung.

Schon zur Zeit der Entdeckung Amerikas (1492) waren Deutsche mit der "neuen Welt" involviert. Die Entwicklung von Globen und Karten durch deutsche Kartographen zeigte die Welt als rund. Das half Columbus. Und 1507 verwendete Martin Waldseemüller den Namen "America"—in der Annahme, daß der berühmte Seefahrer Amerigo Vespucci der Entdecker gewesen sei.

Als die ersten englischen Kolonisten 1608 in Jamestown, Virginia landeten, waren deutsche Handwerker mit dabei. Doch Hunger und Krankheit dezimierten diese Siedlung.

In den nächsten Jahrzehnten folgten Hunderte von Deutschen, unter ihnen der Rheinländer Peter Minnewit (Minuit), der 1626 Manhattan den Indianern abkaufte - jedoch nicht für Deutschland, sondern für die Niederlande. Er nannte das von ihm erbaute Fort und die Siedlung "Neu Amsterdam", später umgetauft in "New York".

Minnewits Rolle erinnert daran, daß zur Zeit des Landerwerbs in Amerika seitens der Seemächte Spanien, England, Frankreich und der Niederlande in Deutschland der Dreißigjährige Krieg (1618-1648) tobte. Rund 20% der Bevölkerung kamen dabei um; das Land war verwüstet, das Reich zerfallen in Hunderte unabhängiger Fürstentümer. Hinzu kam später die mörderische Expansionspolitik des französischen Königs Ludwig XIV, die zur Zerstörung der Pfalz führte. Geschwächt, uneinig und flottenlos war das Reich vom Rennen um Kolonien ausgeschlossen. Wer als Deutschsprachiger nach Amerika kam, war also immer entweder Immigrant oder im Dienst einer Kolonialmacht.

Wie Minnewit, so bleibt auch der Frankfurter Jacob Leisler unvergessen. 1689 zum Nachfolger des britischen Gouverneurs von New York gewählt, wurde er bereits 1691 hingerichtet wegen seiner als hochverräterisch ausgelegten Bemühungen um größere Unabhängigkeit der Kolonien.

"The first Germans to land in Jamestown, the first permanent English settlement in Virginia, arrived aboard the vessels Mary and Margret about October 1st, 1608. These Germans were Glassmakers and Carpenters. In 1620, German mineral specialists and saw-millrights followed, to work and settle in the Viginia colony. These pioneers and skilled craftsmen were the forerunners of the many millions of Germans who settled in America and became the single largest national group to populate the United States." Dr. D. H. Tolzmann

By Professors Eberhard Reichmann and LaVern J. Rippley

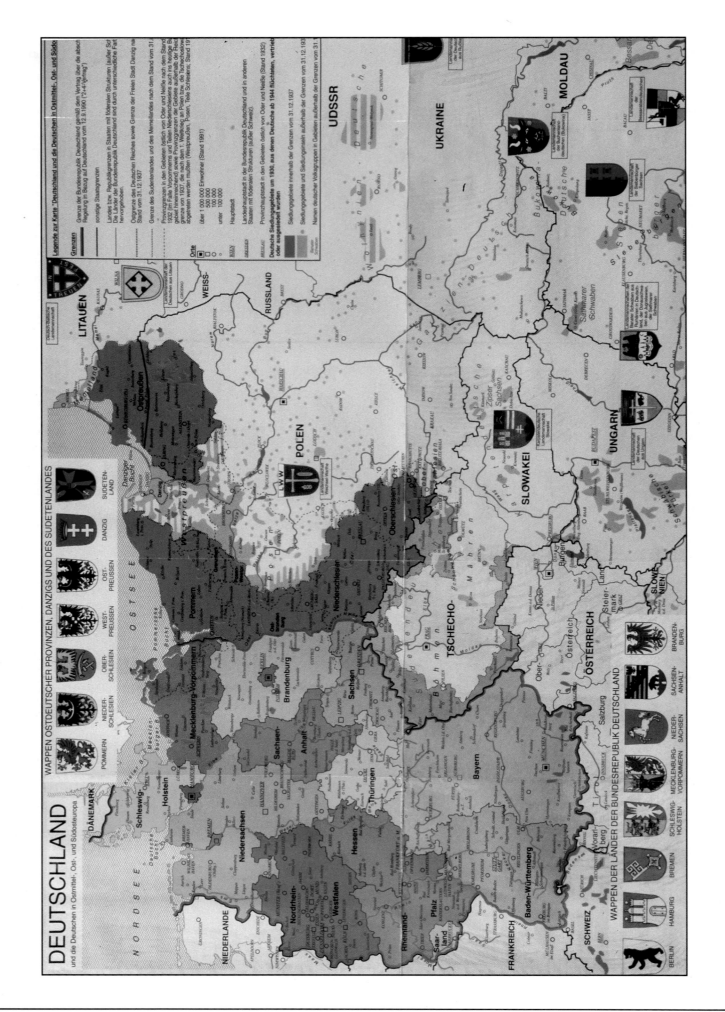

America's First German Town   *Amerikas erste deutsche Stadt*

Germantown, Pennsylvania

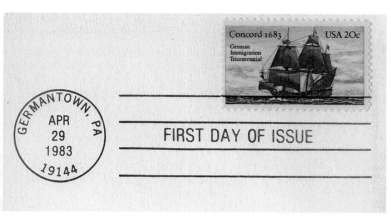

by Profs. E. Reichmann and LaVern J. Rippley

The pious Krefelders who had accepted William Penn's invitation and arrived in Pennsylvania in 1683 aptly called their place Germantown, today a part of Philadelphia. After initial hardships, the guidance provided by Francis Daniel Pastorius, their organizer and first mayor, and the skills of carpenters, weavers and tailors created a prosperous community that grew with new arrivals. As early as 1684, Pastorius set up the first country fair in Philadelphia. The Krefelders' cloth then soon found markets in Boston and New York.

Ten years after its founding, the "German Township" covered 5,700 acres, divided into four sections: Germantown; Kriegsheim—named after the Palatine Quaker's home; Sommerhausen—after Pastorius' Franconian birthplace; and Crefeld—from where the majority of the settlers had come. Recalling their difficult beginnings, Pastorius wrote that some equated their "Germantown" with "Armentown" (town of the poor).

Closely connected to the growing importance of Germantown was William Rittenhouse [Wilhelm Rittenhaus], a 1686 arrival. This first elected Mennonite pastor and bishop also made economic history by founding America's first paper mill (1690). His paper was then also used by another famous Germantowner, Christopher Saur, the printer of the first American Bible (1743). This 1,272 pp. German volume antedates by 40 years the printing of the first English-language Bible in America. The versatile Saur also manufactured printing type and ink, invented optical instruments, improved cast iron stoves, and succeded Ben Franklin's shortlived German-language newspaper with his *Hoch Deutsch Pennsylvanischer Geschicht Schreiber* (1739).

Pastorius and his Germantowners were appalled by the incompatibility of slavery with Christianity. They are credited with the first protest against Negro slavery as early as 1688. Even though this did not change the fate of Afro-Americans in general, it set the standard for German religious communities. None of them would ever engage in slave-holding, and almost all secular German communities lived up to the Germantown declaration as well.

Die frommen Krefelder, die William Penns Einladung gefolgt waren und 1683 in Philadelphia landeten, nannten ihre Gründung passenderweise Germantown, heute ein Teil Philadelphias. Nach schwierigem Anfang und unter Führung von Franz Daniel Pastorius, dem Organisator und Bürgermeister, schafften die Zimmerleute, Weber und Schneider von Germantown eine blühende Gemeinde, die durch Neuzugänge rasch anwuchs. Schon 1684 brachte Pastorius in Philadelphia die erste Warenmesse zustande und bald fand Germantowner Tuch Absatz in Boston und New York.

Innerhalb von zehn Jahren umfaßte das Germantowner Gebiet vier Ortsviertel mit 2300 ha: Germantown selbst; Kriegsheim—benannt nach dem Heimatort der Pfälzer Quäker; Sommerhausen—nach dem fränkischen Geburtsort des Pastorius; und Crefeld—nach der Heimatstadt der mennonitischen Mehrheit. Rückschauend auf die schwierigen Anfänge notierte Pastorius, daß man oft den Reim "Germantown, Armentown" zu hören bekam.

Mit der fortschreitenden Bedeutung Germantowns ist der Name Wilhelm Rittenhaus (anglisiert: William Rittenhouse) eng verbunden. Rittenhaus, der erste gewählte mennonitische Pastor und Bischof, gilt als Vater der amerikanischen Papierherstellung (1690). Seine Mühle lieferte dann auch das Papier für die 1272 Seiten starke erste "Heilige Schrift" der Neuen Welt, gedruckt von dem Westfalen Christoph Saur (1743). Erst 40 Jahre später folgten die ersten englisch-sprachigen Bibeln aus amerikanischen Druckereien. Der vielseitige Saur produzierte auch Drucktypen und Tinten, erfand optische Instrumente, verbesserte den gußeisernen Ofen und gab nach Benjamin Franklins kurzlebiger deutscher Zeitung den "Hochdeutschen Pennsylvanischen Geschichts Schreiber" heraus (1739).

Pastorius und seine Germantowner zogen die Konsequenzen aus der Unvereinbarkeit von Sklaverei und Christentum. Schon 1688 verfaßten sie den ersten Protest im Lande. Obgleich sich dadurch am Schicksal der Afro-Amerikaner wenig änderte, so hat doch danach keine deutsch-amerikanische religiöse Gemeinde Sklaverei praktiziert. Auch fast alle anderen deutschen Gemeinden teilten den Geist der Germantowner Erklärung.

Don't forget the German Language
by Ernst Ott

Several German American Societies have weekend schools, teaching German language, both to children and adults. The Goethe Institute lends a helping hand in this special project as well.

Since the teaching of German in public schools is more and more replaced in favor of Spanish and other major languages, these weekend schools have gained greater significance in promoting the German heritage, but also as a career-asset in the travel, business and professional fields.

The German government supports these efforts by providing teaching aids and sponsoring teacher seminars.

D.A.N.K., for example, maintains a dozen of these schools in Illinois, Wisconsin and Ohio.

Learning and playing together

Vergiß die deutsche Sprache nicht!
Von Ernst Ott

Verschiedene deutschamerikanische Organisationen unterhalten gute Wochenendschulen, wo Kinder und Erwachsene die deutsche Sprache lernen und üben können.

Seitdem die deutsche Sprache mehr und mehr hinter das Spanische und andere Hauptsprachen an den Volksschulen tritt, haben diese Wochenendschulen an Bedeutung gewonnen. Dieses nicht nur um des deutschen Erbes wegen, sondern vor allem als Resume für Geschäfts-, Reise- und andere Erwerbszwecke.

Die deutsche Regierung unterstützt diese Bemühungen mit Lehrmaterial und Lehrerseminaren.

D.A.N.K., der deutschamerikanische National Kongress, unterhält z.B. etwa ein Dutzend solcher Schulen in Illinois, Wisconsin und Ohio.

German Teachers' Workshop

Members of the German Parliament visiting the DANK School at Chicago's "Deutsches Haus".

Starting out young makes it all fun.

Marching in the Steuben Parade

Photos: Ernst Ott

German Language • Die deutsche Sprache

Most newcomers before 1914 had little if any knowledge of the country's language. But once German-speaking settlements and neighborhoods were established, fluency in English was no prerequisite for making a living in the "land of opportunity."

When chain migration made people from a given area follow relatives and friends, their dialect could often be sustained for generations, as with the Palatine dialect continuing in "Pennsylvania Dutch (German)." But when people from different regions settled together, dialect leveling set in. English words crept in for naming previously unfamiliar concepts or things. German words entered English as well, from "burgers" to "sauerkraut" and "Kindergarten."

Immigrants could count on the pillars of the ethnic community: the church parish, the parochial school, the verein (club), the restaurant with its beer garden, and the press. In the ethnic neighborhood, "Deutsch" was it. High German bridged the gap between speakers of Low and Upper German.

Thousands of German churches provided continuity in the ritual and practical use of the language. Long before public schools, there were parochial schools, often taught by clergy and nuns. Catholic, Lutheran, Reformed, Mennonite and Methodist publishing houses produced the textbooks. School subjects were often taught in both German and English, resulting in bilingualism.

German diversity is mirrored in the Vereins: "Two Germans, one verein; three Germans, two vereins; four Germans..." By 1900, Indianapolis had more than 50! Catering to regional origin or personal interest. Some had restaurants, concert halls, stages, gyms and bowling alleys.

Lectures, musical and theatrical performances and fests were as German as "back home." Vereins offered alternatives to church membership. There were "Church Germans" and "Vereins Germans."

In German restaurants, experiences, information, and news from home were shared. While English might have dominated at the work place, the private language remained German.

The German press produced more than 800 dailies, weeklies and monthlies, and everything from children's books to the classics. Its output was greater than that of all other non-English presses combined. Germantown's Christoph Saur printed in 1743 the first Bible in America —in German.

The legend persists that German almost became America's official language. Let's remember: When the U.S. was formed, the German element comprised at most 10% of the white population.

WWI had a devastating effect on the use of German. It never regained its position as the leading foreign language.

By Professors Eberhard Reichmann and LaVern J. Rippley.

Photo: Bert Lachner

Vor 1914 waren die wenigsten Einwanderer mit der Landessprache vertraut. Wo immer es deutschsprachige Siedlungen und Nachbarschaften gab, waren Englischkenntnisse keine Voraussetzung, um es im Land der unbegrenzten Möglichkeiten zu schaffen.

Wenn Kettenwanderung Freunde und Verwandte in der neuen Welt wieder vereinte, konnte sich der mitgebrachte Dialekt oft über Generationen hinweg erhalten. Beispiel: Pfälzisch, das im Pennsylvanisch-Deutsch weiterlebt. Landsmannschaftlich gemischte Siedlungsweise brachte Dialektausgleich. Besonders für vorher unbekannte Sachen und Begriffe bot sich englisches Wortgut an. Deutsch gab dem Englischen auch Lehnwörter, von "Bratwurst" zu "Sauerkraut" und "Kindergarten."

Unentbehrlich für Einwanderer und den Zusammenhalt ethnischer Gruppen waren: die Kirchengemeinden und deren Bekenntnisschulen, Vereine, Wirtshäuser mit Biergärten und die muttersprachliche Presse. Im süddeutsch-plattdeutschen Dialog half Hochdeutsch.

Tausende deutscher Kirchen hielten am rituellen und praktischen Gebrauch der Muttersprache fest. Konfessionsschulen gab es früher als öffentliche Schulen. Geistliche und Nonnen stellten oft die Lehrer. Katholische und protestantische Verlage brachten Textbücher heraus. Schulfächer wurden oft deutsch und englisch unterrichtet, was Zweisprachigkeit förderte.

Deutsche Vielfalt wies auch das Vereinswesen auf: "Zwei Deutsche—ein Verein; drei Deutsche—zwei Vereine; vier Deutsche..." Indianapolis um 1900 hatte über 50 Vereine! Nach Landsmannschaften oder Interessen ausgerichtet. Einige hatten Restaurants, Konzertsäle, Bühnen, Turnhallen und Kegelbahnen. Vorträge, Musik, Theater und Feste gab's wie "daheim." Vereine boten auch Alternativen zur Kirchenzugehörigkeit. Es gab "Kirchendeutsche" und "Vereinsdeutsche."

Im Restaurant teilte man Erfahrungen und Neues aus der Heimat. Wenn Englisch auch bei der Arbeit dominiert haben mag, im Privatleben blieb es beim Deutschen.

Die deutsche Presse brachte über 800 Tages- und Wochenblätter und Monatshefte heraus, Kinderbücher und Klassiker dazu. Sie veröffentlichte mehr als die gesamte nicht-englische Presse. In Germantown druckte Christoph Saur im Jahre 1743 die erste Bibel in Amerika — auf deutsch.

Man hört immer munkeln: "Deutsch wäre beinahe die offizielle Sprache geworden." Bedenk', oh Leser: als USA Realität wurde, stellten die Deutschen höchstens 10% der weissen Bevölkerung.

Durch den 1. Weltkrieg verlor Deutsch seine führende Rolle als Fremdsprache.

Second language of business:	
Spanish 63%	German 4%
Japanese 16%	French 2%
Chinese 11%	

Source: USA Today 4/97

Father Gerold M. Langsch

Faith and Church in the Life of the German-American Immigrants

A person's journey through life is both a family journey and a faith journey. Looking into the life of a German-American family, typically all events of life from birth to death are accompanied by the celebrations, prayers and rites, the customs and traditions of our respective Church community.

The same holds true for the journey of a people or a nation. Whatever happens to us as a people in a particular country, the guiding and comforting hand of God is there. He knows the way, even and especially when history becomes so dark and incomprehensible that we want to say 'He must have forgotten us!'.

As so many of our Danube-Swabian immigrants have experienced in their life, the expulsion from our home was one of those times where Church played a vital role in our survival. As one of Irma Seiler's poems recounts "the people were strong and firm in their faith. While church bells were ringing the whole village gathered at church, never had people shed so many tears there before."

I believe this is a most telling testimony for what Church and faith mean to us. We gather and share before God all of our joyful or painful moments of life with family, neighbors, friends. Church bells ring; together we shed tears of joy and sorrow. But "people were strong and firm in their faith", even though we don't really understand what God is actually doing with us at that time until much later.

Here in the new world, the Church communities have not always been able to be the place where we all gather to share our joys and sorrows with God and each other in order to find strength and support. Yet here in America we are free to practice our religion without restriction or persecution. Many find strength to deepen their personal love relationship with God, to follow their convictions and thus to master life.

The Church provides a home and safe harbor; it offers schooling and an abundance of activities to accompany all walks of life. Whether we sing together in the choir, enjoy a picnic, celebrate anniversaries or weddings or work together on other projects, "Church" stands for practicing our faith, for educating our children, fostering our culture, language and customs. All of these we experience as German immigrants here in our new homeland America.

But I also believe our Churches exert a great influence not only on our personal and family life but also on our social life. There is no season of the year without its particular faith customs. Advent wreaths, Christmas trees, poinsettias or Easter lilies decorate our homes. Nativity scenes are part of almost every place we go. All of those treasures of our faith have found their way into our American culture, just like Santa Claus.

In some areas our various organizations sponsor their own Octoberfest; they participate in the city or nationwide "Fests" of some kind: the Germanfest, Trachtenfest, Polkafest, Gaufest etc. with the food, dances and costumes of their respective region of the homeland.

Or in celebrating a wedding we still see everything connected. The beautiful church celebration is followed by the dances and polkas our bands are playing all night long. Together, young and old enjoy the customs and rituals from of old.

Despite the strong influence of our modern pluralistic society, the German immigrants have kept many of their treasures of faith deeply anchored in their hearts. This I see as a great gift of our heritage to the new world: God and Church are connected with everything we do, enjoy or endure.

"Our faith in God helped us to go on", could be heard from the lips of many of our immigrants; we hear it yet today.

Die Lebensgeschichte einer Person ist immer zugleich eine Familiengeschichte und eine Glaubensgeschichte. Schaut man in das Leben einer deutsch-amerikanischen Familie, sieht man, wie normalerweise alle Lebensereignisse von der Geburt bis zum Tod von den Feiern, Gebeten, Riten, Gebräuchen und Traditionen unserer jeweiligen Kirchengemeinschaft begleitet werden.

Das Gleiche trifft auch zu auf die Geschichte eines Volkes oder einer Nation. Was auch immer unser Volk in einem jeweiligen Land trifft, die führende und tröstende Hand Gottes begleitet uns. Er weiß den Weg, auch und vor allem wenn Geschichte für uns so dunkel und unbegreiflich wird, daß wir sagen möchten, "Er hat uns vergessen!".

Wie so viele unserer donau-schwäbischen Immigranten im eigenen Leben erfahren haben, war die Vertreibung aus unserem Zuhause eine der Zeiten, wo Kirche eine ganz vitale Rolle spielte um zu überleben. Wie eines der Gedichte von Irma Seiler erzählt, "die Leute waren stark im Glauben. So ging es zur Kirche, dem trauten Hort, wo alle versammelt waren vom ganzen Ort. Die Glocken haben geläutet, kein Auge blieb trocken, so viele Tränen wurden noch nie dort vergossen."

Ich glaube, dies ist eines der eindrucksvollsten Zeugnisse für das, was Kirche und Glaube uns bedeuten. Wir versammeln uns, und gemeinsam mit der Familie, den Nachbarn und Freunden bringen wir alle frohen wie leidvollen Ereignisse unseres Lebens zu Gott hin. Die Glocken läuten, es fließen Tränen der Freude wie der Traurigkeit. Aber "die Leute waren stark im Glauben", auch wenn wir jetzt noch nicht verstehen, was Gott mit uns tut.

Hier in der neuen Welt konnten die Kirchengemeinschaften nicht immer der Ort sein, wo wir uns versammeln, Freude und Leid mit Gott und untereinander zu tragen, um darin Hilfe und Kraft zu finden. Aber hier in Amerika sind wir wenigstens frei, unseren Glauben ohne Hindernis und Verfolgung auszuüben. So finden viele dort die Kraft, ihre persönliche Bindung an Gott zu vertiefen, ihren Überzeugungen zu folgen und so das Leben zu meistern.

Die Kirche bietet Heimat und Schutz; sie unterrichtet und hat eine Vielzahl von Aktivitäten für alle Lebensstände. Ob wir miteinander im Chor singen, einen Picknick halten, ob es Jubiläen oder Hochzeiten sind oder ob wir gemeinsam an einem anderen Projekt arbeiten, "Kirche" erleben wir da, wo wir unseren Glauben praktizieren, die Kinder erziehen und Kultur, Sprache und Bräuche pflegen. Alles das erleben wir als deutsche Einwanderer hier in unserer neuen Heimat Amerika.

Aber ich glaube auch, unsere Kirchen üben ihren Einfluß nicht nur auf das persönliche und familienhafte, sondern auch auf das gesellschaftliche Leben aus. Adventskränze, Weihnachtsbäume, Weihnachtssterne oder Osterlilien schmücken unsere Wohnungen. Wo auch immer wir hingehen, finden wir die Weihnachtskrippe. All diese Schätze unseres Glaubens fanden ihren Weg in unsere amerikanische Kultur, so wie der Weihnachtsmann.

In manchen Gegenden halten unsere verschiedenen Vereinigungen ihr eigenes Oktoberfest ab; sie machen mit bei den verschiedenartigen "Festen" auf stättischer oder nationaler Ebene: das Germanfest, Trachtenfest, Gaufest, usw. mit den Speisen, Tänzen und Gebräuchen der jeweiligen Gebiete ihres Heimatlandes.

Oder bei einer Hochzeitsfeier sehen wir, wie noch alles miteinander verbunden ist. Die schöne kirchliche Trauung setzt sich fort in den Tänzen und Polkas, die den ganzen Abend hindurch gespielt werden. Gemeinsam genießen jung und alt die Traditionen und Gebräuche von früher.

Trotz des starken Einflusses unserer modernen pluralistischen Gesellschaft haben die deutschen Einwanderer viele ihrer Glaubensschätze tief in ihren Herzen bewahrt. Das sehe ich als ein großes Geschenk unseres Erbes an die neue Welt an: Gott und die Kirche bleiben verbunden in allem, was wir tun.

"Unser Glaube an Gott hat uns geholfen weiterzumachen!", hörte man von den Lippen vieler Immigranten, man hört es noch heute!

Immigration and Religion

by Profs. E. Reichmann and LaVern J. Rippley

With the onset of the Reformation, religion became a considerable factor in European migration processes. The Augsburg Religious Peace (1555) enabled the princes to determine the faith of their subjects. The Peace Treaty of Westphalia, ending the Thirty Years War (1618-1648), legalized only three confessions: Catholic, Lutheran and Reformed. Sects were outlawed. While minority adherents the "big three" could at least move to duchies of their respective faith, those who rejected child baptism (Anabaptists) and military service had but one choice: emigration. The success of the Mennonite Germantown experiment encouraged other religious dissident groups to seek a new home in Pennsylvania and other colonial states. Virtually forgotten in their home countries today, they not only contributed to America's denominational diversity but just as much to its cultural, agricultural and economic development.

Mennonites, Amish, Moravians, Harmonists, Hutterites, Schwenkfelders, Old Order Baptists, Inspirationists, Salzburger Protestants, and many others were followed by Lutherans and Reformed who chose emigration over Prussia's mandated union of the two churches (1824), and by members of Catholic orders during Bismarck's *Kulturkampf* with the Vatican (1871-1886). The Third Reich made it advisable for Jewish Germans and Jehovah's Witnesses to leave as well.

The perilous crossings and hardships of beginning a new life in a strange environment tended to create meekness and close ties to churches. Beyond ministering to the spiritual needs, the old church tradition of charitable services to the poor, sick, homeless, and orphaned was part of the agenda. This paralleled, but went far beyond, the work of immigrant aid societies which began with the German Society of Pennsylvania (1764) and others at all points of debarkation, and with the Germany-based St. Raphaels Verein that assisted many emigrants before departure, during the voyage, and upon arrival.

Many a famous Methodist and Jewish hospital was started by the religious German immigrant community. Between 1870-1919, Catholic nuns of various national backgrounds built 479 hospitals. The Franciscan sisters, who left Prussia in the 1870s, opened theirs especially in the Midwest.

The survival of the mother tongue was in no small part due to the thousands of German churches. They were, and often still are, centers of their communities. Long before states mandated public instruction, churches operated the schools as well. Lutheran and Catholic schools have always been known for their excellence. Historically, Catholic education is especially indebted to the Benedictine and Franciscan nuns. Totally overlooked in World War I was the fact that German-language instruction and American patriotism always went hand in hand.

Einwanderung und Religion

by Prof. Eberhard Reichmann und Prof. LaVern J. Rippley

Die mit der Reformation aufgekommenen unversöhnlichen Gegensätze machten Religion zu einem wesentlichen Faktor europäscher Wanderungsbewegungen. Der Augsburger Religionsfrieden (1555) gab den Landesherrn das Recht, den Glauben ihrer Untertanen zu bestimmen. Der Westfälische Frieden (1648) begrenzte die Wahl auf katholisch, evangelisch und reformiert. Sekten waren völlig ausgeschlossen und wurden verfolgt. Wer unwillens war entsprechend zu konvertieren, mußte das Staatsgebiet verlassen. Den Anabaptisten (Wiedertäufern), die auch den Militärdienst verweigerten, blieb nur die Auswanderung. Der rasche Aufstieg des mennonitischen Germantown ermutigte etliche Dissidentengruppen in Pennsylvanien und andernorts ihr Heil zu suchen. In ihren Ursprungsgebieten heute fast völlig vergessen, trugen diese Gruppen nicht mur zur religiösen Vielfalt Amerikas bei, sondern auch zu seiner kulturellen, landwirtschaftlichen und industriellen Entwicklung.

Den Mennoniten, Amischen, Mährischen Brüdern, Harmonisten, Hutterern, Schwenkfeldern, Baptisten, Inspirationisten, Salzburger Protestanten u. a. folgten Lutheraner und Reformierte, als Preußen die Union der beiden Bekenntnisse forderte (1824). Bismarcks Kulturkampf mit dem Vatikan (1871-1886) brachte Mitglieder aufgelöster Orden übers Meer. Nach 1933 fanden besonders Juden und Jehovahs Zeugen Rettung durch Auswanderung.

Die Gefahren der Überfahrt und die Härten der Existenzgründung führten mehrheitlich zu starker religiöser Bindung. Die anfänglich wenigen Missionare lebten im Sattel. Über den geistlichen Beistand hinaus galt es in echt kirchlicher Tradition den Armen, Kranken, Obdachlosen und Waisen zu helfen. Das ergänzte in weit größerem Maße die Arbeit der Einwandererschutzvereinigungen, deren erste die Deutsche Gesellschaft von Pennsylvanien (1764) war und die vor allem in den Hafenstädten Hilfe leisteten. Deutschlands katholischer St. Raphaels Verein half vor und während der Reise und nach der Ankunft.

Etliche der bekannten Methodisten– und jüdischen Krankenhäuser waren deutsche Grüdungen. Katholische Schwestern verschiedener Nationalität bauten 479 Krankenhäuser zwischen 1870-1919. Die Franziskanerinnen, die Preußen in den 1870ern verließen, bauten ihre besonders im Mittleren Westen.

Auch für das Weitergeben der Muttersprache spielten Tausende deutscher Kirchen die Hauptrolle. Sie waren– und oft noch heute– echte Gemeindezentren. Und vor dem späten Aufkommen des öffentlichen Schulwesens bestritten die Kirchen auch die Schulen. Heute gewinnt der Erziehungs– und Bildungserfolg der Konfessionsschulen ständig an Beachtung. Geschichtlich sind besonders die Leistungen der lutherischen Schulen und der katholischen Schulen der Benediktinerinnen und Franziskanerinnen bedeutsam. Im Ersten Weltkrieg vergaß man die Tatsache, daß deutschsprachiger Unterricht und Liebe zu Amerika immer Hand in Hand gingen.

A Nation of Immigrants
THE GERMANS

Between 1830 and 1930, the period of the greatest migration from Europe to the United States, Germany sent six million people to the United States—more than any other nation. Their migrations, increasing in numbers after 1850, overlapped the Irish, whose immigration declined.

The Germans were unique among immigrant groups in their wide dispersal, both geographically and occupationally. This was due, at least in part, to the fact that most of them came with some resources, and were not forced to cluster along the Eastern seaboard. Attracted to the United States by cheap public and railroad lands, and later by free homesteads, the German farmer helped to farm the New West and to cultivate the Mississippi Valley; German artisans, much sought after because of their skills, became an important factor in industrial expansion.

Almost every state in the Union profited from their intellectual and material contributions. Hard-working and knowledgeable about agricultural methods, the Germans became propagators of scientific farming, crop rotation, soil conservation. They share with the Scandinavians the credit for turning millions of acres of wilderness into productive farm land.

The urban settlers lent a distinctive German flavor to many of our cities. Cincinnati, then known as "Queen City" of the West, Baltimore, St. Louis, Minneapolis, Milwaukee, all had substantial German populations. Milwaukee has perhaps retained its distinctive German character longer than any of the others.

In these urban centers Germans entered the fields of education, science, engineering and the arts. German immigrants founded and developed industrial enterprises in the fields of lumbering, food-processing, brewing, steel-making, electrical engineering, piano-making, railroading and printing.

A small but significant part of the German immigration consisted of political refugees. Reaction in Germany against the reform ideas of the French Revolution had caused heavy suppression of liberal thought. There was strict censorship of the press, of public meetings and of the schools and universities. Nevertheless, a liberal movement had emerged, nurtured in the universities by young intellectuals. This movement led to unsuccessful revolutions in 1830 and 1848. The United States welcomed a large number of veterans of 1848—men of education, substance and social standing, like Carl Schurz, the statesman and reformer, and General Franz Sigel. In addition, some of the German religious groups established utopian communities in parts of Pennsylvania, Ohio, Indiana, Texas and Oregon.

German immigration reflected all the chaotic conditions of Central Europe after Napoleon: the population growth, the widespread hunger, the religious dissension and oppression. The Germans included Lutherans, Jews and Catholics, as well as freethinkers. Their talents, training and background greatly enriched the burgeoning nation.

To the influence of the German immigrants in particular—although all minority groups contributed—we owe the mellowing of the austere Puritan imprint on our daily lives. The Puritans observed the Sabbath as a day of silence and solemnity. The Germans clung to their concept of the "Continental Sunday" as a day, not only of churchgoing, but also of relaxation, of picnics, of visiting, of quiet drinking in beer gardens while listening to the music of a band.

The Christmas ritual of religious services combined with exchanging gifts around the Christmas tree is of German origin. So, too, is the celebration of the New Year.

The fact that today almost every large American city has its symphony orchestra can be traced to the influence of the German migration. Leopold Damrosch and his son, Walter, helped build the famous New York Philharmonic. Originally composed mainly of German immigrant musicians and called the Germania Orchestra, it became the seed bed of similar organizations all over the country. This tradition was carried to the Midwest by Frederick Stock and to Boston by Carl Zerrahn. Others spread this form of cultural expression to additional urban centers throughout the land.

Community singing and glee clubs owe much to the German immigrant, who remembered his singing societies. The first Männerchor was founded in Philadelphia in 1835; the first Liederkranz was organized in Baltimore in 1836. Their counterparts have been a feature of the German-American community everywhere.

The ideas of German immigrants helped to shape our educational system. They introduced the kindergarten, or "children's play school." They also promoted the concept of the state-endowed university, patterned after the German university. The University of Michigan, founded in 1837, was the first such school to add to the philosophy of general liberal arts education an emphasis upon vocational training. The colonial concept of a university as a place to prepare gentlemen for a life of leisured culture was modified to include training in specialized skills.

The program of physical education in the schools had its roots in the Turnverein, or German gymnastic society. It was adopted and introduced to the American public by the Y.M.C.A.

German immigrant influence has been pervasive, in our language, in our mores, in our customs and in our basic philosophy. Even the hamburger, the frankfurter and the delicatessen, that omnipresent neighborhood institution, came to us via the German immigrants.

Carl Schurz
4c USA

"Yes, we have sauerkraut but we don't call it that anymore."

Although they were mostly Democrats prior to 1850, the Germans broke party lines in the decade before the Civil War and played a prominent part in the formation of the Republican party. They were most united on two issues. They opposed the Blue Laws, and they vigorously fought the extension of slavery into new territories. Indeed, the first protest against Negro slavery came from Germantown settlers, led by Franz Pastorius, in 1688.

During the Civil War they fought on both sides. Following the Civil War, Germans infused the faltering American labor movement with new strength by organizing craft unions for printers, watchmakers, carpenters, ironworkers, locksmiths, butchers and bakers.

Adjusting with relative ease, they did not feel the sting of ethnic discrimination until the outbreak of the First World War, when they became targets of wartime hysteria. This hysteria even caused overardent "patriots" to call sauerkraut "Liberty cabbage" and hamburger "Salisbury steak." Nonetheless, when the United States entered the war in 1917, men of German ancestry entered the armed forces of the United States and served with distinction.

As the Second World War drew near, Americans of German descent faced another test. Only a few joined the pro-Nazi German-American Bund, and many of those left as soon as they discovered its real nature. Again, after the U.S. was attacked, descendants of German immigrants fought with valor in our armed services.

John F. Kennedy, 1917–1963.

New Yorker Staats-Zeitung und Herold

Keimzellen neuer Konflikte

Refruten Verlangt
26. Regiment
Wisc. Volunteers!!

Attention Workingmen!
MASS MEETING
TO-NIGHT, at 7.30 o'clock.

Achtung Arbeiter!
Massen-Versammlung

Fleischmann's
Westinghouse
Oscar Mayer
Weyerhaeuser
STEINWAY & SONS
NEW YORK HAMBURG
HEINZ

Research and Design: Juergen Eichhoff.
Composition: Impressions, Inc., Madison, Wisconsin
A Production of German House Research, Madison, Wisconsin
© 1988 Juergen Eichhoff

For more information on each illustration and a reading list on the history and heritage of German immigration send SASE and $2 to GHR, 3950 Plymouth Circle, Madison, WI 53705.

First published in 1988 in commemoration of the three hundredth anniversary of the Germantown protest against Negro slavery, and the twenty-fifth anniversary of the assassination of John F. Kennedy.

Courtesy of Dr. Jürgen Eichhoff, Pennstate University, PA

Many Reasons for Migration

By Prof. E. Reichmann and Prof. LaVern J. Rippley

During the last 200 years, the U.S. has been the preferred destination for German emigrants. Before that, rather than risking an Atlantic crossing, many more headed overland and eastward into Poland, various Balkan regions, Ukraine, the Black Sea and the middle Volga regions. During the 19th century, Germans also emigrated in large numbers to settlements in South America, Australia, Canada, and to newly acquired German colonies in Africa.

A combination of "push" and "pull" factors underlies these migration processes: "push" — when socio-economic or political conditions at home were in the bad-to-unbearable range; "pull" — when the promise of a better life abroad seemed to justify the hard choice of leaving the **Vaterland**. Reports about the New World, in newspapers, brochures and books, from travelers, American state governments, shipping and railroad companies — all trying to attract settlers and laborers — made information widely accessible. Most trusted and influential, however, were the letters from relatives and friends who had made the big move. This motivated "chain migration" which, in turn, created "little Germanies" in America.

When the exercise of one's religious belief met with an intolerant church and state, America offered a haven of religious freedom not only for the smaller sects but also — during certain periods and in certain regions of the German-speaking countries — for the principal denominations, the Lutherans, Reformed, and Catholics.

When inheritance laws had divided farms into uneconomical mini-farms, America welcomed the land-hungry. For some time, $1.25 bought an acre of land. When economic stagnation, high taxation, potato rot and repeated crop failures brought hunger and despair, America had a need for man power as it built its cities, railroads and canals — and it had no income tax. Some German communities found it more feasible to pay the trip for their poor than to keep the soup kitchen going. For many young men the expectation of lengthy military service was a push factor. Others simply sought adventure. And if two lovers of different denominations couldn't get married at home, America would allow it. Quite a few businessmen wanted to be part of the fast developing economy. By far the greatest number of immigrants came for economic reasons. That included some 800,000 who immigrated after WW II. But once Germany's "economic miracle" had brought about general prosperity in the 1960s, emigration dwindled to a trickle and many migrated back home.

Lack of political freedom in post-Napoleonic times caused thousands to leave Germany, especially after the ill-fated 1848 Revolution. Later, thousands of Social Democrats felt out of place in Bismarck's Second Reich. And anticipating the social/racial/military catastrophes of the Third Reich, over 100,000 intellectuals, writers, artists, actors, musicians — many of whom Jewish-Germans — constituted the greatest "brain drain" in history. German-speaking Europe's losses turned into America's gain.

Warum sie auswanderten

Prof. Eberhard Reichmann und Prof. LaVern J. Rippley

Während der letzten 200 Jahre waren die USA das Vorzugsland deutscher Emigranten. Zuvor war es Ost- und Südost-Europa: Polen, Balkan, Ukraine, Schwarz-Meer und mittlere Wolga-Regionen. Im 19. Jh. zogen viele auch nach Südamerika, Australien, Kanada und in neue deutsch-afrikanische Kolonien.

Diesen Migrationen liegt eine Kombination von Schub- und Anziehungskraft zu grunde — wenn besseres Fortkommen anderswo die schwere Entscheidung zur Auswanderung zu rechtfertigen schien. Berichte über die Neue Welt gab es in Zeitungen, Heftchen und Büchern, von Reisenden, amerikanischen Staatsregierungen, Reedereien und Eisenbahngesellschaften. Man suchte Siedler und Arbeitskräfte. Am einflussreichsten waren jedoch Briefe von Freunden und Verwandten, die den großen Sprung schon gewagt hatten. So kam "Kettenwanderung" zustande.

Für kirchlich und staatlich nichtgeduldete und verfolgte Sekten wurde Amerika zum "gelobten Land". Aber zu gewissen Zeiten und aus gewissen Gebieten suchten auch Evangelische, Reformierte und Katholiken die "Freiheit eines Christenmenschen" überm Meer.

Wenn Erbteilung Bauernland zerstückelte, lockte Amerika mit urbar zu machenden Ländereien. Lange galt dabei 1ha = $3.00. Wenn die Wirtschaft stagnierte, die Steuerlast zu drückend war und Kartoffelfäule und Ernteausfälle Hungersnot und Verzweiflung brachten, brauchte Amerika Arbeitskräfte für schnellwachsende Städte, Eisenbahnlinien und Kanäle. Einkommensteuer? Keine. Manche deutsche Gemeinde fand es vorteilhafter, Armen die Schiffskarte zu kaufen, als Suppenküchen weiterzuführen. Für viele junge Männer war die lange Militärdienstpflicht Grund zum Auswandern, andere packte die Abenteuerlust. Für Geschäftsleute winkten Profitmöglichkeiten. Und das Tabu interkonfessioneller Mischehen trieb etliche Pärchen übers Wasser. Die Aussicht auf Arbeit und Auskommen motivierte mehr Menschen als alle anderen Auswanderungsgründe zusammen. Das gilt auch für die ca. 800,000 der 1950er/1969er Jahre. Der "Wirtschaftswunder"—Wohlstand bewegte dann in den 1960er Jahren viele zur Heimkehr. Die Zeiten der Auswanderung waren damit vorbei.

Die nichtgewährten Freiheitsrechte im Vormärz (1815-1848) und die missglückte Deutsche Revolution (1848) zwangen viele Demokraten nach Amerika; Sozialdemokraten folgten in der Bismarckzeit. Und im Dritten Reich verließen 100,000 Intellektuelle, Politiker, Künstler, Musiker und Schauspieler — viele davon Juden — die Heimat. Das war die größte geistige Abwanderung der Geschichte. Was das deutschsprachige Europa dabei verlor, wurde Amerikas Gewinn.

The German-American Soldier

by Profs. E. Reichmann and LaVern J. Rippley

While clinging to Old World values and traditions in their private sphere, German immigrants have shown to be patriotic Americans in times of peril. From the War of Independence through WW II, they served their new homeland with valor and in great numbers.

In 1776 Pastor Muhlenberg signaled it thus: "Everything has its season. There is a time to preach and a time to fight—and that has come now." He took off his clerical robe and left the pulpit to create the German Regiment of Virginia. General Herkimer also raised 800 men and gave his life in battle. Crucial for the American cause was Baron von Steuben's role as inspector general. He turned the battered colonists into an effective fighting force. Christopher Ludwig was the army's chief baker. And the body guard of General Washington was all German.

As to the Civil War, the statement by the South's General, Robert E. Lee, says it all: "Take the Dutch out of the Union Army and we will easily whip the Yankees." Many of the 1848er revolutionaries who had found exile in America fought for the Union. Its large German-American contingent—several regiments were all-German— had over 5,000 officers, including generals and admirals.

For German-Americans looking back at the War of Independence, the Civil War, and the two World Wars, there is a recurring tragic aspect. In all these wars there were Germans fighting on both sides, brother against brother/relative against relative. The 30,000 Hessian mercenaries, sold by German princes to England, had to be beaten for America to become free. The Germans fighting for the Confederacy had to be beaten to save the Union. America's entry into the European war (1917) caused this country's great hysteria - hysterical Anti-Germanism, leading to the demise of all things German in America. And we will never know how many WW II pilots dropped bombs on ancestral homes.

Ironically, in both World Wars, the commanders-in-chief of the U.S. Armed Forces were of German extraction. Both, Gen. Pershing's and Gen. Eisenhower's forebears (Frederick Pfoerschin/ Johann Nikolaus Eisenhauer) were 18th century immigrants. In WW II German-Americans comprised 30% of those enlisted. Adm. Nimitz commanded the Pacific Fleet. Gen. Spaatz created the Strategic Air Command before becoming the first Air Force Chief of Staff. Germany-born Gen. Krueger led the 6th Army into Japan.

More recently, Gen. Schwarzkopf won the 1991 Blitzkrieg against Saddam Hussein. Grandfather Christian Schwarzkopf had left the Neckar Valley for New York in 1855. His gravestone bears the German inscription of "I know that my Redeemer liveth."

Der deutsch - amerikanische Soldat

von Prof. Eberhard Reichmann und Prof. LaVern J. Rippley

Während das Privatleben deutscher Einwanderer noch stark von mitgebrachten Wertvorstellungen und Eigenarten geprägt blieb,standen sie jederzeit und in großer Anzahl ihren Mann, wenn der neuen Heimat Gefahren drohten.

Pastor Mühlenbergs Haltung bei Ausbruch des Unabhängigkeitskriegs 1776 als Beispiel: "Alles zu seiner Zeit. Es gibt eine Zeit fürs Predigen und eine Zeit fürs Kämpfen. Die ist jetzt angebrochen." Nach diesem Predigtschluß und Ablegen seines Pfarrgewands verliess er die Kanzel in Uniform und hatte in Kürze sein deutsches Regiment von Virginia zusammen. So auch General Herkimer mit seinen 800 Freiwilligen im Staat New York, der sein Leben für die Unabhängigkeit ließ. Überragend war die Bedeutung des preußischen Barons von Steuben, der als Generalinspekteur die angeschlagenen Kolonisten zu tauglichen Soldaten umformte. Den Hunger parierte Christoph Ludwig als Hauptbäcker der Armee. Und dem Schutz General Washingtons diente die aus Deutschen bestehende Leibwache.

Für den Bürgerkrieg (1861-1865) spricht das Wort des konföderierten Generals Lee Bände: "Nehmt die Deutschen aus der Unionsarmee raus, dann schlagen wir die Yankees mit Leichtigkeit." Von den Flüchtlingen der Deutschen Revolution (1848) kämpften viele für die Union. Insgesamt stellten die Deutsch-Amerikaner der Nordarmee über 5000 Offiziere, darunter einige Generäle. Etliche Regimenter hörten auf deutsche Kommandos.

Baron Friedrich Wilhelm von Steuben, born in Magdeburg, September 17, 1730; died near Remsen, Oneida County, NY, November 28, 1794.

Für Deutsch-Amerikaner ist die Kriegsgeschichte der neuen Heimat nicht ohne eine gewisse Tragik. Denn immer wieder kämpften dabei Deutsche gegen Deutsche, Bruder gegen Bruder. 30000 Hessen, von deutschen Fürsten an England verschachert, mußten geschlagen werden, um Amerika frei zu machen. Deutsche, die im Bürgerkrieg für den Süden kämpften, mußten geschlagen werden für den Fortbestand der Union. Amerikas Kriegseintritt 1917 entfachte eine katastrophale anti-deutsche Hysterie. Und wieviele amerikanische Piloten bombten Heimstätten ihrer Vorfahren im 2. Weltkrieg?

Ironie der Geschichte—in beiden Weltkriegen waren die Oberbefehlshaber der U.S. Streitkräfte deutscher Herkunft. Die Vorfahren der Generäle Pershing und Eisenhower [Friederich Pförschin und Johan Nikolaus Eisenhauer] waren im 18. Jahrhundert nach Amerika ausgewandert. 1941-1945 stellten Deutsch-Amerikaner 30% der U.S. Army. Admiral Nimitz war Chef der Pazifischen Flotte. General Spaatz war der Luftkriegstratege und Generalstabschef der Air Force. Der deutschgebürtige General Krüger besetzte Japan mit seiner 6. Armee.

1991 errang General Schwarzkopf im irakischen Konflikt "Desert Storm" einen Blitzsieg über Saddam Hussein. Großvater Christian Schwarzkopf hatte 1855 die Neckarheimat mit New York getauscht. Seine deutsche Grabsteininschrift: "Ich weiß, daß mein Erlöser lebt."

Spirits of 1776
—And 1976

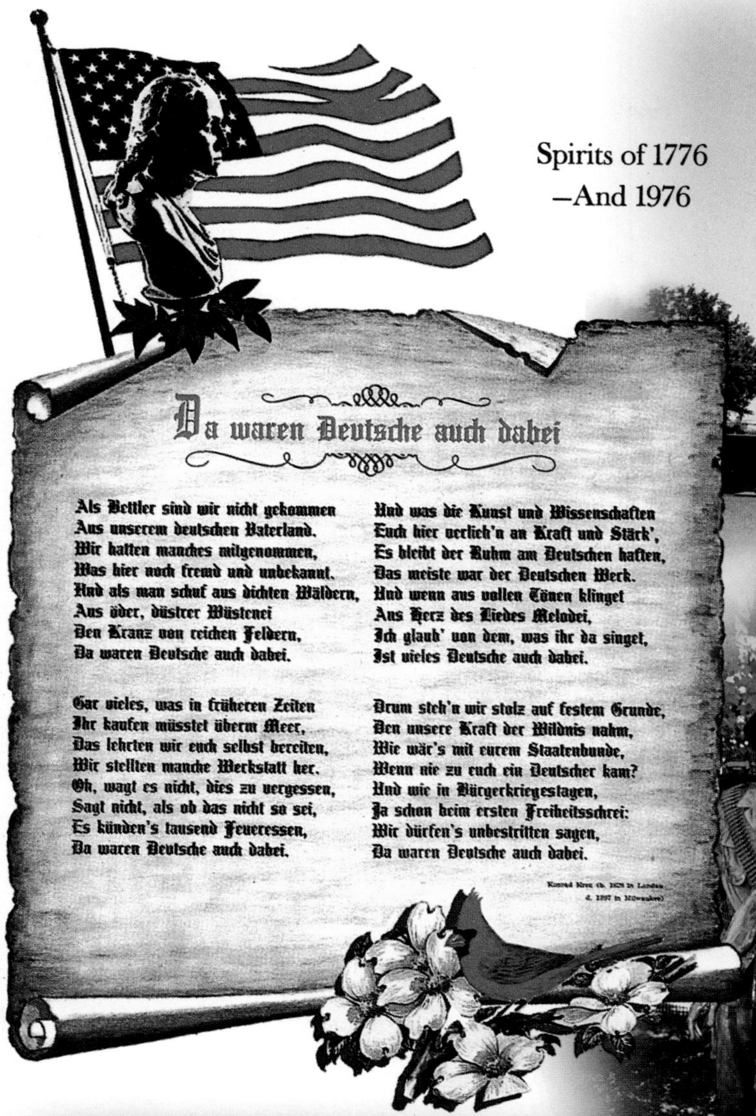

Da waren Deutsche auch dabei

Als Bettler sind wir nicht gekommen
Aus unserem deutschen Vaterland,
Wir hatten manches mitgenommen,
Was hier noch fremd und unbekannt.
Und als man schuf aus dichten Wäldern,
Aus öder, düstrer Wüstenei
Den Kranz von reichen Feldern,
Da waren Deutsche auch dabei.

Gar vieles, was in früheren Zeiten
Ihr kaufen müsstet überm Meer,
Das lehrten wir euch selbst bereiten,
Wir stellten manche Werkstatt her.
Oh, wagt es nicht, dies zu vergessen,
Sagt nicht, als ob das nicht so sei,
Es künden's tausend Feueressen,
Da waren Deutsche auch dabei.

Und was die Kunst und Wissenschaften
Euch hier verlieh'n an Kraft und Stärk',
Es bleibt der Ruhm am Deutschen haften,
Das meiste war der Deutschen Werk.
Und wenn aus vollen Tönen klinget
Aus Herz des Liedes Melodei,
Ich glaub' von dem, was ihr da singet,
Ist vieles Deutsche auch dabei.

Drum steh'n wir stolz auf festem Grunde,
Den unsere Kraft der Wildnis nahm,
Wie wär's mit eurem Staatenbunde,
Wenn nie zu euch ein Deutscher kam?
Und wie in Bürgerkriegestagen,
Ja schon beim ersten Freiheitsschrei:
Wir dürfen's unbestritten sagen,
Da waren Deutsche auch dabei.

Konrad Krez, geb. 1828 in Landau
d. 1897 in Milwaukee.

Translated from the German
original by Dr. Robert E. Ward.

Distributed by D.A.N.K., 27012 Hilliard Blvd.,
Cleveland, Ohio 44145, U.S.A.

At Your Side There Were Germans Too

by Konrad Krez

Not as burdens to these shores we throng,
From our cherished German Fatherland.
Indeed, we have brought so much along,
Unknown to you, yet by our hand.
And when from the dense forestal shields,
and the open wilderness you
wreath'd your vast and verdant fields,
At your side there were Germans too.

So much of that which in earlier days
you brought here from across the sea,
We taught you how to prepare, and ways
to produce more goods, yes, 'twas we.
Dare not forget this, deny it n'er —
Say not that we did not so do,
For a thousand forges witness bear:
At your side there we Germans too.

And though your art and your sciences now
bring their strength and power to this land,
Their fame rests still on the German brow,
'Twas mostly done by German hand,
And when for your songs melodies ring
memories of hearts once so true,
Tis known to me, in the songs you sing
is much put there by Germans too!

Thus, with great pride on this soil we stand,
Which from the wilds our strength bought claim,
Ever wonder then, what kind o land,
'twould be if n'er a German came!
And so we declared in Lincoln's day,
And that day freedom's horn first blew —
Yes, we dare undeniably say:
At your side there were Germans too!

A Book Dedicated to Future Generations

Arlene and Bert Lachner

My sister, who lives in Germany, asked me some time ago: "Herbert, when are you finally coming home?" My answer was quick and from the heart: 'But Christa, I am home!"

Yes, and together with me hundreds of thousands of other Germans who came to this continent in the nineteen fifties and early sixties. I remember it well - in those days we were full of pep and adventurism, but could not find any good opportunities in postwar Germany which had to reshape and reconstruct itself. Thanks to open doors to Canada and the United States, most of us were able to come to this continent without sponsors and resources. As long as we were willing to work and produce we were welcomed.

And did we utilize those opportunities. Just as millions of others had done in harder times before us. We rolled up our sleeves and went to it, attended night schools and completed our education. It was no big deal. We changed jobs frequently to better ourselves or to guide our careers back into the familiar track. After all, at the beginning one took what one could get, as long as it paid well. This would probably have been more difficult in Germany, where papers for everything - certificates, licenses, permits - are required for getting even the simplest job. Eventually, many of us built careers and founded businesses, which not only prospered for ourselves, but we provided work and again opportunities for our employees or partners. Today we are able to pay back some of the generosity this country gave us in the beginning, first as a host, then our home.

Looking from the outside in, we still see some animosity between the regions of Germany, the Bavarians never liked the Prussians, and Berlin has problems with the Saxons, and vice versa, even Cologne prefers to forget

that there is a Düsseldorf. Most evident is the feud between West and East Germany today. Here we are simply Americans...

Americans, who have not forgotten their heritage. Especially Germans, and other Europeans maintain clubs and societies to continue to celebrate the old customs and traditions. This book was designed to introduce many to these organizations in the hope that young and old will have more of an opportunity to communicate, visit and enjoy each others company... from Canada, throughout the United States and even into Mexico.

Its a big continent, I traveled it for the research and support I needed to do this book. And I am grateful to many people, some of them got just as excited about the project as I am. It is a mission that is not over, it will continue as we strive to help the struggling clubs to turn around. Sure it was a lot of work, and sleepless nights and many, many films. Some 60,000 words had to be processed through our computer, in English and German. And if a word or letter is out of place, we hope you will forgive us.

I was amazed how many different clubs and societies there are. Every organization tries to survive and prosper in a different way; just imagine they all knew each other and would share in their experiences. That would breed success.

We must inspire each other and let our young people carry the ball and play the game. They are so much more energetic, understand the new world with its computers and internet. Why not. The world has changed since we left home 40 years ago, and things are not the same in Germany either. Let us make our traditions palatable to the new generation. Speak German, sing German, think German OK, but add the

English language, the American way, a world citizen attitude and really enjoy those customs.

Too bad, the immigration laws are so tough and tight. I bet, a good number of youngsters would love to come to the States today and work and study and build a life here. Unemployment is low, opportunities are plentiful, life is good! Anybody with a little spunk can make it here. You have to work for it, but that's where the satisfaction comes in, to know you have done your best and have done it your way.

I hope this book will help to understand the German character, where we came from, the stock we are made of, who we are and where we are going.

It would be nice if our clubs appealed to our younger families and they in turn saw the clubs as an option to their life style, just like sports, movies, camping, and computers and TV.

Bilingualism is not outdated. It helps when traveling, in business, especially in import/export. It broadens the mind as language is always connected with an other culture and usually a different way of doing things. Its as useful as anything. Starting the children early and keeping them at it will eventually lead to a broader outlook on life. Just like the study of music or any physical skill.

Last but not least, I hope the book will provide many hours of enjoyment to your leisure time. Use it often, refer back to it, make notes in the back of the book and share with friends and the little ones what so preciously we call our heritage.

Thank you for your time, and may God bless you.

James and Deborah Fiddelke with Kevin,
Alexandra Lachner, Christa Fiddelke,
Pat Burland-Lachner and Perry Lachner

Ein Buch, der Jugend gewidmet

Meine Schwester, die in Deutschland lebt, fragte mich kürzlich: "Herbert, wann hommst du denn nun endlich wieder nach Hause?" Meine Antwort kam aus vollem Herzen: "Aber Christa, ich bin doch zu Hause!"

Ja, ich und Hunderttausende von Deutschen außer mir, die in den fünfziger und sechziger Jahren dieses Jahrhunderts hier eingewandert sind.

Damals jung und voller Schwung und Energie, vermißten wir Chancen aller Art im Nachkriegsdeutschland, das sich erst aufbauen und formen mußte. Dank großzügigerer Einwanderungsbestimmungen als heute, konnten viele von uns nach Nordamerika auswandern.

Und wir haben diese Möglichkeiten genutzt! Ebenso wie Millionen anderer Deutscher vor uns, die schon in früheren Jahrhunderten den Weg hierher nicht gescheut hatten. Wir haben die Ärmel hochgekrempelt und zugepackt. Das ging hier leichter als in Deutschland, wo man erst Papiere, Zulassungen und Genehmigungen braucht, um zupacken zu dürfen. Viele von uns haben Karriere gemacht und Betriebe aufgebaut, die nicht nur uns selbst zu Wohlstand verhalfen, sondern wiederum auch anderen Arbeit gegeben haben. So konnten wir die Großzügigkeit unseres erst Gast-, dann Heimatlandes, wieder entgelten. Viele dieser "Entrepreneurs" habe ich in meinen früheren Büchern schon vorgestellt; einige werden hier gezeigt.

In Deutschland gab es - und gibt es immer noch - ständige Konkurrenz und Reibereien zwischen den einzelnen Landsmannschaften: Die Bayern können nicht mit den Preußen, die Berliner nicht mit den Sachsen; die Kölner vergessen gern, daß es ein Düsseldorf gibt - aber hier, in der großen Weite Amerikas, sind wir alle eins - Amerikaner...

Als Amerikaner in der neuen Heimat haben wir aber die frühere nicht vergessen: Hunderte von deutschen Clubs in diesem Lande zeugen davon. Mit diesem Buch möchte ich sie vorstellen: Von "coast to coast", und sogar darüber hinaus - bis nach Kanada und Mexiko hinein.

Es war Freude, Anregung und - jawohl! - auch eine Menge Arbeit dieses Buch zusammenzustellen. Wochenlange Reisen, unzählige Gespräche (persönliche und per Telefon), viele schlaflose Nächte, "X" verknipste Filme und die Mitarbeit vieler freiwilliger Helfer, denen ich sehr dankbar bin.

Die deutschen Klubs und Gesellschaften in Amerika zeigen die ganze Bandbreite, die man mit solchen Vereinigungen darstellen kann: Vom allmonatlichen Bierabend, an dem man endlich wieder mal "heimatliche" Laute hört, über Gesangvereine bis hin zu den größeren Klubs, die keine Kosten und Mühe scheuen, deutsche Kapellen, Künstler, Literaten und Wissenschaftler bei ihren Zusammenkünften einzuladen und zu fördern. Man trifft sich privat, in gemieteten Räumen, oder in eigenen Klubhäusern und Zentren. Es gibt sowohl allgemeine deutsche Clubs als auch spezielle, wie z. B. Berliner, Friesen, Hamburger, Bayern, Schwaben, Donauschwaben, Sudetendeutsche, usw.

Die ursprüngliche Bedeutung dieser Vereinigungen bestand zum größten Teil darin, daß man sein Heimweh bekämpfte, und versuchte, neuen Einwanderern ein familiäres Gefühl zu vermitteln und auch, die alten Sitten und Gebräuche zu bewahren.

Veränderte Einwanderungsbestimmungen haben den Zustrom neuer Deutscher arg beschränkt und damit auch das Durchschnittsalter der (Einwanderer erster Generation) stark heraufgesetzt. Man will seinen

Nachkömmlingen zeigen, wo man selbst und sie herkommen.

Dies ist auch einer meiner Herzenswünsche für dieses Buch, außer daß:

- Es möge informativ sein, d.h. historische, praktische und soziale Leistungen der Deutschen in diesem Lande darstellen und ihre Errungenschaften zeigen.

- Es möge eine Anregung sein, daß Deutsche und ihre Klubs sich gegenseitig kennenlernen und austauschen;

- Es möge jüngere Generationen veranlassen, diese Klubs als alternative Freizeitgestaltung neben Sport, Kino und Computer, anzusehen und

- Die zweisprachige Aufmachung möge ein Vorschlag sein, dieses Buch in Schulen und Universitäten anzuwenden - in Sachen Geschichte, Sitten und Gebräuche sowie im Sprachunterricht.

Ich hoffe, es macht Ihnen, liebe Leser, soviel Spaß, dieses Buch zu lesen und zu verschenken, wie es mir gemacht hat, es herzustellen.

Wir alle sind hier zu Hause. Wir sind Bewohner und Bürger dieses wunderbaren Landes, das uns aufgenommen und uns Entfaltungsmöglichkeiten geboten hat.

Ja wirklich, Christa, Amerika ist unsere Heimat!

Bert Lachner

Aus dem Interview mit Dr. Karin Walter-Spiess

United States

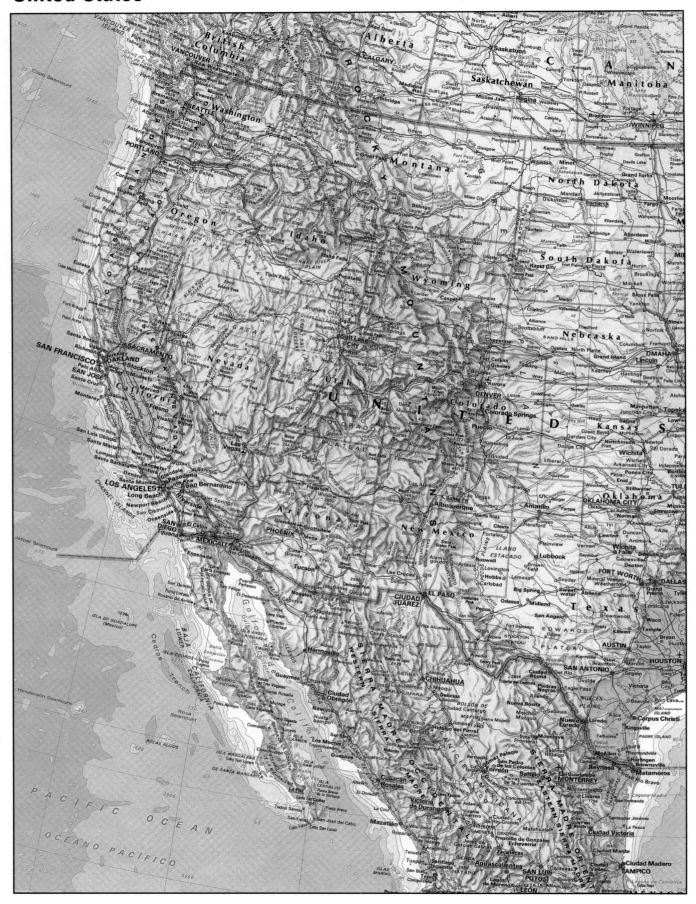

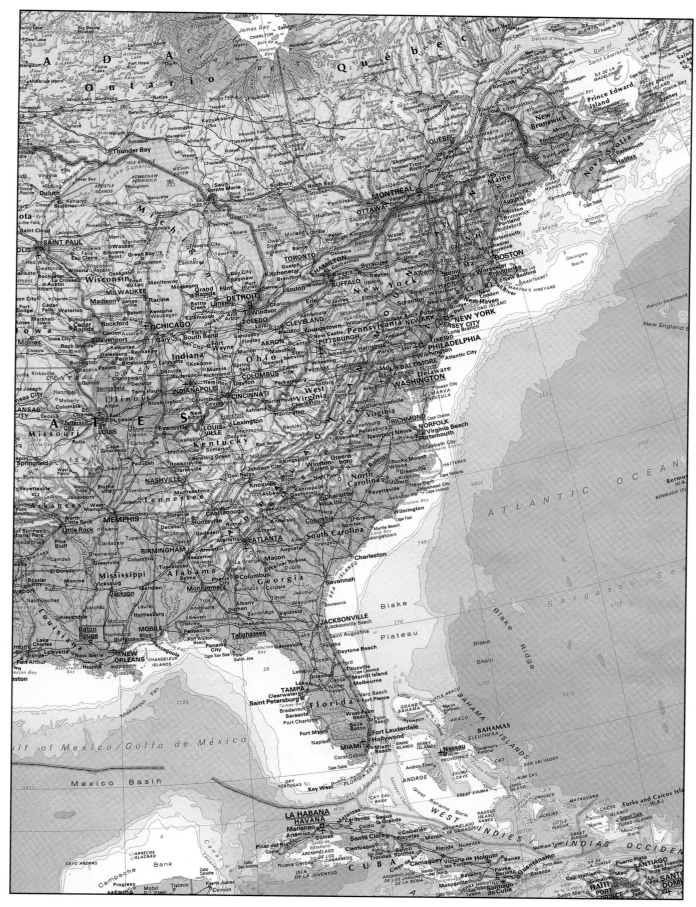

Courtesty of Rand McNally

Europe

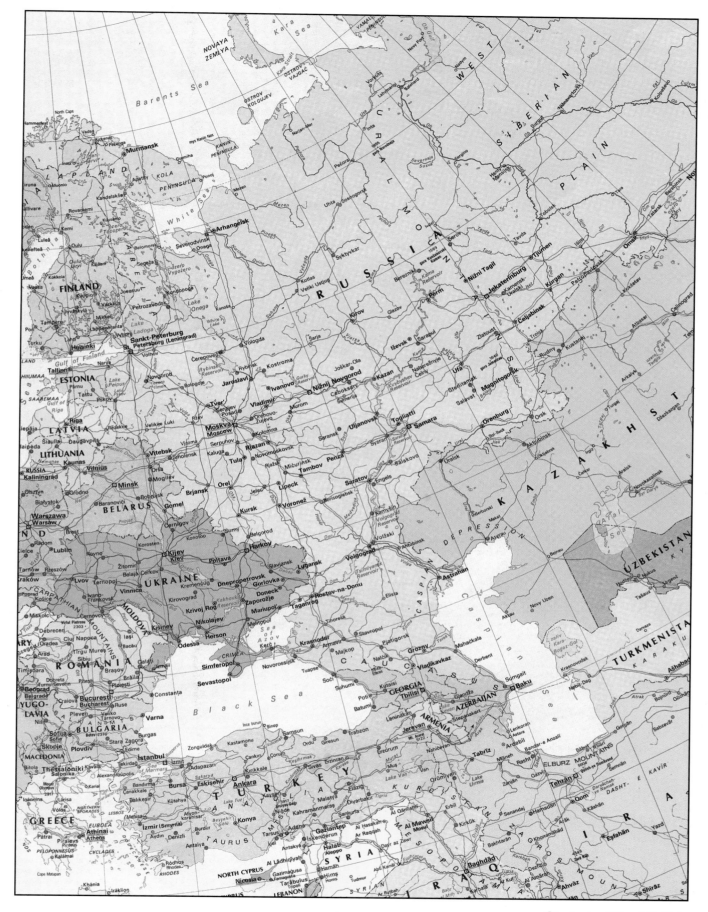

Courtesty of Rand McNally

Almost fifty-eight (58) Million Americans can Claim German Heritage

German-Americans constitute the largest European ethnic group and the historically staunchest supporters of the democratic values. The results of the 1990 U.S. Census indicate that the total U.S. population was 248,709,873 at that time, with the five major heritage groups and their percentages of the total:

Europeans in the United States

Germans	57,947,374	23.3 %
Irish	38,739,518	15.6 %
British	32,655,779	13.1 %
Italian	14,714,939	5.9 %
Polish	9,366,106	3.8 %

Americans of German Heritage by State

State	Total Population	German Pop.	% by State
California	29,760,021	4,935,147	16.58%
Pennsylvania	11,881,643	4,314,762	33.31%
Ohio	10,847,155	4,067,840	37.50%
Illinois	11,430,602	3,326,248	29.10%
Texas	16,986,510	2,949,686	17.36%
New York	17,990,455	9,898,888	16.11%
Michigan	9,295,297	266,179	28.68%
Wisconsin	4,891,769	2,630,680	53.78%
Florida	12,937,296	2,410,257	18.63%
Indiana	5,544,159	2,084,667	37.60%
Minnesota	4,375,099	2,020,975	46.19%
Missouri	5,117,073	1,843,299	36.02%
New Jersey	7,730,188	1,407,956	18.21%
Iowa	2,776,755	1,394,542	50.22%
Washington	4,866,692	1,389,947	28.56%
Maryland	4,781,468	1,218,257	25.48%
Virginia	6,187,358	1,186,056	19.17%
North Carolina	6,628,637	1,110,581	16.75%
Colorado	3,294,394	1,063,694	32.29%
Kansas	2,477,574	968,078	39.07%
Oregon	2,842,321	878,555	30.91%
Arizona	3,665,228	878,088	23.96%
Georgia	6,478,216	810,165	12.51%
Kentucky	3,685,296	798,001	21.65%
Nebraska	1,578,395	794,911	50.36%
Tennessee	4,877,185	724,059	14.85%
Oklahoma	3,145,585	714,184	22.70%
Louisiana	4,219,973	507,453	12.03%
South Carolina	3,486,703	500,089	14.34%
Massachusetts	6,016,425	497,462	8.27%
West Virginia	1,793,477	468,927	26.15%
Connecticut	3,287,116	450,247	13.70%
Alabama	4,040,587	430,442	10.65%
Arkansas	2,350,725	400,234	17.03%
South Dakota	696,004	355,102	51.02%
North Dakota	638,800	324,923	50.87%
Utah	1,722,850	299,414	17.38%
Montana	799,065	285,385	35.71%
Nevada	1,201,833	279,693	23.27%
Idaho	1,006,749	278,615	27.67%
New Mexico	1,515,069	234,000	15.44%
Mississippi	2,573,216	224,674	8.73%
Wyoming	453,588	158,469	34.94%
Alaska	500,043	127,103	23.11%
New Hampshire	1,109,252	118,003	10.64%
Maine	1,227,928	108,859	8.87%
Hawaii	1,108,229	102,714	9.27%
Rhode Island	1,003,464	73,425	7.32%
Vermont	562,758	59,090	10.50%
District of Columbia	606,900	39,218	6.46%
Totals Stats	248,709,873	57,947,374	23.30%

Some Prominent German Americans

Hannah Arendt	1906-1971	Social Philosopher
Wernher von Braun	1912-1977	Rocket Scientist
Walter Percy Chrysler	1875-1940	Automobiles
Marlene Dietrich	1901-1995	Singer, Actress
Everett McKinley Dirksen	1896-1969	Illinois Senator
Albert Einstein	1879-1955	Physicist
Dwight D. Eisenhower	1890-1969	34th President
Clark Gable	1901-1960	Film Star
Henry Louis Gehring	1903-1941	Baseball Player
Oscar Hammerstein II	1895-1960	Lyricist
Milton Hershey	1857-1945	Chocolate Mfgr.
Herbert Clark Hoover	1874-1964	31st President
Grace Kelly	1929-1982	Actress
Henry Kissinger	1923-	Secretary of State
Thomas Mann	1875-1955	Novelist
Chester W. Nimitz	1885-1966	Naval Commander
John Pershing	1860-1948	General WW I
Norman Schwarzkopf	1935-	General Gulf War
Robert Wagner, Jr.	1910-	New York Mayor
Robert F. Wagner	1877-1953	U.S. Senetor
Frank P. Zeidler	1912-	Milwaukee Mayor

For a more complete list of Distinguished German Americans see also the book by Charles R. Haller, Heritage Books, Inc., Bowie, MD 20718, 1995.

German Americans of Today
Who Are They?

By Ernst Ott

When we speak of "German Americans of Today", we refer primarily to first and second generations as well as descendants of older generations. The last census of 1990 revealed that about 57 million Americans stated to be wholly or partially of German descent and German Americans represent the largest European ethnic segment in our country.

Most first generation German Americans (born overseas) have been quickly assimilated in the American mainstream. They established strong roots in their new homeland and America became their new "Heimat".

They often started from scratch, bringing with them only their ingenuity and willingness to work hard. Many were forced from their ancestral homes by the aftermath of World War I and World War II that left Germany dismembered and the German image badly tarnished.

In America, the disastrous consequences of the two wars left the German American community in a rather fragmented state, particularly at the end of World War II. As a result of strong anti-German sentiments, German language teaching in schools was dropped, German institutions closed down, and many German societies dissolved. American citizens of German descent, suspected of pro-German sympathies were, often without due process, interned and kept interned up to 3 years after the war ended. By then even German POWs were already released and shipped back home.

A number of German American societies were able to survive the war, e.g. Gesangvereine as well as cultural and social societies that stressed their strong anti-"Third Reich" sympathies.

It was the large-scale immigration waves of the 50s and 60s that provided the blood transfusion for these societies and led to the formation of new, first generation immigrant organizations such as the German American National Congress (D.A.N.K. = Deutsch Amerikanischer National Kongress), VDAK/USA = Vereinigtes Deutsch Amerikanisches Komitee, and others.

At the time of the Korean and Vietnam wars the immigration influx started to slow down and eventually became just a trickle. Societies' growth began to stagnate. Today, however, it is encouraging to see descendants of older generations becoming more aware and appreciative of their German heritage. Most of the new society members come from, and organizations are formed by these descendants that may not even speak German anymore but want to nurture and promote their heritage.

Much has been written about the early immigrants of colonial times starting with the first organized group of 13 Mennonite settlers from Krefeld in 1683 and the following immigration waves over a period of over 300 years. There is, however, relatively little documentation available that deals with German Americans of the first and second generations or even older generations that today actively cultivate and promote their heritage.

German Americans can be proud of their heritage. They have contributed greatly to the strong cultural and economic fiber of our nation. The present generation is building on the strong foundation our ancestors have laid down.

To these German Americans of today we want to devote and dedicate this book. We want to document their histories, their tribulations and triumphs. We want to honor their contributions to America's society, culture and economy - and their efforts to preserve our heritage.

Deutschamerikaner Von Heute
Wer Sind Sie?

Von Ernst Ott

Wenn wir von den "Deutschamerikanern von Heute" reden dann verstehen wir darunter erste und zweite Generationen (Neueinwanderer sowie die Nachfahren älterer Generationen). Während die Volkszählung vom Jahre 1990 ergab, daß ungefähr 57 Millionen Amerikaner entweder ganz oder teils deutscher Abstammung sind, so befassen sich nur ein Bruchteil davon mit dem Deutschtum. Nichtsdestoweniger stellen sie in unserem Lande die größte Volksgruppe aus Europa dar.

Es wurde bereits viel über die früheren Einwanderer geschrieben, angefangen mit der ersten organisierten Gruppe von 13 Mennoniten Siedlern aus Krefeld im Jahre 1683 sowie den nachfolgenden Einwanderungswellen über mehr als 300 Jahre hinweg. Aber die Dokumentation über die erste, zweite und etwas ältere Generationen, die noch heute ihr Deutschtum pflegen, ist sehr dürftig.

Dar erste und zweite Weltkrieg mit seinen verheerenden Folgen, besonder gegen Ende des zweiten Weltkrieges, waren die Gründe, daß sich die deutschamerikanische Volksgruppe in einem zersplitterten Zustand befand. Die anti-deutsche Einstellung der Bevölkerung führte auch dazu, daß das Lehren der deutschen Sprache in den Schulen eingestellt, deutsch Institutionen geschlossen und viele Organisationen aufgelöst wurden. Amerikanische Staatsbürger deutscher Abstammung und der pro-deutschen Gesinnung verdächtigt, internierte man, oft ohne ein rechtliches Verfahren, zum Tiel bis über 3 Jahre nach Kriegsende hinaus. Zu diesem Zeitpunkt hatte man schon deutsche Kriegsgefangene wieder in ihre Heimat entlassen.

Eine Anzahlt deutschamerikanischer Vereine überlebten den Krieg, z.G. Gesangvereine und Organisationen, die ihre Antipathie gegenüber dem Dritten Reich betonten. Es waren jedoch die großen Einwanderungswellen der 50er and 60er Jahre, die diesen Organisationen eine Bluttransfusion brachten und neue Enwanderervereine gründeten, so z.B. den German American National Congress (D.A.N.K. = Deutsch Amerikanischer National Kongress), Vereinigtes Deutsch Amerikanisches Kommitee usw.

Die Kinder dieser Generation assimilierten sich schnell in die amerikanische Gesellschaft (oder auch "Schmelztiegel genannt). Nur eine kleine Minderheit beschäftigte sich aktiv in den deutsch-amerikanischen Vereinen.

Mit dem Beginn der Korea and Vietnam Konflikte begann jedoch der Einwandererstrom zu verlangsamen und wurde zu einem kleinen Rinnsal. Das Wachstum der Vereine begann zu stagnieren. Es ist aber ermutigend, daß heute die Nachkommen älterer Generationen sich wieder ihrer Herkunft bewußt werden und auf ihr deutsches Erbgut stolz sind. Neue Vereinsmitglieder kommen zum größten Teil aus diesen Generationen, und sie sind es auch die neue Vereine gründen oder jedenfalls Verbesserungen machen. Oft sprechen sie nicht einmal mehr die deutsche Sprache, aber sie wollen ihr Deutschtum weiter pflegen und verbreiten.

Diesen "Amerikanern von Heute" widmen wir dieses Buch. Wir wollen ihre Geschichte, ihre Schwierigkeiten, aber auch Triumphe dokumentieren. Wir wollen ihre Beiträge zur amerikanischen Gesellschaft, Kultur and Wirtschaft, sowie ihre Bestrebungen ihr Deutschtum zu pflegen, anerkennen und ehren.

Gemütlichkeit and Spaß go hand in hand!

Both are favorite German pass times. Gemütlichkeit a little less hectic than Spaß. To have Spaß, means to have fun, an active leisure activity.

Typical Gemütlichkeit is being with friends, talking over a beer or a cup of coffee, usually after work in a cozy atmosphere. Twosomes or more somes are OK, but not a big party.

Germans also like to have lots of Spaß, like at the Oktoberfest, the Wine Fests, Karneval, dancing, picnics and celebrations.

Try it, you'll like it!

From the Office of the Mayor

Dear Friends,

Welcome to Chicago! We are delighted you are visiting our city.

While you are here, you will experience Chicago's marvelous attractions, elegant accommodations, outstanding restaurants, renowned architecture, multicultural neighborhoods and beautiful lake front parks and beaches. More importantly, you will discover Chicago's unsurpassed hospitality which keeps visitors coming back again and again.

Visitors to Chicago will find activities to suit every taste. From lakefront festivals and ethnic parades to outdoor concerts and neighborhood fairs, Chicago offers a variety of exciting events year-round.

Please visit our Information Booth in the landmark Chicago Cultural Center for free brochures and information about our worldclass city. Friendly visitor information representatives will assist you in planning a wonderful Chicago tour.

Enjoy your stay in Chicago; we hope you will visit again soon.

Liebe Gäste,

Willkommen in Chicago! Wir freuen uns sehr, Sie in unserer Stadt begrüßen zu dürfen.

Während Ihres Aufenthaltes werden Sie die herausragenden Attraktionen von Chicago, elegante Unterkünfte, erlesene Restaurants, die berühmte Architektur, multikulturelle Stadtviertel und die wonderschönen Parks und Strände am See kennenlernen. Noch mehr beeindrucken wird Sie aber die beispiellose Gastfreundschaft unserer Stadt, die die Besucher veranlaßt, immer wieder zu uns zurückzukommen.

Besucher unserer Stadt finden Aktivitäten für jeden Geschmack. Von Festspielen am See und Paraden, die die Herkunft ethnischer Gruppen würdigen, bis zu Freiluftkonzerten und Volksfesten in den einzelnen Stadtvierteln bietet Chicago das gane Jahr über eine Vielfalt unterhaltsamer Veranstaltungen.

Besuchen Sie bitte unseren Informaitonsstand im Chicago Cultural Center, einem der Wahrzeichen unserer Stadt, und lassen Sie sich kostenlose Broschüren und Unterlagen über unsere Weltstadt geben. Die freundlichen Mitarbeiter dieser Besucherzentrale werden Ihnen gern bei der Planung einer unterhaltsamen Besichtigungstour helfen.

Ich wünsche Ihnen einen unvergeßlichen Aufenthalt in Chicago und hoffe, daß Sie uns bald wieder besuchen.

Mit freundlichem Gruß

Richard M. Daley
Bürgermeister Mayor

Chicagoland

a world-class Metropolis

U.S. President Bill Clinton greeting Ernst Ott, National President, D.A.N.K. at the White House Oval Office

DANK

The German American National Congress

Marching in the Philadelphia Steuben Parade

D.A.N.K., der Deutsch - Amerikanische National Kongress, hat sich die folgende Ziele gesetzt:

- Zusammenschluß aller Deutsch- Amerikaner.

- Stärkung und Förderung der Freundschaft zwischen USA und Deutschland.

- Eintreten für ein positives Deutschlandbild in USA durch Fernsehen, Presse und in der allgemeinen Öffentlichkeit.

- Kinder und Erwachsene in deutscher Kultur, Sprache und Geschichte zu unterrichten.

- Mitglieder in US-Bürgerrechten zu unterrichten und aktives Interesse für überparteiliche amerikanische Politik zu fördern.

- Stolz für unser Deutsches Erbe zu erwecken.

German Parliament Delegation Visiting D.A.N.K. Weekend School

Honorary National President Willy Scharpenberg and Mrs. Scharpenberg, D.A.N.K. Benefactors

D.A.N.K.

Ernst Ott, right, presenting "Da waren Deutsche auch dabei" plaque to former Bundespräsident Richard von Weizsäcker

D.A.N.K. Chapter Club House in Benton Harbor, Michigan

D.A.N.K. , the German-American National Congress works to:

- Represent, as a nationwide organization, all German-Americans on a national level.

- Foster friendship between the United States and Germany.

- Preserve the German language, customs and culture.

- Educate children and adults in German culture, language and history .

- Instruct D.A.N.K. members in the principles of American citizenship and encourage a general interest in American politics.

- Encourage pride in all German-Americans and interested supporters for the German heritage.

From left: Consul Scholz, German Consulate General, Chicago; Walter Geissler, Chapter President, Milwaukee, WI; Siegfried Reinke, Chapter President Chicago North, and Honorary National President Willy Scharpenberg at the Willy Scharpenberg Museum. All are recipients of the Federal Cross of Merit of Germany.

GERMAN-AMERICAN NATIONAL CONGRESS
4740 N. Western Avenue, Chicago IL 60625
Tel: 773-275-1100   Fax: 773-275-4010

Folk dancers and folk singers, Milwaukee Chapter

Die vollbesetzte Kirche ist ein Zeugnis der Hingabe mit der die Gemeinde ihr Deutschtum pflegt and ehrt.

German American Day in Chicago

While the main focus of German American day has been Washington with its White House and German Embassy and Senate receptions, German Americans throughout the country also celebrated the even in their own dignified fashion.

Chicago, the heartland of the nation has one of the major German American communities that observes German American Day in a festive way.

The "Deutsche Tag Vereinigung" which comprises most German American societies traditionally congregates at the city's St. Benedict's church for a 2 hour program that features, aside from the religious service, a musical program presented by the various choirs as well as speeches by personalities from the state and city governments, the German Consulate General and the German American community.

The standing room only attendance at the church documents the fervor with which Chicago's German Americans treasure their heritage.

Deutschamerikanischer Tag in Chicago

Während das Hauptaugenmerk des deutschamerikanischen Tages in Washington ist mit all den Empfängen im Weissen Haus, dem Senat und der deutschen Botschaft, so feiern Deutschamerikaner im ganzen Lande ebenfalls diesen Tag in ihrer eigenen, würdigen Art.

Chicago, im Herzen Amerikas, hat eine der größten deutschamerikanischen Gemeinden und begeht den German American Day in festlicher Weise.

Die Deutsche Tag - Vereinigung, der die meisten deutschamerikanischen Organisationen in Raume Chicago angehören, versammelt sich in der St. Benedict Kirche zu einem Zweistundenprogramm, das außer dem Gottesdienst, eine musiklaische Einlage der verschiedenen Chöre sowie Ansprachen von Persönlichkeiten der Staats- und Stadtbehörden, dem deutschen Generalkonsulat und der deutschamerikanischen Gemeinde darbietet.

D.A.N.K. Fox Valley - The Fun loving Germans
William Fuchs, President

DANK Chapter Fox Valley 08 was founded in 1967 and covers the Far Western Chicago Suburbs and the Fox River Valley. Activities range from three dances per year, picnics, bus tours, cruises and other fun outings to a German language school, Chapter Newsletter and German video rentals and conversions.
Call us at 630/830-9120

German American Day in Chicago

Text and photos by Ernst Ott

Erich Himmel, President of the Deutscher Tag-Vereinigung, greets his guests, while surrounded by many beautiful flags.

Among the honored guests are Father Bob Heidenreich of St. Benedictine Church; Irene Rotter, Vice President, Deutsche Tag - Vereinigung; Eugene Schulter, Chicago Alderman; Consul General Gabriele von Malsen-Tilborch and Rudi Dick, President, Nordamerikanischer Sängerbund.

Colorful club flags are being presented.

The men's chorus consists of members from many singing societies in the Chicagoland area.

St. Benedict Church on Chicago's North Side.

The ladies, too, come from far and near to sing their beautiful hymns.

UNITED GERMAN AMERICAN SOCIETIES OF GREATER CHICAGO

serving all German Americans since 1920

German Day Association 1997 Front Row from left to right, Helmut Mueller, Irene Rotter, President Erich M. Himmel, Manfred Josellis, Marianne Wehrle, Hans Bernd. Second Row Emil Reiter, John Kraus, Anna Rusheinsky, Joseph Rotter, Inge Himmel, Helga Zettle, Henrietta Baltes, Elizabeth Kraus, Helen Meiszner. Third Row Robert Storch, Bill Blatter, Harold Kekstadt, Carol A. Himmel, Richard Guenther, Bill Milleker, and Joyce Csapo. Not Pictured Nick Kreiling, and Horst Stabenow.

Staging for the Steuben Parade.

A happy crowd at German American Fest, Lincoln and Western Avenues, 1984.

Steuben Parade reviewing stand 1995 from left: Deutsche Tag Vereinigung President Erich Himmel, German Consul Renate Friedemann, Alderman Eugene Schulter with Mayor Richard M. Daley.

United German American Societies

Greetings from the Windy City and the United German American Societies of Greater Chicago

We are the umbrella organization of 78 active Germanic clubs and societies with an estimated membership of 9,600 men, women and children.

The Chicagoland region, about 100 miles by 60 miles in size, is home to about 8 million people, among them 2.3 million inhabitants with German names, 28.75%. More than 400 businesses, dealing with Germany, large and small - industrial, commercial and service companies - are giving this region an industrious and balanced work ethnic. This is indeed a good place to work, live and spend ones quality leisure time.

U.G.A.S. of Greater Chicago coordinates the events calendar of its member clubs and societies and organizes a number of major festivities in the City:

The annual von Steuben Parade is the German American event of the year. It is held the middle of September, when hundreds of participants march, dance, play music or ride the many beautiful floats down Dearborn Avenue. Thousands line the street and join the festivities later at the "Lincoln Mall" German-American Fest.

On October 6th, the German-American Day is celebrated with a solemn service at St. Benedicts Church in nearby North

Chicago in the presence of a forest of club flags and regalia, and to the music of several choirs of men and women and children's groups. A keynote speaker gives the day's celebration a special meaning.

Society meetings are held at the U.G.A.S. headquarter in Niles, every 2nd Monday of the month.

The United German American Societies of Greater Chicago maintain close relations to the German Consulate in Chicago, the Chicago City Government, the Chicagoland and German-American Chambers of Commerce, the press and broadcast media, as well as with German-American clubs and societies in the midwest and from coast to coast.

"It is our hope and prayer that we shall be successful in maintaining our German heritage, customs and culture for many years to come", says Erich Himmel.

We cordially invite all readers of this message and their friends to come to Chicagoland and visit our German American festivals and events, and enjoy our ethnic foods and music.

Auf Wiedersehen! Tschuess!
Ade! Bis bald! See you soon!

Erich Himmel
President
United German American
Societies of Greater Chicago

General von Steuben reenactment.

German American Day celebration at St. Benedicts Church, 1996.

# of Greater Chicago
serving all German Americans since 1920

Deutsche Tag-Vereinigung im Großraum Chicago seit 1920

Grüße aus der Windigen Stadt und von der "Deutsche Tag Vereinigung" aus dem Großraum Chicago.

Wir sind die Dachorganisation für 78 deutschstämmige Vereine mit einer geschätzten Mitgliederzahl von 9.600.

Die "Chicagoland" Region, etwa 160 km Nord-Süd und 100 km breit, ist Heimat von 8 Millionen Menschen, darunter 2.3 Mill. mit deutschen Namen, also 28.75%. Über 400 Firmen aller Größen machen mit Deutschland Geschäfte, einschließlich Industrie -, Handels -, Gewerbe - und Einzelhandelsbetriebe, sowie viele Dienstleistungsunternehmen. Sie alle helfen, dieser Region ein geschäftiges und ausgewogenes Arbeitsklima zu geben. In der Tat ist dieses ein guter Standort zum Leben, Wirken und eine interessante Freizeit zu gestalten.

Die Deutsche Tag Vereinigung von Groß-Chicago coordiniert den großen Vereinskalender und organisiert selbst eine Anzahl von bedeutenden Festlichkeiten in der Stadt:

Die jährliche "Von Steuben Parade" ist das Fest des Jahres der Deutsch-Amerikaner. Es findet immer Mitte September statt, wenn Hunderte von Beteiligten marschieren, tanzen, singen und musizieren oder auf den vielen originellen, bunten Festwagen mitfahren oder diese auf der Dearborn Avenue begleiten. Tausende säumen die Straße und besuchen dann das große German American Fest am Lincoln Mall.

Am 6. Oktober wird der "Deutsch Amerikanische Tag" mit einem feierlichen Festprogramm in der St. Benediktskirche, auch an der Nordseite Chicagos, begangen. Ein Wald von Vereinsfahnen und - Standarten zieren den Raum, mehrere gemischte - und Kinderchöre singen, und ein Gastsprecher gibt dem ganzen Fest eine besondere Note.

Regelmäßig treffen sich Präsidenten und Vertreter der Vereine am 2. Montag im "Deutsche Tag Vereinigung" Hauptquartier in Niles.

Steuben Parade reviewing stand, from right: German Consul General Gabriele von Malsen-Tilborch, Mayor Richard M. Daley and Carol Himmel.

At German American Fest.

Steuben Parade reviewing stand, from left: Announcer George Lieder, UGASGC President Erich Himmel, Chicago Mayor Richard M. Daley, Alderman Eugene Schulter, Irene Rotter, VP, and Ernst Ott, D.A.N.K. National President.

Special words of welcome from Erich Himmel and guests of honor at the German American Fest.

United German American Societies of Greater Chicago serving all German Americans since 1920

continued…

Die "Deutsche Tag Vereinigung' unterhält ein enges Verhältnis mit dem deutschen Konsulat, dem hiesigen Bürgermeisteramt und dem Stadtrat, sowie mit der Chicagoland - und der deutsch-amerikanischen Handelskammer. Natürlich ist man auch mit der Presse und den Radio und Fernseh Stationen bekannt und hält Kontakt mit anderen Vereinen im Mittelwesten und im ganzen Land.

"Es ist unsere Hoffnung und unser ausdrücklicher Wunsch, daß wir erfolgreich sind, das deutsche Erbe, die Sitten und Gebräuche, und unsere Kultur für viele weitere Jahre zu erhalten", sagt Erich Himmel.

Wir laden alle Leser herzlich ein mit ihren Freunden nach Chicago zu kommen und an unseren deutsch-amerikanischen Festlichkeiten und Aktivitäten teilzunehmen und unsere gute deutsche Kost und Volksmusik zu genießen.

Children's Karneval Celebration

Greetings from our Karneval Friends

"Festzelt" at Lincoln Mall

Chicago's First Christkindl Market

Organized by the German American Chamber of Commerce of the Midwest

German Consul Genral von Malsen-Tilborch addressed the visitors during Opening Ceremonies, as did Mayor Richard M. Daley, Nuremberg Mayor Scholz and Christian Röhr, Managing Director of the German American Chamber of Commerce of the Midwest.

35 authentic Nuremberg sales and display stands offered German toys, crafts and food.

At the TV Studios of NDR, Nord-Deutscher Rundfunk, in Hamburg, Sister City of Chicago.

DANK - Spatzen singing for Chicago.

D.A.N.K. - Spatzen singing for Chicago

Chicago greets Hamburg ! The DANK-Spatzen on the floating stage in Hamburg's Harbor, where they delighted thousands of citizens and visitors. with their Chicago voices

... under the joyful leadership of founder Alexandra Pradella-Ott.

Photos by Ernst Ott

Österreichischer gemischter Chor

Eine Gruppe von österreichischen Amerikanern gründeten 1979 einen kleinen Chor, um die österreichischen Volkslieder so zu singen, wie es in den verschieden Provinzen der Heimat üblich war.

So enstand ein netter gemischter Chor mit einer aktiven Mitgliedschaft von etwa fünfzig Sängern. Der Chor bringt außer österreichischen Volksliedern auch leicht klassische Musik, deutsche Lieder und eine kleine Auswahl von englischen Weisen.

Man übt jeden Mittwoch um 20:00 Uhr im Kolping Zentrum an der Elston Avenue in Chicago. Dort heißen wir neue Sänger willkommen, auch ledige Menschen und junge Paare - einige unserer Mitglieder sind Nicht - Österreicher, die auch die Sprache nicht sprechen, aber sich dennoch an dem Singen und der Gesellschaft erfreuen.

Kommen Sie zu uns als Sänger und als Freund.

Austrian Mixed Chorus

Founded in 1979 by a group of Austria - Americans for the purpose of keeping the Austrian folk songs alive as they were sung in the various provinces of their home land.

The idea grew into a viable mixed chorus with an active membership of about 50 singers. The chorus presents in addition to the Austrian folk songs, light classical music, German "Lieder" and a small selection of songs in English.

Practice is every Wednesday at 8 pm at the Kolping Center on Elston Avenue in Chicago. We would welcome new singers, single people and young couples - we have a number of non-Austrians who do not speak the language but enjoy singing and the fun we have as a group.

Join us in song or just for fun !

Trude Nika, Secretary,   Telephone: 630 960 1123
Walter Fleischmann, President, Tel: 847 696 2878

Henry P. Glass, President   *Loretta Fleischmann, Vice President*

THE AMERICAN FRIENDS OF AUSTRIA

an organization
composed of people who are what the name implies.
Americans who have ties to Austria, personal, travel, or cultural.
Our programs strive for a happy balance between entertainment with an Austrian flair
and cultural enrichment through art, music, folklore tradition, and historic interaction.

Our main philanthropic activity is the annual sponsorship of an American student to
study in Austria for a summer. This is funded from the proceeds of a lottery for 2 round
trip tickets to Vienna (donated by Lufthansa) at our annual January
Viennesa Ball with Franz Benteler and his Royal Strings
in the Gold Coast Room of the Drake Hotel — Downtown Chicago

For information about our scholarship fund or attending Viennese Ball,
contact: Loretta Fleischmann
773-583-8288 or 847-696-2878

Berliner Bären
Berlin Bears, Inc.

Berlin Bears

In 1958, the "Berlin Bears, Inc" club was established in Chicago. It was very active for 15 years, but then declined to a hand full of members. Just before the fall of the "wall" in Berlin the club began its renascence, and under the able leadership of President Günter and Secretary Liesel Jacoby, began the club's steady membership growth in October 1990.

With a musical revue in May 1990, under the theme "The Gate Is Open" a new era was born. That fall a new board of directors began a steady campaign for Berlin Bears membership. Today, there are 200 native and "baptized" Berliner Bären which is considered a small wonder in today's club circles.

Scene from the Annual Berlin Revue

Photos: G. Jacoby

At the Berliner Picnic

The Club is well organized with monthly meetings; short business reports and discussions followed by social activities. January has its "Glühwein" (mulled wine) evening; a Berlin Costume dance in February; line dancing lessons in March, etc. Our musical revue rehearsals start in January, and at the Spring Ball, on the first Saturday in May, our guests get one hour of entertainment. A 250 piece raffle always assures many winners. June and July are considered club vacation. It ends with a picnic in August, then an active participation at the Steuben Parade in September. The

blessing of new members with genuine "Spree Water" is a special event, so is the Pork Shank Dinner and Autumn Dance in October. The season ends with a beautiful Christmas Party.

Guests are always welcome at the Berliner Bear functions, everybody can become a member. By the blessing with "Spree Water" everyone can become a Berliner!

We gratefully acknowledge our main sponsors:

Delta Tech Mold, Inc., Klaus Cisliek
John & Christel Limberger
Helm Tool Co., Inc., Helmut Mueller
Spiess Design, Inc., Dr. Karin Walter-Spiess
Country Cast Products Inc., Hans & Elsa Weinert

Der Vereinskalender wird in der "Eintracht" veröffentlicht.

BERLINER BÄREN

Fast vierzig Jahre zurück, in 1958 wurde in Chicago, Illinois der Verein "Berlin Bears, Inc." gegründet und hatte für mindestens 15 Jahre einen Platz im Chicagoer Vereinsleben. Zwischen 1973 und 1989 war die Mitgliedzahl auf eine handvoll zurückgegangen, aber dann im Oktober 1989 begann der neue Aufschwung. Der Fall der "Mauer" hat natürlich sehr dazu beigetragen! Im folgenden Frühjahr fand der erste Ball mit musikalischer Revue statt und unser Motto hies "Das Tor ist auf." Im selben Jahr im Herbst begann mit dem neugewählten Vorstand ein Aufschwung des Klubs mit einem Mitgliederwachstum auf zwei Hundert, und im Vereinsleben Chicago wird dies als ein kleines Wunder betrachtet.

Der Verein ist gut organisiert. Monatliche Treffen bestehen aus kurzen geschäftlichen Sitzungen und dann immer etwas unterhaltsames hinterher: Im Januar Glühweinabend, dann Berliner Kostümfest, kleiner Tanzkursus, usw. Die Revuetruppe beginnt im Januar mit Programmaufstellung und Proben, damit sie

am ersten Samstag im Mai jährlich ihre Gäste zum Staunen und Lachen bringen können. Eine 250-Preis Tombola verspricht immer viele Gewinner.Nach der Sommerpause ist im August das Picknick und eine aktive Teilnahme in der Steuben Parade im September, Spreetaufe/Eisbeinessen/Herbsttanz im Oktober und zum Schluss eine schöne Weihnachtsfeier.

Gäste sind den Berliner Bären immer willkommen, auch zu den Versammlungen und jeder kann Berliner Bär werden; wer nicht echter Berliner ist wird mit Wasser aus der Spree getauft!

Mitteilungsblatt der Berliner Bären
Berlin Bears, Inc.
902 South Robert Drive
Mt. Prospect, IL 60056
Telephone: 847/593-8349

Berliner group at the Steuben Parade

At the dedication of the Willy Scharpenberg Museum

Illinois Governor Jim Edgar receiving book "Chicagoland"
from Chapter President Siegfried Reinke

DANK CHAPTER CHICAGO NORTH

The "Deutsches Haus" is a German American Cultural Center owned and operated by its members. The 6-story building is the focal point of the German-American community in Chicago.

It is the home of the Executive Offices of D.A.N.K., the German American National Congress, the Willy Scharpenberg Museum, a weekend language school, library, large ball room, meeting rooms for over one dozen German American societies and commercial enterprises.

WE ARE PROUD TO SERVE OUR GERMAN- AMERICAN COMMUNITY

Siegfried Reinke,
President and Board.

DANK CHAPTER CHICAGO NORTH Deutsches Haus
4740 N. Western Avenue, Chicago, IL 60625

At a press conference from left Willy Scharpenberg, Siegfried Reinke and Werner Baroni, formally Amerika Woche

Enjoying their company are Alexandra Pradella - Ott, Josef (Jupp) Baumann, Elsbeth M. Seewald, former National President, and Chapter President Siegfried Reinke. All are recipients of the of the Federal Cross of Merit of Germany

Official visit at the D.A.N.K. weekend school

After a performance at the D.A.N.K. Deutsches Haus

Most festive balls of D.A.N.K. Chicago West are the traditional New Years Party ...

...and the May Dance.

GERMAN-AMERICAN NATIONAL CONGRESS

DEUTSCH-AMERIKANISCHER NATIONAL KONGRESS
GRUPPE CHICAGO-WEST & WESTLICHE VORORTE

DANK CHAPTER CHICAGO WEST
Founded 1959

We serve DANK members and friends of Chicago's western suburbs and beyond. Our programs include cultural and social activities. The "Vorstand" meets monthly.

DANK Chicago West enjoys a friendly relationship with other German American societies and supports their activities as well. We also participate in the annual Steuben Parade and German American Day observances.

Our 35th anniversary celebration was a festive event and a milestone in our organization's history..

DANK Chicago West hosted the National Convention of 1993 in Chicago's western suburbs.

DANK CHICAGO WEST INVITES GERMAN AMERICANS AND THEIR FRIENDS TO JOIN US AND PARTICIPATE IN OUR ACTIVITIES.

Siegfried Endlichhofer, President and Board.

GERMAN-AMERICAN NATIONAL CONGRESS
DANK CHICAGO WEST
7431 Arbor Avenue, La Grange, Illinois 60525
630 / 246-6824

A group of D.A.N.K. West members, 1997.

The Board of D.A.N.K. Chicago West, sitting are Marianne Endlichhofer and Margot Bauer, standing from left are Harold Pitz, Siegfried Endlichhofer, Ludwig Schäfer and Annelise Pitz.

Society of Danube Swabians

• Cultural Center •

625 Seegers Road • Des Plaines, IL • 60016 • Tel: 847/296-6172

Youth Group
Jugendgruppe

The Society of the Danube Swabians was organized in 1953 for the purpose of assisting and educating the new immigrants after World War II. Having been evicted or displaced by Communism, the Danube Swabians, a German ethnic minority from Romania, Hungary and the former Jugoslavia, had been living in refugee camps in Germany and Austria after the War until a special immigration law was passed for those refugees to enter into the U.S.A.

Those first immigrants created a Youth Group in which their young could meet and socialize. This proved to be a very successful venture, giving the youth some stability and socialization opportunities. Today the Youth Group participates on many occassions within the Society, the German-American Community and within civic organizations. Their trips nationwide and to Europe are funded through bake sales, brunches and other fundraising activities.

The Society of the Danube Swabians also opened a weekend school in Chicago for the children of the immigrants so that they could associate with their peers and preserve the language, culture and traditions they had learned from their parents. Other activities such as folk dancing, theater playing, singing and performing at cultural and civic functions throughout the city and state also took place. In the early fifties, up to 350 children attended this weekend school.

A successful soccer program was established within the Society which gave the sportsminded youth an opportunity for that popular activity.

Folk Dancing Group
Trachten und Volkstanz Gruppe

A Ladies Group was organized to help raise funds through bake sales, crafts, dinners and cultural functions for the youth group and the weekend school. Over the years it became an important entity, not only for the socializing, but as a support group for all departments within the organization. The ladies run the indespensible kitchen activities, they keep up the Heimatstube and above all, the customs and traditinos of the Danuabe Swabians. They have proven themselves to be the heart and soul of and the driving force within the Society.

There is a fine choral group within the organization for those who like to sing. The Adult Folk Dancing Group, in their traditional costumes, has enriched the activities of the Society, as well as other cultural programs state- and nationwide. At the monthly gatherings of the

Vereinigung der Donauschwaben

The Board of Directors **Der Vorstand**

enior Citizens, retired persons ave a chance to meet their iends, enjoy a delicious meal nd see films or play cards.

Through its newsletter, NACHRICHTEN, the Society has kept its members informed for over 40 years of the activities within the organization, and developments in their former homelands and the history of their rich traditions and culture. It is a valuable link between all Donauschwaben worldwide.

The Society of the Danube Swabians is proud of its achievements over the past 4 decades. Through its community efforts it has contributed and helped all age groups lead a wholesome and productive life, always being mindful of the great opportunities this country has given them. They have proven to be model citizens and have thus enriched this great country by their contributions.

Die Vereinigung der Donauschwaben wurde im Jahre 1953 gegründet, um den Einwanderern nach dem Zweiten Weltkrieg zu helfen, sich in ihrer neuen Heimat einzuleben. Nachdem die Donauschwaben, Auslandsdeutsche aus Rumänien, Ungarn und dem früheren Jugoslawien, ausgewiesen wurden oder geflüchtet waren, lebten viele in Flüchtlingslagern in Deutschland und Österreich, bis ein neues Einwanderungsgesetz ihnen Gelegenheit gab in die U.S.A. einzuwandern.

Diese ersten Einwanderer haben eine Jugendgruppe gegründet um den jungen Menschen Gelegenheit zu geben sich mit gleichgesinnten Jugendlichen zu treffen. Dies war ein guter Zug, denn die Jugendgruppe der Vereinigung der Donauschwaben diente der einge-wanderten Jugend sich gesellschaftlich zu entwickeln und die überlieferten Traditionen weiterzupflegen. Heute nimmt die Jugendgruppe an vielen Programmen der Vereinigung, sowie in der deutsch-amerikanischen Gemeinschaft und bei öffentlichen Organisationen teil. Die Jugendlichen beteiligen sich auch an verschiedenen Aktivitäten um die Unkosten für ihre Reisen im In-und Ausland zu decken.

Bald nach der Gründung der Vereinigung der Donauschwaben wurde auch eine Wochenendschule eröffnet, in welcher die Kinder der Einwanderer ihre Muttersprache und ihre Sitten und Gebräuche pflegen konnten. Durch Volkstanzen, Theaterspielen, Singen und Auftritte bei kulturellen und öffentlichen Anlässen haben die Kinder ihr Volksgut bewahrt und gleichzeitig

Homeland Museum **Heimat Stube**

Vereinigung der Donauschwaben

Mixed Chorus and Ladies Group

Frauen Gruppe und Gemischter Chor

sich sangfreudige Mitglieder anschließen können, Die Erwachsenen Tanz Gruppe, in ihren schönen Trachten, bereichert das kulturelle Programm der Vereinigung und tritt bei Veranstaltungen in- und außerhalb des Vereines auf. Bei den monatlichen Zusammenkünften der Rentnergruppe haben die Ruheständler Gelegenheit ihre Freunde zu treffen, eine gute Mahlzeit zu genießen, Karten zu spielen oder sich einen schönen, deutschen Film anzusehen.

Durch die NACHRICHTEN, die monatliche Vereinszeitung, werden die Mitgliender der Vereinigung nun schon über 40 Jahre auf dem Laufenden innerhalb der Vereinigung gehalten. Ferner laufen Berichte aus der früheren Heimat und geschichtliche Abhandlungen über das donauschwäbische Thema. Die NACHRICHTEN sind ein wichtiges Bindeglied zwischen den Donauschwaben weltweit.

Die Vereinigung der Donauschwaben ist stolz auf die Errungenschaften der vergangenen 4 Jahrzehnte. Durch die Gemeinschaftsarbeit hat die Vereinigung den Einwanderer in allen Altersgruppen geholfen sich an die neue Heimat, dem Land der unbegrenzten Möglichkeiten, anzupassen und ein inhaltsreiches und produktives Dasein zu führen. Sie haben sich als vorbildliche Bürger gezeigt und durch ihren ethnischen Einfluss zur Bereicherung der Vereinigten Staaten beigetragen.

das Donauschwabentum im Ausland gestärkt. In den fünziger Jahren haben über 350 Kinder die Wochenendschule besucht.

Man gründete auch eine er folgreiche Fussballabteilung für die Sportler, die damals den Fussballsport schon zu schätzen wußten.

Die Frauengruppe wurde gegründet, um die Wochenendschule und die Jugendgruppe zu unterstützen. Gelder wurden durch Kuchenverkauf, Handarbeiten und Veranstaltungen erworben. Im Laufe der Zeit entwickelte sich die Frauengruppe zu einer unent-bährlichen Abteilung, nicht nur für die gesellschaftliche Unterhaltung der Frauen, sondern auch als Stütze für alle Abteilungen. Sie führen die anspruchsvolle Aufgabe in der

Küche, erhalten und erweitern die Heimatstube und fördern die Sitten und Gebräuche der Ahnen. Die Frauengruppe ist das Herz, die

Seele und die treibende Kraft in der Vereinigung.

Innerhalb der Vereinigung besteht auch ein Gemischter Chor, dem

Weekend School

Wochenend Schule & Kindergruppe

Our studio is specialized in design and development
of quality gift items in a wide range of applications.

* Corporate executive gifts, customized
* Etched deep-relief metal portraits as awards or recognition plaques
* Minted medallions all sizes and metals
* Lapel pins, pendants of logos and emblems for corporations,
  association, clubs etc.
* Metal etchings of European (16th Century-Merian) and contemporary
  American Cities
* Bar relief or full bust-castings in various metals
* Ethnic flag pins of all nationalities
* Presentation china plates for anniversaries or special events

**Unser Studio ist spezialisiert in Entwurf und
Entwicklung von Qualitäts-Geschenken in
einem weiten Anwendungsbereich.**

* Kunden spezielle Entwürfe
* Tiefgeätzte Relief Portraits
* Geprägte Medaillon, Münzen
* Abzeichen, Anhäger für Firmen, Organisationen, Klubabzeichen
* Metalstiche europäischer Städte 16.Jh (Merian-Stiche)
* Porzelanteller für Jubilare etc.
* Familien-Wappen, Stammbäume
* Ehren, Anerkennungsplaketten
* Führend in Chicago orientierten Geschenken

Collection of typical Mager Metal artifacts
Auswahl von typischen Mager Metal Artikeln

MAGER METAL ART, LTD.

320 S. Cumberland Parkway
Des Plaines, IL 60016

Phone: 847/299-5815 * Fax: 847-299-5802

ST. HUBERTUS
Jagd Club

*Nur jener soll die Büchse tragen,
der nach alter Väter Art
erlernt gerecht zu jagen -
und so zum Jäger ward.*

Der St. Hubertus Club wurde von deutschen
Einwanderern gegründet, um den uralten Beruf zu
Jagen, jetzt ein Sport, auszuüben. Unsere Aufgabe
soll es sein, jagdgerecht zu jagen und die
deutschen Jagdsitten zu pflegen.

The St. Hubertus Club was established by
German immigrants to properly practice the
old vocation of hunting, now considered a
sport. Our objectives are to hunt fair and
safe and to preserve the traditional German
hunting customs.

St. Hubertus Club Vorstand
Board of Directors 1996 - 1997

President....................Gustav Hopp
Vice President...........Wilhelm Antfellner
Protocoll Secretary.....Joseph Uehlein
Schatzmeister ....Walter Boehm
Schießwart ....Armin Hopp
Bummel......................Peter Hopp

Information: 847/297-6894

Weidmanns Heil !
*Gustav Hopp,
President*

Danube-Swabian Cultural Center   Lake Villa, Illinois

Steubenparade

Kindergruppe

Heimatmuseum

American
of German

*D*ie Nachricht von Flucht, Vertreibung, Not und Tod ergriff die
Herzen unserer deutsch-amerikanischen Landsleute sehr schwer, und sie
entschlossen sich ihren Mitmenschen zu helfen. Im September 1944
trafen sich etliche Hauptpersonen von verschiedenen donauschwäbischen
Vereinen, um über die Lage ihrer Landsleute, die Flüchtlinge in den
Lagern in Österreich und Deutschland, zu sprechen und wie zu handeln
ist. Bei diesen Sitzungen wurde beschlossen eine Dachorganisation zu
gründen; diese mußte einen englischen Namen haben, da in 1944 das
Deutschtum in Amerika nicht sehr beliebt war. So enstand die
Entwicklung der AMERICAN AID SOCIETY, eine Hilfsorganisation die
heute noch ihre Pflicht erfüllt und ihrem Namen folglich viele
Unternehmen in allen Erdteilen der Welt unterstützt.

Die Tätigkeit und Leistungen des Vereins, die gute Zusammenarbeit mit
anderen donauschwäbischen Klubs weist auf eine starke
Mitgliederschaft, die immer bestrebt ist die Kultur, Sitten und Gebräuche
der alten Heimat weiter zu erhalten.

Im Vereinsheim an der Milwaukee Avenue in Chicago treffen sich die
Mitglieder jeden 3. Freitag im Monat, sowie die große Kindergruppe,
um ihre deutsche Kultur zu pflegen. Die talentierte Jugendgruppe hat ihr
Beisammensein jeden Freitag, wenn es nötig ist wird auch zweimal in
der Woche geprobt, um die beliebten Volkstänze und Lieder perfekt zu
gestalten. Die Seniorengruppe hat das Vergnügen, sich jeden 2.
Mittwoch im Monat zu unterhalten und über die guten alten Zeiten zu
diskutieren.

Auf dem 15 Acker Picknickgelände in Lake Villa, Illinois befindet sich
das 9 Zimmer große Heimatmuseum, und Bibliothek mit Büchern von
der alten und neuen Heimat. Geliebte Artikel und Gegenstände von
vielen Orten und Städten der Donnauschwaben haben hier ein
liebevolles Heim gefunden. Die Kinder toben sich auf dem Spielplatz
aus, und der Fußballplatz wartet auf eine neue Generation.

Das Nick Pesch Denkmal wurde in den 60ger Jahren für die
Vernichteten, die Gefallenen, die Opfer des 2. Weltkrieges errichtet. An
diesem Platz werden unsere Toten jedes Jahr mit einer Messe,
Kranzniederlegung und sinnlichem Gedenken geehrt.

Die AMERICAN AID SOCIETY OF GERMAN DESCENDANTS
besteht schon 53 Jahre - mehr als ein halbes Jahrhundert unseren
Landsleuten, unserer Kultur, unserem Deutschtum gewidmet

Hans Gebavi, Präsident

ugendgruppe

Aid Society

Descendants

The news of escape, expulsion, need and death deeply touched the hearts of our German-American countrymen and they decided to help their fellow human beings. In September of 1944 numerous leaders from various organizations of Donauschwaben (Swabian settlers on the Danube in Hungary) met to discuss how to respond to the plight of their compatriots, the refugees in the camps in Austria and Germany. In these meetings it was decided to establish an umbrella organization and it had to have an English name, since Germans were not very popular in America in 1944. Thus the AMERICAN AID SOCIETY was created, a benevolent organization that today still fulfills its obligations and, as the name indicates, supports many endeavors in all parts of the world.

The activities and accomplishments of the organization as well as the excellent cooperation with other Donauschwaben clubs indicate a very strong membership. This membership is dedicated to maintaining the culture, traditions and practices of the old country.

The members meet every third Friday of the month at the organization headquarters on Milwaukee Avenue in Chicago. The large children's group also meets here to foster German culture. The talented youth group meets every Friday and when necessary they meet twice a week to rehearse folkdances and songs. The senior group meets every second Wednesday of the month to for a luncheon and to discuss the good old days.

The nine-room heritage museum is located on the 15-acre picnic grounds in Lake Villa, Illinois. The building also houses a library with books from the old and new homeland. Favorite items and objects from many places and cities of the Donauschwaben have found a loving home here. The children play on the playground and the soccer field awaits a new generation.

The Nick Pesch monument was erected in the 1960s to commemorate the destroyed and the fallen: the victims of World War II. Here our dead are honored each year with a mass, a wreath laying ceremony and thoughtful reflection.

Denkmal

The "Future" Marching In The Chicago Steuben Parade

Vorstand und Senioren

The AMERICAN AID SOCIETY OF GERMAN DESCENDANTS has been in existence for 53 years — 53 years dedicated to our compatriots, our culture, and our German heritage.

Hans Gebavi, President

American Aid Society of German Descendants
6540 North Milwaukee Avenue, Chicago, Illinois 60631

The Hamburg - Chicago Club maintains Hanseatic customs, the German language and an active relationship with Hamburg. Its members are encouraged to be good German American citizens and to promote the Sister City program between Hamburg and Chicago.

Der Hamburg-Chicago Klub unterhält hanseatische Bräuche, die deutsche Sprache und eine aktive Verbindung mit Hamburg. Seine Mitglieder sind ermutigt gute deutsch-amerikanische Bürger zu sein und das Partnerschaftsprogramm zwischen den Schwesterstädten Hamburg und Chicago zu fördern.

Hamburg – Chicago's German Sister City
Hamburg – Chicagos deutsche Partnerstadt

Port of Hamburg - 15,000 ocean-going vessels dock in Germany's largest seaport yearly, carrying over 50 million tons of cargo. It is still 65 miles up the Elbe River to the North Sea from here.

Der Hamburger Hafen - 15 000 Ozeanriesen, die über 50 Millionen Tonnen Fracht transportieren, legen Jährlich in Deutschlands größter Hafenstadt an. Von hier sind es noch 104 km weit die Elbe hoch bis zur Nordsee.

Hamburg - interesting, openminded and beautiful. Of this opinion are not only the 1.6 million hanseatic citizens, but also the many visitors who come every year to experience Hamburg.

It may take a little while to discover the charm of this second largest city of the Federal Republic, but it is worth it.

As sister city to Chicago, both metropolis have much in common. Chicago has Lake Michigan, Hamburg the Alster Lake in the heart of the city. Both cities have many bridges, Hamburg more than Venice. Both also feature many green belts and public parks. Hamburg's "Planten un Blomen" for instance, is a 114 acre park only a stone throw from Dammtor Station, a major train and subway stop in the center of the city. This park provides peace and quiet in the bustling downtown area, just like Grant Park does in Chicago.

Hamburg's Hagenbeck Zoo is the darling of all friends of Hamburg, and frequented by young and old.

The harbor, employer of thousands of Hamburgers, prides itself with the most modern container facilities in the world. Hamburg is an expensive but fast harbor, meaning that loading and unloading of ocean vessels occurs around the clock. Freighters are ready to me again in a jiffy.

Hamburg is known as the "Gate to the World", and with 67 consulates, it has the most foreign representative offices of any city in Europe. The international relationship becomes obvious when shopping in the city. Tradition and a contemporary architecture are valued, and so many old department stores and landmark warehouses have changed into elegant shopping centers, offering treasures and rarities from around the world.

More than 2,000 import-export firms keep Hamburg in the vanguard of international trade in the Federal Republic. Industries prominent in Hamburg include space science, aircraft maintenance, shipbuilding, machine tool production, and electronic technology.

Hamburg is the largest media center of Germany publishing several leading newspapers, and magazines, and broadcasting national radio and TV programs. It is home to a number of major advertising agencies.

An international cuisine in many worldclass restaurants caters to discriminating connoisseurs, serving Hamburg's varied specialties, such as "Finkenwerder Scholle".

Hamburg always promoted the arts and cultural events. Its museums, the opera, and many theaters feature world stars, and offer opportunities to young actors and artists, also due to subsidies from the government.

Hamburg has much to offer and it is worth stopping over on your trip through Germany. People are not quite as conservative as told, and the weather is not as bad as some say, just dress for it and you'll be fine.

Hamburg is worth the trip!

View from Lombards bridge across the Inner Alster to the City Hall and Nicolai Church.

Sicht von Lombardsbrücke, die über die Innen-Alster führt, zum Rathaus und zur Nicolaikirche.

HAMBURG - interessant, aufgeschlossen, schön. Dieser Meinung sind nicht nur die 1.5 Mio. Hanseaten, sondern auch die vielen Besucher, die jährlich nach Hanburg kommen.

Es dauert vielleicht etwas Iänger, den Reiz dieser sweitgrößten Stadt der Bundesrepublik zu entdecken, aber es lohnt sich.

Als Partnerstadt von Chicago weisen die beiden Städte viele Ähnlichkeiten auf. Chicago hat den Lake Michigan, Hamburg hat die Alster im Herzen der Stadt. Beide Städte haven viele Brücken (Hamburg hat mehr als Venedig). Beide Städte haven herrliche Grünanlagen und Parks. Hamburg's „Platen un Blomen" z.B., ein 46 ha grosser Park nur einen Steinwurf vom Dammtor Bahnhof entfernt, gibt jedem Besucher Ruhe und Entspannung. Gepflegte Rasen und berrliche Blumenrabatten machen diesen park attraktiv für jedermann.

Hamburg's Zoo „Hagenbeck" das Liebingskind der Hanseaten, zieht Jahr für Jahr Tausende von Besuchern an.

Der Hafen, Arbeitgerber für Tausende von Hambeurgern, hat die modernsten Container-Anlagen der Welt. Hamburg ist als schneller Hafen bekannt. Liegegühren für Schiffe im Hafen sind teuer. Das Be- und Entladen geschieht in 24 Studen rund um die Uhr. In küzester Zeit sind die Schiffe wieder bereit für die nächste Reise.

Hamburg, auch „das Tor zur Welt" genannt, hat mit 76 Konsulaten die meisten ausländieschen Vertretungen in Europa. Die internationale Verbundenheit wird offensichtlich beim Einkaufsbummel. Tradition und zeitgemaesse Architektur haven viele alte Kaufhäuser in elegante „shopping centren" verwadelt. Hier findet man Schätze aus aller Welt.

Über 2,000 Im- und Exportfirmen machen Hanburg zum größten Exportzentrum der Bundesrepublik. Aber auch andere INdustriezweige wählten Hamburg als ihren Standort. Z.B. die Flug- und Raumschiffahrt, Maschienenbau, Elektrotechnik usw. Hamburg ist Deutschland's führendes Media-Zentrum: verschiedene Zeitungen, Magazine, Radio-und Fernsehprogramme sowie Werbefirmen sind heir Zuhause.

Für das leibliche Wohl sorgen die vielen, gepflegten Restaurants. Neben hamburger Spezialitäten, wie Finkenwerder Scholle, bieten sie eine internationale Küche.

Hamburg war schon immer aufgeschlossen gegenüber den Musen. Die Staatsoper und viele Theater verpflichten Weltstars, geben aber auch ungen Künstlern die Gelegenheit, ihr Können zu zeigen. Durch die Subventionen vom Staat haven viele Bühnen die Möglichkeit, zu xperimintieren.

Hamburg has so viel zu beiten. Es lohnt sich wirklich, einige Zeit heir zu erbringen. Die Menschen sind auch gar nicht so reserviert… und das Vetter ist auch nicht so schlecht (man muß sich nur entsprechend kleiden).

When the sun shines it seems like Sunday.

Wenn die Somme scheint, wird jeder Tag zu einem Sonntag.

Der Vorstand - The Board of Directors from left: Ronald Rotter, Erika Erdbeer, Wilhelm Huening, Josef Matuschka(President), Marianne Wehrle, Dale Graf. Not pictured is E. (Cooky) Kraus.

S.T. Prinz Johannes I und I.L. Prinzessin Erika II, Jubiläums- Prinzenpaar, 1990.

One of the oldest Traditions of its kind is the Mardi Gras Society "Rheinischer Verein" of Chicago, which was established by 11 genuine "Kölner" in 1890. First President, also from Köln, was John Cremer. Only people from Köln or the Rheinland were allowed to be members in those days. However, during the immigrationwave of the 50s,there were so many young people who wanted to get in that the rules changed. After all, the club needed new blood and as long as the youngsters maintained the old traditions of Karneval, Fastnacht and Fashing, all was well. The society grew as a fresh breeze invigorated the membership.

Karnevals-Gesellschaft Rheinischer Verein von Chicago, gegründet 1890

Anneliese Jenkins
"Der Weltenbummler"

Text and photos Rheinischer Verein, Chicago

Von der "Karnevalsgesellschaft Rheinischer Verein, Chicago, of 1890" Joe und Susan Matuschka, Siegfried Fischbacher, Erika and Karl-Heinz Brockerhoff, Asim Puskar, Roy-Uwe Horn und Anny Kreidl, beim Besuch nach der phantastischen Siegfried & Roy Show im Mirage Hotel in Las Vegas, Nevada.

Fanfaren Corps des K.G. R.V. Chicago mit Gründer und Corps Leiter Karl-Heinz Brockerhoff

Annemarie and Willy Marx brought the Amazonen Corps to life in 1952. This group and the Fanfare Corps which was established by Karl-Heinz Brockerhoff and five kinsmen in 1957 grew soon by leaps and bounds. They became part of many festivities and are now an established institution in the club world of North America. After all, with the annual custom of Karneval Princes and Princesses, the Princes' Court, the Council of Eleven (Elfer Rath), the Constable, the Storytellers and the Gentlemen's Ballet, the Mardi Gras Society remains loyal to the customs and traditions of the old homeland. With the election of the Princes, the Jester meeting, the Masquerade Ball, the traditional Women's "Fastnacht" night and the celebrations and parades on Rose Monday before Ash Wednesday, thousands of jolly people enjoy Karneval, the fifth season from November 11th until Ash Wednesday from Canada to Arizona and from Chicago, Cincinnati and Milwaukee to Las Vegas. Alaaf and Helau!

Die bekannten Parodisten "Die Prellböck'" Götz Nickel und Karl-Heinz Brockerhoff

Amazonen Corp des Rheinischen Vereins, Chicago

Elfer Rath 1993-94

Karnevals-Gesellschaft Rheinischer Verein von Chicago, gegründet 1890

Mehr als 100 Jahre Karneval in Chicago

Eines der ältesten Kulturträger dieser Art in Amerika ist die K.G.R.V. von Chicago, der 1890 von 11 echten "Kölschen" gegründet wurde. Der erste Präsident war John Cremer, ein gebürtiger Kölner. Damals konnten nur Kölner oder Rheinländer Mitglieder werden. Jedoch mit der Einwanderungswelle in den 50er Jahren kamen viele junge Einwanderer, die gerne Mitglieder werden wollten. Auch der Verein wollte gerne junge Leute aufnehmen, die die Tradition weiter erhalten sollten. So wurde gewählt, die Statuten wurden geändert und nun mußte man nur deutscher Herkunft sein und versprechen, daß man die Traditionen des Karnevals, Fastnacht oder auch Fasching aufrecht erhalten würde. Der Verein wuchs und der "neue Wind" machte sich bemerkbar.

Annemarie und Willi Marx huben 1952 das Amazonen Corps aus der Taufe. Diese Garde und das in 1957 von Karl-Heinz Brockerhoff mit fünf Mannen gegründete Fanfaren Corps wuchsen schnell heran, machten sich mit ihren Auftritten begehrt und sind heute nicht mehr aus der Vereinswelt Nordamerikas wegzudenken. Außerdem, mit den alljährlichen Karnevalsprinzen und -prinzessinnen, Prinzengarde, Elfer Rath, Schutzmann, Büttenrednern und Herrenballett hält die K.G. Rheinischer Verein treu an dem Brauchtum und der Tradition der alten Heimat fest.

Mit Prinzenkürung, Narrensitzung, Maskenbällen, Weiberfastnacht und Rosenmontagsfeier erfreuen sich jährlich tausende von Narren der Fünften Jahreszeit, die zwischen dem 11.11. und Ascher-Mittwoch von Kanada bis Arizona, und von Cincinnati, Chicago und Milwaukee bis nach Las Vegas und Los Angeles gefeiert wird.
Alaaf und Helau!

Christel und Walter Sanders

Prinz Walter, Ehrenmitglied des Schwaben Verein Chicago, war 22 Jahre im Hauptvorstand des Schwaben Verein Chicago, 5 Jahre als Finanzsekretär, 15 Jahre Sekretär und Geschäftsführer und 2 Jahre Präsident. Er wurde in Preßburg, Slowakei, geboren und lebte von 1939 bis 1946, davon 16 Monate als Deutscher inhaftiert im tschechischen Konzentrations- und Arbeitslager Brünn-Brno Malomerice- Borky.

Nach seiner Zwangsausweisung als Deutscher aus der Tschechoslowakei nach Württemberg im Oktober 1946, hat er das Schwabenland zu seiner zweiten Heimat gemacht. Dort hat er auch seine, durch den 2. Weltkrieg zerrissene Familie wiedergefunden, seine Berufsausbildung bekommen und Berufserfahrung gesammelt.

S. T. Prinz Walter II and I.L. Prinzessin Christel 1
Hofmarschall: Dale Graf, Adjutant: Andrew Csapo
Hofdamen: Cynthia Sanders und Sonja Ruppel
Andrea Krauth ist nicht im Bild.
Die Pagen sind Nicole und Alex Anetsberger

Seit Januar 1957, lebt er im Chicago-Raum. Von 1957 bis 1965 hat er hier seinen Lebensunterhalt als Toolroom-Machinist und Toolmaker verdient. Nach seinem erfolgreich beendeten Studium im Jahre 1967, hat er bis zu seinem Ruhestand im Jahre 1994, als Instructor, Engineer und Manager, seiner Familie und sich einen angenehmen Lebensstandart geschaffen.

Seit April 1974 ist er mit seiner hübschen, aus Düsseldorf kommenden Prinzessin Christel verheiratet. Der Präsident des Düsseldorfer Karnevalvereins, Peter Schedler, welcher mit einer Abordnung Düsseldorfer Karnevalisten zu seiner Prinzenkrönung nach Chicago kam, schrieb in einem Brief im Januar 1997 an ihn: "Ihr seit nicht nur ein überrangendes Prinzenpaar, auf das die Stadt Chicago stolz sein kann, sondern auch eine liebenswerte Familie".

H. William Stabenow

Horst William Stabenow, born 1934 in Düsseldorf, emigrated to America in 1954 and started his career in the securities business in 1956. In 1960 he received the certificate in the principals and practices of Investment Finance in Canada. In 1965 he was transferred to New York where he became active in the German-American community. Soon he got involved with Cultural Folk Groups in Germany and has organized tours to America where these groups perform at concerts, picnics and on parades. Among others, he is the past president of the Deutscher Club of Clark, New Jersey, Honorary Grand Marshal of the German American Steuben Parade in New York and on the National Council of the Steuben Society of America.

At his career he is currently Vice President and Treasurer of the NUVEEN Companies in Chicago, where he just celebrated his 20th anniversary. Nuveen was founded in 1898 and today offers a broad range of tax-free and taxable investments designed for

H.W. Stabenow

investors whose portfolios are the principal source of their ongoing financial security, as well as a wide array of municipal and corporate investment banking services.

Horst W. Stabenow

Horst William Stabenow, wurde 1934 in Düsseldorf geboren, wanderte 1954 nach Amerika aus und begann seine Karriere 1956 im Börsengeschäft. Im Jahre 1960 erwarb er sein Diplom in Investment Finanz in Canada. 1965 wurde er nach New York versetzt, wo er in der Deutsch-Amerikanischen Gemeinschaft aktiv wurde. Schon bald arbeitete er mit Volksmusik Gruppen in Deutschland und organisierte Reisen nach Amerika mit Auftritten für Konzerte, auf Picknicks und Paraden. Unter anderem ist er Ehrenpräsident im Deutschen Klub in Clark, New Jersey, Ehren Grand Marshal der Deutsch-Amerikanischen Steuben Parade in New York und im nationalen Forum der Steuben Society von Amerika.

In seiner beruflichen Karriere ist er zur Zeit Vice Präsident und Kassenwart der NUVEEN Firmen in Chicago, wo er gerade sein 20. Jubiläum feierte. Die Firma Nuveen wurde im Jahre 1898 gegründet und bietet heute eine breite Auswahl von Kapitalanlagen für Investoren, deren Anlagen finanzielle Sicherheit im Alter bieten. Im Wirtschftssektor bietet man öffentliche Wertpapiere und Aktien an.

Catholic Kolping Society of America

Kolping Mission Statement

We, the members of the Catholic Kolping Society of America, led by the vision of our founder, Blessed Adolph Kolping, promote the development of the individual and the family by fostering a sense of belonging and friendship through out holistic programs of spiritual, educational, charitable, and social activities.

Adolph Kolping
Gesellenvater

K-olping

Adolph Kolping (1813-1865) was a Roman Catholic priest of the Diocese of Cologne, Germany. His apostolate was directed to the young journeymen of his time. The Society he founded for them in 1849 is now called by his name. It was intended to provide a Christian environment for the young men as they developed their work skills, while at the same time, offsetting the dangers to faith and morals, that were concomitant with the Industrial Revolution.

O-bjectives

Initially, to provide a home-away-from-home for the young men while they learned a trade that would enable them to make a decent and honest living. Even more important, these young men were schooled in the Christian principles that would serve as a guide for their personal, business and community life.The Kolping House, as it later came to be called, was more than a residence. It was a place to relax and have a good time. The priestly presence - in the person of Father Kolping - was the Father-figure and role model. Father Kolping's place within the Society has become the position of the Praeses, and is primarily one of the guidance - teaching by word and example how to live in a secular world without losing or lessening the sacredness of one's life, combining in his ministry the sacred and the secular.

L-eaven

The Society, now open in membership to women, as well as men, to old as well as young, to active Church members, not only Catholic but those in agreement with Catholic teaching and practice.

P-rinciples

As a Society comprised, initially, and even now predominantly, of Catholics, Kolping includes the term "Catholic" in its official title to indicate and proclaim that the principles upon which it is founded and upon which it operates are none other than those taught and proclaimed universally by the Church that has for most all its history been called Catholic.

Adolph Kolping
1813-1865

I-deal

Every Kolping member is to achieve full maturity in Christ so as continually to reach out to become the full person that each of us is called to be in every situation in which we find ourselves.

N-ation

While sponsoring no partisan allegiance, the Society encourages its membership to be active on each level of government, guided always by the Christian principles that each ascribes by the faith in the Lord Jesus.

G-oal

As a means of fostering the wholesome and healthy of the larger community, Kolping is intent in its efforts to encourage and protect the Christian family unit.

Present Chicago Kolping Center, 5826 N. Elston Avenue

The Kolping Society's objectives are:

- to enable its members to demonstrate in today's world their Chistianity in their marriage and family, profession, in their Church, in society and state...

- to give assistance to its members, and society as a whole, and...

- to promote the common good in a Christian atmosphere through its activities and be a decisive influence toward the improvement of society.

Kolping children with St. Nickolaus on December 6th at Kolping Haus.

Group of Kolping members gathered around the flags during a meeting in Philadelphia.

With Cardinal Bernadin, Episcopal Moderator of the National Kolping Society of America, after an appreciation dinner for contributions made by the Kolping Society to the Catholic Seminarians.

Members of the Kolping Society in Chicago after a Communion breakfast meeting at the Chicago Kolping Haus.

BRANCHES OF THE CATHOLIC KOLPING SOCIETY OF AMERICA

BROOKLYN - 6504 Myrtle Avenue
Glendale, New York 11385-6250
Tel: 718/456-7727

BUFFALO - 29 Delphi Drive
Cheektowaga, New York 14227-3605
Tel: 716/668-0018

CHICAGO - 5826 N. Elston Avenue
Chicago, Illinois 60646-5544
Tel: 773/792-2190

CINCINNATI - 10235 Mill Road
Cincinnati, Ohio 45231-1924
Tel/Fax: 513/851-7951

DETROIT - 24409 Jefferson Avenue
Saint Clair Shores, Michigan, 48080-1318
Tel: 810/775-9159

HOLY TRINITY - 226 Harrison Street
Passaic, New Jersey, 07055-6202
Tel: 201/778-9763

LOS ANGELES - 1225 South Union Ave.
Los Angeles, California, 90015-2021
Tel: 213/388-9438

NEW YORK - 165 E. 88th Street
New York, New York, 10128-2241
Tel 212/369-6647

PHILADELPHIA - 1285 Southampton Rd.
Philadelphia, Pennsylvania, 19116
Tel: 217/676-8977

ROCHESTER - 284 Malden Street
Rochester, New York, 14615-2658
Tel: 716/621-3226

SAINT LOUIS - 4035 Keokuk Street
St. Louis, Missouri, 63116-3513
Tel/Fax: 314/776-5312

SAN FRANCISCO - 440 Taraval St.
San Francisco, California, 94116-2530
Tel: 415/753-9542

The Catholic Kolping Society Of Chicago

125th Anniversary 1872-1997

History of the Catholic Kolping of Chicago

Father Adolph Kolping's work did not end with his death. He lived to know that some of his sons had carried his program to the United States. The New World, however, had the old world problem - uprooted young men in strange cities, lacking a home tie.

Kolping House Auditorium 1907-1921

Herman Seibt, a coppersmith and James Ucher, a skilled machinist, had settled in Chicago, Illinois and had known the comforts of a Kolping House. In 1872, they were moved to start a Society in Chicago, it was the year after the Great Fire and a great number of people had been attracted to the rebuilding of the city. Young German immigrants were drawn to the Kolping Society and membership numbered over 200 in a few months. The first Kolping House of Chicago was dedicated in 1874. By 1907, a second house was purchased. By its own merit it was outgrown and was replaced by a larger one in 1921.

"Kolping House" has served thousands of young men from all over the world. It served the strangers who came to Chicago. This is where many got their start when they had nowhere else to begin. We were more than just a home.

There were people who would help us place the boys in jobs and positions, And because we had a lot of volunteer help, we were able to keep the boys until they became established in the community. Newcomers to the house were given free board and room until jobs could be found, and the boys began paying their way.

We were successful largely because we had some great volunteers working for us. Some of our workers were the Senior men, who were really interested in the young. Not in recreating them in their own images, but in helping them make themselves into something good.

In addition to teaching the boys to be good citizens and good Christians, Father Kolping believed boys should be prepared to become the head of the family, with all our boys, you can imagine the place was attractive to girls. Many marriages resulted from our social activities.

Residents at Oakdale have reflected the tensions of the world. Father Fischer, Praeses at the time, recalled: During the Cuban crisis, we were flooded with Cubans, they were among the finest boys I ever met - really the cream of the Cubans. After the revolt in Hungary, the boys were predominantly Hungarian. The House never drew a line at persons of other races or religions.

Two of the persons most active, in our era, in the house were Peter and Mary Hild, who met when Peter was a young resident after his arrival from Germany, and Mrs. Hild was active in the dances and parties given by the auxiliary. Mary Hild was Mother Kolping. She confided that the boys were like sons to her. She recalled just a few of many recollections. One boy from Kerala state, India, is studying for the priesthood in India after a stay here. Two Negro boys from Nigeria are completing their medical studies in Germany before returning to Africa. Mary could go on and on. They were all fine boys, as Mary recalls.

The era at the Oakdale and Halsted location came to close. The difficulties over building code requirements began with the conversion of two six-flat buildings in 1929 and the addition of an auditorium between them. Changing times caused some difficulty for Kolping, Chicago. One of the biggest problems was the lack of money, since Kolping relied solely on contributions and gifts in order to finance its operation. Lack of funds sufficient to keep up with public building standards was one of the big reasons that the Kolping House at

Kolping House 1921 -1968

Halsted and Oakdale was forced to shut down and was sold in 1968.

A new era began. A difficult era. The Kolping Society of Chicago did not have a Kolping House of its own. We had a good Society and we wanted to keep the membership together. We wandered from one meeting place to another. In the meantime a great effort was made to acquire a new permanent Kolping House. After two years this difficult era came to an end and the Kolping Society of Chicago purchased a new House, a Kolping Center at our present location.

Another era began. The new house needed much work and renovation began. Here the true Kolping spirit was shown. Many of our men and women came and worked making this location a beautiful Kolping Center, which we are all very proud of. This was the right location for the Kolping movement to flourish again.

We realized through the changing times, our need for a Kolping Boarding House was not our goal anymore. The Kolping movement changed here and in many locals. Our main objective was to maintain a Kolping Community Center, where we can provide not only for our Kolping members but also for the community.

We have the opportunity to spread our movement to everyone in the community.

DREISILKER ELECTRIC MOTORS INC.

A Father–Son Operation par Excellence!

President Leo Dreisilker and family

Margaret and Henry Dreisilker

Henry Dreisilker, ein deutscher Einwanderer, kam 1954 nach Amerika um eine Zukunft und gute Anstellung zu finden. Harte Arbeit und Rechtschaffenheit besorgten ihm seine erste Stelle in einem kleinen Betrieb, einer Electro Motor Werkstatt in einem Hausgerätegeschäft.

Seine Firma fing an, sich auf moderne Hochleistungsmotor-Reparaturen und den Verkauf zu spezialisieren. Durch das Zusammenfügen von traditioneller Facharbeit und neuester Technik wuchs der Betrieb über die Jahre von drei guten Mitarbeitern auf eine Belegschaft von 120.

Was als eine 75 Quadratmeter große Werkstatt anfing, wurde zu einem der größten und modernsten Elektromotor Verkaufs und Reparatur Zentren Amerikas, auf einer Fläche von 730

Henry Dreisilker, a German immigrant, came to America in 1954 seeking opportunity and gainful employment. Hard work and integrity landed him his first job in a small motor repair and appliance business. Seven months later he purchased the business and founded, Henry Dreisilker Electric Motors and Appliance Service. The company began by specializing in commercial motor repair and sales. Combining old-world craftsmanship with advanced technology the company grew steadily from three employees to over 120.

What started as a 750 square foot facility has grown into one of the largest and most modern 73,000 square foot electric motor sales and repair centers in the USA. The corporate headquarters in Glen Ellyn, IL is supported by 6 other sales locations throughout the state of Illinois.

President, Leo F. Dreisilker, continues to lead the company into the future as a world-class provider of commercial and industrial motors, drives, controls and repair services. "Our business is a totally satisfied customer! For over 40 years the Dreisilker name has stood for a job done right, every time. Whether it is consultation or new equipment, field service or a cost-effective repair, the focus will always be quality, reliability and customer satisfaction," Leo said.

Integrity. Commitment, and, unmatched technical expertise fuel the Dreisilker difference.

Quadratmetern. Das Hauptbüro und die modernen, technischen Anlagen in Glen Ellyn, IL werden von sechs eigenen Verkaufsstellen im Staate Illinois unterstützt.

President Leo F. Dreisilker übernahm und führt heute die Firma in die Zukunft als einen Weltklasse Zulieferer von Betriebs- und Industriemotoren, Antrieben, Schaltwerken und für deren Reparaturdienst.

"Unser Geschäft steht oder fällt mit dem völlig zufriedenen Kunden! Für mehr als 40 Jahre steht der Name Dreisilker für gute Arbeit, garantiert richtig, jeder Zeit! Gleich ob es um Kundenberatung von neuen Anlagen, Kundendienst oder kostengünstige Reparaturen geht, unser Augenmerk gilt der Qualität und Zuverlässigkeit unserer Produkte und der Zufriedenheit des Kunden", sagt Leo Dreisilker.

Rechtschaffenheit, Verpflichtung und unübertroffene Fachkenntnisse sind das Fundament des Dreisilker Mottos.

DREISILKER *Electric* MOTORS

352 Roosevelt Road
Glen Ellyn, IL 60137

Tel: 630/469-7510
Fax: 630/469-3474

SCHWABEN-VEREIN Chicago

Schwaben-Verein, Chicago

Die wohl älteste deutsche Gemeinschaft in Chicago und Umgebung, wurde am 31. März 1878 ins Leben gerufen und dann 1889 als "not for profit Organization" im Staate Illinois inkorporiert. Der Zweck des Vereins wurde damals folgendermaßen angegeben: Die Feste und Brauchtümer der Schwaben vom Schwabenland aufrecht zu erhalten, Grundeigentum dafür zu erwerben und sich gegenseitig zu helfen und zu unterstützen. Auch heute noch ist dieses die Grundlage des Vereins. Seit über 100 Jahren feiert der Schwaben Verein Chicago jedes Jahr sein Cannstatter Volksfest, ein bei der großen, deutschstämmigen Bevölkerung beliebtes Fest, das immer tausende von Besuchern anzieht. Der Schwaben Verein Chicago floriert noch heute mit einer großen Mitgliederzahl; obwohl viele dieser Mitglieder keine Schwaben vom fernen Schwabenland sind, ist und bleibt der Verein den Grundsätzen seiner Gründer treu.

The Schwaben Verein Chicago is probable the oldest German association in Chicagoland. It was founded on March 31, 1878 and incorporated as a 'not for profit organization' in the State of Illinois in 1889. The purpose of the Association is stated as follows:
To maintain the customs and traditions of the Swabians from the Land of Swabia and in support thereof to acquire real estate, and to help and to support each other. These principles of the association are still valid today. And for over 100 years, the Schwaben Verein Chicago has been celebrating its "Cannstatter Folkfest", a favorite among the Americans of German heritage. Each year, the festival attracts over a thousand visitors. Although most members of this Swabian association are not even Swabians, the Schwaben Verein Chicago is growing and prospers as its members remain faithful to the principles of their founders.

Der Schwäbische Unterstützungs-Verein von Chicago

Front row: Dr. Stephen R. Schmid, Secretary; Dietrich Wagner, Vice President; George Boehm, President; Siegfried Hampach, Finance Secretary. Back row: Robert M. Nicholson, Finance Committee; Rudolph J. Iberie, Registrar; Joseph Armonld, Finance Committee; Patrick Shanhan, Finance Committee; Raymond G. Schmid, Treasurer

Der Schwäbische Unterstützungs-Verein wurde 1883 von Mitgliedern des Chicagoer Schwabenvereins ins Leben gerufen, die sich finanziell um ihre Mitglieder sorgten. Heute kann der Verein seinen Mitgliedern finanzielle Unterstützung gewähren, wenn die Notwendigkeit dazu besteht, z.B. bei Krankheiten und auch Todesfällen, um für die Betroffenen und deren Ehegatten zu sorgen. Ein kapitalkräftiges, langfristiges Finanzierungsmanagement des Vereinsvermögen, das aus einer jährliche Mitgliedsgebühr von $24,00 pro Person herleitet, hat eine gut fundierte Rücklage geschaffen, die den Mitgliedern zur finanziellen Unterstützung zur Verfügung steht. Diese Unterstützung besteht aus $60 pro Woche Krankengeld bis zu 10 Wochen jährlich, ein Sterbegeld in Höhe von $300 für Mitglieder, und ein Sterbegeld in Höhe von $75 für den Ehepartner. Heute haben wir eine sehr vitale und relativ junge Liste von fast 60 Mitgliedern, die sich auf diese finanzielle Beihilfe und gesellschaftliche Bereicherung verlassen kann und somit für eine große und begeisterte Teilnahme an den Vereinstreffen und -veranstaltungen sorgt. An einer typischen monatliche Versammlung nehmen über 40% der Mitglieder teil. Jedes Jahr wird mit einem Stiftungsfest und Abendessen die Gründung des Vereins gefeiert. Unser Erbe hat uns bisher gute Dienste geleistet und wird es auch weiterhin bis in das 3. Jahrtausend tun.

Organized in 1883 by some concerned members of the Schwaben Verein of Chicago, the Schwäbisher Unterstützungs-Verein provides its membership today with financial assistance when illness strikes and a death benefit for themselves and their spouses. Sound long-term financial management of the Verein's assets derived from the $24 annual dues each member is assessed has produced an exceptional fund reserve for the benefits enjoyed by the members which are $60 per week sick benefits for ten weeks yearly and a $300 death benefit for members with a $75 spousal death benefit. Today, a very vital and relatively youthful roster of almost 60 members enjoy these dependable financial benefits and the social enrichment of large, enthusiastic turnouts for all Verein meetings and affairs. A typical monthly meeting is attended by over 40% of the membership. Each year a Stiftungsfest is celebrated with a dinner to commemorate the founding of the Verein. Our heritage has served us well and will continue to do so into the third millennium.

Front row: Rudi Kaiser, Secretary; Frank Wimmer, 1st Vice President; Helga Zettl, Treasurer; George Boehm, President; Del Hackl, 2nd Vice President; Rudolph J. Iberle, Finance Secretary; Erich Alex, Collector; Rear row: Peter Steffek, Director; Emil F. Wehrle, Finance Committee; Kurt Gebert, Director; Juergen Trodler, Finance Committee; Karl Ritz, Director; Werner Bayerle, Director; Juergen Kaufmann, Archivar; Rudi Geissler, Director.

Schwäbischer Sängerbund

Schwäbischer Sängerbund Male Chorus

Established upon the need to continue German musical heritage through song in America, and supported by the Schwaben community of Chicago, the Schwäbischer Sängerbund of Chicago was founded on March 4, 1894.

From its initial membership of 18 German-Americans, the group flourished so that by 1939, under its ninth director, H. A. Rehberg, a 100 member chorus won first prize at the prestigious Music Festival of the Chicago Tribune.

The renowned Ludwig Lohmiller guided the chorus from 1941-1979. Having enjoyed the longest tenure with the chorus, his accomplishments include the memorable 1944 concert in Orchestra Hall marking the 50th anniversary, and the 75th concert at Lane High School in Chicago.

Mr. Glen Sorgatz, of a well-respected musical family in Chicago, is the current director. Since 1979, this talented teacher, musician and conductor has not only enhanced the quality of the singing, but has also vigorously recruited younger singers. It was Glen Sorgatz who directed the 100 year anniversary concert, and it is through him that the Schwäbischer Sängerbund will enjoy continued success.

Der Wunsch, das deutsche musikalische Erbe in Amerika durch das Lied fortleben zu lassen, war für die Gründung des Schwäbischen Sängerbundes am 4. März 1894 innerhalb der Schwaben-Gemeinde von Chicago ausschlaggebend.

Von den anfänglichst 18 deutsch-amerikanischen Mitgliedern wuchs die Gruppe schnell an, so daß 1939 unter der Leitung ihres 9. Dirigenten, H. A. Rehberg ein Chor von 100 Sängern auf dem angesehenen Musikfestival der Chicago Tribune den ersten Preis gewann.

Der sehr bekannte Ludwig Lohmiller leitete den Chor von 1941 bis 1979. Er war es, der den Chor am längsten leitete. Zu seinen Erfolgen zählen das unvergeßliche Konzert von 1944 in der Orchestra Hall, als das 50. Jubiläum gefeiert wurde, als auch das 75. Konzert an der Lane Tech High School in Chicago.

Gegenwärtig ist die Leitung in den Händen von Herrn Glen Sorgatz aus einer sehr bekannten musikliebenden Familie in Chicago. Seit 1979 hat dieser talentierte Lehrer, Musiker und Dirigent nicht nur die Qualität des Singens verbessert, sondern er hat auch intensiv weiter nach jungen Sängern gesucht. Glen Sorgatz unterstand die Leitung des Jubiläumskonzertes zum 100jährigen Bestehen, und er wird auch in der Zukunft dafür sorgen, daß der Schwäbische Sängerbund weitere Erfolge verzeichnen kann.

Schwaben-Athletic Club

The Schwaben Athletic Club was founded in Chicago in 1926 by a group of thirteen young "Schwabisch" German Americans that made up their first soccer team. They were an all around Athletic Club in the early years with track and field as well as soccer. In 1969 they began their move to Buffalo Grove, IL by purchasing the first eight acres of land that was to become part of the 18 acre parcel that now makes up Schwaben Center.

Today the club has grown to 350 members and almost 20 soccer teams ranging in age groups from under 8 to over 40 and is active with both boys and girls' teams. The club sends teams to Germany to play against European teams almost yearly.

The Schwaben Athletic Club is a very prestigious name in the soccer world, having won many titles and championships including The U.S. Amateur championship and the Tribune Cup. There have been many Schwaben players that have represented the United States on National and Olympic Teams and have been inducted into the Illinois Soccer Hall of Fame. One member, Rudy Getzinger, has been inducted into the U.S. Soccer Hall of Fame.

The club has three soccer fields at the Schwaben Center and offers quite a social calendar for their members as well. They host three tournaments a year to cover all the age groups, two dinner dances (March and November) and a gala New Year's Eve dinner dance. They have a concession stand on the sideline that offer some great sausages during the games and tournaments.

Der Schwaben-Athletic Club wurde 1926 von einer Gruppen von 13 jungen deutsch-amerikanischen "Schwaben" in Chicago gegründet, die das erste Fußballteam darstellten. In den Anfangsjahren umfaßte der Schwaben-Athletic Club alle Sportarten, auch Leichtathletik und Fußball. 1969 zog der Club um, und zwar nach Buffalo Grove, Illinois, wo man zunächst rund 3.2 Hektar Land kaufte, was später auf 7.2 Hektar erweitert wurde, das heutige Schwaben Center.

Der Club ist bislang auf über 350 Mitglieder angewachsen und hat fast 20 Fußballmannschaften für Altersgruppen von 8 bis über 40 Jahren - für Jungen und Mädchen. Fast jedes Jahr schickt der Club seine Mannschaften nach Deutschland, wo sie gegen europäische Fußballmannschaften spielen.

In der Welt des Fußballs hat sich der Schwaben-Athletic Club einen sehr angesehenen Namen erworben und schon viele Titel und Meisterschaften, einschließlich die U.S. Amateur Championship und den Tribune Cup, gewonnen. So mancher schwäbischer Fußballspieler, der die Vereinigten Staaten im National oder Olympischen Team vertreten hat, wurde in die Fußballehrenliste, Illinois Soccer Hall of Fame, aufgenommen. Und ein Mitglied, Rudy Getzinger, wurde sogar in die U.S. Fußballehrenliste, die U.S. Soccer Hall of Fame, aufgenommen.

CONTINUED ON PAGE 66

Rudy Getzinger
Soccer Hall of Fame

Soccer Team, Schwaben Athletic Club

Schwaben-Atuhletic Club - Cont'd.

Der Club hat im Schwaben Center drei Fußballfelder und bietet seinen Mitgliedern außerdem einen gesellschaftlich sehr aktiven Kalender an. Pro Jahr werden drei Fußballturniere Jahr veranstaltet, um allen Altersgruppen gerecht zu werden, außerdem zwei Tanzabende mit Abendessen (im März und im November) und zu Sylvester gibt es einen Galaabend mit Tanz und Abendessen. Nebenbei, auch bei den Turnieren und Spielen werden hervorragende Bratwürste

The Schwaben Society Charity Fund

Another organization which finds its origins in the Schwaben Verein von Chicago is the Schwaben Society Charity Fund. Founded in 1967 to enable a more efficient and dependable means of assisting charitable organizations through endowment funding, the Fund has distributed earnings of more than $275,000 in financial grants since its inception, over $160,000 in just the past ten years. The Charity Fund has provided sustenance to a host of our less fortunate citizens from newborn infants, to our homeless population and to the aged by funding the organizations which supply such necessary services as housing, soup kitchens, handicapped schools, maternity and infant aid, and other benefits to help these individuals. The Schwaben Society Charity Fund believes in its tradition of caring and has a determined commitment to helping others. You can assist in perpetuating this great tradition by forming your own commitment and sending a contribution to The Schwaben Society Charity Fund today at 2215 W. Estes Avenue, Chicago, IL 60645.

Eine andere Organisation, die ihren Ursprung im Schwabenverein von Chicago gefunden hat, ist der Wohltätigkeitsfonds des Schwabenvereins. Der Fonds, der 1967 ins Leben gerufen wurde, um ein besseres und verläßlicheres Mittel zu schaffen, Wohltätigkeitsorganisationen durch eine Stiftung zu helfen, hat seit seiner Gründung über $275.000 an Erträgen für Fördermittel verteilt, alleine $160.000 innerhalb der letzten zehn Jahren. Mit Hilfe des Wohltätigkeitsfonds kann Unterstützung an die mittellose Bevölkerung, von den Neugeborenen bis zu den Wohnungslosen und Rentnern, erteilt werden, indem man für Pflegedienste, Wohnungen, Suppenküchen, Schulen für Behinderte, Unterstützung für werdende Mütter und Säuglinge und andere Hilfen sorgt. Der Wohltätigkeitsfonds des Schwabenvereins hat sich seiner Mission, anderen zu helfen, vollkommen verschrieben. Auch Sie können dabei helfen, diese großartige Tradition aufrechtzuerhalten, indem Sie sich ihr eigenes Ziel setzen und an The Schwaben Society Charity Fund, 2215 W. Estes Avenue, Chicago, Illinois 60645 heute noch eine Spende schicken.

The Schwaben Center

Located in the Village of Buffalo Grove, a Chicago suburb, is the home of the Schwaben Verein Chicago and the Schwaben Athletic Club, the Schwaben Center. Situated on approximately twenty acres, the Schwaben Center features several well groomed soccer fields and a large Club house. While refreshments during soccer games and tournaments are served from a field house, more formal affairs take place in the club house banquet hall. Managed by a professional chef the banquet hall can seat up to four hundred people for a formal dinner. Available for festive occasions, the Schwaben Center banquet hall has an excellent reputation for the food that is being served there. The Schwaben Center is well known in the area and used by many other German groups for their celebrations.

In Buffalo Grove, einem Vorort von Chicago, liegt das Schwabenzentrum, des Schwaben Vereins Chicago und dem Schwaben Athletic Club. Auf etwa 8 Hektar Land gelegen, hat das Schwabenzentrum einige Fußballfelder und ein großes Klubhaus. Während der vielen Fußballspiele und Turniere werden Getränke von Feldhaus bestellt, aber mehr formelle Anlässe spielen sich im Festsaal des Klubhauses ab. Von einem gelernten Chef geführt, kann der Festsaal bis zu 400 Personen zum Essen bewirten. Für besondere Anlässe auch zu vermieten, hat das Schwabenzentrum einen guten Ruf für eine gute Küche. Das große Schwabenzentrum ist weit und breit bekannt, und wird auch von anderen deutschen Gruppen für ihre Festlichkeiten benutzt. Die Adresse ist 301 North Weiland Road, Buffalo Grove, Illinois

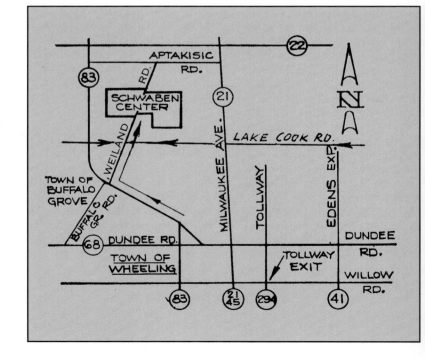

Horst M. Kniesel

- ● A Financial Specialist at Work
- ● A Boy Scout for a Hobby
- ● A Donauschwoab' at Heart

Horst and Heddy Kniesel

The Successful Business Leader

Mr. Kniesel is Vice President and Director of First Chicago NBD's Non-Earning Assets Reduction Program, a position he has held since 1982. This program works through a Non-Earning Assets Team (NEAT), managed by Mr. Kniesel, and comprising the Corporation's C.F.O. and other senior executive management members. It is the mission of the NEA Team to reduce non-earning assets through internal cash management members applications, cost savings initiatives, and revenue generating ideas, thereby increasing overall profits and improving the ROA, ROE, and capital ratios.

Mr. Kniesel has been employed by First Chicago for 36 years and has held various positions of responsibility, including head of the audit function for the Bank's Worldwide activities, head of the Bank's Executive and Professional Banking Division and Private Banking Center, head of the Lending Services Division in the Retail Banking Department, and Auditor's Representative in London and Central Europe. He has been instrumental in helping to establish internal audit and control procedures throughout the Corporation, developing credit policies and loan administration procedures, participating in the Corporation's training programs, and implementing internal cash management techniques. He has also been the catalyst for the Corporation's successful Environmental, Recycling, and Paper Reduction programs.

He is on the Steering Committee and an active participant of the New York Float and Payment Systems Roundtable, and has been a frequent speaker and planning committee member at banking industry conferences.

Mr. Kniesel received his undergraduate degree in financial management in 1965 from Roosevelt university and went on to attend its graduate program. He is a Certified Internal Auditor, and in 1993 was awarded membership in Who's Who Worldwide, listed as a global business leader.

A Dedicated Volunteer

On Thursday, March 21, 1996, at the annual district awards banquet for the Des Plaines Valley Council of the Boy Scouts of America, serving Chicago's western suburbs, Horst Kniesel was honored as one of three recipients with the "District Award of Merit."

This award recognized Horst for his 17 years of Voluntary work as an adult leader and active participant on many of the local and council-wide scouting activities. He was also recognized as a leading chartered organization representative of the Westchester Community Church, since 1990, when the Church Cabinet approved the sponsorship of The Boy Scouts.

Citing some of this accomplishments, Horst was recognized for the "God and Service" award he received from the church on Scouting Sunday in February 1995, and for his 22 years of active participation on many boards and committees in the Westchester Community Church. Horst has been the United Way Campaign Coordinator at The First Chicago Bank, the largest single corporate contributor to The United Way in Chicagoland for the past several years. On January 29, 1996 the bank awarded Horst with the Corporate L.E.A.D. Award, which honors employees who best represent the spirit of leadership, equal opportunity, affirmative action, and diversity.

Horst is this year's chairman of the "Community Campaign" for Friends of Scouting. This is an annual fundraising drive which asks local merchants and individual contributors to provide the much needed financial support for the local scouting programs. Many of his church members voluntarily contribute to this campaign each year.

Horst's wife Hedy Kniesel is a Fine Artist, in the Graphic Arts Department of Elmhurst College. She also does freelance paintings, and desktop publishing assignments under the name of "Alpine Creative Services". Hedy loves to ride and take care of her own horse. Horst was recently promoted to First Vice President of First Chicago NBD. The couple has been happily married for 30 years.

See monument in Ulm and Map of Wiowodina and East Slawonien, Page 293.

Medizin-Technologie - Gestern und Heute

Medical Technology, Yesterday and Today

Einthoven, Roentgen, Semmelweiss, Wien und Heidelberg sind nur einige der wichtigen Namen der Medizin im 19. Jahrhundert.

Während des 20. Jahrhunderts wurden die Vereinigten Staaten führend in der fortschrittlichen Gesundheitspflege und viele deutsche Einwanderer beteiligten sich entscheident an dieser Entwicklung, wie zum Beispiel die Pioniere Müller, Storz, Ritter, Liebel, Spiess, Streifeneder und andere.

Im Jahre 1954 kam der ausgewiesene Einwanderer vom Sudetenland, Karl Hausner, und stellte die Sauna dem amerikanischen Publikum vor. 1959 wurde er Vertreter für medizinische Produkte von Siemens, und trat 1964 bei Siemens als Leiter der medizinischen Produktabteilung ein und wurde gleichzeitig Mitglied des Vorstandes.

1969 kehrte er jedoch mit seiner Gattin Hermine ins eigene Geschäft zurück und gründete die ELMED INCORPORATED, eine Firma die anfänglich prominente Firmen wie Bosch, Martin, Mela und Hüttinger vertrat.

Doch die laufend steigenden Kosten der deutschen Geräte und die vielen Neuerungen die für diesen Markt nötig waren, machten es möglich, eine eigene Forschung, Entwicklung und Produktion auf dem Gebiet der Herzgefäße Diagnose, physikalische Therapie und Chirurgie aufzubauen. Der Weg von vielen Neuerungen, die heute Selbsverständlichkeit sind, wurde von diesen jungen Menschen gebahnt.

ELMED INCORPORATED füllt eine Marktlücke mit hochentwickelten Produkten, beschäftigt Arbeitnehmer aus aller Welt und exportiert 40% seiner Produktion.

Einthoven, Roentgen, Semmelweiss, Vienna and Heidelberg were just some important names in medicine during the Nineteenth Century.

During the Twentieth Century, the United States became the leader in progressive health care and many German immigrants significantly contributed to it, with names like Mueller, Storz, Wolf, Ritter, Liebel, Spiess, Streifeneder and the list goes on. In 1954, the expellee immigrant from the Sudetenland, Karl Hausner, introduced the Sauna to the American public. In 1959, he undertook the distribution of Siemens Medical products and in 1964, he joined the Siemens Corporation as Division Manager and Member of the Executive group.

In 1969, he and his wife Hermine, returned to private business, set-up ELMED INCORPORATED and initially represented prominent German firms such as Bosch Martin, Mela and Huettinger.

The ever increasing equipment cost in Germany and the many innovations which they envisioned, made them start their own research, development and production in the fields of cardiovascular diagnosis, physical therapy and surgery.

Many innovations, which now are part of the standard armamentarium, were pioneered by them.

ELMED INCORPORATED is a high tech niche company with employees from all parts of the world, and now exports over 40% of their production.

ELMED INCORPORATED
60 West Fay Avenue
Addison, Illinois 60101-5106
Telephone: (630) 543-2792 Fax: (630) 543-2102

ASTRO CRAFT, INC.

7509 SPRING GROVE ROAD
SPRING GROVE, ILLINOIS 60081
CALL: 815 / 675-1500
FAX: 815 / 675-1600

Seated: Edward and Otto Dschida,
standing: Ingeborg Lund and Richard Dschida - the new generation.

Carrying on the Tradition: QS

Front of the plant of Astro Craft, Spring Grove, IL

Founded in 1967 by Martin Dschida, Wendel Dschida, the Astro Craft Tradition of Quality began. Our success and growth is due to the preservation of our family tradition - Quality and Service in all that we do.

Today, the second generation is continuing Astro Craft's Tradition of quality and service. Astro Craft provides custom precision machining services for prototypes and production runs to customer specifications. We are a complete service oriented business, providing the customer with consistent, quality products at competitive prices with prompt deliveries.

Over our 20 year history, Astro Craft has established a solid reputation for quality in a wide variety of markets and applications. We have manufactured components for the aerospace, automotive test equipment, communications, health services, packaging, and printing industries.

Our experience in engineering and manufacturing enables us to provide valuable technical service to our customers for efficient components manufacture.

1967 durch Martin Dschida und Wendel Dschida gegründet, begann die Firma Astro Craft ihre Tradition für Qualität. Unseren Erfolg und das Wachstum verdanken wir der Aufrechterhaltung dieser Familientradition - nämlich Qualität und Kundendienst in jeder Hinsicht.

Heute setzt die zweite Generation die Astro Craft Tradition von Qualität und Leistung fort. Astro Craft beliefert seine Kundschaft mit speziell hergestellten Teilen für Modelle und Production. Wir sind völlig auf guten Kundendienst eingerichtet und bedienen unsere Kunden mit hochwertigen Produkten zu wettbewerbsfähigen Preisen und zeitgerechter Lieferung.

Über die letzten 20 Jahre hat sich Astro Craft einen guten Namen für Qualität in weiten Kreisen von Industrien mit verschiedensten Produkten gemacht. Es werden Teile für die Luftfahrt-, Kraftfahrzeug-, Kommunikations-, Gesundheitspflege- und Verpackungsindustrien und für Druckpressen hergestellt. Diese weite Erfahrung hilft uns in der Entwicklung und Produktion und gibt uns die Möglichkeit, unseren großen Kundenkreis mit Rat und Tat zu bedienen.

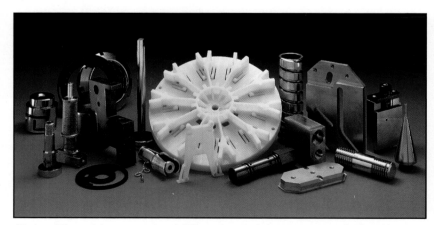

State-of the-art components of different materials are custom designed, engineered and produced on most sophisticated CNC equipment.

DON'T FENCE ME IN

In 1960, after graduating from a Berlin high school, I came to the United States for a year to see the country. Working odd jobs paid for traveling around. Back in Berlin, I studied at the Technical University and graduated as an electronic engineer. Despite good job offers from the big electronic companies, I decided to emigrate to the United States together with my first wife. The Berlin Wall had been erected, and I am an outdoors person who needs space. In America, I worked for four different companies, which all went broke. So I decided to go on my own. There was an opportunity in the optical field. I started to repair medical scopes, and eventually to manufacture them myself. By and by, other products got added. The rest is history: For the last 25 years, SPIESS DESIGN, INC. has been supplying the U.S. and the world with quality medical products, specializing in endoscopic equipment. The company's products can be found in operating rooms all over the United States.

Five years ago, I married my second wife who is also a Berliner, and brought her into the country.

Although my products are made in the USA, I still prefer my wives "Made in Germany".

Joachim Dietrich (Joe) Spiess
Founder and owner of SPIESS DESIGN, INC.

Sperrt mich nicht ein !

1960, nach dem Abitur, ging ich zunächst für ein Jahr in die Vereinigten Staaten, um das Land kennenzulernen. Dort verdiente ich mir mit allerlei Jobs das Reisegeld. Wieder in Berlin, studierte ich an der Technischen Hochschule und machte mein Diplom als Elektronik - Ingenieur. Trotz guter Stellenangebote von etlichen großen Firmen entschloß ich mich, zusammen mit meiner ersten Frau nach USA auszuwandern. Inzwischen war nämlich die Mauer errichtet worden, und ein Naturmensch wie ich braucht eben seinen Raum.

In Amerika arbeitete ich für vier verschiedene Firmen, die aber alle bald eingingen. So entschloß ich mich, auf eigenen Füßen zu stehen. Es ergab sich eine Gelegenheit im optischen Bereich. Ich fing mit der Reparatur von Laparaskopen an und stellte diese schließlich selbst her. Nach und nach kamen andere Geräte dazu. Der Rest spricht für sich selbst: Seit 25 Jahren beliefert SPIESS DESIGN, INC. Amerika sowie alle anderen Kontinente mit medizinischen Qualitätsprodukten, insbesondere Endoskope.

"Unsere Produkte sind in allen Operationssäälen der USA zu finden. Vor fünf Jahren habe ich meine zweite Frau, auch eine Berlinerin, geheiratet und sie in dieses Land gebracht. Obwohl meine Produkte in USA hergestellt sind, bevorzuge ich doch meine Ehefrauen 'Made in Germany'."

Joachim Dietrich (Joe) Spiess
Gründer und Besitzer
SPIESS DESIGN, INC.

Karin and Joe Spiess

Das Ding mit den Namen -

"Joachim" ist ein schöner Name
solange du in Deutschland lebst.
Er wird jedoch zum Zungenbrecher,
wenn nach den USA du strebst.

Dasselbe gilt für Ursula,
für Getrud oder Fritz;
was man hier macht aus deinem Namen,
ist wirklich nur ein Witz.

Für ein paar Jahre denkst du noch,
du kannst vielleicht erzwingen,
daß man den Namen richtig sagt -
doch das will nicht gelingen.

So wird Joachim dann ein Joe,
aus Alfred wird ein Al;
aus Gertrud wird 'ne Goerde hier,
und das geht ziemlich schnell.

"Naja, was soll's", so denkst du dann,
"das ist ja nicht so wichtig.
Wenn auch mein Name flöten geht -
das Leben hier ist richtig !"

The Thing About Names

These Germans, oh my God, please help,
they got the weirdest names !
Call Ursula, Elfriede, Jobst,
instead of Pat or James.

This is too much for any tongue
made in the U.S.A.
So they should change their awful names,
if they intend to stay !

Who can pronounce a name like Jürgen ?
That is ridiculous, is hell !
So make it easy, be just Joe,
and I'll accept you as my pal.

Dr. Karin Walter-Spiess

Spiess Design, Inc.
290 Telser Road • Lake Zurich, Illinois 60047

Merz Apothecary

This old-time apothecary, with its timeless grace and beauty, has been serving the health care needs of Chicagoans since 1875. The stained-glass door chimes as you walk in, and the vast mirrors and glass cabinets framed in dark oak and giant apothecary jars sparkle beneath the brass chandeliers of the oldest pharmacy in the city. The pleasant odor of herbs, European bath soaps, oils and perfumes serves as the perfect environment for this escape into the past. The professional pharmacists will introduce you to natural, herbal, as well as homeopathic alternatives to convential medicine. Experience a touch of Europe and fill your prescription for the past and the present at the *Merz Apothecary*.

Merz Apotheke   established 1875

Merz Apotheke, die älteste Apotheke in Chicago, sorgt seit 1875 für die Gesundheit der Einwohner von Chicago. Beim Betreten dieser alterwürdigen Apotheke von zeitloser Schönheit klingelt die Tür aus Buntglas, und die riesigen Spiegel, die von dunklem Eichenholz umrahmten Glasschränke und die enormen Arzneimittelgefäße funkeln unter den Leuchtern aus Messing. Der angenehme Duft von Kräutern, europäischen Badeseifen, Ölen und Parfüms liefert das perfekte Ambiente für diesen Ausflug in die Vergangenheit. Die erfahrenen Apotheker machen Sie gern mit Kräuterheilmitteln sowie natürlichen und homöopathischen Alternativen zur konventionellen Medizin bekannt. Hier empfinden Sie Glanz und Duft von einst und jetzt aus Europa. Wir laden Sie herzlich ein in die *Merz Apotheke*.

**4716 North Lincoln Avenue
Chicago, Illinois 60625**

**Tel: (312) 989-0900
Fax: (312) 989-8108**

•

Nationwide delivery
Versand ins ganze Land

"SOUND OF EUROPE"

By Gunella Gehrken - Griletz

Now on WJKL 94.3 FM

Gunella Gehrken -Griletz, seit zwanzig Jahren steht die beliebte Moderatorin an der Spitze der Deutschen Radio Programme im Chicagoland. Gunella hat Musik im Blut, lautete schon zu Beginn 1977 das einstimmige Urteil ihrer zahlreichen Radiofans.

"Ich bin eine Frau, die sich hundertprozentig für ihren Job, in diesem Falle meine Radiosendung, einsetzt." Gunella wurde in dem Eifelstädtchen Gerolstein geboren.

1983 wurde der "Sound of Europe" anläßlich der dreihundert Jahrfeier der deutschen Imigration in den Vereingten Staaten von der GACoC für "Outstanding Public Service" ausgezeichnet.

Gunella Gehrken - Griletz

Gunella wechselte im Juni 1997 von WVVX, 103.1 FM, auf WJKL, 94.3 FM. über. Ihre jahrelangen Mitarbeiter sind Ehe- und Showmann Klaus Griletz (Ehemaliger Fußball Profi), der jede Woche 1 - 2 Shows moderiert, Horst-Dieter Groß, Internationaler Bankfachmann aus

Frankfurt, der seit 14 Jahren in regelmäßigen Abständen die Hörer des "Sound of Europe" mit dem Musiktelegramm erfreut. Auch Werner Baroni, bekannter Journalist, mit vielen Auszeichnungen und Gründer der Wochenzeitung "Amerika Woche", der jede Woche die Nachrichten von Hüben und Drüben durchsagt, sowie Cristl Petschke aus Garmisch-Partenkirchen, die dafür sorgt, daß der "Sound of Europe" mit den neuesten CDs versorgt wird.

Gunella ist über 15 Jahre Mitglied der IADM, der Internationalen Assoziation Deutschsprachiger Medien, und wird regelmäßig mit Musikkasetten der Deutschen Welle, Köln bemustert.

"Sound of Europe" - das ist Unterhaltung vom Besten.

"SOUND OF EUROPE"
Gunella Gehrken -Griletz
113 McHenry Road, Suite 233
Buffalo Grove, Illinois 60089
Telephone: 847 / 459 - 1188
Fax: 847 / 459 - 6788

Welcome to Lincoln Square Mall...

International Fashions by
Ingrid

Trachten
Knitwear (Men & Ladies)
Skirts • Blouses
Suits • Dresses
Sizes 8 to 20

4710 N., Lincoln Avenue
Chicago, Illinois 60625

Phone 773/878-8382
Fax 773/878-8148

Deutsche Markenschuhe, hervorragend in Qualität und Paßform.

German Quality Shoes for over 30 years.

SALAMANDER
of Chicago

4762 N, Lincoln Avenue
Chicago, IL 60625
773/784-SHOE • 773/784-7463

**Large Selection
IMPORTED/DOMESTIC**

Sausages • Meat
Cheeses • Fish
Salads • Breads
Cookies • Candies
Juices • Jams • Jellies
Honey • Coffee • Tea
Wine • Liquor • Beer
Champagne
Cosmetics
Household Utensils
Gift Baskets
Party Trays

Delicatessen MEYER

4750 N. Lincoln Avenue
Chicago, Illinois 60625
Tel: 773/561-3377

*Home of
Stiegl
Columbus
Beer*

Phone: 773/561-8281

European IMPORT CENTER

European Crystal • China • Linens and other Imported Gift Items
German Language Magazines • Newspapers and Greeting Cards
4752 N. Lincoln Avenue • Chicago, Illinois 60625

Lincoln Square Mall bietet sich an

*Excellent German &
American Cuisine*

*Live Entertainment
Nightly and Saturday
& Sunday Afternoon*

*Open for
Lunch & Dinner
Closed Tuesdays*

4732-34 Lincoln Avenue
Chicago, Illinois 60625
Tel. 773/784-4444
Fax 773/784-2092

Chicago Brauhaus
RESTAURANT & LOUNGE

Latest Top
European and
Vintage Frames:

– Cazal
– Giorgio Armani
– Hugo Boss
– Neostyle
– Porsche
– Rodenstock
– Silhouette
– Zeiss
– and More...

Board Certified
Opticians

QUALITY OPTICAL
4718 N. Lincoln Avenue
Chicago, IL 60625
Tel: 773/561-0870 Fax: 773/561-4185

Eyes Examined — Children's Vision — Glasses Fitted — Contact Lenses

---

O du fröhliche, gnadenbringende Weihnachtszeit...

Photos: Ernst Ott

The Department of German at UIC

The Department of German at the University of Illinois at Chicago offers a full course of German study that is easily accessible to students in the Chicago area. In addition to basic language courses, we offer the B.A., the M.A., and an intercampus Pd.D. program with the University at Urbana-Champaign. Besides the regular B.A., we offer the B.A. in Teacher Education in German and a new option, the B.A. in German with Business Minor. The latter includes collateral courses taken in the College of Business administration. Study abroad is possible through the University's exchange programs with Vienna and Hamburg. Use of the recently developed modified natural method in basic language instruction enhances student motivation and ensures that communication remains the goal of the undertaking.

We sponsor or co-sponsor many events in the Chicago area, such as screenings of German films, readings by German authors, and lectures by scholars, business executives, artists, authors, and political figures on topics having to do with German and European history, politics, literature, culture, and the German-speaking countries' relations with the U.S. We cooperate closely in arranging events with the German, Austrian, and Swiss consulates and the Goethe Institut (we are now qualified to administer the Zertifikat Deutsch als Fremdsprache) and are seeking to broaden our connections with the German-American community and with German-affiliated businesses. We recently established a memorial fund for Niels Friedrichs, Managing Director of the German American Chamber of Commerce of the Midwest, and we annually dispense student awards from other departmental funds and annual donations. We cooperate closely with the TRIO/Upward Bound program on campus, supplying instruction, guidance, and evaluation for their German offerings. Our Department was among the sponsors of the unusual new elementary school German exchange program at Herbert Spencer Elementary School in the Austin area of Chicago, and two of our alumni have taught there. Each year we invite about 150 high school students from 15 area schools to the campus for German competitions. There are usually several of our alumni teaching in area schools, and several of them are or have been officers in the regional American Association of Teachers of German.

Our predominantly young faculty consists of active scholars on the national and international academic scene, and their expertise ranges from older to contemporary literature and culture and extends to applied linguistics, teaching methodology, and business operations, thus covering most of the major areas of German study. We generally employ about 9 teaching assistants working toward graduate degrees. Our undergraduate and graduate majors produce their own newsletter, and the weekly Kaffeestunde is well attended.

Though our program is small compared to those of the high-demand career fields, our alumni usually praise the individual attention they have received. We believe further, that, in view of changing geopolitical patterns and the trend toward internationalization, the potential for growth in the coming years is strong.

Das Deutsche Institut an der UIC

Das Deutsche Institut an der University of Illinois at Chicago bietet ein vollständiges Deutschstudium an, das für Studenten aus dem Raum Chicago leicht zugänglich ist. Zusätzlich zu elementaren Sprachkursen bieten wir den amerikanischen B.A.-, M.A.- sowie Ph.D.-Abschluß an, wobei letzterer als Programm in Zusammenarbeit mit der University at Urbana-Champaign besteht. Neben dem regulären B.A.-Abschluß ist auch die Möglichkeit gegeben, den B.A. für die Ausbildung zum Deutschlehrer und - neuhinzugekommen -den B.A. in Deutsch mit Wirtschaft als Nebenfach abzulegen. Dieser Studiengang schließt Begleitkurse am College of Business and Administration ein. Durch ein Austauschprogramm der Universität mit Wien und Hamburg wird den Studenten auch ein Auslandsstudium ermöglicht. Die Anwendung der kürzlich entwickelten modifizierten natürlichen Methode im elementaren Sprachunterricht erhöht die Schülermotivation und stellt sicher, daß Kommunikation das eigentliche Ziel des Unterrichts bleibt.

Wir sind Sponsoren und Kosponsoren vieler Veranstaltungen in und um Chicago, wie Vorführungen deutscher Filme, Dichterlesungen deutscher Autoren sowie Vorträge von Wissenschaftlern, Wirtschaftsexperten, Künstlern, Autoren und Politikern, die die deutsche und europäische Geschichte, Politik, Literatur und Kultur sowie die Beziehungen der deutschsprachigen Länder zu den USA zum Thema haben. Bei Veranstaltungen arbeiten wir eng mit dem Deutschen, Österreichischen und Schweizer Konsulat und dem Goethe Institut zusammen (wir besitzen die Qualifikation, das Zertifikat Deutsch als Fremdsprache zu vergeben) und wir sind bestrebt, unsere Beziehungen zu der deutsch-amerikanischen Gemeinde und unsere Verbindungen mit Wirtschaftsunternehmen, die geschäftliche Beziehungen zu Deutschland haben, zu erweitern. Vor kurzem haben wir einen Gedenkfond für Niels Friedrichs, dem Leiter der Deutsch-Amerikanischen Handelskammer für den Mittleren Westen, eingerichtet. Alljährlich werden wir von anderen Institutsfonds sowie jährlichen Spenden Auszeichnungen an Studenten vergeben. Wir arbeiten eng mit dem TRIO/Upward Bound Programm auf unserem Universitätsgelände zusammen und unterstützen dessen Deutsch-Angebote durch Anleitungen, Beratungen und Beurteilungen. Unser Institut war einer der Sponsoren für das ungewöhnliche, neue Deutsch-Austauschprogramm für die Grundschule an der Herbert-Spencer-Grundschule in Chicago-Austin, wo zwei unserer ehemaligen Studenten unterrichten. Jedes Jahr laden wir für Deutsch-Wettbewerbe ungefähr 150 Highschool-Schüler von 15 Schulen aus der Umgebung auf das Universitätsgelände ein. Es unterrichten normalerweise immer mehrere unserer ehemaligen Studenten in den Schulen der Umgebung, und einige von ihnen sind oder waren Mitglieder im Vorstand der regionalen "American Association of Teachers of German".

Unsere überwiegend junge Fakultät setzt sich aus aktiven Wissenschaftlern, die der nationalen wie auch internationalen akademischen Szene angehören, zusammen. Ihr Fachwissen reicht von alter bis zeitgenössischer Literatur und Kulturwissenschaft bis hin zu angewandter Linguistik, Lehrmethoden und Geschäftstätigkeiten, und sie decken damit die Hauptbereiche eines Deutschstudiums ab. Wir beschäftigen in der Regel neun Lehrassistenten, die auf Abschlüsse hin arbeiten. Unsere Deutschstudenten im Grund- und Hauptstudium bringen ihren eigenen Newsletter heraus, und die wöchentliche 'Kaffeestunde' ist gut besucht.

Obwol unser Studienprogramm im Verhältnis zu solchen mit beruflich stark gefragten Bereichen, klein ist, loben unsere ehemaligen Studenten generell die persönliche Aufmerksamkeit, die jedem Studenten zuteil wurde. Wir sind auch davon überzeugt daß angesichts wechselnder geopolitischer Strukturen sowie des Trends zur Internalisierung, ein starkes Wachstumspotential in den nächsten Jahren bestehen wird.

This page was donated to the Niels Friedrichs Memorial Fund, co-author of "Chicagoland", 1994.

University of Illinois in Chicago

USA/FRG
German American Day
Youth Exchange Program

by Elsbeth M. Seewald, former National President, D.A.N.K.

The USA continues to be the country young Germans love to visit. This is reflected in the great number of exchange programs for pupils, students, and young working people. Some 18,000 young people, almost two-thirds from Germany, including the former German Democratic Republic, and one-third from the USA participate every year in government-sponsored programs of various scope and length. The "flagship" of these is the elite Congress-Bundestag Youth Exchange Progam (CBYX), with a visit duration of six to twelve months. There are also Fulbright programs and German-American Partnership exchanges, catering to different program regions and/or ages of exchangees. German funding levels of the programs are numbered in the millions of dollars.

Traveling and making friends are prime objectives of this active Youth Exchange Program

The friendship between Germans and Americans has long since become a fact of life. But it is subject to a permanent process of renewal; it must be experienced and revitalized by all German and Americans, especially the young. This is the task of the bilateral USA/FRG Youth Exchange Council, begun by an initiative of former President Ronald Reagan and FRG Chancellor Helmut Kohl in October of 1986. It was formally established through an exchange of notes between the two governments on February 10, 1988, and held its first meeting the following May.

On August 8, 1990, Bruce S. Gelb, then Director of the United States Information Agency, invited former D.A.N.K. National President Elsbeth M. Seewald to join the Council. She was appointed the USA-Coordinator for a part of the Youth Exchange Program, the specially created German American Day Youth Exchange Program, designed to promote, raise interest in and illustrate the day, celebrated annually nationwide on October 6th.

The program enjoys the strong support of both nations. Both governments have placed a high priority on building bonds of friendship and mutual understanding between their younger generations. The program-inception enhanced the scope of the existing USA/FRG youth exchange programs, and for the first time accorded American and German youths a "grass roots program," an early outreach, enabling them to meet one another at a rather young age. The visits sometimes mark only the first of many future visits back and forth between the countries and deepen the contacts and foster what can become life-long friendships.

As the USA Coordinator, Mrs. Seewald procures all USA host groups, and submits to the German coordinator in Bonn information

about USA youth groups planning to visit Germany. Included in the task are liaison work, such as translations, and program arrangements.

The German American Day Program is administered in the USA by the U.S.I.A., and enjoys the patronage of the German American National Congress, and the financial support of the German American Education Fund. Public funding on the USA side for all exchange programs, and new initiatives, is limited, and Congressional appropriations have been stagnant, making it mandatory for the USA program to rely on private sector resources for financial support.

In Germany the program is sponsored by the Bundesjugendplan, and the Ministerium for Women, Seniors and Youth, and carried out by the International Youth Exchange Visitors Service (I.J.A.B.), an independent agency of the ministerium. The I.J.A.B. matches German youth groups to the wishes and needs of the USA host groups, and also finds suitable host groups for American youths in Germany. The program is financially safeguarded by annual monetary allocations in the FRG budget. German officials consider the program of utmost importance in the context of the international cooperation, and the FRG spends a great deal of money to finance these youth exchange programs, especially the USA/FRG ones.

The FRG pays German host groups per diem stipends for their overseas visitors, and provides health insurance for all American program participants during their stay in Germany. German youth exchangees also receive financial assistance for their flights. American youths must pay for their flights. The other bilateral programs of the FRG receive a different degree of financial assistance.

German authorities would like to welcome more USA youth exchange groups in Germany, but are adamant in their request that "Youth Must Meet Youth," the very reason and intent of the program

Another main criteria of the exchange visits is participation in the annual celebrations of German American Day, on October 6th and German Unification Day, October 2nd.

Photos: Ernst Ott

Musik performances are always welcomed, in the USA and Europe.

The first German youth exchange groups arrived in the USA in October 1990, and in 1993 the first American Youths went to Germany. Regular evaluation meetings with German authorities monitor the scope and success of the program, and see to its constant expansion and financial well-being. It now includes also sport and swimming groups, as well as art performance groups. With the event of German unification in 1990 it also serves an entirely new group of young leaders. It currently gives approx. 175-200 youths annually the opportunity for an exchange visit.

"For more information and a complete list of USA/FRG Youth Exchange organizations, please consult the Addressbook of German-American Cooperation, 4th Edition-1994 (Jütte Druck, GmbH, Leipzig)."

Deutsch-Amerikanischer Jugendaustausch
Sonderprogramm Deutsch-Amerikanischer Tag

von Elsbeth M. Seewald, former National President, D.A.N.K.

Die USA bleibt welterhin das bevorzugte Besuchsland für junge Deutsche. Dieser Trend is reflektiert in der großen Anzahl von Austauschprogrammen für Schüler, Studenten und junge Berufstätige. Etwa 18,000 junge Deutsche und Amerikaner nehmen jährlich an den Regierungs- subventierten Programmen verschiedener Kriterien und Aufenthaltsdauer teil. Ungefähr zwei Drittel kommen aus Deutschland und der damaligen Deutschen Demokratischen Republik, und ein Drittel aus den USA. Das "Flaggschiff" dieser Programme is unbedingt das elitäre **Kongreß- Bundestag Jugendaustauschprogramm** (CBYX). welches Aufenthalte für sechs oder zwölf Monate in beiden Ländern ermöglicht. Andere Programme, wie z.B. die Fulbright Programme und die Deutschamerikanischen Partnerschaftsaustauschprogramme, verfolgen andere Zielrichtungen und beeinschliessen andere Altersgruppen. Deutschland unterstützt alle Jungendaustauschprogramme und gibt Millionen dafür aus.

Die Freundschaft zwischen Deutschen und Amerikanern ist schon lange Tatsache. Aber sie bedarf ständiger Erneuerung; sie muß immer wieder von Deutschen sowie Amerikanern, und ganz besonders von den jungen Menschen beider Länder, vitalisiert und überprüft werden. Es ist die Aufgabe des bilateralen **USA/BRD Jugendaustauschkonzils**, im Oktober 1986 durch eine Initiative des vormaligen **USA- Präsidenten Ronald Reagan und Bundeskanzler Helmut Kohl** ins Leben gerufen, hier zu helfen. Das Konzil wurde am 10. Februar 1988 durch einen formellen Notenaustausch zwischen den beiden Ländern offiziell etabliert, und hielt sein erstes bilaterales Treffen im Mai. 1988.

Getting to know other cultures, language and people makes the Youth Exchange Program so appealing.

Am 8. August 1990 lud **Bruce S. Gelb**, der damalige **Direktor** der **United States Information Agency** (U.S.I.A.) die vormalige **D.A.N.K. National Präsidentin Elsbeth M. Seewald** ein Mitglied des Konzils zu werden, welches sie dann zur USA-Koordinatorin für das neu kreierte **Deutsch-Amerikanischer Tag Sonder-Jugendaustauschprogramm** ernannte. Dieses Sonderprogramm wurde ins Leben gerufen um den jährlich am 6. Oktober in ganz Amerika gefeierten Tag zu illustrieren und immer größeres Interesse und Teilnahme an diesem Ehrentag der Deutschamerikaner zu fördern.

Das Programm wird von beiden Nationen stark unterstützt, und beide Regierungen haben hohe Prioritäten gesetzt für die Verstärkung der bilateralen Freundschaft und gegenseitigen Verständnisses zwischen den jüngeren Generationen ihrer Länder. Die Erstellung des Sonderprogramms **Deutsch- Amerikanischer Tag** steigert die Reichwelte der existierenden Jugendaustauschprogramme, und gibt deutschen und amerikanischen Jugendlichen zum ersten Mal die Möglichkeit, sich schon in relativ jungem Alter in ihren respektiven Ländern zu treffen und kennenzulernen. Diese Erstbesuche schaffen Kontakte und sind oftmals der Beginn lebenslanger Freundschaften und wiederholter Gegenbesuche, und vertiefen die transatlantischen Bindungen.

Als USA-Koordinatorin ist es Frau Seewalds Aufgabe alle amerikanischen Gastgebergruppen für deutsche Jugendgruppen zu beschaffen, und an den deutschen Koordinator in Bonn Informationen über amerikanische Jugendgruppen, die Deutschland besuchen wollen, weiterzuleiten. Ihre Arbeit beeinschließt außerdem komplette Liaisonarbeit wie Übersetzungen, Programmbesprechungen, Telephonbesprechungen, usw. Das **Sonderprogramm Deutsch-Amerikanischer Tag** wird in den USA von der **United States Information Agency (U.S.I.A.)** verwaltet, es steht unter der Schirmherrschaft des **Deutsch- Amerikanischen National Kongresses (D.A.N.K.)** und erhält finanzielle Unterstützung von der **Deutsch Amerikanischen Kulturstiftung (German American Education Fund)**. Öffentliche USA-Geldzuschüsse für alle Jugendaustauschprogramme, inklusive neuer Initiativen, sind sehr begrenzt, und finanzielle USA-Kongress Zuwendungen blieben stagnant. Es wurde deshalb mandatar auf mögliche Hilfsquellen und finanzielle Zuwendungen aus dem Privatsektor zu hoffen.

In Deutschland wird das Programm vom **Bundesjugendplan,** und dem **Ministerium für Frauen, Senioren und Jugend** verwaltet, und durchgeführt vom **Internationalen Jugendaustauschbesucherdienst (I.J.A.B.)**, einer selbständigen Agentur des Ministeriums. Diese Agentur sucht dann im Einklang mit den Wünschen und Notwendigkeiten der amerikanischen Gastgebergruppen passende deutsche Jugendgruppen für die USA-Besuche aus. Gleichzeitig bemüht sich die Agentur auch um passende Gastgebergruppen für die amerikanischen Jugendlichen in Deutschland. Finanziell ist das Programm durch die jährlichen Allokationen im Budget der Bundesrepublik gesichert. Offizielle deutsche Regierungsstellen messen dem Programm äußerste Wichtigkeit im Kontext der internationalen Zusammenarbeit bei, und die Bundesrepublik stellt erhebliche Gelder zur Verfügung, um diese Jugend- Austauschprogramme zu finanzieren, ganz besonders für die USA/BRD Programme.

Die Bundesregierung zahlt ihren deutscen Gastgebergruppen per diem Zuschüsse für deren transatlantische Besucher. Außerdem werden die amerikanischen Besucher für die Dauer Ihres Aufenthaltes in Deutschland in die Soziale Krankenversicherung aufgenommen. Zusätzlich erhalten die deutschen Austauschteilnehmer finanzielle Unterstützung für ihre Flugunkosten, während amerikanische Teilnehmer selbst für ihre Flugkarten bezahlen müssen. Die anderen bilateralen Jugendaustauschprogramme erhalten ebenfalls finanzielle Unterstützung verschiedenen Grades von der Bundesrepublik.

Offizielle deutsche Stellen würden gerne mehr USA-Jungendaustauschgruppen in Deutschland willkommen heißen, aber bestehen absolut darauf, daß, im Einklang mit Absicht und Sinn der Jugendaustauschprogramme bei allen Austauschbesuchen **"Jugend Jugend kennenlernen muß"**.

Ein weiteres Kriterium des Programms sind Teilnahme und Auftritte am 6. Oktober, dem **Deutsch-Amerikanischen Tag** und am 2. Oktober, dem **Tag der Deutschen Einheit**.

Die ersten deutschen Jugendaustauschgruppen kamen im Oktober 1990 in die USA, und in 1993 besuchten die ersten amerikanischen Jugendlichen Deutschland. Reguläre Evaluationstreffen mit den zuständigen deutschen Behörden überwachen den Erfolg und Umfang des Programms, und sorgen für dessen konstante Erweiterung und finanzielles Wohlergehen. Schon jetzt nehmen Sport-, Schwimm- und Gymnastikgruppen, zusammen mit Volktanzgruppen, Chören, musikalischen Gruppen und Jugendorchestern, sowie Vertretern der bildenden Künste am Programm teil. Alle werden in ihrem Gastgeberland mit passenden Gruppen gepaart und zusammen arbeiten. Seit 1990, als West- und Ostdeutschland sich wieder vereinigten, dienen diese Programme auch einer völlig neuen Gruppe junger Führungskräfte. Das Sonder Programm gibt gegenwärtig ca. 175-200 jungen Menschen jährlich die Möglichkeit an einem deutsch-amemrikanischen Austauschbesuch teilzunehmen.

Ammerkung: Eine Liste der Auskunfstellen, Austauschorganisationen in Deutschland und den USA für die Jugendaustauschprogramme kann im **Adressbuch der Deutsch-Amerikanischen Zusammenarbeit**, 4. Auflage - 1994 (Jütte Druck GmbH, Leipzig), eingesehen werden.

The German-American Memorial Association

by Hans J. Beyer, Chairman

Auswanderer Denkmal Bremerhaven war 1996 10 Jahre alt.

Am 5. Juli 1986 wurde das Auswanderer Denkmal in Bremerhaven an einem regnerischen Tag feierlich eingeweiht. Das trübe Wetter und die negativen Berichte in verschiedenen Zeitungen im Bezug auf die Einweihung und das Denkmal selbst haben nur den Sinn des Denkmals vertieft. Die auf dem Sockel stehende Einwanderer Familie sieht optimistisch in die Ferne und Zukunft, so waren sich auch die Erbauer und Initiatoren bewußt, daß dieses Denkmal nicht eine vorübergehende Attrappe sei, sondern für viele Jahre daran erinnern soll, daß viele Menschen, die in einem fernen Land leben, ihre Heimat mit Heimweh und Fernweh verlassen haben. Die Platten mit Einzelpersonen, Vereinen und Spendern erinnern an die Zeit dieser großen Epoche der Auswanderer von Bremerhaven, den Hafen der Tränen, sowie an die vielen anderen Ausgangsorte mit Blick in eine neue Zukunft.

Als dieses Foto von Bert Lachner, dessen Elternhaus nur wenige Kilometer entfernt steht, gemacht wurde, war dieser so sehr beeindruckt, daß er sich entschloß, dieses Auswanderer Denkmal auf dem Einband und der Titelseite dieses Buches zu zeigen.

Ein neuer Anfang:

Landwirtschaftlicher Arbeiter in Wisconsin

von Ernst Ott

Die Musikkapelle spielte "Nun Ade du mein lieb Heimatland" als die letzten Leinen abgeworfen wurden und die U.S.N.S. General C.H. Muir, ein US Truppentransporter, sich langsam von Bremerhaven's Pier löste und seinen Bug in die unruhigen Wogen des Atlantiks drehte.

Es war ein kühler April Tag im Jahre 1952 und an Bord des Schiffes befanden sich ungefähr 1000 Auswanderer, die dem "Land der unbegrenzten Möglichkeiten" und dem Traum ein neues Leben zu beginnen, entgegenfuhren. Sie waren die Glücklichen, deren Einwanderquotennummer aufgerufen wurde und die ein gültiges Visum besaßen.

Ich war auch einer derjenigen die jetzt noch einen letzten Blick auf die schnell am Horizont verschwindende Küste warfen; dann mußte ich mich bei meiner Station melden um meinen Dienst als Dolmetscher für den Ersten Offizier anzutreten.

Noch vor drei Wochen saß ich an meinem Schreibtisch als Einkäufer für die "European Exchange Service", die mit dem Bau und Betrieb von "Snack Bars and Post Exchanges (PX)" für die US Armee in Deutschland beauftragt war. Ich hatte nicht die geringste Ahnung, daß ich wenige Wochen später als Auswanderer und landwirtschaftlicher Arbeiter mich auf dem Wege nach Amerika befinden würde. Aber fangen wir von vorne an.

Ich wurde 1928 in einer kleinen Ortschaft in Siebenbürgen, Rumänien, geboren. Mein Vater war "Reichsdeutscher", ein waschechter Schwabe und Güterdirektor einer deutschen Aktiengesellschaft im Balkan. Dort heiratete er meine Mutter, die aus einer deutschen Gemeinde im damaligen yugoslavischen Banat stammte. Das macht mich was? Na ja, meine Reisepapiere sagten, daß ich deutscher Staatsbürger, geboren in Rumänien, war und daher mit einer rumänischen Einwanderquote nach Amerika kam. (Der entscheidende Faktor war das Geburtsland, nicht die Staatsangehörigkeit). Als die Firma meines Vaters aufgelöst wurde, zogen wir nach Deutschland. Nach meiner Schulausbildung, ich studierte Sprachen und Außenhandel, bekam ich eine Stelle bei der US Militärregierung. Meine Eltern gingen in den Ruhestand auf dem elterlichen Bauernhof meines Vaters, den er geerbt hatte. Es war schon immer mein Wunschtraum gewesen "hinaus in die Ferne zu gehen und die Welt zu sehen", so wie es mein Vater tat. Da ich für eine amerikanische Organisation arbeitete, lernte ich viel über Amerika und sprach ein gutes Englisch. Amerika war meine erste Wahl, aber ein Visum zu bekommen war schwierig; Amerika brauchte keine Dolmetscher.

Eines Tages sah meine Mutter, durch Zufall, in einer landwirtschaftlichen Zeitung eine Annonce die landwirtschaftliche Arbeiter für Amerika suchte. Bewerber sollten sich umgehend bei der landwirtschaftlichen Kommission des Staates Wisconsin in Nürnberg melden. Da ich mit landwirtschaftlichen Arbeiten gut vertraut war, versuchte ich mein Glück und bewarb mich. Innerhalb drei Wochen war ich auf dem Wege nach Amerika.

Meine Vertragsbedingungen waren: ein Jahr Arbeit auf einer Farm, freie Überfahrt zum Arbeitsplatz, Monatslohn $150, freie Wohnung und Verpflegung auf der Farm, aber lange Arbeitsstunden, wie üblich auf der Farm. Nach dem Jahr war ich frei zu tun und gehen nach Belieben. Für einen jungen, 22-jährigen ungebundenen Mann kein Problem. Aber es wurde anders:

Der Farmer in Mineral Point, Wisconsin, dem ich zugeteilt wurde, behauptete er wäre keinen solchen Vertrag eingegangen, der ihn zu einem Monatslohn von $150 verpflichtet. "In seiner Gegend sei das nicht die übliche Bezahlung." Wiederholte Diskussionen führten zu keinem Ergebnis, und wir gingen auseinader; nicht gerade

als Freunde. Aber ich war frei und fuhr nach Milwaukee, wo mehrere meiner Schiffskameraden in Fabriken arbeiteten. Ich fand auch Arbeit als Material-Transportarbeiter in der "Friedhofschicht" (Nachtschicht) der Metallverarbeitungs-Abteilung. Nicht gerade ein Traum Job aber nach dem Fiasko auf der Farm nicht schlecht und die Bezahlung war angemessen. Aber nach fünf Wochen gab es einen Stahlarbeiterstreik der die Fabrik still legte. Die meisten Angestellten, ich eingeschlossen, wurden vorübergehend entlassen. Kaum einen Cent in der Tasche und ohne Arbeit trug ich meinen größten Schatz, meine Rolleiflex Kamera, ins Pfandhaus und bekam $30 mit denen ich meine nächste Monatsmiete bezahlen konnte. Ich hatte wiederum Glück und landete einen Job als Hautöler in einer Gerberei. Wieder Nachtschicht! Der Name besagt alles: Schneiden, ölen. aufkleben der schlüpfrigen Häute auf ein Fließband von Metallplatten ist nicht gerade die bestreichende Arbeit. Nach sechs Wochen endete der Stahlarbeiterstreik und meine frühere Firma stellte mich wieder ein, als Motorenwickler zum Akkordlohn. Ich arbeitete auch an Wochenenden und "machte gut Geld", wie man das so sagt. Ich konnte auch meine geschätzte Kamera wieder einlösen, die ich für meine Tätigkeit als freiarbeitender Photojournalist brauchte.

In der geringen Freizeit die ich hatte, besuchte ich verschiedene deutsche Vereine, wo ich zahlreiche Schiffskameraden wieder traf und auch neue Freundschaften anknüpfte. Mit der Zeit gelang es mir in meine ursprüngliche Berufslaufbahn zurückzufinden und wurde Export Korrespondent in einer großen Maschinenfabrik Nordberg.

Eines Tages erhielt ich in der Post einen sehr offiziell aussehenden Brief. "Grüße von Uncle Sam" (wie man solche Mitteilungen der Regierung nennt). Ich war noch im Einberufungsalter und der Korea Krieg hatte begonnen. Junge Amerikaner wurden schon einberufen und nun ging es auch an die Einwanderer. Gerade als ich wieder in meine "Normalberufspur" zurückfand, stand ich wieder vor einem neuen Umweg. Aber es hätte auch schlimmer sein können. Viele meiner Freunde fanden sich kämpfend - und einige sterbend - in Korea. Ich selbst wurde zurück nach Deutschland und Frankreich versetzt. Es war ein seltsames Gefühl, nach zwei Jahren wieder daheim zu sein - in amerikanischer Uniform.

Nach meiner Ausmusterung aus der Armee konnte meine berufliche Laufbahn endlich Fortschritte zeigen. Aufgrund meiner freiberuflichen Arbeit als Photojournalist, wurde ich in der Werbe- und Pressaebteilung der Firma Outboard Marine, eine der 500 größten amerikischen Firmen ("Fortune 500 Companies"), angestellt. Dort wurde ich dann zum Werbeleiter und Pressechef für die internationale Tochterfirmen, mit Hauptsitz in Nassau, Bahamas, befördert. Nach mehreren Jahren im "Paradies", öffnete sich eine neue Berufschance, die mich nach Frankfurt brachte, als Direktor der europäischen Unternehmen für Jockey International, eine große amerikanische Bekleidungsfirma. Wenige Jahre später nach New York mit größerem Aufgabenbereich und wieder

zurück in den Mittelwesten als Präsident für dieses Internationale Unternehmen und Mitglied des Aufsichtrates von Jockey, Int'l. Nach 10 Jahren in dieser Position ging ich in den Ruhestand, auf Anraten meiner Ärzte, aber letzten Endes wieder ins Berufsleben als Partner einer internationalen Wirtschaftsberatungsfirma. Außerdem bin ich Vorsitzender des Beratungsgremiums der Textil Management Schule der Universität Missouri und Gastdozent an zwei Universitäten.

Ich wurde auch vom Gouverneur Edgar in den Aufsichtsrat der "Illinois State Board of Public Health" berufen.

Meine Betätigung bei DANK begann eigentlich ganz unschuldig. Vor zehn Jahren wurde ich eingeladen an einigen Veranstaltungen im DANK Haus Chicago teilzunehmen. Der Rest ist Geschichte.

Zurückblickend kann ich sagen, daß Amerika gut zu mir war, und es ist für mich meine neue Heimat geworden. Ja, der Anfang war zwar schwer, aber die meisten deutschen Einwanderer hatten ähnliche Erfahrungen. Für mich, und für viele von uns, wurde es "das Land der unbegrenzten Möglichkeiten", aber man mußte darum kämpfen.

A new Beginning:

Farm Hand in Wisconsin

By Ernst Ott

The band played "Nun ade Du mein lieb Heimatland", as the last lines were cast off and the U.S.N.S. GENERAL C.H. MUIR, a US troop transport ship, slowly edged away from Bremerhaven's navy pier and turned her bow into the choppy waves of the Atlantic.

It was a cool April day 1952 and aboard were about 1000 emigrants heading for the land of unlimited opportunities ("Land der unbegrenzten Möglichkeiten") and the dream to start a new life. They were the lucky ones whose quota was called and who had a valid immigration visa.

I was among the ones who cast a last glance back at the rapidly disappearing coast line and then turned to report to my station and commence my duties as interpreter for the ship's first officer.

Only three weeks ago, I was sitting at my desk in Nürnberg as a purchasing agent for the European Exchange Service, a US Army organization commissioned with the building and operation of Snack Bars and Post Exchanges (PX) for the American Armed Forces in Germany. I had not the slightest idea that in less than a month I would be an emigrant, a farm hand, on my way to America. But let's start at the beginning:

I was born in 1928 in a small village in Transylvania, then part of Romania (formerly Hungary). My father though was a "Reichsdeutscher", a "Schwob", and director of a German real estate corporation with responsibility for its Balkan holdings. He met and married my mother who came from the Yugoslavian Banat. That makes me what? At any rate, my passport said that I was a German subject, born in Romania and I came to the US on a Romanian Quota (determining factor was country of birth, not nationality). In 1936 the corporation my father was working for was dissolved and we moved to Germany. After finishing high

school and college where I majored in languages and international trade, I took a job with the US Military Government. My parents eventually retired to father's parental farm which he had inherited.

It was always my desire to "go out and see the world", as my father had done. Having worked for Americans I learned much about the country and spoke English well. Since I majored in languages and international trade America was my first choice but it was difficult to obtain an immigration quota and America was not in need of Interpreters.

One day, by chance, my mother noticed an advertisement in an agricultural tabloid, looking for farm hands in Wisconsin. Applicants had to apply immediately to the agricultural commission of Wisconsin in Nürnberg. Having worked on farms and familiar with the work, I took a chance and applied. Within three weeks I was on my way.

My contract conditions included one mandatory year's work on a farm, free transportation to the place of work in America, a wage of $150. per month, free room and board, but long work hours, as is customary on the farm. After that I was supposed to be free to do as I pleased. For a 22 year young, unattached man, no problem. Well, it didn' t turn out to be this way.

The farmer at Mineral Point, Wisconsin, who I was assigned to, claimed he did not sign such a contract, obliging him to pay $150.

per month "which was not the going rate in his area". The protracted discussions, over a period of two months went nowhere and we finally parted ways, not exactly on friendly terms. But I was free to go and went to Milwaukee where several of my ship mates were working in factories.

I, too, was able to get a job as materials mover in the heat treatment department during the "grave yard shift". Not exactly a dream job, but after the farm fiasco not bad and the pay was adequate. After five weeks, a sudden steel strike shut down the factory; the newest employees, including myself, were laid off. Hardly any money in my pocket and no job I took my treasured possession, a Rolleiflex camera, to the pawn shop and got a $30 loan to pay my next month's room rent. Luck was on my side and I was able to land a night shift job in a tannery as a hide oiler (the term says it all). Cutting, oiling and pasting slippery animal skins on metal sheets is not exactly the sweetest smelling job. Fortunately, the strike ended after six weeks and I was called back by my previous company and promoted to motor winder at piece rate wages, working also weekends and "making good money" as they used to say at that time. I could also reclaim my treasured camera which I needed for my free-lance photo-journalism work.

In the little free time I had, I frequented the various German societies where I met several of my fellow passengers from the ship and made new friends. Eventually I was able to get back into my original professional line of work and was hired as an export correspondent at Nordberg Manufacturing Company, a large Machinery company.

One day, a very official looking envelope arrived in the mail. "Greetings from Uncle Sam". I was still within draft age and the Korean conflict was going on. Young American men were drafted and now they were also calling immigrants.

Just as I was getting "back on track" there was another detour. It could have been worse. Many of my friends wound up fighting, and several dying, in Korea. I was sent back to Germany and France. It was a strange feeling after less than two years being back at home, but in an American uniform.

After discharge from the Army, my professional career finally began to take off. Due to my work as a free-lance photo journalist I landed a position in the advertising and public relations department of Outboard Marine International, a Fortune 500 company, and was promoted to advertising and public relations manger for its international division with headquarters in Nassau, the Bahamas. After several years in "paradise", a new opportunity called and sent me back to Frankfurt, as Director, European Operations for Jockey International, a major American Apparel manufacturer. A few years later, to Connecticut and as Corporate Vice President of Warnaco Inc., another Fortune 500 company with increased responsibilities and then back to the Midwest as President, International Operations and Member of the Board of Directors. After ten years in the position I retired, upon the urging of my doctors (citing "corporate burn-out"), but eventually I went back into professional life as partner of an international management

Ernst Ott, 1954

consulting firm. I am also guest lecturer at two universities and Chairman of the Advisory Board of one. Recently I was appointed by Illinois Governor Edgar to the Illinois Board of Public Health.

My involvement with DANK started innocently enough. About 10 years ago I was invited to attend some functions at the Chicago DANK Haus and the rest is history. I have served the last 6 years as the National President of the German American National Congress, cultivating our German American heritage and representing German American interests on a national level.

In looking back, I have to say that America was good to me and it has become my new "Heimat". Yes, the beginning was tough, but most German immigrants went through similar experiences. For me - and many of us - it has been the "land of unlimited opportunities - but you have to work and fight for them.

Milwaukee - Wisconsin
Heimat in the Heartland

Milwaukee's Lakefront

Photo by Thom J. Beck

TOMMY G. THOMPSON

Governor
State of Wisconsin

TOMMY G. THOMPSON

Gouverneur
Staat Wisconsin

GUTEN TAG!

Welcome to Wisconsin! It is my pleasure to join the people of our great state in extending our best wishes.

Wisconsin combines the excitement of the big city with the wonder of the rustic north woods and the beauty of the Lake Michigan shoreline. We hope that you will have the opportunity to tour our ethnic and historical districts, dine in our world-renowned restaurants, and relax in the serenity of the north woods. Wisconsin also offers an impressive calendar of events, featuring colorful festivals and craft shows, fine theater performances, exciting musical entertainment, and championship professional sports.

In Wisconsin, we are so very proud of our German heritage. We certainly hope you will feel at home with us as you take advantage of all that Wisconsin has to offer.

GUTEN TAG!

Willkommen in Wisconsin! Ich bin sehr erfreut, mich in die Schar derjenigen in unserem großartigen Staat einreihen zu können, die Ihnen viel Glück wünschen.

Wisconsin verbindet das Aufregende einer Großstadt mit dem Zauber der ländlichen Wälder des Nordens und der Schönheit der Ufer des Michigan-Sees. Wir hoffen, daß Sie Gelegenheit haben, unsere ethnischen und historischen Gegenden zu besuchen, in unseren Restaurants von Weltruf zu speisen und sich in der Einsamkeit der Wälder des Nordens zu entspannen. Wisconsin bietet auch einen beachtlichen Veranstaltungskalender mit interessanten Festen und Kunstgewerbemärkten, gelungenen Theatervorführungen, aufregenden musikalischen Veranstaltungen und sportlichen Meisterschaftsaustragungen an.

In Wisconsin sind wir auf unser deutsches Erbe äußerst stolz. Wir hoffen, daß Sie sich bei uns wie zu Hause fühlen, während Sie alle Vorteile genießen, die Wisconsin zu bieten hat.

Wisconsin – Ihr seid unter Freunden!

Sincerely,

TOMMY G. THOMPSON
Governor

Mit freundlichem Gruß

TOMMY G. THOMPSON
Gouverneur

Room 115 East, State Capitol, P.O. Box 7863, Madison, Wisconsin 53707
(608) 266-1212 • FAX (608) 267-8983

Zimmer 115 Ost, State Capitol, P.O. Box 7863, Madison, Wisconsin 53707, TEL: (608) 266-1212, FAX: (608) 267-8983

JOHN O. NORQUIST

Mayor
Milwaukee, Wisconsin

JOHN O. NORQUIST

**BÜRGERMEISTER
MILWAUKEE, WISCONSIN**

Greetings:

The people of the City of Milwaukee take great pride in our community. The beauty of our Lake Michigan shoreline, our celebration of arts and culture, and the industriousness of our workers, all reflect Milwaukee's magnificence.

You might know Milwaukee as America's beer capital because of our respected brewers. Milwaukee is also a top business and manufacturing center in the United States. And every year Milwaukee hosts a series of world-renowned ethnic festivals and America's finest music festival, Summerfest.

Milwaukee's symphony orchestra, ballet, professional theater groups, and art museum make this city a center of culture. Our institutions of higher education, including The University of Wisconsin-Milwaukee, Marquette University and The Milwaukee School of Engineering, make this city an academic center. A wide variety of professional and amateur athletics make this city a center for sports.

This city welcomes visitors with a friendliness that all Milwaukeeans know by the German word "gemütlichkeit".

More residents of Milwaukee claim German heritage than any other ethnic background. We celebrate the cultures of all our forefathers here, and we invite you to feel right at home in Milwaukee.

Sincerely,

JOHN O. NORQUIST
Mayor

City Hall, 200 E. Wells Street, Milwaukee, Wisconsin 53202
Telephone: (414) 286-2200

Viele Grüße!

Die Einwohner der Stadt Milwaukee sind auf unsere Gemeinschaft äußerst stolz. Die Schönheit der Ufer unseres Michigan-Sees, unsere Hochachtung für die Künste und die Kultur und der Fleiß aller unserer Arbeitnehmer: Alles das zeigt die Großartigkeit von Milwaukee.

Sie werden vielleicht von Milwaukee schon einmal als amerikanische Bierhauptstadt wegen unserer angesehenen Braumeister gehört haben. Milwaukee ist aber auch ein Hauptgeschäfts- und Herstellungszentrum in den Vereinigten Staaten. Und in jedem Jahr findet in Milwaukee eine Reihe bekannter ethnischer Feste und das beste Musikfest der Vereinigten Staaten, das "Summerfest", statt.

Das Sinfonieorchester, das Ballett, professionelle Theaterensembles und das Kunstmuseum von Milwaukee machen diese Stadt zu einem Kulturzentrum. Unsere akademischen Institutionen wie "The University of Wisconsin-Milwaukee", die "Marquette University" und "The Milwaukee School of Engineering" machen diese Stadt zu einem akademischen Zentrum. Ein breites Spektrum von Profi- und Amateursportarten machen diese Stadt zu einem Sportzentrum.

Unsere Stadt heißt ihre Besucher mit einer Freundlichkeit willkommen, die alle Einwohner von Milwaukee unter dem deutschen Wort "Gemütlichkeit" kennen.

Die Mehrheit der Einwohner von Milwaukee geben an, von deutscher Herkunft zu sein. Wir gedenken der Kulturen aller unserer Vorfahren hier, und wir laden Sie ein, sich hier in Milwaukee ganz zu Hause zu fühlen.

Mit freundlichem Gruß

JOHN O. NORQUIST
Bürgermeister

Bürgermeisteramt, 200 E. Wells Street, Milwaukee, Wisconsin 53202
Telefon: (414) 286-2200

GERMAN AMERICAN SOCIETIES OF MILWAUKEE, INC.

Founded May 1964

The German American Societies are comprised of the Presidents from 36 German Clubs and Societies. Since 1964, the presidents or the representatives of the Clubs meet on the second Monday of the month. The main function of this President's forum is to coordinate and act as the umbrella organization of the German Clubs in the Milwaukee area.

This organization is responsible for the annual "German American Societies Queen" Contest and the presentation of the Steuben Award to a citizen in the Milwaukee area who has dedicated himself or herself to the preservation of German American culture and heritage. The establishment of German Fest was a result of the combined efforts of all the presidents of the German American Societies. Currently, the Society is the sponsoring organization of the German Sister City relationship between Milwaukee and Schwerin, Capital of Mecklenburg-Vorpommern.

DIE DEUTSCH AMERIKANISCHE VEREINIGUNG VON MILWAUKEE

Im Mai 1964 gegründet

"Die Deutsch Amerikanische Vereinigung" besteht aus den Präsidenten der 36 deutschen Klubs und Vereine. Seit 1964 treffen sich die Präsidenten oder die Vertreter der Klubs jeden zweiten Montag des Monats.

Die Hauptfunktion dieses Präsidenten Forums soll die Dachorganisation sein, die koordiniert und im Namen aller deutschen Klubs und Vereine im Milwaukee-Gebiet handelt.

Diese Organisation ist auch für die Wahl der "Deutsch Amerikanischen Vereinigungs-Königin" verantwortlich.

Außerdem ist die Auswahl und Überreichung der Steuben Auszeichnung an einen Bürger im Milwaukee-Gebiet, der oder die sich besonders der Erhaltung deutsch-amerikanischer Kultur und dem Erbe widmete, Amt des Präsidenten-Forums.

Der gemeinsamen Zusammenarbeit aller Präsidenten der damaligen

"Deutsch Amerikanischen Vereinigung" ist die Gründung des "German Fests" zu verdanken.

Gegenwärtig ist die "Vereinigung" die fördernde Organisation der deutschen Schwesternstadt-Beziehung zwischen Milwaukee und Schwerin, der Hauptstadt von Mecklenburg-Vorpommern.

German-American Societies, Inc.

S71 W12474 Berrywood Lane
Muskego, Wisconsin 53150-3718

First row left to right:

George Weiss, *President,* German Fest
Hans Lange, *Treasurer,* German-American Societies,
    & *President,* Club der Pommern
Elmar Kretschmann, *President,* German-American Societies,
    & *President,* Milwaukee Donauschwaben
George Enders, *V.P.* German-American Societies,
    & *President,* United German Societies of
    Milwaukee (Bavarians)
Franklin Klug, *2nd V.P.* German-American Societies,
    & *President,* Kulturvereinigung
Frank Schmitz, *Secretary* German-American Societies,
    & *President,* Austrian American Societies

Second row left to right:

John Fagan, *President,* (Germany) Philatelic Society
Wilma Giese, Milwaukee Committee of Americans of German Descent
Frank Fink, *President,* Spielmannszug Milwaukee
Heiner Giese, *President,* Deutscher Sprach-und Schulverein
Edwin Günther, *President,* D.A.N.K.
Günther Behre, *President,* Bavarian Soccer Club
Adolph Meinhardt, *President,* Aurora Lodge
Ruth Rehfeld, *President,* Milwaukee Damenchor

Roswitha Schnappup, *President,* Berliner Bären
Roald Faja, *President,* Schlesier Verein
Othmar Dreiseitel, *President,* Milwaukee Liedergranz

Third row left to right:

Reinhold Ellerman, *Fest President,* K.G. Rheinischer Verein
Franz Baszler, *President,* Apatiner Verein
Delano Maisch, *President,* Carl Schurz Memorial Park
Leo Fox, Schwaben Unterstützungsverein
John Schäfer, *President,* D'Oberlandler

Club's 50th Anniversary & Fahnenweihe. Fahnen-Mütter & Paten, left to right: Carol Keidl†, Hedwig Weil, Mary Bittner, and Elfriede Hartung. Flag Bearers: Reinhold Hutz (left) and John Kolupar (right).   †Deceased

Milwaukee Donauschwaben, Inc.
N56 W14750 Silver Spring Dr.
Menomonee Falls, WI 53051

The Milwaukee Donauschwaben

was founded in 1945 to promote the preservation of Donauschwaben traditions and has grown to be the largest German-American club in Wisconsin. The Donauschwaben are ethnic Germans who lived in Hungary, Yugoslavia and Romania.

During the year the Club hosts many events featuring four dance groups, a Frauengruppe, Jägerverein and Stimmung Society.

Donauschwaben

Die "Milwaukee Donauschwaben" schlossen sich 1945 zusammen, um die Erhaltung der Donauschwaben Traditionen zu fördern. Heute sind sie der größte deutsch-amerikanische Landesverband in Wisconsin. Die Donauschwaben sind verwandte Deutsche, die in Ungarn, Jugoslawien und Rumänien lebten.

Während des Jahres organisiert der Klub viele Veranstaltungen. Die Interessengemeinschaften bestehen aus vier Tanz-Abteilungen, der Frauengruppe, dem Jägerverein und der Stimmungs-Society.

President Elmar Kretschmann with the four Vice Presidents. Left to Right: Franz Momirov (VP of Events), Frank Weil (1st VP), Elmar Kretschmann (President), Tim Kretschmann (VP of Public Relations), and Alois Fuchs (VP of Property).

Milwaukee Donauschwaben Officers

Klub der Pommern Inc. Milwaukee

After 1945, America became the homeland for many of the displaced Germans from the Eastern German regions, including Pomeranians and Silesians. Yet, as Jean Paul said: "No one can ban us from the paradise of our memories". Therefore we will not and can not ever forget our homeland. Together, we will remember and preserve our old traditions and customs in the hope that they will be maintained for generations to come.

Mein Pommern-Land,
mein Heimatland

Wo weiße Segel fliegen auf blauer See,
weiße Möwen wiegen sich in blauer Höh',
blaue Wälder krönen weißer Dünensand.
Pommernland, mein Sehnen ist Dir
zugewandt.

Hans Lange, Pres.
313 Bel Aire Drive
Thiensville, WI 53092
414 / 242-1573

Vorstand des Klubs der Pommern

Front row: Margot Paap; Hans Lange, Pres.; Marianne Gottweiss; Ingrid Bensler. Back row: Adolf Bensler; Werner Trippe; Edith Bergner; Waltraut Dreja; Ingelore Wessollek; Edith Dittmar; Ingrid Goeschko; Josef Gottweiss; Harry Wessollek

Pommerscher Verein Freistadt

The Pommerscher Verein Freistadt was organized in 1978 to preserve the history, heritage and culture of Pomerania.

Our annual "Pommerntag" celebration features the music, dances and food of Pomerania. Our genealogy section preserves the family histories of our people. Our computer library lists more than 100,000 Pomerania names.

Pommerscher Verein Freistadt
Box 204
Germantown, Wisconsin 53022

Der Pommersche Verein Freistadt wurde 1978 gegründet um Geschichte, das Erbe und die Kultur Pommerns zu erhalten.

Unser jährlichers Pommerntag Fest wird mit Musik und Tanz sowie heimischen Gerichten aus Pommern gefeiert. Unsere intensive Ahnenforschung bezeugt die Geschichte unserer Familien. Unsere Datenbank enthält mehr als 100,000 Namen aus Pommern.

Schlesier Verein Milwaukee, Inc.

Nach 1945 wurde Amerika die zweite Heimat für viele der aus den ostdeutschen Provinzen Vertriebenen, wie unsere Landsleute aus Pommern und Schlesien. Doch wie schon Jean Paul sagte: „Die Erinnerung ist das einzige Paradies aus dem wir nicht vertrieben werden können." So können und werden wir unsere Heimat nicht vergessen. Gemeinsam denken wir an unsere Heimat zurück, und wir pflegen die Sitten und Gebräuche in der Hoffnung, sie auch für nachfolgende Generationen zu erhalten.

Schlesier Verein   *Gegründet 1965*

Vorstand des Schlesier Vereins, Milwaukee
Von links: Magaret Dale, Roald Faja (Präs.), Ernestine Faja, Erika Kriegisch, Erwin Kriegisch, Elsbeth Bruhnke, Dieter Bruhnke. Sitzend: Henry Becker. Abwesend: Maria Ruch

Mein Schlesierland, mein Heimatland.

Du mein liebes Riesengebirge,
wo die Elbe so heimlich rinnt,
wo der Rübezahl mit seinen Zwergen,
heut' noch Sagen und Märchen spinnt.
: Riesengebirge, deutsches Gebirge,
meine liebe Heimat du.

Roald Faja, Pres.
4222 W. Barnard Avenue
Greenfield, WI 53221
414 / 281-4339

Pommersche Tanzdeel Freistadt

"Pommersche Tanzdeel Freistadt" was organized in 1977 to preserve and disseminate Pomeranian culture through public performances of Pomeranian folk dances and music in authentic colorful native costumes.

Divided into three age groups, ages 6-8, 9-13 and 14 and up, each group has its own dance director. Total membership is over 75.

Pommersche Tanzdeel Freistadt
W 140 N 10829 County Aire Road
Germantown, Wisconsin 53022

VORSTAND
Rheinischer Verein (Board of Directors)

Back Row, from left: Hans Schneider, Charles Guddeck, Erwin Wunn, Reinhold Ellerman, Klaus Fromme, Hans Lux, Rudi Volkert, Willi Massek, Hans Schmidt. Front row, from left: Baerbel Fromme, Renate Wunn, Erika Volkert, Marge Feld, Betty Guddeck, Emmi Lux.

Photos by:
Margrit Lienhard

Fest-Präsident Reinhold Ellerman und Präsident Klaus Fromme

Mardi Gras in Milwaukee ·······························

One of the oldest customs in Germany's Rhineland is Mardi Gras (Karneval), dating back to the middle ages.

To keep this custom alive the Mardi Gras Society of Milwaukee (Rheinischer Verein "Grün-Weiss") was founded in 1964. The club is dedicated to Mardi Gras tradition. Until 1964 the custom of Mardi Gras was relatively unknown in Milwaukee.

The official Mardi Gras season starts around Christmas and ends the day before Ash Wednesday. Certain highlights begin before,

such as the coronation of a Prince and Princess, a colorful gala affair full of pageantry and splendor.

Monthly meetings are held at "Stemmeler's White Coach Inn" in Thiensville, a suburb of Milwaukee. Strong support comes from the Stemmeler family originally from Cologne, Germany.

With the growing popularity of Mardi Gras it became necessary to find more spacious ball rooms to hold some of the major gala affairs. The final move was made to the renowned and elegant "Grand Milwaukee Hotel" where most major festivities are being held now.

The Mardi Gras Society of Milwaukee has become one of the major societies among the local German clubs and has contributed tremendously in keeping Mardi Gras tradition alive.

Wherever Mardi Gras is celebrated there is fun, happiness, and laughter, always gala festivities where pageantry and tradition is in the foreground.

Karnevals Gesellschaft Rheinischer Verein Gruen - Weiss 1964

Mardi Gras Society of Milwaukee, Inc.

Mardi Gras Society of Milwaukee

Eines der ältesten deutschen Brauchtümer, welches seit dem frühesten Mittelalter besonders im Rheinland gepflegt wird, ist Karneval.

Zur Aufrechterhaltung dieses Kulturgutes wurde im Jahre 1964 die Karnevals-Gesellschaft "Rheinischer Verein Grün-Weiss" in Milwaukee gegründet. Hauptziel war, die Tradition des Karnevals zu pflegen, zumal Karneval vor der Gründung des Vereins nur auf kleinerer Basis in Milwaukee gefeiert wurde.

Obwohl die offizielle Karnevalssaison um Weihnachten herum ihren Beginn hat und am Tage vor Aschermittwoch endet, findet die Kürung eines Prinzenpaares bereits im November statt, eine prunkvolle und farbfreudige Galaveranstaltung.

Vereinsversammlungen werden im Vereinslokal, "Stemmeler's Weisse Kutsche" in Thiensville,

einem Vorort von Milwaukee, abgehalten und von der Familie Stemmeler, gebürtige Rheinländer aus Köln, bestens unterstützt.

Mit der wachsenden Popularität des Karnevals wurde es notwendig, sich nach größeren Veranstaltungs-Räumlichkeiten umzusehen, bis man schließlich im renommierten und eleganten "Grand Milwaukee Hotel" den richtigen Rahmen für die prunkvollen Veranstaltungen fand

Über die Jahre hinaus entwickelte sich der Rheinische Verein "Grün-Weiss" zu einem der bekanntesten und größten Klubs im deutschen Vereinswesen und ist maßgeblich daran beteiligt, karnevalistisches Brauchtum zu erhalten.

Wo Karneval gefeiert wird, herrscht Jubel, Trubel, Heiterkeit, immer Gala Festlichkeiten, wo Tradition und Brauchtum im Vordergrund stehen.

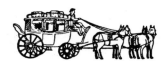

German Fest

Last full Weekend in July!

The Largest Festival...
Das größte Fest...

A group of German-Americans, proud of their heritage and eager to keep alive their traditions and ethnicity, brought together the organizations of the Milwaukee German-American community to provide *Gemütlichkeit* through the display of customs, dance, music and food.

The purpose of the Fest - to promote awareness of German culture and heritage - was realized at a very successful, first German Fest at Milwaukee's lakefront in August 1981. *Gemütlichkeit* was its essence, and it became part of the German Fest logo along with the Milwaukee City Hall.

Thirty-four organizations cooperate to produce an unparalleled, high-quality, ethnic event which each year takes place the last weekend in July.

At a beautiful, 90-acre lakefront park, German Fest features continuous entertainment of ethnic dancing, show and brass bands on nine stages.

Also featured are the popular, eye-catching "Trachtenschau" - a lovely showing of traditional German clothing, a large *Oktoberfest* area, live *Glockenspiel* and a colorful parade which showcases the diversity of this area's German community through ethnic groups, marching bands, floats, dance and singing units.

Participatory events include yodel and tuba playing contests, sheepshead and chess, a piano showcase and special activities for children. These are some of the many offerings at this family-oriented Fest.

Another important part of German Fest is the extensive Culture/Heritage area which includes displays, genealogy assistance, a bookstore, a German Language Center, artisans and videos of Germany.

An extensive *Marktplatz*, a market place, offers a great variety of items of interest, including *Cuckoo Clocks* and *Dirndls*.

But German Fest is much more than a music festival.

n Milwaukee-Wisconsin

of its kind in North America
seiner Art in Nordamerika

Eine Gruppe von Deutsch-Amerikanern, stolz auf ihr deutsches Erbe und darauf bedacht, ethnische Bräuche zu erhalten, brachten die verschiedenen Organisationen der Milwaukee Deutsch-Amerikaner zusammen, um durch Aufrechterhaltung von Bräuchen, Tanz, Musik und Speisen, Gemütlichkeit zu fördern.

Der Zweck des Festes, das Bewußtsein für deutsche Kultur und Tradition zu fördern, wurde im August 1981 zur Wirklichkeit, als man das erste erfolgreiche German Fest in Milwaukees Festival-park am Michigansee feiern konnte.

Gemütlichkeit war die Substanz und wurde zu einem Teil des German Fest Symbols, zusammen mit dem Rathaus der Stadt.

34 Organisationen tragen dazu bei, eine unvergleichliche und erstklassige ethnische Veranstaltung zu produzieren, die in jedem Jahre am letzten Wochenende im Juli stattfindet.

Am wunderschönen, 36 Hektar großen Festpark am Michigansee wird auf neun Bühnen durchgehend Unterhaltung durch ethnische Tänze, Tanz- und Blaskapellen geboten.

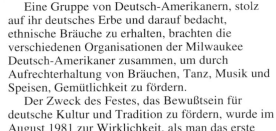

Eine besondere Augenweide ist die populäre Trachtenschau, eine Schau, in welcher traditionelle deutsche Trachten vorgeführt werden. Besondere Anziehungskraft hat der Oktoberfestplatz, ein lebendes Glockenspiel und ein farbenprächtiger Festumzug, der die Vielförmigkeit der deutschen Gemeinschaft Milwaukees durch ethnische Gruppen, Musikkapellen, Schauwagen, Tanz- und Gesangsgruppen zeigt.

An Wettbewerben kann teilgenommen werden wie Jodeln, Tubaspielen, Schafskopf, Schach, Piano- oder Klavierspielen und an anderen besonderen Spielen für Kinder. Dieses sind nur einige der Möglichkeiten dieses familien-orientierten German Fests.

Ein anderer wichtiger Bestandteil des German Fests ist die ausgedehnte Kulturstätte, die Ausstellungen, Ahnenforschung, ein Buchgeschäft, ein deutsches Sprachzentrum, Handwerker und Videos von Deutschland unterhält.

Ein erweiteter Marktplatz bietet eine große Auswahl von interessanten Artikeln, wie Kuckucks-Uhren und Dirndlkleidern.

German Fest ist jedoch mehr als ein Musikfest. Besonderer Wert

Continued on next page!

Glockenspiel

It prides itself in the quality and variety of food offered - such as *Spanferkel,* Chicken, *Sauerbraten,* rib-eye steak sandwiches, *Rollbraten, Rouladen, Bratwurst,* German Potato Pancakes, and, of course, *Sauerkraut.*

The *Konditorei,* one of over 25 food areas, is the best place to enjoy a *Kaffeeklatsch.*

For thirsty souls there are German wine and champagne, famous Milwaukee beers and, of course, our own German Fest *Bier.*

German Fest has become a vital part of the City of Milwaukee and the German-American community. The study of the German language is encouraged and supported through scholarships and educational grants. Participation in fund-raising events, parades and fairs have benefitted local charities and the general public.

Since its inception, German Fest has become well-known throughout the country. 100,000 visitors from around the world experience German Fest *Gemütlichkeit* each year. Tourists from many foreign countries have expressed their delight with such an impressive festival - German Fest!

wird auf die Qualität und die Auswahl der angebotenen deutschen Speisen gelegt, wie Spanferkel, Brathähnchen, Sauerbraten, Rollbraten, Rouladen, Bratwurst, Kartoffel- pfannkuchen und natürlich Sauerkraut.

Die Konditorei, eine der über 25 Imbißbuden und Speiselokale, ist der gegebene Platz, Kaffee und Kuchen zu geniessen.

Für den Durst gibt es importierte, deutsche Weine und Sekte, bekanntes Milwaukee Bier und natürlich das eigene German Fest Bier.

German Fest hat sich zu einem wichtigen Bestandteil der Stadt Milwaukee und der deutsch-amerikanischen Gemeinschaft entwickelt. Das Studium der deutschen Sprache wird durch Stipendien und Spenden ermutigt und unterstützt, ebenso durch Beteiligung an Stiftungsveranstaltungen, Umzügen und Volksfesten, wobei der Erlös lokalen Wohltätigkeitsgruppen und der allgemeinen Bevölkerung zugute kommt.

Seit seinen Anfängen ist German Fest im ganzen Land bekannt geworden. 100,000 Besucher aus aller Welt erleben in jedem Jahr German Fests Gemütlichkeit. Touristen vieler fremder Länder haben ihre Freude über ein solch eindrucksvolles Fest zum Ausdruck gebracht - das ist German Fest!

Die Freistadt Alte Kameraden Band

In 1942, a group of young men from the Freistadt area, Mequon-Wisconsin, with a love for music and fellowship, organized a band, "Die Freistadt Alte Kameraden Band."

This Band is recognized as one of the finest brass bands in America, having performed on four tours of Germany, Austria, in many cities throughout the United States and most of all, locally at our own German Fest here in Milwaukee.

Die Freistadt Alte Kameraden Band has played at German Fest Milwaukee since its founding, at United German Societies Oktoberfest for over 20 years and at many local fests, picnics and celebrations.

The Band has produced a number of cassette tapes and C.D.s.

Im Jahre 1942 formte ein kleine Gruppe von jungen Männern aus der Freistadt Gegend, in Mequon-Wisconsin eine Blaskapelle. Dieses wurde die Freistadt Alte Kameraden Band.

Kiese Kapelle ist als eine der besten Blaskapellen bekannt, auch durch ihre vier Reisen durch Deutschland, Österreich, und viele Städte in Amerika, aber vor allem, hier beim German Fest in Milwaukee, Wisconsin.

Die Freistadt Alten Kameraden haven für das German Fest Milwaukee seit seiner Gründung gespielt, aber auch zum "Vereinten Deutschen Gesellschafts Oktoberfest" für 20 Jahre, und vei vielen heimischen Festen, Picknicks und Festlichkeiten.

Die Freistadt Alten Kameraden haven eine Reihe von Tonbändern und Kassetten produziert.

The director of the Band is Earl J. Hilgendorf, a member since 1949. Master of ceremonies is Elmer Schreiber. Instrumentalists include: Blaine Hilgendorf, Peter Randall, Harold Pipkorn, Steve Siegel, Jerry Borchardt, Franklin Kug, Don Silldorff, Jim Jackson, Curt Wiztlib, Dave Blank, Tom Christie, Wilmer Wetzel, Dave Balsinger, Walter Feutz, Duwayne Wanasek, Wayne Schliewe, Al Jarvis, Koby Scheel, Harold Schoessow, Kelly O'Brien, Dick Blank, Frank Even, Don Boehlke, John Waltee, Wolfgang Voith and Bob Jackson. Singers: Elfriede Häse, Tony Daube. Flag Bearers: Janet Klug, Carol Blank.

Information: Earl Hilgendorf
P.O. Box 304
Germantown
Wisconsin 53022
(414) 242-1397

Der Direktor der Kapelle ist Herr Earl J. Hilgendorf, per Telefon (414) 242-1397 zu erreichen.

Carl Schurz Park

The Austrian American Society was founded in 1980 for the preservation of the Austrian culture and traditions. Adie Binder, and others started the Club, and Adie served as President for the first 10 years. It consists of almost 200 members, who meet monthly. Activities include a spring and fall hike along with a picnic in the summer.

A Winefest is held in the fall, "Krampus" is celebrated in early December, and annual Christmas party provides fun for young and old, the "Gründungsfeier" in March is an annual event, and participation in German Fest is a must, preparing and serving their popular "goulash."

Members and guests meet monthly at the German Fest office, on the second Friday of the month. After a short business meeting, the group enjoys fellowship, coffee and home-made cake or Austrian beer. Often they sing folksongs, play cards or assorted games.

For detailed information call Frank Schmitz at 414/367-2682.

Klub Österreich wurde 1980 gegründet zur Erhaltung der österreichischen Kultur und Bräuche. Adie Binder, und andere startenten den Klub, Adie war Präsident während der ersten zehn Jahre. Der Klub hat etwa 200 Mitglieder, die sich monatlich treffen. Man geht auf Wanderschaft im Frühling und Herbst und hält ein Picknick im Sommer.

Ein Weinfest findet im Herbst statt, dann ist es Zeit für den Krampus Anfang Dezember, die Weihnachtsfeier macht Freude für Jung und Alt, die Gründungsfeier ist ein Jahresereignis im März, und die Teilnahme am German Fest selbstverständlich, wo man das populäre Goulasch kocht und serviert.

Mitglieder und Gäste treffen sich monatlich im German Fest Haus, und zwar am zweiten Freitag des Monats. Nach dem kurzen offiziellen Teil, erfreut man sich der Kameradschaft mit Kaffee und heimgebackenen Kuchen, oder österreichischem Bier. Dann singt man auch Volkslieder, spielt Karten oder auch andere Spiele.

Weitere Einzelheiten von Frank Schmitz 414-367-2683.

The Austrian Club

The Carl Schurz Memorial Park (CSP), a member of the Federation of German-American Societies, was incorporated in 1945 after it operated as a family camp in Grafton since 1936. Members purchased this 26 acre "resort/park" on beautiful spring-fed Moose Lake located in Waukesha County, and designed it after the popular swim and health spas of Germany. Membership is limited to individuals who are sincerely interested in maintaining the park and upholding their German heritage.

There are approximately 200 members who enjoy swimming and fishing, as well as socializing with Skat and Sheepshead card games, dinner dances and picnics with over 100 picnic tables and a pavilion, used also by several guest clubs. Food and beverages are available daily. German dinners are served at noon on Saturdays and Sundays.

German-American Day is celebrated every year on the second Sunday in August with singing, dancing and a parade.

Season opens Memorial Day and continues through Labor Day. For information contact the Park during the summer schedule at 414/966-2841.

Der Carl Schurz Gedächtnis - Park (CSP), ein Mitglied des Bundes deutsch-amerikanischer Vereine, wurde 1945 offiziell eingetragen nachdem er seit 1936 als Sommerlager für Familien gedient hatte. Die Mitglieder kauften diesen schönen, etwa 10 ha großen Resortpark, der am herrlichen Moose See im Kreise Waukesha gelegen ist. Man machte aus dem Park einen Kurort, so wie man ihn in Deutschland finder. Mitgliedschaft nur an Personen, die an der Erhaltung des Parks interessiert sind und die die deutsche Erbschaft pflegen.

Es gibt etwa 200 Mitglieder, die dort gerne baden, angeln und sich sonst die Zeit vertreiben mit Skat und Schafskopf Karten spielen, mit Essen und Tanz und Picknicks.

Der Park verfügt über 100 Picknicktische und einen Pavillon für größere Gruppen, auch für andere deutsche Clubs aus der Nachbarschaft. Es gibt immer zu Essen und Trinken. Am Wochende auch deutsche Gerichte.

Der Deutsch-Amerikanische Tag wird jedes Jahr am zweiten Sonntag im August mit Singen, Tanz und einem Umzug begangen.

Die Saison eröffnet am Memorial Day (Ende Mai) und läuft bis zum Labor Day (Anfang September). Weitere Informationen bitte vom Park 414/966-2841.

Aurora Lodge No. 30 F.&A.M.

Lessing hat einmal gesagt: "Die Freimaurerei ist nichts Willkürliches, nichts Entbehrliches, sondern etwas Notwendiges, das im Wesen des Menschen und der bürgerlichen Gesellschaft begründet ist" ... eine Brudergemeinschaft, die Erlebnisse vermittelt und Menschen formt, eine Art *Selbstverwirklichungsanstalt*.

Top row: Henry Eisenhauer, Adolf Meinhardt, Helmut Godejohan and Ray Ollermann. Bottom row: Richard Reusch, Dieter Damrow, Heinrich Villing, Alfred Mickel, Joachim Diekermann, Gerald Bethke, John Weigel and Günter Heinrich.

The Aurora Masonry Lodge was established 1850 ANNO LUCIS in Milwaukee, and counts today, 147 years later, 63 Brothers, who assemble twice a month and conduct their meetings in the French ritual but in German.

Aurora Lodge # 30 F.&A.M., 517 E. Beaumont Ave., Milwaukee WI

INTERVIEW WITH MAYOR ZEIDLER

Based on an interview with former Milwaukee Mayor Frank Zeidler, at his home on October 17, 1994, by the publisher.

After Mayor Zeidler's account of the German American history in the Milwaukee area, Bert Lachner asked the Mayor his opinion on the lack of assertiveness of Germans in political life.

Bert Lachner: Is it perhaps that Germans, because of both wars, have become afraid to speak out, or speak for other people, since they do not want to appear as little dictators?

Mayor Zeidler: To some extent. But basically it is an instinct of particularly not liking the nastiness of politics. If you were raised as a Lutheran and were taught not to speak evil of your neighbor, it is very difficult to get up and denounce your opponent. Politically, you must be a rascal. That pattern of denouncing people — there is a successful pattern in American politics today, smearing the opponent — must be an instinctive reaction; without it you can't get very far in politics. Therefore, there isn't much of a Germanic representation.

The Germans are in Civil Service. They are detail people and have an ability to operate in this area.

B.L.: When you talked of 41 clubs and societies here, one would get the impression that we have a lot of Germans in Milwaukee. Recent statistics bear this out with more than 50% of the population carrying German names.

F.Z.: Many of the Clubs are small. They tend to be conservative and members belong to the Republican Party. But the Republicans have not been winning in this Municipality. I can think of 2nd tier government people of Germanic extraction, but nobody in the top level.

B.L.: What is the future of the German community, both in business and in the general population? Are we just going into quicksand and fading away, or are we going to be a group of people to be reckoned with?

F.Z.: In my opinion, they won't be group of people to be reckoned with. There might be some people like the Wisconsin Synod Churches, particularly Lutherans. But then there are already four major divisions among the Lutherans. You are seeing the kind of thing that happened in Germany, the Synod splitting off, people like the Mennonites and others going in different directions. It is happening here.

OKTOBERFEST   VOLKSFEST

Be our guest as we celebrate the oldest and most authentic Bavarian Oktoberfest and Volksfest in the Midwest. Enjoy Old World hospitality and Gemütlichkeit at Old Heidelberg Park on the Bavarian Inn grounds. Our Bavarian Inn "Fest Garten" Pavilion seats up to 2,000 people under one roof. Volksfest is celebrated on the 4th weekend in June and Oktoberfest on the three weekends after Labor Day.

Oktoberfest und Volksfest

Bitte sei unser Gast, wenn wir das älteste und urigste Bayerische Oktober-und Volksfest in dem Mittelwesten feiern. Erfreue Dich an der Gastfreundlichkeit der alten Heimat und der Gemütlichkeit vom Alt Heidelberg Park auf dem Bayern Hof. Unser »Bavarian Inn Fest Garten Pavillon" hält 2,000 Gäste unter einem Dach. Volksfest findet am 4. Wochenende im Juni statt. Oktoberfest ist an drei Wochenenden nach Labor Day im September.

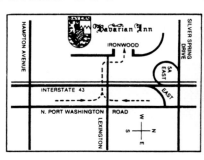

They are comfortable living by themselves - somehow they survive and are prosperous. The largest single gift in the history of the state of a College was given recently to one of the smallest Colleges in the state. Wisconsin Synod Lutheran College of Milwaukee got a $25 million gift. Not even the big Universities ever got a gift like that. These Germans are very quiet, you don't see them out publicly.

B.L.: For instance, we see a split of the Goethe Institut and the Goethe House here in Milwaukee. It seems to me splitting up is a sign of weakness; banding together, doing things together with fewer and larger groups with good management means strength.

F.Z.: That's true. I started the Goethe House in Milwaukee in the Public Library. As Mayor I could do that, but now there are forces trying to push them out. That's indicative of a German Community which does not have political clout - it doesn't have it.

B.L.: This is not unique to Milwaukee, but it's all over the country. In the book "Chicagoland", we list 40 active Clubs under the banner of the German Day Association. However, there are many more, so small and modest, they don't want to be mentioned anywhere.

F.Z.: One of the characteristics of German Clubs in and around Milwaukee is that they consider themselves Pleasure Clubs. These are people who get together for social company, to play cards - often Skat or Schafskopf - to share dinner and traditional customs. In the German community, they are very prominent. On Sunday, they would gather together and some women would bake cakes and serve coffee. Conversation would center around the family, work and of course, reports about trips to Europe and news of relatives there.

B.L.: Do you think that when things are going well, they are doing their own thing. But when there is hardship and anxiety, people band together and try to share their burden?

Also the fact that we can be in Europe within a day has taken away the uniqueness of immigration. Telephone and television keep us in touch and up-to-date so that we feel never far from "home."

F.Z.: There are a number of people who go back and forth frequently. They still feel the difference in culture, here and there. Every trip means an adjustment back to traditional customs, an exciting experience.

B.L.: It seems to me that preserving the old heritage, the customs of their childhood, is what makes them all special. As generations march on and become world citizens, an important aspect of the quality of life may be lost.

Over the last century and a half, much has been written and documented about the history and heritage of the German community. A bibliography follows this chapter at the end of the book for the benefit of your study or entertainment. Enjoy!

Die Deutsch-amerikanische Gemeinschaft von heute!

Aus einem Interview mit dem früheren Oberbürgermeister von Milwaukee, Frank Zeidler, in seinem Domizil am 17. Oktober 1994. Interview vom Herausgeber geführt.

Nachdem Bürgermeister Zeidler über die deutsch-amerikanische Geschichte im Gebiet um Milwaukee erzählt hatte, wurde er von Bert Lachner gefragt, warum die Deutschen seiner Meinung nach nicht die nötige Durchsetzungskraft im politischen Bereich besitzen.

Bert Lachner (B.L.): Hat das vielleicht damit zu tun, daß die Deutschen wegen der beiden Kriege Angst davor haben, den Mund aufzumachen oder für andere einzutreten, weil sie nicht als kleine Diktatoren erscheinen wollen?

Bürgermeister Zeidler (F.Z.): In gewisser Weise. Aber es ist grundsätzlich ein Instinkt, die Schlechtigkeit der Politik zu verabscheuen. Wenn man Lutheraner ist und dazu erzogen wurde, über seinen Nachbarn nichts Schlechtes zu sagen, dann ist es sehr schwer, aufzustehen und seinen Gegner zu denunzieren. In der Politik muß man ein Schlingel sein. Leute zu denunzieren - es gibt ein gutes Muster in der amerikanischen Politik von heute, den Gegner zu beschmutzen - muß eine instinktive Reaktion sein. Ohne sie kommt man nicht weit in der Politik. Deshalb sind so wenig Deutsche vertreten.

Die Deutschen sind im Beamtendienst. Sie sind detailorientiert und haben eine Fähigkeit, gut in diesem Bereich zu wirken.

B.G.T.E.V. D'Holzhacker Buam
Bayerischer Gebirgstrachten Verein - Bavarian Schuhplattling Club

"Sitt' und Tracht der Alten wollen wir erhalten, treu dem guten, alten Brauch. Wenn auch von der Heimat fern, im Herzen denk ich Deiner gern!"

Preserve and treasure we will, the customs and costumes, loyal to good and old traditions. Far away from home - in our hearts we are still one.

The Miesbacher Tracht from Bavaria

Ladies wear a green velour hat with eagle feather. Under the blue wool blend skirt, which is custom made to club patterns, they wear a white cotton slip and bloomers trimmed with lace. A white, short sleeve blouse is worn under a stiff black bodice which is decorated with red silk carnations, silver chain and coins. The blue silk shawl and matching apron complete the costume, together with white opaque stockings and black shoes with strap and buckle.

Men wear a green velour hat with eagle feather, black leather pants with green embroidery, a white long sleeve shirt and blue tie with Edelweiss. The suspenders carry a Bavarian crest of crown and lions.

The wide belt proudly shows the club emblem and features a silver chain and coins. The gray wool coat with green and red trim has deer horn buttons. Split socks covering the foot and calf are custom made. Black shoes with flap complete the costume

More information available by calling 414 / 255-4509

B.L.: Als Sie die hiesign 41 Vereine und Gesellschaften erwähnt haben, erhält man den Eindruck, daß es viele Deutsche in Milwaukee gibt. Die neuesten Statistiken zeigen dies insofern, daß mehr als die Hälfte der Bevölkerung deutsche Namen trägt.

F.Z.: Viele dieser Vereine sind klein. Sie neigen dazu, politisch konservativ zu sein, und ihre Mitglieder gehören der Republikanischen Partei an. Aber die Republikaner gewannen in dieser Gemeinde nicht. Ich erinnere mich an zweitrangige Regierungsleute deutscher Abstammung, aber an niemanden an der Spitze.

B.L.: Wie sieht die Zukunft der deutschen Gemeinschaft aus, im Geschäftswesen sowohl als auch in der allgemeinen Bevölkerung? Werden wir im Treibsand verschwinden oder werden wir zu einer Personengruppe werden, die etwas gilt?

F.Z.: Meiner Meinung nach werden sie nicht zu einer Personengruppe, die etwas gilt. Vielleich, gibt es einige Leute

Former Mayor Frank P. Zeidler

Der frühere Oberbürgermeister Frank P. Zeidler

wie die Synodenkirchen in Wisconsin, vor allem die Lutheraner. Aber dann gibt es schon vier Hauptunterteilungen unter den Lutheranern. Man erkennt das gleiche, was in Deutschland passierte. Die Synode spaltete sich auf, und Leute wie die Mennoniten und andere machten sich in verschiedene Richtungen auf. Das passiert hier.

Sie leben gerne alleine - irgendwie überleben sie und sind wohlhabend. Das größte Geschenk von einer Einzelperson in der Geschichte unseres Staates wurde vor kurzem an eins unserer kleinsten staatlichen Colleges gegeben. Das Wisconsin Synod Lutheran College bekam ein Geschenk von 25 Millionen Dollar. Nicht einmal die großen Universitäten bekamen jemals ein solches Geschenk. Diese Deutschen sind sehr ruhig. Man sieht sie nicht in der Öffentlichkeit.

B.L.: Man sieht diese Aufspaltung am Beispiel vom Goethe Institut und Goethe Haus hier in Milwaukee. Aufspaltung scheint mir ein

Zeichen von Schwäche zu sein, wohingegen Zusammenschluß das gemeinsame Schaffen mit weniger und größeren Gruppen unter guter Führung, Stärke bedeutet.

F.Z.: Ja, das stimmt. Ich gründete das Goethe Haus in Milwaukee in der Öffentlichen Bibliothek. Ich konnte das in meiner Funktion als Bürgermeister machen, aber jetzt gibt es Kräfte, die sie vertreiben wollen. Das ist bezeichnend für eine deutsche Gemeinschaft, die keinen politischen Einfluß hat. Sie hat nun mal keinen politischen Einfluß.

B.L.: Das ist nicht einzigartig für Milwaukee, sondern das passiert überall im Land. In dem Buch "Chicagoland" führen wir 40 aktive Vereine unter der Schirmherrschaft "German Day Association" auf. Es gibt jedoch noch so viele andere, die so klein und so bescheiden sind, daß sie nirgends aufgeführt werden wollen.

F.Z.: Eine der Eigenschaften der deutschen Vereine in und um Milwaukee herum ist, daß

sie sich selber als Vergnügungs-
vereine ansehen. Die Leute kommen
zusammen, um ein geselliges Leben
zu führen, um Karten zu spielen - oft
Skat oder Schafskopf - zusammen
Abend zu essen und die traditionellen
Sitten zu pflegen. Sie sind in der
deutschen Gemeinschaft sehr
bekannt. Sie treffen sich gewöhnlich
an Sonntagen, und einige Frauen
backen Kuchen und schenken Kaffee
ein. Man redet über die Familie, die
Arbeit und natürlich über Reisen
nach Europa und Neuigkeiten der
dortigen Verwandten.

B.L.: Glauben Sie, daß man alles
allein erledigt, wenn es einem gut
geht, aber daß man sich zusammentut
und sein Leid klagt, wenn es
Probleme und Furcht gibt?

Auch die Tatsache, daß man in
Europe binnen eines Tages sein kann,
hat der Einwanderung das
Einzigartige genommen. Telefon und
Fernsehen halten uns in Verbindung
und auf dem neuesten Stand, so daß

wir uns nie von "zu Hause" entfernt
fühlen.

F.Z.: Es gibt viele Leute, die
häufig hin - und herfahren. Sie fühlen
immer noch den kulturellen
Unterschied, den es hier und dort
gibt. Jede Reise bedeutet eine
Rückanpassung an die traditionellen
Sitten, die eine aufregende Erfahrung
darstellt.

B.L.: Mir kommt es so vor, als ob
das Bewahren des alten Erbes, der
Sitten der Kindheit, das Besondere
darstellt. Mit jeder weiteren
Generation eines Weltenbürgers
verlieren wir möglicherweise einen
wichtigen Aspekt der Lebensqualität.

Im Laufe der letzten 150 Jahre
wurde viel über die Geschichte und
das Erbe der deutschen Gemeinschaft
geschrieben und veröffentlicht. Eine
Kurzbibliographie schließt sich
diesem Kapitel am Ende des Buches
zu Studienzwecken oder zum
Vergnügen an. Viel Spaß!

WISCONSIN
A Century and a Half of German Immigration

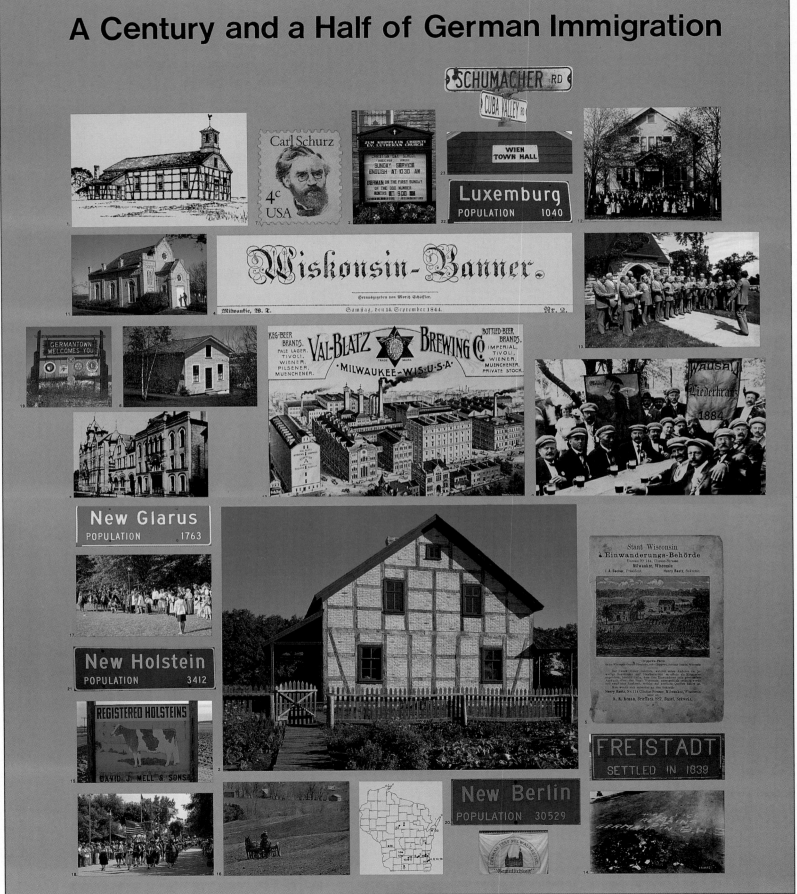

Compliments of Professor Jürgen Eichhoff

In Freud und Leid zum Lied bereit.

Photo: Milwaukee Liederkranz

Milwaukee Liederkranz

Im Jahre 1878 wurde der "Milwaukee Liederkranz" unter dem Vorsatz gegründet, die deutsche Musik, den Gesang, die deutsche Sprache und die Geselligkeit zu pflegen.

Obwohl sich im Laufe der Jahre der Lebensstil weitgehend veränderte, versuchen wir, die Sänger des Milwaukee Liederkranz, diesem Grundsatz treu zu bleiben.

Milwaukee Liederkranz Sänger

<u>Front row from left:</u>

John Gebhardt, Dr. Jim Kestly, Dietrich Bendzka, Manfred Dill, Franz Schmidt, Werner Stöhlker, Frank Schmitz, Rudolf Zerbel, John Van Uxem, John Magnus

<u>Middle row from left:</u>

Heinz Glienke, Leonard Schweigert, John Jahn, Jr., Walter Greis, Robert P. Hefter, Charles Wagner, Erwin Kriegisch, Les Lund, David Herrmann, Edward G. Langer

<u>Top row from left:</u>

Othmar J. Dreiseitel, Karl Lethmate, Carl Schmitt, Jr., Günther Greis, Richard Kuenn, Alex Tietz, Steven L. Joyal, Hermann Tewes, Rolf Hoffmann, Andrew F. Grosch, Ivan Konings, Ron Friedel

<u>Missing:</u>

Henry Becker, Fred Cramer, Ken Field, Gordon Greis, Norbert Greis, Gene Gross, Joel Johannes, Heinz Krüge, Geoffrey Kroening

Activity Highlights:

January:	Stiftungsfest
March:	Wisconsin Sängerbezirk Kommer's
April:	Frühjahrskonzert
May:	"Nord-Amerikanischer Sängerbund" Sängerfest
June:	"Wisconsin Sängerbezirk" Sängerfest
July:	German Fest, Milwaukee
August:	German American Day, Carl Schurz Park, Family Picnic
September:	Liederabend
December:	Singing at Nursing Homes Weihnachts-Konzert Vereinigte Chöre von Milwaukee

Milwaukee Liederkranz,

Mitglied des Deutschen Sänger Bundes
Besitzer der Zelter Plakette

Chorleiter: Steven L. Joyal - President: Othmar J. Dreiseitel

The Main House of the Karl Hausner Farms.

Karl and Hermine Hausner at one of their Farms.

Milchproduktion in Wisconsin ist harte Arbeit und erfordert Liebe zur Sache.

Die Karl Hausner Höfe in der Nähe von Sauk City, etwa 80 km nordwestlich von Madison, WI, sind typisch - aber dennoch mit menschlicher Hand geführt.

Mehrere Höfe gehören und arbeiten zusammen; so gibt es Farmen auf denen das Vieh zu Hause ist, wo es gefüttert und gemolken wird. Und wo täglich Kälber geboren und die trächtigen Kühe gepflegt werden oder sich ungestört erholen können. Die Stallungen sind solide, sauber und ordentlich, und nach neuesten Erfahrungen gebaut. Licht, Temperatur und sauberes Lager sind genau so wichtig um gute Milch zu geben, wie das richtig gemischte Futter. Jede Farm hat ihre Besonderheit nach Lage und Boden und produziert je nach dem Luzerne, Heu oder Mais.

Die Belegschaft der Hausner Farms besteht aus drei Managern, den Viehbetreuern und Futterexperten, und einer Gruppe von Studenten. Alle bemühen sich sehr um gute Leistung und humanen Umgang mit den Tieren. Das macht sich auch für sie bezahlt.

In der kleinen Kapelle auf dem Herrenhof wird der Besucher an die schrecklichen Schicksale deutscher Familien im "Osten" erinnert und auf das Glück in der neuen Heimat aufmerksam gemacht.

Dairy Farming in Wisconsin is Hard Work, but a Labor of Love.

The Karl Hausner Farms near Sauk City, about 50 miles NW of Madison, WI, are just that, but with a touch of extra human care.

Several farms make up the operation. There are feed farms where the 680 plus cows are housed, fed and milked three times a day. There is special housing for pregnant cows and for their calves. The buildings are solid, well maintained and designed according to latest scientific knowledge: gentle light, temperature, clean bedding and the very best feed. Each farm, according to its location and soil, produces different feed such as alfalfa, hay, corn and other products. The balanced mix and additions of vitamins are very important for the quality of milk.

The Karl Hausner staff benefits from the proper care of the farms and its animals. There are 3 managers, experts to handle the cattle and farmhands to work the fields, as well as some international students, doing their apprenticeship. All live in the houses of the various farms.

A small Chapel on the mainfarm reminds the visitor of a difficult past in the old country, and of the blessings we can count in this beautiful new world.

Calves are housed in comfortable open air shelter.

Photos by Bert Lachner

The EXPELLE Memorial Chapel welcomes visitors.

Karl Hausner's Main Farm, Sauk City, WI

Wisconsin Farming

At the end of the Twentieth Century, only 4% of the population is involved in farming, and the average family spends about 16% of its income for food. Since most of the food is processed and a lot of it is consumed in restaurants, the farmer gets less than five per cent of the food dollar.

Agriculture, due to improved plant and animal genetics, improved fertilization and advanced technology, has been the most cost effective branch of the economy. It contributes the greatest share to the export economy of the United States.

The majority of Americans have no conception about farming and food production, since most of our city folks buy processed food, which is very remote from the original crops. Some even believe that farming is extremely lucrative, because they are told that out of one kernel of corn, the plant produces 60, 80 or even 100 kernels. Thus, they think of a one hundred fold profit.

The relatively large investment in land, buildings, machinery and livestock, in addition to the risks caused by unfavorable weather, illnesses and losses of livestock, yield only modest returns.

Most farmers are good stewards of the land, because it is their greatest investment. They subscribe to common sense, protection of the environment, avoiding erosions and pollution of our water supply. Wisconsin, which was settled by mostly German farmers, became the largest milk producer in the nation. The Karl Hausner farm produces high quality Grade A milk and earns quality bonuses. Our cattle is our lifeline and thus, we try to provide optimal conditions and care.

We protect the heritage of this region by conserving old buildings and bringing them into harmony with productive new structures.

Both of our ancestors were farmers in the Sudetenland for centuries until we were expelled in 1946. Thus, agriculture is in our bloodstream

We are blessed with a dedicated group of people, who feel like we do. We also have an International Exchange Program of Agricultural Students with various universities and agencies.

Karl and Hermine Hausner

Wisconsin Dairyland

(Official State Centennial Song)
Original by Henry C. Spears, 1948

Let's sing a song of Dairyland,
Rare beauty over hill and lake;
To other states we gave our hand
In eighteen hundred forty-eight;
With orchard fruit and prairie grain,
With winter sports to entertain,
With products of man's hand and brain:
Wisconsin Dairyland.

It is with pride we sing our song
Of min'rals, leather, furs and wood;
The school and church with spirit strong
Contribute to the common good;
With fishes in a thousand rills,
With cattle on a thousand hills,
With workers in a thousand mills:
Wisconsin "Heimatland".

Fair Badgerland amid the lakes,
Progressive hope of pioneers,
Vacationland of all the states,
For us the future holds no fears;
So on and up Wisconsin goes,
To gain more friends and lose its foes;
What heights we'll reach nobody knows:
Wisconsin Badgerland.

Sing to the hymn of ...
"Lift up your heads, ye mighty gates;
Behold the king of Glory waits!"

Nur das Beste ist gut genug ! Während eines offiziellen Besuches in Deutschland, schenkte Wisconsins Gouverneur Tommy Thompson "Miller Genuine Draft" Bier aus, und zwar in der Mutter Hoppe Bar in Berlin. Dieses Wisconsin Bier wurde Anfang 1997 zum meisten von Amerika eingeführten Bier in Deutschland ernannt.

Offering nothing but the best. During a recent trade mission to Germany, Wisconsin Governor Tommy Thompson served Miller Genuine Draft to consumers at Mutter Hoppe, a Berlin pub. Miller Genuine Draft, Wisconsin's hometown brew, was recently named the No. 1 imported American beer in Germany.

Adolf and Markus Meinhardt

A & M Tooling Co., Inc.

- Founded in 1980
- Manufacturer of precision machine parts, fixtures and gages for a variety of industrial applications and for customers throughout the Midwest.
- Builder of special machines for any type of application.
- Manufacturer of precision Broadheads used for hunting Big Game.

elmass® NORTH AMERICA, INC.

- Founded in 1988
- Exclusive import organization for United States, Mexico and Canada.
- The ELMASS Keyway Cutting System is for cutting precise keyways and splines in BLIND and thru holes faster and with closer tolerances.
- The ELMASS System was invented in Schaffhausen, Switzerland which is also World Headquarters.
- Primary Markets: Gear Manufacturers, Agriculture, Aerospace, Automotive, Mining, Farming and Food Processing.
- Some better known customers of ours include: APV Crepaco, Emerson Electric, Baldor Electric, Dana Corporation, Parker Hannifin, McDonnel Douglas, Westinghouse Electric, Sunstrand, Falk, etc.

A & M Tooling Co., Inc.

N115 W19012 EDISON DRIVE
414/255-5644

GERMANTOWN, WI 53022 USA
FAX 414/255-6509

KOHLER CO. of Kohler, Wisconsin,

is a global family of diverse but related businesses with 37 manufacturing sites and more than 16,000 associates worldwide. Its mission is to improve the level of gracious living for all who are touched by its products and services.

John Michael Kohler, an Austrian immigrant, founded Kohler Co. in 1873. His small foundry and machine shop located in Sheboygan, Wisconsin, produced farm plows and other agricultural implements.

Today, Kohler is a world leader in kitchen and bath products, engines and generators. It is the parent company of Baker Furniture, McGuire Furniture and Ann Sacks Tile & Stone. It operates The American Club, the only five diamond resort hotel in the Midwest, and Blackwolf Run, whose River Course has been cited as the third highest rated public access golf course in the United States by GOLF Magazine.

Kohler Village, 55 miles north of Milwaukee and headquarters for Kohler Co., is a community created to blend the best of residential living with an exceptional array of recreational, cultural and social activities. An attractive year-round resort destination that is often referred to as a garden at industry's gate, its orderly growth is guided by a 50-year plan created under guidelines established by the Frank Lloyd Wright Foundation.

KOHLER CO. in Kohler, Wisconsin,

ist ein weltweites Familienunternehmen mit verschiedenartigen aber doch verwandten Firmen, 37 Fertigungsstätten und mehr als 16.000 Mitarbeitern weltweit, deren Firmenphilosophie darin besteht, das Leben derer, die mit ihren Produkten und Dienstleistungen in Kontakt kommen, zu verschönern.

Der aus Österreich eingewanderte John Michael Kohler gründete die Kohler Co. im Jahre 1873. In seiner kleinen Gießerei und Reparaturwerkstatt in Sheboygan, Wisconsin, stellte er Pflüge und landwirtschaftliche Geräte her.

Heute ist Kohler weltführend in Küchen- und Badarmaturen und -vorrichtungen, Maschinen und Generatoren. Zudem ist Kohler die Muttergesellschaft von den Möbelfirmen Baker Furniture und McGuire Furniture und von Ann Sacks Fliesen. Kohler ist auch Besitzer des *The American Club*, dem einzigen Fünf-Sterne Hotel im Mittelwesten, und *Blackwolf Run*, dessen Golfkurs am Fluß entlang von der Zeitschrift GOLF, als der drittbeste, öffentliche Golfplatz in den Vereinigten Staaten angeführt wurde.

Der Ort Kohler, fast 90 km nördlich von Milwaukee, wo sich die Hauptverwaltung der Kohler Co. befindet, ist eine Gemeinde, die etabliert wurde, um eine Kombination von bester Wohngegend mit einer außergewöhnlichen Auswahl an Erholungsmöglichkeiten, Kultur und Unterhaltung zu schaffen. Ein attraktiver Erholungsort, der das ganze Jahr geöffnet ist und der oft als Garten am Tor der Industrie beschrieben wird. Die Landschaftsgestaltung ähnelt der eines französischen Gartens und basiert auf einem 50-Jahresplan gemäß den Richtlinien für Landschaftsgestaltung der Frank Lloyd Wright-Stiftung.

The "Vintage" Suite from KOHLER

provides a unique blending of Victorian flavor and modern flair, offering fixtures that are reflective of Kohler's distinctive products from the early 1990s. The Vintage free-standing bath with golden oak trim and the Vintage pedestal lavatory are shown here in white. Faucets, in polished brass, are from the Antique line.

Das "Vintage" Bad von KOHLER

zeigt eine außergewöhnliche Kombination des Victoria Stils und der modernen Wohnkultur. Die Einrichtung und Armaturen sind ein Beispiele der Kohler Produkte aus den frühen 1990ger Jahren. Die freistehende "Vintage" Badewanne, mit goldener Eichenholz -Verkleidung, und das "Vintage" Waschbecken sind hier in weiß gezeigt. Die Armaturen, hier in poliertem Messing, sind typish für die "Antique" Ausführung.

KOHLER

Generators

A large KOHLER standby generator undergoes testing before delivery.

Ein großer KOHLER Reserve Stromerzeuger wird vor der Anlieferung technisch freigegeben.

Steaming through Boone & Scenic Valley

Wir heißen Sie willkommen in den Prärie Staaten Iowa und Minnesota. Kommen Sie, und haben Sie Teil an unseren vielen Pfaden der Pioniere, unseren historischen Stätten, den lebendigen Hauptstraßen und dem Geschenk von Mutter Natur, der unberührten Landschaft.

Lassen Sie uns zusammen unser Erbe erforschen, unser schönes Land genießen und unsere freundlichen Bürger erleben.

Amana Colonies, Iowa Tourism

Welcome to the Prairie States, Iowa and Minnesota. Come and share our unique bounty of pioneer pathways, inspiring historic sights, vibrant main streets and nature's gift of pristine landscapes.

Let us share with you our colorful heritage, our beautiful land and crafty, friendly people.

German Americans in and around Davenport, Iowa

The American Schleswig-Holstein Heritage Society (ASHHS) assists in geneology, promotes tourism and maintains the "Platt-Deutsch" language.
A library of German books has been established in Walcott, Iowa, and the ASHHS participates in local parades with its unique and award-winning "Glockenspiel".

For more information call
319 / 843-2867

Die amerikanische Schleswig Holstein Erbschafts Vereinigung (ASHHS) hilft in der Geneologie, fördert den Reiseverkehr und pflegt die plattdeutsche Sprache. Ein Bücherei mit deutschem Lesematerial wurde in Walcott, Iowa eingerichtet und die ASHHS nimmt teil an den festlichen Umzügen der Stadt mit einem preisgekrönten Glockenspiel.

Mehr ist zu erfahren über
319 / 843 - 2867

Prairie States

Iowa, Minnesota

The Prairie States span a fascinating land of rolling prairies, tranquil river valleys, small and some large cities, huge ranches and farms, and broad stretches of wheat fields.

Their remarkable diversity also includes wildlife refuges, recreational lakes, and vast expanses of national monument forests to welcome adventurous tourists who enjoy getting close to nature.

The largest cities are Des Moines in Iowa and Minneapolis in Minnesota, both with fairly large populations of Germans and Scandinaviens.

Die Prairie Staaten umfassen eine großartige Landschaft von wogenden Prairien, stille Flußtäler, viele Dörfer und einige schöne Großstädte, sehr große Viehherden auf den Ranches und reiche Bauernhöfe mit weiten Streifen von Weizen. Naturschutzgebiete bieten dem Wild eine gesunde Umwelt, und es gibt große National Parks, die dem abenteuerlichen Wanderer die Möglichkeit geben, nahe der Natur zu sein.

Die größten Städte sind Des Moines in Iowa und Minneapolis in Minnesota; beide haben eine ansehnliche Einwohnerzahl von Deutschen und Scandinaviern.

Photos: Minnesota Office of Tourism

Houseboating is a popular past time on the many lakes and rivers of Minnesota.

The cosmopolitan skyline of down-town Minneapolis

Canoeing in the solitude of the Wilderness Waters on the Canadian border.

The historic Armory Building

The Brown County building and monument, depicting "Pioneers of Brown County" showing a Sioux Indian and German Hunter. The monument was erected in 1949, for the 100th anniversary of statehood.

Many headstones show German names.

Photos by Bert Lachner

Prairie grass and flowers

Views of New Ulm

The Gag Home. Ida Gag was a well known celebrity.

The Gag Stone testifies that life was often short lived.

Grave marker of August and Anna Schell, founders of the Schell Brewery

Greetings from . . .

NEW ULM
MINNESOTA

New Ulm's 1897 statue of Hermann the Cheruscan towers over the city and its internationally known Concord Singers.
New Ulms Statue von Hermann dem Cherusker von 1897 überragt die Stadt und deren international bekannte Concord Sänger.

DISCOVER GERMANY IN MINNESOTA

Heritagefest, hospitality and history of New Ulm

German traditions continue to thrive in New Ulm, MN, nearly 150 years after the first settlers established a model community, where freedom of ideas could flourish. Their ethnic heritage is evident in every facet of city life, from the orderliness of the original plat to an insatiable appetite for music and festivals, from the warm maintenance of Sister City relations with Ulm and Neu Ulm to the work ethic that attracted such industrial giants as 3M, Kraft and Caterpillar.

Boisterous German music, flowing morning to evening from downtown speakers all year, lifts the spirits of clerks and shoppers alike on streets speckled with specialty shops bearing German names. Tidy neighborhoods bespeak the Germanic penchant for cleanliness and order. A sense of history embellishes a landscape dotted with monuments and historic sites.

New Ulm abides by many slogans, never disappointing travelers who are invited to "Discover Germany in Minnesota" because there is no more German community in the U.S. It is the "City of Charm and Tradition," marked by Old World courtesy and friendliness, where only real evergreen trees and boughs, never plastic, decorate downtown at Christmas. And it is the "City of Festivals," where musicians seem always polishing their instruments or rehearsing for parades, concerts and celebrations.

Chief among these crowd-pleasing events is **Heritagefest**, drawing 40,000 people from across the U.S. and foreign countries on the second and third weekends every July. Ranked among the Top 100 Events in North America, Its lure is continuous family entertainment featuring bands from Europe as well as New Ulm's own Concord Singers. This male chorus, established in 1931, has performed its festive German music around the U.S. and in Europe.

The Concord Singers also are featured entertainers during the city's other major annual festivals, including Fasching just prior to Ash Wednesday, the Minnesota Festival of Music in April (New Ulm is home to the Minnesota Music Hall of Fame), and Oktoberfest, held the first and second weekends in October.

Religious murals and gold ornamentation grace the arched ceilings inside New Ulm's Cathedral of the Holy Trinity. A strong German baroque influence is evident throughout the interior.

Statue of its namesake greets visitors to New Ulm's Martin Luther College.

Although festive by nature, the community takes its heritage seriously, maintaining and adding more monumental tributes noteworthy by their uniqueness. Hermann the Cheruscan, erected atop a viewing tower in 1897, provides a panoramic view of the city. The Defenders' Monument solemnly recalls the 1862 Dakota Conflict which nearly reduced the village to ashes and took hundreds of pioneer and Dakota lives.

In recent years, New Ulm has expanded its treasure of attractions. A generous benefactor led a drive to build a free-standing glockenspiel, in 1980, now a "don't-miss" stop for tour buses. In 1984, the German-Bohemian Heritage Society was formed to maintain the unique culture and heritage of the German-speaking people who lived in Bohemia and helped settle New Ulm. Seven years later, the society unveiled a sculpture memorializing German-Bohemian immigrants, designed by Bohemia-born sculptor Leopold Hafner of Passau, Germany. The society also fields a talented musical group and publishes books to preserve their culture.

Immigrants, active within German Turnvereins, chose and colonized New Ulm in 1856. The town site was begun in 1854 by another German group. The first Turner Hall was completed in 1858 only to see it destroyed in the 1862 conflict. Turner Hall remains a social and cultural focal point in New Ulm. Turner Hall Park, Main Hall and an 1873 annex containing a Rathskeller are on the National Registry of Historic Sites.

One survivor of the Dakota Conflict was Schell's Brewery, founded by August Schell in 1860 and still operated by his descendants today. Schell's is a well-known New Ulm symbol, linking the nearly 14,000 residents of this prosperous modern community to a colorful past marked by the struggle of German immigrants against adversity.

MINNESOTA
CONVENTION & VISITORS BUREAU

P.O. Box 862
New Ulm, MN 56073
(507) 354-4217
Toll Free: 1-888-463-9856

IHR KLEINES DEUTSCHLAND IN MINNESOTA

"Heritagefest", Gemütlichkeit und Geschichte New Ulms

New Ulm's 45 foot Glockenspiel, built in 1980, plays three times daily.
Dreimal am Tag hört man New Ulms 13,5 m hohes, 1980 errichtetes Glockenspiel.

Überblick über New Ulm, Minnesota

In den 150 Jahren nach der Gründung einer Modell-Gemeinschaft, in der Ideen frei diskutiert werden sollten, lebt die deutsche Tradition in New Ulm, im US-Bundesstaat Minnesota, fort. Der Bezug zum deutschen Erbe drückt sich in allen Aspekten des Lebens aus, zum Beispiel in der Regelmäßigkeit des ursprünglichen Stadtplans, der schier unstillbaren Vorliebe für Musik und Feste, des Festhaltens an den Beziehungen zwischen den Partnerstädten Ulm und New Ulm sowie dem Arbeitsethos, durch den Industriekonzerne wie 3M, Kraft und Caterpillar zur Anlage von Fabriken bewogen wurden.

Die von morgens bis abends aus den Lautsprechern in der Innenstadt tönende deutsche Blasmusik erhöht die Lebensfreude von Ladenangestellten und Einkaufenden gleichermaßen, und in den betreffenden Straßen reihen sich Läden mit deutschen Spezialitäten aneinander, die alle deutsche Namen tragen. Gutgepflegte Stadtbezirke setzen die Tradition deutscher Sauberkeit und Ordnung fort. Die Landschaft um den Ort herum ist voll von historischen Denkmälern, so daß man sich einem besonderen Sinn für Geschichte nicht entziehen kann.

New Ulm wird mit vielen Slogans beschrieben und enttäuscht niemals eine Reisenden, die dazu eingeladen sind, "Deutschland in Minnesota" kennenzulernen, weil es in den USA keine deutschere Stadt gibt. Als Stadt des Charmes und der Tradition" verkörpert New Ulm außerdem die Höflichkeit und Freundlichkeit der alten Welt. Die

Weihnachtsdekoration besteht aus echten Tannenbäumen und -zweigen, und nicht aus Plastikimitationen derselben.

Schließlich ist New Ulm auch die "Stadt der Feste", in der Musiker immer ihre Musikinstrumente zu pflegen scheinen oder für Paraden, Konzerte und Feierlichkeiten proben. Das wichtigste dieser die Menge begeisternden Ereignisse ist

das **Heritagefest**, das am zweiten und dritten Wochenende eines jeden Juli bis zu 40 000 Menschen aus allen Teilen der USA und aus dem Ausland anzieht. Hier folgt eine für Familien geeignete Musik-veranstaltung der anderen, und es wird als eines der 100 "Top Events" in den Vereinigten Staaten eingestuft. Musikkapellen aus Europa wie auch New Ulms eigene "Concord Singers" gestalten das

German-Bohemian immigrants helped settle New Ulm, and 350 of their surnames are inscribed on this monument.
Deutsch-böhmische Einwanderer halfen bei der Besiedlung von New Ulm mit, und 350 ihrer Familiennamen werden mit diesem Denkmal der Nachwelt bewahrt.

Programm. Letzterer Männerchor wurde 1931 gegründet und ist schon überall in den USA und in Deutschland mit seinem Programm deutscher festlicher Musik aufgetreten.

Die Concord Singers stehen auch während der anderen größeren Veranstaltungen der Stadt im Mittelpunkt, wie etwa dem Fasching vor Aschermittwoch, dem Minnesota Festival der Musik im April, welches New Ulm als Heimatstadt der "Minnesota Music Hall of Fame" gestaltet, und dem am ersten und zweiten Oktoberwochenende stattfindenden Oktoberfest.

Neben diesen Festen nimmt die Stadt ihr geschichtliches Erbe in anderer Weise ernst, indem sie ihre in den USA einzigartigen, sehenswerten Denkmäler pflegt und gelegentlich auch neue hinzufügt. 1897 wurde eine Statue von Hermann dem Cherusker auf einem Aussichtsturm errichtet, von wo aus man auch heute noch einen wundervollen Blick über die

Five acres of flowers, deer, roaming peacocks and meandering paths provide a quiet setting for visitors to Schell's Brewery in New Ulm.

Schell's Brewery Company in New Ulm hat einen großen Park mit wunderhübschen Blumen, Wild, herumstolzierenden Pfauen und sich durch die Landschaft schlängelnden Pfaden als ruhige Erholungsstätte für Besucher der Brauerei geschaffen.

German architecture of New Ulm's former post office contributes to the city's "Old World" charm. The building now is a museum, which devotes a room to displays from Ulm, Germany.

Die deutsche Architektur des früheren Postamts von New Ulm trägt zum "Old World"-Charme der Stadt bei. Das Gebäude dient jetzt als Museum, in welchem ein Raum Ausstellungsstücke aus Ulm in Deutschland zeigt.

gesamte Stadt genießen kann. Das "Denkmal der Verteidiger" ("Defenders' Monument") erinnert feierlich an den schrecklichen sogenannten "Dakota-Conflict" von 1862, in dem das Dorf New Ulm niedergebrannt wurde und viele hundert Pioniere und Dakota-Indianer ihr Leben verloren.

In den letzten Jahren hat New Ulm dem allen noch mehr Attraktionen hinzugefügt. Ein großzügiger Stifter veranlaßte eine Geldsammlung, die 1980 den Bau eines freistehenden Glockenspiels ermöglichte, welches New Ulm endgültig zu einem feststehenden Ziel entsprechender Bustouren machte. 1984 bildete sich die "German-Bohemian Heritage Society" zur Pflege des distinkten Kulturerbes der Deutschböhmen, die bei der Besiedlung von New Ulm eine große Rolle gespielt hatten. Sieben Jahre später weihte die Stadt eine dieser deutsch-böhmischen Auswanderer gedenkende, von dem von Deutschböhmen abstammenden Bildhauer Leopold Hafner aus Passau in Deutschland geschaffene Skulptur ein. Die deutsch-böhmische Gesellschaft bewahrt ihr kulturelles Erbe außerdem durch eine Musikgruppe und die Veröffentlichung von Büchern.

Auf Wiedersehen in New Ulm!

Als Ort für eine neue Pioniersiedlung wurde die Gegend von New Ulm durch in der deutschen Turnerverein-Bewegung aktiven Einwandern ausgewählt, die auch die 1854 beginnende Kolonisation anführten und 1858 die erste Turnerhalle errichteten, nur um mitansehen zu müssen, wie sie 1862 im Krieg mit den Dakota-Indianern zerstört wurde. Die dann wieder aufgebaute "Turner Hall" ist immer noch einer der gesellschaftlichen und kulturellen Mittelpunkte von New Ulm. Der "Turner Hall Park", die "Main Hall" und ein 1873 für einen "Rathskeller" hinzugefügter Anbau befinden sich auf der Liste der historischen Denkmäler in den USA ("National Registry of Historic Sites").

Nicht zerstört allerdings wurde die von August Schell 1860 gegründete Brauerei, "Schell's Brewery", die von den Nachkommen noch heute betrieben wird. "Schell's" ist ein bekanntes New Ulmer Symbol, eine Verbindung zwischen der modernen prosperiereden Stadt mit fast 14 000 Einwohnern und der farbigen Vergangenheit, in der die deutschen Einwanderer sich mühsam durchsetzen mußten.

New Ulm Chamber of Commerce
1N Minnesota St. PO Box 384
New Ulm, MN 56073
Ph: 507-354-4217
nuchamber@ic.new-ulm.mn.us
www.newulmweb.com
http://www.ic.new-ulm.mn.us
Toll-free 1-888-463-9856

August Schell Brewing Co.
P.O. Box 128
New Ulm, MN 56073
Ph: 507-354-5528
schells@ic.new-ulm.mn.us

New Ulm Sister City Commission
c/o City of New Ulm
100 N. Broadway
New Ulm, MN 56073

German-Bohemian Heritage Society
P.O. Box 822
New Ulm, MN 56073
Ph: 507-354-2763
lalgbhs@newulmtel.net
http://www.rootsweb.com/~gbhs/

Heritagefest
P.O. Box 61
New Ulm, MN 56073
Ph: 507-354-8850
hfest@newulmtel.net
http:www.newulmtel.net/~hfest

Turner Hall
102 S. State St.
New Ulm, MN 56073
Ph: 507-354-4916
nuturner@newulmtel.net
http:www.newulmtel.net/~nuturner

Concord Singers
P.O. Box 492
New Ulm, MN 56073
Ph: 507-354-8850
concords@newulmtel.net
www.newulmtel.net/~municipa concords

Main Street, New Ulm, Minnesot

Old Main at St. Olaf College

Old Main is the focal point of teaching and learning languages at St. Olaf College.

Faculty offices are organized according to eight foreign languages taught at St. Olaf. On the first floor, Russian and Chinese are to the North and Norwegian to the South. The second floor is home to the Romance languages of French and Spanish. The third floor houses the classics department, Greek and Latin to the North and German to the South.

The architecture of Old Main is typical of the era when it was dedicated in 1878. Recently, it was renovated to its original state.

Professor LaVern J. Rippley has taught German here for many years and at the same time published numerous books. He travels frequently, often with his students, to Europe, including Germany, Poland, Russia and the Baltic States.

For further information contact:
The Old Main, St. Olaf College
1520 St. Olaf Avenue
Northfield, Minnesota 55057-1098
Phone: 507/646-3233   Fax: 507/646-3732
E-mail: RIPPLEYL@STOLAF.EDU

"Old Main", das alte Hauptgebäude ist der Blickfang und das Sprachzentrum der Hochschule St. Olaf College.

Die Räumlichkeiten der Fakultät sind in acht Gruppen aufgeteilt, und zwar ist Russisch, Chinesisch und Norwegisch im Paterre, im ersten Stock die romantischen Sprachen Französisch und Spanisch und oben im zweiten Stockwerk die klassischen Sprachen Griechisch, Latein und Deutsch.

Die Architektur des alten Gebäudes ist für seine Zeitepoche um 1878 typisch, und so wurde es auch wieder neu hergestellt.

Professor LaVern J. Rippley lehrt hier seit vielen Jahren deutsch, und brachte gleichzeitig eine Reihe von Büchern heraus. Er reist viel, oft mit seinen Studenten, hauptsächlich nach Europa, einschließlich Deutschland, Polen, Rußland und die baltischen Staaten.

Weitere Informationen erhalten Sie über:
The Old Main, St. Olaf College
1520 St. Olaf Avenue
Northfield, Minnesota 55057-1098

Prof. LaVern J. Rippley at Old Main

WHERE GERMAN ROOTS RUN DEEP

Germans first came to America in large numbers in the 1720s, when many settled in Pennsylvania. A second and much larger wave began in the 1830s and lasted until 1930, with most going to the Midwest and the upper Plains states. In 1790, only 7 percent of the American population was of German descent. Today, people who list German ancestry first on the census form make up 23 percent of the population.

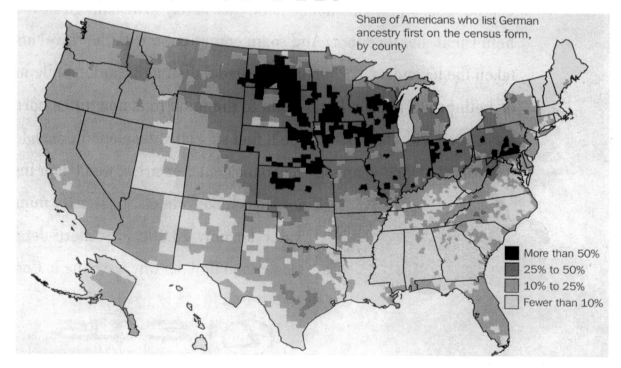

Share of Americans who list German ancestry first on the census form, by county

More than 50%
25% to 50%
10% to 25%
Fewer than 10%

USN&WR–Basic data: 1995 estimate based on U.S. census data.

MAP BY RODGER DOYLE FOR USN&WR

Have you seen a "typical" German-American?

By Profs. Eberhard Reichmann and LaVern J. Rippley

"Why, yes: 'You can always tell a German, but you can't tell him much.'" This is but one of many stereotypical labels that abound in multicultural America. But as with legends, there is often a kernel of truth behind it— a character trait, a behavioral style more prevalent in one group than in others. The "stubbornness," implied above, was also observed by Siegmund Freud along with "thrift" and "orderliness." Yes, "Order is half of life" (German proverb), and "Our God is a God of Order," (Constitution of the first Lutherans in Frankenmuth, MI). And thrift shines through in "going out Dutch" = each pays for himself, or in "Take as much as you want, but eat all you take" = waste not.

Labels pale or change over time. In the 18th century, Germans were summarily called "Palatines," because immigrants from the Palatinate were most numerous. Pennsylvania Germans became the "Pennsylvania Dutch," for "deutsch" was hard to pronounce by their neighbors. "Dutch" became widely used, so did the nickname "Kraut," from the German "sauerkraut." Baden-Württemberger were called "Schwabs," and North Dakota Germans from Russia became "Rooshians." German mercenaries fighting for England in the Revolutionary War came to be known as "Hessians"— not always a term of honor. Also relating to war (1917) was the low blow characterization of all Germans as "Huns."

Ben Franklin and other Anglos had mixed opinions of the Dutch: good farmers, yes, but a threat to the English language and culture. Germans were seen as more spontaneous, less reserved, fond of amusement, less interested in fashion, but superior in love of music and the arts. Journalists also praised the Germans' opposition to slavery and to prohibition, their pioneering work in music in the schools, and in physical and vocational education. The German apprenticeship system, although producing master craftsmen and work with the quality label "Made in Germany," was too exacting a concept and incompatible with the freedom enjoyed by the trades in America. Nor did the German notion that "Work makes life sweet" make the hit parade of American proverbs.

Because of the much admired German universities and the "brain drain" arrivals in the early Hitler period and after WW II, Germans were also highly regarded in the arts and sciences.

An American writer predicted long ago that in the end "The German character—there are enough of the nation among us to do it—will affect the American community by his blood and his ideas. The resultant will be neither Yankee nor German, it will be American." Meanwhile, we know that the Germans are the largest numerical contributors to the American composite, and their decisive influence in procreating the American character is out of the question.

In today's America the German qualifies as a happy-go-lucky beer drinker who knows moderation. He in Lederhosen, she in a Dirndl may mark them at best as Bavarians or Austrians. They are spreading Gemütlichkeit at clubs and festivals and produce the finest Bratwurst, Sauerkraut and Black Forest Cake.

Gibt's den "typischen" Deutsch-Amerikaner?

"Natürlich: 'Man kann's gleich sagen, ob's 'n Deutscher ist, aber viel sagen kann man ihm nicht.'" So eines von vielen Klischees im multikulturellen Amerika. Doch wie bei Legenden, so steckt auch in solchen Verallgemeinerungen meist ein Stückchen Wahrheit—ein Charakterzug, der einer Gruppe besonders zu eignen scheint. Das im Zitat angedeutete "eigensinnig" hat schon S. Freud—neben "sparsam" und "ordentlich" vermerkt. Tja, "Ordnung ist das halbe Leben." Die Satzung der frühen ev. Gemeinde von Frankenmuth/ Michigan begann mit: "Unser Gott ist ein Gott der Ordnung." "Sparsam" scheint durch in "Dutch" ausgehen = getrennte Kasse für sie und ihn.

Etiketten wechseln wie Moden. Im 18.Jarhundert. nannte man Deutsche einfach "Palatines" = Pfälzer, weil die am stärksten vertreten waren. Aus "Pennsylvania Germans" wurden "Pennsylvania Dutch", weil sich "deutsch" schlecht aussprechen liess. "Dutch" verbreitete sich überall wie auch der weniger schmeichelhafte Spitzname "Kraut". Südwestdeutsche und Donauschwaben waren "Schwabs", und Nord-Dakota-Deutsche aus Russland waren "Rooshians". Der Name "Hessen" für die im Unabhängigkeitskrieg unter englischer Flagge kämpfenden Deutschen war kein Kompliment. Ebenso kriegsbedingt (1917) war die niederschmetternde Bezeichnung der Deutschen als "Hunnen."

Benjamin Franklin u.a. kam mit den "Dutch" nicht ganz zurecht. Er schätzte sie hoch als Bauern, fürchtete aber ihren Zuwachs als Gefahr für englische Sprache und Sitte. Die "Dutch" zeigten ein ungezwungeneres Verhalten, Unterhaltsamkeit, doch weniger Interesse an Moden als an Musik und Kunst. Journalisten lobten die Opposition der Deutsch-Amerikaner gegen Sklaverei und Alkoholverbot, ihre Leistungen in der Schulmusik, in Leibeserziehung und Berufsbildung. Das für den Erfolg der "Made in Germany" Produkte grundlegende System der Lehrlingsausbildung war jedoch zu rigide für das vom Innungszwang freie amerikanische Handwerk. Auch die Vorgabe, daß Arbeit das Leben süß mache, schaffte nicht die Hit Parade amerikanischer Sprichwörter.

Die hochgeachteten deutschen Universitäten und die Abwanderung des Geistes im 3. Reich und danach brachten deutscher Wissenschaft und Kunst große Anerkennung.

Vor langem schon sagte ein amerikanischer Schriftsteller voraus, daß angesichts der großen Anzahl Deutscher und deren Ideen das Endresultat weder der Yankee noch der Deutsche sein werde, sondern der Amerikaner. Inzwischen steht fest, daß die Deutschstämmigen zahlenmäßig das größte ethnische Element aus Europa darstellen. Daß sie auch bei der Formung des amerikanischen Charakters mit am einflußreichsten waren, steht außer Frage.

Im heutigen Amerika sieht man im Deutsch-Amerikaner gerne den unbeschwerten Bierfreund, der weiß, was er verträgt. Er in Lederhosen, sie im Dirndl. Ganz au oberbayerisch-österreichisch, mit viel Oktoberfestgemütlichkeit und immer noch die besten Hersteller von Bratwürsten, Sauerkraut und Schwarzwälder Kirschtorte.

Some Prominent German Americans

Hannah Arendt .1906-1971. Social philosopher
John Jacob Astor . . . . .1763-1848. Financier and fur trader
Maximillian Berlitz . . . . . . .1852-1921. Founder of language school
Wernher von Braun . . . . .1912-1977. Rocket/Space Scientist
Walter Percy Chrysler . . . . .1875-1940. Automobile maker
Moses Cleveland . . . . .1754-1806. Founded Cleveland, Ohio
George Armstrong Custer . . . . .1839-1876. Civil War General
Everett McKinley Dirksen . . . . . . .1896-1969. U.S. Senator, Illinois
Marlene Dietrich . . . . .1901-1995. Singer, Actress
Albert Einstein . . . . .1879-1955. Physicist
Dweight D. Eisenhower . . . . . . .1890-1969. Thirty-fourth President
Clark Gable . . . . .1901-1960. Film star
Henry Louis Gehrig . . . . .1903-1941. Baseball player
Oscar Hammerstein . . . . . . .1847-1919. Producer of grand opera,
vaudeville and musical comedies
Oscar Hammerstein II .1895-1960. Lyricist
Friedrich Hecker . . . . .1811-1881, Political orator. Civil War
Henry J. Heinz .1844-1919. Food packer
Milton S. Hershey . . . . . . .1857-1945. Founder, Hershey Chocolate
Michael Hillegas . . . . .1729-1804. First Treasurer of the U.S.
Herbert Clark Hoover . . . . .1847-1964. Thirty-first President
John Kalb (Baron de Kalb) . . . . .1721-1780. War General
Grace Kelly . . . . .1929-1982. Actress and Princess of Monaco
Henry Kissinger . . . . .1923- . Secretary of State
Lotte Lehmann . . . . .1888-1976, Stage star
Thomas Mann . . . . .1875-1955. Novelist, essayist
Ottmar Mergenthaler . . . . . . .1854-1898. Inventor of Linotype Print
Henry Muhlenberg . . . . . . .1711-1787. Father of Lutheran
Church in America
Thomas Nast . . . . .1830-1902. Artist
Chester W. Nimitz . . . . .1885-1966. Naval Commander
Francis Daniel Pastorius . . . .1651-1719. Founder of Germantown,
Pennsylvania
John Pershing . . . . .1860-1948. World War I General
"Molly Pitcher" . . . . .1754-1832. Revolutionary War Heroine
John Roebling . . . . .1806-1869. Builder of Brooklyn Bridge
Karl Schurz . . . . .1829-1906. Secretary of Interior
Margarethe Schurz . . . . . . .1832-1876. First "Kindergarten" U.S.
Norman Schwarzkopf . . . . .1935- . Gulf War General
Baron von Steuben . . . . .1730-1794. Inspector General of
George Washington's Army
Levi Strauss . . . . .1829-1902. Originator of Levi Jeans
Robert Wagner, Jr. . . . . .1910- . Mayor, New York City
Robert F. Wagner . . . . .1877-1953. U. S. Senator
Frank P. Zeidler . . . . .1912- . Mayor, Milwaukee

For more information, we refer to another book:

Charles R. Haller
"Distinguished German-Americans"

ISBN # 0-7884-0193-9
Heritage Books, Inc.
1540-E Pointer Ridge Place
Bowie, Maryland 20716
Telephone: 301 / 390-7709

From My Cultural Heritage to America:

We've heard of the American Revolution from here to Sheboygan,
and its great hero, German General, Frederick von Steuben,
When the rush for gold sent us out west,
German designed covered wagons were best.
The solid blue jeans you wear around the house,
were designed by German, Levi Strauss.

When the truth is told, he made them so we could pan for gold,
the Roebling, whose first name was Johann,
designed the Brooklyn Bridge that so many could go on.
Also Henry Villard, a German who was terrific,
connected his coast to coast railway, the Northern Pacific.

Clement Studebaker, a German car maker,
was for the American auto, a mover and a shaker.
Now when Christmas seems to come too fast,
the States see Santa as designed by German, Thomas Nast.
Making the melody of Christmas sound just right,
hear the strains of Franz Gruber's, Silent Night.
Just remember when you trim that tree,
the idea comes from Germany.

Whenever your sweet tooth cries for mercy,
it can be satisfied with famous chocolate by Hershey.
When you attend an American baseball game,
remember Lou Gehrig, a German-American athlete of fame.
To add extra flavor to your brat,
ketchup by Heinz adds a lot.

If you prefer a piano to play the fine way,
purchase one built by German, Heinrich Steinway.
If you look to math and science skills to keep you in line,
examine the life of German, Albert Einstein.
We've heard about the moon landing all about town,
and the Saturn rockets that led to this by Wernher von Braun.

For contributions, this is far from all,
yet from what I see, we can stand tall.
Study your contributions, it helps you to live,
All German-Americans had something to give.

Sr. Frances C. Ault

Golden Wheatfields in Nebraska
Nebraska DED.

Farm in North Dakota
Bob's Photo, North Dakota Tourism

Corn Palace
South Dakota Tourism

Fort Peck Lake near Big Dry
© Travel Montana, DoC

Wagon Train, Bayard, Nebraska
Nebraska DED.

Visit the old West, as you travel through endless fields of amber grain. Pass Omaha, Nebraska, and Lincoln, where the Pony Express preceded the Railroad. Buffalo Bill's Ranch and Rodeos – yes, the legendary West is very much alive.

Kommt den "Wilden Westen" zu besuchen; Weizenfelder von Horizont bis Horizont. Farmen so groß wie ein kleiner Kreis in Deutschland, Trecker mit Rädern größer als ein Mann mit Hut. Erleben Sie Nord und Süd Dakota, wo viele Deutsche aus Rußland leben und ihre Höfe bestellen. Ja, der Westen lebt!

Western Adventure on Horse Back
South Dakota Tourism

Lonely cabin near Sawtooth Mountain, Idaho
Idaho Department of Tourism

Mount Rushmore
South Dakota Tourism

Sky Country

Bisons at Custer State Park
South Dakota Tourism

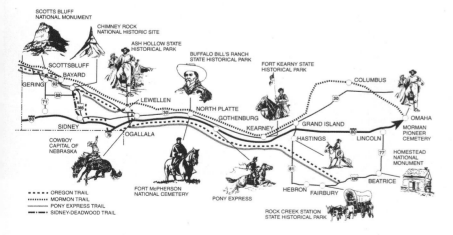

SCOTTS BLUFF
NATIONAL MONUMENT
CHIMNEY ROCK
NATIONAL HISTORIC SITE
ASH HOLLOW STATE
HISTORICAL PARK
BUFFALO BILL'S RANCH
STATE HISTORICAL PARK
FORT KEARNY STATE
HISTORICAL PARK
SCOTTSBLUFF
BAYARD
GERING
92
LEWELLEN
NORTH PLATTE
GOTHENBURG
COLUMBUS
SIDNEY
OGALLALA
KEARNEY
GRAND ISLAND
OMAHA
COWBOY
CAPITAL OF
NEBRASKA
HASTINGS
LINCOLN
MORMAN
PIONEER
CEMETERY
HOMESTEAD
NATIONAL
MONUMENT
FORT McPHERSON
NATIONAL CEMETERY
PONY EXPRESS
HEBRON FAIRBURY
BEATRICE
ROCK CREEK STATION
STATE HISTORICAL PARK

- - - - OREGON TRAIL
.... MORMON TRAIL
———— PONY EXPRESS TRAIL
– · – SIDNEY-DEADWOOD TRAIL

Come Visit The Old West

Sundown over Nebraska
Nebraska Dept. of Economic Development

Heimat Tänzer der German-American Society

Herzlich willkommen im
Deutsch-amerikanischen Klub, Omaha, Nebraska

Der Deutsch-Amerikanische Club in Omaha, Nebraska ist eine der größten ethnisch Deutschen Organisationen im Mittleren Westen mit mehr als 1500 Einzel- und Familienmitgliedern. Der Club wurde 1966 durch Zusammenschluß des Turnvereins, Musikvereins und des Deutsch-Amerikanischen Clubs geschaffen. Letzterer hatte sich aus dem Plattdeutschen Vereen gebildet. Die Gründung des Plattduetschen Vereens im Januar 1884 erlaubt den heutigen Mitgliedern auf 113 Jahre kultureller und anderer Aktivitäten zurückzublicken. 1966 wurden die drei alten Gebäude der Clubs verkauft. Ein großzügiges, attraktives Clubhaus wurde 1968 am damaligen Stadtrand Omahas errichtet. Ein Anbau 1984 bringt die Sitzkapazität für Mahlzeiten auf 550. Ein Ratskeller und Klassenzimmer im Untergeschoß bieten Platz für kleinere Gruppen.

Unterorganisationen und Aktivitäten sind der Sängerchor, die Heimattänzer (Trachten), Die Gymnastik, die Heimatfreunde (Damen), die Deutsche Sprachschule für Erwachsene und Kinder, die Bären (Herren), der Freundschafts Tanzclub, die Singenden Wanderer, Rosen (Damen), Kulturverein (Filme), Braunschweig Schüleraustausch, Schützengilde, Skatclub, Narren und Männerballett während der Karneval Saison. Ein Museum steht in der Planung und eine öffentliche Radiostation bietet an Sonntagen ein Deutsches Programm, das vom Club unterstützt wird. Eine Statue von Friedrich Schiller auf dem Gelände erinnert die Mitglieder an die wichtige Geschichte des Dichtens und Denkens die wir unser Eigen nennen können.

Der jährliche Deutsche Tag am ersten Sonntag im September zieht viele Mitglieder und andere Deutschstämmige an. Mehr als 50% der Bewohner Nebraskas haben Deutsche Ahnen. Meist spielt eine Kapelle aus Deutschland für dieses Ereignis und tausende von Bratwürsten, Schnitzel, Torten, Bier und andere Getränke werden vertilgt. Der Club nimmt auch an der ethnischen Weihnachtsfeier in einem früheren Bahnhof teil, der zum Western Heritage Museum umgebaut wurde. Ein Essen mit Tanz an zwei Samstagen des Monats zieht etwa 500 Tänzer an, während sich an

zwei Freitagen Mitglieder abends gemütlich im Ratskeller zusammen finden. Es gibt kaum einen Abend, an dem nicht eine Gruppe das Gebäude benutzt.

Zwei frühere Vorsitzende, Reinhold Fürstenau und Heinz Olk, haben das Bundesverdienstkreuz für ihre Führung des Clubs erhalten, und für ihren Anteil am Vertiefen der Freundschaft und besseren Verstehens zwischen Bürgern der U.S.A. und Deutschlands. Zwei Brüder, William und Joseph Schuette, wurden 1996 für 70-jährige Mitgliedschaft geehrt!

"Von den Deutschen, für die Deutschen"
Klubhaus, erbaut 1968-69, erweitert 1984

Es ist eines der Ziele des Clubs, weiterhin den Respekt und die Ehre unserer Deutschen Geschichte zu erhalten und dieses Erbe an unsere Nachkommen weiterzugeben.

Sängerchor der German-American Society

Welcome to the
German – American Society, Omaha, Nebraska

The German-American Society of Omaha, Nebraska is one of the largest ethnic German organizations in the Midwest with more than 1,500 individuals and families as members. The Society was formed in 1966 by the merger of the Turnverein, Musikverein and G.-A. Society which had developed from the Plattduetsche Vereen. The founding date of the Plattduetsche Vereen in January 1884 lets the current member of the Society look back to 113 years of cultural and other activities. In 1966 the three old buildings of the three clubs were sold and a spacious, attractive clubhouse was constructed at the then outskirts of Omaha in 1968. An addition in 1984 brought the seating capacity for dinner to 550. A Ratskeller and education rooms at the lower level allow room for smaller groups.

Suborganizations and activities include the Sängerchor, Heimattänzer, Gymnastics, Heimatfreunde (ladies), German Language Classes for children and adults, Baers (men's group), Freundschafts Tanzclub, Die Singenden Wanderer, Rosen (ladies), Kulturverein (movies), Braunschweig Student Exchange, Schützengilde, Skatclub, Narren and Männerballet during the Carnival Season. A Museum is in the planning stages and a public radio station airs a German program sponsored by the club every Sunday. A Friedrich Schiller Statue on the grounds reminds members of the important heritage of thought and poetry we can count as our own.

The annual German Day on the first Sunday in September attracts many members and other ethnic Germans. More than 50% of the people of Nebraska have some German ancestry. Normally a band from Germany plays for the event and thousands of Bratwurst, Schnitzel, Torten, Beer and other drinks are consumed. The club also participates in the ethnic Christmas celebration at a former railroad station which was converted into the Western Heritage Museum. A dinner dance on two Saturdays a month regularly attracts close to 500 dancers, while on two Friday evenings members assemble for Gemütlichkeit in the Ratskeller. There is hardly an evening on which not at least one group has an activity on the grounds.

Two former presidents, Reinhold Fuerstenau and Heinz Olk, received the Bundesverdienstkreuz for their leadership in the Society and for their part in furthering friendship and understanding between citizens of the United States and Germany. Two brothers, William and Joseph Schuette, were honored in 1996 for 70 years of membership!

It is one of the goals of the Society to continue the celebration of and respect for our German heritage and to pass it on to the next generations.

German-American Society, Inc.
3717 South 120th Street
Omaha, NE 68144
Telephone: 402 333 6615 • Fax: 402 498 0730

My First Christmas in America

By: Gerda Anna Linkert

In the fall of 1956 I arrived in the United Stated and began work as an au pair for my sponsors. I must admit I had never ever in my life seen such an elegant home. For the first time ever I admired the most beautiful oriental carpets. Even the staircase to the basement was carpeted. Without a doubt, the basement alone was at least as large as the apartment which in 1956 my parents shared with ten people: my parents, siblings, my oldest sister, her husband and their two toddlers. Actually, it had not been that long ago that 28 of us had to share one large room in a refuge camp. No matter where one tried to look, to the right or to the left, one simply could not avoid meeting another set of eyes. But now I was alone in this magnificent house all day long, since the lady of the house was working in her husband's factory as office manager. All my life long I had been miserably cold, but now I even had the luxury of leaving the windows open in the bathroom when it turned cold outside. The entire house was heated, from the basement to the top floor. What a delightful feeling.

We spent my first Thanksgiving in the U.S. with friends of the family in New Jersey and I marveled at the size of my first turkey. Incessantly I would ask about the different dishes that were quite new to me and occasionally even quite exotic. The only sweet potatoes I had known in my previous life were frozen potatoes. But I was quick to learn and it was an absolute delight to live like a human being. I even had my very own room!

Immediately after Thanksgiving we got busy writing Christmas cards. I was put in charge of addressing, stamping and sealing over 200 envelopes. The next undertaking was decorating the house for Christmas. Carton upon carton was hauled from the attic until the whole house looked as if the movers were at work. Despite all the activities, the head of the house not only sang Christmas carols happily, but also told jokes even when ordered with a stern summons of "Emil" to put everything in its rightful place.

Indeed, all the toil and labor paid off, because I stood silently as I beheld the miraculous wonder of our brightly lit house and the beautifully decorated neighborhood. It looked like a picture from a fairy tale. Our Christmas tree, which was set up in the party room in the basement, was glistening and sparkling almost as brightly as our Christmas trees back home in Pomerania where I lived as a child and where I took pleasure every year anew in the light shed by real candles on our trees. However, never before had I seen so many brightly wrapped presents that were piled under and around the Christmas tree. Friends of the family, all German immigrants, who had no other relatives in the United States, had been invited. It was a merry group; cocktails were served and I relished my first taste of shrimps. We also had Swabian potato salad and cold cuts and sausages had been ordered from Ehmer in New York. On Christmas day we had roast beef for dinner and it reminded me of the story they tell about the old Cossacks who would place the meat under saddles and ride with it until it was tender enough to eat (without knife and fork). In any case, our table setting was most elegant with all the silver that I had polished, with all the beautiful china and crystals. I had yet to master all this splendor, but by the time the next Christmas came around, I was quite accomplished in the art of preparing an elegant menu.

Mein erstes Weihnachten in Amerika

By: Gerda Anna Linker

Ich kam im Herbst 1956 in Amerika an und arbeitete für meine Bürgen als Haushaltshilfe. Ich muß gestehen, daß ich bis dahin noch kein so elegantes Haus gesehen hatte: Ich sah zum estenmal die schönsten orientalischen Teppiche meines Lebens, sogar die Treppe zum Keller hatte Teppiche: Der Keller selbst war gewiß so groß wie die Wohnung meiner Eltern 1956, wo wir mit 10 Menschen hausten, die Eltern, Geschwister, die älteste Schwester mit Mann und 2 kleinen Kindern. Aber waren wir nicht schon mal vor garnicht so langer Zeit 28 Menschen in einem großen Raum im Flüchtlingslager gewesen? Wo man immer einem Augenpaar begegnete ob man nach links oder rechts schaute. Und jetzt war ich in diesem herrlichen Haus, den ganzen Tag alleine, denn auch die Frau des Hauses arbeitete, sie führte das Büro ihres Mannes, der eine Fabrik besaß. Obwohl ich für viele Jahre meines Lebens erbärmlich gefroren habe, konnte ich jetzt in Amerika sogar das Fenster im Bad offen lassen als es kalt wurde. Das ganze Haus war geheizt, vom Keller bis in den 2. Stock! Was für ein angenehmer Luxus.

Thanksgiving verbrachten wir bei Freunden der Familie in New Jersey, und ich bestaunte den ersten riesengroßen Turkey meines Lebens. Und meine Fragen waren immer wieder: Und was ist das? Alles neue Gerichte, manche recht exotisch für mich. Die einzigen Süßkartoffeln die ich kannte, waren angefrorene Kartoffeln gewesen. Aber ich lernte schnell. Und es war eine Wonne, wie ein Mensch zu leben. Ich hatte ein Zimmer ganz für mich alleine!

Nach Thanksgiving wurde sofort mit der Weihnachtspost angefangen. Ich muße helfen die Adressen zu schreiben. Es waren über 200 Briefe, die frankiert und zugeklebt werden mußten. Und dann kamen die Weihnachtsdekorationen dran. Es wurden Kartons vom Boden geholt und es sah so aus, als wenn jemand beim Umzug wäre. Und ganz ehrlich, bei all dieser Arbeit hat der Hausherr nicht nur Weihnachtslieder gesungen sondern er hat auch gescherzt, als er all die Dinge an dem richtigen Platz anbringen sollte - dann kam die Stimme der soliden Hausfrau: „Emil!"

Aber all die Mühe und Plage hatte sich ganz gewiß gelohnt, denn als das Haus dann hell erleuchtet war, und die Nachbarschaft ähnlich geschmückt war, da stand ich stumm vor diesem Wunder. Es sah aus wie eine Märchenlandschaft. Der Weihnachtsbaum war im Party-Raum im Keller aufgestellt, und er glänzte und funkelte fast so schön wie unsere Tannen in Pommern, als ich noch ein Kind war und jedes Jahr aufs Neue mich am Kerzenschein erfreute. Ich hatte noch nie so viele bunt verpackte Geschenke gesehen, hochgestapelt und um den Baum, nicht nur unter dem Baum. Freunde der Familie waren eingeladen, alles deutsche Immigranten, die weiter keine Familienangehörigen in Amerika hatten. Es war eine fröhliche Runde, es wurden Cocktails serviert, und ich probierte zum ersten Mal Shrimps - es war ein Genuß. Es gab schwäbischen Karoffelsalat und alle Wurst und Würstchen kamen von Ehmer in New York. Am Weihnachstag gab es Roastbeef und ganz ehrlich, es erinnerte mich an die Geschichte, daß die alten Kosacken ihr Fleisch unter dem Sattel weichritten damit sie sie essen konnten (ohne Messer und Gabel). Jedenfalls war es ein eleganter Tisch, der da gesetzt war, mit all dem Silber, das ich putzen mußte, mit all dem schönen Porzellan und Kristall. All die Herrlichkeiten mußte ich erst erlernen, aber beim nächsten Weihnachtsfest wußte ich ganz genau, wie ein elegantes Menü zubereitet wird.

This is the place where Lawrence Welk grew up.
Hier wuchs Lawrence Welk auf.

The historic Ludwig Welk homestead makes the past come alive in *Strasburg, North Dakota*

Lawrence Welk,
the Master at home

Reservations: 701/336-7519

The Main House   Das Herrenhaus

The Barn   Die Scheune

The historic Ludwig Welk homestead makes the past come alive.

Restoration of the Ludwig and Christina Welk Homestead began in 1990, and the six-acre site opened to the public on May 15, 1991.

Many of the original furnishings have been placed in the sod house along with other antiques from the 1920s. Restored outbuildings - the summer kitchen, carriage house, blacksmith shop, privy - are much as they were when renowned band leader Lawrence Welk was born and grew up on the farm. The barn is slated to be restored in the future, but the loft already features a young Lawrence practicing his accordion overlooking the farmyard.

Pioneer Heritage, Inc. has a 99-year lease from the Schwab family on the property, and the goal is to build a Germans from Russia Heritage Center.

Tour groups and individuals are welcome at the site from May 15 through September 15, and off-season tours can be arranged.

Special thanks to the volunteers and contributors who have made the Ludwig and Christina Welk Homestead restoration possible.

Hier war Lawrence Welk zuhause, auf der Farm der Eltern in Strasburg, North Dakota.

Die Farm von Ludwig und Christina Welk wurde restauriert und am 15. Mai 1991 der Öffentlichkeit zugänglich germacht.

Viele der alten Möbel wurden in dem Sodenhaus mit anderen Geräten aus dem 1920er Jahren untergebracht. Die Gebäude, einschließlich der Sommerküche, der Wagenschuppen, die Schmiede und das Klo, sind wieder so wie der berühmte Kapellmeister es erlebte, als er auf der Farm aufwuchs. Die Scheune zeigt den jungen Lawrence beim Üben des Accordeon Spielens.

Pioneer Heritage, Inc. hat eine 99 Jahre Pacht von der Schwab Familie, und hofft in nächster Zukunft ein Museum für Deutsche aus Rußland auf dem 2.5 Hectar Land zu bauen.

Who Are The Germans From Russia?
PRESERVING A HERITAGE

Who are the Germans from Russia? This is an often asked question and why did they leave Germany and go to South Russia and then come to America? People in Germany were experiencing hard times during the 17th and 18th centuries. Parts of the country were devastated by wars, and poor economic conditions plagued the people. A great number of Germans felt depressed and discouraged, and many of them experienced persecution. An invitation was extended to these Germans in 1763 by Catherine the Great. This invitation brought many Germans to the Volga region. A second invitation of Manifesto was extended in 1804 by Czar Alexander I, which brought many Germans to settle the Black Sea shores in South Russia to colonize the vast empty parts of this area. There were many provisions included in this Manifesto. After enjoying the privileges inherent in the Manifest over a period of approximately 150 years, the Russian Government began to revoke most of the privileges and freedoms granted these people and were conscripting the young men into the military.

It is common knowledge, of course, that the United States Homestead Act of 1862 became the prevailing reason for these

people to leave South Russia and come to America where free land was to be claimed. The railroad companies in the United States were extending their tracks westward and seeking more business. So they, too,

The wedding mass for Carrie & Doug Gefro at St. Mary's Catholic Church in Hague, ND June 8, 1996. Family ties are strong. *Photos: Katie Wald*

became actively involved in the effort to bring these immigrants to the United States and Canada. The railroads began a rather intensive advertising campaign during the late 1800s for German Russians to come to America and ride the rails to the great plains and file a claim under the Government Homestead Act for the initial 160 acres.

In 1972 a small group of descendants of Germans from Russia formed an organization to be headquartered at Bismarck, North Dakota for the purpose of collecting and preserving the history of their ancestors. The name chosen for this non-profit organization was the North Dakota Historical Society of Germans from Russia and was chartered with approximately 200 members. Several years later the Society expanded to international status and was reorganized as the Germans from Russia Heritage Society (GRHS).

It is an ever expanding organization always striving to obtain new materials and ways to help their members in the United States, Canada and several foreign countries. Membership in the Society entitles you use of the GRHS Library located in Bismarck, North Dakota, two newsletters and four issues of the Society's official publication, Heritage Review. The first issue of each year is called Der Stammbaum, which is the annual genealogical issue, containing surname lists, cemetery records, church records, lists of passengers and other valuable research assistance. A convention is held annually during the month of July with predominant emphasis on genealogy workshops employing exceptional researchers and speakers from throughout the United States, Canada and abroad.

Due to the scarcity of records from Russia research can be very difficult. In researching your family history, you should have no trouble with the first two generations, but after that you may need more help. If your ancestors are Germans from Russia the staff at GRHS will assist you in the use of the thousands of surnames and obituaries on file at Headquarters. In addition, many

Four young men who were guests at the Wald house, August 25, 1995, are members of the band Musikverein Jesingen, Bavaria.

Members of our local GRHS Chapter - putting on our Annual Christmas program along with a light lunch at the local Strasburg Nursing Home.

passenger lists from 1800s and 1900s may contain names of the families you are seeking. These lists contain names of immigrants and their families who migrated to America. Other genealogical information can also be obtained from the many family histories, church records and publications housed at GRHS Headquarters and is used by a large number of visitors each year. Books and publications are available and can be purchased from the GRHS bookstore.

For further information contact Germans from Russia Heritage Society located at 1008 East Central Ave., Bismarck, ND 58501. Telephone (701) 223-6167.

Reprinted from Northern Plains
Who are the Germans from Russia?
Preserving a Heritage by Clarence Bauman,
President GRHS (1988-1991)

Wer sind die Deutschen aus Rußland?

Diese Frage, und der Grund warum Deutsche ihr Heimatland im 18. Jahrhundert verließen, um nach Süd-Rußland zu strömen, um dann im 19. Jahrhundert nach Amerika auszuwandern, wird oft gestellt.

Die Menschen in Deutschland erlebten harte Zeiten in der Vergangenheit. Zum Teil war das Land durch Kriege verwüstet oder schlechte wirtschaftliche Verhältnisse plagten sie. Viele waren niedergeschlagen und entmutigt, und andere wurden verfolgt. Jedenfalls, als Katharina die Große 1763 diese Deutschen einlud, freies Land in der Wolga Region zu beziehen, wanderte man gerne aus.

Eine zweite Einladung des Czar Alexander I 1804 brachte weitere Deutsche ins Schwarze Meer und auf die Krim, um die großen, fruchtbaren Gebiete dort zu besiedeln und zu bewirtschaften. Es gab viele Vorteile in dem Manifesto, dem Grundgesetz. Und es war gut für 150 Jahre, aber dann begann die russische Regierung viele von den Previligien zurückzuziehen, die Menschen wurden weniger frei behandelt, und schließlich wurden viele junge Männer ins Militär eingezogen.

Als dann in U.S.A. die "Homestead Act" 1862 Gesetz wurde, kamen viele dieser unglücklichen Menschen aus Rußland nach Amerika, wo wiederum freies Land zur Verfügung war.

Die Eisenbahnen in den Staaten legten ihre Schienen nach dem Westen um mehr Geschäfte zu machen. Und so wurden sie aktiv, Einwanderer in die Vereinigten Staaten und Kanada zu locken. Man machte große Werbung in den späten 1800er Jahren, um Deutsche aus Rußland auf ihren Schienen in den Westen zu bringen. Ein freies, gutes Standardgrundstück war etwa 65 Hektar groß.

1971 begann eine kleine Gruppe von Abstämmigen der Deutschen von Rußland, eine Vereinigung mit Sitz in Bismarck, North Dakota zu gründen, um die Geschichte zu bewahren. Man nannte die Organisation die North Dakota historische Gesellschaft der Deutschen von Rußland, und man ließ sich mit 200 Mitgliedern offiziell eintragen. Später wurde diese Vereinigung ausgebaut und bekam internationalen Status, und einen neuen Namen: "Germans from Russia Heritage Society, GRHS".

GRHS, 1008 E.Central Avenue, Bismarck ND 58501
Inforamtion: 701 / 223-6167

CHAPTERS

Alberta (Calgary, AB Area)

Black Hills (Rapid City, SD Area)

"Black Sea" German Heritage Group (Minneapolis, MN Area)

British Columbia (BC Area)

Dakota Pioneer (Bismarck, ND Area)

"Das Schwarze Meer" Stammhalter Verein (Emmons/Kidder County, ND Area)

Deutsche Freunde (New Leipzig, ND Area)

Deutsche Kinder (Grand Forks, ND Area)

Deutsche Leute (Dickinson, ND Area)

Deutscher Kultur Verein (Aberdeen, SD Area)

Die Deutsche Freiheit (Java, SD Area)

Die Deutschen Glieder (Pierre, SD Area)

Die Deutschen Stammhalter (Beulah, ND Area)

Gas City & District (Medicine Hat, AB Area)

Heart of America (Rugby, ND Area)

James Valley (Jamestown, ND Area)

Landsleute (Minot, ND Area)

"North Eastern Germans from Russia" Heritage Society & Research Center (Lebanon, OH Area)

Northern California (Sacramento, CA Area)

Prairie Heritage (Mandan, ND Area)

Puget Sound (Summer, WA Area)

Red River (Fargo, ND Area)

SoDak Stamm (Menno, SD Area)

South Central North Dakota (McIntosh/Logan County, ND Area)

Vorväters Kinder (Hebron, ND Area)

Wheatland (Allan, SK Area)

Leavenworth
WASHINGTON

Es gibt mehr als den dramatischen östlichen Hang der "Cascade Mountains" hinter dem Stevens Pass. Da ist Leavenworth - und viel, viel mehr.

Jeder Zeit ist es schön am Lake Wenatchee, Fish Lake, Plain und im Chumstick Tal. Von Leavensworth nur 20 bis 30 Minuten mit dem Auto.

Die ganze Umgebung ist sehenswert. Leavenworth selbst ist ein reges Bayerisches Dorf mit aller Gemütlichkeit der alten Heimat. Besuchen Sie auch das Rumpelstilzchen Cafe am Highway 2.

Leavenworth Chamber of Commerce
Informationen: 509 / 548-5807

Bavarian
Leavenworth, Washington

There is more to the east slope of the Cascade Mountains after Stevens Pass. There is Leavenworth. And much more.

For all-season fun and escape, try Lake Wenatschee, Fish Lake, Plain and the Chumstick Valley. From Leavenworth 2 to 30 minutes by car. Use Highway 2 through Tumwater Canyon, Highway 207 to Lake Wenatchee, the Beaver Valley Road to Plain and the Chumstick Road back to Leavenworth. A short drive, but if you stop for all the sights to see, you need more time.

There is plenty to do and every opportunity for all-season outdoor recreation, from fishing to hiking, cross country skiing, sleigh riding and snowshoeing.

Welcome to Leavenworth !

Photos by Robert S. Smith

Orca Whale watching in San Juan Islands
Washington Tourist Development

Day-Hikers enjoy the thrills on Mt. Rainier
Washington Tourist Development

Pacific Northwest

Seattle Skyline
Washington Tourist Division

Photo: Bert Lachner

Main House of the Manfred Vierthaler Winery & Restaurant on the way to Mt.Rainier.

The Pacific Northwest offers great nature adventures from the beautiful mountains of Mt. Rainier and St. Helen, to the rainforests and the coastline of the Pacific Ocean. Seattle, Washington and Portland, Oregon are major metropolitan areas with a sizeable German American population.

Die Nordwest Passage Amerikas bietet viele Naturschönheiten, von den Bergen Mt. Rainier und St. Helen, durch das Dschungelregen Gebiet bis an die Küste des Pazifischen Ozeans. Der Hafen Seattle, Washington und Portland, Oregon sind Großstädte mit einer größerer Anzahl von Deutschamerikanern.

Trails on Sol Duc Fall provide visitors with Rain Forest Thrills
Washington Tourism Development

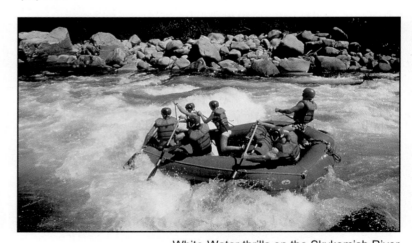

White-Water thrills on the Skykomish River
Washington Tourism Development

Seattle, Washington

Home of BOEING... a German Name Flies Around the World!

Plattduetscher Vereen

The "Plattduetsche Vereen" Men's Club was founded in 1907 under the motto: "Jungs, holt fast!" Two years later the Plattduetsche Women's Club was organized under the slogan: "Deerns, laht nich los!" Plattdeutsch, lower German, was spoken. Both clubs flourished over the years. Now they have members of all nationalities, and plattdeutsch? Both clubs merged and now host monthly dances and go on a day cruise each year.

Austrian Club of Washington

The Austrian Club of Washington was founded in 1976. Inge Waltz became first president and remained for several years. Later also a Tacoma club was formed. In 1997, Erwin Wimmer was elected president of the Seattle Club with 210 members and with him a highly motivated board who are willing to steer the club towards the year 2000 and beyond.

The club has supported a child at Kinderdorf near Gmunden in Austria. The club participates in the "World Fest at the Northgate Mall" and the "International Dance" every February.

*The **German House** in Seattle has been registered as a "National Historical Monument" since 1972 and became a "City of Seattle Historical Landmark" in 1983, because of the Assay-Office, where once all the gold from Alaska was checked and transferred.*

Gesangverein "ARION"

Already in 1884 a German Singing Society was in existence. On October 10, 1910 Gesangverein "ARION" was founded. In 1926, ARION merged with "Seattle Liedertafel," which originated in 1892.

The name ARION was taken from the Greek mythology. Arion was a Greek poet and player of the Lyre in the seventh century BC. According to legend, while returning from a successful musical contest in Sicily, he was robbed by sailors and cast into the sea, but was saved by a dolphin which had been attracted to the ship by Arion's music.

Arion is part of the "North Pacific Saengerbund" which includes 12 other German Choirs, several from Canada. The ARION is one of the most active and versatile German Societies in the Pugent Sound area.

Frohsinn Männergesang-Verein

Was it an escape? Revolution? Aggression? Or just the longing for: Männer unter sich? Well, whatever... In 1984 the male chorus "Frohsinn" was formed mostly by men of the "ARION", and they soon became a success, no - a sensation!

The Continental Club and Berghaus

The Continental Club was founded in 1961 by a small group of young and family oriented immigrants from Europe who had a strong desire to preserve and support the Germanic cultural heritage. In 1961 they started a very successful Charter Flight Program for thousands who visited Europe and relatives coming to Amerika. They also had the idea to build a German Retirement Home which we know today as the Berghaus near Hyak. This is not only a day lodge but in a second building 100 beds provide over-night accommodations.

The 100 member strong Continental Club runs the Annual Sommerfest, formerly known as the Pig Roast, and a Winter Tour, the New Years Party and Fashing, which all have become traditions and are well attended.

The German Retirement Home

As early as 1930, there was a German Old Peoples Home in the State of Washington. Theatrical performances of the Drama Club, the Sewing Bees, Turnverein, Arion Singing Society and others made it financially possible to purchase the 1st Home in 1937. During the war, it was leased to war workers. In 1975 it was sold and in 1977 a new home was dedicated. Today, the German Retirement Home is open to all nationalities and is known for the best operated one in the State of Washington.

In Seattle "**International Showcase**" with hostess Hedy Lachmann is aired each Saturday morning on KBLE with music around the world, features, interviews, bulletin board, community news, and in Tacoma "**Gisela's Original German Hour**" is on the air at the same time.

*Thank you, **Hedy Lachmann** for your assistance in providing text and photos for these Seattle pages.*

Deutsch-sprachige Kirche in Seattle
Mangelnde englische Sprachkenntnisse, Heimweh und der gleichen mehr waren der Schlüssel zur Gründung der Deutschen Kirche im Jahre 1881. Es ist die älteste Kirche in Seattle.

Other Groups include:
Love to "Tanz" Club
"Enzian" Schuhplattler
Alpentänzer
Regenbogen Dancers

Typical Chateau Bianca Wine Label

Chateau Bianca Wine Selection

Chateau Bianca
"Producers of Premium Varietal Wines"

The owners, Helmut and Liselotte Wetzel, operate the winery and vineyard with their two children Andreas and Bianca. The Wetzel family's wine roots began when Helmut's Grandfather started producing wine in the famous wine growing region of Würzburg, Germany. Both Helmut and Lilo were born and reared in Hamburg, Germany, which is a very large seaport in the northern part of the country. As time went on and he immigrated to the United States his love for wine never left his mind.

Chateau Bianca Winery was first conceived as a family operation in the mid-80's. As is typical of most Oregon wineries the annual production is very small but committed to high quality. Types of wines currently bottled are: Riesling, Gewürztraminer, Pinot Noir, Pinot Blanc and, Chardonnay, in addition to a Blush wine, two types of Champagnes and a hot spiced wine produced from an old family recipe.

As demand grows for this family run operation, production and acreage of the vineyards will be increased as well. The family has plans to grow to a maximum 20,000 case annual production so that tight quality controls can be maintained.

Chateau Bianca, Inc.
"Producers of Premium Varietal Wines"
17485 Highway 22 - Dallas, Oregon
Tel: (503) 623-6181 * Fax: (503) 623-6230

The End of the Oregon Trail

Hecata Head
Lighthouse

Photos from Oregon Tourism

Timberline Lodge at Mt. Hood

Portland
Rose Garden

Golden Gate Bridge, San Francisco

Family outing at Big Bear Lake

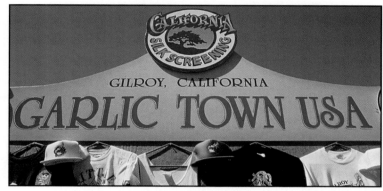

Gilroy Garlic Festival, San Francisco

The Golden State
CALIFORNIA

California Wild Flowers

Photos:
Robert Holmes
California Div. of Tourism

Napa Valley Wine Country

Mission San Diego de Alcala

Agua Caliente Festival, Palm Springs

Los Angeles Skyline at dusk

Vernal Falls, Yosemite National Park

STATE OF CALIFORNIA

Early settlers of California have looked to the region in search of unlimited opportunities—the land of gold, oil, beauty, fame and fortune. Tourists can understand when they see historic sites and missions, ocean seascapes, beaches and coves, as well as grape vineyards, fruit orchards, mountains, deserts, giant redwoods, skyscrapers, amusement parks, high-tech industries, and mild climates. Indeed, there is something for everyone in this state of cosmopolitan cities, small villages, productive farms, 1,200 miles of Pacific Ocean coastlines, 800 state parks, 8 national parks, and a progressive outlook on amusements, recreation, careers, and life in general.

"Blow, boys, blow - to Californio ..."

New Port Beach, Orange County

Golfing in Carmel Valley

Apricot Drying Operations, Patterson

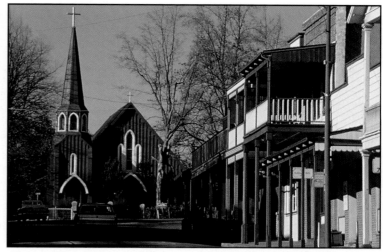

Historic Church in a charming town: Sonora, Gold Country Region

Die Pioniere, die nach Kalifornien drangen, sahen dieses Land voller unbegrenzter Möglichkeiten - Gold, Öl, Naturwunder, Ruhm und Glück. Man kann es verstehen, wenn man heute die historischen Stätten und die Missionen besucht, das weite Meer sieht, mit den Stränden und Buchten, Weinberge und Obstplantagen, die Bergketten, die Wüste und riesigen Tannenwälder, Hochhäuser und Vergnügungsparks, Hi-Tech Industrien - und ein wunderschönes, sonniges Klima.

Ja es gibt in diesem Staate wirklich von allem und für jedermann etwas: Lebendige Großstädte und kleine idyllische Dörfer, schmucke Bauernhöfe, 2,000 km Küste entlang dem Pazifischen Ozean, 800 regionale Naturparks und acht bundeseigene, wunderbare Naturschutzgebiete, die Film- und Fernsehindustrie - und Disneyland. Die Bevölkerung hat einen fortschrittlichen Ausblick bezüglich Umwelt, Beschäftigung und Freizeitgestaltung, und einen flotten Lebensstil allgemein.

Heavenly Valley, Lake Tahoe

Desert Dunes at Stovepipe Wells, Death Valley

Mount Shasta, Shasta Cascade Northern California

PHOENIX CLUB

PHOENIX ENTERTAINMENT CENTER
Phoenix Club, Inc.

Men and women of German heritage established a community in Orange County, California, for the purpose of maintaining our German language, culture, customs and traditions and this association had agreed to honor all religious confessions and all parties.

With this purpose in mind, the Phoenix Club was founded in 1960. The association opened its first club house surrounded by orange orchards in April 1965 in Anaheim. During the first ten years, 18 different interest groups evolved within the Phoenix Club: bowling, soccer, a mixed choir, a German School for adults, youth groups, a hobby group for ladies, young marksmen group (revolver and rifle), carnival group, competitive skat group, chess club, Schafskopf game, Schuhplattler dancing, adult marksmen, gliders, skiing, table tennis, SOS groups to help members in time of need. The Phoenix Club opened its new home on 11 acres of land in November of 1992. Known as German-American Entertainment Center, the Phoenix Club in Southern California is located only a few miles from John Wayne Airport in Santa Ana. It is surrounded by the most renowned and best hotels in the U.S. and it is located about 5 minutes from Disneyland and many other amusement parks. As the pride of its members it has become a tourist attraction for many guests from the U.S. and Germany. The main entrance, adorned with the proverb "Please enter, here you are among friends" that needs no further explanation, will continue to greet many more guests. The beautiful building with its elegant Ballroom, the Heritage room, the Bierstube, the Loreley Restaurant and the splendid park accommodating 3000 visitors have thus become the heart of the German Oktoberfests with many local and German bands, the Phoenix Club offers weekly two evenings of ballroom dancing and two evenings with German dance music. Throughout the year, this full program is enhanced by group events. Hundreds of volunteers help at the summer events and man the many different sales booths and stands. The fare includes German pea soup from the original field-kitchen, potato pancakes, bratwurst and beer. The 2000 families within that community still have the same sense of belonging to the

Die Schützengruppe

Die gemütlichen Schuhplattler des Phoenix Clubs

Phoenix Club Karnevals Gesellschaft

Community in California. Our chefs in the kitchen have been trained in Hamburg and in Baden-Baden and they make sure that the patrons can enjoy many specialities from home. From small snacks in the Bierstube to the most elegant dinners in the Loreley Dining Room to festive banquets for 600 guests in the Ballroom, consistent quality is assured.

In addition to the permanent annual events, such as the Easter bazaars, German Fests, Carnivals, May festivals, children festivals, Village fairs that last for 3 days and the well-known Phoenix Club, just as they did 37 years ago. It is the mission and vision of the board of directors to continue supporting and promoting the ideas of the founders of the Phoenix Club. The board is composed of President Erwin Simons, Vice President Willi Gerstner, Corporate Secretary Richard Roth, Treasurer Rudi Gräf, Assistant Treasurer Hildegard Helmbrecht, Assistant Manager Manfred Walter, Secretary Jürgen Picard, Board Members Albert Helmbrecht responsible for maintenance, and Alex Hertfelder responsible for Decorations.

Deutscher Verein in Orange County

Zur Erhaltung unserer gemeinsamen deutschen Sprache, Kultur, Sitten und Gebräuche haben Männer und Frauen deutscher Herkunft sich in Orange County, Kalifornien, zu einer Gemeinschaft zusammen gefunden, die ausschließlich und gemeinnützig diesem Zwecke dienen soll. Die Gemeinschaft verpflichtet sich außerdem zu überkonfessionellem und überparteilichem Verhalten.

Der Phoenix Club gemischte Chor

Mit diesem Vorsatz wurde im Jahre 1960 der Phoenix Club gegründet. Im April 1965 eröffnete der Klub sein erstes Klubhaus umgeben von Orange Hainen in Anaheim. In den ersten zehn Jahren entwickelten sich 18 verschiedene Interessen Gruppen im Phoenix Club:

Bowling, Fußball, Gemischter Chor, Deutsche Schule für Erwachsene, Jugendgruppe, Hobby-Gruppe für Damen, Jungschützen (Pistole & Gewehr), Karnevals Gruppe, Preisskat, Schach, Schafkopf, Schuhplatter, Schützen, Segelflieger, Skat, Skifahrer, Tischtennis, SOS Gruppe hilft aus bei notleidenden Mitgliedern. Im November 1992 eröffnete der Phoenix Club sein neues Haus auf 4.5 ha Land. Nur einige Meilen entfernt vom John Wayne Flughafen in Santa Ana, umgeben von den bekanntesten und besten Hotels Amerikas, etwa 5 Minuten von Disneyland und vielen anderen Vergnügungsparks liegt der Phoenix Club als German American Entertainment Center in Süd-Kalifornien. Ein Stolz aller Mitglieder und heute bereits als ein Touristen Anziehungspunkt vieler Gäste aus USA und Deutschland. Der Spruch im Haupteingang: "Tritt ein, hier bist Du unter Freunden", spricht für sich selbst und wird auch weiterhin die Begrüßung vieler Gäste sein. Das schöne Gebäude mit seinen eleganten Festsaal, Heritage Saal, Bierstube, Loreley Restaurant sowie einem herrlichen Park für 3000 Gäste, ist somit der Mittelpunkt des Deutschtums in Kalifornien geworden.

Die gute Küche mit unseren in Deutschland ausgebildeten Köchen,

Die Phoenix Club Fußballgruppe

aus Hamburg und Baden-Baden, garantieren dem Besucher alle Spezialitäten der alten Heimat. Vom Kleingericht in der Bierstube, zum feinsten Menü im Loreley Diningroom bis zum 600 Personen Festbankett im Saal, eine beständige hohe Qualität wird immer garantiert.

Neben den festliegenden jährlichen Veranstaltungen, Oster-Bazaar, Germanfest, Schützenfest, Mai- und Kinderfest, Village Fair für 3 Tage, und den bekannten Oktoberfesten mit vielen hiesigen und deutschen Kapellen, bietet der Phoenix Klub Ballroom wöchentlich 2 Abende für Ballroom Dancing und 2 weitere Abende für deutsche Tanzmusik. Gruppen Veranstaltungen während des Jahres, erweitern dieses volle Programm. Bei allen Sommer Verantstaltungen arbeiten hunderte von freiwilligen Mitgliedern an den verschiedenen Verkaufsständen und anderen Positionen: Von Erbsensuppe aus der original Gulasch Kanone, von Reibekuchen bis zur Bratwurst und Bierausschank. Das Zugehörigkeits Gefühl, der 2000 Familien zum Phoenix Club ist heute noch wie es vor 37 Jahren war. Die Aufgabe des heutigen Vorstandes, bestehend aus Präsidenten Erwin Simons, Vize Präsident Willi Gerstner, Geschäftsführer Richard Roth, Finanzleiter Rudi Gräf, stellvertretende Finanzleiterin Hildegard Helmbrecht, stellvertretender Geschäftsführer Manfred Walter, Protokollführer Jürgen Picard, Vorstandsmitglieder Albert Helmbrecht, Instandhaltung, und Alex Hertfelder, Dekorationen, wird auch weiterhin sein den Phoenix Club im Sinne der Gründer zu unterstützen und zu fördern.

Gedeckte Tische für private Anlässe

Phoenix Entertainment Center
Phoenix Club, Inc.
1340 Sanderson Ave., Anaheim, CA 92806

Viel Platz im Innenhof

Phone: 714-563-4166 • Fax: 714-563-4160 • International Web page: www.phoenixentctr.org • E-mail: phoenix@phoenixentctr.org

Vereinigte Deutsch-Amerikanische Gesellschaften von San Francisco und Umgegend, Inc.
United German-American Societies of San Francisco and Vicinity, Inc.

The Organization was founded in 1890 in order to achieve cooperation among the more than 60 German clubs that existed in the Bay Area.

From the start it has been the U.G.A.S. mission to honor and celebrate October 6, 1683 as the day the first German people arrived in America. This tradition continues with the active cooperation of the 17 member organizations and other German groups from the Bay Area. GERMAN DAY IN SAN FRANCISCO is held every year on or around October 6th. Festivities include a banquet and a public music and dance festival in Golden Gate Park.

Every member connected to this organization remembers with pride the 100th Anniversary Celebration of the U.G.A.S. in 1990. The high point of this 2-weekend event was the big Parade up Market Street to the Civic Auditorium in San Francisco. 33 German-American groups from the Greater Bay Area as well as individuals participated in the parade and the festival; something that had not been done since before WWII. The fact that the German Reunification occurred right between the two weekends gave our celebration a special meaning and a big boost in attendance from both the German community and the American public.

Der Verband wurde 1890 gegründet um das Zusammenwirken unter den 60 deutschen Mitgliedsvereinen, die in der Bay Gegend ansässig waren, zustande zu bringen und zu fördern.

Von Anfang an war es die Aufgabe der Vereinigten Deutsch-Amerikanischen Gesellschaften (V.D.A.G.) den 6. Oktober 1683 zu ehren und zu feiern, als den Tag an dem die ersten Deutschen in Amerika landeten. Diese Tradition besteht weiter mit der Zusammenarbeit der heutigen 17 Mitglieder- Organisationen und anderen deutschen Gruppen vom Raum der San Francisco Bay. Der Deutsche Tag in San Francisco wird jedes Jahr am oder um den 6. Oktober begangen. Das Programm schließt gewöhnlich das Festmahl und ein Musik- und Tanzfest im Golden Gate Park ein.

Jedes Mitglied, das mit den Organisationen verbunden ist, erinnert sich mit Stolz an das 100jährige Jubiläum der Vereinigten Deutsch-Amerikanischen Gesellschaften im Jahre 1990. Der Höhepunkt des 2-Wochenend-Ereignisses war der große Umzug auf der Market Street hinauf zum Civic Auditorium in San Francisco. 33 deutsch-amerikanische Vereine von der Bay Gegend sowie Einzelpersonen beteiligten sich an dem Aufmarsch und dem Fest, etwas was nicht seit vor dem zweiten Weltkrieg stattgefunden hatte. Die Tatsache, daß gerade zu diesem Zeitpunkt die deutsche Wiedervereinigung stattfand, gab dem ganzen Fest eine besondere Note und einen Auftrieb in der Beteiligung aus deutschen Kreisen, aber auch aus der amerikanischen Bevölkerung.

Der Vorstand:
The Board:

Heinz Paletzki
Präsident

Erich Eberle
1. Vize Präsident

Ingeborg Stottmeister
2. Vize Präsident

Wolfgang Hirdt
Schatzmeister

Hermann Harjes
Sekretär

Organisationen:
Member Organizations:

Allgemeiner Deutscher Frauen Hilfsverein

Arbeiter Bildungsverein

Concordia Sport Club

Damenchor Liederkranz

Deutsche Schule von Marin

Deutsche Schule - San Francisco

Deutscher Musik Verein

Freundschaft Liederkranz

Germania Verein, Inc.

German-American Society of Marin

Golden Gate Blaskapelle

Harmonie Singing Society - Belmont

Redwood Empire Chor

San Francisco Männerchor

S.F. Männerchor - Damen Verein

San Francisco Schwaben Verein

Schwäbischer Frauen Verein

United German American Societies of San Francisco and Vicinity

Gesselligkeit, verbunden mit Wandern, Camping, Touring

Roswitha Paletzki — President
Wolfgang Hirdt — Vice President

Tel. (415) 461-3312

SEIT

San Francisco Schwaben-Verein
und
Schwäbischer Frauen Verein

Neue Mitglieder von Baden-Wuerttemberg Herzlich Willkommen!
Versammlungs-Abend: Jeden Zweiten Donnerstag im Monat,

2355 OCEAN AVENUE • SAN FRANCISCO, CA 94127

1881
INFO: 415-334-3351

SAN FRANCISCO MAENNERCHOR und DAMEN VEREIN

2nd and 4th Tuesday, 8:00 p.m.
First United Lutheran Church
6555 Geary Blvd., San Francisco

Hermann Harjes, President
675 6th Ave., San Francisco 94118
(415) 221-4520

German Ladies' General Benevolent Society
Allgemeiner Deutscher Frauen-Hilfsverein

Helping Women and Children of
German Descent in the Bay Area since 1870
donations are tax deductible

P.O. Box 27101, San Francisco, California 94127   (415) 391-9947

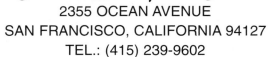
Concordia Sport Club

FOUNDED
2355 OCEAN AVENUE
SAN FRANCISCO, CALIFORNIA 94127
TEL.: (415) 239-9602

1963
Ein gemütlicher Treffpunkt für Alle

WORKMEN'S EDUCATIONAL ASSOCIATION
(ALLGEMEINER ARBEITER BILDUNGS–VEREIN)

440 TARAVAL STREET
SAN FRANCISCO, CALIFORNIA 94116

Ingeborg Stottmeister
President   (415) 386-3885

HARMONIE SINGING SOCIETY, INC.

* Mixed chorus devoted to German music
* Rehearsals: Every Friday, 7:30 - 9:30 p.m.
                Lind Hall, 621 Masonic Way, Belmont
* Contact: Annemarie Krueger
                2036 Monroe Ave., Belmont 94002
                (415) 591-0525, FAX (415) 342-5162

Damenchor Liederkranz

Singstunde:
Montags
19:30–21:30
Zion Lutheran
Church
9th Ave. & Anza
San Francisco, CA

1936

Herzlichst
Willkommen!
Information:
Astrid Holder,
Präsident,
Phone/Fax:
(415) 697-3982

Singe wem Gesang gegeben

DEUTSCHE SCHULE von MARIN
PO BOX 4172, SAN RAFAEL, CA 94913
TEL. (415) 898-1709

Die Deutsche Schule von Marin wurde 1967
von einigen Eltern gegründet, die sehr darauf
bedacht waren die deutsche Sprache und Kultur
hier zu Lande aufrechtzuerhalten. Kinder und
Erwachsene besuchen seitdem unsere Samstagschule.
Frau Elizabeth Esmerian ist seit 1970 die Rektorin.

Freundschaft   Liederkranz
seit   1925

Treffpunkt jeden Montag 7:30pm
St. Matthews Church ▪ 3281-16 Street ▪ San Francisco
Ludwig Rumbucher Präsident   (415) 664-8597

In our picture, DAV President Hans Schneider, left, presents the Certificate of the 125th Anniversary of the Turner Society of Los Angeles to their President Dennis F. Fredricks.

DAV Präsident Hans Schneider, links, überreicht die Urkunde an den Turner Präsidenten Dennis F. Fredricks zum 125 Jahre Bestehen der Los Angeles Turner Gemeinschaft.

Gegründet 1905

Deutsch-Amerikanischer Verband
P.O. Box 6081
Torrance, CA 90504

Zweck und Ziel des Verbandes
DAS ZUSAMMENGEHÖRIGKEITS GEFÜHL ALLER PERSONEN DEUTSCHER ABSTAMMUNG ZU ERWECKEN, UND DIE ERHALTUNG UNSERER GEMEINSAMEN DEUTSCHEN SPRACHE, KULTUR, SITTEN UND GEBRÄUCHE ZU FÖRDERN.

ALPINE VILLAGE CORP.
AUSTRIAN AMERICAN CLUB
CALIFORNIA FUNKEN
CLUB HEIDELBERG
DEUTSCH-AMERIKANISCHER VEREIN SANTA MONICA
DEUTSCH-AMERIKANISCHER SCHULVEREIN
DONAUSCHWÄBISCHE VEREINIGUNG
FROHSINN DAMEN CHOR
GERMAN CRUSADERS
GERMAN-AMERICAN MARDI GRAS ASSOCIATION

GERMAN SOUTH BAY CLUB
GESANGVEREIN FROHSINN MÄNNER
G.T.E.V. D'OBERLANDLER
KOLPING SOCIETY
LOS ANGELES SCHWABEN VEREIN
LOS ANGELES SOCCER CLUB
LOS ANGELES SPORT CLUB
LOS ANGELES STAMM #252
LOS ANGELES TURNERS, INC.
MUSIC FOUNDATION OF HOLLYWOOD
PHOENIX CLUB, ANAHEIM
TIROLER & BAYERN ZITHER CLUB
WORKMENS BENEFIT FUND

Induction of the DAV Flag, May 1995   Fahnenweihe der DAV Fahne

---

California Staats=Zeitung
MIT SAN FRANCISCO SEITEN
und Neue Zeitung

American German Weekly   since 1890

Just because ...

I have been with the paper for about 8 years and cover San Francisco and surrounding area - intent on keeping our German culture and traditions alive - getting involved as much as possible. Through the media you can reach a lot of people and as an American Citizen I can stand up for my beliefs and have a voice in the voting of same.

My childhood was spent in Berlin-Koepenick - the only child - my father was a Police Officer who died at an early age in 1938. We were totally bombed out and my mother had to start all over. She passed away in 1962, and they would not let her coffin across the wall because of the conditions in Berlin at that time. So she was buried in Hamburg where my Dad's sister lived.

I came to the US to be with an Aunt, a spinster in Chicago, and got transferred with my job there later to Texas, then to California where I met my husband who passed away in 1977. I later remarried - have two children, and now three grandchildren.

Lore Warren received the Friendship Pin and Letter of the Federal Republic of Germany from Consul R. Henatsch on May 14th, 1996

Dennoch ...

Seit 8 Jahren bin ich bei der Zeitung und schreibe über San Franzisko und Umgebung - um die deutsche Kultur und Tradion zu pflegen und kümmere mich so weit es mir möglich ist. Durch die Media erreicht man viele Menchen, und als amerikanischer Staatsbürger kann ich meine Meinung vertreten und habe auch eine Stimme, die gehört wird.

Meine Kindheit verbrachte ich in Berlin-Köpenick - als einziges Kind - mein Vater war ein Polizist, der 1938 als junger Mensch starb. Wir wurden völlig ausgebombt und meine Mutter mußte wieder von vorn anfangen. Sie verstarb 1962, und man ließ ihren Sarg nicht die Mauer passieren, so war es damals in Berlin. Also wurde sie in Hamburg beigesetzt, wo die Schwester meines Vaters lebte.

Ich kam in die Staaten um bei einer Tante, einer ledigen Frau in Chicago, zu sein, wurde dann aber durch meine dortige Arbeit später nach Texas und dann nach Kalifornien versetzt. Hier lernte ich meinen Mann kennen, der jedoch 1977 verstarb. Später heiratete ich wieder - und habe zwei Kinder, und heute drei Enkel.

Lore Warren wurde mit der Freundschafts-Nadel und dem Brief der Bundesrepublik Deutschlands am 14. Mai 1996 aus den Händen des Konsuls R. Henatsch gebührend ausgezeichnet.

Lore Warren enjoys the "universal language," music and especially her accordion.

Germania Hall, San Jose, California

San Jose, located at the most southern part of San Francisco Bay, is the center of the California high-tech industry. Already 150 years ago, German settlers came and stayed, lured by the mild climate and the fertile soil. Today, as it always was, the Germania Club is the meeting place of the German people. At present, we have 393 members. The club offers interesting activities for everyone through its various interest groups:

◆ The **Mixed Choir** has 32 active members, who pratice weekly. In the spring and during the Christmas season the choir performs at concerts. In addition, the members take part at the yearly choir festival of the Pacific Singing Federation.

◆ The **Ladies' Auxiliary**, where men are welcome, gets together for social hours during Kaffeeklatsch, followed by Bingo. Excursions lead us into the country or to Reno, now and then, as well as Sunday luncheons with music and dance.

◆ The **Marksmen** are a relatively new chapter, they are very active and draw many new members. This year a representative group went to Hanover, Germany, to attend the largest German Marksmen's Fest.

◆ The **Germania Singles** get together for dinner and to exchange ideas and discuss opinions.

◆ The **"Skat" Card Players** take their matter seriously. They even play at international competitions.

◆ Monday nights, German is taught and learned in the **Language Department**. At the Language Fest pupils have a chance to converse with German natives.

◆ The **Hiking Group** meets once a month on Sunday, to wander into the mountains or to the beach, to enjoy the fresh air and the beautiful views.

In addition to the Chapters, which are designed for the members enjoyment and entertainment, there are a number of committees, which work together with the board of directors for the benefit of all members:

• **Aiello** keeps the leased premises rented and in top shape.

• **Building** does the renovation, repair and remodeling; no small task in a 103 year old Clubhouse.

• **Refreshments** sees to it that all meetings are supplied with food & beverages as needed.

• **"Germania Nachrichten"** is the club's newsletter, which is published every second month in German and English.

Das Vereinshaus wurde 1892 als Musik- Konservatorium gebaut; seit mehr als 80 Jahren ist es der Treffpunkt der Deutschen und Vereinseigentum.

The Club House was built in 1892 as a music hall; it has been the meeting place of Germans for over 80 years since its acquisition by the Germania.

Die neue Vereinsfahne wurde von unseren Mitgliedern durch persönliche Beiträge finanziert und in Deutschland angefertigt.

The new Club Flag was financed by personal contributions of our members and handmade in Germany.

Der Vorstand — 1996 — The Board

Vorne, von links   Front row from left
Ilse Boldt: Vorsitzende . . . . *Director*
Irmgard Hunter: Präsidentin . . .*President*
Frida Sönkson: Vorsitzende . . . .*Director*

Zweite Reihe, von links   Second row, from left
Jerry Prosek: Secretär . . . .*Secretary*
Reinhold Schneidereit: Vorsitzender .*Director*
Lee Suess: Vizepräsident . . .*Vice President*
Dennis Mueller: Vorsitzender . . . . . .*Director*
Fred Perhson: Schatzmeister . . . .*Treasurer*

$\mathfrak{Germania}$ $\mathfrak{Club}$, San Jose, California   1856

Der Weihnachtsmann kam auch zu den Kindern in die Germania-Halle. Mit Gesang, Tanz und Klavierspiel trugen die Kinder dazu bei, ein Fest zu gestalten, welches noch lange in Erinnerung sein wird.

Santa Claus visited the children at Germania Hall. With song, dance and piano playing, the children had a ball, which will long be remembered.

- **Liaison** makes sure that all is well between the Lessee of the restaurant and the "Verein".

- **Public Relations** informs News Media about festivities, events and Club life in general.

- **"Sunshine"** visits with elderly, sick and mourning members of the Club and often brings a little gift.

- **"Vergnügen"** (enjoyment) is responsible for festivities, picnics, tours, etc., which are sponsored by the Club.

For those who spent an extraordinary amount of time and labor, there is the possibility to be named an honorary member. Presently, Germania has eight honorary members.

. . . .

Members of the Germania Club, together with the San Jose Fire Department, visited the fire department of Linderte near Hanover in 1994. This friendship bridge has since been strengthened by reciprocating visits.
Mitglieder des Germania Vereins, gemeinsam mit der San Jose Feuerwehr waren 1994 zu Gast bei der Feuerwehr in Linderte bei Hannover. Diese Brücke der Verständigung hat sich in den letzten Jahren durch gegenseitige Besuche noch verstärkt.

San Jose, am südlichsten Zipfel der San Francisco Bucht gelegen, ist das Zentrum der Hightech Industry. Schon vor 150 Jahren ließen sich hier, vom milden Klima und dem fruchtbaren Boden angezogen, deutsche Siedler nieder. Heute, so wie damals, ist der Germania Verein Treffpunkt der Deutschen.

Zur Zeit haben wir 393 Mitglieder. Der Verein bietet durch seine Unterabteilungen für jeden etwas:

◆ Der **gemischte Chor** hat 32 aktive Sänger/ Sängerinnen, die sich wöchentlich zur Probe treffen. Im Frühling und zur Weihnachtszeit gibt der Chor ein Konzert. Außerdem beteiligen sich die Mitglieder einmal im Jahr am Kommers des Pazifik Sängerbundes.

◆ Die **Damenabteilung** (Männer sind willkommen) trifft sich für gemütliche Stunden zum Kaffeeklatsch. Anschließend wird Bingo gespielt. Ausflüge ins Grüne oder nach Reno stehen hin und wieder auf dem Programm, sowie Sonntags Luncheons mit Musik und Tanz.

◆ Die **Schützen** sind eine verhältnismäßig neue Abteilung, die sehr aktiv ist, und viele neue Mitglieder anzieht. In diesem Jahr reiste sogar eine Vertretung nach Hannover zum größten deutschen Schützenfest.

◆ Die **Germania Single**s treffen sich beim Stammtisch zur Unterhaltung und zum Gedankenaustausch.

◆ Die **Skatspieler** nehmen ihre Sache ernst. Sie beteiligen sich sogar an internationalen Wettbewerben.

◆ In der **Sprachabteilung** wird montagabends deutsch gelehrt und gelernt. Beim Sprachfest haben die Schüler Gelegenheit sich bei einem Imbiß mit deutschen Einwanderern zu unterhalten.

Eine Vertretung unserer Schützen 1996 in Hannover beim größten Schützenfest Deutschlands.
A representation of our Marksmen at the largest marksmen fest in Germany, 1996 in Hanover.

Germania Verein, San Jose, California 1856

◆ Die **Wandergruppe** trifft sich an einem Sonntag im Monat, um in den umliegenden Bergen oder am Strand die reine Luft und die schönen Aussichten zu genießen.

● ● ● ● ● ● ● ● ●

Außer den Unterabteilungen, die zur Weiterbildung und zum Vergnügen der Mitglieder bestimmt sind, haben wir Komitees, die gemeinsam mit dem Vorstand zum Wohl und Besten aller Mitglieder arbeiten:

- **Aiello** ist für die Vermietung und Instandhaltung der separaten Räumlichkeiten verantwortlich.

- **Bau** führt die Renovierungsarbeiten durch, die bei unserem 103 Jahre alten Vereinshaus viel Mühe erfordern.

- **Erfrischung** sorgt bei Versammlungen und dergleichen für das leibliche Wohl der Anwesenden.

- **Germania Nachrichten** sind unsere Vereinsnachrichten, die jeden zweiten Monat in deutscher und englischer Sprache herausgegeben werden.

- **Liaison** bemüht sich die Harmonie zwischen dem Pächter des Restaurants und den Klubmitgliedern zu erhalten.

- **Public Relations** informiert die Zeitungen über Feste, Veranstaltungen und das Vereinsleben im allgemeinen.

- **Sonnenschein** besucht die älteren, kranken und trauernden Mitglieder des Vereins und überreicht eine kleine Aufmerksamkeit.

- **Vergnügung** ist für alle Feste, Picknicks, Touren u.s.w., die vom Hauptverein veranstaltet werden, verantwortlich.

Für soviel Mühe und Arbeit besteht die Möglichkeit nach Jahren zum Ehrenmitglied ernannt zu werden. Zur Zeit haben wir acht (8) Ehrenmitglieder.

Germania - Mitglieder bei einer bunten, internationalen, kulturellen Veranstaltung in San Francisco.

Germania members at a colorful, international and cultural event in San Francisco.

Am 9. September, 1995 fand die feierliche Fahnenweihe in unserer historischen Halle statt.

On September 9th, 1995, our new flag was consecrated at a solemn ceremony at renowned Germania Hall.

Die ältere Garde beim wohlverdienten Plauderstündchen.

Seniors enjoying a much deserved rest at Kaffeeklatsch.

Der gemischte Chor gibt ein Weihnachtskonzert.

The mixed chorus performs a Christmas concert.

A Little History of California, San Francisco, San Jose

California at the west coast of the United Sates was the destination for many adventurers among them Germans, who literally were following the call: "Go West Young Man." Many of these Germans did much to help the growth of this state. And here are a few examples:

John August Sutter, born 1803 in Kandern, Baden. The first gold was discovered on his land in 1848.

The **Seal of California** was designed by Alfred Kuhner, who was born on October 9, 1819 in Lindau.

The first map of California was drawn up by Karl Preuss, born 1803 in Höscheid-Waldeck.

Eschscholtzia Californica has been California's state flower since 1903 and was named after Dr. Eschscholtz, naturalist, who was born in 1793 in Germany.

In 1857, 50 Germans moved south from San Francisco and founded the town of Anaheim, today the home of Disneyland.

"The City by the Bay" San Francisco, in Northern California.

Golden Gate Bridge: Joseph Strauss, designer and chief engineer; born in 1870 in Cincinnati, Ohio, where his parents had settled, who originally had come from Strassbourg.

Hermann Oelrich, agent for the Norddeutsche Lloyd Schiffahrtsgesellschaft; builder of the **Fairmont Hotel**, Number One Hotel since 1907.

Palace of Fine Arts; Bernhard Maybeck, architect, son of a German cabinet maker; born in 1862 in New York.

The Palace of the Legion of Honor, the **Band Shell in the Golden Gate Park** and the Spreckel Villa we owe to the Spreckels Family. Klaus was born in 1828 in Lamstedt near Hanover.

San Jose, Capital of Silicon Valley. Here also German pioneers made history during the 19th Century.

Karl Weber from Homburg was the first German who came in 1841 to San Jose. He founded Stockton and opened the first Bank in the San Joaquin Valley.

Adolph Pfister came in 1848 from Strassbour. In his house the idea was born to open a Germania Club, which became a reality in 1856. In 1872 he was elected Mayor. He built the first hotel, opened the first resort and founded the first free public library.

In the 1860 a "Germania Club Orchestra" existed which later became the "San Jose Symphony."

John Balbach, born in Bad Mergentheim in 1820, manufactured the first plow on the West Coast in 1852.

The Lenzen brothers, specialists in the building trade, came from Cologne around 186. To San Jose and surrounding they gave many beautiful buildings.

Photo: pen Pictures from the Garden of the World. 1888

John Balbach

The Band Shell in the Golden Gate Park, San Francisco

Photo: Sourisseau Academy, SJSU

Adolph Pfister

Pfister Block, Downtown, San Jose

Etwas Kalifornien, San Francisco, San Jose Geschichte

Kalifornien, an der Westküste der Vereinigten Staaten gelegen, war das Ziel vieler Abenteurer die den Ruf: „Go West young Man", wörtlich nahmen und folgten. Unter ihnen waren viele Deutsche, die zur Entwicklung dieses Staates beitrugen.

John August Sutter, geb. 1803 in Kandern, Baden. Auf seinem Grund und Boden wurde 1848 das erste Gold entdeckt.

Das Kalifornische Siegel ist das Werk von Alfred Kuhner, geboren in Lindau am 9. Oktober 1819.

Die ersten Landkarten von Kalifornien wurden von Karl Preuss aufgezeichnet, geb. 1803 in Höscheid-Waldeck.

Eschscholtzia Californica, seit 1903 Kalifornias Staatsblume, benannt nach Naturforscher Dr. Eschscholtz; geb. 1793 in Deutschland.

1857 zogen 50 Deutsche von San Francisco südlich und gründeten den Ort Anaheim, wo jetzt Disneyland zuhause ist.

San Francisco, „die Stadt an der Bucht" im Norden Kaliforniens.

Golden Gate Brücke: Joseph Strauss, Entwerfer und chief engineer, geb. 1870 in Cincinnati, Ohio, wo sich seine Eltern, aus Straßburg stammend, niedergelassen hatten.

Hermann Oelrich, Agent der Norddeutschen Lloyd Schiffahrtsgesellschaft; Erbauer des **Fairmont Hotels**; seit 1907 das erste Hotel am Platze.

Palace of Fine Arts; Bernhard Maybeck Architect, Sohn eines deutschen Schreiners; geb. 1862 in New York.

Place of the Legion of Honor, die **Konzertmuschel im Golden Gate Park** und die Spreckels Villa verdanken wir der Familie Spreckels. Klaus wurde 1828 in Lamstedt bei Hannover geboren.

My sincere gratitude to Maria and Walter Brand for their diligent work in providing this information.
Bert Lachner

San Jose, Hauptstadt von Silicon Valley. Auch hier machten deutsche Pioniere im 19. Jahrhundert Geschichte.

Karl Weber aus Homburg, kam 1841 als erster Deutscher nach San Jose; gründete Stockton und eröffnete die erste Bank im San Joaquin Tal.

Adolph Pfister kam 1848 aus Straßburg. In seinem Hause wurde die Idee, einen Germania Verein zu gründen, geboren, welche dann 1856 verwirklicht wurde. 1872 wurde er zum Bürgermeister gewählt; baute das erste Hotel, öffnete den ersten Badeort und gründete die erste freie Leihbücherei.

In den 1860 Jahren gab es ein „Germania Vereins Orchester" aus welchem später die „San Jose Symphony" hervorging.

John Balbach, 1820 in Bad Mergentheim beboren, fabrizierte 1852 den ersten Pflug an der Westküste.

Gebr. Lenzen, Meister im Baugewerbe, kamen um 1860 aus Köln, gaben San Jose und Umgebung viele der schönsten Gebäude.

Eschscholtzia Californica,
California's State Flower.

Golden Gate Bridge and Park

General John A. Sutter

Fairmont Hotel, San Francisco

Palace of Fine Arts, San Francisco

Reporting for "Deutsches Fernsehen in Amerika" DFA™, Dr. Pierre A. Kandorfer

EuroChannel

Televising European TV Programs on Int' Channel - Cable & AlphaStar "small dish" DBS digital satellite USA nationwide

DFA - German TV in America now six years on the air USA nationwide.

DFA survived "against all odds" and is now a major information source for German-Americans across the continent.

Do you want to watch daily German news on nationwide US TV? No problem if you have a regular satellite dish - or cable and live in one of the 200 US cities offering ICN (International Channel Network) with DFA - Deutsches Fernsehen in Amerika (German TV in America), provided by EuroChannel Broadcasting Inc. (Los Angeles). ICN is available on the satellite F1/24 anywhere in the US and in most major US markets such as Boston, New York, Washington, Philadelphia, Dallas, Houston, Seattle, S.F. Bay Area, Los Angeles, San Diego, etc .On cable, too. This means a potential audience of over 20 million people. Check your local cable set-up for "International Channel Network".

Starting in 1997, all EuroChannel programs are available on the "small dish" DBS digital Satellite "Alpha Star" anywhere in the US, too.

In five years from 29 to over 200 cable stations . . .

German TV in America started in 1991 with a variety of German, Austrian and Swiss TV programs. Later on DFA became the major rebroadcaster of Deutsche Welle TV programs such as the news magazine "Journal" and other information and entertainment shows. In just a few years - DFA grew from just 29 US cable systems to over 200 North American cable affiliates in the USA, Central America and the Caribbean (Costa Rica, El Salvador, Guam, Honduras, Martinique, Nicaragua, Panama, Virgin Islands, Venezuela).

Reaching over one million people every day . . .

Today, DFA reaches over one million actual viewers every day. Sadly, despite this "American dream" of success, there was little support for this unique venture of promoting German language, culture and business in the US. Just a few major German advertisers such as 4711 and Henkel took advantage of this unique advertising opportunity to reach millions of "ideal" US customers for their

products and services at a fraction of the regular price for nationwide TV advertising. Even during the live broadcast of the Soccer World Cup 1994 in the US (sponsored by a major US phone company), no German advertisers or sponsors wanted to participate. No American was able to understand this.

Have the Germans already lost the game in the US?

DFA management learned that most German companies in the US just do not advertise. Additionally, no German-American organizations were interested in supporting DFA and promoting "German culture and language in the US" on a broad basis. All other ethnic programs on ICN get a lot of advertising and sponsorship support by their ethnic communities.

This did not surprise Dr. Pierre A. Kandorfer, DFA president: "Considering the fact that most members of German Clubs in the US are 60 and older, many of them are not able or not interested in attracting younger people enough to continue promoting German language and culture.

Co-founder Helga Kandorfer is checking the final version of the show before the daily broadcast.

In five or ten years from now, many of the German Clubs will no longer exist. They have already lost the game because they are absolutely out of touch with today's youth."Kandorfer points out that there is a dramatic decline in German students in American high schools and universities. In many German Clubs across the continent English is the only language all the members understand. Kandorfer states: "DFA could help, but no German Clubs we talked to are really interested. Nobody seems to care…"

DFA is now just a part of the "European package" . . .

After losing a huge investment, the corporation operating DFA was dissolved in 1996, and most of the German language programs were discontinued. EuroChannel Broadcasting Inc. took over the remaining German news magazine "Journal", and the rest of German TV in America became a part of the "European programming package" on ICN.

DFA's daily news magazine "Journal" (via satellite from Deutsche Welle Berlin) is the current "center piece" of the German language programs. This show presents the latest national news from Germany as well as comprehensive coverage of all important international news events. For millions of German or Yiddish speaking people in the US this is the most important European information source in America.

Free Calling Card and Lowest Phone Rates to Germany . . .

Under the new European umbrella, the programs are expanding rapidly. EuroChannel offers a variety of services such as free basic membership, lowest rates on international calls to and from Germany, and best flight rates and travel packages to Europe, provided in cooperation with a major European tour operator in the US.

EuroChannel information is available on Internet, too. On the world wide web (address: www. eurochannel.com/usa) you can find the complete programming, cable and other information such as "EuroChannel TeleShopping" on Internet and "European-American Business Guide" with a directory of important German and other European organizations in the US.

Offering free basic membership to everyone . . .

For a free copy of the "EuroChannel News" containing all relevant schedules, programming and cable information please contact: EuroChannel Broadcasting Inc. P.O. Box 4328, West Hills, CA 91308. Tel. (818) 883-8529, Fax (818) 883-8801. If you are interested in specific services such as free calling card, low-cost calls to or from Germany, or in European flights and tour packages, you can use the nationwide toll-free membership and order line at 1-800-For-Euro (367-3876).

An Interview with

Eric Braeden

The following short interview was conducted by Ernst Ott in March, 1990 during the founding ceremonies of the German American Heritage Society, St. Louis, MO. which was also attended by Mr. Braeden.

Ernst Ott with Eric Braeden

Eric Braeden came to America from Kiel, as Hans Gudegast, and eventually wound up in Hollywood where he became a famous actor and played in many movies and TV series. He currently stars in the CBS Soap Opera series "The Young and the Restless".

EO: You are a successful actor, what motivated you to become active in promoting the German Heritage here in America?

EB: If you have lived here for over 30 years, as a German, as a proud German, and you see how narrow and superficial the projected image of a German is - mostly limited to the period of Hitler's reign - and when you see the German being viewed as a caricature and not as a human being, you recognize the need to initiate an enlightenment process, a historical enlightenment. You have to make clear to the Non-German, that Germans have the same feelings as other beings.

EO: Do you believe German Americans have been passive for too long?

EB: We have been too passive for much too long. It is time, high time, that we speak up and be noted. Every other minority is active and recognized. We are not, we are the "docile" Germans. I am not a "docile" German.

EO: It is very admirable and commendable that you personally take such an active role in standing up for our German heritage. The recent events in Europe and particularly the former East Germany, we feel, should help to boost the German image.

EB: In general, yes. However, I have to say that I am very much disturbed and enraged when I read various editorials in certain American papers. Then I read some articles where German sentiments are expressed not only in a cynical but also very superficial way. As a free man in the Western world I have the same rights as everybody else and I like to see the caricature of the German image being corrected.

EO: Since you are a public personality, have you ever been attacked because of your pro-German position by unfriendly people or organizations?

EB: To be honest, no, and for the following reason. I am rather conciliatory and I am not a revisionist when it comes to history. I see history in a clear and realistic way and say, yes it happened. But this tragic episode of the German history cannot be undone. I also take pains not to be misunderstood because it is time we Germans have a dialogue with Jewish groups so that they realize we Germans also feel pain about those times. True, some suffered more personally, however, I have suffered too - we all have suffered. Today, the differences between us are not as many as one assumes and we do have much in common. But we must have a dialogue with each other.

The NEUE PRESSE (USPS 001603) is published weekly for $36.00 (incl. tax in CA) per year by NEUE PRESSE 2331-D2 East Avenue S, #127, Palmdale, CA 93550 Phone (805) 266-1818 - Fax: (805) 274-0212

THE WEEKLY GERMAN LANGUAGE NEWSPAPER
Heimatverbunden - Unabhängig - Überparteilich

Periodical Postage paid at Palmdale, California and additional mailing offices
POSTMASTER: Send address changes to NEUE PRESSE 2331-D2 East Avenue S, #127, Palmdale, CA 93550

NEUE PRESSE

Die aktuelle deutschsprachige Wochenzeitung für Nordamerika

USA $1.50 • California $1.00 • Canada $1.75

Neue Presse is Americas modern German Language Newspaper. About 100,000 people in all 50 US-States frequently read the Neue Presse. Founded in 1986, our paper today has regional offices and newsrooms in Atlanta (Georgia), San Diego and San Francisco (California). Our main office and newsroom is located in Palmdale near Los Angeles.

Neue Presse offers everything demanding readers could possibly expect from a modern German Weekly: news and information about the old and new world, commentaries and features, entertainment and sports, classified ads and coverage of the German language communities in the metropolitan areas of the United States.

Neue Presse is the product of professionals who were trained in Germany and the United States. Every year we have interns from Germany that we train up to our high standards. Critical, independent and non-partisan coverage is what **Neue Presse** stands for. "There is no better German Language newspaper in the US" - is what our readers frequently tell us.

Try us - we'll be happy to send you a four week subscription free of charge.

Norbert Schreiber, Neue Presse

NEUE PRESSE

The German Language Newspaper in North America

Herausgeber: Norbert-Hartmut Schreiber

2331-D2 East Avenue S, # 127
Palmdale, CA 93550
Telefon (805) 266-1818
Telefax (805) 274-0212
e-mail: neuepresse@CompuServe.com
e-mail: http://www.neuepresse@earthlink.com

Die Neue Presse ist Amerikas aktuelle deutschsprachige Wochenzeitung mit fast 100 000 Lesern in allen 50 US-Bundesstaaten. 1986 gegründet, verfügt die Zeitung über Redaktionsbüros in Atlanta (Georgia), San Diego und San Francisco (Kalifornien). Die Zentralredaktion befindet sich in Palmdale bei Los Angeles.

Die Neue Presse bietet anspruchsvollen Lesern all das, was sie von einer modernen deutschen Wochenzeitung erwarten können: Nachrichten und Informationen aus der alten und der neuen Heimat, Kommentare und Hintergrundberichte, Unterhaltungs- und Sportseiten, Kleinanzeigen und US-Stellenmarkt sowie Lokalberichte aus den deutschsprachigen Gemeinden der amerikanischen Metropolen. Die NP ist kein Amateurprodukt, sondern wird von Journalisten gemacht, die ihr Handwerk "von der Pike auf" in der Bundesrepublik und den Vereinigten Staaten gelernt haben. Praktikanten und Volontäre aus Deutschland schauen bei uns im Rahmen von Fortbildungsmaßnahmen Jahr für Jahr regelmäßig hinter die Kulissen.

Kritische, überparteiliche und unabhängige Berichterstattung sind unsere Markenzeichen.
Es gibt keine bessere deutschsprachige Zeitung in U.S.A. - so sagen unsere Leser.
Warum überzeugen Sie sich nicht selber? Ein vierwöchiges Probe-Abo senden wir Ihnen gerne kostenlos zu, Anruf, Fax oder e-mail genügt.

MESSAGE TO MY FELLOW GERMAN-AMERICANS

by

The Honorable Johan Klehs

Chair, California State Board of Equalization

Heartfelt greeting to me 57 million Americans of German descent who contribute to our country's greatness. From the landing of the Concord in 1683 when the first German stepped on what would become American soil through the quilt of history, some of America's greatest citizens have been of German-American descent. Among those who have contributed in so many ways to America's greatness are Baron von Steuben, Molly Pitcher, Levi Strauss, Carl Schurz, Alfred Bierstadt, John Peter Altgeld, Babe Ruth, Hannah Arendt, Albert Einstein, Marlene Dietrich, Dwight Eisenhower, Henry Kissinger, Oscar Hammerstein, and Wernher von Braun.

In the postwar world, PResident John F. Kennedy linked the futures of Germans and Americans in his steadfast defense on the freedom of Berlin. That joint American and German effort led to the defeat of communism and the ultimate and peaceful unification of Germany.

Growing up in San Leandro, California, my brother, Karsten, and I were taught the value of community service by our parents' example. Our father served in the U.S. Army during World War II. He was president of his carpenter's union local and a leader of our Boy Scout troops. My father helped neighbors build the community park where he and my mother had decided to settle. Our mother was just as dedicated to service in her new American community. She served as president of the local PTA, was active in our schools and served as a Camp Fire Girls leader even though she had no daughters. She also taught German at home to neighborhood children and participated in numerous community activities.

At home we also learned important lessons of history. My parents taught us never to forget the injustices of past totalitarian governments and never again to allow any government to trample on the rights, freedoms, and liberties of its people. They instilled in us the idea that the best way to insure the freedom of all was active participation in our government and in our communities.

As an American of German descent, I am proud of my heritage and mindful of the lessons of history and the teachings of my parents. Having served as a city council member, a state legislator and now as an elected member of the California State Board of Equalization performing my duties as a tax commissioner, I appreciate the courage it took to fight for no taxation without representation. That is why we value our rights as citizens. We remember why those immigrants came over on the Concord and ultimately fought for independence in the first place.

EINE BOTSCHAFT FÜR MEINE DEUTSCH-AMERIKANISCHEN MITBÜRGER

der Honorable Johan Klehs

Vorstand des Grundbesitzausgleichamts, Bundesstaat von Kalifornien

Auf das herzlichste möchte ich die 57 Millionen Amerikaner deutscher Herkunft begrüßen, die das ihrige taten, unser Land in ein großartiges Land zu verwandeln. Von dem Zeitpunkt in 1683 an, an dem die Concord die amerikanische Küste erreichte und die ersten Deutschen das Land betraten, das sich im Laufe der Geschichte durch vielerlei Einwirkungen einmal in americaknischen Boden verwandeln sollte, waren einige der bedeutendsten amerikanischen Bürger deutsch-amerikanischer Herkunft. Unter denen, die dazu beitrugen, dieses großartige Land zu schaffen, befinden sich Baron von Steuben, Molly Pitcher, Levi Strauss, Carl Schurz, Alfred Bierstadt, John Peter Altgeld, Babe Ruth, Hannah Arendt, Albert Einstein, Marlene Dietrich, Dwight Eisenhower, Henry Kissinger, Oscar Hammerstein, und Wernher von Braun.

In seinem unnachgiebigen Kampt um die Freiheit Berlins in der Zeit nach dem 2. Weltkrieg, verknüpfte Präsident John F. Kenndy die Zukunft der Deutschen mit der Zukunft Amerikas. Es war dieses gemeinsame amerikanisch-deutsche Unterfangen, das zum Sieg über den Kommunismus und zur endgültigen und friedlichen Wiedervereinigung Deutschlands führte.

Mein Bruder Karsten und ich wuchsen in San Leandro, Kalifornien auf und unsere Eltern lehrten uns durch ihr gutes Beispiel, den Sinn für den Gemeindedienst. Der Vater diente während des 2. Weltkrieges als Angehöriger der U.S. Armee. Er war Vorstand der Tischlergewerkschaft und Führer einer Pfadfindertruppe. Mein Vater hatte daran teil, mit den Nachbarn zusammen einen Gemeindepark dort aufzubauen, wo er und meine Mutter sich niedergelassen hatten. Unsere Mutter war dem Dienst ihrer neuen amerikanischen Gemeinde genauso ergeben. Sie wurde Elternvertreterin an unserer Ortsschule, nahm aktiv am Schulwesen teil und wurde Leiterin einer Pfadfinderinnentruppe, obwohl sie gar keine Töchter hatte. Zu Hause erteilte sie den Kindern der Nachbarschaft Deutschunterricht und nahm im allgemeinen an den Gemeindeaktivitäten teil.

Zu Hause war es auch, wo wir einen wichtigen Teil der Geschichte mit auf den Weg bekamen. Meine Eltern lehrten uns, niemals die Ungerechtigkeiten der totalitären Regierungen der Vergangenheit zu vergessen und es niemals zuzulassen, daß die Rechte, Freiheit und Gleichberechtigung der Menschen von einer Regierung jemals wieder mit Füssen getreten werden. Sie flößte in uns die Idee ein, daß eine aktive Teilnahme an der Regierung und in unseren Kommunen, der beste Weg sei, die Freiheit aller zu gewahren.

Als Amerikaner deutscher Herkunft bin ich stolz auf meine Vergangenheit und ich werde niemals die Lehren der Geschichte vergessen, die uns unsere Eltern mit auf den Weg gaben. Als ehemaliger Stadtrat und Mitglied des Parlaments meines Bundesstaates und jetzt als gewähltes Vorstandsmitglied des Grundbesitzausgleichamts von Kalifornien, für das ich das Amt eines Steuerkommissars innehalte, kann ich es sehr wohl verstehen, daß viel Mut dazu gehörte, um "taxation wihtout representation", also Besteuerung ohne Vertretung, zu kämpfen. Ein guter Grund, warum wir unsere Rechte als freie Bürger zu schätzen wissen. Wir werden es auch nie vergessen, warum die Einwanderer auf der Concord nach Amerika kamen und später die Ersten waren, die um Unabhängigkeit kämpften.

The Honorable Johan Klehs

Dittmer and Margaret Bubert with their children Mark and Petra Silva.

Octoberfest every day of the year!

Dittmer Bubert from Hamburg and wife Margaret from Westfalia operate their "Gourmet Meats and Wurst-Haus" in Mountain View , CA together with their grown children Mark and Petra.

Unique is their awardwinning, innovative selection of delicatessen and sausages from different countries and parts of USA, to name a few:

✳ Weisswurst, Bratwurst, Knackwurst, coldcuts

✳ Kassler Rippchen, Leberkaese, Landjaeger,

✳ Sheboygan Brats, Polish Sausage, Swedish Potato Sausage, Corned Beef, Steak Tatar

✳ Beef, lamb, pork, veal, venison and poultry

✳ Variety of cheeses, spices and condiments

✳ Chocolates, cookies for Easter, Christmas

✳ Party Plates for all occasions!

✳ Call **(415) 941-3800**

Oktoberfest an jedem Tag des Jahres!

Dittmer Bubert aus Hamburg und Frau Margaret aus Westfalen bewirtschaften eine feine Fleischerei und Wurst-Haus in Mountain View, Kalifornien, zusammen mit ihren erwachsenen Kindern Mark und Petra.

Die ausgezeichneten Spezialitäten des Hauses sind weit und breit beliebt. Hier einige der Delikatessen und Wustwaren:

✳ Weißwurst, Bratwurst, Knackwurst, Aufschnitt

✳ Kassler Rippchen, Leberkäse, Landjäger Wurst

✳ Sheboygan Brats, Polish Sausage, Schwedisch Potato Sausage, Corned Beef, Sülze, Hack

✳ Rinder-, Lamm-, Scheine- und Kalbfleisch,

✳ Wildbret und Geflügel, auch Konserven

✳ Auswahl von Käse, Zutaten und Gewürze,

✳ Schokoladen, Gebäck und andere Leckerbissen.

✳ Kalte Platten für jede Festlichkeit!

Come and get it!   **DITTMER'S**   *Guten Appetit!*

High Tech
Silicon Valley, California

Als Peter Breidbach 1957 Deutschland verließ und nach Amerika auswanderte, wurde dies zu einer Lebensaufgabe. 1932 in Bremen geboren, studierte der junge Peter Breidbach Fertigung und verbrachte 4 ½ Jahre in der Lehre. 1954 heiratete er Waltraut Krellwitz, und das junge Paar entschied sich, durch die Nachkriegsjahre enttäuscht, nach Kanada auszuwandern. Vier Jahre in der Luftfahrt-Industry und Englisch lernen waren genug um seine ganze Familie nach San Fransisco Bay zu versetzen. Das was 1961.

"Um uns selbst zu lehren, sprach die ganze Familie englisch zu hause", erklärt Peter Breidbach, der erstaunt war zu sehen, daß Amerikaner ihn trotz seiner begrenzten Sprachkenntnisse einstellten. "Ich sprach wenig Englisch und dennoch wurde ich als Gleicher behandelt".

Er bekam einen Job in der Werkzeug- und Zubehör- Entwicklung in einer kleinen Werkstatt, Edwards Enterprises, die durch die Gebrüder Les und John Edwards in San Carlos gegründet war. Nach nur einem Jahr bekam Breidbach die Schlüssel in die Hand und wurde beauftragt, die kleine sechs-Mann Firma zu leiten. Die Firma entwickelte und baute Produkte für die Flugzeugindustrie. Unter Peter Breidbachs Führung wuchs Edwards Enterprises auf eine Belegschaft von zwanzig und erfreute sich einem Ruf von Kreativität und Neuerung.

Peter Breidbach wurde 1966 amerikanischer Staatsbürger. Als Vater von vier Kindern, paßte er seine Familie an den amerikanischen Lebensstil an. "Ich schätze die Hilfe, die mir hier in USA zu Teil wurde. Amerikaner sind großzügige Menschen und gewillt, anderer Ideen als fair zu akzeptieren". Aber er gibt zu, daß sein Erfolg auf der alten-Welt-Überzeugung basiert, seine Belegschaft voll zu unterstützen.

" Wir haben die besten Leute in der Industrie", sagt er stolz, "das beneidet der Wettbewerb am meisten". "Wir haben als Firma durch überlegenes Talent im Ingenieurswesen überlebt".

Heute, mit $ 34 Millionen Umsatz und 150 fleißigen Beschäftigten, ist die Firma immer noch von der selben kreativen Kultur, als eine der modernsten Fertigungsstätten Kaliforniens bekannt. Seit 1987, als ernannter Präsident und Geschäftsführer von Erwards Enterprises, hat Herr Breidbach in den

letzten 35 Jahren geholfen, diese erfolgreiche Firma in einen einflußreichen Branchenführer umzuwandeln, der heute Produkte für Flugzeug- und Komputerfirmen entwickelt und herstellt.

"Ich habe eines in U.S.A. gelernt", erklärt Herr Breidbach, "wer gewillt ist hart und klug zu arbeiten, wird erfolgreich sein".

Peter B. Breidbach, President & CEO, Edwards Enterprises, Newark, California.

When Peter Breidbach left his native Germany for North America in 1957, he embarked on the journey of a lifetime. Born in Bremen in 1932, Mr. Breidbach studied manufacturing in a German technical school and spent 4-1/2 years practicing his trade. In 1954, he married Waltraut Krellwitz and the young couple, disillusioned with the aftermath of World War II, decided to emigrate to Canada. After four years working in Canada's aircraft industry and perfecting his English, Mr. Peter Breidbach moved his family to the San Francisco Bay Area of California in 1961.

"To teach ourselves, our family decided to speak only English at home," explained Mr. Breidbach, who says he was surprised at the willingness of Americans to hire him with his limited language. "I barely spoke English and yet was treated as an equal."

Photo: Rubiolo

Mrs. & Mr. Peter Breidbach

He landed a job in tool and fixture design at a small machine shop, Edwards Enterprises, founded by brothers Les and John Edwards in San Carlos. After only a year, Mr. Breidbach was handed the keys and asked to run the six-person shop, which designed and built products for the aircraft industry. Under Mr. Breidbach's leadership, Edwards Enterprises soon grew to 20 employees and earned a reputation for creativity and innovation.

Mr. Breidbach became a U.S. citizen in 1966. The father of four children, he was happy to assimilate his family to the American way of life. "I really appreciate the help I was given here in the U.S. Americans are very generous people and willing to accept other people's ideas as fair." But he credits his own success with the old country conviction that supporting and educating your employees is paramount to success. "We have the best people in the industry," he proclaims proudly. "It's what our competitors envy the most. We've survived as a company because of better engineering talents."

While his $34 million company now employs over 150 people, the same innovative culture is present in one of the most modern manufacturing facilities in California. Named president and chief executive officer of Edwards Enterprises in 1987, Mr. Breidbach has spent the past 35 years helping to build this successful company into an influential industry leader that today designs and manufactures products for aerospace and semiconductor companies.

"I found out one thing in the U.S.," explains Mr. Breidbach, "If you're willing to work hard, you will be successful."

Edwards Enterprises
8455 Cabot Court, Newark, CA 94560

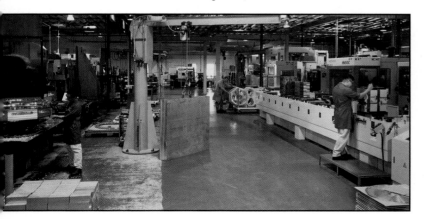

... and Every Morning a New Day! ... und jeden Morgen ein neuer Tag!

Gertrude Czikus

I like to recall my early childhood. Father had been a "Seesoldat", a marine. He was sent to Peking in 1912 to protect the German Ambassador to China. In 1914, he was sent to Tsingtao, a German colony by the Yellow Sea in China, to help defend this small seaport from invading Japanese. He then spent eight years in a Japanese prisoner of war camp. In 1922 the International Red Cross sent a ship around the world to pick up stranded people in order to return them to their homelands. Father could tell wonderful stories about far away countries such as China, Japan and Indonesia. He could speak some Japanese and also knew much about the stars, moon and oceans.

At the age of 12, I was fortunate to be one of 30 students in Frankfurt to receive a scholarship to attend high school where I started learning English.

Then came the time we like to forget, but I can still remember walking through the burning city after school, scrounging for food, water and coal. Mother had always been sickly and died when I was 16. Both father (53 then) and brother (15 then) returned from the front and life slowly became normal.

Colleges and universities had been bombed out, so my desire to become a teacher vanished. I started an apprenticeship in accounting. My monthly salary was just enough to buy a loaf of bread.

When I was 19, I married Robert. He had been drafted at the age of 17 into the German army as an Infantryman and served for 3 years at the Russian front. He suffered from frostbites and wounds to his face, neck and back.

Postwar Germany was not the best of places to try to remold shattered lives. Conditions were hard and living accommodations almost impossible to find. But we were young and eager to catch up with living.

In 1948 I started working for the American Quartermaster in Frankfurt. Because of my knowledge of English, I was sent to management school (the only woman among 25 men) and then given the job of Supply Manager. I was responsible for acquiring, purchasing and distributing all the perishable food. This was a difficult job, but great experiences.

In 1953, my husband and I sold all our belongings, which was basically our motorcycle, left Frankfurt and Germany, and boarded one of those old troop transporters that had been converted to an emigrant ship bound for Quebec, Canada.

In Toronto I found work in bookkeeping, but Robert could not get a job in his trade. In Germany, he had been a machinist and the company provided the tools. In Canada, employees had to bring their own tools. Therefore, he had to take menial jobs until he learned some English and we saved money for tools. On the ship coming over to Canada, I wanted to teach him some English, but his response was that if the ship sank, he would have learned for naught.

We would walk miles to save the dime for the streetcar and managed pretty well for three years. I changed jobs once, spent evenings studying and as a result was promoted. Also I helped my husband with his technical manuals so he could pass his government tests and begin work at his trade.

Then we visited a new mining town being built in the middle of the northern Ontario bush, Manitouwadge, and decided to relocate there. Marvelous times followed; long, cold winters with winter sports, and short, mosquito and black-fly plagued summers. But what an experience it was for the adventure-hungry young. In the winter the town looked like a Christmas card. In the summer there were lakes on which to enjoy fishing and boating. I worked for the Hudson's Bad Company,

Ich erinnere mich gerne an meine frühe Kindheit. Mein Vater war „Seesoldat". Seine Truppe wurde 1912, zum Schutz der deutschen Botschaft in China, nach Peking geschickt. Als 1914 der erste Weltkrieg ausbrach wurde er nach Tsingtao versetzt um diese kleine deutsche Handelsniederlassung am Gelben Meer in China, gegen die Japanische Invasion, zu verteidigen. Acht Jahre folgten in Japanischer Kriegsgefangenschaft. 1922 schickte das Internationale Rote Kreuz ein Schiff in alle Weltteile um gestrandete Menschen nach ihren Heimatländern zurück zu bringen. Vater konnte interessante Geschichten über China, Japan und Indonesien erzählen. Er hatte etwas Japanisch gelernt, und wußte viel über Sterne, Mond und Ozeane.

Zusammen mit 30 andern ausgesuchten Schülern aus der Stadt Frankfurt bekam ich als 12 jährige ein Stipendium für die Real Schule und konnte unter anderem Englisch lernen.

Dann kam die Zeit, die wir vergessen möchten, doch erinnere ich mich immer wieder als ich nach der Schule durch die brennende Stadt lief und wir dann später Essen, Wasser und Kohlen suchten. Mutter war immer kränklich, sie starb als ich gerade 16 war. Mein Vater (mit 53 Jahren) und mein Bruder (mit 15 Jahren) kamen von der Front zurück, und langsam nahm das Leben wieder seinen normalen Weg.

Mein Wunsch Lehrerin zu werden mußte ich aufgeben, da alle Schulen geschlossen waren (oft ausgebombt). So trat ich eine Lehre als Buchhalterin an. Mein monatliches Gehalt war gerade genug für ein Laib Brot.

Robert und ich heirateten als ich 19 Jahre alt war. Er wurde schon mit 17 Jahren zur Wehrmacht eingezogen und diente 3 Jahre lang in Russland. Mit erfrorenen Füßen, Verletzungen am Gesicht, Hals und Rücken kehrte er heim.

Nachkriegs Deutschland hatte nicht die besten Voraussetzungen um ein neues Leben zu gestalten. Es war fast unmöglich für junge Leute eine Wohnung zu bekommen. Aber wir waren begierig ein neues Leben anzufangen.

1948 trat ich eine Stelle beim Amerikanischen Hauptquartier an und auf Grund meiner Englisch Kenntnisse wurde ich als einzige Frau unter 25 Männern auf eine Manager Schule geschickt. Dann erhielt ich die Stelle als Versorgungs Manager und war verantwortlich für den Einkauf und Verteilung verderblicher Lebensmittel. Das war eine grosse Verantwortung für mich, aber eine gute Lehre.

1953 verkauften wir unsere gesamten Habseligkeiten (was eigentlich nur ein Motorrad war) und verliessen Frankfurt und Deutschland, und schifften uns auf einem zum Emigranten Schiff umgebauten alten Truppen-Transporter nach Kanada ein.

In Toronto fand ich Arbeit in der Buchhaltung, aber Robert konnte in seinem Beruf nicht arbeiten. In Deutschland stellt die Firma die zur Arbeit benötigten Werkzeuge zur Verfügung, während die Arbeiter in Kanada ihr eigenes Werkzeug mitbringen müssen. Deshalb mußte er niedrigere Arbeit annehmen bis er Englisch lernte und wir genügend Geld zum Kauf von Werkzeug hatten. Auf dem Schiff nach Kanada hatte ich versucht mit ihm Englisch zu lernen, aber er war der Meinung, wenn das Schiff sinkt, wäre diese Anstrengung umsonst gewesen.

Um das Geld für die Straßenbahn zu sparen, liefen wir meilenweit, und so ging das Leben ganz gut für die nächsten 3 Jahre. Abends studierte ich noch um mein Wissen zu erweitern, und bekam dadurch eine bessere Position. Ich half auch meinem Mann mit den englischen technischen Büchern damit er seine Staats-Prüfung bestehen konnte, und endlich in seinem Beruf arbeiten konnte.

Im Urlaub besuchten wir eine neue Bergwerks Ortschaft im Nord Ontario Busch, Manitouwadge, und entschieden uns dorthin zu ziehen. Das waren wunderschöne Zeiten; lange, kalte Winter mit Wintersport und kurze Sommer, mit Mücken und Black Flys geplagt. Aber was ein Erlebnis für Abenteuer-lustige junge Menschen. Im Winter sah das Dörfchen aus wie das

managing accounting, personnel and administration. Meanwhile I kept working on my education by taking university correspondence courses.

By 1958 we had saved enough to return to Europe, visiting London, Paris, Brussels and stayed two weeks with our families. We found that we big city kids longed to get back to the bush country.

But after five years in the "bush" we began looking for a permanent home. We sold all our belongings (except tools) and once again headed west. As we crossed the border to the USA at Duluth, the immigration officer asked where we were headed. The reply was "California". He said that we needed to be more specific; in case immigration tried to find us. The first name that came to mind was, "Sacramento". I must admit we knew very little about California, but we dutifully drove to Sacramento. We did not like the heat (coming from the cold country), so we continued on, settling in the San Francisco bay area.

To obtain our immigration visa we had to provide a health certificate and prove that we either had a job to go to, or had enough money to support ourselves for one year, so we would not need welfare. Since we had no problem finding jobs, we were able to use our saved money for our dream, our own home.

From 1961 to 1971 I worked at two different companies, paper product manufacturing and health care. Again I managed finance, administration and data processing departments. Here I was able to take college courses in business management and business law.

A very interesting ad for an accountant caught my eye in 1971. ROLM, a start-up company in electronics was looking for an accountant. I applied, was hired and became employee #35, among all engineers and the four founders. This was during the early days of computers and high-tech companies in Silicon Valley. Lots to learn again about computers, new impressions, new words and their meanings: motherboards, interfaces, memories, etc.

As the company grew and matured I grew with it. My employment dossier paralleled the milestones of the company's growth. From different positions in finance, accounting, administration I was moved up to Computer Division Financial Controller and finally International Controller.

I helped start up wholly owned subsidiaries in Germany, England, Hong Kong, Japan and a production facility in Mexico. There were so many complicated issues in dealing with the many countries in Asia, South America, Mexico and the Middle East. Knowledge in international law, contracts, foreign currencies, banking, economic and political environments was needed. It was necessary to work long hours and I traveled a great deal.

Before I retired in 1988, I had the incredible experience of spending a year in Hong Kong to help with the business in China. I traveled to Beijing, (and imagined the years my father spent there), Shanghai and Hangzhou. At that time ROLM had grown to around 10,000 employees. My manager told me that I was capable of performing all of the functions in the division with the exception of engineering. Well, I suppose that was true, but I did have a lot of help.

I am grateful that I had a husband who was always understanding when I worked long hours or traveled, and he stood by me with help and advice.

I am grateful that I always had a mentor at ROLM who would prod me to reach higher.

Being a woman never interfered with my work or goals. I did my job and enjoyed every minute of it. It must have been my initiative, enthusiasm for the job, perseverance and high energy which put me into key positions. Very often I was the only female at top management meetings.

Being a German immigrant never held me back. It may have helped me to be successful, as I had a better understanding of other countries and business environments and people.

I am very proud of my accomplishments. I've met many wonderful people all over the world and I still remain friends with many of them.

My husband of 47 years died of cancer in 1994. I still enjoy traveling and am pursuing new interests.

Bild auf einer Weihnachtskarte. Rundherum waren Seen, da hatte man im Sommer viel Spaß mit angeln und Klepper Boot fahren. Ich arbeitete für die Hudson's Bay Company, war verantwortlich für alle Buchhaltung, Personal und Verwaltung. Und nebenbei studierte ich immer noch durch Korrespondenz Kurse.

Bis 1958 hatten wir genug Geld gespart für den ersten Europa Besuch, London, Paris, Brüssel und 2 Wochen bei der Familie in Deutschland. Doch wir Großstadtkinder waren froh, als wir wieder in den „Busch" kamen.

Nach 5 Jahren in Manitouwadge war es Zeit ein festes Heim zu finden. Wieder mal verkauften wir alles (ausschließlich der Werkzeuge) und zogen nach Westen. An der Grenze in Duluth fragte der Immigration Offizier wohin wir wohl ziehen würden. Unsere Antwort war „Kalifornien". Er meinte, wir müßten das etwas genauer angeben, im Falle daß man uns suchen wollte. Das erste was mir einfiehl war „Sacramento". Ich muß zugeben, wir wußten sehr wenig über Kalifornien, aber wir fuhren pflichtbewußt nach Sacramento. Doch die Hitze dort gefiel uns nicht (kamen doch gerade aus der kalten Zone). Dieses Mal ließen wir uns in der San Francisco Bay Gegend nieder.

Wir mußten einige Tests bestehen bevor wir das Visum für USA bekamen. Ein Gesundheitsbeweis war nötig; auch mußte man eine Arbeit oder genug Geld nachweisen, damit man dem Staat nicht zur Last fiel. Da wir keine Probleme hatten, Arbeit zu finden, konnten wir mit unserem gesparten Geld unseren Traum verwirklichen, ein eigenes Haus anzuzahlen.

Von 1961 bis 1971 hatte ich Stellungen in zwei verschiedenen Betrieben, Papier Produkte und im Gesundheitswesen. Wieder war ich Manager in Buchhaltung, Finanzen, Verwaltung und nun auch Datenverarbeitung. Hier konnte ich weiter College Kurse nehmen in Geschäftsverwaltung und Rechtskunde.

Im Jahre 1971 wurde ich auf eine sehr interessante Stellenanzeige aufmerksam. Eine junge Firma in Electronics, ROLM, suchte einen Buchhalter. Ich wurde eingestellt als Arbeitnehmer #35, alle waren Ingenieure, auch die vier Gründer.

Das war die Zeit der ersten Computer und High Tech Firmen in Silicon Valley. Wieder so viel zu lernen über Computer, neue Eindrücke, neue Worte und ihre Bedeutung: Motherboards, Interfaces, Memories, etc. So bin ich mit der Firma herangewachsen. Meine Laufbahn reflektierte die Meilensteine des Wachstums der Firma. Ich wurde dann Financial Controller der Computer Abteilung und später Controller für die Auslands Abteilung.

Bei der Gründung von Tochter Gesellschaften in Deutschland, England, Hong Kong und Japan war ich beteiligt, und dann auch als wir eine Fabrik in Mexico aufbauten. Da waren so viele komplizierte Geschäfte zu verhandeln in vielen Ländern in Asien, Süd Amerika, Mexico und im Mittel Osten. Man mußte gute Kenntnisse haben über Internationale Konventionen, Kontrakte, Währungen, Bankwesen, wirtschaftliche und politische Verhältnisse. Es war nötig lange Stunden zu arbeiten, und ich war viel auf Reisen.

Bevor ich 1988 in Rente ging, hatte ich das wunderbare Erlebnis, ein Jahr in Hong Kong zu leben und mit dem Geschäft in China zu helfen. Ich reiste nach Peking (und dachte an die Zeit als mein Vater dort war), Shanghai und Hangzhou. Zu dieser Zeit war ROLM bis auf 10,000 Angestellte gewachsen. Mein Vorgesetzter sagte immer, dass ich fähig war alle Funktionen in der Abteilung (außer den Ingeneuren) ausführen zu können. Ja, ich denke schon daß es stimmte, aber ich hatte auch immer viel Hilfe.

Ich bin sehr dankbar, dass ich einen Lebensgefährten hatte, der viel Verständnis hatte als ich lange Stunden arbeitete oder auf Reisen war. Er stand mir immer zur Seite mit Hilfe und guten Ratschlägen.

Ich bin sehr dankbar, dass ich immer einen Mentor bei ROLM hatte, der mich anspornte höher zu reichen.

Daß ich eine Frau bin hat mich nie daran gehindert meine Arbeit oder gesetzten Ziele auszuführen. Ich habe meinen Job gemacht und hatte jede Minute Freude daran. Wahrscheinlich war es meine Initiative, Begeisterung für meine Beschäftigung, Beharrlichkeit und Energie, die mir zu guten Stellungen halfen. Sehr oft war ich die einzige Frau bei Management Sitzungen.

Auch hat es mich nie zurück gehalten, dass ich ein deutscher Immigrant bin. Es kann mir sogar zum Erfolg geholfen haben, da ich ein gutes Verständnis hatte für andere Länder, Leute und Wirtschaft.

Ich bin sehr stolz auf das was ich erreicht habe. Ich habe so viele liebe Menschen überall in der Welt getroffen, und halte noch viele Freundschaften aufrecht.

Nach 47 Jahren Ehe, in 1994, starb mein Mann an Krebs. Ich habe immer noch viel Freude am Reisen und finde neue Interessen.

Josef Vierhaus at work.

AMERICAN MONUMENTAL COMPANY

It was his desire for adventure that actually led my father, Josef Vierhaus, to the United States in 1960. Born in 1932 in Velen, Westfalen, into a farmers' family, Josefs childhood was affected by World War Two. After finishing his school years my father served a woodcarving apprenticeship and became journeyman. The rebuilding of Germany brought about a huge demand for stonework and prompted Josef to begin an additional apprenticeship with a stonemason.

After earning the master craftsman diploma [Meisterprüfung], my father emigrated to America. Initially, in October of 1960, he settled in Fon du Lac, Wisconsin. There he heard about Colma, a small town situated between San Francisco and South San Francisco. Even though its population then was a mere 100, it boasted 18 cemeteries with roughly one million graves, namely, because in the twenties San Francisco had prohibited the excavation of any more graves within its city limits. Thus began the great exodus into the surrounding communities, where Colma became the chief beneficiary of the thriving grave and monumental business.

No wonder my father wanted to move to the place where he saw great work opportunities for a stonemason. He relocated to San Francisco, where he instantly found employment with the California Cut Stone Company. Soon thereafter, however, orders ceased to come in and he found himself forced to work temporarily in a bakery, Fosters Bakery. In 1962 the old established American Monumental Company offered my father employment. He worked there for seven years and then transferred to Donhoe & Carroll Monuments, where he worked for three years. In 1972 my father used his savings to open Josefs Memorials in the no longer existing Danelaz Monument Works Company. He renovated the property and, over the next 8 years, made quite a name for himself in the local monument industry with his high quality work and good prices. In 1980 he went into partnership with Russell Antrocolli, the new owner of the American Monumental Company. However, Russell passed away in 1984, and thus my father became its sole owner. In 1985 he moved the firm's location to the grounds of the old Berlin Monument Works. Once again, he completely renovated and practically rebuilt from the ground up the new property and its outdated workshops.

Because my father had always maintained an even balance between wholesale and retail, he could see the American Monumental Company prosper up to his retirement in 1993, when he handed the firm over to me. To this day, my father still participates actively in our family business, standing by my side with advice or, if need be, with elbow grease.

Es war eigentlich reine Abenteuerlust, die meinen Vater Josef Vierhaus im Jahre 1960 in die Vereinigten Staaten brachte. 1932 in Velen, Westfalen, als Sohn eines Landwirts geboren, war seine Kindheit vom zweiten Weltkrieg geprägt. Nach der Schule machte mein Vater eine Lehre und wurde Holzbildhauergeselle. Wegen des unwahrscheinlich großen Bedarfs an Steinarbeiten beim Wiederaufbau Deutschlands begann er anschließend eine weitere Lehre bei einem Steinmetz.

Nachdem er die Meisterprüfung in diesem Beruf abgelegt hatte, wanderte er nach Amerika aus. Im Oktober 1960 ließ er sich zunächst in Fon du Lac, Wisconsin nieder. Dort hörte er von dem kleinen Städtchen Colma, das zwischen San Francisco und South San Francisco liegt. Die Stadt hatte damals nur 100 Einwohner, dafür aber 18 Friedhöfe und etwa eine Millionen Gräber. In den 20er Jahren hatte die Stadt San Francisco nämlich neue Gräber innerhalb der Stadtgrenzen verboten. Deshalb begann der große Exodus in die Vororte, und besonders in Colma florierte das Geschäft mit Gräbern und Grabmalen.

Kein Wunder, daß es meinen Vater, den Steinmetzmeister, dorthin zog, wo er sich gute Arbeit versprach.. Er ging also nach San Francisco und erhielt gleich eine Anstellung bei der Firma California Cut Stone. Doch bald darauf hatte das Unternehmen keine Aufträge mehr, so daß mein Vater vorübergehend bei Foster's Bakery in der Backstube arbeiten mußte. 1962 stellte ihn die American Monumental Company, ein alteingesessenes Grabmalunternehmen, ein. Für diese Firma arbeitete mein Vater über sieben Jahre lang. Dann wechselte er zu Donhoe & Carroll Monuments, wo er drei Jahre blieb.

American Monumental Company, Colma, California

Nachdem er genug Geld gespart hatte, eröffnete er 1972 Josef's Memorials in dem alten Gebäude der nicht mehr existierenden Firma Danaluz Monument Works. Mein Vater renovierte das Anwesen und wurde in den folgenden acht Jahren in der lokalen Grabmalindustrie für seine Qualitätsarbeit und für seine fairen Preise bekannt.

Mit dem neuen Besitzer der American Monumental Co., Russell Antrocolli, ging er dann 1980 eine Partnerschft ein. Russell verstarb jedoch 1984, und so wurde mein Vater Alleineigentümer. 1985 übersiedelte die Firma auf das Anwesen der alten Berlin Monument Works. Noch einmal wurde der neue Besitz mitsamt der schon existierenden Werkstatt von Grund auf renoviert und umgebaut.

Da mein Vater stets ein Gleichgewicht zwischen Groß- und Einzelhandel gehalten hatte, konnte er bis zu seiner Pensionierung im Jahre 1993, als er mir die American Monumental Co. übertrug, das Geschäft blühen sehen. Heute ist mein Vater noch immer in unserem Familienbetrieb aktiv und steht mir ratgebend zur Seite oder legt, wenn nötig, noch selbst Hand an.

AMERICAN MONUMENTAL COMPANY • 1351 El Camino Real • Colma, California 94014

A Family Operation from the Word Go!

H. Horn   H. Koehler   G. Horn

When we, the Horn brothers, came from Netphen Westfalia, Germany, to San Francisco, Hermann (19) in 1957, Theo (19) in 1959 and Guenther (19) in 1960, we all three were so lucky as to immediately find employment in our trained trade.

Hermann worked as a sheet-metal mechanic, Theo as tool and die maker, and Guenther as a lathe operator and machinist.

After having worked in the steel industry for several years, Guenther found employment in the ceramics industry at Wesgo in Belmont, California. Because Wesgo was very happy with Guenther's performance, the company also hired Theo as tool and die maker.

It did not take long for Guenther to figure out that the ceramics industry had a very good future.

After several years of working, learning, saving and learning English, Guenther and Theo decided to open their own business. In 1974 Guenther bought a grinding machine and shortly thereafter, Theo bought a drilling and milling machine. They housed these machines with a friend in San Carlos, and at night, after their day shift, they worked on these machines.

It did not even take a year and the many orders allowed them to purchase more machines, which, of course, meant, they needed more space. Thus, they rented a small shop in San Carlos, and for Guenther the time had come to quit his job and work fulltime in his own shop.

In 1976, together with Tom Burke, a former co-worker, they founded B & H (Burke & Horn). After Theo also started to work fulltime for B & H, Tom Burke left the company. In July of 1978, they hired Ed Daubenmire as their ceramics specialist. Years ago, Ed and Guenther had worked together at Wesgo. Today, 18 years later, Ed is still working with us.

On July 26, 1978, we had the great misfortune of losing our brother, Theo Horn, who died after a short illness. Now the company needed another tool and die maker and as luck will have it, our friend, Helmut Koehler, also a trained tool and die maker, was willing to assume Theo's place and he was hired in October 1978 as partner in B & H.

Then on December 1, 1978, Hermann Horn also joined us as a partner, fulltime. With the help of these four people, our business went well for the next several years. Those were good years for the ceramics industry and especially for us, because we are located in the Silicon Valley.

On May 15, 1989, our dream became reality, and we moved into our very own building at 306 Industrial Way in San Carlos, California. By now, we have 20 people working for the company.

Of course, much luck and much help is needed for each success story. And B & H had much help from certain individuals, particularly during the first few years, for which we are still very grateful.

We would like to thank Mark Campo and Gilbert Seavey of Veller in Santa Clara, California, and Harry Richter and Hans Weber of Wesgo in Belmont, and all the others, too numerous to mention. We will always remember them in gratitude.

Ein Familienbetrieb von Anfang an!

Als wir Gebrüder Horn, Hermann (19) im Jahre 1957, Theo (19) 1959 und Günther (19) schließlich 1960 von Netphen Westfalen in Deutschland nach San Franzisko kamen, hatten wir alle drei das Glück sofort in unseren gelernten Berufen Arbeit zu finden. Hermann arbeitete als Blechschlosser, Theo als Werkzeugschlosser und Günther als Dreher-Maschinist.

Nach einigen Jahren in der Stahlindustrie fand Günther eine Stellung in der Keramic-Industrie bei der Firma Wesgo in Belmont, CA. Da die Wesgo Firma mit Günthers Leistungen sehr zufrieden war, stellten sie Theo sofort als Werkzeugmacher ein.

Es dauerte nicht lange bis Günther wußte, daß die Keramic-Industrie eine sehr gute Zukunft bringen kann.

Nach einigen Jahren Arbeit, Lernen, Sparen und Englisch lernen kamen Günther und Theo auf die Idee sich selbständig zu machen. 1974 kaufte Günther eine Schleifmaschine und kurz darauf Theo eine Bohr- und Fräsmaschine. Diese Maschinen wurden bei einem Freund in San Carlos untergestellt. Abends, nach täglicher Schicht, wurde dann an diesen Maschinen gearbeitet.

Es dauerte kaum ein Jahr bis die vielen Aufträge es möglich machten noch mehr Maschinen zu kaufen, und natürlich brauchten wir mehr Platz. Wir mieteten in San Carlos eine kleine Halle - und für Günther war die Zeit gekommen, seinen Posten aufzugeben um im eigenen Shop volltägig zu arbeiten.

Zusammen mit Tom Burke, einem früheren Arbeitkollegen, wurde dann 1976 die Gesellschaft B & H (Burke & Horn) gegründet. Als Theo so weit war, auch volltäglich bei B & H zu arbeiten, trat Tom Burke von der Firma ab. Im Juli 1978 wurde Ed Daubenmire als Keramik Spezialist eingestellt. Ed und Günther hatten vor Jahren zasammen bei Wesgo gearbeitet. Heute nach 18 Jahren arbeitet Ed noch immer mit uns zusammen.

Am 26. Juli 1978 traf uns das Schicksal, als unser Bruder Theo Horn nach kurzer Krankheit verstarb.

Nun brauchte unsere Firma einen neuen Werzeugmacher und zu unserem Glück war unser Freund Helmut Köhler, auch ein gelernter Werkzeugmacher, bereit und willig Theos Platz zu übernehmen. Helmut wurde dann im Oktober 1978 als Teilhaber von B & H eingestellt.

Am 1. Dezember 1978 kam Hermann Horn als Teilhaber auch volltägig nach B & H. Mit vier (4) Personen lief die Gesellschaft für einige Jahre recht gut. Diese Jahre waren sehr gut für die Keramik-Industrie und für uns, besonders, da wir zum Silicon Valley gehören.

Am 15. Mai 1989 wurde ein Traum zur Warheit: Wir zogen in unser eigenes Gebäude ein - 306 Industrial Way in San Carlos, California. Inzwischen arbeiteten 20 Personen in unserer Gesellschaft.

Natürlich gehören zu jedem Erfolg viel Glück und viel Hilfe. B & H hat besonders in den Anfangsjahren viel Hilfe von gewissen Leuten bekommen, wofür wir auch heute noch sehr dankbar sind.

Mr. Mark Campo und Mr. Gilbert Seavey von der Firma Veler in Santa Clara, CA und den Herren Harry Richter und Hans Weber von der Firma Wesgo in Belmont danken wir recht herzlich - sowie vielen anderen Leuten, die man nicht alle nennen kann, bleiben wir immer dankbar.

B & H Technical Ceramic Inc. 306 Industrial Way • San Carlos, CA 94070

Actuellus typico Ritterburg, a. U. 138

Schlaraffia AHAmerika

*I*m ganzen Land, sogar weltweit
gibt es Schlaraffen jeder Zeit:
Seßhafte Ritter, Junker, Knappen
und Würdenträger mit bunten Wappen.
Sie tragen Namen wie einst zuvor
und sprechen fremd aber lustig hervor.

*S*ie tragen vor und haben Spaß
Erstaunt fragt man: Was ist denn das?
Sie begrüßen sich mit "Lulu"
und ehren den weisen Uhu.
Sie leben und wirken in Reychen,
rechnen die Zeit in Monden und Teilchen.
Eine lustige, ehrenvolle Runde
wirklich, die haben noch Gold im Munde.

Herbertus Hahachner
Allgemeino Spritana

Das Blaue Buch

eyne Fechsung von Ritter Orofex Reych 229, Losangela

Profan bin ich sehr oft auf Reise und ziehe durch das ganze Land
ich kenn die Welt auf meine Weise bin auch selbst nicht unbekannt
Doch wenn am Abend im Hotele alleine ich den Schlaf dann such
dann hab ich dabei für alle Fälle das wunderschöne Blaue Buch.
In diesem Buche sind zu lesen Addressen vieler Freunde mein
und ich bin wirklich nicht vergessen, nein ich fühl mich wie daheim.

Selbst meine Burgfrau hat empfohlen: Nimm ja das Buch mit lieber Mann
dann mache ich mir weniger Sorgen und Du bist nicht alleine dann.
Das Blaue Buch es ist ein Wunder gefüllt mit Kunst, Freundschaft, Humor
und wenn man in den Seiten blättered dann kommt man sich behagen vor
und ist der Ort den ich besuche auch wieder eine fremde Stadt
so ist es doch sehr gut zu wissen dass man gute Freunde hat.

Freunde die im Uhuversum gebunden durch Schlaraffen Pflicht
Freunde die das Ideale pflegen soetwas vergißt man nicht.
Und gibt es dann noch eine Chance einzureiten in ein Reych
dann wird aus der profanen Reise ein echter Freudentag zugleich
denn das Atzen und das Laben mit Sassen grosse Freude macht
und man kann den Kantus hören Klingen bis zur späten Nacht.

Mit Lulu's die dann erschallen vergeht der Abend viel zu schnell
und bevor ich mich versehen bin ich wieder im Hotel
Doch der Abend dieser Sippung bleibt in der Erinnerung bestehn
und es wird nicht lange dauern bis sich gute Freunde wiedersehn
Wohin mich Flugross, Stinkross führen in dieser unsrer profanen Welt
In dem Uhuversum kann man fühlen Freundschaft die zusammen hält.

Schlaraffen hört wenn ich vereise hier in AHAmerika
oder gar in Germaniens Gauen eines ist Euch sicher klar
wo ich mein Haupt hernieder lege zum Anfang einer langen Nacht
Hab ich die Stammrolle der Schlaraffen, das Blaue Buch auch mitgebracht.
Dort ist dann ganz leicht zu finden zwischen Reychen fern und nah
Freunde die der Geist vebindet, der Geist der Schlaraffia.

LULU, Denvera am 8.Ostermonde a.U.136

Desert Riding

Sheep Herding

Navajo Children

The Desert States
- Arizona, Nevada and New Mexico -
bring together vast open spaces, parched desert areas, rugged mountain passes, hollow yet breathtaking canyons cutting deep into red rocks, forsaken mining towns, and lively retirement retreats or places of recreation and amusement.

Reminders of the Old West like Spanish Missions, sleepy cow towns and trading posts are gradually giving way to current life-styles, exemplified by the population explosion since the mid 40's.

Mexican Plaza, Old Tucson Studios

ARIZONA™
GRAND CANYON STATE

Spring in the Sonoran Desert

Die Wüstenstaaten
Arizona, Nevada und New Mexico
bestehen aus weiten Landstrichen, ausgedörrter Wüste, schroffen Bergpässen, hohlen und atemberaubenden Canons die tief in die roten Felsen greifen, verlorene Dörfer ausgedienter Bergwerke, und lebendige Städte voller Ruheständler oder Orte des Vergnügens und der Freizeitgestaltung.

Die Zeichen des "Wilden Westens", wie die spanischen Missionen oder ruhigen Kuhdörfer, verschwinden langsam und machen dem neuen Leben Platz, wo das warme, sonnige Klima einen modernen Lebensstil bietet.

Las Vegas Strip at Dusk

View of Hoover Dam

Historic Route 66

Cowboy Kids Having Fun in the Sun

Sunset over the Grand Canyon
by Jessen Associates

Photos courtesy of the Arizona Office of Tourism and Nevada Tourism

Deutscher Karneval in Arizona

German American
Mardi-Gras Society
of Arizona

Die German American Mardi-Gras Society of Arizona (G.A.M.S.A.) wurde im April 1993 von Horst Wolf und seinen Freunden in Sun City gegründet.

Der nun von nahezu 200 Mitgliedern, hauptsächlich aus Ruheständlern von ganz Amerika, bestehende Verein, feiert den traditionellen, deutschen Karneval vom 11.11. bis Aschermittwoch. Angeschlossen auch an die German American Mardi-Gras Association of America (G.A.M.G.A.), erfreut sich dieser Verein auch an den gegenseitigen Besuchen im Südwestlichen Amerika.

Karneval Prominenz auf der Bühne

Arizona Funken

Photos: Horst Wolf

Leiterin: Ellen McNeill

Horst Wolf und seine Freunde, die auch die Deutsch-Amerikanischen Vereine in Phoenix und Umgebung, zusammengebracht haben, feiern nun alle Feste miteinander nach einem von allen Vereinen gesetztem Kalender.

Mit finanziellen Überschüssen werden auch wohltätige Gesellschaften unterstützt.

G.A.M.S.A.
German American Mardi-Gras Society of Arizona
10515 Bayside Road, Sun City AZ 85351

Das erste Prinzenparr 1993
S.T. Prinz Eckhard I. I.L. Prinzessin Lisa I.

Die Gründer von G.A.M.S.A.
(Der erste Elfer Rat)
Sitzend von links: Heinz Fischbeck, John Mischitz, Reinhard Freiwald, Herbert Schreck
Stehend: Adam Gossler, Siegfried Böhnke, Horst Wolf, Ulrich Dalken, Steve Swanberg, Tom Shue, Julius Kölln. Nicht auf dem Bild: Don Paige, Adi Büchel, Erich Kirchberg und Mark Fleck

uftritt in Las Vegas Das Prinzen Paar S.T. James I. und I.L. Johanne I. mit Hofmarschall
lans Schacke

The German American Mardi-Gras Society of Arizona (G.A.M.S.A.) was founded in Sun City, AZ in April 1993 by Horst Wolf and his friends.

The Society has about 200 members, mainly retirees from all over America. It celebrates the traditional German Karneval from 11.11. at 11:11am until Ash Wednesday. G.A.M.S.A. is a member of the German American Mardi- Gras Association of America (G.A.M.G.A.).This Club enjoys visiting with other Societies in the Southwest.

Horst Wolf and his friends, who have also formed an alliance of all German Clubs in Phoenix and surrounding area, celebrate all festivals, according to a common Club Calendar.

Any financial surplus is used also to support benevolant societies.

Gemeinsames Picknick der Deutsch- Amerikanischen Vereine
Knieend die Präsidenten:
Werner Jacker: DANK
Betty Gossler: Frohsinn M.C.
Wolfgang Reinke: Historische Schützen
Ingeborg Wilm: Deutsch-Amerikanischer
   Freundschafts Club
Horst Wolf: G.A.M.S.A.
Stehend vierter von rechts:
Alfred Beallis: Spielmannszug

German-American Friendship Club
Sun City, Arizona

Sitting left to right: Founders: Margarete Arlt, Karoline Kuhn, George Kuhn, Maria Biri and Anna Kipper

Standing left to right VP Earl Matter, Pres. Ingeborg Wilm, Sec. Joan Freiwald, Corresp. Sec. Virginia Micetich, Treas. Erna Hahn, Trustees: Theresia Seick and Kurt Malsch

German-American Friendship Club
Sun City, Arizona 85351

The German-American Friendship Club is the oldest and largest bilingual club in the Valley. Over 200 members enjoy a monthly dinner and dance at the Lakes Club in Sun City. Members are from Sun City, Sun City West, Peoria, Glendale, Phoenix and even Chandler. The majority of the members are of German heritage or ancestry. Our main goal is to keep the German traditions and customs alive. The club will be celebrating its 21st club anniversary in November 1997.

Our original founders alive today are: Anni Kipper, Magarete Arlt, George and Karoline Kuhn and Maria Biri. The deceased members Andy Kipper, Bill Arlt and the above mentioned members started the club by having a get together and some remarked: "Well we have enough people here to form a Board, how about starting a German Club". With this in mind the word spread and a month later about 130 people showed up at the former Greenbriar Restaurant, now Nancy's Cupboard Restaurant, and the rest is history.

The German-American Friendship Club has participated for 13 years at the Bank One Centers International Christmas.

Der deutschamerikanische Freundschafts Klub ist der älteste und größte zweisprachige Verein im Phoenix Tal. Mehr als 200 Mitglieder erfreuen sich am monatlichen Dinner-Tanz im "Lake Club" in Sun City. Man kommt von überall, von Sun City, Sun City West, Peoria, Glendale, Phoenix und sogar von Chandler. Die meisten im Klub sind deutscher Herkunft und Abstammung. Unser Hauptziel ist es, unsere deutsche Tradition und Sitten zu erhalten. Der Freundschafts Klub feiert im November 1997 sein 21. Jubiläum.

Gründer des Klubs unter uns sind Anni Kipper, Margarete Arlt, George und Karoline Kuhn und Maria Biri. Diese haben damals zusammen mit Andy Kipper und Bill Arlt bei einem gemütlichen Beisammensein scherzhaft gemeint: "Wir sind genug Leute um einen Vorstand zu wählen, warum gründen wir nicht einen deutschen Klub". Und so sprach es sich herum und einen Monat später trafen sich 130 Interessenten im frühren "Green Briar Restaurant", heute Nancy's Cupboard Restaurant - und der Rest ist Geschichte.

Der deutsch-amerikanische Freundschaftsklub beteiligt sich seit 13 Jahren an den Weihnachtsfeierlichkeiten im "Bank One Center".

Contact: Ingeborg Wilm 602/972-4245

Frohsinn M.C.

GERMAN-AMERICAN MIXED CHORUS
OF THE SUN CITIES, ARIZONA

"Frohsinn" Mixed Chorus of the Sun Cities, Arizona

Frohsinn M.C.
German-American Mixed Chorus
of The Sun Cities, Arizona

The Frohsinn Mixed Chorus, as it is known today, became a Mixed Chorus in the mid 1980's. The first elected President was Bernhard Gerhards who came from Wisconsin. Fifty plus active members rehearse every Monday night at Ritter's Chalet (formerly Milwaukee) to keep the German Songs and other German Music alive. All the hard work ends with a Spring Concert in March or April in Sun City. The public is invited to this and interested persons are always welcome. The Chorus has been singing at the International Christmas Downtown at Bank One for many years, treating citizens to German Christmas Songs. The Chorus has been invited and performed in other States. Our current President is Elizabeth Gossler.

Der gemischte Chor "Frohsinn", wie er heute heißt, wurde in den Mitte 80er Jahren ins Leben gerufen. Der erste gewählte President war Bernhard Gerhards aus Wisconsin. Mehr als 50 aktive Mitglieder kommen jeden Montagabend im Ritter's Chalet (auch von Wisconsin) zusammen, um deutsche Lieder zu singen und andere deutsche Musik zu proben. Alle Vorbereitung gilt dem Frühlingskonzert im März oder April in Sun City. Die Bevölkerung ist eingeladen und interessierte Menschen sind im Chor willkommen. Der Chor singt jährlich beim großen internationalen Weihnachtsfest im Bank One Zentrum in Phoenix Innenstadt, und begeistert die Menschen mit schönen deutschen Weihnachtsliedern. Der Chor hat wiederholt in anderen Staaten gesungen. Die heutige Präsidentin ist Elizabeth Gossler.

Contact: Betty Gossler

Spielmannszug, Arizona

"Spielmannszug" Arizona Drum and Bugle Korps & Karnevalgruppe, was founded in 1982 by Erich Kirchberg and Willi Ritter. We proudly maintain our German traditions.

Der Spielmannszug Arizona Drum & Bugle Korps und Karnevalgruppe, wurde 1982 durch Erich Kirchberg und Willi Ritter gegründet. Man pflegt mit Stolz die deutsche Tradition.

Neue Mitglieder und Gäste sind immer willkommen.
New members and visitors are always welcome.
Please contact Elfried Moore at 602 / 972-9704 or
Alfred Biallas at 602 / 991-2632.

Spielmannszug Arizona, Box 154, Sun City, AZ 85372

Deutsch Amerikanisch Historische Schützen

Unser Motto ist: Glaube, Sitten, Heimat
Unser Glaube an den allmächtigen Vater, der den Menschen zum Nutzen der Erde geschaffen hat. Unsere Sitten sind die Garantie und ein Maßstab zum Nutzen der Menschheit.Diese starken Grundsätze beschützen unsere Heimat und sind das Symbol aller Völker.

Our motto: Faith, Tradition and Homeland are guidelines of our Club. Faith in the everlasting Father who created us to serve and preserve mother earth. Our traditions are a guarantee and granite cornerstone for the existence of mankind. These strong principles protect our homeland and are the hallmark of all people.

D.A.N.K
Deutsch-Amerikanischer National Kongress

DANK Mitglieder Versammlung 1997

Back row from left: Daniel Paul - Merle Pipho - Gisela Leonard - Marga LaMaire - Heinz Giese - Adolf Buechel - Gudrun Chafen - Helen Pipho - Else Radtke - Bob LaMaire
Front from left: Manfred Deurer - Manuela Deurer - President Werner Jacker - Anni Schmidt

D.A.N.K. Phoenix # 48
German American National Congress

1982 setzten sich einige DANK Mitglieder in Phoenix, Arizona zusammen um eine Gruppe zu gründen. Auf Anfrage im Hauptbüro in Chicago, schickte man eine Liste mit den Namen der Mitglieder, die im Laufe der Jahre nach Arizona gezogen waren.

30 Mitglieder erschienen zur ersten Versammlung im Deutschen Haus. Diese Leute entschieden die DANK Gruppe # 48 zu gründen. Gegenwärtig hat die Gruppe 250 Mitglieder.

In 1982 a few DANK members came together in Phoenix to form their own chapter. A request for information from DANK headquarters in Chicago resulted in a list of retirees, who had moved to Arizona. For the first meeting, 30 people showed up at the "Deutsche Haus", and formed Chapter #48. Today the DANK group Phoenix has 250 members.

D.A.N.K Chapter # 48, Phoenix, Arizona
For Club and membership information contact:

President: **Werner Jacker   602/979-1325**
5352 W. Yucca Street
Glendale, AZ 85304

Vice President: **Merle Pipho   602/838-0254**
2028 E. Pegasus
Tempe, AZ 85283

Ritter's Chalet

A fine Restaurant featuring European Cuisine and a meeting place for German Americans in Sun City, Arizona.

It started back in the 50s, after Willi Sr. was released from P.O.W. camps. He was a highly decorated Master Sergeant, and came to the United States in 1950, where he met Emma in 1951.

First he worked in a tannery in Milwaukee and bar tendered at the Forest Keller, later at Jefferson Hall. In 1964 they bought a small tavern in a modest area, mother spent all day in the kitchen and father in the bar: it was the beginning of Ritter's Inn.

In 1956 Willi Jr. was born and with his older brother Edward, they enjoyed their childhood in the beautiful German district of western Milwaukee.

Emma and Willi Sr. at Ritter's Inn, 1969

With time the neighborhood deteriorated and in 1976 Ritter's sold the Inn. The new owner kept things as they were and today is established in Brookfield.

Willi Sr. retired in 1976 and moved back and forth between Milwaukee and Sun City, AZ. Got to know the area and the people, and finally opened up Ritter's Chalet in 1978. Father, mother and son together, they liked the climate, the peaceful town and made it their home.

Willi, the father, passed away in 1993. He was a member of the Milwaukee German Krieger Verein, the Austrian War Veterans, Schwaben Männer Chöre and Unterstützungsverein and a founding member of the Spielmanns Zug. He supported the German clubs and activities as much as possible, grateful for the assistance he received in the early years. Brother Edward lives with his family in Hartland, Wisconsin.

In 1980 in Sun City, Willi Sr. helped to found the Frohsinn Männer Chor, and the Spielmanns Zug in 1981 which he supported with money for uniforms, instruments, etc.

Today, Ritter's Chalet is the Clubhouse for the Spielmanns Zug, Singers, and GAMSA meetings. Willi keeps up the heritage and follows in his father's tradition. He appreciates what his parents have given him, and the opportunity to continue and do well for the community.

Ritters Chalet

ein feines Restaurant mit Europäischer Küche, und ein Treffpunkt für Deutsch-Amerikaner in Sun City, Arizona.

Es fing in den 50er Jahren an, nachdem Vater Willi aus der Gefangenschaft kam. Er war ein hoch ausgezeichneter Feldwebel, und als er 1950 in die Staaten kam, fand und heiratete er Emma in 1951.

Zuerst arbeitete er in einer Gerberei in Milwaukee, und bediente abends hinter der Theke im Forest Keller, später in der Jefferson Halle. 1964 kauften sie eine kleine Kneipe in einer bürgerlichen Gegend. Mutter war den ganzen Tag in der Küche, Vater in der Bar: Es war der Anfang von Ritters Inn.

1956 wurde Willi Jr. geboren, und zusammen mit seinem älteren Bruder Edward, verlebten diese ihre Kindheit in der schönen deutschen Wohngegend in West Milwaukee.

Mit der Zeit verfiel die Nachbarschaft, und so verkauften die Ritters den Gasthof 1976. Die neuen Besitzer führten alles so weiter, und sind heute im guten Viertel Brookfield ansässig.

Always festive with dancing nightly and European atmosphere - Ritter's Chalet

Brother Edward with Family, Willi Jr., Emma and Willi at a special dinner cruise.

Willi Sr. ging 1973 in den Ruhestand, und zog hin und her zwischen Milwaukee und Sun City, AZ. Er lernte die Gegend und die Menschen kennen und eröffnete bald darauf Ritter's Inn in 1978 . Vater, Mutter und Sohn zusammen, ihnen gefiel das Klima, die friedliche Umgebung und sie machten es zu ihrem zu Hause.

Willi, der Vater, starb 1993. Er war Mitglied des Milwaukee Deutscher Krieger Verein, den Österreichischen Kriegsveteranen und bei den Schwaben Männer Chören und dem Unterstützungsverein. Im Jahre 1980 half Willi Sr. den Frohsinn Männer Chor zu gründen, und der Spielmannszug folgte 1981, den er dann mit Geld für Uniformen und Instrumente unterstützte. Er hat alle deutschen Klubs und ihre Aktivitäten so gut wie möglich unterstützt, weil er für die Hilfe, die ihm am Anfang zu Teil war, dankbar war. Bruder Edward lebt mit seiner Familie in Hartland. Wisconsin.

Heute ist Ritter's Chalet das Klubhaus für den Spielmannszug, die Sänger und für GAMSA Treffen. Willi Jr. pflegt das deutsche Erbe und folgt dem Vater in seiner Tradition. Für immer dankbar, für was die Eltern ihm gegeben haben und für die vielen Möglichkeiten, Gutes für die Gemeinschaft zu tun.

Ritter's Chalet
13232 North 111th Avenue
Youngtown, Arizona 85363
Telephone: 602 / 933-6023

European Bistro

Traditional German Speciality Restaurant and European Cuisine *Best of Phoenix* Master Chef Eduard Stemrowitz prepares all dishes from scratch according to his recipes brought to Phoenix straight from Germany.

Tasty, hearty and reasonably priced German fare in an uncommon neighborhood. There's a marvelous herring appetizer, and familiar, well prepared entries from the homeland. Wiener Schnitzel, Sauerbraten and delicious Rinderroulade are particularly noteworthy.

Lunch and Dinner from Tuesday to Sunday, 10 am until 10 pm

European Bistro
2530 W. Camelback Rd., Phoenix AZ 85017
Phone: 602 249-1123 Fax: 602 249-1169
Internet: www.European-Bistro.com

Old Heidelberg Bakery - established 1969– on Opening Day February 7, 1997 at this location

Open daily: Tuesday - Saturday
Oven fresh Bread, Rolls and Cakes
Large selection of cheeses,
Fine sausages and food imports.
Freshly brewed Coffee to enjoy in our cafe or to go!
Imported Chocolates and Candy
Brand name Cosmetics, Gifts and Cards
German Newspapers and Magazines

Old Heidelberg Bakery + Euro Market
2210 E. Indian School Road
near Squawpeak Parkway, Phoenix AZ 85016
Call: 602 224-9877

Fresh sausage made daily on our own premises. Wide variety of cold cuts and lunchmeat.

Imported german chocolates, Bahlsen Keks, selection of cheese, pickled items, canned fish and german magazines. We also carry bread and cakes.

German Sausage Co.
Fritz Scherz & Son
4900 E. Indian School Rd.,
Phoenix AZ 85018
Phone: 602 840-6032 Fax: 602 840-8925

A restaurant offering German "Gemütlichkeit" in a traditional setting. Family style food from German kitchen includes your favorite dishes.

Live entertainment and dancing on weekends. A place to meet and enjoy.

Rooms available for business meetings, weddings and other occasions.

German Corner
Michael Ulmer, Manager

4900 E. Indian School Road
Phoenix AZ 85018
Phone: 602 840-7838 Fax: 602 840-7415

Felsen Haus, 1008 E. Camelback, Phoenix 602-277-1119

European Bistro, 2530 W. Camelback Rd., Phoenix, Arizona

169 E. Wickenburg Way, Wickenburg, AZ 520-684-5044

Edelweiss German Deli, 13439 N. Cave Creek Rd., Phoenix

Papago Trackers celebrated 52 Years since the Escape from POW Camp in Phoenix, in 1997.

Friendship binds Ex-POWs and their Captors in this picture during 1985 Reconciliation Event. The greatest escape by Axis prisoners from the Papago compound took place during the night of December 23, 1944 when 25 German Submarine Sailors made their way through a 178 foot long makeshift tunnel. After years of communications and interaction, the Papago Trackers are a group of friends from America and Germany, sharing in this historic event.

PAPAGO TRACKERS, P.O. Box 34422, Phoenix, Arizona 85067
"Renewing in Friendship an Association Commenced in Anguish"

Text by Lloyd Clark and Heinz Gies

The End of World War II -

A German-American Experiences D-Day 1944

by Elsbeth M. Seewald

How does it feel to be an American? Offspring of people who came from a country called Germany - a country which you are now at war with - which you are about to occupy? Does ethnicity really enter into it? We thought we would ask a German-American just these questions. Here is EUGENE (at home they call him "Gene") WEIDENBACH'S story.

It is now long a part of the past and history, that day in June, 1944. Was it the 22nd, or 23rd, when Gene came ashore as a member of the 533rd ORDINANCE HEAVY TANK MAINTENANCE COMPANY at the little village of St. Marie-Eglise near Cherbourg in the French Normandy region. An area, which was to occupy a place of prominence in history forever after, and which would become famous as OMAHA BEACH - the D-DAY landing site.

Gene was a young man then, fresh from South Dakota, 23 years of age, who had been called upon to fight a war in far away Europe, against enemies which he only knew indeterminably, and of whom he nevertheless was an inseparable part, because of his German ethnic cultural heritage.

He tells of the old records in the family bible, and of his great-great-grandfather, his great-grandfather, and their families who came from Albertsweiler in the Palatinate in Western Germany, and emigrated to Russia, and helped to cultivate and settle the southeast region of that country, where homesickness made them give their new villages beloved names remembered so well: Worms, Rohrbach, Johannistal, Waterloo, etc. Then in 1873, when his grandfather was a mere ten years old, they came to America, and homesteaded in South Dakota, which in those days was called the "Dakota Territory", and was a wild land, home only to the indigenous Indian tribes.

And now this offspring of a family with German roots landed on Omaha Beach in those June days of 1944, bringing ashore the first Sherman tanks from England to assist General Patton in his thrust to invade Germany. Gene recalls that these tanks were specially armed with bigger guns, 10.5 cm instead of the regular 75mm. The reason being that the 75mm's were not able to penetrate the 4" armor of the German tanks. Neither was life for him exactly " the life of Riley"... it was extremely dangerous then... even for the men of the maintenance and supply corps. He remembers that on landing at Omaha Beach the tide was out, which meant that Gene and his comrades had to sleep in the tanks on the ship. The heavy armory which could not be beached for another 12 hours, until the choppy wind-blown channel waters reached the beaches again, presented an easy target for German aircraft.

But then he and the 32 men in his unit put their 16 tanks ashore, fired them up again, and delivered them to General Patton at the front line in Normandy - the German line of defense. Gene recalls that they had to drive the tanks on the open roads, in danger of being fired upon by airplanes and artillery, because of the many hedges so much native to Normandy, and all the North-European countries. A nuisance, however, he considered them in those days - and a dangerous one at that.

Back and forth it was - but mainly they stayed in that little village on the windy northern French Coast. All throughout the summer and autumn; they continued to unload and get tanks ready for the battles.

Because of the nature of their work, Gene and his fellow maintainers did not see actual battles. They left the village next March, and when the 1945 spring offensive started Gene followed the tank unit into Elsace Lorraine, and entered Germany in that same month. Since he spoke the German language fluently, Gene Weidenbach became an official US-Army interpreter.

He remembers coming to Palatine and the city of Zweibruecken, and talks about this first encounter with some German POWs. "They looked so drawn and hungry", he recalls. "One could plainly tell that they were famished and totally undernourished. There was no more fight left in them. They just wanted out and see the war end." They were sent back to a main POW reception camp - and there the war was finally over for them.

His personal feelings? What is it like to occupy a country from which your ancestors, whose blood still curses in your veins, set out into distant lands? A land left behind so long ago..."It was an awful war and an awful time - all this death and destruction - to me it became particularly evident when I came to Cologne - the city was in a terrible condition - no living thing or beast visible anywhere - mountains, endless mountains of rubbish - the sorry tale of yet another war and its consequences - the finely smashed and powdered remains of the humans habitats of happier times - destruction everywhere - everything was burned out - I just stood there and cried and cried, and thought how lucky I was, and how safe my dear loved ones at home in far away South Dakota were."

Asked about his feelings as an American of German descent, fighting on the American side, he explains: "When you are young, and a soldier, you just want to get the war over and go home. I was an interpreter, and got to more German people than maybe some of my comrades, but despite all that I was very much aware of my German forefathers, and the long ago time when they trekked to Southeast Russia, and later immigrated to the United States, and thought, how entwined all our lives and existences really are, and what a waste it is to annihilate one another. Here I was, fighting in Germany, and in the ancient city and region of my German ancestors, irresolvably a part of them forever, their very blood in me! I can't say, that I felt particularly German, or that my presence in this land disturbed me because of my family's past - I felt our cause was just. My family and I, we have been Americans for so long. Strangely though, I certainly felt an innate sense of belonging - it was spooky to stand on this earth of the beginning. I felt the inhumanity of that war so very much, when I was in Zweibruecken and Cologne, and became such an immediate witness - and even a mediator of human disasters - through my translations. War is just horrible.

Yes, wasn't it? After Gene arrived in Zweibruecken it started to rain, and he and his comrades had to find a place whole enough to enable them to stay dry. They found a shoe factory, he recalls, with just one large hall and a much war-damaged roof on it. Bombs and artillery - shelling had affected even Zweibruecken. It was a miserable night after a long and miserable day. War was rough even on the victors.

But, eventually his tour of duty ended, and Gene went home after the war. Incredulously he did see Zweibruecken and the Palatinate again. Guess what, his son became stationed with the US-Army in Zweibruecken 32 years later, and Gene visited him there in 1977. He

A Time for Healing!

Zeit der Heilung –

Der Mann, der Hunderte Soldaten rettete.

Dr. Günther Süttgen war der Mititärarzt, der unmögliche Hilfe ermöglichte, kurze Waffenstillstände vereinbarte und damit Hunderten von verwundeten deutschen und amerikanischen Soldaten im Zweiten Weltkrieg das Leben rettete. Dafür wurde er, zusammen mit seinem Arztkollegen Dr. Bedford Davis, 1996 in Harrisburg, PA geehrt.

"Es spielten sich bei der Schlacht grausame Szenen ab, die ich nie vergessen werde", erzählt der heute 77jährige Wilmersdorfer. Insgesamt verloren 68,000 Soldaten ihr Leben in der "Hölle von Hürtgenwald". Mit Raketenwerern und Panzerkanonen wurde im Wald aufeinander geschossen. In den umliegenden Eifel-Dörfern wurde Mann gegen Mann gekämpft. "In Absprache mit meinem Kommandeur, Oberst Rössler, habe ich Feuerpausen ausgehandelt, um die Verletzten bergen und behandeln zu können". Bei den Verhandlungen zeigten sich die Amerikaner immer als fair und erlaubten Versorgung der Verletzten.

Grave of Lt. Friedrich Lengfeld who fell trying to save an American soldier.

Photos by Heinz

A Time For Healing by Robert M. Nisley

The acrylic painting "A Time for Healing" by Hummelstown PA, artist Robert M. Nis was commissioned by the Governor's Committee For World War II Commemoration.The resulting choice was what is called by military historians "The Incident On The Kall Trail." It was there in November 1944 during the Battle of the Huertgen Forest in which the Pennsylvania 28th Division was fighting the German 89 Division for the towns of Schmidt-Kommerscheidt that a series of truces were arrang between the Germans and the 28th Division's 112th Infantry Regiment. During the truces, German and American medical personnel aided each other in bringing in the wounded, who were bleeding and freezing to death in the worst German winter in 50 years. The collection centered around the 112th Infantry Regiment's 1st and 3rd Battalion's forward aid station, which was in no-man's land.

It is this humanitarian effort that is pictured here.

D-Day cont'd.

came in at night and did not recognize anything at first. What a difference since his war-days. His son helped him find that old shoe factory once again. It had been rebuilt, and was in full working operation. Odd to realize again that a part of one's ancestors came from this pat of Germany, from an area close to Zweibruecken. Odd, and yet so intimate, to find some of their graves in the old cemeteries, and their names in the record books of the churches...The long gray line - family - belonging - who can even deny its innate power...?

Gene is now a semi-retired farmer in South Dakota, in an area where many Germans from Russia settled. He calls himself a "Schwoab", and still speaks perfect German. He lives with his wife Lorene, (also a German-American - her maiden name was

Behl) whom he married 48 years ago, in September of 1946, after he returned from the great war, and his five children: Jeanette, Linda, Lyle, Paul and John, all married with families, in Scotland, S.D. All of them retain their cultural heritage and speak some German. Life, at least for Gene, and his family, has become tranquil and serene again on the South Dakota plains.

He is a member of the International Board of the GERMANS FROM RUSSIAN HERITAGE SOCIETY, with headquarters in Bismarck, N.D., and the current president of the SODAK STAMM HERITAGE SOCIETY OF TRIPP, S.D., a DANK affiliate, and a participant in the GERMAN AMERICAN YOUTH EXCHANGE PROGRAM since its inception.

Tornado Fighter Bomber

Tactical Training Commando of the German Air Force USA

On May 1st, 1996 the German Air Force Tactical Training Center, USA was formally activated by Federal Minister of Defense Volker Rühe and US Secretary of Defense William Perry.

Twelve *Tornado* aircraft and more than 300 German servicemen have been stationed at Holloman to perform 2,500 flying hours of national training annually.

Taktisches Ausbildungskommando der Luftwaffe USA

Am 1. Mai 1996 wurde auf Holloman AFB, New Mexico das Taktische Ausbildungskommando der Luftwaffe USA durch den Bundesminister der Verteidigung Volker Rühe und den amerikanischen Secretary of Defense William Perry in Dienst gestellt.

12 Lfz *Tornado* und über 300 deutsche Soldaten wurden in Holloman stationiert um 2500 Flugstunden nationaler *Toranado-* Ausbildung im Jahr zu erbringen.

Tornado Besatzungen können im Rahmen nachfolgender Ausbildungslehrgänge, Tiefflug bis 100 Fuß, scharfer Bombenabwurf, usw. vermittelt werden. Diese sind im dichten und stark reklementierten Luftraum über der Bundesrepublik Deutschland nicht möglich.

Die Tornado-Ausbildung beim Taktischen Ausbildungskommando besteht aus:

- Durchführung von 2 Waffenlehrerlehrgängen *Tornado* pro Jahr (3 Crews/Lehrgang) in Form von lehrgangsgebundener Ausbildung

- Durchführung Taktischer Verbandsausbildung *Tornado* als Hochwertausbildung. Im Rotationsverfahren sollen bis zu 8 Luftfahrzeugbesatzungen der deutschen *Tornado* Verbände für 3¹/₂ Wochen in Holloman üben.

Zur Realisierung dieses Vorhabens, wurden Infrastrukturmaßnahmen in Höhe von 62 Mio. DM erforderlich

Des weiteren befindet sich bereits seit 1992 die F-4 Phantom-Ausbildung auf Holloman AFB

US Secretary of Defense William Perry and Federal Minister of Defense Volker Rühe

Holloman Air Force Base
New Mexico

This training consists of:

- two course-based Tornado weapon system instructor training courses (3 crews per course), and

- high-value advanced tactical unit training for Tornado fighter- bomber crews. On a rotating schedule, up to eight German Tornado aircraft crews undergo training at Holloman AFB for 3¹/2 weeks.

Infrastructure measures totaling 62 million deutsche mark were necessary to realize this project.

Furthermore, F-4 "Phantom" training has been going on at Holloman AFB since 1992.

Holloman Air Force Base
1021 Fifth Street
Holloman AFB, NM 88330-8040
Tel: 505 / 475-2259
DSN: 505 / 867-2259
Fax: 505 / 475-7245

F-4 Phantom Fighter

The Committee

Desert Landscapin

At the Mall

At the Lak

SUN CITY, AZ *Impressions*

photos by Bert Lachner

Kaffee Runde

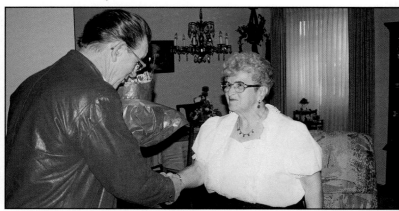

Happy Birthda

Camel Back Boulevard

Ghost Tow

The Lone Star State

Texas, called the Lone Star State is the second largest state in the Union, after Alaska. It is 2-1/2 times larger than Germany by encompassing 267,440 square miles (692.600 sq.km) as it extends 773 (1,200 km) miles from east to west. Everything about it is big in this sprawling and diversified region of vast wealth and power. Texans are justifiably proud of their state, and are not bashful about letting everybody know about it in their 300 major museums.

Having a population of 16,825,000, it has ten major cities with a population of more than 100,000. There is plenty to do and see in each city, as well in the vast stretches of land surrounding them.

Principal Cities

Houston is the fifth largest city in the country, a deep-water port, with contemporary towering buildings of glass and steel dotting the skyline. It has its own symphony orchestra, ballet, and opera house enjoying a national reputation. Houston has three world-class museums and a famous zoo.

It is also the home of Rice University and the Texas Medical Center where the first successful heart transplant was performed. Located 25 miles south of town is the Lyndon Johnson Space Center of the National Aeronautical Space Administration, (NASA) known chiefly for its outer space mission control complex.

Dallas is the state's second largest city and home of some major corporate oil, financial and distribution headquarters, located in numerous impressive skyscrapers. As the state's cultural center, it has five major museums as well as its own symphony orchestra and civic opera.

Natural Wonders

Texas has numerous national and state parks which enable the state to successfully compete with the traditional states of California and Florida for attracting millions of visitors annually. In addition to hundreds of artificial rivers, it includes the majestic Rio Grande which borders on Mexico, and the Colorado River, Texas' longest waterway running throughout the entire state. There white water rafting is enjoyed by fun loving tourists throughout the year. What is more, there are 625 miles of Texas beaches along the Gulf of Mexico.

One of its largest national parks is Big Bend National Park where 810,000 acres of natural beauty include canyons, rivers, deserts, wilderness, numerous animals, and 430 species of birds. Near Corpus Christi is the Padre Island National Seashore, a beachcomber's paradise stretching 80 miles along the Gulf of Mexico. The Davey Crockett National Forest of 161,500 acres provides 19 miles of trails for hiking enthusiasts. Guadalupe Mountain National Park encircles the unique remnants of an ancient forest thrusting outward from the desert.

Texas – Horses, Wranglers and Mountains

Commerce and Industry

After the discovery of oil in Texas in 1901, the "black gold" has been the state's chief export and main source of phenomenal wealth for many Texans. Petroleum deposits have netted 8 billions of barrels, 1/3 of the United States' supply. The Texas Panhandle region is the source of one of the world's greatest gas reserves.

Because of the state's mild climate throughout the year, Texas leads the nation in beef cattle output, with 14 million heads. Agricultural products such as oranges and red grapefruit are the state's third largest export. Texas leads the nation in growing cotton, as it has become its second most valuable export. Forestry and mining are also important natural resources, contributing substantially to the state's economical development.

In the last several decades, manufacturing emphasis has been in diversification and expansion, particularly because of the drop in the state's oil production. Manufacturing now includes nonelectrical machinery, transportation equipment, fabricated metals, boats and mobile homes. Austin itself has become the home of major branch plants for many of the country's leading electronic firms.

German Immigration into Texas: *The Last Wave.*

German immigration into Texas in the 20th century never reached the numerical proportion of the previous century. Prosperity combined with upward mobility in the industrialized nation of Germany made emigration no longer a necessity. In the decades following World War II, German immigration into the United States, and Texas, picked up slowly in the early 1950s with the arrival of German brides of American servicemen and of displaced persons from areas that formerly were German possessions. Still, the number of Germans leaving their country remained relatively low over the next decades when Germany enjoyed an unprecedented economic recovery (Wirtschaftswunder) with abundant job opportunities and prosperity enjoyed by all.

That Germans would choose to come to Texas is attributed in part to the mystique that the Lone Star State holds, a mystique also perpetuated by past as well as present-day German writers. Texas conjures up images of wide open spaces, oil, cowboys and Indians, cattle and rodeo, country music and NASA. The other aspect that makes the state attractive is its business climate. Among other things, Texas opens avenues to other business centers in Central and South America.

The German newcomers to Texas in recent decades are a more random cross-section that ever before. Also, they are better informed which makes them better prepared for the transition to their new home; for the most part they are highly educated and trained professionals

Reprinted courtesy of the Fort Bend Museum Association.
Photos taken at George Ranch Historical Park, Richmond, Texas.

in the manufacturing sector, the petro-chemical industry and the medical and gastronomic fields; they are more cosmopolitan; they work in the city and live in suburbia, consequently, they blend in quickly with the overall population. If they wish to retain their ethnic identity, they have to work at it. German enclaves have disappeared in Texas towns and cities and, for all practical purpose, so have the German-language press, broadcast and church services. A focal point where some German ways are still observed are the German clubs and the singing societies throughout the state, organized by an earlier generation. Generally, new arrivals from Germany are not as much concerned about their past, nor are they concerned over the loss of their self-identification. Not so the third or fourth generation German-Texan who now follows conscientiously his forebears traditions by staging the Maifest, Oktoberfest and Christkindlmarkt (Christmas bazaar). In recent years a new trend has been observed in the Texas Hill Country. This is the arrival of the German "snow birds" retirees who discovered the German-Texan ambiance as well as the joys of the pleasant Texas climate while Germany is in the grip of King Frost.

Wolfram M. Von-Maszewski
George Memorial Library
Richmond, Texas
January 1997

Die jüngste deutsche Einwanderungswelle nach Texas.

Die Zahl deutscher Einwanderer nach Texas im 20. Jahrhundert ist weit unter der des letzten Jahrhunderts geblieben.

Wohlstand und steigende Mobilität im hochindustrialisierten Deutschland ließ Auswanderungspläne unnötig werden. Erst nach dem Zweiten Weltkrieg, in den frühen 50er Jahren, erlebten die Vereinigten Staaten und auch Texas eine weitere kleine deutsche Einwanderungswelle. Deutsche Bräute amerikanischer Soldaten und Offiziere sowie Vertriebene aus ehemaligen deutschen Gebieten suchten den Weg in eine neue Heimat. Nichtsdestotrotz blieb alles in allem die Zahl deutscher Auswanderer in die USA während der nächsten Jahrzehnten relativ gering. Grund dafür war eine bis heute nicht wiederholte wirtschaftliche Entwicklung, das sogenannte Wirtschaftswunder, die der deutschen Bevölkerung reichlich Jobmöglichkeiten und hohen Wohlstand bescherten. Die Faszination vieler Deutscher für Texas hängt teilweise mit dem Mythos zusammen, den dieser US-Staat in sich birgt, ein Mythos, den sowohl ältere aber auch zeitgenössische Autoren heraufbeschwören und verewigt haben. Mit Texas verbinden sich Bilder von weiter Prairie, Öl, Cowboys und Indianer, Rinderherden und Rodeo, Country Musik und NASA. Ein anderer Aspek der diesen Landtei attraktiv macht, ist sein ausgezeichnetes Geschäftsklima. Unter anderm öffnet Texas Wege zu anderen Geschäftszentren i Zentral- und Südamerika. Die deutschen Neuankömmlinge, die in den letzten Jahrzehnten nach Texas gekommen sind, haben im Unterschied zu den früheren deutschen Siedlern ein sehr breit gefächertes Erfahrungsspektrum. Sie sind außerdem besser informiert, was die Integration in ihre neue Heimat wesentlich erleichtert. Zum größten Teil sind sie sehr gebildet und haben fundierte berufliche Erfahrungen, die sie hauptsächlich in der Ölindustrie, im medizinischen oder gastronomischen Bereich anwenden. Sie sind kosmopolitisch, arbeiten in der Stadt und leben in Vororten, was ihnen wiederum das Zusammenleben mit der durchschnittlichen amerikanischen Bevölkerung erleichtert. Wollen sie ihre ethnische Identität und ihre Tradition beibehalten, müssen sie heutzutage was dafür tun, sind doch fast alle ehemaligen deutschen Enklaven in texanischen Städten und Dörfern verschwunden. So gibt es fast kein deutsche Presse, keinen deutschen Rundfunk und auch fast keine in deutscher Sprache gehaltenen Gottesdienst mehr. Nur in einigen verbliebenen deutschen Clubs und Sängervereinen, die von früheren Generationen gegründet wurden, sir deutsche Gebräuche und die deutsche Sprache noch vorzufinden. Im allgemeiner sind die Neuankömmlinge aus Deutschland nicht sonderlich um ihre Vergangenheit und ihre Indentität besorgt. Im Gegensatz zu den Deutsch-Texanern, die in der dritten und vierten Generation in Texas leben, und mit Maifest, Oktoberfest und Christkindlmarkt ihre Herkunft dokumentieren wollen. In den letzten Jahren ist ein neuer (Einwanderungs-) Trend in der Gegend um Austin, im sogenannten Texas Hill Country, zu beobachten. Deutsche Rentner, liebevoll deutsche "snow birds" (Schneevögel) genannt, haben das deutsch-texanische Ambiente für sich entdeckt und genießen das milde und angenehme Klima während in Deutschland "Väterchen Frost" herrscht.

Eva-Maria Kruse
und
Wolfram M. Von-Maszewski

Im Dienste der Freundschaft

Consul Gershon Canaan

Service with a Smile

Gershon Canaan wurde 1917 in Berlin geboren. Seine Familie zog 1933 nach Palestina aus, und 1938 bestand er seine Abschlußprüfung als Architekt vom „Technion" Haifa. 1947 trat er in die amerikanische Frank Lloyd Wright Stiftung ein. Er lehrte „Design" an der Universität von Texas in 1950-51, wo er auch seine Meisterprüfung in Architektur ablegte und gleichzeitig sein Studium für Stadt Planung beendete.

Canaan gründete 1958 eine private Praxis in Dallas. Danach wurde er zum besonderen architektonischen Ratgeber und zum landesweiten Berater in Sachen Planung und Entwurf der amerikanischen Wohnungsbau-Behörde ernannt. 1964 wurde er mit einer Auszeichnung des Präsidenten für seine hervorragenden Beiträge geehrt.

Während des zweiten Weltkrieges diente er freiwillig in der Britischen Armee, wo er durch seinen Einsatz in Palestina, Afrika und Italien zum „Garrison-Engineer" aufstieg. Schon 1948 trat er der Israelischen Armee bei, um im Unabhängigkeits-Krieg zu kämpfen. Er kam in die U.S.A. zurück und wurde 1958 amerikanischer Staatsbürger.

Mr. Canaan amtierte in Dallas als Konsul der Bundesrepublik Deutschlands für 25 Jahre, von 1962 bis 1987. Er war 1963 bei der Gründung des jährlichen „German Day in Texas" Festes maßgeblich beteiligt und war Vorsitzender dieser Versammlung von 1963 bis 1972. Als Anerkennung seiner großen Erfolge und seiner dynamischen Leitung, wurde ihm 1972 die erste „Goldene Medaille" des „German Day in Texas" verliehen.

1964 gründete er das Dallas Goethe Zentrum und diente diesem als sein Präsident bis 1971. Er unternahm den ersten Schritt und drückte 1964 die Verkündigung durch den amerikanischen Präsidenten des „Von Steuben Tages" durch. Seine Arbeit um den „German American Day", an jedem 6. Oktober, hat sich inzwischen längst gelohnt. Unter seinen vielen Auszeichnungen befinden sich das Große Verdienstkreuz und das Verdienstkreuz 1. Klasse der Bundesrepublik Deutschlands, die Verdienstmedaille des „Instituts für Auslandsbeziehungen" Stuttgart, die Ehrentafel der Stadt Frankfurt, und die Medaille fürs Amerikanertum der D.A.R. Er wurde 1964 Freundschaftsbotschafter unter Gouverneur John Connally ernannt, und er ist Ehrenbürger von Texas; Dallas,

Fort Worth, Fredericksburg, Houston und San Antonio. Er ist Autor des Buches „Rebuilding the Land of Israel" , Wiederaufbau des Landes Israel, 1954, und Mitautor von „German Days in Texas", deutsche Tage in Texas, 1972.

Konsul Canaan ist im "World Jewry" verzeichnet, im Verzeichnis „South", Süd, und „Southwest", Südwest, des Who's Who.

Er ist ein Mitglied des „American Institute of Architects", dem amerikanischen Instituts der Architekten, der „Texas Society of

At Villa Hammerschmidt, 1980 in Bonn: Son Dr. Robert Ernst, Hon. Consul Canaan, Bundespräsident Karl Carstens, and Doris Canaan, Hon. Konsul von Monaco in Texas.

Architects", dem „American Council on Germany", des Rates der Amerikaner über Deutschland, des Corps der Konsulare von Dallas und Amerika, der „International Trade Association of Dallas", dem internationalen Handelsverband von Dallas und der Loge No. 760 & K.C.C.H., 32°.

Architekt Canaan heiratete Doris Smith 1954, sie haben einen Sohn namens Robert Ernst.

Konsul Canaan spielte eine entscheidende Rolle in der Einführung einer Briefmarke zur Erinnerung an die 300. Jahresfeier der ersten deutschen Immigranten im Jahre 1983. Er entwarf das Ersttagscouvert herausgegeben von Fleetwood, U.S.A. Es war eine gemeinsame Ausgabe zwischen den Vereinigten Staaten und Deutschland.

Im Jahre 1988 hat er erfolgreich Spenden für den deutsch-amerikanischen Freundshaftsgarten in Washington, DC aufbringen können.

Die Wiedervereinigung Deutschlands hat ihn nicht verwundert. Er sagte: „ Es mußte irgendwann passieren, aber es ist trotzdem wunderbar, daß es noch zu unseren Lebzeiten kam, wie seiner Zeit die Mondlandung".

Diesem ausgezeichneten deutschen Konsul und Architekten, durch dessen unermüdliche Arbeit die Bande der Freundschaft, Kultur und

menschlichen Verbindungen zwischen Deutschland und den Vereinigten Staaten gefestigt wurden, gebührt der Dank weiter Kreise unserer Gesellschaft.

★

Consul Canaan was born in 1917 in Berlin. His family moved to Palestine in 1933, and in 1938 he graduated in Architecture from the "Technion", Haifa. In 1947 he became an apprentice with the Frank Lloyd Wright Foundation in the United States. He taught Design at the University of Texas in 1950-51, where he also received the M.A. in Architecture and the B.A. in City Planning.

Canaan established a private practice in Dallas in 1958. He was appointed special Architectural Advisor and National Design Consultant to the U.S. Housing Administration (HUD). He was awarded a Presidential Citation for his outstanding contribution in 1964.

During World War II he volunteered for the British Army and advanced to garrison engineer while campaigning in Palestine, Africa and Italy. In 1948 he joined the Army of Israel to fight in the War of Independence. He returned to the U.S.A. and became a citizen in 1958.

Canaan served as Honorary Consul of the Federal Republic of Germany for 25 years, 1962-1987. He was instrumental in establishing in 1963 the annual celebration, "German Day in Texas", and was chairman of the Council from 1963-1972. In recognition of his great achievements and dynamic leadership, he was awarded the first "Gold Medal" of the "German Day in Texas" in 1972.

In 1964 he founded the Dallas

Goethe Center and served as its president until 1971. As initiator, he brought about the U.S. President's "Von Steuben Day" proclamation of 1964. His efforts regarding a "German American Day", every October 6th, have long born fruits. Among his many honors are the Commanders Cross of Merit and the Officers Cross of Merit of the Federal Republic of Germany, the Medal of Merit of the Institute of Foreign Relations, the Honor Plaque of the City of Frankfurt, and the Americanism Medal of the D.A.R. He was named Ambassador of Goodwill by Governor John Connally in 1965, and he is an Honorary Citizen of Texas, Dallas, Fort Worth, Fredericksburg, Houston and San Antonio. He is the author of "Rebuilding the Land of Israel", 1954, and co-author of "German Days in Texas", 1972.

Consul Canaan is listed in the *Who's Who in World Jewry* , and *Who's Who in the South and Southwest.* He is a member of the American Institute of Architects, Texas Society of Architects, American Council on Germany, Dallas and National Consular Corps, International Trade Association of Dallas, and Lodge No. 760, K.C.C.H., 32°.

Architect Canaan married the former Doris Smith in 1954. They have one son, Robert Ernst.

Consul Canaan played an instrumental part in the adaptation of a stamp commemorating the 300th anniversary of the first German immigrants in 1983. He designed the "First Day Cover" of the stamp by Fleetwood U.S.A. It was a joint issue between the United States and Germany.

In 1988, he successfully raised funds for the German American Friendship Garden in Washington, DC.

Unification of Germany did not surprise him; he said he was confident it would happen at some point: "It's a wonderful thing that happened in our lifetime, just like the moon landing".

This distinguished German Consul and Architect, through whose untiring efforts the bonds of friendship, culture and humanitarian ties between Germany and the United States are strengthened, deserves the gratitude of large circles of our society.

Measurement Conversions / Umrechnungstabellen

METRIC SYSTEM

ENGLISH SYSTEM

Units of Length

Metric					English			
Meter	=	1.903	yards		Yard	=	0.9144	meter
	=	3.281	feet		Foot	=	0.3048	meter
	=	39.370	inches		Inch	=	0.0254	meter
Kilometer	=	0.621	mile		Mile	=	1.609	kilometers

Units of Area

Square Meter	=	1.196	square yards		Square yard	=	0.836	square meter
	=	10.764	square feet		Square foot	=	0.092	square meter
Square centimeter	=	0.155	square inch		Square inch	=	6.45	square centimeters
Square kilometer	=	0.386	square mile		Square mile	=	2.590	square kilometers
Hectare	=	2.471	acres		Acre	=	0.405	hectare

Units of Volume

Cubic meter	=	1.308	cubic yards		Cubic yard	=	0.764	cubic meter
	=	35.314	cubic feet		Cubic foot	=	0.028	cubic meter
Cubic centimer	=	0.061	cubic inch		Cubic inch	=	16.387	cubic centimeters
Stere	=	0.275	cord		Cord	=	3.624	steres

Units of Capacity

Liter	=	1.056	U.S. liquid quarts or		U.S. liquid quart	=	0.946	liter
	=	0.8880	English liquid quart					
	=	0.908	dry quart		Dry quart	=	1.111	liters
	=	0.264	U.S. gallon or		U.S. gallon	=	3.785	liters
	=	0.220	English gallon		English gallon	=	4.543	liters
Hectoliter	=	2.837	U.S. bushels or		U.S. bushel	=	0.352	hectoliter
	=	2.75	English bushels		English bushel	=	0.363	hectoliter

Units of Weight

Gram	=	15.432	grains		Grain	=	0.0648	gram
	=	0.032	troy ounce		Troy ounce	=	31.103	grams
	=	0.0352	avoirdupois ounce		Avoirdupois ounce	=	28.35	grams
Kilogram	=	2.2046	pounds avoirdupois		Pound	=	0.4536	kilogram
Metric ton	=	2204.62	pounds avoirdupois		Short ton	=	0.907	metric ton
Carat	=	3.08	grains avoirdupois					

DECIMAL SCALE TABLE

10 millimeters	=	1 centimeter
10 centimeters	=	1 decimeter
10 decimeters	=	1 meter
10 meters	=	1 decameter
10 decameters	=	1 hectometer
10 hectometers	=	1 kilometer
10 kilometers	=	1 myriameter

DECIMAL SCALE PREFIXES

Deca	=	10
Hecto	=	100
Kilo	=	1000
Myria	=	10000

NOTE: The above prefixes apply to meters, liters and grams.

ROMAN NUMERALS

I	=	1
II	=	2
III	=	3
IV	=	4
V	=	5
VI	=	6
VII	=	7
VIII	=	8
IX	=	9
X	=	10
XX	=	20
XXX	=	30
XL	=	40
L	=	50
LX	=	60
LXX	=	70
LXXX	=	80
XC	=	90
C	=	100
D	=	500
M	=	1000

TEMPERATURE

To convert Centigrade* into Fahrenheit:

Multiply Centigrade degrees by 9, divide by 5, add 32.

To convert Fahrenheit into Centigrade:

Subtract 32 from degrees of Fahrenheit and multiply by 5, then divide by 9.

	Fahrenheit	Centigrade
Water freezes	32°	0°
Water boils	212°	100°
Absolute zero	−459.6°	−273.1°

(Hypothetically the lowest possible temperature at which all motion would cease)

*Centigrade also known as "Celsius"

FEVER CHART

Fahrenheit	Centigrade
105°	40.5°
104°	40°
103°	39.4°
102°	38.8°
101°	38.3°
100°	37.7°
98.6°	37° (normal)
97°	36.1°

WEATHER CHART

Fahrenheit	Centigrade
110°	43°
100°	37.8°
90°	32.2°
80°	26.7°
70°	21.1°
60°	15.6°
50°	10°
40°	4.4°
32°	0°
20°	−6.7°
10°	−12.2°
0°	−17.8°
−10°	−23.3°
−20°	−28.9°

★ Capital of Texas
Austin
The Lone Star State

Texas Capitol

The German-Texan Heritage Society

Founded in 1978, the German-Texan Heritage Society mission is to promote awareness and preservation of Texas' German cultural heritage. Membership includes a journal, newsletter and book and meeting discounts. The Society's headquarters is located in Austin in the Old German Free School.

President: Rodney C. Koenig
Executive Director: Teresa Schwausch Chavez
Journal Editor: W. M. Von-Maszewski

German-Texan Heritage Society,
507 East 10th Street, Austin, Texas 78768
Tel: (512) 482-0927 * Fax (512) 482-8809

German Free School Building 507 E. 10th Street, Austin, Texas

Photos by Bert Lachner

The "Sängerrunde" Men's and Ladies' Choruses sing regularly at the Scholz Garten, built in 1866, located at 1607 San Jacinto Avenue in Austin, Texas

1996 Sängerfest in Fredericksburg, Texas

Photo: Classic Panoramics

Vereinskirche Fredericksburg Convention and Visitor Bureau

Kurort, Resort, Retirement Community

Fredericksburg, Texas

named in honor of Prince Friedrich Ludwig Wilhelm von Hohenzollern, was founded in 1846 by German Settlers. Its Charm and Heritage Endure to this Day.

Wide streets are lined with picturesque homes of native limestone, German Fachwerk, and Victorian gingerbread. Residents take immense pride in the beauty and safety of their community, as seen in the well-kept homes, neat, colorful yards and gardens. To this day, you can still hear German dialect used to conduct everyday business on the streets and in the stores.

A greeting from the Mayor:

"It is with great joy that I extend to you a most hearty welcome to Fredericksburg in the beautiful German Texas Hill Country…"

Linda Krauskopf Lagerhans
Bürgermeisterin
Fredericksburg, Texas

Im Jahre 1846 durch deutsche Siedler gegründet, ist Fredericksburg heute immer noch ein Zeugnis deutscher Gastfreundschaft und Herkunft.

Breite Straßen mit bübschen Häusern aus einheimischem Sandstein, deutschem Fachwerk und englischem Knusperhäuschenstil beherrschen das Stadtbild. Die Bürger sind stolz auf ihre schöne und sichere Gemeinschaft, wie man an den schmucken Häusern und den ordentlichen und farbfreudigen Höfen und Gärten sehen kann. Auch heute noch kann man die deutsche Art am Dialect auf der Straße und in den Läden erfahren.

Fredericksburg, Texas
1997 Hauptveranstaltungen
(approximate dates after 1997)

Januar: 1. IVV-AVA Volksmarsch (s. IVV Mitternacht Wanderung, 12.31.) **10.-11.** Kreis 4-H & FAA Vieh Schau & Versteigerung. **8.-19.** Edelstein & Mineral Austellung

Februar: 2. Hochschul Kapellen Bankett-Konzert. **8.** Fasching-Markenball, Turnverein Halle. **8.-9.** Gun & Knife Schau

März: 2. St. Franz-Xavier Gemeinde Kirmes, Stonewall; Turnverein Schwein-Spießbraten Fest. **21.-23.** Country Peddler Handarbeit Austellung & Verkauf. **22.** Frank V. van der Stucken Gedächtnis-Konzert; Nimitz Museum Programm "Massacre of German Texas Unionists"; Frühlings Handarbeit Verkauf. **29.** Osterfeuerfest-Freilicht Pageant

April: 5.-6. Gun & Knife Schau. **18.-20.** Frühling Kraut & Gewürzfest. **9.** Freiwillige Feuerwehr Fischbraten Fest, Marktplatz. **19.-20.** Frühlings Echte Antiquitäten Austellung & Verkauf. **26.** Hospital Wildblumen Lauf & Wanderrung (5K + 10K)

Mai: 3. Cinco de Mayo Fiesta; **151.** Gründungs-Tag Feier, Pionier Freilicht Museum Festplatz.

23.-24.-25. Friedrichsburg-Comanche Indian Pow Wow & Tanz-Wettbewerb celebrating 1847 Peace Treaty Never Broken, Fort Martin Scott. **26.** Memorial Day Services & Parades.

Juni: 7.-8. Küstler Austellung & Verkauf. **13.-15.** Country Peddler Handarbeit Schau. **14.-15.** Pari-mutuel Pferderennen Saison beginnt. Fairgrounds Track; IVV-AVA Laufen-Schwimm-Fahrrad Internationales Volkssportverein Fest. **20.-21.** Pfirsich Fest & Rodeo, Stonewall. **28.-29.** Antique Tractor & Engine Austellung.

Juli: 4. Fourth of July Parades & Programs. **4.-6.** Pari-mutuel Pferderennen, Fairgrounds; Night in Old Fredericksburg Sommerfest (Deutsch, Country Western), Fairgrounds. **19.-20.** Pari-mutuel Pferderennen Fairgrounds. **20.** Schützenbund Vorfest. **25.-27.** Hill Country Auto Swap Meet & Antique Car Exhibition.

August: 2.-3. Bundesschützenfest. **9.-10.** Pari-mutuel Pferderennen, Fairgrounds. **23.** Gillespie County Fair Parade 10:00 am. **22.-23.-24.** Kreis-Gillespie County Fair & Pari-mutuel Pferderennen.

September: 19.-20.-21. Kom' mit Friedrichsbürger & Bürgermeisterin Frau Linda Krauskopf-Langerhans nach Montabaur, Westerwald, Rheinland Pfalz - Partner Stadt Fest (Reiseplan Info: 830-990-8849). **27.** Hospital, Wellness

Center & Kurgelände Gala. **28.** Gebirgs-Bundes Sängerfest, Gastgeber: Arion Männerchor & Hermann Söhne Gemischter Chor.

Oktober: 3.-5. Oktoberfest, Marktplatz. **10.-12.** Texanische Mesquite Wood Artesian Festival & Verkauf, Marktplatz. **11.-12.** Nimitz Museum Symposium. **25.** Essen & Wein Fest, Marktplatz. **25.-26.** Katholische St. Marien Gemeinde Kirmes & Truthahnfest.

November: 7.-8.-9. Die Künstler von Friedrichsburg Austellung & Verkauf, St. Joseph Halle. **15.-16.** Echte Antiquitäten Schau & Verkauf, Fairgrounds. **28.** Gebirgsregion Weihnachtsbeleuchtung beginnt. **28.-29.** Country Peddler Handarbeit Schau & Verkauf.

Dezember: 6. St. Nikolaus Tag Kinderfest, Freilichtmuseum; Santa Klaus Parade 10 am. **7.** Nimitz Museum Pearl Harbor Symposium. **12.-13.-14.** Christkindlmarkt. **13.** Candlelight Tour of Homes & Historic Buildings, 14:00 bis 20:00 Uhr. **14.** Lions Club Weihnachts-Programm: Musik und singen auf Deutsch, Englisch, Spanisch. **26.** Zweites Weihnachten Party, Freilicht Museum. **31.** Silvester Tanz, Fairgrounds. IVV-AVA Jahresend Volksmarsch (11:00 am) & Mitternachts Taschenlampen Wanderung (23:00 Uhr).

Montabaur Castle in Fredericksburg's
Sister City, Montabaur, Westerwald

Historic May Tree
Der Lebensbaum

North Sea Chanti Chorus performing in the Biergarten of the Fredericksburg
Brewery.

Sunday Houses *Sonntagshäuser*. Many pioneers lived on farms and ranches,
and came into town on weekends for business, church and enjoyment.

More than 40 restaurants and biergartens provide a wide choice of food and
fun for Fredericksburg's 1 million annual visitors.

Chomanche Chief, warriors and princess returned to celebrate 150 years of
the German - Comanche Peace Treaty of 1847.

German Limestone House in the natural "Enchanted Rock" State Area.

It's fun to be German in Fredericksburg, Texas!

Best Western Sunday House Inn, German-American Restaurant, Conference & Celebration Center,
501 E. Hauptstrasse, Fredericksburg: 830-997-4484, 1-800-528-1234. Kerrville: 210-896-1313. Kenneth & JoAnn Kothe.

Fredericksburg German Club Leaders & German Language Institute
Luncheon meetings each Thursday, at the Sunday House German-American Restaurant… seated l to r: Carol Woitalla, Cathy Weidmann, Elsie Burrer, and Paula Hein. standing l to r: Marge Bennack, Horst Woitalla (instructor), Kenn Knopp, John O'Malley, Bob Weidmann, J.D. & Joyce Jordan, John Kothmann, Rev. Milton Bierschwale, and Jan Carr.

Oakwood RV Park Resort,
Rt 2 - Box 8B, 830-997-9817. New park, shade of stately oaks, full hookups, cable TV, concrete patios, 30 & 50 Amp Service, paved roads, level sites, telephone jacks, laundry, large swimming pool, basketball court, rally building. Irwin & Erburga Schilling.

Hill Country Memorial Hospital & Medical Center Krankenhaus & Kurgeländ Kurverwaltung – Wellness Center "Office provides health evaluation and accepts professional referrals for especially designed health and wellness packages of any length of stay any time of the year."
HCMH Wellness Center

Fischer & Wieser Specialty Foods, Inc.
Makers of specialty jams, jellies & mustards. Visit the shops of Fischer & Wieser: das Peach Haus on Hwy. 87S, the Epicurean Shop at 315 E. Main St. & Kaffee Klatsch at 138 E. Main . Call for a complete brochure & catalog 1-800-369-9257. Left to right: Case Dietz Fischer, Case Dietz Fischer, Jr., Ellen Kate Fischer, Deanna Leigh Fischer.

The Grasshopper & Wild Honey,
113 E. Hauptstrasse, 830-997-5012, Biersteins, nutcrackers and many other German imports, wildlife, western sculpture, crystal, and porcelain figurines. Mike Sedgewick.

Fredericksburg Convention & Visitor Bureau, 106 N. Adams
Front (L-R) Penny C. Reeh (Director), Alma Ramirez.
Back (L-R) Joe Kammlah, (Executive Director, COC),
Peggy Crenwelge, Basilia Martinez, Christine S. Heimann

Call: 830/997-9523

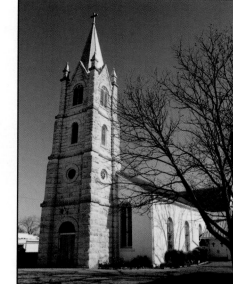

Zion Kirche

Zion Lutheran Church
first congregation to build its
own edifice in the 1850s.

Der Lindenbaum Restaurant & Biergarten,
312 E. Hauptstrasse, 830-997-9126. Fredericksburg's award winning, Rhineland-style
German Cuisine, Live entertainment in the Biergarten weekends. Ingrid Jünger-Hohmann, chef-owner, from the Eifel.

Gästehaus Schmidt Bed & Breakfast Reservation Service,
231 W. Hauptstrasse, 830-997-5612, Email:gasthaus@ktc.com;
Internet:www.ktc.com/GSchmidt. Serveral hundred outstanding B&B's in town & in
the countryside. Catalog on Request. Donna Bruchs-Mittel.

Showcase Antiques,
119 E. Hauptstrasse, 1-800-663-5505, 830-997-5505. Fax: 830-997-0220.
Fredericksburg's premier antique dealers since 1970 specializing in fine porcelain, cut
glass, furniture, including an outstanding selection of reference books on antiques.
Ronald L. & Jane Woellhof.

Crenwelge Motors...
Hunsrück descendants of 1846, three generations and 56 years of Automotive Trust in
the Texas Heartland, three locations: Fredericksburg: 413 W. Hauptstrasse (Chrysler,
Plymouth, Jeep, Eagle), & 307 E. Hauptstrasse (Buick, Oldsmobile, Aurora); Kerrville:
301 Main St. (Chrysler, Plymouth, Jeep, Eagle, Dodge, Dodge Trucks & GMC Trucks).
1-800-880-5616. Pictured l to r: Tim, Milton, and John Crenwelge.

Fredericksburg Herb Farm, 402 Whitney St., Fredericksburg, TX 78624. Tel.: 830 997-8615. Tea Room, Health Spa, Bed & Breakfast, featuring the beautiful star-shaped Working Herb Garden.

Germania Haus, International Books and Gifts, 239 Hauptstrasse, Fredericksburg, TX 78624. Tel.: 830 997-3388, located in the Edelweiss Markt in the heart of the Historic District.

Sunday House Fine Collectables, 107 N. Adams, Fredericksburg, TX 78624. Tel.: 830 997-9733, in the Stadtzentrum across from the Adelsverein Halle in Marktplatz Park. Featuring M.I. Hummel, Gardinen, Gnomes, European Table Lace, collections of all kinds.

John O. Meusebach

When affairs of the colony became desperately muddled as a result of Prince Carl of Solms-Braunfels's autocratic methods and nonexistent accounting, the society chose a well-educated, wealthy and idealistic young jurist to succeed him. Baron Ottfried Hans von Meusebach was a perfect choice - intelligent, learned and practical. The day he sailed for Texas he dropped his noble title and started in the new land as plain John O. Meusebach. Arriving at Galveston in April 1845, he had spent most of the society's available funds to free Prince Carl from his creditors. At every stop he found the affairs of the colony in worse shape. The settlers were disgruntled, unwilling to work, poorly provisioned and inadequately housed. And he new more boatloads were on their way from Germany. Meusebach straightened out the tangled

finances of the colony, established credit in Texas and prepared to expand the Adelsverein holdings to make room for the oncoming flood of immigrants.

John O. Meusebach

Signing of the Meusebach-Comanche Treaty   *Courtesy of Paul Camfield, Gillespie County Historical Society*

Comanche Treaty 1847

The immigrant's goal of settling on the Fisher-Miller property was blocked by hostile Indians. John O. Meusebach made peace, with the less-war-like Waco tribe, then set out to deal with the fierce Comanches. In January 1847 he left with 40 men for the Comanche camps on the San Saba River. When the time came for negotiations to begin, Meusebach rode into the Comanche camp emptying his rifle so that the Indians would know that he was unarmed and unafraid. He won their respect with his courage and their confidence with his frankness. The Comanches agreed to allow the Germans, to explore the territory, and on March 2, 1847, signed a treaty which allowed them to enter the grant and make settlements. This remarkable treaty was the only one negotiated by white men and Indians in Texas which was kept rigorously in tact on both sides.

Robert Justus Klegberg

"Santa Gertrudis Ranch" building, constructed in 1852, was once one of the main houses on the ranch. It serves today as a museum on the King Ranch, west of Kingsville, approx. 40 miles SW of Corpus Christi, Texas.

Robert Justus Kleberg

The German who established one of the most famous Texas ranching families, Robert Justus Kleberg, was one of the thousands inspired to settle in Texas by Friedrich Ernst's glowing letter. A well-to-do young lawyer, Kleberg left his native Westphalia in 1834 with a group of immigrants, including many of his wive's relatives, the wealthy and titled Von Roeders. After being shipwrecked off Galveston Island, they underwent numerous hardships before settling on a league 14 miles out of San Felipe near Ernst and Fordtran. The settlement of Germans which grew up around them is known today as Cat Spring.

At the outbreak of the revolution, Kleberg and his men joined the Texas army and gave a good account of themselves at San Jacinto. Their women mounted horses and drove their cattle to Louisiana until the war was over. After the war Kleberg served on the Board of Land Commissioners for Austin County and as justice of the peace and chief justice. He moved to DeWitt County in 1847 and served as chief justice there in 1853 and 1855. He was a leading rancher in that area until his death in 1888. His descendants today own and operate the famous King Ranch, 1,250,000 acres in Nueces, Kennedy, Kleberg and Willacy Counties.

Ranger Stiles, ret., is the historian on todays King Ranch, explaining the art and applications of branding irons to the publisher.

Possibly the largest Cattle Operation in the US, the King Ranch sprawls over more than 100,000 acres and four counties, providing ideal grazing for their cattle and visiting deer alike.

Corpus Christi

German Society of the Coastal Bend
Corpus Christi, Texas

Mixed Choir "Heimatmelodie", 1997

GERMAN SOCIETY OF THE COASTAL BEND, INC.

The German Society of the Coastal Bend was founded in 1989 as a tax-exempt, non-profit corporation for the advancement of cultural and educational exchanges.

Membership in the Society is open to all persons who are interested in the German language and culture.

The Society hosts annual festivities such as the Fasching (Mardi Gras) party in February, and Oktoberfest in the fall, participates in multicultural programs in conjunction with the city, such as the annual multicultural Festival at Heritage Park during either Buccaneer Days or Bayfest, a Christmas celebration, and a trip to the Wurstfest at New Braunfels.

Through its educational committee, the Society sponsors speakers at area schools, seminars, and workshops appropriate to the topic of German-Texan heritage and strives to promote and enhance German-American relationships. The Society established an annual scholarship fund.

The Society Choir "Heimatmelodie", a mixed choir, was formed in 1989, they have performed at Heritage Park on several occasions, sing at several of the Nursing Homes at Christmas, and participate in

Sängerfests at New Braunfels, Fredericksburg and San Antonio. They were the first new group to join the Texas Gebirgssängerbund in 46 years. Heimatmelodie are also members of the Nordamerikansicher Sängerbund, Southern District.

Our meetings presently are on the second Monday of each month.
For more information on the Society or our other events, contact Friedel Paddack, at 512/993-0263.

Die deutsche Gesellschaft von "Coastal Bend" wurde 1989 als eine gemeinnützige Organisation für den kulturellen und Studenten Austausch gegründet.

Mitgliedschaft in der Gesellschaft ist allen Personen offen, solange sie an der deutschen Sprache und Kultur interessiert sind.

Die Gesellschaft veranstaltet jährliche Festivitäten, wie den Fasching im Februar, ihr eigenes Oktoberfest mit deutscher Musik, Tanz, Essen und Trinken und beteiligt sich an multikulturellen

Programmen der Stadt, wie am jährlichen Volksfest im Heritage Park während der Buccaneer Days oder Bayfest, einer traditionellen Weihnachtsfeier,

und einer Fahrt zum Wurstfest nach New Braunfels.
Durch das Bildungskommittee unterstützt die Gesellschaft Sprecher in den lokalen Schulen, Seminaren und Lehrgängen im Zusammenhang mit Themen über die deutsch-texanische Geschichte und versucht das deutsch-amerikanische Verhältnis zu fördern und zu stärken. So hat die Gesellschaft eine Stiftung für Stipendien gegründet.

Der gemischte Vereinschor "Heimatmelodie" wurde 1989 ins Leben gerufen. Die Gruppe ist verschiedentlich im Heritage Park aufgetreten, sie hat in Altenheimen zu Weihnachten gesungen, und beteiligt sich an Sängerfesten in New Braunfels, Fredericksburg und San Antonio. Sie sind die erste neue Gruppe, die dem Texas Gebirgssängerbund in 46 Jahren beigetreten sind. "Heimatmelodie" ist außerdem Mitglied des Nordamerikanischen Sängerbundes und des Southern Districts.

Man trifft sich jeden zweiten Montag im Monat. Weitere Informationen erhalten sie von Frau Friedel Paddack unter 512 / 993 - 0263.

President Maria Greenwell with Club Flag

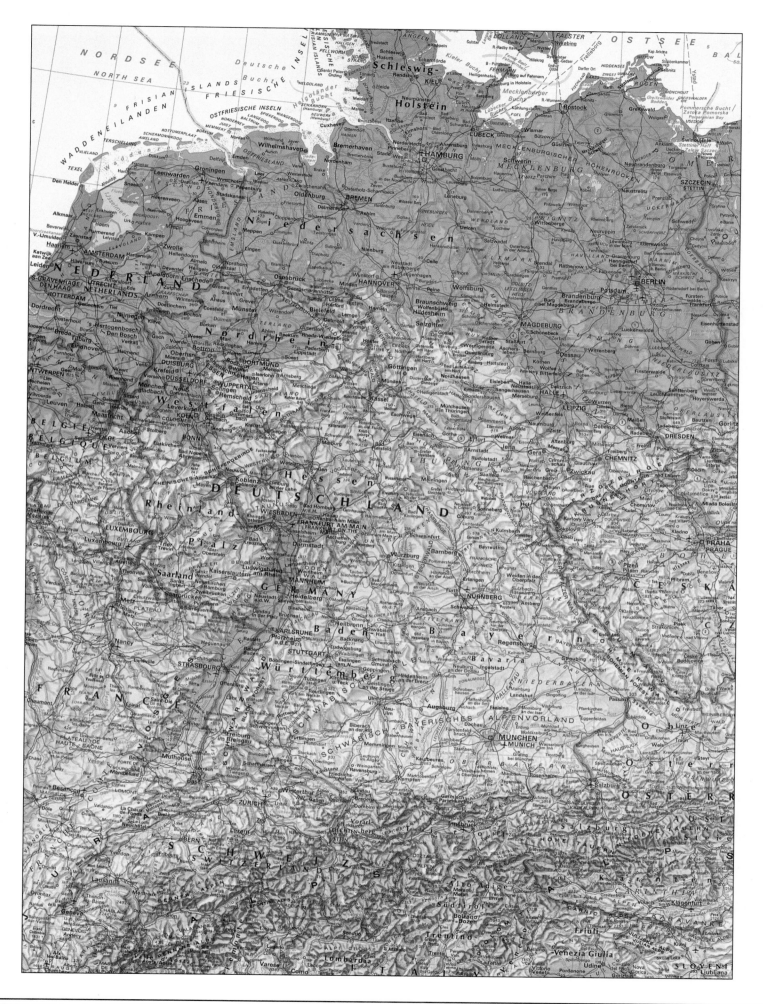

Houston

Home of the
German Gulf Coast Association

Houston Christkindl Market

At Rudi Lechner's Restaurant
In the back, holding the book:
Michael Ritter

German Organizations In Houston/Texas

Organization	Contact	Phone
German Gulf Coast Association (1986)	President: Michael Ritter	281/350-601
German-Texan Heritage Society (1978)	State Pres.: Rodney Koenig	713/651-533
Houston - Leipzig Sister City Association (1993)	President: Stephen Braun	713/861-090
Houston Liederkranz (1925)	President: Erich Schoennagel	713/957-900
Houston Saengerbund/Soccer/Skat (1883)	President: Richard McGinty	713/944-095
Houstoner Karnevalverein '81	President: Joachim Modlich	713/721-817
Stammtisch at Rudi Lechner's Restaurant	Chair: Karin Ramsey	281/531-882
Texas German Society, Houston Chapter (1983)	Pres: Norm Uhl, TV-Ch.11	281/370-580
Texas German Society, North Harris County (1995)	President: Roger Wunderlich	281/353-461
Deutsche Samstagsschule (1986)	Principal: Dr. Ute Eisele	713/666-812
Deutsche Welt USA/"Musical Trot with Liselott'	Producer: L. Babin (25 years)	713/721-727

NASA

Lyndon B. Johnson Space Center

Outer Space Mission Control
and Training Complex in Houston, TX,
where famous German rocket and space
scientist Wernher von Braun was among
the first to build the U.S. space program.

Michael and Kristina Ritter at Degeno Show Room in Houston

Dregeno Products:

- Nutcrackers
- Pyramids
- Incense Smokers
- Music Boxes
- Schwib Bows
- Angel Selection
- Candle Holders
- Minatures
- Wooden Toys
- Carved Trees
- Ornaments

ERZGEBIRGE IN HOUSTON

Dregeno, USA

It all started about 400 years ago when silver mining subsided in the German Erzgebirge (Ore Mountain) and silver miners turned to toy making in order to make a living.

They developed extraordinary wood carving skills that were inherited from generation to generation. Such items as the Nutcracker and the incense burning folklore figures were created in that region during the last century.

Common and noble men alike enjoyed them, poets wrote fairy tales about them (E.T.A. Hoffmann) and Tschaikowsky composed the renown Nutcracker Suite. The Fürchtner family created the original Nutcracker.

Over 140 family enterprises from the village of Steiffen and surrounding area have created a collection of more than 4,000 different items, from music boxes, pyramids, schwib bows, trees, toys and miniatures of all kinds to Christmas - and Easter ornaments and figurines. This cottage industry is united by the cooperative **"Dregeno Steiffen e.G."**

The first traditional nutcracker was created by the House of Fürchtner in Steiffen.

In the United States, Dregeno has established a representative office with showroom in Houston, Texas. Call **Michael Ritter at 281 350-6012** or fax him at 281 355-1490 for details and/or a catalog.

Frank B. Helgard and Brigitte Suhr

Suhr Photo

Die Schlitterbahn in New Braunfels ist

America's #1 Water Park. Open April - September.

Helgard Suhr came to New Braunfels in 1962. She volunteered for many things. In 1978 she was co-founder of the German American Society and its President for 10 years. She is a member of the Rotary Club, of three historical Organizations, and belongs to the local Chamber of Commerce. She received the Achievement Award from the City of New Braunfels. In 1994 she was honored again by being awarded the Federal Cross of Merit from President of the Federal Republic Roman Herzog.

Helgard Suhr kam 1962 nach New Braunfels und hat sich dort als Voluntär einen Namen gemacht. Sie war 1978 Mitbegründerin der deutsch-amerikanischen Gesellschaft und 10 Jahre Präsidentin. Sie gehört zum Rotary Club, drei historischen Vereinen, zur Handelskammer u.a. Sie erhielt die höchste Auszeichnung der Stadt New Braunfels: Besserung Award. 1994 bekam Sie das Bundesverdienstkreuz von Bundespräsident Roman Herzog.

Hummel Museum downtown New Braunfels.

German American Society was founded in 1978.

Wurstfest building at New Braunfels.

We promote our heritage and culture by sponsoring musical groups from Germany, operating a booth at Wurstfest, have a Maskenball, a Mai Fest and the Christmas Party.

A "Mai Baum" was erected by the society to commemorate the 150 year founding of our city in April 1995. City of New Braunfels established and dedicated a plaque showing the route taken by the German immigrants who landed at Indianola, TX and tredged to New Braunfels to settle this city in complete wilderness. The route included Victoria, Cuero, Gonzales and Seguin.

Die deutsch-amerikanische Gesellschaft fördert das Erbe und die Kultur durch die Unterstützung von Musik Gruppen aus Deutschland, einen Stand auf dem Wurstfest, einen Maskenball, das Mai Fest und die Weihnachtsfeier. Ist Sponsor einer deutschen Radiosendung und unterrichtet deutsch für Erwachsene.

Ein Maibaum wurde zum 150. Jubiläum durch die deutsch-amerikanische Gesellschaft im April 1995 aufgestellt. Gleichzeitig weihte die Stadt eine Gedenktafel ein, die bezeugt, daß Einwanderer in Indianola landeten, um über Victoria, Cuero, Gonzales und Seguin nach New Braunfels zu kommen, welches sie in der Wildnis besiedelten.

Wurstfest Helpers – Rotary Club

Wurstfest Performers from North Germany

Main Plaza

Hauptplatz in New Braunfels

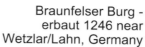

Braunfelser Burg - erbaut 1246 near Wetzlar/Lahn, Germany

Sophienburg Memorial Museum and Archives

401 West Coll Street

 200 N. Seguin Ave.
New Braunfels, Texas 78130

Open daily until 5:00 p.m.

Memorial Museum and Archives

Greater New Braunfels Chamber of Commerce

New Braunfels, a German Heritage Center of Texas, is set amidst the meandering waterways and lush green belts of Central Texas. The rugged beauty of the famous Texas Hill Country begins in this oasis which was founded by Prince Carl of Solms, Braunfels, Germany and is known as the "City of a Prince". It is ideally located on Interstate 35 between two major Texas Cities, only 45 minutes away from Austin, the capital of the state, and just 30 minutes from San Antonio, home of the Alamo.

The founding of New Braunfels had a major impact upon the immediate area and opened West Texas to a civilized economy. The many artisans and craftsmen among the 6,000 settlers generated industry and commerce for the entire central Texas area. From this town grew a tenacious German heritage that consisted of wine and beer making, beekeeping, gardening and celebrations with massive dinners.

Visitors to New Braunfels can experience this German heritage through a walking tour of the community. Many of the businesses still carry the German influence in their names such as Wurstfest, Schlitterbahn Water Park, the Plant Haus or Opa's Haus and Oma's Haus Restaurant.

New Braunfels, die deutsche Wiege Texas, liegt im schönen Gebiet der grünen Weiden und Gewässer in Zentral-Texas. Die rauhe Schönheit der Texas Hügellandschaft fängt bei dieser Oase, die durch Prinz Carl von Solm gegründet wurde, an. Ideal gelegen an der Autobahn 35 zwischen den Metropolen Austin, der Hauptstadt, und San Antonio mit der historischen Festung Alamo.

Die Gründung von New Braunfels hatte einen schnellen Einfluß auf die ganze Umgebung und machte West-Texas zu einem Wirtschaftszentrum. Die vielen Künstler und Handwerker unter den 6,000 Siedlern förderten Industrie und Wirtschaft.
Aus dieser Stadt wuchs die deutsche Gesellschaft, die aus Winzern und Brauereinen, Bienenzucht, Landwirtschaft, und Festen mit großen Gelagen, bestand.

Besucher können auch heute noch die deutsche Art, durch einen Bummel durch die Stadt, erkennen. Viele der Namen sind deutsch, wie Wurstfest, Schlitterbahn, Oma's Restaurant und Opa's Haus, Hummel Museum, Lindheimer Haus und Sophienburg.

Greater New Braunfels Chamber of Commerce
P. O. Box 311417, New Braunfels, TX 78131
Tel: (800) 572-2626 * Fax (210) 625-7918

Photos by Bert Lachner

Lindheimer House
The New Braunfels Conservation Society also includes the Baetge House

---

Museum of Texas Handmade furniture
managed by the
Heritage Society of New Braunsfels, Texas

Handmade Texas Furniture Museum

"Alamo... The Price of Freedom"

San Antonio – Today

Beethoven Ha

Was ist Gemütlichkeit?

1. When people are gathered together
In a warm and friendly way
Enjoying conversation and
Passing the time of day,
"Das ist Gemütlichkeit!"

2. When we all go to the Saengerhalle
At any time of the year
And we raise our glasses on high
With "Ein Prosit", "Salude", "Good Cheer",
"Das ist Gemütlichkeit!"

3. When we join hands across the sea
With relatives and friends
Enjoying good times together
Instead of fighting, make amends,
"Das ist Gemütlichkeit!"

4. When Oma and Opa and all the rest
Gather around the hearth
And sing around the Christmas tree
"Peace to men of good will on earth-"
"Das ist Gemütlichkeit!"

5. When your "Schatzie" takes you in his arms
To the tune of Johann Strauss
And dances the whole night through with you
The time? - - Das macht nichts aus.--
"Das ist Gemütlichkeit!"

6. When your little grandson comes around
And climbs upon your knee
Puts his arms about your neck -
"Oh Gee!"
"Das ist Gemütlichkeit!"

7. Hospitality, friendship, togetherness,
Warm or cordial or close,
Can't quite define that German word
But they all come a little close:
"Das ist Gemütlichkeit!"

8. It's a feeling that comes from experiencing
Many of these words combined
A word you learn from within your heart
Not with your mind,
"Das ist Gemütlichkeit!"

by Dollie Seidel

Texanischer
Gebirgssängerbund

GEGRÜNDET 1892
SAN ANTONIO LIEDERKRANZ

Marker of the Historical Survey Committee

Comfort, Texas

"Treue der Union"

Dieses deutschsprachige Denkmal, welches 1866 errichtet wurde, ehrt die 68 Männer (meistens Deutsche) aus dieser Gegend, die der Union während des Zivilkrieges treu waren.

Als sie verzweifelt versuchten ihre "U.S. Federal" Truppen über Mexico zu erreichen, wurden 40 von ihnen durch rachsüchtige "Confederates" getötet, mit dem Ziel sie auszurotten in der Schlacht von Nueces am 10. August 1862 und in einem späteren Gefecht am 18. Oktober.

Die Überreste der Toten und der beim Schwimmen durch den Rio Grande Ertrunkenen waren nicht begraben worden.

Ein paar Deutsche sammelten die Knochen ihrer Freunde auf und beerdigten diese an dieser Stelle im Jahre 1865.

Loyalty to the Union

This German language monument, erected 1866, honors the memory of 68 men (mostly Germans) from this region who were loyal to the Union during the Civil War.

Trying desperately to reach U.S. Federal Troops by way of Mexico, about 40 of the men were killed by vengeful Confederates bent on annihilating them, in the battle of the Nueces (on Aug. 10th, 1862) and a later fight (Oct. 18).

The bones of the slain and those who drowned swimming the Rio Grande were left unburied.

A group of Germans gathered the bones of their friends and buried them at this site in 1865.

Great Plains States

The Great Plains is where "East Met West" in the early railroad expansion days to accommodate the cattle drives to markets. Here in the South Central part of the country, major food and fuel producing regions were established. Green, fertile, and hilly lands are dotted by woods and streams, where vast wheat and grain fields abound. Beef cattle graze on the flat plains and low hills. Thousands of oil and gas wells operate in many areas. In this region, grain storage and oil storage structures compliment each other over the sweeping landscape.

Natural Wonders

Arkansas: Hot Springs National Park is one of the country's oldest (1832) and most popular national parks, promoting its 4,700 acres. One million gallons of thermal water flow from its 47 natural springs, averaging 143 degrees F. The spring water is distributed over insulated pipes to the nearby bath houses frequented by health seekers.

Oklahoma: Great Salt Plains State Park/Salt Plains National Wildlife Refuge draws tourists from around the world, largely because visitors can keep the selenite crystals they dig up in the park's salt flats.

Kansas: El Dorado State Park consists of 4 areas, totaling over 4000 acres of rolling hills, wooded valleys, and open prairies, plus 1,100 campsites. El Dorado Lake, 8,000 acres, is within the park environment, and it offers considerable swimming, boating, and fishing conveniences.

Missouri: Lake of the Ozarks State Park, with its 1,375 miles of Lake Ozark shoreline, offers almost unlimited recreation for visitors to enjoy swimming, fishing, boating, and camping.

Commerce and Industry

Arkansas' poultry industry is number one in the country with 750 million birds produced yearly, providing employment for 50,000 Arkansans. Other agricultural enterprises yield 15 million acres of crops such as peaches, watermelons, and rice, among others. The state manufactures paper and chemical products, electronic aerospace equipment, steam boilers, steel plate, and plastic pipes.

Oklahoma benefits from 600 energy and energy-related firms employing over 30,000 people. Since oil dominates the economy, oil well equipment is produced here, as well as aircraft and auto parts, tires, furniture, glass, and clay products. Wheat and cotton are grown in Oklahoma, plus peanuts and hay. Petroleum, liquefied petroleum gases, and natural gas are an important factor in the state's business.

Kansas manufactures oil and mining machinery, aircraft parts, petroleum products, and food products. Chief agricultural products encompass beef cattle, hogs, milk, corn, flour, wheat, and soybeans.

Missouri manufactures shoes and clothing, airplanes and space craft, railroad cars, and processes flour, beer, chemicals, and specialties. Cattle, hogs, corn, cotton, and soybeans are main agricultural products. The state's mines yield clay, coal, iron, and limestone.

Arkansas, Oklahoma, Kansas, Missouri

Monument in Hays, Kansas (KS):The German-Russians (also called Volga-Germans) came to Kansas from Russia in the 1870s and 1880s in search of freedom and religious tolerance.

(Photo Kansas Travel & Tourism)

Caldwell portrays the Chisholm Trail with silhouettes depicting the original cattle drives.

(Photo Caldwell C of C/KS)

Old Cowtown Museum in Wichita, KS

(Photo Keith Philpott)

In Topeka, KS: The Heritage House of pioneer Karl Menninger, is today an elegant bed & breakfast and fine dining establishment.

(Photo Craig Thompson)

The Flint Hills Overland Wagon Train

(Photo Jon Hardesty)

Fort Scott, KS features a Victorian-era downtown with a variety of specialty shops.

(Photo Ray Brecheisen)

Anheuser-Busch Brewery, St. Louis, Missouri

(Photo Missouri Division of Tourism)

St. Louis Arch, Gateway to the West

(Photo Missouri Division of Tourism)

Oktoberfest in Hermann, Missouri

(Photo Missouri Division of Tourism)

"Prosit" from Bruno Romes and Herb Schmid of the N.W. Arkansas German-American Club at June 1996 Picnic at Blowing Springs Park, Bella Vista, AR.

Members of the German-American Club dancing at Springfest 1997. President Lyn Schmid, front left.

German American Club-Bella Vista, Arkansas

Our club was formed back in 1988 by several German-Americans in Bella Vista, who wanted to get together with some of their contemporaries and enjoy German conversation, fellowship and meals. It evolved very quickly from the original group of six to around 25 and when Herb and I came in 1990, it soon became too large to have in someone's home and we started meeting in restaurants. Since I took over as president some four years ago, I have tried to vary the format somewhat.

We still meet once a month, either at a restaurant for fellowship, or the Springfest and Oktoberfest which are held at our local country club, or picnics at various parks. Occasionally, we take a group to Tulsa or Kansas City to a function the German Clubs there are putting on, as Herb and I are members of both of these city's clubs.

We specifically attend the Oktoberfest in Tulsa, Oklahoma for the weekend, as this is known as the fifth largest in the world, and we all have a very good time.

Our club has over 120 members at present. We enjoy our "Gemütlickheit" and since s many people from the upper Midwest sectio of the country are moving to this area, many to retire, we have a lot of people with Germa backgrounds who are interested in what we have to offer, which is mainly "fellowship."

Lyn Schmid, President
German-American Club
Bella Vista, Arkansas 72714

December 1996 Christmas Party at VFW Hall in Bella Vista of members, NW Arkansas German American Club

Lyn Schmid, President, NW Arkansas German-American Club, at Picnic 1996.

Tulsa, Oklahoma
Oktoberfest for Families
"mit allem drum und dran!"

A Festival for the Whole Family

Families come first in Tulsa, so our Oktoberfest offers great fun for every age. Special children's areas offer arts and crafts activities, entertainment from jugglers, clowns, and yodelers, and a professionally-operated amusement park. Everyone enjoys the authentic German food and other European treats, music from bands imported from Germany, and high-quality arts and crafts from European and American artists. Huge tents host televised European sporting events, ethnic dances from around the world, and plenty of polka music. Held mid-October. Admission free. Call 918 / 596-2001 or write: Oktoberfest c/o River Parks, 707 S. Houston, Ste. 202, Tulsa, Oklahoma 74127-9033

Ein Fest für die ganze Familie

Die Familien werden in Tulsa groß geschrieben, und so bietet unser Oktoberfest etwas für jedermann und jedes Alter.

Es gibt Kinderspielplätze mit Malerei und Basteln, auch Clowns, Jodler und Jongleure, und ein Platz mit Karussells, Schaukeln und Buden. Alle essen gerne die gute deutsche Küche und andere europäische Köstlichkeiten. Da ist Musik von deutschen Kapellen und eine Kunst - und Gewerbe-Ausstellung europäischer und amerikanischer Künstler.

Unter großen Zelten sieht man europäisches Sport-Fernsehen und Volkstänze von der ganzen Welt, und auch die Polka Musik kommt nicht zu kurz. Mitte Oktober- Freier Eintritt.

Familie Fred Losch, Kansas City

Warum ich die USA als meine neue Heimat gewählt habe.

Als gebürtiger Ostpreuße war ich am Ende des Krieges 17 Jahre alt. Glücklicherweise war ich unverletzt. Am 3. Mai 1945 geriet ich in Gefangenschaft und wurde in die damalige Soviet Union verschleppt. Die Zeit war nicht leicht, aber ich glaube, sie hat mich stärker gemacht. In den spärlichen Briefen, die mich damals erreichten erfuhr ich, daß meine Eltern jetzt in Holstein wohnten. Sie schrieben mir auch, daß mein amerikanischer Onkel mich nach der Entlassung in die USA eingeladen hat. Diese Nachricht half mir, das Elend der Gefangenschaft besser zu ertragen. Nach 2 Jahren und 7 Monaten kehrte ich heim, etwas angeschlagen, aber lebendig.

Es war nicht möglich, gleich in die USA zu kommen. Zuerst mußte ich mich auf einem Bauernhof, woman schon wieder gut essen konnte, aufpäppeln. Dann erlernte ich den Polsterer Beruf. Im November 1951 erhielt ich ein Visum und kam per Boot nach den USA

In den ersten Monaten gab's viel zu lernen. Mein Englisch wurde besser aber ich informierte mich immer noch von deutschen Zeitungen. Darin las ich, daß sich alle männlichen Immigranten unter 25 Jahren zum Wehrdienst melden sollten. Bei Nichtbefolgung könne man des Landes verwiesen werden. Im August 1952 trat ich in die USAF ein. Ich wurde Bordfunker und verbrachte 4 Jahre in Neufundland. Dort traf und heiratete ich meine deutsche Frau. Auch besuchte ich Universitätskurse und studierte Mathematik und andere vorgeschriebenen Kurse. Daneben hatte ich die einmalige Möglichkeit, die Arktik zu befliegen, was damals nur wenigen Menschen möglich war.

Danach sah ich die Welt in den Riesentransportern (C-124). Im Norden flogen wir bis nach Nordgrönland, im Süden bis nach Neu Seeland, im Westen bis nach Thailand und im Osten bis nach Pakistan. - Anschließend durfte ich das Lehrbuch für mein Fachgebiet schreiben. In derselben Zeit erhielt ich auch mein Bachelors Degree.

Dann zogen wir alle, wir hatten inzwischen drei Kinder, nach Libyen, wo ich für die US Botschaft arbeitete. Wir waren dort während der Revolution. Danach waren wir drei Jahre in Deutschland, das wir viel bereisten. Deutschland war schön, aber wir merkten, daß wir Amerikaner geworden waren. Wir kehrten zurück, erst nach Missouri, dann für fünf Jahre auf eine Militär-Akademie nach Alabama. In 1980, nahm ich meinen Abschied von der USAF und wir zogen zurück nach Missouri, wo ich einen guten Job fand

Im Alter von 65 Jahren trat ich in den Ruhestand. Ich arbeite immer noch als Voluntär in einer deutschen Schule. Daneben machen wir viele Touren durch's Land. Jedes Jahr besuchen wir Deutschland um die Verbindung mit unsrer Familie aufrecht zu erhalten. Ich weiß, ich werde nicht nach Ostpreußen zurückgehen. Jetzt leben dort andere Menschen. Hier haben wir ein Heim und sind zufrieden mit dem Klima des mittleren Westens. Unsere Kinder, die beide Sprachen beherrschen, wollen auch hier wohnen und wir wollen in ihrer Nähe bleiben.

Good Soldiers Never Die!

Why I chose the United States as my new Homeland.

Born and raised in Eastprussia, I was 17 years old at the end of the war. Fortunately I was not injured. On May 3, 1945, I became a POW and a few weeks later I was with many other young soldiers on a train to the then "Soviet Union." Life there was not easy , but I think it made me stronger. In the sparse letters I received from my parents, now living in Holstein, I heard that my American uncle would like to sponsor me once I had returned from Russia. That information gave me the will to survive. After two years and seven months I returned to Germany, frail but alive.

I was unable to emigrate to the USA right away. First I had to recuperate by working on a farm where food was plentiful. Next I found a place to learn a trade, upholstering. In November 1951 I received a visa and arrived in the USA by boat.

The first few months were a learning experience. My English got better but I still got my information from German newspapers. There I read that all male persons under 25 had to report to a draft board. If they failed to do so they could be expelled from the USA. I followed the call and joined the USAF in August 1952. Recruit training was easy after my previous military experiences. I became a radio operator and spent four years in Newfoundland. There I met and married my German wife. Through evening classes in the University of Maryland program I studied Math and other required subjects. As a flightcrew member I had the opportunity to fly the Arctic. What a thrill it was for me to view the great expanses of the North where few men ever had trod

Mr. and Mrs. Fred S. Losch with Poodle.

On my next assignment I saw the world flying with the big C-124 transporters. We flew as far north as northern Greenland, south as far as New Zeeland, West as far as Thailand and east as far as Pakistan. - When I quit flying I was chosen to write the training manual for my careerfield. At that time I also was able to complete my bachelors degree.

After that the whole family (we had three children by now) went to Libya for duty with the US Embassy. There we experienced the Libyan revolution. Then we spent three years in Germany where we were able to see all of Germany and we looked at our options. Germany was beautiful, but we had become Americans now. We returned to Missouri, then served five years in Alabama with a military academy. After 27 years of service with the USAF I retired in 1980 and moved back to Kansas City where I found a job.

At 65 I retired for good. Today I still work as a volunteer in a German language school. And we do travel a lot through these our United States. However, every year we visit Germany to keep our family ties alive. I know I will not return to Eastprussia. Other people call it their homeland now. Here we own our home and enjoy the climate of the Midwest. Our children who are bi-lingual also prefer to live in this country. Naturally we want to be close to them.

Deutsche Vereine in Kansas City

Germania Klub in Kansas City

Der Germania Klub in Kansas City wurde 1967 gegründet, und hat seitdem in jedem Jahr Karneval gefeiert, um diese altdeutsche Tradition zu erhalten.Die Krönung des Prinzenpaares findet immer im frühen November statt, und die Karneval Saison hat ihren Höhepunkt mit dem Maskenball im Februar. Die etwa 500 Mitglieder des Klubs veranstalten jährlich ein Maifest und ein Oktoberfest. Der Verein hat einen sehr aktiven Frauenkreis. Öfter wird zu Dinner- und gesellschaftlichen Abenden im Germania Klubhaus in Nord Kansas City eingeladen.

Deutsch Amerikanischer Bürgerverein, e.V.

Unsere deutsch - amerikanische Gemeinde hat sich erstmals und formell im Jahre 1858 organisiert. Viele Änderungen haben sich über die Jahre ergeben, aber heute ist der deutsch-amerikanische Bürgerverein stolz auf seine Rolle, die deutsche Tradition und Kultur in Kansas City und Umgebung aufrecht zu erhalten.

Man sieht sich als Brücke zwischen der alten Welt und der neuen, und beehrt sich, das deutsche Erbe im Herzen Amerikas zu fördern.

Karneval Society

Trachten Gruppe

Germania Club of Kansas City

The Germania Club of Kansas City was founded in 1967 and, in each year since, has celebrated Karneval in keeping with German traditions. The Coronation of the Prinzenpaar takes place each year in early November and the Karneval season culminates with a Maskenball in February. The Club's 500 members organize a Maifest and an Oktoberfest each year and the Club has a very active Ladies Circle. Frequent dinners and social gatherings are held at the "Germania Klubhaus" in North Kansas City.

For information:
Contact the **Germania Club of Kansas City**,
1611 Swift Street, North Kansas City, MO 64116
Telephone: 816 / 421 - 4287.

German American Citizens Association, Inc.

Our German American community first formally organized itself in the year 1858. Many changes have occurred throughout the years, but today, the German-American Citizens' Association is proud of its role in upholding German tradition and culture in the Kansas City metropolitan area.

We stand as the bridge between the old world and the new, and are honored to promote our German heritage in the Heartland of America.

For information:
German American Citizens Association, Inc.
Deutsch-Amerikanischer Bürgerverein, e.V.
302 Manor Court, Belton, MO 64012
Telephone: 816 / 331 - 3441

A Healthy Sense of Duality: Growing up Bilingual

by Jill Metzler for *German Life* Magazine

Sitting with her parents on the back patio of her childhood home in Liberty, Missouri, Annette Petty recalls long family trips, packed into the back of the station wagon with her older brother, off to destinations across America. Like many on vacation, Annette's family sang songs to pass the time in the car. What set this family apart, however, was that their songs were often in German. Many of their favorites, in fact, were traditional German Wanderlieder (hiking songs).

"My dad had this harmonica…" says Annette, rolling her eyes at the memory. Her father, Joachim Brill, takes the teasing easily. "We sang whatever we knew, whatever language," says Annette's mother, Jutta Brill. And since Annette and her brother were raised speaking both English and German, they had twice as many songs in their repertoire to keep themselves entertained.

Between bites of her mother's authentic Apfelkuchen, or apple cake, and sips of hot tea, Annette describes how her bilingual upbringing has shaped her interests, her perspective of the world, and who she is now at 25. Growing up as a child of German parents, but having American friends and schoolmates, Annette says she learned early that there are many ways of doing things. "The Americans had a different way of going about life than we did," she says. "I'm just not as easily shocked when I come across something that is different."

In a country where people have little incentive to learn about other lands and traditions, a bilingual upbringing seems to encourage multicultural tolerance and enlarge a person's world view. Mike Vukosavich, whose Austrian mother taught him German, grew up in an area of Chicago where he says about 75 percent of his schoolmates spoke a language besides English at home. "If you come from a multicultural environment, you get a bigger perspective and scope," he says. "You learn

there's another world outside of here." Cindy Zorn, whose German-born parents raised her bilingually, and who has traveled to Europe 15 to 20 times in her life, says her bilingualism, coupled with a strong sense of her own German heritage, allows her to better understand other people "who are strongly into their background." Differences, bilingual people often learn, are to be celebrated, not feared.

Annette's family tried not to impose the use of German at home too strictly. Instead, they allowed her to pursue other interests and other languages, and to see where her background and abilities in German would lead her. Annette decided to

Jutta and Joachim Brill with their daughter, Annette Petty

study French in high school and discovered that her understanding of German helped her in learning French. "I found it a little bit easier to learn another pronunciation," she says. "A different sound wasn't as strange to me as maybe it would be to someone who wasn't used to hearing any foreign sounds."

Kenji Hakuta, professor of education at Stanford University and a leading researcher of bilingualism, agrees that bilinguals are often at an advantage when attempting a third language later in life. One example of this advantage, he says, is that bilinguals often "have a higher level of awareness about the arbitrariness of language." They

know, for instance, that inconsistencies occur in grammar, and they aren't as intimidated when they encounter another language.

In addition, bilinguals may behave differently in a third language than someone learning a foreign tongue for the first time. American-born Lorenz Huelsbergen, whose first language was German, and who spent a lot of effort as a child ridding himself of his German accent in English, says his bilingualism had an unpredictable influence when he tried to learn Dutch. After two years of study, Lorenz traveled to Holland to test his new skills. To his surprise, he had a difficult time, particularly in

Amsterdam, getting anyone to respond to him in Dutch; but instead of assuming he was an American traveler and speaking English to him, the Dutch he encountered mistook him for a native German. Lorenz speculates that perhaps his accent or syntax—or maybe his clothes, he jokes—led people to believe he was a German, not an American tourist.

Much of the research that has been done on bilingualism looks at how proficiency in two or more languages affects cognitive skills. Fewer studies look at the sociopsychological realm, probably because it's difficult to quantify how the bilingual experience affects such things as cultural sensitivity and identity. It

makes sense, though, to presume that growing up in a bilingual family is likely to instill certain characteristics, such as an interest in studying and traveling abroad and in learning more about one's own heritage.

After having spent a summer in Germany with her relatives, Annette became even more interested in learning about German culture and decided to spend an academic year abroad. She took correspondence courses and summer classes in order to graduate from high school a year early, and through a Youth For Understanding program, spent a year at a German high school, called a Gymnasium, in Hanover. She went on to major in German and journalism at the University of Kansas.

Her experience is not unusual. Mike Lindenberg spent much of his childhood in Reading, Pennsylvania, where his family was very active in Reading's large German community. After high school, he decided to attend a Kochlehre program, a cooking traineeship, in Villingen-Schwenningen in southwestern Germany, where he studied hotel and restaurant management. Harvey Morrell, who lived on a U.S. military base in Germany when he was a child, eventually majored in German area studies, international relations, and economics at American University. After attending law school, he worked as a research fellow at the Max Planck Institute in Munich and is now a foreign/international law librarian at the University of Baltimore Law Library.

Higher education goals and international careers aside, the mere popularity of such things as German clubs, folk costumes, and oom-pah bands attests to the desire of people to learn about and celebrate their heritage. Researcher Kenji Hakuta says that people raised in a bilingual environment where the two languages and cultures are not in conflict with each other (conflict occurs, for example, when

Ein gesundes Gefühl für Dualität: Zweisprachig aufwachsen

von Jill Metzler aus der Zeitschrift *„German Life"*

immigrants are encouraged to learn a new language at the expense of their first) generally emerge with "a healthy sense of duality."

Cindy Zorn has found opportunities all her life to explore this duality. Although her high school didn't offer German classes, she was active in clubs and participated in many activities. As a teenager, she won a "Miss Deutscher Club" title, and as a graduate student she was the Cornflower Queen in the New York Steuben parade, for which she got to travel around Germany as a kind of goodwill ambassador. She currently maintains a World Wide Web site on the Internet that links viewers to information about German clubs, German restaurants, historical facts, and upcoming events, and other sites of German-American interest. (Her site can be found at: <http://mars.superlink.net/czorn/>.)

While the term "German-American" is a phrase people of German heritage often use to describe themselves, many raised in German-speaking homes tend to reserve the title for those who, like themselves, truly have a sense of what German culture is all about. "I get a little roused when people claim they're Irish-American or Italian-American, but they don't know what that means," says Mike Vukosavich. Mike Lindenberg shares the sentiment. "I do consider myself a German-American, because I know the language and the culture," he says. "It's very important. If you say 'I'm German-American,' you should know something about the culture."

Annette's parents obviously believed this as well, which accounts not only for their trips to Germany every few years, but also for the miles they logged together, touring the United States. "We had friends who went back (to Germany) every year," says Annette's mother, Jutta. "We were afraid if we went back so often, we wouldn't

get to see as much of the States."

"For us [it was important] to get to go to Virginia and see the Civil War battlefields, and to go to the Atlantic Ocean, and to Hilton Head…" Annette's father continues, lost in reminiscence. Their friends, who went home to Germany every year, couldn't ever understand what it is to grow up in America, he says. " You want to be a part of this country, too."

Annette and her brother got a taste of it all, German and American culture, as they sat snugly in the back of the station wagon, singing Wanderlieder from Missouri all the way to the Grand Canyon.

Annette Petty sitzt mit ihren Eltern auf der Terrasse ihres Elternhauses in Liberty, Missouri, und erinnert sich und die langen Ferienreisen mit ihrer Familie, als sie und ihr älterer Bruder hinten in den Kombiwagen verstaut quer durch Amerika fuhren. Wie so viele, die auf Reisen gehen, sangen sie dabei Lieder, um sich die Zeit zu vertreiben. Was aber diese Familie von den anderen unterschied war, daß sie oft deutsche Lieder sangen. Ja, eigentlich waren einige ihrer Lieblingslieder deutsche *Wanderlieder*.

„Mein Vater hatte diese Mundharmonika… " sagt Annette und rollte bei der Erinnerung daran mit den Augen. Ihr Vater, Joachim Brill, lacht gutmütig dazu. „Wir sangen, was uns gerade in den Sinn kam, egal in welcher Sprache", fügt Annettes Mutter, Jutta Brill, hinzu. Und da Annette und ihr Bruder in beiden Sprachen aufwuchsen, war ihr Repertoire an Liedern, mit dem sie sich unterhielten, zweimal so groß.

Während sie sich ein Stück ihrer Mutters selbstgebackenen Apfelkuchen in den Mund schiebt und dazu heißen Tee trinkt, erzählt Annette davon, welchen Einfluß ihre zweisprachige Erziehung auf ihre Interessen und ihre Weltanschauung ausgeübt hat und wer sie eigentlich heute als 25jährige ist. Wenn man

als Kind deutscher Eltern aufwächst, aber amerikanische Freunde und Schulkameraden hat, lernt man von früh auf, daß man viele Dinge auf viele verschiedene Arten und Weisen machen kann. „Die Amerikaner haben eine ganz andere Art, mit dem Leben fertig zu werden", sagt sie. „Es schockiert mich also nicht, wenn etwas andersartig ist."

In einem Land, in dem die Menschen kaum Anreiz erhalten, sich mit anderen Ländern und Kulturen auseinanderzusetzen, hilft eine zweisprachige Erziehung nicht nur, anderen Menschen und Sitten gegenüber toleranter zu sein, sondern sie vermittelt auch eine globale Weltanschauung. Mike Vukosavich, der von seiner österreichischen Mutter Deutsch gelernt hatte, wurde in Chicago groß, wo, wie er behauptet, 75% seiner Klassenkameraden außer Englisch auch noch eine andere Sprache sprachen. "Wenn man in einer multikulturellen Umgebung groß geworden ist, ist man weitsichtiger als andere", behauptet er. "Man lernt, daß da draußen noch eine andere Welt existiert." Cindy Zorn, deren in Deutschland gebürtigen Eltern sie zweisprachig erzogen haben, und die schon 15 oder 20 mal in ihrem Leben in Deutschland war, meint, daß Zweisprachigkeit und ein starker Sinn für das deutsche Erbe es ihr erlauben, andere Menschen besser verstehen zu können, "die sich stark mit ihrem eigenen Erbe identifizieren." Andersartigkeit, so stellen zweisprachige Menschen oft fest, sollte gepriesen und nicht gefürchtet werden.

Annettes Familie hatte nicht darauf bestanden, den Gebrauch der deutschen Sprache zu Hause streng durchzusetzen, sondern man gab ihr genügend Spielraum, ihren eigenen Interessen nachzugehen und andere Sprachen zu lernen, um selbst entscheiden zu können, welche Richtung sie mit ihrer Erziehung und ihren deutschen Sprachkenntnissen einschlagen solle. So entschied sich Annette, in der Oberschule Französisch zu lernen, und sie stellte dabei fest, daß ihre deutschen Sprachkenntnisse es ihr erleichterten, eine andere Fremdsprache zu lernen. " Ich fand

es schon ein bißchen leichter, mich mit einer anderen Aussprache auseinander zu setzen", sagt sie. „Für mich war der Klang einer anderen Sprachen nicht so fremd, wie für jemanden, der nicht daran gewöhnt ist, eine andere Sprache zu hören."

Kenji Hakuta, Pädagoge und Professor an der Stanford Universität und führender Forscher für Bilingualismus, war ebenfalls der Meinung, daß zweisprachige Menschen es später beim Lernen einer dritten Sprache leichter haben. Zum Beispiel sind sich Zweisprachige der „Willkür von Sprachen besser bewußt", wie zum Beispiel Ungereimtheiten in der Grammatik, und sie werden nicht so schnell von einer anderen Sprache eingeschüchtert.

Außerdem kommen Zweisprachige mit einer dritten Sprache ganz anders zurecht als jemand, der zum ersten Mal eine Fremdsprache lernt. Der in Amerika geborene Lorenz Huelsbergen, dessen erste Sprache Deutsch ist, und der sich als Kind viel Mühe gab, seinen deutschen Akzent abzulegen, weiß, daß seine Zweisprachigkeit es ihm sehr erleichtert hat, Holländisch zu lernen. Nach zwei Jahren Holländisch reiste Lorenz nach Holland, um dort seine Holländischkenntnisse auszuprobieren. Zu seiner größten Überraschung konnte er keinen finden, der ihm auf Holländisch antwortete, ganz bensonders nicht in Amsterdam. Ja, und da die Holländer annahmen, er sei ein deutscher und nicht ein amerikanischer Tourist, sprach auch keiner Englisch mit ihm. Lorenz glaubt, daß es vielleicht an seinem Akzent oder seinem Syntax lag, oder vielleicht an seiner Garderobe, wie er lachend meint, da die Holländer ihn irrtümlicherweise für einen Deutschen hielten.

In der Forschung über Bilingualismus befaßt man sich weitgehend damit, wie sich die Fähigkeit, zwei oder mehr Sprachen zu sprechen, auf die Wahrnehmungsfähigkeit auswirkt. Viel weniger Zeit wird in der Forschung für den soziophychologischen Bereich aufgewendet. Vielleicht liegt das an der

Ein gesundes Gefühl für Dualität: Zweisprachig aufwachsen

von Jill Metzler aus der Zeitschrift *„German Life"*

Schwierigkeit, die zweisprachige Erfahrung und ihre Auswirkung auf kulturelle Empfindsamkeit und Identität in Zahlen auszudrücken. Aber zweifelsohne ist das Aufwachsen in einer zweisprachigen Familie sicherlich für bestimmte Merkmale verantwortlich, wie zum Biespiel das Interesse, im Ausland zu studieren und zu reisen und der Wunsch, mehr über die eigene Herkunft zu erfahren.

Nachdem Annette einen Sommer lang bei Verwandten in Deutschland verbracht hatte, vertiefte sich ihr Wunsch, mehr über die deutsche Kultur zu lernen, und so kam es, daß sie ein Jahr in Europa studierte. Um ihren Abschluß in der High School ein Jahr früher zu schaffen, machte sie ein Fernstudium und belegte außerdem Sommerkurse. Durch ein *Youth For Understanding* Programm besuchte sie dann ein Jahr lang eine deutsche Oberschule, ein sogenanntes Gymnasium, in Deutschland, und zwar in Hannover. Danach studierte sie Deutsch und Journalistik an der Universität von Kansas.

Ihr Werdegang ist nichts ungewöhnliches. Mike Lindenberg verbrachte seine Kindheit in Reading, Pennsylvania, wo seine Familie in der großen deutschen Gemeinde sehr aktiv war. Nach Abschluß der *High School* machte er eine Lehre als Koch in Villingen-Schwenningen im Südwesten Deutschlands, wo er Hotel- und Restaurantmanagement studierte. Harvey Morrell, der als Kind mit seinen Eltern auf einem Militärstützpunkt in Deutschland lebte, studierte später an der Amerikanischen Universität, *Deutsch, International Relations und Wirtschaft*. Nach seinem Jurastudium arbeitete er als Forschungsstipendiat am Max-Planck-Institut in München und ist heute Bibliothekar der Internationalen Rechtsbibliothek an der Universität von Baltimore.

Aber abgesehen von einer akademischen Ausbildung und einer internationalen Karriere, ist die Tatsache, daß solche Dinge wie deutsche Clubs, Trachten, und Balskapellen sich großer Beliebtheit erfreuen, ein Beweis dafür, daß man

über seine Vorfahren mehr erfahren will und sich mit seinem Erbe identifizieren möchte. Der Forscher Kenji Hakuta, ist der Meinung, daß Menschen, die in einer zweisprachigen Welt aufwachsen, in der zwei Sprachen und Kulturen nicht miteinander in Konflikt geraten (und ein Konflikt entsteht, wenn Einwanderer eine neue Sprache auf Kosten der alten lernen), mit einem „gesunden Sinn für Dualität" ausgestatten werden.

Cindy Zorn hat ihr Leben lang immer wieder Gelegenheiten gefunden, diese Dualität zu erforschen. Obgleich ihre Oberschule keinen Deutschunterricht angeboten hatte, so war sie doch aktiv in Clubs tätig und beteiligte sich an vielen deutschen Veranstaltungen. Als Teenager wurde sie zur „Miss Deutscher Club" gewählt und als Universitätsstudentin wurde sie zur Kornblumenkönigin der New Yorker Steubenparade ernannt. In dieser Eigenschaft bereiste sie als eine Art Goodwill-Botschafterin ganz Deutschland. Jetzt hat sie eine Seite auf dem World-Wide-Web im Internet unter: <http://mars.super-link.net/czorn/>, mit Informationen über deutsche Clubs, deutsche Restaurants, Geschichtshinweise und Veranstaltungen und mit Hinweisen auf andere Seiten, die für Deutsch-Amerikaner von Interesse sein können.

Obgleich viele Amerikaner deutscher Herkunft sich mit „Deutsch-Amerikaner" bezeichnen, behalten sich andere der deutschsprechenden Amerikaner diese Bezeichnung für diejenigen vor, die, wie sie selbst, einen echten Sinn für die deutsche Kultur besitzen. „Es irritiert mich, wenn Menschen behaupten, sie seien z.B. Irisch-Amerikanisch oder Italienisch-Amerikanisch, können aber überhaupt nicht verstehen, was das eigentlich bedeutet", sagt Mike Vukosavich. Und Mike Lindenberg teilt seine Meinung. „Ich betrachte mich als Deutsch-Amerikaner, weil ich die Sprache und die Kultur kenne", sagt er. „Es ist sehr wichtig, daß, wenn man behaupten will, man sei 'Deutsch-Amerikaner', man auch etwas von der Kultur versteht."

Annettes Eltern haben das

anscheinend auch so gesehen, denn sie fuhren alle paar Jahre nach Deutschland, und sie unterließen es auch nicht, viele Meilen in den Vereinigten Staaten zurückzulegen. „Wir haben Freunde, die jedes Jahr zurückgingen (nach Deutschland)", sagt Annettes Mutter, Jutta. „Aber wir machten uns Gedanken, daß, wenn wir so oft nach Deutschland reisen würden, wir nicht viel von Amerika sehen würden."

„Für uns war es wichtig, nach Virginia zu reisen, um die Schlachtfelder des amerikanischen Bürgerkrieges zu besuchen, den Altantischen Ozean und Hilton Head…", fährt Annettes Vater fort, und verliert sich in Gedanken. Ihre Freunde, die jedes Jahr nach Deutschland reisten, können es gar nicht richtig verstehen, was es bedeutet, in Amerika groß zu werden", sagt er. „Man sollte sich doch auch in dieses Land integrieren".

Annette und ihr Bruder haben viel von der deutschen und der amerikanischen Kultur mit auf den Weg bekommen, als sie hinten in den Kombiwagen gepackt und deutsche Wanderlieder singend von Missouri bis zum Grand Canyon reisten.

German-American Krankheit

Ein Mann, der war erkrankt, you know,
War schwer verstopft und couldn't go,
A fever came dann noch hinzu
Und obendrein a chill or two.

He felt himself entsetzlich schlecht,
As if he had all night gezecht.
Er war ganz blaß, sein face war gray.
He had to stay im Bett all day.

He moaned and groaned und stöhnte lau
The pain was there da gabs kein doubt.
Er war erschöpft, extremely schlaff,
Das ist zuviel; he's had enough.

Mann rief den Doktor right away,
Zu sehen, what he had to say.
Mit einem stethoscope and so
Checked er den Mann from head to toe.

Dann sagt der Arzt: "Just have Geduld!
The rotten weather is dran schuld.
In kurzer Zeit, I quarantee,
Bist du gesund. Now pay me fee!"

The patient tat as he was told
Und schluckte Pillen for his cold,
Frühmorgens schon und every noon
And felt tatsächlich besser soon.

So helped the doctor and the pills,
Für seine Krankheit and the chills;
Auch die intestines wurden klar,
Und everything was wunderbar.

He's made it through auch diesesmal;
In Zukunft he would wear a Schal
To save himself against the draught,
Sodaß er bleibt the last who laughed.

St. Louis, Missouri

Honoring Alexander von Humboldt, Germany's great humanist, on his 225th Birthday, in St. Louis, MO,
Tower Grove Park, September 12, 1994. Arrangements by the German - American Heritage Society,
George S. Hecker, Chairman; Anna Lea Kerckhoff, President; George L. Stemmler, Founder.

Photos by Bert Lachner

Saint Louis
German/American Committee, Inc.

St. Louis German/American Committee, Inc.

Josef J. Hammes
President

Egon Matschke
Vice-President

Betty J. Fritz
Corresponding Secretary

Ruth Umhoefer
Recording Secretary

Norman Cleeland
Treasurer

The purposes for which this organization has been organized are…
To create and maintain strong cohesive and viable German/American cultural ties;
To maintain and enhance the relationship between German and American cultural activities;
To encourage and help retain the German/American cultural spirit in the geographical area;
To educate and work with other cultural organizations as to methods of improving the German/American relationship;
To promote and organize events to educate the general public regarding the German/American heritage.

Der Zweck für die Gründung der Organisation ist…
um: die Lebensfähigkeit der deutsch-amerikanischen Kultur zu erhalten
um: die Aktivität der deutsch-amerikanischen Kultur zu erhöhen und aufrecht zu erhalten
um: den deutsch-amerikanischen kulturellen Geist in dem geographischen Gebiet zu fördern
um: die deutsch-amerikanische Kultur organizatorisch zu bilden, planmässig zu steigern und zu verbessern
um: die deutsch-amerikanische Bevölkerung durch kulturelle Veranstaltungen ihre deutsche Abstammung zu erhalten and zu verbessern

• Participating Organizations •

Badischer Unterstützungs Verein
Founded Josef J. Hammes, President
1885 (314) 647-6291

Deutscher Kulturverein
Founded German Cultural Society Hall
1945 3652 S. Jefferson
St. Louis, MO

Deutscher Männerchor, St. Louis
Founded Richard Fischer, President
1986 (314) 638-4499

Deutscher Schulverein
Founded Andrew Roeslein, President
1962 (314) 892-7798

G.T.E.V. D'Fröhliche Schuhplattler
Founded Betty Fritz, President
1976 (314) 544-4409

Honorary Consul of the Federal
Republic of Germany

Anna Mayer Beck
49 Orange Hills Drive
Chesterfield, MO 63017
Telephone: (314) 576-4786
Fax: (314) 576-6956

German-American Heritage Society
Founded Anna Lea E. Kerckhoff, President
1990 (314) 862-1733

Eden Klub
Founded Egon Matschke, President
1927 (314) 843-1827

Harmonie Sängerbund
Founded 1885 Joe Ruppe, President

Liederkranz Singing Society
Founded Norman Cleeland, President
1870 (314) 225-7332

St. Charles German-American Heritage Society
Founded Joe Daues, President
1973 (314) 946-6828

St. Louis Bayern Verein
Founded George Gansner, President
1883 (314) 544-1335

St. Louis Strassenfest Corporation
Founded Michael J. Wendl, President
1959 (314) 849-6322

St. Louis-Stuttgart Sister Cities, Inc.
Founded Roy E. Leimberg, President
1960 (314) 781-5665

St. Louis Schützenverein
Founded Norman Waterwiese, President
1961 (314) 838-8566

Schwäbischer Sängerbund
Founded Bruno Erben, President
1903 (314) 892-7567

Steuben Society of America
Founded Betty Gardner, Chairman
1919 (314) 464-3749

Goethe-Institut, St. Louis
German Cultural Center
Dr. Birgit Schweckendiek
326 N. Euclid
St. Louis, MO 63108
Telephone: (314) 367-2452
Fax: (314) 367-9439
E-mail: geothes/@attmail.com

St. Louis
Badischer Unterstützungs Verein

Josef J. Hammes, President   (314) 647-6291
Walter Lindemann, Vice-Pres.   (314) 481-1745

On December 20, 1885 German immigrants from Baden, Germany residing in St. Louis, Missouri formed the above-named organization for the purpose of providing sociability and support for immigrants from Baden who are in need and especially to our survivors.

Deutscher Männerchor
of St. Louis

Norbert R. Cook, President   (314) 638-5890

The Deutscher Männerchor (German Men's Chorus of St. Louis) was founded in January, 1986, as an umbrella organization for four smaller choruses – the Eden Club, the Harmonie Singing Society, the Schwäbischer Sängerbund, and the Swiss Singing Society which all retained their identity as a smaller singing society. The purpose of the organization is to promote and maintain German music and songs.

Deutscher Schulverein

Andrew Roeslein, President   (314) 892-7798

The German School Association of Greater St. Louis is a non-profit, independent non-denominational organization. The school year is from September through May. The German School Association offers an opportunity for children and adults to get acquainted with the German language. Children: 6-14 Beginners and up to the 4th class. Adults: Beginners - Intermediate and Advanced. All classes are designed (comprehension) speaking, reading and writing.

Steuben Society of America

Betty Gardner, Chairman   (314) 464-3749

We are a non-partisan, patriotic organization. The name of our Society is in honor of General Friedrich Wilhelm von Steuben, Major General and Inspector General of the Army of George Washington. We work on a national level to maintain the independence of the United States and the uphold the constitution.

Liederkranz Singing Society

Norman Cleeland, President   (314) 225-7332

The Liederkranz Singing Society was 125 years old in 1995. It is the oldest German mixed chorus west of the Mississippi. We have Men's, Ladies' and Mixed Choruses. We sing both German and English music from classical to Broadway show tunes, as well as the old German favorites and German folk songs.

Schützenverein — St. Louis von 1961

Established in 1961, the St. Louis Shooting Club d.b.a. Schützenverein St. Louis, is a not-for-profit organization. Their mission is to enhance German-American relationships by providing fellowship and education through mutual social interest in German Schützenverein traditions and competition. Air rifle competition and meetings are held on a monthly basis. The club also sponsors two dances each year. The Königs-Ball in January and the Hubertus dance in October are open to the public. Please call Norman Waterwiese at (314) 838-8566 or Karl Seibert at (314) 843-5206 for more information.

Im Jahre 1961 gegründet, ist der Schützenverein eine gemeinnützige Organisation. Die deutschen und amerikanischen Mitglieder pflegen die Tradition der deutschen Schützenvereine in der neuen Heimat. Der Verein benutzt Luftgewehre die den Regeln der Internationalen Schützen Union entsprechen. Ferner hat der Verein zwei Tanzabende im Jahr. Der Verein pflegt auch den Kontakt zu anderen Schützenvereinen in den U.S.A. und Deutschland durch gegenseitige Besuche und Teilnahme an Veranstaltungen der anderen Vereine. Für weitere Informationen rufen Sie Norman Waterwiese (314) 838-8566 oder Karl Siebert (314) 843-5206 an.

The not-for-profit St. Louis Strassenfest Corporation coordinates entertainment, concessionaire, and logistics related activities of the three-day weekend Strassenfest (street festival) celebration. The Strassenfest is held on the first weekend in August in a five square block area in downtown St. Louis across from City Hall. The Strassenfest features four entertainment stages including a children's stage with clowns and jugglers, dancers, polka bands, and visiting German brassbands. Delicious food and beverages are available. Enjoy the arts/crafts, game booths, and rides for children and adults. All food, beverage and game booth operators are members of civic, cultural, educational or charitable organizations from the St. Louis metropolitan area. Strassenfest started some 35 years ago, has raised millions for charitable causes and has become one of the largest German festivals in Mid-America.

Die St. Louis Strassenfest Corporation koordiniert Unterhaltungen, Verkaufswaren, Verpflegungswesen, und andere Verantwortlichkeiten betreffend des drei-Tage langen Strassenfestes. Das grosse Strassenfest wird gefeiert am ersten Wochenende im August auf einer Parkanlage von fünf Häuserblocks in der Innerestadt St. Louis vor dem Rathaus. Das Strassenfest wird gestaltet von vier Unterhaltungsbühnen einschließend einer Kinderbühne, die Unterhaltungskünstler, Tänzer, Polkakapellen, und auch deutsche Blaskapellen prominieren. Geschmackvolles Essen und Getränke werden serviert. Genießen sie die Kuntswerke/Handwerke, Spielbuden, und Ringelspiele für Kinder und Erwachsene. Die Bedienung (Beteiligungspersonal) sind Mitglieder von Stadt, Kultur, Schul, und Wohltätigkeitsvereinen aus der St. Louis Umgebung. Das Strassenfest wurde vor 35 Jahren gegründet und hat mehrere Millionen Dollar für diese Vereine erworben und ist eines der größten deutschen Feste von ganz Nord-Amerika.

Back Row (l.t.r.) : H. Eisele, J. Hediger, J. Wittenberg, J. Worzer, P. Littlefield, R. Villaire
Front Row (l.t.r.) : G. Andres, L. Mueller, M. Wendl (Pres), B. Betancourt, N. Cleeland
Missing from Picture : M. Sherman, A. Meyer-Beck

St. Louis Strassenfest

Ein Prosit

Freeman R. Bosley, Jr. - Mayor of St. Louis, Missouri
Manfred Rommel - Lord Mayor of Stuttgart, Germany
Michael J. Wendl - President, St. Louis Strassenfest Corp.

Stuttgarts Oberbürgermeister Manfred Rommel besuchte St. Louis

Im Zusammenhang des 35jährigen Bestehens der Schwesterstädte Stuttgart-St. Louis, Missouri, stattete Oberbürgermeister Manfred Rommel einen Besuch mit 20 Handelsabgeordneten in St. Louis ab.

Das Foto zeigt: v.l. St. Louis Mayor Bosley, Oberbürgermeister Rommel and Strassenfest-Präsident Michael Wendl, der einen Porzellanteller der berühmten "Mottahedeh" Hersteller an Bürgermeister Rommel von dem St. Louis Strassenfest Komittee überreicht.

The German American Heritage Society
Saint Louis, Missouri

GAHS Board
of Directors

The Society supports the German-American Archives at the St. Louis Public Library, made possible by a grant from Anheuser-Busch Foundation. It also sponsors cultural exchanges between Germany and the U.S. and participates in restoration of German monuments such as the statue of Alexander von Humboldt, General Franz Sigel and "The Naked Truth." Membership by election is open to Americans of descent from Germany, Austria, Switzerland and Alsace Lorraine.

The German-American Heritage Society was founded in 1990 by St. Louis advertising and public relations executive, George L. Stemmler, Jr., and Strassenfest founder, Eberhard Gress. Sponsors were German Ambassador Juergen Ruhfus and DANK leaders, Elsbeth Seewald and Ernst Ott. The charter was presented to the president, George Hecker, St. Louis attorney and great grandson of German freedom fighter Friedrich Hecker, by Governor John Ashcroft at the St. Louis Racquet Club.

DANK President Ernst Ott presents a historic scroll to GAHS Chairman George Hecker and Founding Director George L. Stemmler.

Der Deutsche Kulturverein
St. Louis, Missouri

German Cultural Society, 3652 South Jefferson Avenue, St. Louis, MO 63118   314 / 771-8368

The German Cultural Society

has its origin in the St. Louis Chapter of the American Aid Society, which was founded in 1945 to help German refugees from the East who fled to Germany and Austria. When it became possible to immigrate to this country, many who came to the St. Louis area joined the Society, as did many other immigrants from all parts of Germany and Austria.

The members of the Society set as their goal the preservation of their cultural heritage. To more accurately reflect these aspirations, the organization changed its name to "German Cultural Society" in 1969.

By becoming active in the various groups, members of all ages can contribute to the preservation of their rich and varied traditions in accordance with their interests and talents. In 1982, the Society started the construction of its Center, which is today the site of events of the German Cultural Society and that of most of the other German Organizations in St. Louis.

The Officers, Executive Committee and Fest Committee
The Society has benefited from the dedication and hard work of its member in general and that of the officers and committees in particular

Photos: Joe Unterreiner

The weekend KINDERGARTEN is an early effort by the Society to involve families in the activities of the organization. Pictured above are some of the little "angels" at the "Weihnachtsfeier".

The "SCHUHPLATTLER" are first and second generation Americans who enjoy dancing and entertaining their many followers. The children in the "Kindertanzgruppe" are beginning their participation in the cultural progra of the society.

The 'DAMENCHOR', the Ladies' Choir, has been acclaimed by German audiences for their outstanding vocal talent and repertoire of favorite musical selections. The annual Fall Concert is a popular event for their many admirers.

Der Deutsche Kulturverein,

früher ein Teil der amerikanischen Hilfsvereine, wurde in 1945 in St. Louis gegründet, um den donauschwäbischen Flüchtlingen in Deutschland und Österreich zu helfen.

Als viele von diesen Familien später nach Amerika kamen, haben sie sich, wie so viele andere Einwanderer aus Deutschland und Österreich, dem Verein angeschlossen.

Sie machten es sich zur Aufgabe, ihr kulturhistorisches Erbe zu bewahren und zu pflegen. Um die Tätigkeit des Vereines besser zu beschreiben, wurde in 1969 der Name auf "Deutscher Kulturverein" geändert.

Die Mitglieder wirken in den verschiedenen Gruppen mit, je nach Alter und Begabung, und tragen so zur Erhaltung der Sitten und Gebräuche der alten Heimat bei.

In 1982 wurde mit dem Bau der Vereinshalle begonnen und heute finden dort die Veranstaltungen des Deutschen Kulturvereines und der meisten deutschen Vereine in St. Louis statt.

"Wir laden Sie ein, uns zu besuchen und sich uns anzuschließen"

The "DEUTSCHMEISTER BLASKAPELLE" Founded in 1963, the talented musicians of this group are known throughout the region and have provided the entertainment at many festivals.

The 'TRACHTENGRUPPE" takes great pride in performing folk dances in their traditional colorful Danube-Swabian costumes. The group is involved in many activities that foster the preservation of the traditions of the "old country".

Many of the current members of the 'JUGENDGRUPPE" are the second generation to have belonged to the group. Since its founding in the early fifties, many friendships have been formed that will last a lifetime. The high point at the annual "Kirchweihfest" in late summer is their presentation of folk dances.

ST. LOUIS AND STUTTGART SISTER CITIES SINCE 1960

Representatives from St. Louis, Missouri, USA, and from Stuttgart, capital of the state of Baden-Württemberg, Germany, met on March 10, 1960, to sign official documents uniting the two cities in a sister city relationship and committing each to ongoing activities which encourage people-to-people and government-to-government interaction. The affiliation was formed under the guidelines of Sister Cities International, Inc., an organization founded by former U.S. President Dwight D. Eisenhower to promote world peace through mutual understanding. St. Louis-Stuttgart Sister Cities, Inc., a non-profit organization of volunteers, was founded in St. Louis to maintain communication with the director of sister cities programs in Stuttgart and to manage the activities which achieve the goals set forth in the partnership agreement.

A first for St. Louis

The sister city alliance with Stuttgart was the first for St. Louis and has been followed by a succession of ties with cities in Africa, Asia, Europe and South America. The linking of cities is based on similarities which offer opportunities for exchange. St. Louis and Stuttgart share corresponding characteristics and resources: both are located on major rivers and are inland ports; are important transportation hubs; are major centers of automobile manufacturing; and are rich in educational and cultural institutions. The two cities have drawn from all of these sectors for over thirty-five years, lending and borrowing ideas, personnel and resources to build a rich and strong association.

For all citizens of all ages

Student exchanges are important springboards to reciprocal interchange on other levels; bringing together young counterparts in the sister cities not only promotes friendships which may last a lifetime but introduces youth to the concept of international exchange as a means to cultural understanding. St. Louis and Stuttgart have sponsored educational exchanges at high school and university levels, as well as business internships and teacher exchanges. Sports competitions have played a major role in bringing German and American youth together and the camaraderie surrounding matches adds an additional dimension to the experience for both the young participants and members of the community. The link between the cities has encouraged involvement of art and cultural institutions in both St. Louis and Stuttgart; major art collections, as well as amateur and children's art, have been displayed by museums and galleries. Performances of adult and youth symphony orchestras have brought

appreciative audiences to concert halls; world renown ballet, modern and folk dance troupes have dazzled sister cities spectators. Theater groups and a variety of music and choral groups have participated in festivals and competitions. Mayors representing both cities have led official delegations to promote trade and tourism; groups of citizens have made mutual visits, always with opportunities for personal contact to reinforce the sister city relationship. A unique and important factor in exchanges of visitors is the homestay tradition, giving guests the opportunity to become a member of a family and learn about day-to-day life in another culture.

An international and a civic organization St. Louis-Stuttgart Sister Cities, Inc. functions as a civic as well as an international organization, keeping a high profile in the St. Louis community by participating in local ceremonies, conventions, parades and festivals. The organization is united with St. Louis' other sister city groups and international associations through the office of the St. Louis Center for International Relations.

In order to support a full calendar of activities and to provide scholarships and grants for exchange groups and hospitality to visitors, St. Louis-Stuttgart Sister Cities, Inc. organizes two major fund raising events each year. Winterball, a Fasching season gala, launches the year's calendar of activities and brings together members, supporters and groups from the surrounding metropolitan area who are also affiliated with cities in Germany. Oktoberfest, a two-day outdoor festival, with music by a visiting brass band from Stuttgart, celebrates the music, the food and the customs of Germany.

Lasting family ties

A sister city relationship reaches beyond the organized exchanges of people and goods to the interest of individual citizens in the economic, political and social health of their twin city. Elections of officials, upward and downward trends in currency and economy, domestic and foreign affairs are followed with interest on both sides of the Atlantic. When disastrous floods inundated the Midwest in 1993, the citizens of Stuttgart, following developments in the media, were quick to extend financial assistance to St. Louis flood recovery organizations. This empathy has roots in a relationship which began decades ago and has matured into a legacy to be handed down from generation to generation.

St. Louis-Stuttgart Sister Cities, Inc. is a membership organization open to anyone interested in joining and participating in activities.

Anna Mayer Beck
Honorary
German Consul

Manfred Rommel
Lord Mayor
City of Stuttgart

Roy E. Leimberg
President
Sister Cities, Inc.

Freeman R. Bosley, Jr.
Mayor
City of St. Louis

St. Louis und Stuttgart sind Partnerstädte seit 1960

Am 10. März, 1960 trafen sich Vertreter der Stadt St. Louis, Missouri, USA und Stuttgart, Hauptstadt des Landes Baden-Württemberg, um die offiziellen Dokumente, die die zwei Städte in einem Partnerschaftsverhältnis verbindet, zu unterzeichnen. Hierbei verpflichteten sie sich zu weiterführenden Tätigkeiten, die "People to People", und Regierungen mit Regierungen verbinden. Der Zusammenschluß wurde nach den Richtlinien von Partnerstädte International durchgeführt. Dies ist die von dem U.S. Präsidenten Dwight D. Eisenhower gegründete, uneigennützige, von Freiwilligen getragene Organisation mit dem Ziel, den Weltfrieden durch gegenseitige Verständigung der Menschen untereinander zu fördern. Die St. Louis-Stuttgart Partnerstadt, Inc. wurde in St. Louis gegründet, um die Verbindung mit dem Leiter des Partnerstädteprogramms in Stuttgart aufrecht zu erhalten, und um die in der Vereinbarung festgelegten Ziele, zu verwirklichen.

Die erste Partnerstadt für St. Louis

Die Partnerstadtverbindung mit Stuttgart war die erste in St. Louis. Ihr folgten eine Reihe von Vereinbarungen mit Städten in Afrika, Asien, Europa, und Süd-Amerika. Die partnerschaftliche Verbindung von Städten beruht auf Gemeinsamkeiten, die einen sinnvollen Austausch ermöglichen. Die beiden Städte St. Louis und Stuttgart haben vergleichbare Eigenschaften: beide liegen an Flüssen und haben Binnenhäfen, beide sind wichtige Verkehrsknotenpunkte, beide haben große Automobilfabriken, beide verfügen über zahlreiche Bildungs- und Kulturstätten. Auf allen diesen Gebieten haben beide Städte während der letzten fünfunddreißig Jahre Ideen und Resourcen, aber auch Personen ausgetauscht, um die Grundlage für eine enge und haltbare Zusammenarbeit zu schaffen.

Für Bürger jeden Alters

Schüler- und Studentenaustauschprogramme sind wichtige Ausgangspunkte für weitere Kontakte auf anderen Gebieten. Die Zusammenführung gleichaltriger junger Menschen in den Partnerstädten fördert nicht nur lebenslange Freundschaften, sondern macht junge Menschen mit der Idee des internationalen Austausches als ein Mittel zu kultureller Verständigung bekannt. St. Louis und Stuttgart unterstützten Schüler- und Studentenaustausch sowie Gewerbe und Industrie Praktikanten und Lehreraustausch. Eine beträchtliche Rolle spielen Sportwettkämpfe, die deutsche und amerikanische Jugendliche zusammenbringen. Das kameradschaftliche Verhältnis, das sich dabei entwickelt, bringt eine zusätzliche Dimension in die Erfahrungen der jungen Teilnehmer und der Bürger von Ort. Die Verbindung zwischen den Städten hat die Zusammenarbeit zwischen Kunst- und Kulturinstitutionen begünstigt. Bedeutende Kunstsammlungen, sowie die Werke von Hobby-Künstlern und Kindern wurden von Museen und Galerien ausgestellt. Konzerte von

Berufsmusikern und Jugendorchestern brachten begeisterte Zuhörer in die Konzerthallen. Weltberühmte Ballett-Ensembles, moderne Tanz- und Volkstanzgruppen haben Zuschauer der Partnerstädte begeistert. Theater-Gruppen und eine Vielfalt von Musik-und Sängergruppen nahmen an Festen und Wettbewerben teil. Die Bürgermeister der beiden Städte kamen mit offiziellen Delegationen, um Handel und Fremdenverkehr zu fördern. Reisegruppen besuchten einander immer mit der Möglichkeit zum persönlichen Kontakt und somit das Partnerstadtverhältnis stärkend. Ein besonderer Aspekt bei diesen Gegenbesuchen ist die Gastfamilientradition, die den Besuchern die Gelegenheit gibt, als Mitglieder einer Familie das alltägliche Leben der anderen Kultur zu erleben.

Bürgerorganisation mit Internationalität

Die St. Louis-Stuttgart Partnerstadt, Inc. hat die Funktion einer internationalen und gleichzeitig einer lokalbürgerlichen Organisation, da die Mitglieder an Stadtfesten, Versammlungen, Festzügen, und anderen Festivals teilnehmen. Die Organisation arbeitet in Gemeinschaft mit den anderen St. Louis-Partnerstädte-Organisationen durch das "St. Louis Zentrum für Internationale Verständigung".

Um die alljährlichen Tätigkeiten und Veranstaltungen abzudecken, und um Austauschprogramme, Stipendien, und gastfreundschaftliche Aktivitäten zu ermöglichen, muß die Organisation zwei jährliche Spendeaktionsveranstaltungen durchführen. Der Winterball, eine Gala Faschingsveranstaltung, beginnt die alljährlichen Tätigkeiten und bringt Mitglieder, Förderer und Unterstützer, sowie Mitglieder anderer mit Deutschland verbundenen Partnerstädte zusammen. Das zweitägige Oktoberfest im Freien, mit Musik von einer Stuttgarter Band, stellt Musik, landesübliche Gerichte und deutsche Lebensart in den Vordergrund.

Dauernde Familienverbindungen

Eine Städtepartnerschaft will über den organisierten Austausch von Menschen und kulturellen Gütern hinaus auch das Interesse des einzelnen Bürgers an dem wirtschaftlichen, politischen und gesellschaftlichen Wohlergehen der jeweiligen Partnerstadt zu fördern. Auf beiden Seiten des Ozeans werden politische Wahlen, Währungsschwankungen, innen-und außenpolitische Verhältnisse mit Interesse verfolgt. Als 1993 die furchtbaren Fluten den Midwesten überschwemmten, kamen die Bürger Stuttgarts mit schnellem finanziellen Beistand den St. Louis- Hilfsorganisationen zu Hilfe. Dieses Mitgefühl hatte seine Wurzeln in dem engen Verhältnis, das vor 35 Jahren begann, und das sich zu einer Tradition entwickelte, das von Generationen zu Generationen weitergereicht werden kann.

St. Louis-Stuttgart Partnerstadt, Inc. ist eine Organisation jedem offen, der beitreten und sich aktiv beteiligen will.

ANHEUSER-BUSCH Companies

More than four million people of Germanic origin immigrated to the United States between the years 1830 and 1900. With them they brought an industrious nature, a seriousness of purpose, and a love for social companionship that centered around sports, music and the beverage of their choice—beer.

Kingsmill Business and Recreation Center, Williamsburg, VA

While certain cities developed a predominately Germanic flavor, such as Milwaukee, Cincinnati and St. Louis, there was no area of America that did not have German settlers. Wherever these German immigrants called home, they soon established breweries to brew their lager beers, which had a lower alcohol content and a milder, smoother taste than English ales or stouts.

Among the smallest of the St. Louis brewers was the Bavarian Brewery, owned by a local soap maker named Eberhard Anheuser. In 1869 Anheuser's son-in-law, Adolphus Busch, became his partner, forming the name that would become synonymous with beer worldwide... Anheuser-Busch.

As the Industrial Revolution took hold of America, the brewing industry experienced rapid growth through such technological innovations as pasteurization, artificial refrigeration, refrigerated rail cars, and a coordinated system of railroad distribution.

Adolphus Busch had the foresight to recognize what impact these technological developments could have on the industry, and was the first brewer to apply them on a major scale.

American Oktoberfest at Busch Gardens

Today, decades later, Anheuser-Busch remains true to its German heritage. An unwavering commitment to quality is at the heart of every aspect of the business, from brewing to packaging to marketing a family of more than 30 brands of beer that includes Budweiser, Michelob and Busch.

Innovation has been a long-standing strategy at Anheuser-Busch. This company remains the pace setter in product quality, environmental responsibility, community partnerships, and alcohol awareness and education. As the world's largest brewer, Anheuser-Busch works hard to encourage responsible drinking among adults who choose to drink, and to fight alcohol abuse, drunk driving and underage drinking.

The German-American love for social companionship is fulfilled at the Anheuser-Busch Theme Parks, which include Busch Gardens Tampa Bay, Busch Gardens Williamsburg and four Sea World parks in Orlando, San Diego, San Antonio and Aurora, Ohio. More than 20 million guests visit the company's nine theme parks each year. True to its Bavarian heritage, the Busch Gardens parks feature "Das Festhaus," a German festival hall where an "oompah" band and dancers greet guests with a festive atmosphere. For the brave of heart, the Gardens feature some of the most fierce steel roller coasters in the world,

Lochness Monster at Busch Gardens

answering to names like "Drachen Fire," the "Lochness Monster," and "Kumba."

Anheuser-Busch has become a leader in the world of sports marketing. The company was one of only 10 official Centennial Olympic Games Partners of the 1996 Summer Olympic Games in Atlanta. Budweiser is the official sponsor of the U.S. men's and women's National and Olympic soccer teams, Major League Soccer, and the 1998 World Cup in France.

From its humble beginning, Anheuser-Busch now aggressively taps the global market for growth, making inroads from China to Argentina, from Ireland to Japan, and in more than 80 countries in between. As Anheuser-Busch grows domestically and expands globally, the company credo continues to guide its behavior. "Making Friends Is Our Business" remains at the heart of brewing, packaging and family entertainment at Anheuser-Busch.

Budweiser is now available in more than 80 countries.

ANHEUSER-BUSCH Unternehmen

In den Jahren 1830 bis 1900 wanderten mehr als vier Millionen Menschen deutscher Abstammung nach Amerika aus. Sie brachten Fleiß, Entschlossenheit und eine Vorliebe für geselliges Zusammensein rund um Sport, Musik

Budweiser Clydesdales

und ihr beliebtes Getränk, Bier mit. Bestimmte Städte entwickelten einen speziellen deutschen Charakter, wie zum Beispiel Milwaukee, Cincinnati und St. Louis, aber es gab keinen Flecken in Amerika, der keine deutschen Siedler hatte. Wo auch immer sich diese deutschen Immigranten niederließen, errichteten sie bald Brauereien, um ihr helles Bier zu brauen, das einen niedrigeren Alkoholgehalt und einen milderen, weicheren Geschmack hatte als das englische Ale und Starkbier.

Visit with Hummel master Artisan at Busch Gardens.

Zu den kleinsten Brauereien in St. Louis zählte die Bayerische Brauerei, die Eberhard Anheuser,

einem ansässigen Seifenhersteller, gehörte. 1869 nahm er seinen Schwiegersohn Adolphus Busch zum Partner, und so entstand der Name, der in der ganzen Welt für Bier stehen sollte...Anheuser-Busch.

Als die industrielle Revolution auf Amerika übergriff, erlebte die Brauerei-Industrie durch technologische Innovationen wie Pasteurisieren, künstliche Kühlung, Kühlwaggons und ein geordnetes Vertriebssystem mit Hilfe der Eisenbahn ein rapides Wachstum. Adolphos Busch besaß Weitblick und erkannte, welche durchschlagende Wirkung diese technologischen Entwicklungen für die Industrie haben könnten. Er war der erste Brauer, der sich dieser Innovationen im großen Ausmaß zunutzen machte.

Fun at Busch Gardens, Williamsburg

Bis heute bleibt Anheuser-Busch seinem deutschen Erbe treu. Kompromißloser Einsatz für Qualität liegt in jedem Unternehmensbereich, vom Brauen über das Packen bis hin zum Marketing von mehr als 30 Biersorten, zu denen Budweiser, Michelob und Busch gehören.

Innovation heißt seit langem die praktizierte Strategie bei Anheuser-Busch. Dieses Unternehmen bestimmt bis heute das Tempo, wenn es um Produktqualität, Verantwortung gegenüber der Umwelt, Zusammenarbeit der Gemeinden sowie Alkohol, seine Bewußtmachung und Aufklärung, geht. Als größte Brauerei der Welt setzt sich Anheuser-Busch sehr dafür ein, Erwachsene zu einem verantwortungsvollen Umgang mit Alkohol zu bewegen und Alkoholmißbrauch, Alkohol hinter dem Steuer sowie Alkoholgenuß bei Minderjährigen zu bekämpfen.

Die deutsch-amerikanische Vorliebe für geselliges Zusammensein findet in den Anheuser-Busch-Vergnügungsparks seinen Ausdruck. Zu ihnen gehören Busch Gardens Tampa Bay, Busch Gardens Williamsburg sowie vier Sea World Parks in Orlando, San Diego, San Antonio und Aurora, Ohio. Mehr als 20 Millionen Gäste besuchen alljährlich diese firmeneigenen neun Vergnügungsparks. Getreu der bayrischen Herkunft befindet sich in den Busch Garden Parks "Das Festhaus", ein deutsches Festzelt, wo eine Blaskapelle und Volkstanzgruppen die Gäste in einer festlichen Atmosphäre begrüßen. Für ganz Mutige bieten die Gardens einige der wildesten Achterbahnen der Welt, die solche Namen tragen wie "Drachenfeuer", "Lochness Monster" und "Kumba".

Anheuser-Busch ist führend in der Welt des Sport-Marketing. Das Unternehmen gehörte zu den lediglich zehn offiziellen Centennial Olympic Games Partner der Olympischen Sommerspiele 1996 in Atlanta. Budweiser ist der offizielle Sponsor der nationalen und olympischen Damen- und Herren-Fußballmannschaft der USA, der Major League Soccer und des World Cup 1998 in Frankreich.

Im Gegensatz zu seinen bescheidenen Anfängen erschließt Anheuser-Busch heute aggressiv den globalen Markt in Hinblick auf Wachstum und ist von China bis Argentinien, von Irland bis

This Bud's for you!

Japan und in mehr als 80 Ländern dazwischen vertreten. Während Anheuser-Busch im eigenen Land wächst und weltweit expandiert, bestimmt das Credo des Unternehmens weiterhin das Verhalten. "Freunde Machen ist Unser Geschäft" liegt Anheuser Busch beim Brauen, Vertrieb und der Unterhaltung für die ganze Familie auch weiterhin am Herzen.

G & W Bavarian Style Meat and Sausage Company

Native Bavarian brothers Helmut and Henry Wanninger started the business 30 years ago. Today, sons Bob and Gerhard with Katy Wanninger own and operate the wholesale and retail market where German is the favorite language and that heritage can be tasted. 30 kinds of sausages are made on premises, all fresh and delicious.

Prime meat specialties have customers coming from miles away. G & W also carries packaged German imported food items, breads and a wide selection of cheeses.

You will like it ☺

Gebrüder Helmut und Henry Wanninger aus dem schönen Bayern begannen die Fleischerei vor 30 Jahren. Heute sind es die Söhne Bob und Gerhard mit Katy, die das Geschäft übernommen haben, und auch jetzt noch Gro-ßund Eizelhandel betreiben, viel in gutem Deutsch, man kann es beinahe schmecken. Dreizig Wurstsorten werden im Haus selbst gemacht, sie sind immer frisch und köstlich. Fleischspezialitäten bringen Kunden von nah und fern. Und es gibt bei G & W auch vieles Eingeführtes, wie Konserven, Schokoladen und Süßigkeiten, usw. Auch manche Sorten Brot und eine Menge Käsearten sind erhältlich. Rufen Sie an unter 314 / 352-5066 oder kommen Sie nach 4828 Parker Avenue, St. Louis, Missouri 63116. Sie werden es nicht bereuen.

4828 Parker Avenue • St. Louis, MO 63116
(314) 352-5066

wGNU 920 Khz / 24 Hrs.

The oldest German Radio Program in St. Louis, one of the first in the U.S. broadcasted in 1949 with host Eugen Geissler on station KSTL690.

Name of the show and all rights were brought by Goerlichs Delikatessen in 1971 and the program was continued until today under the name "Deutsche Schlagerparade."

You can tune in to the "Deutsche Schlagerparade" every Sunday on WGNU920AM and listen to musical greetings, popular older and modern music and songs, news from the old country and updates from St. Louis and its area.

Since 1965, Mr. & Mrs. Alfred Goerlich have also operated the leading German Delikatessen Store with delicious food specialties and beverages as well as gift items from Germany, Austria and Switzerland.

The community is grateful to Mr. & Mrs. Alfred Goerlich in St. Louis for their support of the German heritage in this region.

Das älteste deutsche Radioprogramm in St. Louis ist auch eines der ältesten deutschen Radio Programme in Amerika. Es war die "Original deutsche Stunde" auf KSTL 690AM seit 1949 damals von Eugen Geissler gerbacht.

Der Name und alle Rechte des Programms wurden von Goerlichs Delikatessen in 1971 aufgekauft, und seitdem gibt es die "Deutsche Schlagerparade" - bis zum heutigen Tage.

Die Deutsche Schlagerparade hören Sie jeden Sonntag auf WGNU 920 AM mit vielen musikalischen Grüßen und den beliebten älterer und neuen Liedern. Außerdem hören Sie Nachrichten aus der alten Heimat und Kurznachrichten von St. Louis und Umgebung.

Herr und Frau Alfred Goerlich führten das deutsche Delikatessen-Geschäft mit Speisen und Getränken, sowie Geschenke aus Deutschland, Österreich und der Schweiz. Damit haben Herr und Frau Goerlich in St. Louis und Umgebung dem Deutschtum sehr geholfen.

275 Union Blvd. • St. Louis, MO 63108
(314) 454-6660 • (618) 451-9950

Mrs. Anita Fink

Autohaus of Clayton

Mr. and Mrs. Willi (Anita) Fink came to America in 1957 from Hamburg, Germany. For three and one-half years, Mr. Fink was employed by a company. In 1961, he opened his own business — a foreign car repair shop. In 1964, Mr. Fink became a Porsche dealer and by 1967 included BMWs at his Webster Groves, MO, store. By 1975, the business had grown so large that it outgrew its Webster Groves location and moved to Sunset Hills. Three years later, the Autohaus as it was called then and continues to be called now, once again outgrew its space and moved to its present location in Clayton, MO. Thus, the Autohaus became known as the Autohaus of Clayton. Mrs. Anita Fink, currently president and owner of the company, took over for her husband when he became ill. Mr. Willi Fink, the founder of the company, died in 1981 of cancer at only 50 years of age. Without any interruption to the BMW dealership, Anita and her daughters continue to run the business. Autohaus of Clayton is the oldest and only exclusive BMW dealer in the State of Missouri and surrounding area. The business continues to grow and prosper and has won several BMW Factory President's Awards.

Autohaus of Clayton

Autohaus von Clayton

Willi und Anita Fink kamen 1957 aus Hamburg in die Staaten. Für 3-1/2 Jahre war Herr Fink bei einer Autofirma beschäftigt. 1961 eröffnete er sein eigenes Geschäft für importierte Autos. 1964 wurde Herr Fink ein Porsche Händler und 1967 auch BMW Vertreter in Webster Groves, MO. Das Geschäft wuchs so sehr, daß die Firma sich 1975 vergößerte und von Webster Grove nach Sunset Hills umsiedelte.

Drei Jahre später war das "Autohaus", wie es damals und auch heute noch genannt wird, wieder aus seinem Rahmen gewachsen, und zog in die neuen Rümlichkeiten nach Clayton, MO um. So wurde es das "Autohaus of Clayton". Frau Anita Fink, heutige Presidentin und Eigentümer, übernahm das Geschäft von ihrem Mann, als er krank wurde. Herr Willi Fink, Gründer der Firma starb 1981 an Krebs im jungen Alter von 50 Jahren.

Ohne Unterbrechung der BMW Händlerschaft, haben Frau Anita und ihre Töchter das Geschäft weitergeführt. "Autohaus of Clayton" ist der älteste und einzig exclusive BMW Händler im Staate Missouri und Umgebung. Das Geschäft wächst weiter und hat über die Jahre mehrere von BMW Präsidenten gestiftete Fabrikpreise gewonnen.

Autohaus of Clayton • 8455 Maryland Ave. • 2 Blocks East of I-170 on Ladue Road • 314 / 727-8870

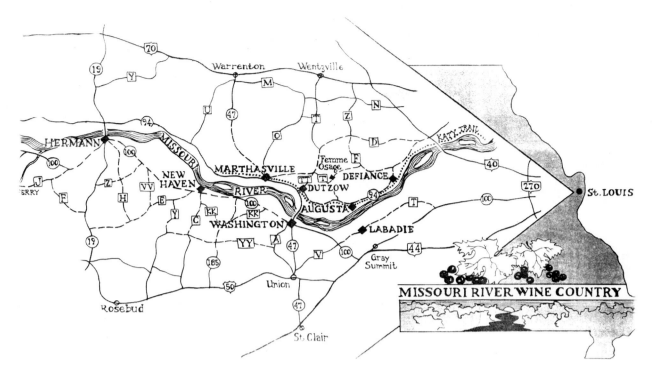

A Celebration in St. Louis

On the official day, October 6,1990, three days after the "Day of German Unity", the German-American Committee of St. Louis celebrated in the large hall of the Kulturverein the German-American Day 1990. More than 400, mostly German guests, came to this sold out hall, beautifully decorated with flowers, flags and garlands.

The President of the "German-American Committee", Josef J. Hammes, greeted the German-American organizations and guests. In his remarks he pointed proudly to the many letters of congratulations by President George Bush, from Governor of Missouri John Ashcroft, from the Mayor of St. Louis Vincent Schoemehl, Jr. and from Germany Consul General Günter Wasserberg.

Highpoint of this festive evening was the colorful speech by Consul General Wasserberg and the following presentation of the "Order of Merit" to Mr. Hammes for the efforts in bringing and keeping together the local German Clubs, and for the promotion of understanding between Germany and the United States. The award was given on behalf of Richard von Weizsäcker, President of the Federal Republic of Germany.

Moved by the event, Josef J. Hammes gratefully acknowledged the high award and humbly pointed out in his special way, that he was not alone and had a lot of help from members of the German Clubs, supporting and promoting the German heritage and unity.

Eine Feier in St. Louis

Am offiziellen Datum, dem 6. Oktober, drei Tage nach dem "Tag der deutschen Einheit", veranstaltete das "German/American Committee of St. Louis" im großen Veranstaltungssaal des Deutschen Kulturvereins feierlich den Deutsch-Amerikanischen Tag 1990. Über 400, größtenteils deutschstämmige Gäste, kamen in den mit Blumen, Fahnen und Wandgirlanden festlich geschmückten, ausverkauften Saal.

Der Präsident des "German/American Committee", Josef J. Hammes, gegrüßte die deutsch-amerikanischen Organisationen und alle Gäste herzlich. In seiner Ansprache verwies er mit Stolz auf die zu diesem besonderen Tag eingetroffenen Glückwunschschreiben von Präsident George Bush, vom Gouverneur des Staates Missouri, John Ashcroft, vom Bürgermeister von St. Louis, Vincent Schoemehl Jr., und von Generalkonsul Günter Wasserberg.

Höhepunkt des festlichen Abends war die launige Ansprache von Generalkonsul Günter Wasserberg mit der anschließenden Überreichung des Bundesverdienstkreuzes an Herrn Hammes, das dieser wegen seiner Verdienste um den Zusammenhalt der örtlichen Vereinigungen und um die deutsch-amerikanische Verständigung von Bundespräsident Richard von Weizsäcker verliehen bekam.

In bewegten Worten dankte Josef J. Hammes für diese besondere Auszeichnung und meinte bescheiden wie es seine Art ist, daß nicht nur er allein sich jahrelang für diese Zusammenarbeit eingesetzt hätte, sondern auch viele Mitglieder der deutschen Vereine mithalfen, daß das deutsche Brauchtum und der Zusammenhalt erhalten geblieben ist.

Consul General Günter Wasserberg and President of the German-American Committee Josef J. Hammes at German American Day 1990.

Stone Hill Cellars

Main Hous

Stone Hill Winery *Missouri's Most Popular Winery Destination*

Nestled among the rolling hillsides of the Missouri River, in a countryside reminiscent of Germany's Rhine Valley, is the little town of Hermann. Perched prominently on one of these hills, with a commanding view of the village, is Stone Hill Winery.

Established in 1847, Stone Hill grew to be the third largest winery in the world and second largest in the United States. The wines were world- renown, winning gold medals in eight world fairs, including Vienna in 1873 and Philadelphia in 1876. By the turn of the century, the winery was shipping 1,250, 000 gallons of wine per year.

Unfortunately, the advent of Prohibition in 1920 killed the wine industry in Missouri, and the winery's spectacular arched, underground cellars (the largest series of vaulted cellars in America) were used to grow mushrooms.

In 1965, Jim and Betty Held, with their four small children bought the winery and began the long process of restoring its picturesque buildings and vaulted underground cellars, which had fallen into disrepair after Prohibition. Today, Stone Hill is Missouri's largest and most awarded winery. In 1995

Award winners.

Stone Hill produced 150,000 gallons of wine, using state of the art equipment and the latest technology.

Three of the Held's four children hold a degree in enology and viticulture, and along with the winemaker David Johnson, they produce wines that are receiving international acclaim, winning 138 awards in 1993 and 181 medals in 1994 - making Stone Hill the third most awarded winery in the country for two consecutive years! Stone Hill achieved national prominence when it was named Missouri's Small Business of the Year in 1982, featured on the Today Show in 1994 and in Nations Business Weekly in 1995. For the Held's this recognition had been gratifying, but only incidental to their primary task: producing and marketing the finest wines that can be made and putting Hermann back on the map as a world-class wine producing area.

Bon Appetite!

Stone Hill Winery
Rt. 1, Box 26
Hermann, MO 65041

800-909-9463

Jim and Betty Hel

Die Winzerei Stone Hill

Missouris beliebtester Ausflugsort unter den Winzereien

Die kleine Stadt Hermann schmiegt sich an die sanften Hügel des Missouri-Tals, einer Landschaft, die an das deutsche Rheintal erinnert. Auf einem dieser Hügel befindet sich an bevorzugter Stelle, von der man das Dorf voll im Blickfeld hat, die Winzerei Stone Hill.

Gegründet im Jahre 1847, entwickelte sich Stone Hill zur drittgrößten Winzerei der Welt und zur zweitgrößten in den Vereinigten Staaten. Die Weine hatten Weltgeltung, wurden auf acht weltweit beschickten Fachmessen, einschließlich Wien im Jahre 1873 und Philadelphia im Jahre 1876, mit Goldmedaillen ausgezeichnet. Um die Jahrhundertwende hat die Winzerei pro Jahr nahezu 4,8 Mill. Liter Wein versandt.

Leider hat die im Jahre 1920 eingeführte Prohibition die Weinindustrie in Missouri vernichtet, und die spektakulären, unterirdischen Kellergewölbe (die größten zusammenhängenden Kellergewölbe in Amerika) wurden zur Pilzzucht verwendet.

Im Jahre 1965 haben Jim und Betty Held mit ihren vier kleinen Kindern die Winzerei gekauft und mit dem langwierigen Unterfangen begonnen, die malerischen Gebäude und die unterirdischen Kellergewölbe, die nach der Prohibition verfallen waren, zu restaurieren. Heute ist Stone Hill Missouris größte, mit den meisten Auszeichnungen versehene, Winzerei. Im Jahre 1995 hat Stone Hill mit dem neuesten Stand der Technik entsprechender

Ausstattung und der modernsten Technologie nahezu 570.000 l Wein produziert.

Drei der vier Held-Kinder haben ein Diplom in Önologie und Weinbaukunde. Zusammen mit dem Winzer David Johnson produzieren sie Weine, die sich internationalen Ansehens erfreuen und die im Jahre 1993 138 Auszeichnungen und im Jahre 1994 181 Medaillen erhielten - wodurch Stone Hill in zwei aufeinanderfolgenden Jahren zur Winzerei mit den drittmeisten Auszeichnungen in Amerika wurde. Stone Hill hat durch seine Ernennung zu „Missouri's Small Business of the Year" (Missouris Kleinbetrieb des Jahres) im Jahre 1982, der Vorstellung in der *Today Show* im Jahre 1994 und im Magazin *Nations Business Weekly* im Jahre 1995 einen nationalen Bekanntheitsgrad erlangt. Für die Familie Held war diese Anerkennung befriedigend, jedoch was ihr Hauptziel anbelangte, allerdings nur nebensächlich: Produktion und Vermarktung des bestmöglichen Weins, wodurch Hermann wieder einen Platz auf der Landkarte als Produzent von Spitzenweinen einnehmen würde.

Wenn Sie weitere Auskünfte wünschen, rufen Sie bitte folgende Telefonnummer an:
Stone Hill Winery
Rt. 1, Box 26
Hermann, MO 65041
1-800-909-9463

Deutschheim, Hermann, Missouri

Dr. Erin Renn,
Curator

Pommer-Gentner House

Strehly House & Winery

Pommer-Gentner House
108 Market Street

This is the finest remaining 1840 German Neoclassical (Klassizismus) house standing in the Midwest.

1820s-1840s Fine Biedermeier Furniture

Chinese and German Porcelains

1830s Kitchen Garden with unusual and rare heritage vegetables and flowers, woven fencing, and straw beehives

Temporary and Traveling Exhibits in the Gallery

Strehly House & Winery
130 West Second Street

Two outstanding examples of German Vernacular architecture, once common and now found only in a few places in the United States, built from 1842 to 1869. Half timbered, stone, and brick.

Winery:
- Last Surviving Carved Wine Cask, signed and dated 1875
- 19th Century German Peasant Arts and Crafts
- Wedding Customs and Other Folkways

House:
- 1860s-1880s Furnishings
- Colors throughout
- Authentic German interior

Garden:
- 1850s Wine Grapes, still bearing
- 1880s Flower Garden, with rare roses and other heritage plants
- Extensive Herb Garden

Hecker Troop on their departure to Amerika, Spring 1992

On Liberty's Trail
German Group retraces Friedrich Hecker's life in America

Who is Friedrich Hecker ?
Friedrich Hecker was one of the most prominent figures of the 1848 democratic movement in Germany and for a long time after that continued to be a symbol for the struggle for freedom on both sides of the Atlantic Ocean. He was born in 1811 in Eichtersheim, Baden (southwest region of Germany), studied law and history and established himself as a lawyer. A liberal deputy of the 2nd "Badische Kammer" (regional parliament) since 1842, he became famous throughout Germany as a fighter for the Republic.

When, in 1848, the first democratic German parliament ("Vorparlament") came together in Frankfurt to discuss events in revolutionary Germany, Hecker and other radical democrats demanded that the Republic be proclaimed. However this was declined. Back home in Baden, Hecker then instigated an armed rebellion to enforce his policy. Starting from Constance, he set out towards Karlsruhe with about 5,000 men and, having advanced only as far as the Black Forest, was defeated by troops under Prussian command.

Hecker in North America
To escape political persecution, Hecker fled to the United States via Switzerland in October 1848. Upon his arrival in New York, Hecker

was given an enthusiastic reception by thousands of people. In other cities, the fighter for freedom was appropriately honored with torch-light processions and banquets. Hecker even inspired a full-fledged "Hecker-cult", which included imitating his beard, his dress and his "Hecker-Hat". In the American Midwest, near Belleville, Illinois, he settled down as a cattle-breeder and vineyard owner. Because of his education, like some of his neighbors, he was nicknamed "latin farmer". Hecker continued to take part in the affairs of public life in North America. For instance, he was one of the founding members of one of the first "Turnvereine" (athletic clubs) and was an active member of the Republican Party. Like many of his former comrades-in-arms from the 1848 revolution (who were called "forty-eighters" in North America), he actively supported the Union during the Civil War and the abolition of slavery. Although F. Hecker was wounded at the battle of Chancellorsville, he continued to give political speeches after the war. He died in St. Louis in 1881.

A monument of Friedrich Hecker stands in St. Louis, MO. Descendants of Friedrich Hecker still live in St. Louis and George Hecker, a prominent lawyer, has been serving for several years as Chairman of the German American Heritage Society of St. Louis.

Back in Singen, Germany, a group of German citizens formed the "Hecker Troop" which in Spring 1992 retraced Friedrich Hecker's trail in America. Their trip took them to Washington, Chicago and St. Louis where they met with George Hecker. In Chicago they were hosted by the German American National Congress and visited historic sites.

Auf dem Weg der Freiheit

Photo: Ernst Ott, DANK

George Hecker, right, with General Ronald Fogleman.

Wer war Friedrich Hecker?

Friedrich Hecker war eine der bekanntesten Gestalten der demokratischen Bewegung 1848 in Deutschland und noch lange danach auf beiden Seiten des Atlantiks ein Symbol für das Streben nach Freiheit. Er wurde 1811 in Eichtersheim, Baden geboren, studierte Jura und Geschichte und ließ sich als Rechtsanwalt nieder. Als liberaler Abgeordneter der 2. Badischen Kammer (seit 1842) machte er sich bereits in ganz Deutschland einen Namen als Verfechter für die Republik.

Nachdem 1848 in Frankfurt in der St. Pauls Kirche das "Vorparlament" zusammengetreten war um über das Schicksal des revolutionären Deutschland zu beraten, verlangten Hecker und andere radikale Demokraten die Ausrufung der Republik. Dies wurde jedoch abgelehnt und Hecker begann im heimatlichen Baden einen bewaffneten Aufstand zur Durchsetzung seiner Ziele. Von Konstanz aus zog er mit etwa 5,000 Leuten Richtung Karlsruhe, wurde aber schon im Schwarzwald von Truppen unter preußischer Führung geschlagen.

Hecker in den Vereinigten Staaten

Daraufhin emigrierte Hecker über die Schweiz im Oktober 1848 in die USA. Bei seiner Ankunft in New York wurde er von Zehntausenden begeistert empfangen. Auch in anderen Städten des Landes feierte man den Vorkämpfer der Freiheit mit Fackelzügen und Banketten. Es entwickelte sich ein richtiger "Hecker-Kult", sein Bart und seine Kleidung ('Hecker-Hut') wurden nachgeahmt. Im amerikanischen Mittelwesten, in

der Nähe von Belleville, Illinois, bewirtschaftete Hecker als Viehzüchter und Weinbauer eine Farm; aufgrund seiner Bildung wurde er wie einige seiner deutschen Nachbarn als "Latin Farmer" bezeichnet.

Hecker nahm auch in den USA am öffentlichen Leben teil. So war er an der Gründung einer der ersten Turnvereine in Amerika beteiligt; vor allem wirkte er auch in der Republikanischen Partei mit. Wie viele seiner ehemaligen deutschen Mitkämpfer (z.B. Carl Schurz) aus der 1848er Revolution, in den USA "Forty-eighters" genannt, trat er im Bürgerkrieg aktiv für die Union und die Abschaffung der Sklaverei ein. In der Schlacht bei Chancellorsville wurde Hecker verwundet. Nach dem Krieg hielt er weiterhin politische Vorträge. Friedrich Hecker starb 1881 in St. Louis.

Ein Denkmal Friedrich Heckers steht in St. Louis, Missouri. Nachkommen Heckers leben heute noch in St. Louis, und George Hecker, ein prominenter Rechtsanwalt war mehrere Jahre Präsident der German American Heritage Society of St. Louis.

In dem Städtchen Singen bei Schaffhausen bildete eine Gruppe die "Hecker Truppe", die im Frühjahr 1992 Heckers Spuren in Amerika folgte. Die Reise führte sie nach Washington D.C., Chicago und St. Louis, wo sie sich mit George Hecker trafen. In Chicago waren sie Gäste des German American National Congress und besuchten historische Stätten.

Wegbereiter Der Freien Lande

Schon hundert Jahr und vier Dekaden
Seit demokratischer Aktion.
Karl Friedrich Hecker und Kam'raden,
Sie kämpften für des Volkes Lohn.

Sie kämpften für die Wahlregierung,
Verdammten Königsmacht und Thron.
Sie wollten Parlamentsregierung,
Nicht Herrschermacht dem Volk zum Hohn.

Neunzehnt' Jahrhundert achtundvierzig,
Demokratie war Wunsch und Ziel.
Die Kirche Pauls bestimmt besinnt sich,
Die Neuverfassung blieb ein Spiel.

Schurz, Sigel, Hecker und Mitstreiter
Entkamen Preußen nur mit Not.
Amerika war Wegbegleiter
Für neue Freiheit und für Brot.

Als gleichgesinnte Freiheitskämpfer
Abe Lincoln wählten sie zum Held.
Das Sklaventum ward Freiheits Dämpfer,
Der Bruderkrieg war nicht bestellt.

Zweihundertzwansigtausend Schützen,
Rekruten bis zum General,
Nordstaaten Regimenter Mützen,
Die Deutschen hatten keine Wahl.

F. Hecker dient als Kommandeur,
Südstaaten soll er mürbe schlagen.
Bei Chancellorsville trifft ihn Malheur,
wird rasch vom Felde fortgetragen.

Am Grab' von Hecker sollt ihr schreiben:
"Wer hier ruht, oh vergeßt es nie.
Amerika soll frei uns bleiben -
und Deutschland, durch Demokratie".

Eberhard W. Gress
Sarasota, Florida

River Boat on the Mississippi

St. Louis Arch - Gateway to the West

Missouri River Boat, 1870, Hermann, MO

Maritime Museum, 1871, was then
German School in Hermann, MO

Charles D. Eitzen, Benefactor

Starkenburg Church has many German Caves

Views of St. Louis and Hermann, Missouri, September 1994

Hermann Homes

Deutschleim's Beehives still busy and buzzing

The Strehly House, an Historical Landmark
and Museum

Quilt Made by Hermann Women

Hermann Mansion

Author and Photographer Bert Lachner on the
Katy Trail

Florida Journal is the award winning German language magazine about Florida.

Manfred Behr
Publisher

Florida Journal ist die einzige preisgekrönte deutschsprachige Florida Zeitschrift.

Florida Journal was founded in 1993 in Fort Myers, Florida by the Behr family and has been growing tremendously ever since. The Publisher, Manfred Behr says that "The interest for instance in Southwest Florida alone is just incredible, from a mere 22,000 German visitors in 1988 to over 200,000 in 1996." That is a lot of people that need to have literature in their own language. So what makes Florida Journal so successful? "We are always looking for ways to serve Florida's German visitors better. Our content ranges from exciting travel features to in-depth real estate, immigration and investment law articles".

In February of 1997, FLORIDA JOURNAL received the "gold addy" for best illustrations from the Southwest Florida Advertising Federation.

Florida Journal is published quarterly (January, April, July and October) and has a distribution of 45,000 per quarter, 180,000 annually. What makes the distribution so unique is that it is available on the newsstands at airport, train stations, and bookstores in Germany, Austria and Switzerland. Florida Journal is also on LTU Airline flights from Germany to Florida and free of charge at over 500 locations within Florida.

Please call us for subscription or advertising information:

Für alle Florida-Freunde (und solche, die es werden wollen) gibt es nur eins: das FLORIDA JOURNAL. Das durchgehend farbig aufgemachte Magazin unterhält seine Leserinnen und Leser mit Reiseberichten, Reportagen, Immobilien-und Rechtsartikeln sowie aktuellen Trends.
Gegründet im Jahre 1993 in Ft. Myers von Familie Behr, ist die Auflage ständig gewachsen. "1988 zählte man 22.000 deutsche Besucher, im Jahre 1996 waren es bereits mehr als 200.000", berichtet Herausgeber Manfred Behr. "Die Zahl bestätigt uns, daß es genau der richtige Zeitpunkt war, ein deutschsprachiges Magazin für das deutsche Publikum auf den Markt zu bringen.

Im February 1997 verlieh uns die Southwest Florida Advertising Federation den "Gold Addy" für beste Gestaltung".

FLORIDA JOURNAL erscheint vierteljährlich (Januar, April, Juli, Oktober) mit einer Auflage von 45.000 Exemplaren pro Quartal, 180.000 Hefte pro Jahr. Auch in Sachen Vertrieb sind wir führend. Unser Magazin erhalten Sie in Deutschland, Österreich und der Schweiz auf jedem Flughafen und Bahnhof sowie im ausgewählten Zeitschriftenhandel. Außerdem haben wir das Exklusiv-Recht an Bord der LTU auf jedem Flug von Deutschland nach Florida. Im Sunshine State selbst, bekommen Sie das Heft an über 500 verschiedenen Stellen.

Bitte rufen Sie uns an für Abonnement oder Anzeigen:

6238 Presidential Court, Suite 6, Fort Myers, FL 33919
Tel: (941) 481-7511 or Fax: (941) 481-7753
E mail:behr@floridajournal.com • http://www.floridajournal.com

Subscription price is $6.75 within the Continental USA, foreign subscriptions are $29.50 (DM49,-)
Jahresabonnement $6.75 in den USA, außerhalb den USA $29.50 (DM 49,-)

Die Vereinte Deutsch-Amerikanische Gesellschaft von Florida

See more of Disney World's Epcot on page 219

German American Society, Central Florida, Casselberry

German American Society, Pinellas Park

All location photos by Bert Lachner

German American Social Club of Cape Coral

Im May 1990 hatte John Lange, Präsident vom Amerikanisch-Deutschen Verein von Palm Beach, alle Deutschen Vereine in Florida benachrichtigt mit dem Vorschlag eine Vereinigung zu gründen. Der Vorschlag wurde von 10 Vereinen angenommen, und während der Versammlung entschied man sich auf den Namen "Vereinigte Deutsch-Amerikanische Society of Florida", die dann auch gesetzmäßig am 30 August, 1991 eingetragen wurde.

Innerhalb von 2 Jahren kamen 17 neue Anträge und die Vereinigung vergrößerte sich auf 27 Vereine. Einer der ersten Vorschläge, der einstimmig angenommen wurde, war einen jährlichen Deutschen Kulturtag zu veranstalten, der letzteich am 9. März, 1997 im Coliseum von St. Petersburg abgehalten wurde.

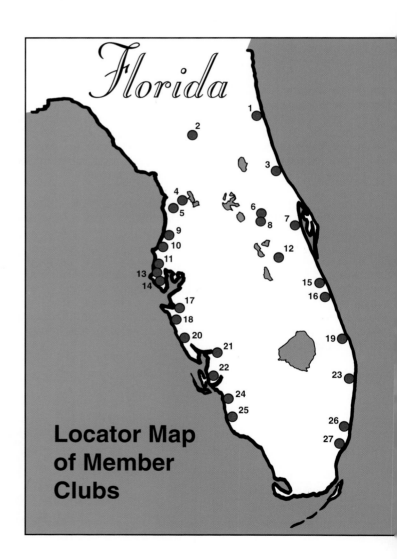

Florida

Locator Map of Member Clubs

United German-American Society of Florida

In May of 1990, John Lange, then President of the American-German Club of the Palm Beaches, contacted members of all German American Clubs of Florida. The intent was to suggest a unification of all clubs under one charter.

The offer and suggestions was accepted by 10 clubs and the new organization chose the name "United German-American Societies of Florida," and was incorporated as such on August 30, 1991.

Within two years, the United German-American Society of Florida added 17 more clubs representing a total of 27 German American Clubs throughout the State of Florida.

One of the first resolutions passed by the new organization was to hold a "German Heritage Day" and the latest was held on March 9, 1997 in the St. Petersburg Coliseum.

1. German American Club of St. Augustine, Inc.
2. German American Society of Gainsville
3. German American Society , Daytona Beach
4. German American Club of West Central Florida, Beverly Hills
5. Steuben Society of America Karl Schumacher Unit # 55
6. German American Society, Central Florida, Casselberry
7. German American Social Club, Brevard
8. Greater Beneficial Union GBU of Pittsburgh
9. German American Club, Spring Hill
10. German American Club, New Port Richey
11. Gulf Coast Enzianer Schuhplattler, Dunedin
12. Osceola German American Club
13. Steuben Society of America, John Ringling   Unit # 813
14. German American Society, Pinellas Park
15. German American Club, Barefoot Bay
16. German American Club, Vero Beach
17. German American Club of Manatee County
18. German American Social Club of Sarasota
19. German American Club of the Treasure Coast, Port St. Lucie
20. German American Friendship Club of Venice
21. German American Club, Charlotte County
22. German American Social Club of Cape Coral
23. American German Club of the Palm Beaches, Lantana
24. German American Club, Bonita Springs
25. German American Club "Harmonie", Naples
26. German American Society, Greater Hollywood
27. German American Society, Greater Miami

**Presidents of the
United German American Society of Florida**

1990 to 1991   John Lange (absent)
1991 to 1993   Klaus Kohl   (left)
1993 to 1995   Hannelore Crothers (middle)
1995 to 1997   Fritz Eggerts (right)

American German Club of the Palm Beaches, Lantana

German American Society, Greater Hollywood

German American Society, Greater Miami

German American Society
Daytona Beach, Florida

Joe Binder, Sigart Eisermann, Fritz Eggerts

The German-American Society of Daytona Beach, established in 1969 for the purpose to preserve and further develop German customs and traditions, plans, organizes and holds social functions and recreational activities, and takes part in programs of the United German-American Society of Florida.

Der Deutsch-Amerikanische Verein von Daytona Beach wurde 1969 gegründet, um deutsche Gebräuche und Kultur zu erhalten und zu fördern. Dazu veranstaltet der Verein eine Reihe von gesellschaftlichen und unterhaltsamen Festlichkeiten. Man nimmt auch Teil an den Programmen der "United German-American Societies of Florida".

Das Bild zeigt die Übergabe des neuen Vereinsbanners, ein Geschenk vo. Mitgliedern zum 25th Jubiläum, übergeben von den Hauptsponsoren (v.l. Joe Binder und Sigart Eisermann an den derzeitigen Präsidenten Fritz Eggerts.

In the picture we whitness the presentation of the new Club Banner, a present from members for the 25th Anniversary, presented by the organizers (f.l.) Joe Binder and Sigart Eisermann to the then presiding President Fritz Eggerts.

German American Society of Daytona Beach, Inc. • P.O. Box 5194, Ormond Beach, FL 32175

German-American Club of the Treasure Coast
Founded in 1973 - Our 25th Anniversary 1998

We are active from September through May with

- Fasching Ball
- Anniversary Party
- Bock Bier Fest
- Oktoberfest
- Schlachtfest
- German Christmas Party
- And functions of the United German-American Society of Florida

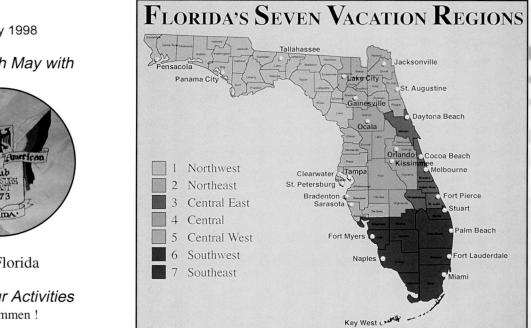

FLORIDA'S SEVEN VACATION REGIONS

1	Northwest
2	Northeast
3	Central East
4	Central
5	Central West
6	Southwest
7	Southeast

Everyone is Invited to Participate in our Activities
Sie sind alle herzlich eingeladen und willkommen !

German American Club of the Treasure Coast
P.O. Box 8076, Port St. Lucie, FL 34985
President: Werner Sorsch

Unser Haus in Lantana

The American-German Club of the Palm Beaches *Welcomes You*

Der "American-German Club" wurde gebaut um, bei gutem Essen und Trinken, beim Tanz oder einem Glas Bier, die bayerischen Gebräuche und deutsche Gemütlichkeit zu pflegen. Überzeugen Sie sich miteinem Besuch in unserem Haus, Sie werden es nicht bereuen.

Auch Sie können unser Haus für Ihre Ereignisse benutzen, ob Hochzeit, ein Jubiläum oder ein Empfang, unser "Haus" - der American-German Club - bietet komfortablen Raum für jede Gelegenheit, drinnen im bayerischen Stil, in der gemütlichen Stube oder auf dem großen Saal, oder auf dem Picknick Gelände unter schattigen Bäumen.

Der "American-German Club" ist bekannt durch gutes Essen, Tanz, Unterhaltung und Gemütlichkeit.

Ob große Festlichkeiten oder kleine Gruppen - Sie werden alle die Athmosphäre genießen, der Festsaal hat eine Kapazität bis zu 500 Personen.

When the American-German Club was built, the intent was to create an authentic hall, where people could eat, drink, dance and continue the customs of Old Bavaria - and invite the public to do likewise. We invite you to call and make arrangements to hold your event like weddings, anniversaries and other receptions at our "Haus".

Our "Haus" - the American - German Club - offers a beautiful setting, the finest facilities, and spacious picnic grounds to help make your event a success!

The reputation of the American-German Club for providing excellent food, drink, dancing, and socializing is unquestionable.

Whether a small gathering or large group - you will enjoy all our facilities. Our beautiful Banquet Hall accommodates up to 500 people.

American-German Club of the Palm Beaches
5111 Lantana Road
Lake Worth, Florida 33466

Bier Stube

Tanz Saal

Picnic Grounds

Willkommen zum German American Club in Pinellas Park

Welcome!

In der Nachbarschaft von St. Petersburg, FL an der Hauptstraße 66 liegt das Heim der "German American Society, Inc. in Pinellas Park", ein sauberes, schmuckes Klubhaus auf einem Gelände von ca. 1.2 ha. Seit 1951 heißt es im Klubbüchlein, daß Freundschaft, Gemütlichkeit und Unterstützung unserer Nächsten immer ein überragendes Ziel dieser Gesellschaft war.

Als eine seit 1953 eingetragene öffentliche Körperschaft, bietet der Klub wöchentlichen Tanz mit Abendessen, samstags von 20 bis 24 Uhr. Außerdem gibt es verschiedenene, der Zeit entsprechende Anlässe zu feiern, wie den Kaffeeklatsch an jedem 2. Mittwoch, das fröhliche Muttertag Festessen und die schöne Weihnachtsfeier im Dezember. Im Februar macht der Klub "Karneval am Rhein" und beteiligt sich später am internationalen Volksfest. Im September-Oktober ist die ganze Stadt zum Oktoberfest eingeladen.

Auch Sie sind eingeladen. Rufen Sie uns an unter 813 / 541-6782 für weitere Informationen.

German American Club House in Pinellas Park

Near St. Petersburg, FL on Route 66 lies the home of the "German American Society Inc. Of Pinellas Park", a tidy and well maintained clubhouse on a 3 acre site. Since 1951, "friendship, sociability and charitable deeds toward our fellow men were always the paramount objectives of this Society."

A not-for-profit corporation since 1953, the Club offers weekly dinner - dances on Saturdays from 8 to 12 pm, and a number of special events on Sunday afternoons, such as the Cake and Coffee Circle every 2nd Wednesday, and the Mothers Day Banquet and the beautiful Christmas Party. In February, the Club celebrates Mardi Gras "Karneval am Rhein" and participates in March in the International Folkfair and invites the community to their annual Oktober Fest on two weekends in September-October.

You are also invited. Call 813/514-6782 for details.

German American Society, Inc. 8098 66th Street North, Pinellas Park FL 34665

Clubhouse in Miami

Club History

The German American Social Club of Greater Miami, Inc. was established in 1949 by a small group of Germans who were interested in getting together to share German social activities. For many years the meetings and social gatherings took place at various restaurants and ethnical and religious social halls. Outdoor picnics were held monthly at Crandon Park and large auditoriums were rented to sponsor large festive Oktoberfest events. After acquiring a five acre parcel of land on Miller Drive in the early 1970's, the members purchased bonds and supplied mortgage money so that a

The German-American Social Club of Greater Miami, Inc.

Clubhouse could be constructed in 1974 at its present site. Frugal management and hard working volunteer members helped to pay off the sizeable debt incurred as well as maintaining our Clubhouse and grounds today. Through the Club, individuals with varying interests have formed additional activities, including the Original Auerhahn Schuhplattler, the Deutsche Volkstanz Gruppe, the Edelweiss Jungend Schuhplattler, and the new Schützenverein.

Club Activities:

The German American Social Club holds monthly theme dances on Saturday evenings from 6:30 p.m. Sunday Brunches are scheduled on the 1st and 3rd Sunday of each month, from 11:00 to 2:00 the fourth Sunday of the month is the membership Birthday party and afternoon Tea Dance from 2:00 p.m. COME JOINS US!!

The German-American Social Club
11919 S.W. 56 Street (Miller Road)
P. O. Box 650972
Miami, Florida 33156   Phone: (305) 552-5123

Der Deutsche Pavillon im Schaukasten der Welt in Epcot®

Der Deutsche Pavillon im Schaukasten der Welt in Epcot (R) Ein Dorf wie dieses gibt es nirgendwo in Deutschland, ein Kaleidoskop mannigfaltiger Stile, inspiriert von den Dörfern des Rheingebiets, Norddeutschlands und Bayerns, dessen Gebäude uns an Altstädte so unterschiedlich wie Frankfurt, Freiburg und Rothenburg und Stade erinnern; eine Szene voller Charme, mit Zinnen, Balkone und Treppenstufendächern und Arkaden, über den Gehsteigen versetzt, wie in einem Märchenland. Besonders in der lustigen Spätaufführung ist die Stimmung in der Bierhalle am Ende des Dorfes fast so groß wie in den Bierzelten auf dem berühmten Münchner Oktoberfest.

In den Läden verlocken Waren aller Art, von Wein und Süßigkeiten zu Keramik und Kuckucksuhren, sowie Spielzeug, Bücher, und sogar Kunstwaren zum Einkauf. Eine Schilderung der verschiedenen Elemente, die den Deutschland Pavillon ausmachen, erfolgt in West-Ost-Richtung, also gegen den Uhrzeigersinn, rund um den im Zentrum gelegenen kopfsteinbepflasterten Sankt Georgs-Platz, der nach der auf der Platzmitte stehenden Statue benannt wurde. Diese Statue stellt Sankt Georg dar, den Schutzpatron der Soldaten, mit dem Drachen, den er der Legende nach auf einer Pilgerreise in das Heilige Land getötet hatte.

"Wir heißen Sie herzlich im deutschen Pavillon willkommen. Hier können Sie stündlich das Glockenspiel vom Turm beobachten. Auch die

Guests enjoying entertainment at "Germany" Pavilion

Biergarten Musiker werden Sie erfreuen, besonders in den Abendstunden. Bringen Sie Kinder und Freunde zu einem fröhlichen Erlebnis am St. Georgsplatz."

Volkskunst - Shopping

German Pavilion at the World Showcase in Epcot®

There are no villages in Germany quite like this one inspired variously by towns in the Rhine region, Bavaria, and in the German north, it boasts structures reminiscent of those found in urban enclaves as diverse as Frankfurt, Freiburg, and Rothenburg. There are stair-stepped roof lines and towers, balconies and arcaded walkways, and so much overall charm that the scene seems to come straight out of a fairy tale. The beer hall to the rear is almost as lively as the one at Munich's famed Oktoberfest, especially during the later show. The shops, which offer a range of merchandise from wine and sweets to ceramics and cuckoo clocks, toys, and books -and even art- are so tempting that it's hard to leave the area empty-handed. The various elements that constitute the Germany pavilion are described here as they would be encountered walking from west to east (counter-clockwise) around the cobblestone-paved central plaza, which is formally known as the St. Georgsplatz, after the statue found at its center. St. George, the patron saint of soldiers, is depicted with the dragon that legend says he slew during a pilgrimage to the Middle East.

"Let us welcome you at the German Pavilion at World Showcase in Epcot® Hear and see the Glockenspiel at the Tower on the hour, and enjoy the strolling beergarden musicians, especially in the evening hours. Bring children and friends for the time of your life."

St. Georgsplatz at "Germany" Pavilion, Epcot

Photos © DISNEY ENTERPRIZES, INC.

Helen, Georgia

Es war 1968, als ein Geschäftsmann den Künstler John Kollock aus
Clarkesville, GA fragte, ob er eine Idee hätte die Geschäftshäuser in
Helen, GA neu zu gestalten. John Kollock fotografierte die alten
Gebäude in Helen und machte Skizzen und legte schließlich die
"bayerischen" Aquarelle der Dorfvätern vor. Als John nach Helen kam,
um sich die Häuser anzusehen, hatte er schon eine Idee: Er erinnerte
sich an die Zeit in der amerikanischen Armee in Bayern, und wie schön
die Läden und Geschäftshäuser waren in ihrem alpinen Stil, mit viel
Holz gebaut, bunt begemalt mit fröhlichen Bildern der Natur und reich
mit Blumen verziert. Auch die Landschaft hatte viel ähnliches, die
Hügel und Wälder und mit bunten Blumen besähten grünen Flächen,
wo Vieh graste.

Die Begeisterung war groß und der nette Jim Wilkens von der Orbit
Fabrik stellte sein Gebäude als erster zur Verfügung.

Heute ist die ganze Innenstadt renoviert. Das Rathaus wurde saniert und
bietet nun Platz für die Gemeindeverwaltung, Polizei und Feuerwehr,
und ein neues Willkommen Zentrum. Alle Schnitzereien und Fassaden
wurden von zwei Bauherren gemacht: Ray L. Sims und J.S. Chastair
nahmen einfache Skizzen und übertrugen sie in Holz, Stein und Gips.

Alle Kosten der Umbauten ihrer Geschäftshäuser mußten die Besitzer
selbst bezahlen. Die Stadt kommt für die Parkanlagen, Blumenkörbe
und Straßenbeleuchtung auf, so wie es im Bayerischen Tradition ist.
Auch wurden alle Strom- und Telefonleitungen unterirdisch verlegt,
was einen sauberen und ordentlichen Eindruck macht. Viele neue
Arbeitsplätze wurden gewonnen, neue Geschäfte siedelten sich hier
an und der Tourismus blüht.

Durch seinen guten Ruf wird Helen weiter wachsen, aber nie
seinen "bayerisch-amerikanischen" Reiz verlieren.

Helen liegt in the Nordost Ecke von Georgia in den wunderschönen
Blue Ridge Mountains, 30 km westlich von Toccoa (am GA
Highway #23).

Kommen auch Sie und besuchen Sie uns in **Helen, Georgia!**

Today, the whole town is renovated and looks gorgeous. The townhall was rebuilt and now facilitates the Town Council, the Police and Fire Department, and there is a new Welcome Center. All carvings and fascades were made by two contractors: Ray L. Sims and J.S. Chastair, who simply took the sketches and converted them into real wood, stone and stucco. All costs for the renovation of their businesses had to be born by the owners. The City handles the park, roads and flower decorations, as well as the street lighting. Also, all power lines were re-installed, underground. This makes for a clean and tidy appearance of the inner city. Many new work places were created, as new companies moved into the area and tourism started to pick up. Due to its marvelous reputation, Helen will continue to grow, but it will never give up its "Bavarian-American" Charm.

Photo by Bob Rogers

Helen is located in the Northeast corner of Georgia, approx. 20 miles west of Toccoa (on GA Highway 23).

In 1968 Helen businessmen asked the artist John Kollock from Clarkesville, GA if he had any idea how to give the businesses and buildings in Helen a facelift. When John came to Helen, GA to see the buildings, he already knew what he was going to propose. He vividly remembered his time in the Army in Bavaria, and how impressed he was with the alpine style of the buildings there, made of wood and plaster, nicely painted with murals of nature and decorated with flowers everywhere. Even the landscape was similar, the rolling hills, forests and flower covered meadows with roaming cattle.

John Kollock photographed the buildings in Helen and made sketches and then presented the colorful watercolor paintings to the town council. They were well received and when the popular Jim Wilkens led the way with renovations, the project was soon under way.

Come and visit us in Helen, Georgia!

Write us at:
Box 730, Helen, GA 30545 or call 706 / 878-2181

"Das Fenster"

"Das Fenster" is America's oldest and most popular German language magazine providing a wide variety of interesting reading on any number of different subjects. Regular monthly features include Our Health, Garden Friends, Science and Technology and a Culture section. German crossword puzzles are also a popular feature as well as a humor section and the children's page, "Hallo Kinder"! A serialized novel runs on a continuing basis every month and travel articles and short stories appear on a regular basis.

"Das Fenster" actually started in 1904 as "Die Deutsche Hausfrau" and catered to the large population of Germans in America, especially the German housewife. The name was subsequently shortened to "Die Hausfrau" and continued with that name until the early 1990's. The need for another name change became apparent because of a gradual change in the editorial content of the magazine. Over the years the magazine has evolved into a general interest publication, not only focused on the housewife or on the home but also giving both men and women an excellent variety of quality reading material in the German language. Because of this interesting variety, students of the German language find "Das Fenster" an exciting addition to their study programs.

"Das Fenster" is available mainly through subscriptions but a few stores in some of the larger cities do carry it. The number of subscribers is growing with a current total of approximately 18,000 subscribers and a readership of over 70,000. Offices of the publication are located at 1060 Gaines School Rd, Suite B-3, Athens GA 30605 and can be reached by phone at 1-800-398-7753.

"Das Fenster" ist Amerikas älteste und beliebteste Zeitschrift in deutscher Sprache und bietet eine große Auswahl interessanter Artikel, Berichte und Erzählungen. Für die Gartenfreunde und Tierliebhaber sowie Rätselfans gibt es besondere Seiten. Auch an die Kinder wurde gedacht. Man erfährt das Neueste in Wissenschaft und Forschung, über kulturelle Dinge in Europa and USA sowie Interessantes aus aller Welt. Außerdem gibt es Reiseberichte und einen unterhaltsamen Fortsetzungsroman.

"Das Fenster" enstand eigentlich 1904 unter dem Namen "Die Deutsche Hausfrau" als Service für die vielen deutschen Emigranten, besonders die deutschen Hausfrauen. Der Name wurde dann in "Die Hausfrau" abgewandelt. Anfang der neunziger Jahre wurde es eine dringende Notwendigkeit, den Titel noch einmal zu ändern, da der Inhalt der Zeitschrift nicht mehr nur auf Frauen zugeschnitten war. Der interessante Lesestoff ist für Leute jeden Alters, Männer oder Frauen, gleichermaßen geeignet.

Deutschlehrer und Studenten der deutschen Sprache benutzen die Zeitschrift gerne als unterhaltsamen zusätzlichen Lehrstoff.

"Das Fenster" wird hauptsächlich von Abonnenten gelesen; aber einige Geschäfte in Großstädten bieten die Zeitschrift zum Verkauf an. Die Anzahl der Abonnenten steigt; zur Zeit sind es ca. 18,000. Die Zeitschrift wird von über 70.000 Personen gelesen. Herausgegeben wird diese Zeitschrift in Athens Georgia: 1060 Gaines School Rd, Suite B-3, Athens GA 30605. Telefonisch über 1-800-398-7753 zu erreichen.

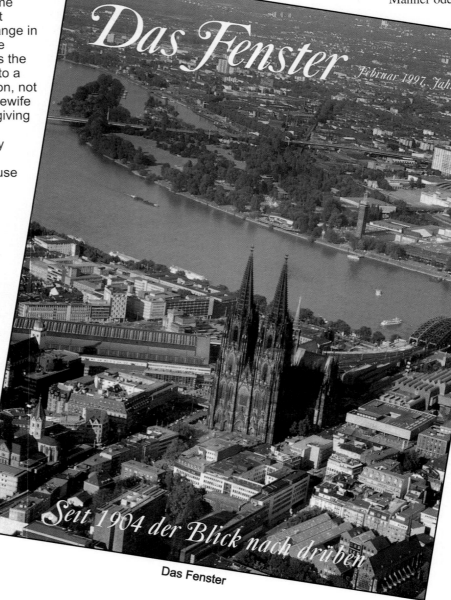

Das Fenster

The Mercedes-Benz Visitors and Training Center (in the forefront) with the M-Class All-Activity Vehicle manufacturing facility pictured in the background. The Visitors Center, which houses entertaining exhibits detailing the history of Mercedes-Benz including its products, technology and commitment to safety.
Photo : MBUSI photo by Barry Fikes

MERCEDES-BENZ

Something Old, Something New

Mercedes-Benz US International at Tuscaloosa, Alabama

The M-Class is destined to create new traditions, because it has firm roots in the old traditions - of quality, performance and durability.

It is being built to the exacting quality standards that have come to define Mercedes-Benz - standards that have become a way of life for Team Members within the Mercedes-Benz M-Class Unit at the Tuscaloosa County, Alabama engineering, marketing and production facility. These standards have also been adopted by the systems suppliers who have become working partners in the development of the M-Class. In addition to engineering and production of the M-Class, the M-Class Unit is tasked with penetrating new market, price and customer segments, while maintaining Daimler-Benz standards and providing a learning field for Mercedes-Benz worldwide.

World-class performance on and off-road is assured with such innovative features as four-wheel Electronic Traction System

(4-ETS); full-time four-wheel drive; high ground clearance; raised passenger seating and substantial towing capability.

And, of course, every component has been designed to exemplify the legendary durability that defines Mercedes-Benz. M-Class owners will appreciate the same level of service as Mercedes-Benz passenger car owners, as the new vehicle will be fully integrated into the current service programs.

So what's the cost of this strict adherence to tradition That's the real beauty of the M-Class. The distinguishing feature of its new tradition will be: value. Through extremely efficient manufacturing processes and strict adherence to value engineering, along with offering a number of accessory items, the M-Class can be offered at competitive pricing and still satisfy the Sport Utility Vehicle owner's need for personalization.

Mercedes-Benz M-Class has plenty of room.

Photo: Mercedes-Benz U.S. International

BMW fertigt Z3 Roadster nur in Amerika

Im Juni 1992 machte man bei BMW die große Entscheidung, die einzige USA Fertigungsstätte auf einer Fläche von 420 ha zwischen den Südkarolina Städten Greenville und Spartanburg zu errichten. Der Bau begann im April 1993 und die ersten in USA gefertigten BMWs wurden schon im März 1995 an Kunden ausgeliefert. Das war ein Meisterstück und die kürzeste Bauperiode für ein Werk bis zur Fertigung in der Geschichte der Automobilindustrie. Heute rollen täglich etwa 255 Wagen vom Band der BMW Manufacturing Corporation.

BMW Manufacturing Corp. Spartanburg, South Carolina

In June of 1992, BMW made a landmark decision to locate its only United States manufacturing facility on a 1,039-acre site, midway between the South Carolina cities of Greenville and Spartanburg. Construction began in April of 1993, and the first American-made BMWs were shipped to customers in March 1995. It marked the fastest construction to production build-up in automobile manufacturing history. Now, more than 255 cars a day are rolling off the production line at BMW Manufacturing Corp., BMW's first full manufacturing facility in the United States.

The South Carolina plant moved to all-roadster production in August 1996 to meet the market demands for the all-new Z3. Built exclusively at the Spartanburg plant, the Z3 is exported to more than 73 countries worldwide.

To date 2,000 associates work at the 1.2 million-square-foot plant, where all the manufacturing functions are housed under one roof. By late 1999, a $200 million expansion will add more than 3.5 million square feet and increase plant capacity form 300 to 400 units a day.

Text and photos BMW Manufacturing Corp.

Line-up of Z3 Roadsters, ready for delivery.

Die Südkarolina Fabrik baut seit August 1996 nur noch Roadsters, weil dieser Typ, Z3, so gefragt ist. Da der Z3 nur in Spartanburg gebaut wird, ist es gleichzeitig ein begehrter Exportartikel, der nach 73 Ländern, weltweit, ausgeführt wird.

Es ist eine Belegschaft von 2,000 in der 120,000 qm großen Fabrikanlage unter einem Dach beschäftigt. Man plant eine $ 200 Millionen Erweiterung bis Ende 1999, die die Ausmaße auf 350,000 qm bringen soll und damit die Fertigungskapazität auf 300 bis 400 Wagen am Tag steigert.

Duke of Gloucester Street
Williamsburg, Virginia
(Virginia Tourism Corporation)

Wild and wonderful waters
West Virginia Mountain Stream
(Photo by Steve Shaluta, Jr., WV Div. Of Tourism)

Washington Harbor in Georgetown
(Washington , DC Convention Assn.)

Community Day, AG. Museum
(Delaware Tourism Office)

Rehoboth Beach Boardwalk
(Delaware Tourism Office)

Colonial Region and U.S. Capital Washington D.C.

White House, South Lawn
(Washington, DC Visitors' Assn.)

U.S. Capitol at dusk
(Washington, DC Visitors' Assn.)

Pride of Baltimore under sail in Annapolis
(Photo: Tom Darden, Maryland, Office of
Tourism Development)

Calvert Marine Museum, Solomons
(Maryland Office of Tourism)

U.S. Naval Academy, Annapolis
(Maryland Office of Tourism)

A.G.A.S.

Vereinigung der deutsch-amerikanischen Gesellschaft im Raume Washington, D.C.

Die Vereinigung der deutsch-amerikanischen Gesellschaft des Raumes Washington, D.C., eine gemeinnützliche Körperschaft, die 1963 gegründet wurde, unterstützt zwei große Feste im Jahr, hilft die deutsche Kultur zu fördern, und ist Schirmherrschaft für viele deutsch- amerikanische Gesellschaftsvereine, historische Kreise und Musik- und Tanzgruppen in der Gegend von Washington.

A.G.A.S. hilft auch Personen und Organisationen passende regionale Kontakte zu finden. A.G.A.S. Mitgliedsvereine bieten eine große Palette von Aktivitäten an, einschließlich gesellschaftliche Tätigkeiten, Lehrprogramme, Tanz- und Musikfestlichkeiten im Umkreis, sowie Ahnenforschung.

United Church (Vereinigte Kirche)

Member Clubs	**Mitgliedsvereine**

1 S.u.G.T.V. Washingtonia (Bavarian folk dance)

2 German Speaking Damen Club (social and cultural)

3 G.T.E.V. Alpenveilchen (Bavarian folk dance)

4 German European American Society (social and cultural)

5 Alpine Dancers (German and Austrian folk dance)

6 Deutscher Klub   (Northern Virginia Community College)

7 German Club of Northern VA Inc.   (social and cultural)

8 Tidewater German-American Society (social and cultural)

9 The Continentals of Washington, D.C. (Polka band)

10 Heidi und Hans Band (musical duo-trio)

11 Blaskapelle "Alte Kameraden" M.V. (brass band)

12 The Edelweiss Band (dance band)

13 The German Heritage Society of Greater Washington, DC (historical research)

14 Mid-Atlantic Germanic Society (genealogical research)

15 Regiment von Donop (18th Century reenactment Hessen Soldiers)

German-American Friendship Garden designed by Wolfgang Oehme

1 and 3 Bayerische Volkstänze

2,4,7,8 Gesellschaft und Kultur Vereine

5 Deutsche und österreicher Volkstänze

6 Hochschule der Gemeinde Virginia Nord

9 to 12 Musik- und Tanz Gruppen

13 Herkunftsforschung

14 Ahnenforschung

15 Kampfspiele der Hessen Soldaten aus dem 18. Jahrhundert

Not shown are: US Capitol Dome was designed by German born Walter U. Thomas, the Library of Congress Building and Healy Building at Georgetown University by German-American Architects John L. Smithmeyer and Paul J. Pelz.

Das alte Steinhaus in Georgetown wurde 1766 von Deutschen gebaut.

rts and Industries Building of the Smithsonian Institution by Adolph Cluss

The Association of German-American Societies of Greater Washington, D.C., a non-profit corporation established in 1963, sponsors two major festivals a year, helps promote Germanic culture, and is the umbrella organization for many metropolitan area German-American social clubs, historical societies and musical / dance groups.

A.G.A.S. also helps individuals and organizations find appropriate regional contact. A.G.A.S. member societies offer a wide range of activities including social functions, educational programs, area dance and musical performances and genealogical research.

A.G.A.S. Vereinigung der deutsch-amerikanischen Gesellschaft im Raume Washington, D.C.

German American Day Festival

Franklin School by Adolph Cluss

Photos by Eva Nanni, Pres. AGAS

Charles Sumner School & Museum by Adolph Cluss

Residence of the German Ambassador in Georgetown, Washington, D.C.

Ältestes Haus in Washington wurde 1766 von Deutschen gebaut

Submitted by Ingeborg Miller, German Heritage Society of Greater Washington, DC

Es steht soweit fest, daß das "Old Stone House", das einzig noch stehende Haus aus der Vorrevolutionszeit im District of Columbia ist. Im Jahre 1764 begann das Einwandererehepaar Christopher und Rachel Layman (auch Leyhman und Lehmann geschrieben) mit dem Bau des Hauses. Die Laymans hatten das Grundstück an der damaligen Bridge Street, jetzt 3051 M Street, am 11. Juni 1764 für ein englisches Pound und zehn Shillings erworben.

Christopher Layman ist wahrscheinlich zu Beginn der sechziger Jahre über Pennsylvania nach Georgetown gekommen. Man nimmt an, er sei ein Tischler gewesen, da sich in seinem testamentarischen Nachlaß unter anderem deutsche Bibeln, Werkzeuge und Kiefernplanken befanden.

Der untere vordere Raum des Steinhauses ist jetzt als Werkstatt eingerichtet und enthält die typischen Werkzeuge eines Tischlers. Im 18. Jahrhundert hatten viele der Häuser in Georgetown einen Laden oder eine Werkstatt. Die Wohnräume befanden sich gewöhnlich im oberen Stock. Der zweite Besitzer des Hauses, eine Frau Chew, ließ weitere Räume an den hinteren Teil des Hauses anbauen. Der zum Haus gehörende, schön gepflegte, langgestreckte Garten war ursprünglich ein Gemüsegarten.

Ende des 18. Jahrhunderts kamen viele deutsche Familien aus Pennsylvania, Delaware und anderen Teilen Marylands nach Georgetown, das zu jener Zeit zum Frederick County von Maryland gehörte. Als Georgetown 1751 aufgeteilt wurde, hatte man für die am Rock Creek und Potomac wohnenden deutschen Lutheraner ein besonderes Stück Land bestimmt. Dort entstand 1769 die erste deutsche lutheranische Kirche. Am selben Platz, 1556 Wisconsin Avenue, befindet sich die jetzige historische Georgetown Lutheran Church. Diese Kirche besitzt noch immer eine 1730 in Tübingen gedruckte deutsche Bibel für die Kanzel. Sie ist eine der wertvollen Schaustücke der Kirche.

The oldest house in Washington was built by Germans in 1766

Submitted by Ingeborg Miller, German Heritage Society of Greater Washington, DC

The "Old Stone House" has, thus far, been declared the only building dating back to the pre-revolution era in the District of Columbia. On the 11th of June, 1764, immigrants Christopher and Rachel Layman, (also spelled Leyhman and Layman) purchased the site at the former Bridge Street, now 3051 M Street, for one English pound and ten shillings. In the same year, they began with the construction of the house.

Christopher Layman presumably arrived in Georgetown in the early sixties via Pennsylvania. German bibles, tools and pine planks found in his estate lead to the conclusion that he had been a carpenter.

The front room on the ground floor of the stone house is now furnished as a workshop and contains typical carpenter tools. In the eighteenth century many houses in Georgetown contained a store or a workshop. Living quarters usually were located on the upper floor. The second owner of the house, Mrs. Chew, had more rooms added to the rear of the house. It is beautifully kept. The long garden was originally a vegetable garden.

At the end of the eighteenth century many German families left Pennsylvania, Delaware and other regions in Maryland, and headed for Georgetown, then part of Frederick County, Maryland. When Georgetown was divided in 1751, a special parcel of land was set aside for the German Lutherans living on the Rock Creek and Potomac. There they erected in 1769 the first Georgetown Lutheran Church. On the same site, 1556 Wisconsin Avenue, stands today's historical Georgetown Lutheran Church. A German bible printed for the pulpit in Tübingen in 1730, remain in the possession of this church and is one of its most prized showpieces.

We the Immigrants

With dreams we came,
with highest expectations.

For centuries we came
to this New World,
we called it: "Land of Gold",
this Land of endless Opportunities.

We are no different now
from those who came
three hundred years ago -
those first to look for better lives,
fleeing from hunger, wars,
and persecution.

We, the immigrants, still arrive
from all corners of the world
From Europe, Asia, Africa,
the continents,
East, West, South, North,
searching for freedom,
looking for our own land.

The first Germans
were craftsmen here,
built houses, tables, beds,
wagons and ships,
carried their dreams
across the seas.

They were the pioneers,
those woodcutters, farmers,
tailors and printers, teachers,
adventurers.

"Bring me the unfortunate,
the willing", America said,
America the rich, the open-hearted
and unexplored.

The Germans flocked
along with many others.
Bringing their language,
culture and their own skills.

They tilled the savage soil,
grew wheat, rye and corn,
beets, cabbage and potatoes,
helped from this land
in science, business,
and the arts.

So, sing your song,
you German Americans.
Sing of your ambitions,
your dreams and desires.
Sing of freedom, equality,
and liberty forever.

© Ingeborg Carsten-Miller,
Presented April 9, 1994,
the 10th Anniversary of the
German Heritage Society
of Greater Washington, DC
Eva Nanni, President

Germany
and German-Americans

By Ernst Ott

After World War II, with the resumption of regular diplomatic relations between the USA and Germany, both German-Americans and German governmental agencies started to explore avenues for mutual cooperation. This relationship remained, for many years, at a state of catching up with the aftermath of the war, legal, commercial, organizational and personal matters that needed to be dealt with.

With the resurgence of German-American societies and their national growth, Germany began to recognize the fact that Americans of German descent still are the largest ethnic group in America and a factor of importance. Vice versa, Germany's emergence as a vital NATO partner of America, the change of its image from former foe to new ally and friend also enhanced the image of German-Americans. The many initiatives on both sides of the Atlantic, e.g. the People-to-People programs, student and various other exchange programs contributed to a strengthening of the friendly ties between the two nations.

While the German government, its embassy and consulates initially retained an arms-length relationship to the German-American societies, the cooperation began to intensify in the 1980s. Some of the most important contributions while the embassy of the Federal Republic of Germany made to the strengthening of the German-Americans were the diplomatic support of the efforts to establish German American Day bringing together the major German-American organizations which then formed the German American Joint Action Committee (GAJAC).

The embassy was also instrumental in obtaining from the "Wirtschaftsrunde," a group of German companies and banks with offices in Washington, initial financial support for GAJAC. High ranking German government officials attended the German-American Day celebrations at the White House, US Senate, the Friendship Garden and Embassy. The German Government began to recognize and honor prominent German-Americans for cultivating their German heritage and promoting American-German friendship. German political and cultural personalities, during their visits to America are often guests of German-American societies. German-Americans likewise are their guests during their trips to Germany.

German-Americans are bridge builders, promoting the vital relationship between the United States and Germany. Through its embassy, consulates, Goethe Institutes, Chambers of Commerce and other agencies, Germany also provides Americans of German descent a link to the country of their heritage, giving the American people an opportunity to get to know and appreciate the new Germany as a friend and partner in preserving world peace.

Deutschland
und die Deutschamerikaner

von Ernst Ott

Nach Beendigung des 2. Weltkrieges und der Aufnahme normaler diplomatischer Beziehungen zwischen den USA und der Bundesrepublik Deutschland begannen Deutschamerikaner sowie bundesdeutsche Regierungsbehörden Wege zur Zusammenarbeit zu erforschen.

Diese Bemühungen beschränkten sich anfänglich auf das Bearbeiten von Folgen des Krieges, diplomatische, kommerzielle und bürgerliche Angelegenheiten. Mit dem Wiederaufleben der deutschamerikanischen Vereine und ihr Anwachsen auf nationaler Ebene, begann Deutschland zu erkennen, daß Amerikaner deutscher Abstammung immer noch die größte ethnische Volksgruppe und ein wichtiger Faktor darstellen. Anderseits war es auch für Deutschamerikaner vorteilhaft, daß mit der Entwicklung Deutschlands von ehemaligem Feind zum wichtigen NATO Partner das Image Deutschlands sich wesentlich verbesserte.

Die zahlreichen Initiativen beiderseits des Atlantiks, wie z.B. das "People-to-People" Programm, Studenten und Jugend Austauschprogramme, trugen wesentlich zur Stärkung der freundschaftlichen Beziehungen der beiden Nationen bei. Während anfangs die deutschen diplomatischen Vertretungen ein auf Distanz gehaltenes Verhältnis zu deutschen Vereinen hielten, begann dieses sich in den 1980er Jahren zu intensivieren.

So waren einige der wichtigsten Beiträge der deutschen Botschaft zur Stärkung der Deutschamerikaner die diplomatische Unterstützung für die Bemühungen den Deutschamerikanischen Tag ins Leben zu rufen und die stärksten deutschamerikanischen Vereine zusammenzubringen, die dann das "German American Joint Action Committee" (GAJAC) gründeten. Es war auch weitgehend der Botschaft zu verdanken, daß die "Wirtschaftsrunde," eine Gruppe deutscher Firmen und Banken mit Sitz in Washington, GAJAC anfänglich finanziell unterstüzten.

Hohe deutsche Regierungsvertreter nahmen an den German American Day Feiern im Weißen Haus, US Senat, Botschaft und Freundschaftsgarten teil. Die Bundesregierung begann auch prominente Deutschamerikaner für ihre Bemühungen zur Erhaltung und Förderung des Deutschtums sowie Beitrag zur deutsch-amerikanischen Freundschaft mit der Verleihung des Bundesverdienstkreuzes zu ehren. Deutsche politische und kulturelle Persönlichkeiten sind oft bei deutschamerikanischen Organisationen zu Gast und Deutschamerikaner erwidern diese Besuche bei ihren Deutschlandreisen.

Deutschamerikaner sind Brückenbauer, die die wichtigen Beziehungen zwischen den Vereinigten Staaten und der Bundsrepublik Deutschland fördern. Deutschland wiederum, durch seine Botschaft, Konsulate, Goethe Institute, Handelskammern und andern Institutionen bieten Amerikanern deutscher Abstammung eine Verbindung zum Lande ihrer Vorfahren und geben dem amerikanischen Volk die Gelegenheit, das neue Deutschland als Freund und Partner zur Erhaltung des Weltfriedens besser kennenzulernen.

October 6th
German American Day
By Ernst Ott

It took many years and persistent struggle for German Americans to achieve the national recognition that was long overdue. Finally in 1987, a Joint House/Senate Resolution was passed and President Reagan issued his Proclamation, declaring October 6, 1987 German American Day, honoring the many contributions of German Americans to the freedom and prosperity of America.

True, German immigrants and their descendants have held German Day celebrations way back in colonial times but they were mostly of local or regional character. In 1889, German Americans in Cleveland decided to commemorate the many achievements of America's German-speaking immigrants. Over 100 German organizations formed a "German Day Association" which held its first German Day celebration August 4, 1890. It has been observed ever since in June every year.

During the 1950s and 60s, with the influx of new immigrants and the resurgent pride of German heritage more German Day Associations were formed and German Day celebrations held. There were several attempts to organize national German Days but they never got off the ground.

In Dallas, Texas, Berlin-born Gershon Canaan, an architect, student of Frank Lloyd Wright and later Honorary Consul of the German Federal Republic of Germany, promoted a German American Day in 1963 with a turnout of 1600 people at a banquet at the city's Memorial Auditorium. It was also through Mr. Canaan's efforts that a resolution to designate October 6 as German American Day was introduced in Congress by Rep. Joe Pool of Dallas six times, in the years 1964 through 1969. In 1964 he also persuaded then President Lyndon Johnson to declare September 17th of that year "Von Steuben Day".

Profs. Eberhard and Ruth Reichmann and Dr. Don Heinrich Tolzmann, who drew up the original "German American Day" proclamation.

Only in 1986 did serious discussions on a National German American Day start the ball rolling again. Dr. Ruth Reichmann and Dr. Don Heinrich Tolzmann of the Society of German American Studies discussed the possibility of drafting and introducing into Congress a *German American Day* resolution. Dr. Tolzmann then drafted the resolution which was submitted to Congress through Rep. Thomas Luken of Cincinnati and Senator Lugar of Indiana. It

failed to muster the required votes to pass. It did pass, however, in 1987 when the German American National Congress with then National President Elsbeth M. Seewald mobilized German Americans and German American organizations nationwide to urge their legislators to support the Senate and House resolutions. Both Mrs. Seewald and Dr. Tolzmann attended this historic event when President Reagan, in a Rose Garden ceremony, signed the first Presidential Proclamation declaring October 6, *German American Day*. Also in attendance were Senator Lugar as well as the former West German President Karl Carstens; President of the German Bundestag, Dr. Phillip Jenninger; Ambassador Guenther Van Well; Howard Backer, Chief of Staff of the White House and members of the Presidential Cabinet and the German embassy.

In subsequent years, the Washington celebrations of *German American Day* were attended by high ranking German and American government members including President of the Bundestag Dr. Rita

After the Ceremony 1993, from right: German Foreign Minister Kinkel, then House Speaker Foley and D.A.N.K. National President Ernst Ott.

Süssmuth, Vice President Klein, Foreign Minister Kinkel and members of the German Parliament (Bundesrat and Bundestag). Receptions at the U.S. Senate and German Embassy followed the Presidential proclamations at the White House and ceremonies at the German American Friendship Garden. They were festive events

In 1988, the three largest German American societies, the German American National Congress, the United German American Committee of the U.S.A., and the Steuben Society of America, with the support of the German Embassy founded the German American Joint Action Committee (GAJAC) with the main objective of promoting future German American events in Washington and nationwide. Such promotions included, aside from the Washington celebration, educational material for schools, German American Day instruction material for the governors, mayors and German American societies.

Today, October 6, *German American Day* is celebrated throughout the country. State and local governments issue proclamations and German American societies hold celebrations. German teachers in schools instruct students on the contributions of German Americans to America's culture and independence.

6. Oktober -
Deutsch-amerikanischer Tag *von Ernst Ott*

Es brauchte viele Jahre und hartnäckiges Ringen der Deutschamerikaner um die längst überfällige nationale Anerkennung zu erhalten. Endlich, im Jahre 1987 wurde eine Gemeinschaftsresolution des Senates und Abgeordneten Hauses verabschiedet und vom Präsidenten Reagan eine Proklamation erlassen, die den 6. Oktober 1987 zum *German American Day* erklärten und damit die vielen Beiträge der Deutschamerikaner zum Wohlstand Amerikas and Erkämpfung der Unabhängikeit ehrten.

Zwar hielten deutsche Enwanderer und ihre Nachkommen schon zur Kolonialzeit "Deutsche Tag" Feiern, aber diese hatten meist nur lokalen oder regionalen Charakter. 1889 entschieden die Deutschamerikaner in Cleveland die Errungenschaften der deutsch-sprechenden Einwanderer zu würdigen. Über 100 deutsche Organisationen gründeten die "German Day" Association die ihren ersten "German Day" am 4. August 1889 feierte. Er wurde seitdem jährlich im Monat Juni begangen.

Während der 1950er und 60er Jahre wurden durch den Zuwachs neuer Einwanderer und das Wiederaufleben des Stolzes auf die deutsche Herkunft, weitere "German Day Associations" gegründet und "German Days" gefeiert. Es wurden auch mehrere Versuche unternommen nationale German Days zu organisieren aber diese konnten nicht verwirklicht werden.

In Dallas, Texas, organisierte 1963 der in Berlin geborene Gershon Canaan, Architekt und Schüler von Frank Lloyd Wright, und später Honorar Konsul der Bundesrepublik Deutschland, einen German American Day mit einem Bankett im City Memorial Auditorium an dem 1600 Personen teilnahmen. Es war aufgrund der Bemühungen von Mr. Canaan, daß der Kongress Abegeordneter Joe Pool von Texas sechsmal im Kongress in den Jahren 1964-1969 Resolutionen einbrachte um den 6. October zum German American Day zu erklären. Er überredete auch den damaligen Präsidenten Lyndon Johnson den 17. September 1964 zum "Von Steuben Day" zu erklären.

Erst wieder 1986, als ernsthafte Diskusionen um einen nationalen *German American Day* stattfanden, kam der Stein wieder ins Rollen. Dr. Ruth Reichmann und Dr. Don Heinrich Tolzmann der Soeiety German American Studies diskutierten die Möglichkeit eine German American Day Resolution zu entwerfen und im Kongress vorzubringen. Diese wurde dann auch von Dr. Tolzmann angefertigt und im Kongress vom Abegeordneten Thomas Luken von Cincinnati und Senator Lugar von Indiana unterbreitet. Sie erreichte nicht die erforderliche Stimmenzahl. Im folgenden Jahre 1987 jedoch war sie erfolgreich, nachdem der Geman American National Congress mit ihrer damligen National Präsidentin Elsbeth Seewald die Deutschamerikaner und Vereinigungen auf nationaler Ebene mobilisierte und sie aufforderte ihre Gesetzgebenden um Unterstützung der Resolution anzusprechen. Sowohl Frau Seewald als auch Dr. Tolzmann wohnten der historischen Begebenheit bei als Präsident Reagan in einer Rosengarten Zeremonie die erste Proklamation zum 6. Oktober als German American Day unterschrieb. Anwesend waren auch Senator Lugar, der Präsident des deutschen Bundestages Dr. Phillip Jenninger, Botschafter Van Well, Chief of Staff des Weissen Hauses Howard Baker sowie Mitglieder des Cabinets und der deutschen Botschaft.

The GAJAC delegation with President Bill Clinton at the Oval Office after the 1996 Ceremony. See the actual Proclamation on pages 10 / 11.

White House staff photo.

In den folgenden Jahren kamen hohe Mitglieder der deutschen sowie amerikanischen Regierungen zu den *Geman American Day* Feierlichkeiten, einschließlich Bundespräsidentin des durtschen Bundestages Dr. Rita Süßmuth, Vize Präsident Klein, Außenminister Kinkel und Mitglieder des Bundesrats sowie Bundestags. Empfänge im US Senat und der deutschen Botschaft folgten der Präsidenten Proklamation in einer Weissen Haus Zeremonie sowie im German American Friendship Garden. Es waren festliche Ereignisse.

1988 gründeten die 3 größten deutschamerikanischen Organisationen, der German American National Congress, das United German American Committee of America und die Steuben Society of America, mit Unterstützung der deutschen Botschaft, das German American Joint Action Committee (GAJAC). Sie machten es sich zur Hauptaufgabe zukünftige *Deutsch Amerikanische* Tag Programme in Washington und auf national Basis zu organisieren und zu fördern. Solche Programme umfassen auch Verbreitung von Informationsmaterial für Schulen, Gouverneure, Bürgermeister und Deutsch-Amerikanische Vereine.

Heute wird der 6. Oktober, *Deutsch Amerikanischer* Tag, im ganzen Lande gefeiert. Staats- und lokale Behörden erlassen Proklamationen und deutschamerikanische Vereine begehen ihre Feierlichkeiten. In den Schulen unterrichten Deutsch-Lehrer die Studenten über die Beiträge der Deutschamerikaner zur Erkämpfung der Unabhängigkeit und amerikanischen Kultur.

The German American Friendship Garden in Washington, DC

By Ernst Ott

The Nation's capital has an abundance of monuments and museums depicting and documenting America's diverse ethnic fibers that have molded the character of our country. Aside from the Steuben monument, erected in 1910 across from the White House, the other major German American fixture and of more recent history is the *German American Friendship Garden* (Freundschafts Garten), located at the base of the Washington Monument on Constitution Avenue.

Annually the German American Friendship Garden serves as the location where, in spirit, we unite ourselves with the multitude of local celebrations of *German-American Day* taking place in states, cities, and towns throughout these United States.

How the Garden was created.

The Presidential Commission for the German-American Tricentennial, celebrated in 1983, described "The Friendship Garden" in a colorful brochure in these terms: "The lasting German-American contributions to our nation, and the continuing friendship between the United States and the Federal Republic, will be endearingly symbolized in a Friendship Garden. The location of the magnificent garden, in the Mall area, is one of our nation's most treasured sites, within walking distance of the Washington Monument, the Lincoln and Jefferson memorials".

The path to its dedication was not always certain and was longer than anticipated. Contributions to fund the design and construction costs were donated by the German American community. For a time, however, it appeared that this project never would be completed because of the lengthy and complex decision-and-approval process requiring concurrence by many agencies of the federal government and of the District of Columbia. The German-American community responded to these circumstances and demonstrated that we were a constituency that cared about the delays and would not tolerate abandoning the project to fittingly commemorate "... the constructive contributions of German-Americans in government, industry, education and the arts, entertainment, engineering and science".

All German Americans may rightly take pride in the fact that the *German American Friendship Garden* bears witness to our love of country, our gratitude for the opportunity our country has afforded us and that the *German American Friendship Garden* has fully integrated its beauty into the magnificence of our national mall. The Garden's benches and fountains welcome the visitor to tarry, rest, and drink in the spectacle of America's finest vistas.

Flags and spirits fly high at the dedication ceremony

Der deutschamerikanische Freundschaftsgarten

von Ernst Ott

Die Haupstadt Amerikas hat eine Vielzahl von Denkmälern und Museen, die die ethnische Diversität Amerikas und die Fasern, die den Charakter unseres Landes bilden, dokumentieren.

Abgesehen von dem Steuben Denkmal das 1910, gegenüber vom Weißen Haus errichtet wurde, ist das andere deutschamerikanische Merkmal neueren Datums, der *deutschamerikanische Freundschaftsgarten* am Fuße des Washington Denkmals, an der Constitution Avenue.

Der *deutschamerikanische Freundschaftsgarten* ist der Ort an dem wir uns jährlich mit den zahlreichen deutsch-amerikanischen Tag Feiern die in vielen Staaten, Städten und Ortschaften Amerikas gefeiert werden, im Geiste vereinigen.

Die Gründung des Freundschaftsgartens

Die Präsidentschaftskommission zur 300 jährigen Einwanderung, gefeiert 1983, beschreibt den Freundschaftsgarten in einer bunt illustrierten Broschüre folgendermaßen: "die beständige deutschamerikanische Beiträge zu unserer Nation und die fortdauernde Freundschaft der Vereingten Staaten von Amerika und der Bundesrepublik Deutschland sind in diesem Freundschaftsgarten in inniger Freundschaft symbolisiert. Der Standort dieses wunderschönen Gartens ist der "MALL". Eines der heiligsten Orte der Nation und in Fußgänger-Entfernung vom Washington Denkmal sowie den Lincoln und Jefferson Denkmälern.

Der Werdegang der Einweihung des Gartens war oft eine unsichere Sache und dauerte länger als erwartet. Spenden für den Entwurf und die Baukosten wurden von den deutschamerikanischen Organisationen aufgebracht. Eine zeitlang schien es jedoch als ob das Projekt niemals vollendet werden könnte, wegen dem langwierigen und komplexen Entscheidungsprozeß, der die Genehmigung einer Vielzahl von Behörden der Bundesregierung sowie des Districts of Columbia benötigte. Die deutschamerikanische Gemeinde nahm diese Umstände mit in Kauf und zeigte, daß wir eine Gemeinde sind, die solch ein Projekt, das die Beiträge de Deutschkamerikaner zur Regierung, Industrie, Erziehung, der Künste, Unterhaltung, Technik und Wißenschaft würdigt, nie aufgeben würde".

Alle Deutschamerikaner können mit Recht stolz darauf sein, daß der Freundschaftsgarten Zeugnis unserer Liebe zur Nation und Dankbarkeit für die uns gegebenen Chancen ist, und daß die Schönheit des *deutschamerikanischen Freundschaftsgarten* in die Herrlichkeit der nationalen Ehrenmals eingegliedert wurde. Die Gartenbänke und Blumen laden die Besucher ein zu weilen, sich auszuruhen und das Schauspiel Amerikas schönster Aussichten zu genießen.

German American National Observances

By Ernst Ott

The National events celebrated annually across the country are the Steuben Parades, German American Day and Volkstrauertag (Day of National Mourning), with the Steuben Parades having the longest tradition.

Steuben Parade Celebrations

They have become one of the focal points of German American pride and are held throughout the country, in New York for 40 years in 1997, Chicago 32 years, and Philadelphia 27 years, observed in September each year. They have become popular international occurrences with international participation as well.

General Friedrich Wilhelm von Steuben was born in Magdeburg, Germany in 1730. He was a Prussian officer under King Frederick II, traveled to America in 1778 on the recommendation of Benjamin Franklin. His job was to drill some efficiency into the "civilians in uniform" as he once jokingly called George Washington's troops. Von Steuben recognized that the poor state of the troops was due to a complete lack of organization, order and discipline. He saw great moral strength in the soldiers' willingness to sacrifice themselves and in their dedication to the cause of freedom and felt that with this strength even the greatest of difficulties could be overcome. His military knowledge, his untiring commitment and his sense of justice earned him the respect and acknowledgment of his troops.

Within a few months, von Steuben succeeded in transforming the chaotic troops into a disciplined army of mobile fighting men. He was appointed Inspector General of the Army with the rank of a major general. He played a decisive role in the victory over England and the resulting independence.

As "Drill Instructor" of the Continental Army, von Steuben wrote "Regulations for the Order and Discipline of the Troops of the United States." Although this manual has been modified - it still remains the basic guide for discipline and drill of the Army.

His memoranda reveals a general with military vision and the format of a statesman. He devised a system of national defense and inspired the establishment of a military academy. The famous U.S. Military Academy at West Point is the result of this initiative. As a committed democrat and advocate of humanitarian behavior, von Steuben dedicated himself to the needy when he left the army; he became chairman of the Deutsche Gesellschaft in New York, which provided aid to indigent immigrants, and was elected to the board of New York University. In recognition of his services, Congress presented him with a gilded sword on which were engraved the words: "The United States to Major General Baron von Steuben, 15th April 1784, for Military Merits". He died in 1794.

While the Steuben Parades enjoyed a resurgence after World War II, one of the most significant parades took place December 7, 1910 in Washington, D.C. on the occasion of the unveiling of the Von Steuben statue in Lafayette Park, opposite the White House. The following extract from Washington's "Evening Star" describes the memorable celebration:

"Nation's Tribute to Von Steuben - Bronze Statue of Washington's great Drillmaster unveiled in Lafayette Park"

"In weather perhaps as bleak as that which enfolded the cheerless camp of the great commander in chief at Valley Forge, when barefoot Colonials tracked their course in blood over the pitiless snow, the United States of America, 133 years later, this afternoon, at the Capital of the Nation, unveiled the statue of Frederick William Augustus Henry Ferdinand, Baron von Steuben, the Adjutant General of the armies of Frederick the Great, the friend of George Washington, and the great inspector of the Colonial Army that wrested its independence from the British Crown.

Surrounding the tribute of bronze were thousands of von Steuben's countrymen, proud of heart and exultant at the honor conferred upon their great representative, who, in his time, conferred honor upon their adopted country and gave to it all the force of his military wisdom and skill in its fight for liberty. Not the barefoot and disorganized stragglers of the patriotic Army of long ago, but officers and troops of an Army and Navy second to none in Christendom, were gathered with them, while on all sides Americans to the manner born joined with all in the tribute to the memory of the great man who yet lives in the proudest annals of their native land.

Representative Bartholdt's address was followed with one by Dr. Charles J. Hexamer, president of the National German American Alliance; a song by the Northeastern Singers' Association, and an address by the German ambassador, Count J.H. von Bernstorff.

The statue was unveiled by Miss Helen Taft, daughter of the President, while the German singing societies, accompanied by the Marine Band, sang "The Star Spangled Banner," and a salute was fired by Battery E, of the Third Field Artillery.

The statue stands at the northwest corner of Lafayette Square, opposite the White House. The statue is bronze, surmounting a granite pedestal, and is so highly regarded as a work of art that Congress has provided for the presentation of a bronze replica to the German emperor in partial recognition of his gift to the United States of a statue of Frederick the Great. The Steuben Statue is the work of Albert Jäger of New York.

After the introduction of the sculptor, who received an ovation, President Taft, who was presented by Secretary Dickinson, spoke in praise of von Steuben.

Following the President's address, the benediction was pronounced by Rev. Dr. William T. Russell, pastor of St. Patrick's Catholic Church, and the military and civic parade then started. It was reviewed by the President and special guests. It is estimated there were 10,000 men in line."

Today Steuben Parades are held in larger German American communities throughout the country, the three major being New York City, Chicago and Philadelphia. They are colorful events and are attended by the German American societies, Germanic Societies from the "Old Country", luminaries from the cultural, political and religious spectrum as well as many military and high school marching bands. Here is a photographic kaleidoscope from Chicago, Philadelphia and New York.

Nationale deutsch - amerikanische Gedenktage

Von Ernst Ott

Nationale Gedenktage die jährlich in ganz Amerika begangen werden sind hauptsächlich: die Steuben Paraden; German American Day, 6. Oktober; und der Volkstrauertag im November, wovon die Steuben Parade die längste Tradition hat.

Steuben Paraden

Steuben Paraden sind ein Fokus deutschamerikanischen Stolzes und werden seit vielen Jahren in ganz Amerika im Monat September abgehalten; in New York in diesem Jahr seit 40, Chicago 32 und Philadelphia seit 27 Jahren. Sie haben sich sogar zu populären Ereignissen mit internationaler Beteiligung entwickelt.

General Friedrich Wilhelm von Steuben wurde im Jahre 1730 in Magdeburg geboren. Er diente als preußischer Offizier unter Kaiser Friedrich II, und reiste 1778 auf Empfehlung von Benjamin Franklin nach Amerika. Seine Aufgabe war es den "Zivilisten in Uniform", wie er in humoristischer Weise George Washington's Truppen nannte, Tüchtigkeit einzurichtern. Von Steuben erkannte, daß die armselige Verfassung der Truppen auf eine komplette Unorganisation und Disziplinlosigkeit zurückzuführen war. Er sah aber die moralische Kraft und die Bereitschaft der Soldaten sich für die Freiheit aufzuopfern und fühlte, daß mit dieser Stärke auch die größten Schwierigkeiten überwunden werden konnten. Seine militärischen Kenntnisse, seine unermüdliche Hingabe und sein Gerechtigkeitssinn ernteten ihm den Respekt und die Anerkennung seiner Truppen.

Innerhalb weniger Monate verwandelte er die chaotischen Truppen in eine disziplinierte Armee mobiler Kämpfer. Er wurde zum General Inspekteur der Armee, mit dem Rang eines General Majors, ernannt. Er spielte eine entscheidende Rolle beim Sieg über England und der Erkämpfung der Unabhängigkeit.

Als "Ausbilder" der Continental Army schrieb von Steuben die "Vorschriften über Ordnung und Disziplin der Truppen der Vereinigten Staaten". Obwohl dieses Handbuch inzwischen modifiziert wurde, ist es immer noch die Grundlage für Disziplin und Ausbildung der Armee.

Seine Aufzeichnungen enthüllen einen General mit dem Format eines Staatsmannes. Er entwickelte ein nationales Verteidigunssystem und die Idee zur Errichtung einer Militärakademie. Die berühmte US Militärakademie West Point ist das Ergebnis dieser Initiative. Als ein treuer Demokrat und Verfechter humanitären Verhaltens widmete sich von Steuben, nach seinem Ausscheiden aus der Armee, den Bedürftigen. Er wurde Vorsitzender der Deutschen Gesellschaft in New York, die Einwanderer mit Unterstützung versorgte. Er wurde auch zum Aufsichtsrat der New York University erwählt. In Anerkennung seiner Verdienste übergab ihm der Kongress einen vergoldeten Degen mit der Inschrift: "Die Vereinigte Staaten an General Major Baron von Steuben, 15. April 1784, für Militärische Verdienste". Er starb im Jahre 1794.

Nach dem zweiten Weltkrieg erhielten die Steuben Paraden einen neuen Auftrieb, aber eine der bedeutendsten Paraden fand am. 7. Dezember 1910 in Wahsington DC statt, zum Anlaß der Einweihung der von Steuben Statue im Lafayette Park, gegenüber vom Weißen Haus. Folgender Auszug aus Washington's "Evening Star" beschreibt diese denkwürdige Feier:

"Tribut der Nation an von Steuben - Bronze Statue des großen Drill Meister Washington's im Lafayette Park eingeweiht".

"Bei einem Wetter, das vielleicht genau so trostlos war wie im Lager des berühmten Kommadeurs bei Valley Forge, als barfüßige Kolonisten ihre Blutspuren im erbarmunglosen Schnee hinterließen, enthüllten die Vereinigte Staaten von Amerika, 133 Jahre später, heute Nachmittag in der Hauptstadt, die

Statue des Frederick William Augustus Henry Ferdinand, Baron von Steuben, General Adjudant der Armeen von Friedrich dem Großen, Freund von George Washington, und dem großen Inspekteur der Kolonial Armee, die sich ihre Unabhängigkeit von der britischen Krone erkämpfte.

Dieses Zeichen der Anerkennung in Bronze war umringt von Tausenden von Steuben's Landsleuten, im Herzen stolz und jubilierend über die Ehre, die ihrem großen Verteter zu Teil wurde, der zu seiner Zeit seinem adoptierten Land Ehre brachte und auch die gesamte Stärke seines militärischen Wissens und Talentes im Kampfe um die Freiheit bewies. Mit ihnen standen nicht die barfüßigen und unorganisierten Kämpfer der patriotlischen Armee aus früheren Zeiten, sondern Offiziere und Truppen einer Armee und Marine, einzigartig im Christenreich und Amerikaner jeder Gattung die mit allen anderen ihre Anerkennung an die Erinnerung des großen Mannes, der in den Annalen ihres Heimatlandes weiterlebt.

Der Rede von Kongress Abgeordneten Barthold folgte eine weitere von Dr. Charles J. Hexamer, Präsident der National Geman American Alliance, ein Gesang der Northeastern Singers Vereinigung und eine Ansprache vom deutschen Botschafter Graf J. H. von Bernstorf.

Die Statue wurde enthüllt von Miss Helen Taft, Tochter des Präsidenten, während deutsche Gesangvereine, begleitet von der Marine Kapelle das "The Star Spangled Banner" sangen und die E Batterie der Third Field Artillery Salutschüsse abgaben. Die Statue steht an der Norwest Ecke des Lafayette Square, gegenüber vom Weißen Haus. Die Bronze Statue steht auf einem Granitsockel und ist als Kunstwerk so geschätzt, daß der Kongreß eine Kopie dem deutschen Kaiser übergab, als Gegenleistung seines Geschenkes einer Statue des Friedrich dem Großen. Die Steuben Statue ist das Kunstwerk von Albert Jäger aus New York.

Nachdem der Bildhauer vorgestellt wurde und großen Beifall erhielt, präsentierte Staatsminister Dickinson den Präsidenten der Vereinigten Staaten Taft, der die Verdienste von Steuben lobte.

Nach der Ansprache von Präsident Taft hielt Rev. Dr. William T. Russel, Pastor der St. Patrick's Katholischen Kirche ein Dankesgebet und dann begann die Militär und Bürgerparade, abgehalten vom Präsidenten und den Ehrengästen. Man schätzte 10,000 Teilnehmer.

Heute werden Steuben Paraden in den größeren Städten des Landes abgehalten, die größten in New York, Chicago und Philadelphia. Es sind farbenprächtige Veranstaltungen an denen deutschamerikanische Vereine, deutsche Vereine aus "der alten Welt", Persönlichkeiten aus dem Kultur, Politik und dem Religions Spektrum sowie Militär und Schulkapellen teilnehmen.

Denkmal des Generalmajors Friedrich Wilhelm von Steuben in Washington.

Von Albert Jäger.

Former President George Busch with children at a German American celebration in Washington, DC

VOLKSTRAUERTAG
(Day of National Mourning)

By Ernst Ott

Germany observes its annual day of mourning on the 3rd Sunday in November when it remembers its soldiers that perished during the last World War.

The United States maintained several Prisoner of War Camps throughout the country, housing captured German soldiers who were put to work on a variety of jobs e.g. in agriculture and forestry. Those who died while in captivity were buried in military installations such as Fort Sheridan, Illinois; Fort Custer National Cemetery, Michigan and the cemetery at Fort Meade, Maryland. U.S. Military authorities maintained the graves and later some German American societies looked after them as well. In conjunction with the U.S. Armed Forces, which extended military honors to their former enemy, the German Consulates and the German societies conducted Memorial Day ceremonies.

Here are three of these cemeteries where recent *Volkstrauertag* observances were held.

The Cemetery at Fort Meade: Remembrance, Recording the Past, and Reconciliation
by Merl E. Arp

It was a sunny Sunday morning at Fort Meade, a U.S. Army post just south of Baltimore, Maryland. The sun shone down on a small but manicured cemetery, surrounded by an iron fence and flanked by silent trees. As I walked among the grave markers, it became apparent that this cemetery was different. Certainly it is a typical military cemetery with rows of identical semi-rectangular white stone graves markers. But on closer examination one sees that many of the names on the grave markers are not those of Americans. Here one finds an Italian name, with the Italian word "Soldado", or soldier, below the name of the interred. More frequently one finds German names, with German military ranks below the names.

My examination of grave markers was interrupted by the arrival of an olive drab military bus at the cemetery gate. Out of the bus stepped military officers, officers of the German navy, and the well dressed ladies accompanying them. The German group, led by Captain Lutz-Uwe Gloeckner, Chief Naval Attaché at the German Embassy in Washington D.C., was greeted on arrival by Colonel Robert Morris, U.S. Army garrison commander at Fort Meade. The two ranking officers, Gloeckner and Morris, exchanged pleasantries and then led the entire group down the central walkway, past a waiting U.S. Army band, to the northeast corner of the cemetery. There they halted and turned to face a single grave marker bearing the following inscription: Werner Henke, Korvettenkapitän, German Navy.

The military band played the national anthems of the Federal Republic of Germany and of the United States of America. Then the ranking German officer placed a wreath at the grace marker of Henke honoring the war dead of both Germany and the U.S. The ceremony was completed and this element of *Volkstrauertag* had been observed at Fort Meade with reverence to the past and honor to those on both sides who had fallen in that terrible war.

At Fort Sheridan military cematary

Fort Sheridan, Illinois

Nine German soldiers, formerly American POW's, rest in the Fort Sheridan's Soldiers Cemetery in north-eastern Illinois. They found their final resting place far from home, and far from their loved ones, but rest in the company of fellow soldiers - American soldiers. Friend and foe are united here forever - all earthly battles and conflicts have been fought. Eternity and God's realm are at peace forever.

Fort Sheridan, however, is no longer the busy place filled with military personnel. It is said, that plans are underfoot to convert the property into a housing project. But that will not affect the graves of the nine German POWs, and those of their American comrades, in the cemetery at the far northern part of the fort. Four of the German POWs were killed in a truck accident, and transferred to Fort Sheridan, and five died of natural causes. In those early days German graves received no care, quite different from the American ones. The Army and local Veterans groups tended to them. The little cemetery will remain where it is, even if the land is sold.

DANK Chapter Waukegan, IL, has tended to these graves since —, and, together with the Chicago Consulate General and U.S. Army representatives, conducts the annual memorial service.

Volkstrauertag at Battle Creek, Michigan

The 43rd Annual German National Memorial Service - *Volkstrauertag* was observed at the Fort Custer National Cemetery, Battle Creek, Michigan, on November 17, 1996. The service honored twenty-six German soldiers, who died between 1943-1946, while prisoners of war and interred at the prison camp at Fort Custer.

The ceremony has been an annual event since 1953, and promoted by Battle Creek American Legion Post #54. Featured in the program was a welcome by Ft. Custer National Cemetery Director Robert E. Poe and a memorial address given by Juergen Mews, from Detroit, Consul, Federal Republic of Germany.

Memorial service of the Donauschwaben · *Trauerfeier*

While the Schwaben Male Chorus from Toledo sang "Ich hatt' einen Kameraden", presentations of wreaths were made by various representative German organizations, including the German-American Club, Grand Rapids; German-American Club, Kalamazoo; G.A.G., Toledo; German Club, Detroit; and Benton Harbor D.A.N.K. Chapter 13, and St. Joseph Kickers Sport Club. Honor and color guards with a gun salute, and playing "taps" concluded this impressive memorial service.

The 250 spectators, who were cold and wet but not complaining, were all invited to the American Legion Post #54 Hall where refreshments were served, hospitality enjoyed, and new acquaintances made.

Memorial Day of the Donauschwaben

The Donauschwaben of Amerika and their affiliated American Aid Society of German Descendants observe their own day of mourning when they remember their loved ones who died in their ancestral home lands, particularly in the former Yugoslavia, Romania and Hungary.

Annually, in May, various Donauschwaben organizations from the Midwest gather at the American Aid Society home and picnic area at Lake Villa, Illinois for their traditional memorial service. Representatives of the national Donauschwaben umbrella organization, as well as other German American societies participate in paying tribute to the victims of the horrible massacre of ethnic Germans.

Similar observances are held in Cleveland and other cities where the Donauschwaben, Siebenbürger Sachsen and other Germans from the Balcans, Silesia and Pommerania (now Poland) and former Czechoslovakia have settled after the war.

Volkstrauertag

von Ernst Ott

Deutschland begeht seinen alljährlichen Volkstrauertag am 3. Sonntag im November, an dem es sich an seine Soldaten erinnert, die während des zweiten Weltkrieges starben. Die USA unterhielten mehrere Kriegsgefangenen Lager im Lande in denem die Insassen in der Landwirtschaft, Forstwirtschaft und mit anderen Arbeiten beschäftigt wurden. Jene, die während der Gefangenschaft starben wurden in den Militärinstallationen, wie Fort Sheridan, Illinois; Fort Custer National Cemetary Michigan; und Fort Meade, Maryland, Friedhöfen beerdigt. Die US Militärbehörden pflegten die Gräber und später nahmen sich auch deutschamerikanische Vereine ihrer an. Zusammen mit den US Armed Forces, die ihren früheren Feinden die militärische Ehre erwiesen, halten die deutschamerikanischen Vereine die Volkstrauertagsfeiern ab.

Der Friedhof von Fort Meade: Erinnerung, Dokumentation der Vergangenheit und Versöhnung.
von Merl E. Arp

Es war ein sonniger Sonntag Morgen in Fort Meade, eine US Armee Installation südlich von Baltimore, Maryland. Die Sonne schien auf einen kleinen aber gut gepflegten Friedhof mit einem eisernen Zaun und umrahmt mit stillen Bäumen. Als ich an den Grabsteinen vorbei ging wurde offenbar, daß dieser Friedhof doch irgendwie anders war. Es war natürlich ein militärischer Friedhof mit Reihen von identischen, halbrechteckigen weissen Grabsteinen. Beim genaueren Hinsehen jedoch sah man, daß viele der Namen auf den Grabsteinen keine amerikanischen Namen waren. Man finde einen italienischen Namen mit dem italienischen Wort "Solado", oder Soldat unter dem Namen des Beerdigten. Aber noch öfters findet man deutsche Namen mit dem deutschen Militärrang.

Meine Studie der Gräber wurde durch die Ankunft eines Militärbusses, in matter Oliven farbe, am Friedhofstor unterbrochen. Aus dem Bus stiegen Offiziere der deutschen Kriegsmarine, begleitet von elegant gekleideten Damen. Die deutsche Gruppe, angeführt von Kapitän zur See Lutz-Uwe Glöckner, Chef Marine Attache der deutschen Botschaft in Washington, D.C., wurde bei ihrer Ankunft von Colonel (Oberst) Robert Morris, Kommandeur der Garnison Fort Meade begrüßt. Diese ranghöchsten Offiziere, Glöckner und Morris, tauschten militärische Höflichkeiten und führten die gesamte Gruppe entlang dem Hauptweg, vorbei an der schon wartenden US Militär Kapelle zur Nordost-Ecke des Friedhofes. Dort angekommen, hielt sie vor einem Einzelgrab mit folgender Inschrift: Werner Henke, Korvettenkapitän, Deutsche Kriegsmarine.

Die Militär Kapelle spielte die Nationalhymen der Bundesrepublik Deutschland und der Vereinigten Staaten von Amerika. Der ranghöchste deutsche Offizier legte dann einen Kranz am Grabe von Henke nieder und ehrte damit die Gefallenen Deutschlands sowie Amerikas. Somit war die Volkstrauertagsfeier in Fort Meade, die an die Vergangenheit erinnerte und die Gefallenen des schrecklichen Krieges ehrte, beendet.

Fort Sheridan, Illinois

Neun deutsche Soldaten führe Kriegsgefangene, ruhen im Soldatenfriedhof von Fort Sheridan in Nordosten des Staates Illinois. Sie fanden ihren Ruheplatz, fern der Heimat und fern ihrer Geliebten, aber sie fanden ihn in der Gemeinschaft von Kameraden - amerikanischen Soldaten. Hier sind Freund und Feind für ewig vereint, nachdem alle irdischen Kämpfe und Konflikte gefochten waren. Ewigkeit im Reiche Gottes ist Friede, ewiger Friede.

Memorial Service at Fort Sheridan

Photos by Ernst Ott

Fort Sheridan, jedoch, ist nicht mehr der geschäftige Ort, überlaufend mit militärischem Personal, der es einmal war. Es sollen Pläne entworfen werden ihn zu einem Wohnkomplex umzuwandeln. Diese Pläne betreffen aber nicht die Gräber der neun gestorbenen deutschen Kriegsgefangenen und ihren amerikanischen Kameraden, die sich im nördlichen Teil der Forts befinden. Vier der deutschen Kriegsgefangenen wurden bei einem Lastwagen Verkehrsunfall getötet und nach Fort Sheridan überführt; fünf starben eines natürlichen Todes, in früheren Zeiten wurden die deutschen Gräber nicht gepflegt, im Gegensatz zu den amerikanischen Gräbern. Die Armee und Kriegsveteranen Gruppen nahmen sich später ihrer an. Der kleine Friedhof wird bestehen bleiben selbst wenn das Land einmal verkauft wird.

Das DANK Chapter Waukegan, Illinois hat seitdem diese Gräber gepflegt - und zusammen mit dem deutschen General Konsulat in Chicago und Vertreter der US Armee, halten diese jährlich die Volkstrauertagfeiern ab.

Volkstrauertag Battle Creek, Michigan

Am 17. November 1996 fand im Fort Custer National Cemetary, Battle Creek, Michigan die 43. jährliche Volkstrauertagfeier statt. Diese Gedenkfeier ehrte 26 deutsche Soldaten, die in den Jahren 1943-1946 während ihrer Gefangenschaft im Fort Custer starben. Sie wird seit 1953 von der Battle Creek American Legion Post abgehalten. Am Programm nahmen teil u.a. der Direktor des Fort Custer national Friedhofes Robert E. Poe und Konsul Jürgen Mews vom deutschen Konsulat in Detroit der auch die Ansprache hielt.

Während der Schwaben Männerchor von Toledo das Lied "Ich hatt' einen Kameraden" sang, legten verschiedene Vertreter deutscher Vereine, darunter der German American Club Grand Rapids Michigan; German American Club, Kalamazoo, Michigan; GAG, Toledo, Ohio; German Club, Detroit, Michigan; Benton Harbor, Michigan DANK Chapter 13 und St. Joseph, Michigan Kickers Sport Club, Kränze nieder. Ehren und Flaggen Garden gaben Gewehr Salut und ein Zapfenstreich beendete diese beeindruckende Zeremonie.

Nach deren Beendigung wurden die 250 Teilnehmer, zwar frierend und naß vom Regen aber ohne zu klagen, von der American Legion Post 54 zu ihrem Klubhaus eingeladen wo ihnen Erfrischungen serviert und auch neue Bekanntschaften gemacht wurden.

Volkstrauertag bei den Donauschwaben

Der Donauschwaben Verein von Amerika und die assoziierte American Aid Society halten ihren eigenen Volkstrauertag ab, an dem sie aller ihrer Lieben gedenken die in den Heimatländern, hauptsächlich im vormaligen Yugoslavien, Rumaenien und Ungarn ihr Leben ließen.

Im Mai versammeln sich die verschiedenen Vereine aus dem Kreis Chicago auf dem Klubgelände bei Lake Villa, Illinois zu ihrem traditionellen Gedenktag. Vertreter der nationalen Dachorganisation sowie befreundeten deutschamerikanischen Vereinen nehmen teil und gedenken der Opfer der schrecklichen Massakrierungen an den Volksdeutschen.

Solche Gedenktage werden auch in anderen Städten wie z.B. Cleveland, Ohio so sich viele Donauschwaben, Siebenbürger Sachsen und andere deutschstämmige Einwanderer aus den Balkanländern, Schlesien, Pommern und der früheren Chechoslovakei niederließen, abgehalten.

Sister Cities International

Building Community Partnerships Worldwide

SCOPE: Sister Cities International (SCI) is the premier organization for citizen diplomacy in the United States. SCI represents the sister cities programs of more than 1200 US cities and their 1,900 partners in 123 countries worldwide.

OBJECTIVE: SCI leads the national movement for local community development and volunteer action in the global arena. SCI motivates and empowers municipal officials, volunteers, and youth to conduct long-term programs of mutual benefit and interest with their sister city counterparts.

GOALS:

- to develop municipal partnerships between US towns, cities, counties, states, and similar jurisdictions in other nations;

- to create opportunities for the citizens of member cities to experience and explore other cultures though long-term municipal partnerships;

- to create an atmosphere in which economic development and trade can be developed, implemented and strengthened;

- to stimulate environments through which municipal partnerships can creatively learn, work and solve problems together; and

    to collaborate with organizations in the United States and other countries that have similar goals.

AGREEMENTS: SCI is unique in that it officially links municipalities from the United States with foreign cities through sister city agreements signed by the respective mayor of each city and ratified by each city council, or its equivalent. To be official, a sister city relationship must have the endorsement of the local authorities, who support the efforts of community volunteers. This dynamic process empowers all sectors of a community to participate in the global arena, thus unleashing citizen diplomacy at the grassroots level.

HISTORY: Sister city affiliations between the United States and other nations began shortly after World War II and developed into a national initiative when President Dwight D. Eisenhower proposed the people-to-people program at a White House Conference in 1956. Originally housed as part of the National League of Cities, SCI became a separate, not-for-profit organization in 1967 due to the tremendous growth and popularity of the US program. President Eisenhower's intention was to involve people and organized groups at all levels of US society in personal, citizen diplomacy with the hope that people-to-people relationships, fostered through sister city affiliations, would lessen the chance of future world conflicts.

MISSION: Sister city relationships in the Western Hemisphere offer a network through which to implement the goals of the United Nations Conference on Environment and Development (UNCED) and the North America Free Trade Agreement (NAFTA). Dr. Joseph Duffey, director of the United States Information Agency (USIA), remarked during his keynote address at the Summit of the Americas in 1994, "SCI has and should continue to be an essential tool in helping countries in this hemisphere address the common goals and concerns we face in this moment… nothing can replace the personal contact that results from exchanges between sister cities."

VOLUNTEERS: SCI supports and serves an expansive network of volunteers dedicated to promoting citizen exchange and community-based leadership. This network includes:

- State Coordinators, who serve in a voluntary capacity in each state providing program development assistance as field staff to local-level sister city committees;

- Local committee leaders and municipal officials, who represent the vast volunteer network in over 1,200 cities throughout the United States; and

- Community volunteers, who number in the hundreds of thousands at the grassroots level and who are members of the local sister city programs.

SUPPORT: SCI staff and local sister city committees administer a wide variety of innovative grant programs which provide new ideas and direction to the national sister cities movement. Recent programs have included support for municipal education and training, youth community service learning, technical assistance, trilateral exchanges, and independent newspaper management.

FUTURE: As previously isolated nations become increasingly interdependent, global cooperation is crucial to social and economic vitality. To further meet the needs of its network, SCI has expanded its leadership role by: providing training and support to municipal officials from newly emerging democracies; strengthening its global communications capabilities; and supporting multiculturalism and cultural diversity initiatives that help address common social issues and improve the quality of life in communities consisting of highly diverse populations.

Sister Cities Internaional
120 South Payne Street
Alexandria, Virginia 22314
http://www.sister-cities.org
info@sister-cities.org

Sister Cities International

Weltweiter Aufbau kommunaler Beziehungen

UMFANG: Sister Cities International (SCI) ist die bedeutenste Organisation für Diplomatie auf zwischenmenschlicher Ebene in den USA. Der Verband vereinigt unter seinem Dach die Partnerstadt-Programme von 1.200 US-Städten, mit denen 1.900 Partnerstädten in 123 Ländern rund um die Welt verbunden sind.

ZIEL: Der SCI bildet die Speerspitze für den amerikanischen Beitrag zur Entwicklung von kommunalen Gemeinschaften und Freiwilligeneinsätzen auf weltweiter Ebene. Der SCI motiviert und ermächtigt städtische Beamte bzw. Angestellte, Freiwillige und Jugendliche zur Durchführung von Langzeitprogrammen, die zum gegenseitigen Vorteil sind und im gemeinsamen Interesse der eigenen und der jeweiligen Partnerstädte liegen.

ZIELE IM EINZELNEN:

- Die Entwicklung kommunaler Partnerschaften zwischen US- Kleinstädten, Städten, Landkreisen, Bundesstaaten und ähnlichen Verwaltungseinteilungen in anderen Ländern.

- Es den Bürgern von Mitgliedsstädten zu ermöglichen, andere Kulturen durch langfristige kommunale Partnerschaften vertieft kennenzulernen.

- Eine Atmosphäre herzustellen, in der wirtschaftliche Entwicklung und Handel initiiert, durchgeführt und verstärkt werden können.

- Bedingungen zu fördern, unter denen kommunale Partnerschaften kreativ voneinander lernen und miteinander arbeiten sowie ihre Probleme gemeinsam lösen können.

- Die Zusammenarbeit mit Organisationen in den USA und anderen Ländern, die ähnliche Ziele verfolgen.

VERTRÄGE: Der SCI ist insofern ein einzigartiger Verband, als er US-amerikanische Gemeinden mit fremden Städten durch von den jeweiligen Bürgermeistern der Städte unterschriebene und dem Stadtrat bzw. dessen Entsprechung ratifizierte Verträge als Partnerschaftsstädte verbindet. Offiziell gilt diese Verbindung zwischen Partnerschaftsstädten nur, wenn die die Bemühungen der Freiwilligen aus den Gemeinden unterstützenden kommunalen Behörden ihr Plazet gegeben haben. Dieses dynamische Verfahren ermöglicht es allen Teilen der jeweiligen Gemeinden, am globalen Bereich Anteil zu nehmen, so daß sich dadurch die Bürgerdiplomatie als Bürgerbewegung konstituiert.

GESCHICHTE: Amerikanische Städte begannen kurz nach dem Zweiten Weltkrieg, potentielle ausländische Partnerstädte anzusprechen. Zu einer landesweiten Kampagne entwickelte sich diese Bewegung. Als Präsident Dwight D. Eisenhower 1956 auf einer Konferenz im Weißen Haus die Erweiterung dieser zwischenmenschlichen Kontakte anregte, entwickelte sich daraus eine landesweite Bewegung. Ursprünglich unter dem Dachverband der National League of Cities gegründet, wurde der SCI 1967 aufgrund des enormen Anwachsens und der Popularität seines Programms davon getrennt und in eine gemeinnützige Organisation umgewandelt. Präsident Eisenhower hatte beabsichtigt, Menschen und organisierte Gruppen auf allen Ebenen der amerikanischen Gesellschaft in diese persönlich Bürgerdiplomatie einzubeziehen, in der Hoffnung, daß zwischen menschliche, durch partnerstädtische Bindungen kultivierte Beziehunge Weltkriege in der Zukunft unwahrscheinlicher werden lassen würden.

ROLLE DES SCI: Beziehungen zwischen Partnerstädten in der westlichen Hemisphäre knüpfen ein Netz, durch welches die Ziele der Umwelt- und Entwicklungskonferenz der Vereinten Nationen (UNCED) und des Nordamerikanische Freihandelsvertrags (NAFTA) durchgesetzt werden können. Dr. Joseph Duffey, Direktor der United States Information Agency (USIA), sagte 1994 während seiner Grundsatzrede auf dem Gipfeltreffen der nord- und südamerikanischen Staaten: "Der SCI ist weiterhin ein ungemein wichtiges Instrument, da es Ländern in dieser Hemisphäre dabei hilft, die uns allen gemeinsam bevorstehenden Ziele und Probleme anzugehen.. . . Nichts kann den persönlichen Kontakt ersetzen, der sich aus dem Austausch zwischen Partnerstädten ergibt."

FREIWILLIGE: Der SCI unterstützt und erhält ein ausgedehntes Netz von Freiwilligen, die den Bürgeraustausch und die gemeinschaftsbezogene Leitung fördern. Zu diesem Netz gehören:

- in jedem Staat freiwillig tätige Staatskoordinatoren, die als von außen hinzu kommende Mitarbeiter den kommunalen Partnerstadt-Komitees bei der Programmentwicklung behilflich sind.

- kommunale Komitee-Vorsitzende und städtische Beamte bzw. Angestellte die in über 1.200 Städten das Gros des Freiwilligennetzes in den ganzen Vereinigten Staaten ausmachen.

- Helfer aus den Gemeinden, deren Bürgerbewegung aus Hunderttausenden von Menschen besteht und die Mitglieder der kommunalen Partnerstadt-Komitees sind.

UNTERSTÜTZUNG: Die Mitarbeiter des SCI und die kommunalen Partnerstadt-Komitees verwalten eine große Vielfalt innovativer Stipendienprogramme, die neue Ideen kreieren und der Bewegung hin zu Partnerstädten neue Richtungen weisen sollen. Kürzlich durchgeführte Programme galten zum Beispiel der Unterstützung der kommunalen Ausbildung und dem Training, Lernprogrammen für Jugendliche über den Dienst an der Gemeinde, technischer Hilfe, der Durchführung von dreiseitigen Austauschverfahren und der unabhängigen Leitung von Zeitungen.

ZUKUNFT: Da inzwischen viele noch vor kurzem ziemlich isolierte Bundesstaaten zunehmend unabhängig werden, ist die globale Kooperation für deren gesellschaftliche und wirtschaftliche Entwicklung entscheidend. Um auch weiterhin den Bedürfnissen seines Netzes nachkommen zu könne hat der SCI seine Führungsrolle dadurch erweitert, daß er kommunalen Beamten bzw. Angestellten aus den neu entstehenden Demokratien Training und Unterstützung zukommen läßt, seine globalen Kommunikationsfähigkeiten verstärkt und multikulturelle Initiativen sowie Initiativen im Hinblick auf kulturelle Unterschiede unterstützt, durch welche gemeinsame soziale Probleme angesprochen und die Lebensqualität in Gemeinden verbessert werden sollen, die aus sehr unterschiedlichen Bevölkerungsteilen bestehen.

Sister Cities International
120 South Payne Street
Alexandria, Virginia 22314

German – USA Cities
February 1997

German Towns	US Partners
Aachen	Arlington County, VA
Altenberg	Western Piedmont, NC
Ansbach	Bay City, MI
Apolda	Rapid City, SD
Augsburg	Dayton, OH
Bad Königshofen	Arlington, TX
Bad Zwischenahn	Centerville, OH
Berlin	Los Angeles, CA
Berlin [Spandau]	Boca Raton, FL
Bexbach	Goshen, IN
Billerbeck	Englewood, OH
Bingen am Rhein	White Salmon, WA
Bissendorf	Huntingburg, IN
Braunfels	New Braunfels, TX
Braunschweig	Omaha, NE
Budingen	Tinley Park, IL
Coburg	Garden City, NY
Cologne	Indianapolis, IN
Crailsheim	Worthington, MN
Cranzahl	Running Springs, CA
Dorfen	Constantine, MI
Dortmund	Buffalo, NY
Dresden	Columbus, OH
Eberbach	Ephrata, PA
Eichstatt	Lexington, VA
Eisenach	Waberly, IA
Emmerich	Kirkland, WA
Erfurt	Shawnee, KS
Esslingen	Sheboygan, WI
Eutin	Lawrence, KS
Freiburg im Breisgau	Fryburg, PA
Friedrichshafen	Peoria, IL
Füssen	Helen, GA
Garbsen	Farmers Branch, TX
Garmisch Partenkirchen	Aspen, CO
Gau Algesheim	Redford, MI
Gedern	Columbia, IL
Gera	Fort Wayne, IN
Geissen	Waterloo, IA
Gotha	Gastonia, NC
Gottelfingen	Botkins, OH
Greifswald	Bryan-College Station, TX
Grunstadt	Bonita Springs, FL
Gunzenhausen	Frankenmuth, MI
Hamburg	Chicago, IL
Hamm	Chattanooga, TN
	Santa Monica, CA
Helmstedt	Albuquerque, MN
	Oxford, MS
Herford	Quincy, IL
Hof	Ogden, UT
Holzerlinger	Crystal Lake, IL
Ingelheim	Ridgefield, CT
Kaiserslautern	Davenport, IA
Kleve	Fitchburg, MA
Koblenz	Austin, TX
Königs Wusterhausen	Germantown, TN
Krefeld	Charlotte, NC
Kubelstein Stadt Schesslitz	Victoria, KS
Kusen	Marietta, OH
Leinfelden-Echterdingen	York, PA
Leipzig	Houston, TX
Lengerich	Wapakoneta, OH
Leonberg	Seward, NE
Lichtenfels	Vandalia, OH
Linz Am Rhein	Marietta, GA
Lübeck	Spokane, WA
Ludinghausen	Deerfield, IL
Ludwigsburg	St. Charles, MO

German Towns	US Partners
Ludwigshafen Am Rhein	Pasadena, Ca
Lutherstadt Wittenburg	Springfield, OH
Mainz	Louisville, KY
Malsch	Dinuba, CA
Mannheim	Manheim, PA
Marbach am Neckar	Washington, MO
Marl	Midland, MI
Melsungen	Elmira, NY
Memmingen	Glendale, AZ
Messtetten	Toccoa, GA
Montabaur	Fredericksburg, TX
Morzheim	Frederick, MD
Mühlacker	Tolleson, AZ
Munich	Cincinnati, OH
Münster	Fresno, CA
	Radcliff, KY
Neckargemünd	Missoula, MT
Neu Ulm	New Ulm, MN
Neusaess	Redwood Falls, MN
Neustadt an der Waldnaab	Hays, KS
Nienburg	Las Cruces, NM
Ofterdingen	Dexter, MI
Osnabrück	Evansville, IN
Paderborn	Belleville, IL
Passau	Hackensack, NJ
Pfaffenweiler	Jasper, IN
Pforzheim	Williamsville, NY
Pinneberg	Rockville, MD
Porta Westfalica	Waterloo, IL
Postdam	Sioux Falls, SD
Rastatt	New Britain, CT
Ratingen	Vermillion, SD
Regensburg	Tempe, AZ
Rheinsberg	Huber Heights, OH
Rodental	Eaton, OH
Saarbrücken	Pittsburgh, PA
Schaumburg	Schaumburg, IL
Schifferstadt	Frederick, MD
Schorndorf	Tuscaloosa, AL
Schwerin	Milwaukee, WI
Schwieberdingen	Belvidere, IL
Seevetal	Decatur, IL
Soltau	Coldwater, MI
Stade	Swarthmore, PA
	Lakewood, CO
Stuttgart	St. Louis, MO
Sulzfeld	El Cajon, CA
Schwäbisch Gmünd	Bethlehem, PA
Tegernsee	Ketchum, ID
Tirschenreuth	Santa Fe Springs, CA
Trier	Fort Worth, TX
Trossingen	Beavertown, OR
Tübingen	Ann Arbor, MI
Ulm	New Ulm, MN
Villingen-Schwenningen	Great Bends, KS
Walldorf	Astoria, OR
Wasserburg	Vincennes, IN
Wesel	Hagerstown, MD
Wiernsheim	New Harmony, IN
Wiesloch	Strugis, MI
Wilhelmshaven	Norfolk, VA
Winterlingen	Shiner, TX
Wittmund	Simsbury, CT
Wolfach	Richfield, OH
Wolfenbüttel	Kenosha, WI
Worms	Mobile, AL
Würzburg	Rochester, NY
Zittau	Portsmouth, OH
Zweibrucken	York County, VA

Panorama Deutschland

1997 feiert die Zeitschrift *German Life* ihr dreijähriges Bestehen

Durch die Präsentation der deutschen Kultur abseits aller Stereotypen und in ihrer ganzen Breite versucht die Zeitschrift *German Life*, Deutschland und seine weitreichenden Bindungen an die USA für ihre Leser zu analysieren und ihnen verständlich zu machen.

German Life erscheint alle zwei Monate und wendet sich an Leser, die sich für die verschiedenen Ausprägungen der deutschen Kultur in Geschichte und Gegenwart interessieren sowie für die Art und Weise, in der der deutsche Einfluß die Vereinigten Staaten geprägt hat. Ein Viertel der amerikanischen Bevölkerung stammt von deutschen Einwanderern ab, und viele Leser aus diesem Kreis haben einen bestimmten Informationsbedarf, dem die Zeitschrift gerecht zu werden sucht. Insofern werden in jeder Ausgabe deutsche und deutsch-amerikanische Themen etwa gleichgewichtig behandelt.

Obwohl ihr Name es kaum vermuten läßt, hat die Herausgeberin, Lisa Fitzpatrick, deutsche Vorfahren und kam so auf den Gedanken, die Zeitschrift zu gründen. Nach etlichen Jahren Berufserfahrung im Zeitungswesen war Frau Fitzpatrick an einer der Berichterstattung über Deutschland gewidmeten Zeitschrift interessiert. Da sie eine solche Zeitschrift auf dem Markt nicht finden konnte, gründete sie selbst eine.

Natürlich erwies sich die Gründung nicht so leicht, wie das vielleicht klingen mag. Zunächst gab es da die normalen, mit der Neugründung einer Zeitschrift verbundenen Schwierigkeiten, denn schließlich gehen im US-Zeitungsmarkt neun von zehn Neugründungen unter, nur jede zehnte überlebt. Außerdem gab es auch anfänglichst von mehreren Seiten Widerstände gegen die Idee einer sich nur mit Deutschland und seinem Umfeld befassenden Zeitschrift. Obwohl der letzte der beiden Weltkriege, in denen Deutschland eine so prominente Rolle gespielt hat, jetzt über fünfzig Jahre zurückliegt, sind Themen, die sich mit Deutschland befassen, bei vielen Menschen in den Vereinigten Staaten noch verpönt.

Obwohl *German Life* kontroversen Themen, wie etwa dem Holocaust, keineswegs aus dem Wege geht, stellt die Zeitschrift Deutschland insgesamt dar, und zwar von den verschiedensten Blickpunkten aus. Ausgaben erschienen zu sozialen Problemen wie der Armut in Deutschland und politischen Themen wie etwa den rechts radikalen Parteien, aber daneben auch Reiseberichte über Städte wie Augsburg, Berlin und Weimar. Darüber hinaus informiert *German Life* ihre Leser auch über Saisonereignisse wie etwa das Münchner Oktoberfest in der Herbstausgabe und den Karneval in der Winterausgabe, gibt in der Frühlingsausgabe dem Reiseteil etwas mehr Gewicht und diskutiert im Spätsommer Bildung und Politik.

In seinen Rubriken konzentriert sich *German Life* auf besondere Aspekte de Lebens von Deutschen und Deutsch-Amerikanern in Geschichte und Gegenwart. An Kunst interessierte Leser können durch die "Galerie" blätter und Buch-, Film- und Musikliebhaber die "Bibliothek" aufsuchen. Die Rubrik "Zuhause" enthält Ratschläge zum Kochen, zur Wohnungseinrichtur und sogar zur Haltung von Haustieren. Schließlich enthält jede Ausgabe auc einen besonderen Werbeteil mit einem Verzeichnis von Kauf- und Versandhäusern, bei denen die Leser deutsche Produkte bestellen können, ohne erst eine aufwendige transatlantische Reise antreten zu müssen.

Die Leserschaft von *German Life* zeigt großes Interesse an "ihrer" Zeitschrift. Die gegenwärtig Auflage beträgt etwa 40.000 Exemplare, wozu im voraus bezahlte Abonnements, Verkäufe an Kiosken und Zeitungsständen in Buchläden sowie die Verteilung in deutsch-amerikanischer Betrieben und Organisationen beiträgt. Das Leserprofil der Zeitschrift zeigt, daß die Leser i allgemeinen gebildet sind, viel reisen und zu über 80 % von deutschen, österreichischen oder schweizerischen Vorfahren abstammen. Um Leserwünschen nachzukommen, wird *German Life* neben der traditionellen Betonung deutsche Probleme in allernächster Zukunft auch Themen aus Österreich und der deutschsprachigen Schweiz ihren gebührenden Platz einräumen.

Nach der erfolgreichen Gründungsphase ist die Zeitschrift jetzt so positioniert, daß sie auf den Ausbau ihrer Leserschaft und ihrer internationalen Kontakte hinarbeiten kann.

Heidi L. Whitesell
Redakteurin

Weitere Auskünfte erhalten Sie bei *German Life*,
Telefon-Nr.: (800) 314-6843
[diese Telefonnummer ist nur in den USA gebührenfrei]

Am Ende des Zweiten Weltkrieges

Deutschamerikaner halfen notleidenden Deutschen

Von Ernst Ott

Als am Ende des verheerenden Krieges viele deutsche Städte in Schutt und Asche lagen und Millionen von Flüchtlingen und Vertriebenen aus den Ost- und Südostländern Europas nach Westdeutschland strömten, waren Deutschamerikaner unter den ersten, die ein Hilfsprogramm einleiteten.

Während CARE, die Quakers, kirchliche Organisationen usw. große humanitäre Anstrengungen unternahmen, begannen auch viele der deutschamerikanischen Vereine unter ihren Mitgliedern Lebensmittel und Spenden zu sammeln, um den notleidenden deutschen und österreichischen Familien zu helfen.

Sie waren auch unter den ersten, die Bürgschaften für Einwanderer übernahmen und ihnen bei der Ankunft in Amerika, ihrer neuen "Heimat", auf die Beine halfen. Ihrer selbstlosen Bereitschaft, bedürftigen Verwandten, Freunden und selbst totalen Fremden zu helfen, gebührt unsere Anerkennung und Dankbarkeit.

At The End of World War II

German Americans Helped Needy Germans

By Ernst Ott

When many German cities lay in ruins at the end of the disastrous war and millions of refugees from the eastern and southeastern lands of Europe crowded into what was called West Germany, German Americans were among the first to initiate aid and relief programs.

While large-scale humanitarian efforts were undertaken by CARE, the Quakers, religious organizations etc., many of the German American societies started their own food and financial help drives among their members to alleviate the sufferings of German and Austrian families.

They were also among the first to provide sponsorships for immigrants and helped getting them established once they arrived in America, their new "Heimat". Their unselfish readiness to assist their relatives, friends and even total strangers in need deserves the recognition and gratitude of all of us.

Surveying the German Panorama:

German Life Magazine Celebrates Three-year Anniversary in 1997

Going beyond stereotypes and into the broader issues behind German culture, *German Life* magazine seeks to explore and understand Germany and its extensive connections to the United States.

A bimonthly written for all interested in the diversity of German culture, past and present, and in the various ways that the United States has been shaped by its German ties, *German Life* fills an information gap for its readers, many of whom are Americans of German ancestry and who thus come from one-fourth of the U.S. population. In each issue, the magazine strikes a delicate balance between coverage of Germany and of German-American issues.

Though her last name may not reflect it, the magazine's publisher, Lisa Fitzpatrick, is of German heritage, which influenced her decision to launch the project. After years of working in the publishing business, Lisa was interested in a magazine devoted to coverage of Germany. Not finding such a magazine on the market, she founded her own.

Of course, the establishment of *German Life* was not quite that easy. Besides the expected challenges of starting a magazine in a market where nine out of ten new launches do not survive, the notion of a publication devoted to German-related issues encountered initial resistance on various sides. Some fifty years after Germany's prominent role in two World Wars, topics regarding the country still carry a stigma in many people's minds.

While *German Life* does not, by any means, ignore controversy-engendering topics like the Holocaust, for example, the magazine portrays all aspects of German life–in all its diversity. Past issues have included topics ranging from social issues such as poverty in Germany to political issues like the rightwing parties and travel features on the cities of Augsburg, Berlin, or Weimar. Moreover, *German Life* follows seasonal topics, such as the Oktoberfest in the fall issue, carnival festivities in the winter, a greater focus on travel of for the spring, and a look toward education and politics in the late summer months.

In its departments, *German Life* focuses on specific aspects of German and German-American historical and present-day living. The artistically inclined might peruse the Gallery and the book, film, or music connoisseur the Library. The At Home department shares insights into cuisine, home design, and even household projects. In addition, each issue contains a special advertising directory of retail and mail-order companies giving readers access to German products without the fuss of international travel.

German Life's readers maintain an active interest in the magazine. Current circulation is approximately 40,000, including paid subscriptions, newsstand/bookstore sales, and distribution to German-American businesses and organizations. The publication's readers show themselves to be well educated and well traveled; more than 80 percent have German, Austrian, or Swiss roots. To satisfy readership requests, the publication will soon be including broader coverage of not just Germany, but also Austria and German-speaking Switzerland.

Springing forward from a successful start, *German Life* now looks forward to building its readership and international exposure.

For more information, contact *German Life* at (800) 314-6843.

Heidi L. Whitesell, Editor

Zeitgeist Publishing, 1 Corporate Drive, Grantsville, MD 21536 • Fax: 301-895-5029

German Corner™

Your Resource Guide to German Goods in the US

Webpage on Internet
www.germancorner.com / www.german-usa.com

The German Corner (http://www.german-usa.com or http://www.germancorner.com) is a home port for all Germans or German-Americans/Canadians living abroad. This website, written in English, contains a nationwide resource guide for German goods and services in the USA and Canada, a club index, as well as a monthly bi-lingual magazine, a German recipe and poetry collection, an events calendar, free personal ads, and much more. The German Corner doesn't limit itself just to Germans - they also include Swiss, Liechtensteiners, Austrians and other Germanic people.

Creator and founder Katharina Davitt came to the US in 1992 and found herself longing for some of the German goods and German culture she was used to. Her husband, having slightly more basic needs, missed his German beer. After her unsuccessful search for those 'homey' items, she started a web page on the Internet; after all, her technical background is in computer science.

To date the website has evolved from its small beginnings into a professional site, which counts Alpentraum, Amerika Woche, Der Buchwurm, European Classics, Freie Zeitung, German Music Import, Landmark Books Unlimited, and Neue Presse among it's customers. The German Corner is presently comprised of more than 800 pages, over 4000 business addresses, over 1000 subscribers to the monthly e-mail newsletter, and welcomes more than 4000 visitors each month, thus creating the first and largest German-American magazine and resource guide nationwide. Companies and organizations trying to reach a German-American audience will find a true home here.

The **Monthly Magazine** contains both German and English columns and deals with our German heritage. Some of the columns are written by professional writers. For instance, "Notes of an Outlander" by Ortrun Wenzel-Gates is a column about German Americans. Elisabeth Castleman, a professional food writer, features a column "Culinary Roots of the '90's" presenting a Germanic food and cuisine topic every month. Mary Ann Lindner Allen, a true Germanic homemaker born in the US, writes "Memories of Days Gone By", a historical perspective. Continuing through the magazine you will find news (provided by

the German Information Center), descriptions of famous German-Americans and German traditions, questions from the US citizenship test (fun for citizens and non-citizens alike) and a craft page. Also represented are various poets with at least one of their best known poems. The travel pages alternate with suggestions for trips through Germany or the United States. While the columnists write in English, the travel page and some of the other pages mentioned already are written in German. The magazine is still growing and Mrs. Davitt is always interested in suggestions and/or articles about the activities or history of clubs and societies.

The magazine is not the only thing you will find on this site. Here is a snapshot of other services provided:

- **Resource Guide** - provides a listing in Yellow Page format of German goods and services.
- **Cultural Pages** - information about clubs, radio shows, events and bands.
- **Travel section** - information about regions, towns, national parks and other attractions in North America and Europe.
- **Educational Information** - tips about student exchanges and language information.
- **Kitchen Corner** - conversion charts, recipes and other useful tips.
- **Personal Ads** - a free place for anyone to place an ad.
- **Chat room** - a place were interested parties meet twice a month on the Internet to talk about German-American related issues, or just for fun.

The German Corner recently added a **Small Shopping Mall**, where German goods are sold at a special discount to the readers. This promotion is done in conjunction with known German-American companies. The offers change bi-monthly.

As the German Corner forges ahead into the future, we invite you to become part of our family.

www.german-usa.com or **www.germancorner.com**

Visit often, list your clubs or businesses with us. If you are running a business dealing with Germanic goods, consider advertising on this our site and thus reach a whole new generation of German-Americans.

Be part of the future!

Deutsche Ecke

Die deutsche Ecke, **German Corner** (http://www.german-usa.com oder http://www.germancorner.com) ist ein Heimathafen für alle Deutschstämmigen in den USA und Kanada. Die German Corner umfaßt nicht nur Deutsche, sie schließt auch Schweizer, Liechtensteiner, Österreicher, Deutsch-Amerikaner/Kanadier und alle die am Deutsch-Amerikanertum interessiert sind, ein. Auch Leute, die keinerlei Verbindung zu Deutschland haben, werden die Seite aufschlußreich und anregend finden. Die Webseite, der Einfachheit wegen auf Englisch geschrieben, enthält ein landesweites Branchenbuch für deutsche Produkte und Dienstleistungen in den USA und Kanada, ein Vereins-Verzeichnis, sowie eine monatliches zweisprachiges Magazin. Unter anderem auch eine deutsche Rezept- und Gedichtesammlung, einen Veranstaltungskalender, ein Anschlagbrett für persönliche Anzeigen, um nur einige aufzuzählen.

Die Herausgeberin Katharina Davitt kam im Jahre 1992 mit ihrem Mann in die Vereinigten Staaten, und bekam Sehnsucht nach den gewohnten deutschen Gegenständen und der Kultur. Ihr Ehemann hatte einfachere Sorgen, er vermißte eigentlich nur das deutsche Bier. Da sie in ihrem Beruf als Computertechniker täglichen Umgang mit Computern hatte, dachte sie bald daran, das Internet als "Auskunftsbüro" für ihre Bedürfnisse zu benutzen und baute so ihre erste Webseite.

Das war damals. Heute können Sie Firmen wie Alpentraum, Amerika Woche, Der Buchwurm, European Classics, Freie Zeitung, German Music Imports, Landmark Books Unlimited, und Neue Presse auf der German Corner finden. Diese Webseite hat gegenwärtig mehr als 800 Seiten, über 4000 Firmenaddressen, über 1000 Abonnenten des monatlichen electronischen Rundschreibens, und begrüßt mehr als 4000 Besucher pro Monat. Damit hat sich die German Corner zur ersten und größten landesweiten deutsch-amerikanischen Webseite entwickelt. Vereine und Organisationen die ein deutsch-amerikanisches Publikum erreichen möchten, finden hier eine wahre Heimat.

Das **monatliche Magazin** ist Heimat für deutsche und englische Artikel, die sich hauptsächlich mit deutschen Themen in Amerika beschäftigen. Einige Seiten werden von bekannten Verfassern geschrieben. Zum Beispiel, "Notes of an Outlander" von Ortrun Wenzel-Gates. Sie schreibt diese Spalte über Deutsch-Amerikaner. Elisabeth Ciacon Castleman, eine Küchenexpertin und kulinarischere Beraterin bietet monatlich, durch Culinary Roots of the '90's", deutsche Küche und Rezepte an. Mary Ann Lindner Allen, eine Hausfrau deutscher Abstammung, aber in Amerika geboren, schreibt "Memories of Days Gone By" aus geschichtlicher Perspective.

Von aktuellen Nachrichten aus Deutschland (zur Verfügung gestellt von dem German Information Center), Schilderungen berühmter Deutsch-Amerikanern und von deutschen Traditionen, einer Reise- und Bastelseite, bis zu Informationen über amerikanische Staatsbürgerschaft, das Magazine ist eine Fundgrube für jedermann. Frau Davitt ist ständig auf der Suche nach Interessanten Neuigkeiten oder Klubnachrichten, die sie gerne kostenlos bekanntmachen wird.

German Corner hat mehr zu bieten. Hier ist ein Schnappschuß:

Resource Guide - dieses Branchen-Verzeichnis ist eine Auflistung von deutschen Waren und Dienstleistungen.

Cultural Pages - die Kulturseiten geben Auskünfte über Vereine, Radiosendungen, Ereignisse und Musikgruppen.

Travel Section - ein Reiseplaner gibt Auskünfte über Regionen, Städte, Nationalparks und andere Anziehungspunkte in Nordamerika und Europa

- **Educational Information** - Tips über Sprache und Studentenaustausch
- **Kitchen Corner** - Umrechnungstabellen, Rezepte und andere nützlichen Tidbits.
- **Personal Ads** - eine freie Anzeigentafel für jedermann.
- **Chat Room** - ein Treffpunkt für Interessenten, zweimal im Monat trifft man sich im Internet, redet über deutsch-amerikanische Angelegenheiten, oder nur zum Spaß.

Die **German Corner** laded sie herzlich zu einen regelmäßigen Besuch ein. Frau Davitt steht Ihnen gerne mit Rat und Tat zur Verfügung, falls Sie ihre deutschen Waren oder Dienstleistungen anzubieten haben und eine ganz neue Generation von Deutsch-Amerikanern erreichen wollen. Nehmen auch Sie an der Zukunft teil!

German Corner
Davitt Publications,
Box 1116
Jessup, MD 20794
Phone: 410 / 519-1749   Fax: 410 / 519-1184
Webaddress: http://www.german-usa.com
E-mail: davitt@german-usa.com

~~~~~~~

Blaskapelle "Alte Kameraden"

Die Blaskapelle "Alte Kameraden" aus Fairfax, Virginia hat bei Festlichkeiten, Konzerten und anderen feierlichen Anlässen sein Publikum seit über 20 Jahren mit flotten Märschen und anderer Bayerischer Volksmusik unterhalten. Es gibt vier gute Kassetten Aufnahmen.

For over 20 years, the "Old Comrades" of Fairfax, VA have treated American audiences to the sound of European village bands, entertaining, with four recordings, and frequent performances at Washington's embassies, ethnic festivals, and community events.

Contact "Kapellmeister" Samuel Laudenslager at 703 / 978-8642

Size comparison Federal Republic of Germany vs United States

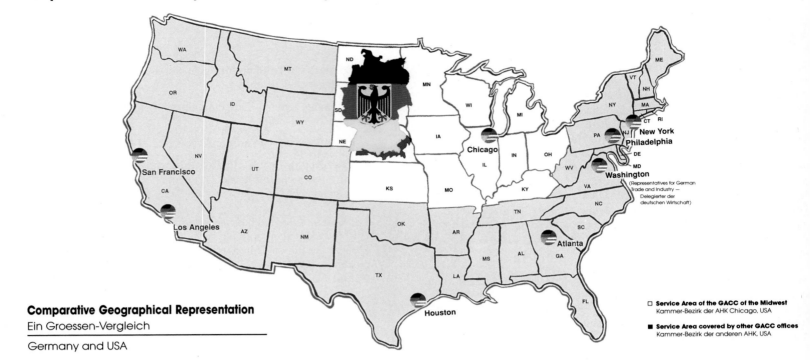

Comparative Geographical Representation

Ein Groessen-Vergleich

Germany and USA

□ **Service Area of the GACC of the Midwest**
Kammer-Bezirk der AHK Chicago, USA

■ **Service Area covered by other GACC offices**
Kammer-Bezirk der anderen AHK, USA

German American Chambers of Commerce

Atlanta: Thomas Beck, Managing Director
3340 Peachtree Rd., Suite 500 Tel: (404)239-9494
Atlanta, GA 30326 Fax: (404)264-1761
E-Mail Address: 74672.3117@compuserve.com
States Served: Alabama, Florida, Georgia, North Carolina,
South Carolina & Tennessee

Chicago: Christian J. Röhr, Managing Director
401 N. Michigan Ave., Suite 2525 Tel: (312)644-2662
Chicago, IL 60611-4212 Fax: (312)644-0738
E-Mail Address: 106025.402@compuserve.com
States Served: Illinois, Indiana, Iowa, Kansas, Kentucky,
Michigan, Minnesota, Missouri, Nebraska, North Dakota, Ohio,
South Dakota & Wisconsin

Houston: Friedhelm Kuhlmann, Managing Director
5599 San Felipe, Suite 510 Tel: (713)877-1114
Houston, TX 77056 Fax: (713)877-1602
E-Mail Address: gacchou@flex.net
States Served: Arkansas, Louisiana, Mississippi, Oklahoma &
Texas

Los Angeles: Michael Krieg, Managing Director
5220 Pacific Concourse Dr., Suite 280 Tel: (310)297-7979
Los Angeles, CA 90045 Fax: (310)297-7966
E-Mail Address: 104165.3056@compuserve.com
States Served: Arizona, California (south of Fresno), Colorado,
Nevada (southern part - Las Vegas), New Mexico & Utah

New York: Werner Walbröl, President & CEO
40 W. 57th Street, 31st Floor Tel: (212)974-8830
New York, NY 10019-4092 Fax: (212)974-8867
E-Mail Address: 72700.3042@compuserve.com
States Served: Connecticut, Maine, Maryland, Massachusetts,
New Hampshire, New Jersey*, New York, Pennsylvania*, Rhode
Island, Vermont, Virginia, Washington DC, West Virginia &
Puerto Rico
* except GACC-Philadelphia region

Philadelphia: Barbara Afanassiev, Managing Director
1515 Market Street, Suite 505 Tel: (215)665-1585
Philadelphia, PA 19102 Fax: (215)665-0375
E-Mail Address: 104753.426@compuserve.com
States Served: Delaware, New Jersey (south of 178, west of US
206 and JU 571/525/539), Pennsylvania (eastern)

San Francisco: Lawrence A. Walker, Managing Director
465 California St., Suite 506 Tel: (415)392-2262
San Francisco, CA 94104 Fax: (415)392-1314
E-Mail Address: 76375.1513@compuserve.com
States Served: Alaska, California (north of Fresno), Hawaii,
Idaho, Montana, Nevada (northern part - Reno), Oregon,
Washington & Wyoming

Washington, DC: Jakob Esser, Representative
Representative for Tel: (202)659-4777
German Trade & Industry Fax: (202)659-4779
1627 I Street, NW, Suite 550
Washington, DC 20006
E-Mail Address: 104075.1540@compuserve.com
Representative Office

German Weeks In Washington, D.C.

Reprinted from Deutschland Magazine, October 1996

Washington's great Union Station is one of the largest railroad stations in the world, with a length of 760 feet and a width of 343 feet. It is an imposing Beaux Arts building which hosts not only commuters every day but a large number of visitors: the station acts as a crossroads for some 70,000 people a day, not a bad place if you're looking for attention. German business used the ambience of America's most beautiful railroad terminal in presenting a major exhibition: The first weeks in October 1996, where the first "Deutsche Wochen," or German Weeks, in the United States, celebrated under the banner, "From Germany...To You."

From October 1st to 11th, people experienced first hand those inventions "Made in Germany" without which everyday life would be no longer imaginable: the first automobile, the first bicycle, the first telephone; the first television, the first refrigerator, the first printed book: The list of German innovations which overran the world is very long indeed. The exhibition was concentrated at the heart of the terminal, the waiting room, which is modeled after the great central hall in the Baths of Diocletian in Rome. Here, on more than 20 exhibition islands, the public saw how German inventions of long ago, such as the Otto or Diesel engines, still form the basis of Germany's best products today.

Visitors also marvelled at newer German inventions, such as the superfast Transrapid train, which uses a video in inviting onlookers to take a cyberspace journey from Hamburg to Berlin.

In the shopping mall, 70 retailers offered traditional German brand names: Apart from brands already well-established on the American market, such as Nivea, Dresden china, and Underberg - the new in-drink at bars in the countryside - newcomers made the leap across the Pond. With the advice and help of the German-American Business Association, 15 firms from the new federal states presented their goods for the first time on the American market. This initiative was being sponsored by the German Federal Ministry of Economics, which also organized the whole event..

Washington's famous Union Station was decorated with American and German Flags.

Photos by Ernst Ott

"From Germany...To You", the Concordia Youth Band from Kiel plays favorite German and American tunes.

One of the highlights of German Weeks was a quiz about Germany, run up on an old printing press. This will allow everyone to test their knowledge about Germany and even learn something new.

But "German Weeks" were not made up solely of product exhibitions. A program of arts rounded out the entire happening. There were musical performances ranging from the classical to modern jazz; there was entertainment by a musical corps of the Bundeswehr, and, of course, some original Bavarian "Schuhplattler.." The German movie industry was presenting both amusing and intellectual offerings and, most importantly, the world exhibition in Hanover, Expo 2000, was a central attraction.

The Press and Information Office of the Federal Government had its own information area set up in one of the terminal's main halls where the public had its questions answered by representatives of the German Embassy, the Ministry of Economics, and the German Tourism Office. An Internet cafe was an additional source of information, providing direct connections to home pages of all those institutions and companies taking part. And in order to do justice to the historical relationship between Germany and the United States, the Bundeswehr had organized an exhibition titled "Paths to Friendship", with pictures and documents from over four centuries.

Apart from the official opening and closing celebrations for invited guests from the worlds of politics and business, the general public also had an opportunity to join in the fun. Doffing a hat to the Oktoberfest, the weekend of October 5th-6th, German American Day, was celebrated in all the restaurants at the station, with wine, beer, sausage, and of course, music from Germany. Ambassador Jürgen Chrobog who, with his team, came up with the overall idea and has had chief responsibility for "German Weeks," hopes that the event will be supported by the entire German community in the United States, in order to ensure that "From German - To You," will continue into the future.

Deutschamerikanischer Bürgerverein von Maryland, Inc.

The German-American Citizens Association of Maryland

The German Festival at Baltimore's Inner Harbor

Founded May 9, 1900 and incorporated April 8, 1904, it strives for a closer union of German clubs, organizations and citizens of German descent in the promotion of German culture, language, gymnastics and soccer through cultural education, social and charitable endeavors.

The **Deutschamerikanischer Bürgerverein von Maryland** is an "umbrella" association consisting of 15 German-American organizations within the State of Maryland. The "Bürgerverein" represents the German ethnic community and is the spokesman of it and its members on a city, state and national level.

The **"Bürgerverein"** serves as a coordinating and facilitating body for its membership and the community as a whole by providing a forum for matters of concern. A community *"Calendar of Events"* is maintained by the Bürgerverein to prevent date and activity conflicts among its member organizations.

The **"Bürgerverein"** plans and promotes all major cultural and educational activities and exchanges with the primary objective of maintaining and enhancing German customs, traditions and culture within its own community as well as maintaining good relations with the German Embassy and groups abroad and at home.

DEUTSCHAMERIKANISCHER BÜRGERVEREIN

VON MARYLAND 1900

Participating Clubs & Societies

Arion Gesangverein
Baltimore Kickers
Blob's Park
Club Fidelitas
Deutsche Geselligkeit
Edelweiss Club
G.T.V. Annapolis Bavarians
G.T.V. Immergrün
General German Aged People's Home
German Radio Klub
German Society of Maryland
Maryland Oktoberfest
Schlaraffia Baltimora
Society for the History of Germans in MD
Verein Deutscher Trachten

Am 9. Mai, 1900 gegründet und am 8. April 1904 eingetragen, strebt der Bürgerverein eine enge Verbindung mit den deutschen Klubs, Organisationen und Bürgern deutscher Herkunft an, um die deutsche Kultur, Sprache, Gymnastik und Fußball durch Schulung, Geselligkeit und Fürsorge zu fördern.

Der Deutschamerikanische Bürgerverein von Maryland ist ein Dachverband der aus 15 einzelnen deutsch-amerikanischen Vereinen im Staate Maryland besteht.

Der Bürgerverein vertritt die deutsche Gemeinschaft und ist Sprecher für sie und seine Mitglieder auf Stadt, Land und nationaler Ebene.

Der Bürgerverein dient als koordinierendes und ausführendes Organ zwischen seiner Mitgliedschaft und der Gemeinde allgemein. Ein Aktivitätskalender wird für alle Beteiligten geführt, um mögliche Überschneidungen zu vermeiden.

Der Bürgerverein plant und fördert alle größeren, kulturellen und festlichen Anlässe, mit dem Zweck die deutschen Sitten, Traditionen und Gebräuche zu pflegen und zu fördern. Außerdem ist man bemüht ein gutes Verhältnis mit der Botschaft und anderen Gruppen, in Übersee und daheim zu unterhalten.

Bob Sheppard, President

Deutschamerikanischer Bürgerverein von Maryland, Inc.
Post Office Box 22367, Baltimore, Maryland 21203, Phone: 410/522-4144

The German American Dilemma

By Ernst Ott

In order to understand the dilemma of the German Americans and their often voiced reluctance to become involved in the political process we have to go back a bit into the history of the last 90 years.

The anti-German sentiment by a large segment of the population can be traced back to the fact that America was, during that time, involved in two wars with Germany. In America you had both pro and anti-imperial (1914-1918) and pro-and anti-Hitler camps (1933-1945). In the two World Wars, Germans were fighting Germans on opposite sides. Even during the Revolutionary War, German colonists in Washington's army were fighting Hessian mercenaries in the service of the British Crown.

On April 5th, 1994, the German American Studies Program of the University of Cincinnati and the Ohio Historical Society documented the extent of the anti-German hysteria with an exhibit in connection with the dedication of a historic marker. Ohio Governor George V. Voinovich also issued a proclamation as a tribute to those who suffered from prejudice and hate. The following account, as documented by Dr. Don Heinrich Tolzmann and excerpts from the American press, gives a shocking testimony of the hate propaganda during World War I.

The Anti-German Hysteria
German-American Life on the Home Front

"In the United States the declaration of the war in Europe in 1914 signaled the beginnings of a hysterical crusade to seek out and destroy any- and everything remotely connected to America's German heritage. The Anti-German Hysteria reached its height in April 1918, but continued into the 1920s.

One needs only to read reports of the events of the day in the New York Times, or a local newspaper such as the Cincinnati Enquirer to gauge the level of the anti-Germanism. Family names were changed, business and organization names were changed, street names were changed, words disappeared from the language, German-Americans were interned; even a bird was interned for the duration. Library books and textbooks were censored and burned. German-Americans could expect to be visited by vigilantes, who dragged them out of their homes, usually at night, and forced them to parade around the city and kiss the flag, or similar. Some were then tarred and feathered, or hung. Flags were nailed to buildings of "pro-Germans." Buildings or monuments or people were painted yellow. Some monuments were removed. In Chicago, Bible passages in German on a church wall were whitewashed over. German-Americans were dismissed from jobs because of their ancestry.

In 1918 rumors of sabotage and spying by German-Americans were rampant and accepted as fact. For example, in a speech in Chicago March 1, 1918, the international president of the Rotary Club stated

that there were 110,000 German agents in the U.S. The Federal Food Administrator for Pennsylvania suggested in a speech in Philadelphia that 10,000 German propagandists in that state should be "hanged to telegraph poles and shot full of holes."

In both world wars, there were numerous wrongs and injustices suffered by German-Americans. They suffered for no other reason than because of their heritage. Over 75 years have passed since the street names were changed in Cincinnati, and although the war hysteria is over, the street names have not been restored. On April 5, 1994 a historic plaque was placed in Fairview Park, overlooking Over-The-Rhine, to recall the original names of the streets."

After World War I, with the German Imperial Government defeated and Germany in political and economic turmoil, a new wave of German immigrants washed ashore. But the rise of Hitler's regime with all its disastrous consequences soon caused another round of anti-German sentiment which culminated in America again going to war against Germany. At the end of World War II many German American organizations were largely decimated or had disappeared completely.

While the "Morgenthau Plan" advocated, as a severe punishment, a partial dismemberment, political and economic restrictions and long military occupation of Germany, the rapidly developing threat of Communism and the aggressive posture of Russia made it imperative for the "West" to reestablish a strong West-Germany, both economically and militarily. "The Marshall Plan", private help institutions e.g. Quakers, Care, etc. were instrumental in a quick recovery. The European Community and NATO with Germany as a partner built a strong defense against Russia and the Warsaw Pact."

Dr. Don H. Tolzmann

America Calling

The post-war economic boom in America, and the shifting into high gear of the industrial complex, required a labor pool that could only be provided by opening the door to large scale immigration, particularly from Europe. Millions of displaced persons, refugees and expellees from Communist countries were languishing in Germany and Austria. They represented an available resource ready to be tapped. For these displaced person (called DPs), emigration was the great hope for a new start in life. Australia and South America opened their doors as well but it was America and Canada that most wanted to go to.

Those who had relatives, friends or professional contacts in these countries often received valuable assistance and sponsorships to obtain the necessary immigration visa and quota to speed up the process. But even those without connections had opportunities to make the trip to the "New World". American industry and agriculture were searching for skilled and even unskilled labor; the Midwestern states in particular reached out to Europe's potential resource. Pennsylvania's steel mills, Indiana's and Wisconsin's heavy machinery and foundry industry and the large Midwest farm belt, they all sent scouting commissions to Germany and Austria to recruit their badly needed work force. To the chosen they offered immediate jobs and immigration quota, even free transportation and housing upon arrival. Offers that were hard to refuse. (Yours truly came as such a farm hand to Wisconsin).

There were other private initiatives as well; such as churches, cultural and ethnic organizations that took an interest in attracting new blood from the "old country". Thus thousands of today's German Americans, came to America and Canada and received their new start in life.

For many it was a tough start; learning the language, becoming used to a completely different life style etc. but it was a good change, compared to what they left behind. Yes, there were instances where these newcomers, "Greenhorns", were taken advantage of, but eventually they were able to extract themselves from these adverse conditions.

Those post-war immigrants that came to urban or even rural areas that had German American families or societies quickly found "Anschluß" and a "home away from home", where they could converse in their mother tongue or meet other Germans or German Americans to associate with. Those surviving World War II societies were also eager to embrace the new arrivals. Where there was an organizational void, the newcomers bounded together and started their own clubs, and societies. Germans are very good at that! Thus, many new societies were founded by these first generation immigrants.

The large, post World War II immigration waves took place in the early 50s and 60s but were slowed down at the outbreak of the Korean and Vietnam wars, when particularly draft-age young men preferred to emigrate to Canada and other countries not involved in a war.

Germans in the American Armed Forces uniform? Less than 10 years after the war? "Uncle Sam" was very pragmatic about it. "YOU came to America, received the benefits of American citizens but you also have to share the responsibilities and obligations." To be frank, not more than fair. When the Korean and Vietnam wars started and young Americans were called to arms, why not legal residents and aspiring citizens?

Yours truly also received "Uncle Sam's greetings" a little after a year in America and followed his call. Yes, there was some arm twisting in the "invitation" in the form of a statement that "refusal to honor the draft could result in a denial to be granted citizenship." However, there were also obvious advantages. Draftees could apply for citizenship while in the Armed Forces rather than having to wait 5 years before becoming eligible. In my own case, I became a citizen after less than 2 years in America with all the veterans' educational, insurance and other benefits. Your employer had to guarantee taking you back after completing active service. Not bad at all. From most accounts I know of, Germans were treated fairly in the Armed Forces, accepted as equals and promoted just like other American-born soldiers. There was a good camaraderie among GIs. Many German inductees were even lucky enough to serve in Germany.

Plattduetscher Vereen and Altenheim

Franklin Square, Long Island, N.Y.

Photos by Jack Williams

With the large-scale post war immigration, the German American communities in America began to grow but with rather different implications. While the established World War II surviving organizations benefitted from the addition of new immigrant members, American-born ethnic Germans were slow in returning to the old societies. Even today, the majority of the active societies' members are first generation immigrants. Also, most of the new societies were founded by these immigrants. The two largest national umbrella organizations, the Deutsch Amerikanischer National Kongress, DANK (German American National Congress) and the Vereinigte Deutsch Amerikanische Kommittee, VDAK, (The United German American Committee of the USA), were both founded in the late 50s and early 60s.

In large metropolitan areas, such as New York, Chicago, Milwaukee, Philadelphia, Pittsburgh, Cleveland, St. Louis, etc. where large immigrant waves settled, new ethnic German centers and neighborhoods developed. German restaurants, clubs, shops, newspapers, etc., began to flourish. The dream of many Germans to own their own home out in the suburbs or country, with a garden or spacious backyard and flowers, a cottage at the lake or in the woods, became reachable. Slowly at first, but then at an accelerated pace, Germans moved away from the inner cities into the suburbs. Traditional German neighborhoods began to thin out. In the absence of new German immigrants, other ethnic groups moved in. Soon the major German sections of New York (Yorkville), Chicago's Lincoln Ave., etc. lost much of their German flavor. Many German clubs followed their members to the suburbs as well.

The audience enjoys singing and dancing

German country bands are always popular

German American Celebrations

Always a full house when German-Americans meet in the Trump Taj Mahal on the Boardwalk at Atlantic City, New Jersey.

The German Festival in May, the October Fest in the Fall and the Christkindl Festival in December are among the favorite celebrations at this elegant and extravagant resort-hotel-casino on the East Coast.

Super stars and attractions from the States and Germany's film and sound stage will keep the audience in awe, singing and dancing, and having a good time. Excellent Germanic food and a wide selection of gifts and souvenirs make a trip to these festivals in Atlantic City a great experience.

Deutsch-amerikanische Feste

Immer ein volles Haus, wenn sich echte Deutschamerikaner im Trump Taj Mahal auf dem Boardwalk in Atlantic City treffen.

Das "German Festival" im Mai, das Oktoberfest im Herbst und das "Christkindl Fest" zur Weihnachtszeit sind unter den beliebtesten deutschen Feiern im eleganten und superlativen Hotel - Casino an der Ostküste.

Superstars und Künstler, Kapellen und Schausteller aus den Staaten und Deutschlands Film und Musikwelt bringen die Besucher in fröhliche Stimmung, wo singen und tanzen an der Reihe sind.

Gute deutsche Küche und eine reichliche Auswahl an Geschenken, Musikkassetten und Souvenirs machen es immer wieder eine Reise nach Atlantic City wert.

Award presentation on the main stage

Many groups, such as this, visit from Europe

1000 Boardwalk, Atlantic City, NJ 08401
Information: 609 / 449 - 5230 Gisela Lewis

The Fritz Reuter Lifecare Community Celebrated Its 100th Anniversary June 1, 1997

The Fritz Reuter Altenheim, a continuous care retirement community, will be celebrating its 100th Anniversary with a Gala Dinner and Dance on Sunday, June 1, 1997, in the Grand Ball Room of Schuetzen Park, Bergen Turnpike (32nd Street) and Kennedy Boulevard, North Bergen, New Jersey.

Perhaps no activity in human affairs is more noble than to provide loving care to the elderly. The Fritz Reuter Altenheim has accomplished this mission as a non-profit, charitable organization with devotion and excellence since 1897. It is especially noteworthy that funding is supported in large part by voluntary efforts, donations and bequests. This benevolence has enabled the Altenheim (Home of the Aging) to admit many residents on a charitable basis during its 100 years of operation.

The centennial celebration will have as its guest speaker, Minister Dr. Arthur Caliandro (successor to Norman Vincent Peale) of the Marble Collegiate Church, New York City.

We look forward to the participation of the general public on the occasion of this historic event. Further details regarding reservations, donations and general information regarding applications for admission to our home may be obtained by writing to the Fritz Reuter Altenheim, 3161 Kennedy Boulevard, North Bergen, New Jersey 07047 or calling (201) 867-3585

The Origin of the name "Fritz Reuter"

The Fritz Reuter Altenheim derives its name from the Plattduetsche (North German) novelist and poet Fritz Reuter who was born on November 7, 1810 in Stavenhagen. He died on July 12, 1874. His father was a prosperous farmer who also served as Mayor. An activist for social justice,

The exercise room is enjoyed under the supervision of a qualified staff instructor.

Mr. Reuter's great service to mankind along with Klaus Groth and John Brinckmann was the revival of Plattduetsch as a literary language. Reuter, who was greatly influenced by Charles Dickens, excelled in character-ization and his works, like Dickens, exhibit a similar blend of humor, seriousness, and sentimentality, combined with a sincere ethical purpose.

The Past and Present

The Fritz Reuter Altenheim became a reality in 1897, when Henry Kroeger, President of the Plattduetsche Volksfest-Vereen of New York and New Jersey and delegates of the various Plattduetsche organizations voted to build a home for aging Germans that needed a place to live out their golden years. The cornerstone of the home was laid in 1898 and one year later, on June 15, 1899, the first occupants moved into the Home, which had beautifully furnished living quarters, a chapel, dining room, kitchen and other utility rooms. Today, the Fritz Reuter Life Care Retirement Community is a place for all, with a fully staffed nursing unit, a residential facility, and independent living apartments. Admission to any of these units is not limited to German speaking individuals but people of other ethnic origins as well.

The Home is managed by a Board of Trustees, House Committee, and Marketing Committee. A great deal of assistance to the residents and the home in general is rendered by the Frauen Verein des Fritz Reuter Altenheim (the women's auxiliary).

The greatest asset to the Fritz Reuter Altenheim is "peace of mind" knowing that one will be taken care of for life and will never have to transfer to a nursing home. Interested persons are invited to visit the home and to receive information regarding your retirement at our Life Care Retirement Community.

Die Fritz Reuter Lifecare Community feierte am 1. Juni 1997 ihr hundertjähriges Bestehen

Das Fritz Reuter Altenheim, eine Versorgungs- und Pflegegemeinschaft für Senioren, wird am 1. Juni 1997 ihr hundertjähriges Bestehen im großen Ballsaal des Schützen Parks (am Bergen Turnpike und Kennedy Boulevard) in North Bergen, New Jersey, feiern.

Kaum eine Tätigkeit im humanitären Bereich verdient größeren Respekt als die liebevolle Fürsorge für unsere älteren Mitmenschen. Das Fritz Reuter Altenheim, eine gemeinnützige, karitative Einrichtung, hat seit 1897 diese Aufgabe mit Hingabe und Auszeichnung erfüllt. Es ist besonders erwähnenswert, daß die Finanzierung zu einem großen Teil durch freiwillige Hilfe, Spenden und Vermächtnisse getragen wird. Durch diese Wohltätigkeiten war das Altenheim in der Lage, während der letzten hundert Jahre seines Bestehens eine Vielzahl von Bürgern auf karitativer Grundlage zuzulassen.

Pfarrer Dr. Arthur Caliandro (Nachfolger von Norman Vincent Peale) von der Marble Collegiate Kirche in New York wird als Gastredner auf der Jahrhundertfeier sprechen.

Wir freuen uns auf die rege Teilnahme der Bevölkerung, um dieses historische Ereignis mit uns zu feiern. Für weitere Informationen bezüglich Reservierungen, Spenden sowie Anträgen für die Aufnahme in unser Haus können Sie sich schriftlich an das Fritz Reuter Altenheim, 3161 Kennedy Boulevard, North Bergen, New Jersey 07047 wenden oder anrufen (201) 867-3585.

Wer war "Fritz Reuter"?

Das Fritz Reuter Altenheim leitet seinen Namen von dem niederdeutschen Romanschriftsteller und Dichter Fritz Reuter ab, der am 7. November 1810 in Stavenhagen geboren wurde und am 12. Juli 1874 starb. Sein Vater war ein wohlhabender Großbauer, der gleichzeitig das Amt des Bürgermeisters innehatte. Fritz Reuter setzte sich für soziale Gerechtigkeit ein, doch sein größter Dienst an der Menschheit bleibt zusammen mit Klaus Groth und John Brinckmann die Wiederbelebung des Plattdeutschen als Literatursprache. Reuter war stark von Charles Dickens, seinen Personendarstellungen und Werken, beeinflußt, und wie er stellte Reuter eine ähnliche Mischung aus Humor, Ernsthaftigkeit und Sentimentalität, verbunden mit einer aufrichtigen, ethischen Absicht heraus.

Damals und Heute

Die Idee für das Fritz Reuter Altenheim wurde 1897 Realität, als Henry Kröger, Vorsitzender des Plattduetschen Volksfest-Vereens von New York und New Jersey sowie Abgeordnete verschiedener plattduetscher Organisationen für den Bau eines Heims für ältere Deutsche, die einen Ort brauchten, wo sie den Rest ihres Lebens verbringen konnten, stimmten. Ein Jahr später wurde der Grundstein

gelegt, und am 15. Juni 1899, zogen die ersten Bewohner in das neue Heim ein. Es war mit schön eingerichteten Wohnbereichen, einer Kapelle, einem Speiseraum, einer Küche und weiteren Nutzräumen ausgestattet.

Heute ist die Fritz Reuter Life Care Retirement Community ein Ort für jeden. Sie beinhaltet eine voll ausgestattete Pflegeabteilung, eine Wohnheimanlage sowie individuelle Apartments. Die Annahme in eine dieser Einrichtungen ist nicht auf Deutschsprachige beschränkt und schließt auch Personen anderer Kulturkreise ein.

Das Heim wird durch ein Kuratorium, einen Heimausschuß und einen Marketing-Ausschuß verwaltet. Ein großer Teil der Hilfe für die Bewohner und für das Heim generell wird vom Frauen Verein des Fritz Reuter Altenheims geleistet.

Das wichtigste Gut des Fritz Reuter Altenheims ist der "Seelenfrieden". Man weiß, daß man für den Rest seines Lebens versorgt ist und nie in ein Pflegeheim wechseln muß. Jeder Interessierte ist eingeladen, sich das Heim anzusehen und sich Informationen über den Lebensabend in unserer Life Care Retirement Community einzuholen.

Dining pleasure with fellow residents of the Fritz Reuter Lifecare Retirement Community.

FRITZ REUTER
Lifecare Retirement Community
3163 Kennedy Boulevard
North Bergen, New Jersey 07047
(201) 867-3585

Deutscher Schul- & Gesangverein, Inc.
"Germania Park"

Gegründet 1895 von deutschen Arbeitern in der Gegend von Geithain, Sachsen, die in Dover bei Paul Günther in der Strumpfwaren Fabrik ihr Geld verdienten.

Heute ist es unser Ziel, weiterhin die deutsche Sprache und den Gesang zu pflegen. Unsere jährlichen Oktoberfeste, die wir mit Kapellen aus Deutschland feiern, helfen uns unser Heim zu erhalten.

Wir danken allen, die uns dabei unterstützen.

Freitags und Samstags ist das Clubhaus geöffnet, jederman ist willkommen. Jeden 2. Freitag im Monat ist Versammlung.

Wir grüßen alle Leser.

Arnold Lange,
Präsident

Conger Street, Rackaway TWP. near Dover
Information: 366-9693

Established in 1895 by workers from the Geithain, Sachsen area, who earned their money at Paul Guenther's stocking goods factory in Dover.

Today it is our aim to maintain the German language and music.

Our annual October Fests, which we celebrate with bands from Germany, help us to keep our Clubhouse in shape. We are grateful to all who support us.

The Clubhouse is open on Fridays and Saturdays and everybody is welcome. Every 2nd Friday is Meeting night.

Best regards to all readers.

Arnold Lange,
President

Founded 1935. "The Oasis for German Americans in New Jersey." Dance music every Saturday night with German American bands. Kitchen is open on Friday & Saturday nights and Sunday afternoons. German dinners available. German beers, wines and liqueurs at the bar. Shady grove ideal for outdoor festivals. Visiting bands from Germany. One of New Jersey's outstanding German cultural and social organizations. German language is encouraged.

Ladies Division - a strong supporter of the Club. Contact to various German Clubs in friendship and harmony. New members welcome!

Deutscher Club of Clark, Inc.

Gegründet 1935. Die Oase des Deutschtums in New Jersey. Jeden Samstagabend Tanzmusik mit deutsch-amerikanischen Musikkappellen. Küche Freitagabend, Samstagabend und Sonntagnachmittag geöffnet. Deutsche Speisen erhältlich. Deutsche Getränke im Ausschank. Ideales Gelände für Veranstaltungen im Freien. Besuch von Musikvereinen aus Deutschland. Reichhaltiges kulturelles Programm für Mitglieder. Erhaltung der deutschen Sprache.

Damenbteilung unterstützt Verein tatkräftig. Freundschaftliche Beziehungen zu anderen deutschen Organisationen werden gepflegt. Neumitglieder herzlich willkommen!

Deutscher Club of Clark, Inc.
787 Featherbed Lane • Clark, New Jersey 07066
(Garden State Parkway Exit 135)
Tel. (732) 574-8600

Freie Zeitung, Inc.

(FREE PRESS)
An American Newspaper printed in the German Language
Founded 1858 by Benedict Prieth

The "Freie Zeitung" (formerly New Jersey Freie Zeitung) looks back on an almost 140-year tradition.

The first edition of the "New Jersey Freie Zeitung" was published in Newark on April 26, 1858 upon the initiative of Benedict Prieth and appeared daily until 1932 and weekly after that.

After Louis Fischer of Fischer Travel Bureau, Irvington, took over the newspaper after World War II and served as the publisher, it again became an important instrument, serving as a bridge to the old homeland.

Max Richter became Editor-in-Chief, and Theo E. Daurer was a sports reporter and also became chief editor. He took over from Max Richter, before the NJFZ was purchased from Louis Fischer in 1963.

Theo Daurer passed away shortly afterwards and again, a sports reporter followed in his foot steps: Helmut Heimsch took every effort to keep the newspaper in circulation for the German-Americans and connected organizations. Heimsch died in 1978.

Eberhard Schweizer (Helmut Heimsch was his stepfather) was encouraged and asked by numerous clubs and organizations to continue the newspaper for the German American community. Improvements were made in the format, and the printing system was modernized.

The newspaper includes reports about politics, economics, sport and culture. Club news keep readers informed about German organizations. They appreciate to find information about German speaking and other European countries, which the American media usually ignores. Reporters contribute articles about large German events, like the German Heritage Festival, the Steuben Parade and others on a voluntary basis.

The change of the name to "Freie Zeitung" seemed appropriate, since subscriptions on the entire East Coast and especially in Florida increased tremendously.

The newspaper in the German language is a link to the old homeland for the majority of the readers and they appreciate the politically neutral, yet objective position. The editor and his staff are making every effort to preserve this as long as possible.

Die "Freie Zeitung" (früher New Jersey Freie Zeitung) erfreut sich fast 140-jähriger Tradition

Die erste Ausgabe der "New Jersey Freie Zeitung" erschien am 26. April 1858 in Newark auf Initiative von Benedict Prieth und wurde bis 1932 täglich und später einmal wöchentlich veröffentlicht. Als Louis Fischer (Fischer Reisebüro, Irvington) nach dem 2. Weltkrieg das Zeitungswesen übernahm, wurde die "Freie Zeitung" wieder ein wichtiges Organ als Brücke zur alten Heimat.

Max Richter war als Chef-Editor und Theo E. Daurer als Sportsreporter tätig; Theo wurde später ebenfalls Chef-Redakteur und löste Max Richter ab, bevor er die NJFZ 1963 von Louis Fischer kaufte.

Kurz nach der Geschäfts-übernahme verstarb Theo Daurer und wieder war es ein Sports-berichterstatter, der ihm nachfolgte. Helmut Heimsch machte es sich zur Lebens-aufgabe, die NJFZ für Deutsch-Amerikaner und angeschlossene Organisationen zu erhalten. Leider verstarb er allzu früh in 1978. Eberhard Schweizer (Helmut Heimsch war sein Stiefvater) wurde von Vereinen und Organisationen ermuntert und gebeten, die Zeitung dem Deutsch-Amerikanertum zu erhalten. Er führte ein neues Format ein und modernisierte das Drucksystem. Die Zeitung beinhaltet aktuelle Berichte über Politik, Wirtschaft, Sport und Kultur. Durch Vereinsberichte werden die Leser über die verschiedenen Organisationen auf dem laufenden gehalten. Als beliebtes Sprachrohr empfinden

Eberhard Schweizer, Verleger und Herausgeber (Bildmitte)
George Krueger, Anzeigendirektor (l.) Christa K. Wimmer, Vertriebsleiterin (r.)

die Leser die "Freie Zeitung", in der sie Informationen über die deutschsprachigen Länder und ganz Europa finden, welche von den amerikanischen Median meist nicht berücksichtigt werden. Freiwillige Mitarbeiter berichten über deutsche Großveranstaltungen (German Heritage Festival, Steubenparade, usw.).

Die Namensänderung auf "Freie Zeitung" wurde vorgenommen, da die FZ an der ganzen Ostküste von Amerika und in letzter Zeit besonders stark in Florida vertrieben und gelesen wird.

Viele Leser betrachten die Zeitung als ein Stück Heimat und schätzen das unpolitische, aber objective Verhalten sehr, und die Redaktion ist weiterhin bemüht, ihnen ihre "Freie Zeitung" noch möglichst lange zu erhalten.

Freie Zeitung, Inc.
500 South 31st Street, Kenilworth, NJ 07033
Tel: 908 245-7995 • Fax 908 245-7997

Carlstadt Turn Hall at Broad Street

Carlstadt Turnverein, Inc.
Founded 1857

Der Carlstadt Turnverein wurde 1857 gegründet. In diesem Jahr feiert der Verein sein 140ig jähriges Bestehen im eigenen Heim, zusammen mit seinen zwei Abteilungen, der **Carlstadt Mixed Chorus** und die **Carlstadt Active Turners.** Die Gründungsmitglieder sahen die Notwendigkeit einer Schule, nicht nur für den Körper wie die Turnhalle, sondern auch für die

Allgemeinheit der Familien und somit legten sie den Grundstein für die erste **Volksschule** in ihrem neuen Heimatort Carlstadt.

Info and photo: Ingeborg Wendler

Carlstadt Turnverein, Inc.
500 Broad Street, Carlstadt, N.J. 07072
Tel: 201/438-9644

Float and Band of the 1996 von Steuben Parade, Yulan, NY

Photos from Charles F. Gutekunst and Fred Reber

Yulan von Steuben Parade *by Jack Williams*

The Annual **von Steuben Parade & Germanfest** is usually held on the 3rd Saturday of September in Yulan near the Tri-State borders of New York, New Jersey and Pennsylvania.

The parade is named in honor of Baron Frederick Wilhelm von Steuben who came to this country as a volunteer, offering his services to the embattled General George Washington.

The purpose and aim of the von **Steuben Parade** is to demonstrate historic events on colorful floats to provide our neighbors and our leaders with a visual picture of the part played by Germanic immigrants and their descendants in the development of our country.

The participating clubs include:
- German-American Society of the Tri-States, NY
- Honesdale German-American Club, Pennsylvania

- Lake Wallenpaupack German-American Club, PA
- German-American Club of Middletown, New York

The **von Steuben Parade** is sponsored by the Highland Chamber of Commerce and benefits the Breast Cancer Detection Program at Mercy Community Hospital in Port Jervis, New York.
For more information call: **914 / 557-8600.**

German Society Services

Immigration and advisory services

Social services

Job placement services

Financial assistance

Estate and Trust Administration

as permitted by law

". . . to assist German immigrants and to afford relief to distressed Germans and their descendants . . ."

Dienstleistungen der Deutschen Gesellschaft

Einwanderung und Beratungsdienst

Allgemeine Hilfeleistungen

Arbeitsnachweis

Finanzielle Unterstützung

Testamentsvollstreckung und

Nachlassverwaltung

im Rahmen der Gesetzgebung

German Society of the City of New York

The German Society of the City of New York is the oldest chartered charity in the State of New York. Founded in 1784 to protect German immigrants from unscrupulous exploiters operating in the ports of arrival. In the course of its long history The German Society has lent a helping hand to countless numbers of German immigrants in need.

Today, as a modern social service agency, each year it continues serving hundreds in the German American community, who require assistance due to old age or infirmity. It renders vocational counseling and job placement without charge. It also offers technical assistance in immigration and naturalization matters, and gives competent advice or referrals concerning personal problems.

The German Society of the City of New York
6 East 87th Street, New York, N.Y. 10128
Telephone: 212 / 360 - 6022
A Social Service Organization Founded in 1784

Die Deutsche Gesellschaft der Stadt New York ist die älteste eingetragene Hilfsorganisation im Staate New York. Sie wurde 1784 gegründet, um deutsche Immigranten vor skrupellosen Ausbeutern im Hafen der Ankunft zu schützen. Im Laufe der langjährigen Geschichte hat dieses Hilfswerk zahllosen deutschen Einwanderern in Not eine helfende Hand gereicht.

Heute, als eine moderne Wohlfahrtsorganisation, wird Hunderten von Bedürftigen weitergeholfen, besonders wenn diese im Alter oder bei Krankheit Hilfe benötigen. Man gibt auch kostenlos beruflichen Ratschlag und Arbeitsnachweis. Auch bietet man praktische Hilfe bei der Einwanderung und Einbürgerung. Außerdem gibt die "German Society" kompetente Auskunft und Nachweis an Experten betreffend verschiedener, persönlicher Angelegenheiten.

The Liederkranz of the City of New York was founded on January 9, 1847 by 25 German immigrants as a male singing society. From this humble beginning, it developed into an organization which has contributed much to the musical, cultural and social life of the City of New York.

In the early 1880's a beautiful clubhouse was constructed on East 58th Street just east of Park Avenue in Manhattan. Here, German charity and elegant dress balls were held regularly. These were considered the highlight of New York's social season. The period before the First World War was the Golden Age of the Liederkranz. Its membership stood at 1500, and its male chorus at 250. The highly regarded chorus and orchestra toured the United States and performed at the White House. Following WWII the original clubhouse at East 58th Street was sold, and replaced by the stately clubhouse at East 87th Street, its present location.

This new building was acquired through the generosity of a loyal membership who were determined to preserve the German musical heritage of the Liederkranz in New York City. On April 18, 1948 the Liederkranz Foundation, Inc.

"Polyhymnia"

Presented by the L. K. Damen Verein on the 50th Anniversary of the Liederkranz on January 8th, 1897

The Liederkranz

was established as a charitable, tax exempt organization with the purpose of providing financial support to young singers and musicians to further their careers.

The 87th Street Clubhouse is owned by the Foundation, but operated by the Liederkranz Club which provides the day-to-day staffing. The building has several dining areas and rooms for meetings, corporate seminars, lectures and recitals, all of which may be engaged by contacting the Club's manager. The Club also employs a full-time German chef, serving delicious meals for members and guests, often in conjunction with operatic or orchestral performances.

The Liederkranz Foundation and the Liederkranz Club with a rich tradition of musical excellence for over 150 years look forward to a greatly expanded membership and a prosperous future supporting artistic endeavors, good fellowship and the traditions of its German musical heritage.

The Liederkranz
6 East 87th Street • New York, NY 10128
(212) 534-0880

Zion - St. Mark's Lutheran Church

Yorkville's German Church

Zion Lutheran Church
1892

The beautiful Munich style windows on the South side of the Church.

St. Mark's Lutheran Church
1847

Zion - St. Markus Lutheran Church is an old German Church located in Yorkville on 84th Street near 1st Avenue, in the renown German section of New York.

The Church sponsors year 'round German heritage fests and hosts the German Film Club, as well as special concerts. It has a bi-lingual choir and a German language school.

It is building an ever growing historical exhibit, for which it is seeking material, featuring the Churches, Olde Yorkville and the Slocum Disaster. Books on these topics are sold at the Church.

German Service is held Sundays at 11:00 am and English Service at 5:00 pm. Both are followed by popular coffee hours.

St. Mark's, founded in 1847, became well known because of the tragic 1904 Slocum Ferry Boat disaster, where 1021 parishioners, half of them from St. Marks, perished in the largest fiery maritime catastrophe. It stunned the world and became a sad part of New York's history.

By 1945, the dwindling congregation of St. Mark's, brought a large dowry, including its altar furniture, to its subsequent marriage with Zion Evangelical Lutheran Church. Today, Zion - St. Marks, with its modest but dedicated congregation is also famous for its beautiful rare Munich style windows and its Fenton Organ match-funded in 1912 by philanthropist Andrew Carnegie.

Please call the 24-hour hot line # 212 / 650-1648 for monthly events and more information.

*Das Portal der Deutschen Ev. Kirche
in Yorkville, 339 East 84th Street, New York.*

Presented with thanks to Kathryn A. Jolowicz for her deligent research on Yorkville.

Die Zion - St. Markus Kirche ist ein Leuchtfeuer in der deutschen Gemeinde von New York.

Die deutsche, evangelisch lutherische Zion - St. Markus Kirche ist im historischen Yorkville, dem bekannten Viertel der Deutschen in New York, gelegen.

Die Kirche gibt das ganze Jahr lang deutsche Feste, beherbergt den deutschen Film Klub und veranstaltet besondere Konzerte. Sie hat einen zweisprachigen Chor und eine gute deutsche Sprachschule. Die Kirche ist auch Mittelpunkt der deutschen Geschichte in New York und deshalb immer auf der Suche nach antiken Ausstellungs-Stücken, die sich mit den früheren Kirchen, dem "olde Yorkville" und dem Slocum Unglück befassen. Entsprechende Bücher sind in der Kirche zum Verkauf.

Nach dem deutschen Gottesdienst um 11 Uhr und dem englischen um 17 Uhr am Sonntag gibt es ein gemütliches Kaffeetrinken hinterher.

St. Markus, 1847 gegründet, wurde durch das furchtbare Slocum Unglück, 1904, in der die Hafenfähre kenterte, bekannt, als 1021 Kirchenmitglieder, davon die Hälfte von St. Markus, ertranken oder verbrannten. Die ganze Welt war erschüttert, und das Unglück wurde zu einem traurigen Teil der Geschichte New Yorks.

1945 brachte die kleiner werdende Gemeinde der St. Markus Kirche ihr Hab und Gut, einschließlich der Altar Möbel, und vereinte sich mit der Zion evangelisch lutherischen Kirche. Heute ist die Zion - St. Markus Kirche mit seiner kleinen aber treuen Gemeinde bekannt für seine schönen, kostbaren München-artigen Fenster und ihre Fenton Orgel, die 1912 mit Hilfe von Philantrophist Andrew Carnegie angeschafft wurde.

Mehr Auskunft erhalten Sie über die 24-stündige Beantwortung 212 / 650-1648.

The "Slocum Ferry Disaster, 1904"
from the Claude Rust Collection in Yorkville, New York.

Köstliche Leckerbissen

Culinary Tidbits

Elisabeth A. Castleman, international food writer, culinary historian and consultant, is the creator of "Culinary Roots of the 90's," a monthly column accessible through the Internet at www.german-usa.com. She provided this short culinary dictionary:

Krabbensalat	Shrimp cocktail
Sauerfleisch	Marinated meat stew
Eisbein	Corned leg of pork
Gänseschmalz	Goose fat spread
Franzosensuppe	Beef stock vegetable soup
Himmel und Erde	Mashed potatoes, blood sausage, apple sauce
Plaaten in de Pann	Pan fried potatoes and sausage
Kutteln	Tripe dish
Knödel und Spätzle	Egg flour dumpling
Zwiebelkuchen	Onion quiche
Rote Grütze	Fruit jelly
Nürnberger Lebkuchen	Honey ginger bread
Dresdner Stollen	Christmas fruit bread
Bismarck Hering	Marinated herring
Matjes Hering	Herrings preserved in salt brine
Sauerbraten	Wine marinated beef roast
Rouladen	Boneless meat rolls
Kohlrouladen	Rolled-up cabbage leaves
Königsberger Klopse	Ground meatballs with caper gravy
Hamburger Frikadellen	Hamburg ground meat patty
Frankfurter	Wiener / pork-veal-beef sausage
Knackwurst	Thick and short pork-beef-veal smoked sausage
Bratwurst	Smoked pork and veal sausage
Blutwurst	Blood sausage

Braunschweiger	Liver sausage
Sülze	Head cheese
Leberkäse	Liver-meat loaf
Sauerkraut	Green cabbage pickled in salt
Zwiebelkuchen	Onion pie
Kartoffelpuffer	Raw shredded potatoes pan fried
Marzipan	Ground almond honey paste
Bienenstich	Yeast dough cake with filling
Berliner-Krapfen	Deep fried jam filled donuts, also called Bismarcks
Glühwein	Sweet spiced red wine
Feuerzangenbowle	Sweet spiced mulled wine
Bowle	Wine punch with fruits
Eierliqueur	Egg nog
Jägermeister	Herb liquor
Obstler	Clear fruit liquor
Schnaps	Hard liquor
Weinbrand	Brandy
Semmel, Brötchen	Wheat bread roll
Wiener Schnitzel	Breaded boneless cutlet
Muas-Müsli-Knödel	Breakfast cereals
Gugelhupf	Bund cake
Sacher Torte	Jam filled chocolate cake
Linzer Torte	Cake lined with red fruit jam
Schwarzwälder Torte	Rich chocolate cake
Kaiserschmarren	Shredded raisin pancake

"Yorkville" New York's German District around 86th Street and 2nd Ave.

Prominente Ehrengäste
im "German Film Club, N.Y.":
Nach der Vorführung einer ihren vielen Operettenfilme stellte Mr. Joe Pasternack (rechts) die Sängerin und Schauspielerin Marta Eggerth und Sohn Marjan Kiepura vor.

Stammtisch

Bei Franz' Stammtisch trifft man sich monatlich am ersten Freitag und dritten Mittwoch um 19:30 im Yorkville Inn, 1701 Second Avenue (88th Street). Essen, Trinken und Gemütlichkeit - es wird nur deutsch gesprochen.

Heidelberg Restaurant, 1648 2nd Ave., New York
(between 85th & 86th Street) Call 212 / 628-2332
Gute deutsche Küche - Treffpunkt mit Gemütlichkeit

Founded in 1974, the "German Film Club of New York" provides rare entertainment of classic films at the Zion - St. Markus Church in Yorkville. You are invited to experience these "Oldies" from the 1930s and 1940s in the historic environment of this German Church. For more information call 212 / 369-7114 and ask for Joe Pasternack, New York's famous German News Correspondent.

1974 gegründet, zeigt der "Deutsche Film Klub in New York" seltene Filme aus den 30er und 40er Jahren in der Zion - St. Markus Kirche in Yorkville, nahe 84. Straße und 2. Avenue. Sie sind eingeladen, diese schönen, alten Filme zu erleben. Rufen Sie 212 / 369-7114 an und fragen Sie nach Herrn Pasternack, New York's bekannten deutschen Nachrichten Korrespondenten.

New York Radio by Hostess Marion Ockens presents

WFUV 90.7 FM
Public Radio from Fordham University, Bronx, New York
(Reklamefreies Programm)

WVOX 1460 AM
Westchester Community Radio
New Rochelle, New York

Grüße aus der Heimat
Jeden Sonntag 16:00 bis 18:00 Uhr

* Bekannte Musik aus der Klassik und populäre Weisen.
* Kultur- und Vereinskalender
* Nachrichten und Berichte

Heimatgrüße
Jeden Sonntag 13:00 bis 14:00 Uhr
* Bunte, beliebte Musikpalette
* Kurzberichte: Englisch/Deutsch
* Anzeigen: Firmen, Vereine, usw.

Hostess/Producer **Marion Ockens**

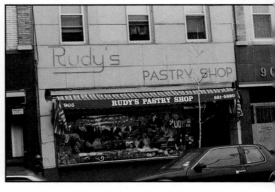

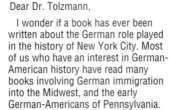

Dear Dr. Tolzmann,

I wonder if a book has ever been written about the German role played in the history of New York City. Most of us who have an interest in German-American history have read many books involving German immigration into the Midwest, and the early German-Americans of Pennsylvania.

By the way, I am extremely disturbed by the fact that the Pennsylvania Dutch region of Pennsylvania is referred to as such. It should be renamed Deutsch Country. This may sound a bit off the wall, but wouldn't it be wonderful if heads of various German-American organizations started such a campaign. Maybe they could begin by contacting very large and famous Pennsylvania Deutsch bakeries and candy manufacturers, perhaps if they could be persuaded to change their labeling, it would set a trend and spread slowly on an even smaller level; such as small gift shops, restaurants and etc.

It's really heartbreaking that such a place exists in this country that actually represents what German-Americans stand for, such as: devotion to God, family, love, a well enjoyed cuisine, outstanding artistic talents, etc., has the misfortune of being misnamed. This would have been a perfect promotion of the German-Americans as the positive and loving people that they truly are. No thanks to the conspirators in Hollywood who do all they can, and then some, to ensure that Germans are only perceived as negative characters.

I am twenty-eight years of age, and I was born and raised by a German Mother and a Father of German extraction. I have to admit that I had become very envious of other strong ethnic groups in our city. I have watched friends of other groups enjoy a strong and thriving ethnic community, and then I would turn to my own community and all I would see

was a community that was crumbling away year after year.

Our community is known as Glendale and Ridgewood, Queens. This community was founded in the 1800's, every brick was laid by German immigrants. We are proud to boast that two German restaurants exist that date back to those early days of old New York: Gebhardt's and Niederstein's Restaurants.

We are also the home to one of the largest and oldest Lutheran Cemeteries in the state. 99% of the tombstones are from the turn of the century and are almost entirely written in the German language. This neighborhood still offers church services in German, I believe there are three churches to be exact. One of the largest Wurst manufacturers: Karl Ehmer is in operation, not to mention all of the other wonderful smaller Pork stores dotted in and around the streets of this town. One of the things I enjoy doing is sampling all of the imported German beer that can still be found at the many German Bierstubes. As far as restaurants go, here can be found really authentic specialties and an old world atmosphere.

In the past 10 years it has all started to take a downward turn. I have done all I can possibly do to try to save the area on my own small level. I started first by creating a map of the area, a sort of guide. I then proceeded to create a very large mailing list which contained the addresses of organizations and people who I believed would be interested in passing out these maps. I started sending them out by the thousands. I even went so far as to stand on the corner of 86th Street and 2nd Avenue in Manhattan to pass out these maps to Germans who still traveled to this area. (86th Street was once the center of German culture in Manhattan).

appear to be a bright future for the preservation of our heritage in this area. My idea with this map was to perhaps attract Germans from other areas to come and shop here to at least keep the business related to German culture alive.

My dream is to see a book written about this section of New York, so that if this place must die, there will still remain a book written that will explain in complete detail the importance that this area had in New York for the German immigrants, it would also prove that this area was in fact in existence and was just as important to the growth of our city as were the Italian, Irish and Jewish communities, etc. I really hope that by writing this letter to you, some positive result occurs. A book should be written now while hundreds of living people in the area can still tell the story, and while photos still exist. There is still time to write this history down with detailed accuracy.

I am not a skilled writer, it must be assembled by an absolute expert from the community.

If you are in no way capable at this time to assemble such a book, I would be grateful if you would pass the idea along to D.A.N.K. or the Steuben Society or perhaps the German National Committee.

It has been a deliberate oversight on the part of the New York historians to delete, the German presence from New York City history as well as nationally, or at least that is my opinion. Thank you for the opportunity of making your books available through the Heritage Book Company. The one that I have read thus far is an excellent account of American history. I am looking forward to reading another one. Also, thank you again, for the role you have played in the fight against this unjustified prejudice, of which millions of innocent German-Americans suffer through year after year.

Sincerely yours,
Jack Williams
Member: Steuben Society
Harmony Lodge #199

This letter appeared in Dr. Don-Heinrich Tolzmann's Column in the September 1995 issue of the German American Journal, the official newspaper of the German American National Congress, D.A.N.K. .

Reprinted with permission.

I have been doing this non-profit publicity work for little more than two years now, I am not even sure if it has accomplished anything. Since German immigration has dropped down to zero, and with the old Germans slowly departing, there doesn't

Christine and Jack Williams

Glendale, N.Y. German Queens

By Jack Williams

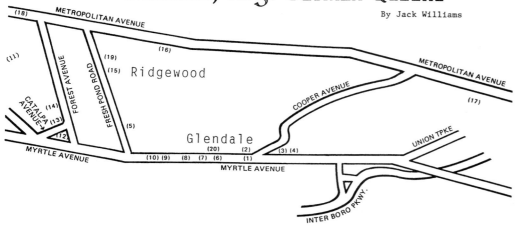

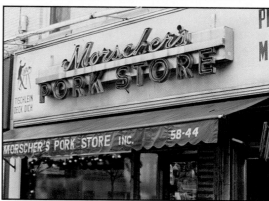

(1) **"Zum Stammtisch"** 69-46 Myrtle, Glendale

(2) **Glendale Pork Store,** 70-03 Myrtle, Glendale

(3) **Von Westerhagen's Restaurant,** 71-28 Cooper

(4) **Eddie's German Meats & Salads,** 72nd & Myrtle

(5) **German American School,** 70-01 Fresh Pond,
Language School for kids & adults since 1892

(6) **Wolf Jewelers,** Watchmaker, 69-31 Myrtle

(7) **Gebhardt's Restaurant,** since 1933, 65-08 Myrtle

(8) **Hans Gasthaus,** 64-04 Myrtle, Glendale

(9) **Glendale Health Foods,** 62-24 Myrtle, Glendale

(10) **Alster Pavilion,** 62-14 Myrtle, Glendale
Imported gifts, tapes & records, etc.

(11) **Martin's Lounge,** 675 Woodward, Ridgewood

(12) **Morscher's Pork Store,** 58-46 Catalpa

(13) **Karl Ehmer,** meats & deli, 68-38 Forest

(14) **Forest Pork Store,** various foods, 66-39 Forest

(15) **Karl Ehmer,** wholesale, 63-35 Fresh Pond

(16) **Niederstein's Restaurant,** est.1845, fine food
69-16 Metropolitan Avenue

(17) **Chalet Alpina,** restaurant, live music
98-35 Metropolitan Avenue

(18) **German Sports Club,** 60-60 Metropolitan

(19) **Glendale Brauhouse,** good food and drink
68-05 64th Place, Glendale

(20) **Glendale Pork Store,** German & Austrian 67-17
Myrtle, Glendale

Cozy Corner, *restaurant and bar*,
60-01 70th Avenue
Ridgewood

Rudy's Konditorei, *delicious pastries*
905 Seneca Ave.
Ridgewood

Steuben Society of America
(preserve heritage)
67-05 Fresh Pond
Ridgewood

Emmaus Evangelical Church,
German *9am Sun*
60-10 67th Ave.
Ridgewood

Trinity Reformed Church,
German *9am Sun.*
66-30 60th Place
Ridgewood

R.C. Church of Mathias, German *8:30 am Sun*
58-15 Catalpa
Ridgewood

Gottscheer Klubhaus, *"Heimat Club"*
657 Fairview Ave.
Ridgewood

Photos by Bert Lachner

The Steuben Society of America
A National, Fraternal and Patriotic Society

The Steuben Society of America was founded in 1919, when U.S. citizens of German heritage were sorely in need of political leadership. A small group of men in New York City created this national, fraternal and patriotic organization to arouse in Americans of Germanic descent a greater sense of their civic and political duties and their rights as citizens. The Society fosters citizen participation in public affairs and in the paths of public service. It is independent of political parties; not meant to dictate to its members how to vote, yet, it is to provide a forum for the edification of its members. Duty, Justice, Charity and Tolerance are the cornerstones upon which the Steuben Society of America is built.

"The Steuben News" and Literature explaining policy and activities of the Steuben Society of America. In the background replica of Jensen's Steuben Statuette and National Chairman's gavel.

While continuing its educational, cultural and public affairs activities, the Society is composed of local Units and higher Councils that act on local, regional and national levels. Annual visits are made by the Public Affairs Committees to brief legislators and ask for action when such is desired. Among recent recommendations for action from federal representatives is that our government make plans for the tenth anniversary of the dedication of the German-American Friendship Garden in Washington DC, in 1998; that the Garden's general appearance as a symbol of German-American Friendship be improved; that the National Park Service be prompted to create and distribute visitor information pamphlets that inform about the meaning and history of the Garden.

Along with its public affairs activities, the Society has also kept up its scholastic awards programs for meritorious achievements in German language and American history, honoring students and teachers at high schools, colleges, and military academies. Steubenites have supported patriotic activities, such as the German-American Friendship Garden Project, the Statue of Liberty Restoration Project, and preservation of historic sites relating to Friedrich Wilhelm von Steuben and other great German-Americans. The Society's members participate in the annual parades held in honor of their patron in New York, Philadelphia and Chicago. The Society publishes Steuben News as a communication for members and friends. Membership is open to all U.S. citizens of Germanic derivation.

To prepare for the future, to create greater awareness of German contributions to America, and to attract younger Americans to the Society, efforts are underway to share our history through various activities at colleges and universities and with organizations like the Boy Scouts of America.

Die Steuben Society of America
Eine bundesweite, patriotische Brüder- und Schwesternschaft

Die Steuben Society of America wurde 1919 gegründet; in einer Zeit, in der die amerikanischen Bürger deutscher Herkunft dringend politischer Führung bedurften. Eine kleine Gruppe solcher Bürger in der Stadt New York legte damals den Grundstein für diese bundesweite, patriotische Brüderschaft, um Amerikaner deutschen Ursprungs zu intensiverer Teilnahme an öffentlichen Angelegenheiten und zur Wahlbeteiligung anzuregen, aber auch, um sie auf ihre Rechte als Bürger hinzuweisen. Die Steuben Society fördert die Bestrebungen derer, die sich für öffentliche Angelegenheiten einsetzen, und auch jene, die im Staatsdienst ihre Karriere suchen. Die Society ist parteipolitisch unabhängig und schreibt ihren Mitgliedern nicht vor, wie sie wählen sollen, obwohl sie durch Vorträge und öffentliches Forum zur Erbauung ihrer Mitglieder beiträgt. Bürgerpflicht, Gerechtigkeit, Benevolenz, und Toleranz sind die Grundsteine der Organisation.

Die Society führt auch weiterhin ihre instruktiven, kulturellen und politischen Tätigkeiten aus. Dies geschieht in den lokalen Einheiten (Units), und in regionalen Ratsversammlungen (Councils), sowie im Nationalrat (National Council). Die Mitglieder des Komitees für

"Steuben Society of America" float at the New York Steuben Parade

öffentliche Angelegenheiten kommen zumindest einmal jedes Jahr mit den Gesetzgebern zusammen, um das Programm der Society zu erklären, und um in gewissen Angelegenheiten Gesetzgebung zu ersuchen. Derzeit geht es unter anderem darum, die Regierung zu Plänen für eine Feier des 10. Jahrestages des Deutsch-Amerikanischen Freundschafts-Gartens in Washington, D.C., im Jahre 1998 anzuregen, und die Anpflanzungen in diesem Garten, einem "Symbol deutsch-amerikansicher Freundschaft", diesem Zweck mehr gerecht werden zu lassen. Auch wurde der National Park Service darum ersucht, Informationsbroschüren über den Freundschaftsgarten zu drucken und diese der Öffentlichkkeit zugänglich zu machen.

Die Society unterhält auch weiterhin ihr Programm der Leistungs-Auszeichnung von Schülern und Lehrern in Oberschulen, Kollegien, und Universitäten, einschließlich der Militärakademien, die sich dem Studium der deutschen Sprache und Kultur, und dem Studium der amerikanischen Geschichte widmen. Die Mitglieder der Steuben Society haben sich in den vergangenen Jahrzehnten an patriotischen Projekten wie dem Deutsch-Amerikanischen Freundschaftsgarten, der Restaurierung der Freiheitsstatue,

und an den Feiern zum 6. Oktober als Tag der Deutsch-Amerikaner beteiligt. Die Mitglieder der Society sind auch Teilnehmer an den Paraden, die zu Ehren von Steuben's alljährlich in New York, Philadelphia und Chicago statt finden. Die Society gibt die Steuben News als ein Mitteilungsblatt für Mitglieder und Freunde heraus. Mitgliedschaft steht allen Amerikanern deutscher Herkunft offen.

Um auch in Zukunft die Bewußtheit des Deutschtums in Amerika und der deutschen Beiträge am Aufbau Amerika's wach zu halten, und die Amerikaner der jüngeren Generationen zur Mitarbeit einzuladen, hat die Society die Zusammenarbeit an Schulen und höheren Lehranstalten, und auch mit den Boy Scouts of America begonnen.

Steuben Society of America

6705 Fresh Pond Road, Ridgewood, NY, 11385
Telephon 718 381-0900   Fax 718/ 628-4874
Internet: http://www.steuben.org
Nationalrats Vorsitzender: Heinz Obry, Chairman
Natioalrats Sekretärin: Ilse Hoffmann, Secretary

GOETHE-INSTITUT

The Goethe-Institut is a worldwide nonprofit organization, privately founded in Germany in 1951 and publicly funded a short time thereafter. Our mission is to foster appreciation for the German language and culture in our host countries, to contribute to international understanding, and to enhance the intercultural dialog with other countries. There are some one hundred-seventy institutes in eighty countries around the world. Our fifteen centers in North America are seeking cooperation with leading educational, cultural and arts organizations to co-present and address aesthetic, social, and critical issues in contemporary Germany, Europe, the US and Canada.

Das Goethe-Institut ist eine weltweite gemeinnützige Organisation, die 1951 in Deutschland privat gegründet und bald danach durch öffentliche Mittel unterstützt wurde. Unsere Aufgabe ist es, die deutsche Sprache und Kultur in unseren Gastländern zu fördern, zum gegenseitigen internationalen Verständnis beizutragen und den interkulturellen Dialog mit anderen Ländern zu pflegen. Es gibt circa 170 Institute in 80 Ländern der Welt. Unsere 15 Zentren in Nordamerika suchen die Zusammenarbeit mit führenden Organisationen in den Bereichen Erziehung, Kultur und Kunst und sprechen ästhetische, soziale und kritische Themen aus dem heutigen Deutschland, Europa, den Vereinigten Staaten und Kanada an.

- We provide a forum for the discussion of current German issues.
- We are interested in cultural similarities and differences.
- We organize and co-sponsor with our local communities films, concerts, exhibitions, theater and dance performances, conferences and panels.
- We facilitate and co-produce radio, TV and computer projects.
- We are setting standards for German as a foreign language.
- We help develop the latest teaching material for German.
- We teach German to 100,000 students in 80 countries every year.
- We help you to go to Germany, the best and fastest way to learn German.
- We foster over 700 school partnerships between secondary schools in the US and Germany.
- We offer internationally recognized examinations.
- We conduct and co-host workshops for teachers of German.
- We offer you free access to our library network.
- We provide extensive and current information about Germany.
- We are on line: http://www.goethe.de

Photo © Guenter Wehrwann

Das Goethe Institut New York an der Museumsmeile der 5. Avenue
The Goethe-Institut New York on Fifth Avenue's Museum Mile

- Wir bieten ein Forum zur Diskussion aktueller deutscher Themen.
- Wir sind an kulturellen Gemeinsamkeiten und Unterschieden interessiert.
- Wir organisieren und unterstützen zusammen mit Institutionen vor Ort Filmvorstellungen, Konzerte, Ausstellungen, Theater- und Tanzaufführungen, Konferenzen und Diskussionen.
- Wir ermöglichen und koproduzieren Radio-, Fernseh- und Computer-Projekte.
- Wir setzten die Standards für Deutsch als Fremdsprache.
- Wir unterstützen die Entwicklung der neuesten Lehrmaterialien für Deutsch als Fremdsprache.
- Jedes Jahr lernen 100,000 Studenten in 80 Ländern die deutsche Sprache.
- Wir helfen Ihnen, nach Deutschland zu gehen, dem besten und schnellsten Weg, Deutsch zu lernen.
- Wir betreuen über 700 Schulpartnerschaften zwischen Sekundarschulen in den USA und Deutschland.
- Wir bieten international anerkannte Prüfungen an.
- Wir führen Fortbildungsveranstaltungen für Deutschlehrer durch.
- Wir bieten Ihnen freien Zugang zu unserem Netz von Bibliotheken an.
- Bei uns finden Sie ausführliche aktuelle Informationen über Deutschland.
- Wir sind im Netz: http://www.goethe.de

Goethe-Institut United States

Ann Arbor, MI: (313)996-8600
Atlanta, GA: (404)892-2388
Boston, MA: (617)262-6050
Chicago, IL: (312)329-0915

Cincinnati, OH: (513)721-2777
Houston, TX: (713)528-2787
Los Angeles, CA: (213)525-3388
New York, NY: (212)439-8700

San Francisco, CA: (415)391-0370
Seattle, WA: (206)622-9694
St. Louis, MO: (314)367-2452
Washington, DC: (202)289-1200

Goethe-Institut Canada

Montreal, PQ: (514)499-0159
Toronto, Ont.: (416)924-3327
Vancouver, BC: (604)732-3966

Colorful Costumes from Germany • Farbfrohe Trachten

arin Gottier in Sunday dress from the Palatine.
elson Gottier in North German dance suit.
arin Gottier in Festtracht aus der Pfalz.
elson Gottier in Tanztracht aus
ord-Deutschland.

Richard Scheller of the Hartford Sängerbund Dancers (Newington, CT) in North German dance custume.
Richard Scheller von den Hartford Sängerbund Tänzern (Newington, CT) in nord-deutscher Tanztracht.

Mrs. Helene Tank in festival dress from the island of Fohr. Mrs. Tank is a member of the Amrumer Damen Verein, Franklyn Sq. LI, NY.
Frau Helene Tank in Festtracht von der Insel Föhr. Frau Tank ist Mitglied des Amrumer Damen Vereins, Franklyn Square LI, NY.

Richard Scheller of the Hartford Sängerbund wearing his 60th birthday present.
Richard Scheller vom Hartford Sängerbund, trägt sein Geburtstagsgeschenk zum 60.

Hamburger water carrier.
Steuben Parade, New York City

artford Sangerbund Dancers. Men in North-German costumes, women in costumes from the Palatine.
artford Sängerbund Tänzer. Herren in nord-deutschen Tanztrachten, Damen in pfälzer Tracht.

Brenna Gottier wearing "Borta" and "Kranzl" of the costume for single girls as worn in Topporz, Zips area of the High Tatras, Slovakia. A large part of the Zipser community in Manchester, CT, came before and after the first Wold War to work in a silk and brokade Mill. After the second World War the German population of the Zips was expelled. Many came to Manchester to join relatives already there. Most of the women who came after 1945, managed to bring some of their native dress with them.

Students from James Madison University, Harrisonburg, VA in a Palatine costume from the area of Hordt, dancing in a Vintner Festival at the American Museum of Frontier Culture, Staunton, VA.
Studenten der James Madison Universität, Harrisonburg, VA, in einer Tracht aus der Gegend um Hördt, Pfalz. Die Gruppe tanzt bei einem Weinlese Fest auf dem deutschen Hof aus Hördt, in dem Museum für Amerikanische Frontier Kultur, Staunton, VA.

'Chlause Laufe'. Reenactment of Swiss Chirstmas custom at the Christkindlmarkt of the Hartford Sangerbund, Newinton, CT.
'Chlause Laufe', ein schweizerischer Weihnachtsbrauch zum Christkindlmarkt des Hartford Sängerbundes, Newington, CT.

From L to R: Karin Gottier and Anne Weiss in Zipser Tracht.
(Von links nach rechts: Karin Gottier und Anne Weiss in Zipser Tracht)

The Hartford Sangerbund Dancers (Newington, CT) in a Friesean costume.
Mitglieder der Hartford Sängerbund Tänzer in einer friesischen Tracht.

Mettenlicht" taken to Christmas Eve Mass midnight in Austria.

'Chlause Züüg': gingerbread given to children by their Godparents in the Canton of Appenzell, Switzerland. The gingerbread is collected and displayed during Advent. The display is part of the 'Christkindlmarkt' of the Hartford Sängerbund.

"Friesenbogen" decorated with gingerbread, apples and candles. These structures were used in place of pinetrees on the Friesian islands along the North Sea coast. Part of the exhibit at the Christkindlmarkt of the Hartford Sängerbund.

Advent table decoration and traditional fruit and "Stollen".

St. Nikolaus Day with Friesian wooden shoe.
St. Nikolaus Tag mit friesischen Klompen.

All photos and text provided by **Karin Gottier**

Benefit Street, Providence RI

Photo: C. Browning, RI Tourism

Photo: Vermont Travel Division

Barnet Center, Montpelier VT

New England

Connecticut, Maine, Massachusetts, New Hampshire, Rhode Island, Vermont

New England is not just a place, it is also a state of mind. The individualistic residents are justly proud of their colonial heritage as they extol the beauty in what is old and true in what is simple, such as the simple church steeples, red and white barns, picket fences, stately homes, covered bridges, and lighthouses. That also includes the old fishing villages, village greens, valley brooks, sheltered coves, and rugged coast lines.

Bearskin Neck, Rockport Mass.
Photo: Kindra Clineff, 1995

Covered Bridge, Franconia Notch
Photo: New Hampshire Tourism

Edgartown Lighthouse, Martha's
Vineyard, MA.   *Photo: Kindra Clineff*

Herring Cove Beach, Provincetown, Massachusetts.   *Photo: Kindra Clineff*

Hammersmith Farm, Newport RI
Photo: P. Browning, RI Tourism Div.

Portland Head Light
Maine Office of Tourism

Marlborough, New Hampshire
Photo: Paul Spezzaferri, NH Tourism

German immigrants have come to these shores since 1630 and made an impact in almost all walks of life. In Maine, the town of Waldoborough was founded in 1743 and became the center of the shipbuilding industry. In Massachusetts, South of Boston, "New Germantown" was founded at the same time and attracted a great number of Rhinelanders. In the City of Boston Germans, for over 350 years, substantially influenced education, science, music, philosophy, and the arts. Glass factories, textile mills and other

commercial establishments, mainly in Lowell, Lawrence and Holyoke, as well as in Manchester, New Hampshire, attracted many German immigrants in the 1800s.

Since 1873, German artisans, silver workers, cabinetmakers and jewelers came to Providence, Rhode Island, where they greatly furthered the jewelry- and cabinetmaking industries due to their exceptional skills. German cultural and social clubs as well as Aid Societies have been in existence in New England for over

160 years. Some of them, however, were founded later in the 1950s and '60s by the new wave of German immigrants having arrived after WW II.

Although contributions by German immigrants in New England and the country have been substantial, the assimilation of German Americans, of all nationalities, probably has been the most complete. We need to continue to show our heritage and maintain our culture.

by Rose-Mary Kemper

Faneuil Hall, Boston, Massachusetts
Photo: Kindra Clineff, MA Tourism

Maine Office of Tourism

Schooner off Rockland Breakwater

Associated German Societies of New England

Celebration of German-American Heritage Day.

Member Organizations

* Boylston Schul-Verein
* German American Club of Cape Cod
* Deutsche Kulturverein of Bristol County
* Deutsches Altenheim
* German Aid Society
* German-American Club of Berkshire County
* German-American Club of the North Shore

* German-American Ladies Society
* German Cultural Club of Lowell
* Germania Social Club of Worcester County
* German Dramatic Society, Providence RI
* German Ladies Society
* Goethe Society of New England, Inc.
* Holy Trinity (German) Catholic Church
* Sängerchor Boston

Originally founded in 1930, when there were 21 German Clubs in the Greater Boston area, the AGSM was known as the "Verband Deutscher Vereine in Massachusetts". It functioned informally until 1946, observing "Deutscher Tag" each year in October, and was revitalized in 1983, the tercentenary of Germans in America. A concentrated effort was made to bring existing German clubs in the area together under one "umbrella" to coordinate, share and foster interest in their individual activities and to preserve our German heritage. AGSM was incorporated in 1983, and presently 15 member clubs of Massachusetts and Rhode Island collaborate in sponsoring the following annual functions: Selecting a "Miss German-American" to encourage interest in the German culture and language among young people; participating in the New York City "Steuben Parade"; celebrating "German-American Day" on October 6th, having a German cultural / educational exhibit in the 6-day Boston International Festival with a '96 attendance of 78,000, including 40,000 school children from the whole Northeast, and paying tribute to 20 German POW's at a military Memorial Service at Fort Devens, MA.

The AGSM is governed by a "Vorstand" of seven officers annually elected at the General Meeting. Three Delegate Meetings are scheduled additionally. A periodical, the AGSM NEWS, is published four times a year.

Erstmals 1930 gegründet, umfaßte

dieser Verband 21 deutsche Klubs in der Boston Umgebung. Als AGSM bekannt, bestand dieser „Verband Deutscher Vereine in Massachusetts" inoffiziell bis 1946. Er feierte den „Deutschen Tag" im Oktober jeden Jahres.

1983 wurde er wiederbelebt aus Anlaß des 300 jährigen Jubiläums der deutschen Einwanderung. Mit vereinten Kräften wurden die bestehenden deutschen Vereine der Umgebung unter das Dach gebracht, um den Aktivitäts-Kalendar zu co-ordinieren, gemachte Erfahrungen zu teilen und solche Interessen zu fördern, die unserem deutschen Erbe zu Gute kamen. 1983 ließ man sich eintragen und heute gibt es 15 Mitglieds-Vereine in Massachusetts und Rhode Island. Diese wählen zusammen die „Miss German-American", um auf die deutsche Tradition aufmerksam zu machen und die deutsche Sprache unter jungen Leuten zu fördern. Man nimmt auch an der „Steuben Parade" in New York teil, feiert den „German American Day" am 6. Oktober, beteiligt sich am Boston International Festival mit einer Lehr- und Kulturausstellung, zu der 1996 sage und schreibe 78,000 Menschen, darunter 40,000 Kinder aus dem ganzen Nordosten kamen. Im November ehrt man die Deutschen, die als Kriegsgefangene hier gestorben sind, mit einer militärischen Trauerfeier in Fort Devens, MA.

Unser Dank gilt Frau Rose-Mary Kemper, die nicht nur dieses Material zusammengetragen hat, sondern uns auch das „Profil von New England", Seite 268 und den Artikel „Einwanderung deutscher Frauen", Seite 274, schrieb.

ASSOCIATED GERMAN SOCIETIES OF MASSACHUSETTS
P. O. Box 207 • Walpole, Massachusetts 02081
Tel. (617) 244-0343 & (617) 444-4709

Boylston Schul-Verein, Massachusetts

The Boylston Schul-Verein, chartered in 1874, is the largest German club in Massachusetts. Its modern club house is situated on 10 acres of partly wooded land, southwest of Boston. A lively social calendar offers monthly dinner dances, a cabaret, Stammtisch, hunters- and skat club. The outdoor pavilion is used for our Sommerfest, Oktoberfest and other functions.

The Boylston Schul-Verein also supports a "Sonnabend-Schule" for children, ages 5 to 17, and for

adults at three different levels.

The club represents a "German Oasis" in Eastern Massachusetts!

Der Boylston Schul-Verein, 1874 gegründet, ist der größte deutsche Verein in ganz Massachusetts. Seine modernen Klubräume sind auf einem 4 Hektar großen, bewaldeten Grundstück gelegen, ca. 30 km südwestlich von Boston. Ein aktiver Kalender bietet monatliche Dinners, Tänze, ein Kabaret, den Stammtisch, den

Auerhahn Jagdklub und die Skat Runde. Der Garten Pavillon wird für unser Sommerfest, Oktoberfest und andere Gelegenheiten benutzt.

Der Boylston Schul-Verein unterstützt auch die "Sonnabend Schule" für Kinder 5 bis 17 Jahre alt, und Deutschunterricht für Erwachsene in drei Stufen.

Der Klub ist eine deutsche Oase in Ost-Massachusetts !

BOYLSTON SCHUL-VEREIN
8 County Street (Route 109)
P. O. Box 207
Walpole, MA 02081
Tel. (508) 660-2018

Our gratitude goes to Mrs. Rose-Mary Kemper who not only provided the information for these pages, but also wrote the "Profile of New England", page 268 and the "Women's Point of View", page 274.

Deutsches Altenheim in Boston

Deutsches Altenheim

German Home for the Aged

2222 Centre Street
West Roxbury, MA 02132-4097
Phone (617) 325-1230 Fax (617) 323-7523

Serving the elder German-American community since 1914, Deutsches Altenheim with its 124 beds now provides an array of long term and rehabilitative services from its location in residential West Roxbury, including post-hospital recuperative care, outpatient therapy services, adult day health, and skilled nursing. The Altenheim also offers exceptional care to persons suffering from dementia.

Seit 1914 bemüht sich dieses Altenheim um die deutsch-amerikanische Gemeinde. Das Deutsche Altenheim hat 124 Betten, und bietet eine Reihe von Langzeit- und Erholungsdiensten in seinem Haus in West Roxbury - einem ruhigen Wohnviertel.
Das schließt auch die Pflege nach einem Krankenhausaufenthalt, ambulante Dienstleistungen, Tagesaufenthalt für Erwachsene und ärztliche Krankenhilfe ein. Dieses Altenheim ist auch auf Dementia spezialisiert.

Deutsche Kulturverein *of Bristol County*

The "Deutsche Kulturverein" of southeast Massachusetts, incorporated in 1985, exemplifies the goal of preserving our cultural heritage. Commensurate with our pride, the German flag was raised over the International Plaza at Government Center, Fall River, in 1990.

Der Deutsche Kulturverein von Südost Massachusetts, 1985 grgründet, ist ein Musterbeispiel für die Erhaltung unseres kulturellen Erbes. Dem Deutschen Kulturverein ist es zu verdanken, daß die deutsche Fahne seit 1990 über dem International Plaza in Fall River, MA fliegt.

German Flag over International Plaza in Fall River, Massachusetts.

P. O. Box 347 • Swansea, MA 02777 • (508) 672-8574

German-American Club of Cape Cod

The Club was founded in 1974. By way of social gatherings and functions, club members strive to preserve and promote the cultures of Germany as manifested in its language, music, dress, food and festivals.

Dieser Klub wurde 1974 ins Leben gerufen, um durch Gesellschaft und Festlichkeiten die deutsche Kultur, Sprache, Musik, Trachten und kulinarischen Bräuche zu erhalten und zu fördern.

P. O. Box 187 • Hyannis, MA 02601 (508) 255-3326

German American Ladies Society

Founded in 1975 as an auxiliary of the Boylston Schul-Verein, its 50 members sponsor a Christmas Bazaar, a Children's Christmas Party, two dinner-dances, and grant scholarships to college students focusing on the German language.

1975 als ein Unterstützungs-Mitglied des Boylston Schul-Vereins gegründet, halten die 50 Damen den Weihnachtsbasar, das Kinderweihnachtsfest, zwei Dinner-Tänze ab, und geben Stipendien an solche Studenten, die die deutsche Sprache lernen.

8 County Street • Walpole, MA 02081 • (508) 660-2018

GERMAN AID SOCIETY OF BOSTON

In 1997 the German Aid Society of Boston is celebrating its 150th Anniversary. The Society was founded in 1847 to extend financial assistance and advice to needy German Americans in the Boston area and to the Deutches Altemheim in West Roxbury, MA.

We are proud of our 150 years of support to immigrants, who came to Boston, some of whom may have included your ancestors.

Then, as today, the German Aid Society responds to those in need.

Our membership and the Board of Directors are dedicated volunteers. Please help us to help others with your tax deductible donation and/or by joining our large membership   (dues are $5.00).

Our motto is simple: "Founded by Germans to help Germans"!

DEUTSCHER HILFSVEREIN VON BOSTON

1997 feiert der "Deutsche Hilfsverein von Boston" sein 150. Jubiläum. Der Verein wurde 1847 gegründet, um finanzielle Hilfe und Rat an bedürftige Deutsch-Amerikaner und an das Deutsche Altenheim in Boston zu geben. Wir sind stolz auf unsere 150 Jahre Hilfestellung an Einwanderer, unter denen auch Vorfahren von Ihnen auf der Durchreise durch Boston gewesen sein mögen. Damals sowohl wie heute springt der Deutsche Hilfsverein von Boston bei unerwarteten Notfällen ein.

Unsere Mitgliedschaft und der Vorstand sind freiwillig für Sie da. Bitte helfen Sie uns anderen zu helfen, mit einer steuerfreien Spende oder Ihren Beitritt.

Unser Motto ist: "Deutsche helfen Deutschen!"

8 County Street • Walpole, MA 02081 • Tel. (508) 668-8827

Goethe Society of New England • Holy Trinity German Parish, Boston

The Goethe Society of New England is dedicated to fostering German culture and language. Founded in 1963 as a non-profit corporation, the Society offers cultural and social programs from September to May, with opportunities to hear and speak in German. There is an annual Christmas celebration and a membership meeting / reception each May.

Die "Goethe Society of New England" bemüht sich deutsche Kultur und Sprache zu fördern. Seit 1963 gemeinnützig, gibt es viele intersessante kulturelle und gesellschaftliche Programme von September bis Mai.

Goethe Society of New England, Inc.
170 Beacon Street
Boston, MA 02116
(617) 262-8413

Es kann Deutsch gehört und gesprochen werden. Eine Weihnachtsfeier und ein Offenes Haus im Mai sind die größeren Ereignisse.

The Holy Trinity German Catholic Church,
140 Shawmut Ave.,
Boston, MA 02118
(617) 426-6142.

Christmas Concert by Sängerchor Boston at Holy Trinity German Church

The only national German Catholic church In New England - known as the Christmas Tree Parish - where parishioners worship, sing German hymns; home to community programs and the Christian Arts Series Committee that hosts national and international musical events. Holy Trinity is the designated church in the Boston Archdiocese where the 1962 Latin Tridentine Mass is celebrated at Noon every Sunday.

Die einzige, nationale Deutsch Katholische Kirche in New England - auch als Weihnachtsbaum Gemeinde bekannt - wo Kirchgänger den sonntäglichen deutsch-amerikanischen Gottesdienst besuchen und deutsche Hymnen singen. Die Kirche ist Heim für hilfreiche Nachbarschaftsprogramme und die christliche Kunstgemeinschaft, die jährlich nationale und internationale Musikfeste veranstaltet.

Holy Trinity ist die in Boston erwählte Archdiocese, wo die lateinische Tridentine Messe von 1962 jeden Sonntag um 12:00 Uhr gefeiert wird.

Sängerchor Boston

This 40-member mixed-voice chorus of German-Americans from Eastern Massachusetts specializes in German folk and art music. Annual activities include 3 dinner-dance- concerts, 3 Christmas concerts and participation in the annual "Prize-Song" competition of the Connecticut Sängerbund.

Ein gemischter Chor mit 40 deutsch-amerikanischen Stimmen vom östlicher Massachusetts singt deutsche Volks- und Kunstlieder. Jährlich gibt es drei Dinner-Tanz- Konzerte, drei Weihnachtskonzerte sowie Teilnahme am Wettbewerb-Singen vom Connecticut Sängerbund.

Sängerchor Boston • 8 County St. (Route 109) • Walpole, MA 02081 • (508) 660-2018

Memorial Garden for German soldiers who died as Prisoners-Of-War at Fort Devens, MA. In November, a military Memorial Service is held to honor the fallen with the participation of all AGSM member clubs.

The German cultural and educational exhibit, sponsored by AGSM, at the Boston International Festival was coordinated by Rose-Mary and Albert Kemper. Pictured on Rose-Mary's right is Carolyn Beierlein who coordinated the German Food Booth.

Participation at New York's Steuben Parade

New Era

Monument and Benevolent Association, Inc.

1991 marked the 100th Anniversary of the NEW Era Monument and Benevolent Association.

The New Era was a 1340-ton packetship, built at Bath, Maine, launched in April 1854 and destroyed by a storm off what is now Asbury Park on November 13, 1854 with great loss of life. The New Era had left Bremen September 19 under the command of Captain Henry with a crew of 30, a full

cargo of freight and 385 passengers, mostly German immigrants. After stopping at Liverpool, England, she ran into foul weather which persisted during the 55-day crossing. Gales whipped the clipper ship so fiercely that the superstructure was badly damaged. Finally the ship bit into a sand bar near Sandy Hook and became stuck as though cemented to the bottom. Many of the passengers were washed overboard by giant waves and drowned. Others died of Cholera. Of the 415 persons who boarded the ship in Bremen, only 132 reached the shore alive.

A simple wooden cross was put up on the site. In 1891, however, a group of people of German descent organized the New Era Monument Association and collected $700.00 for a granite monument which was dedicated at the cemetery the following year. The Association still takes care of the graves.

In Newport, Rhode Island

The 5th Annual WJAR-10

Oktoberfest

You never SAUSAGE an event!
Missing it would be the WURST.

The WJAR-10 **Oktoberfest** of Rhode Island offers the public an authentic German celebration with lively Bavarian music, delicious German food, *Biergarten, Weingarten*, and a special *Kindergarten* tent for children.

In addition to the food and celebration, the event is a vehicle for many non-profit organizations to raise funds. Included are the major recipients, The Arthritis Foundation and Kiwanis Club of Newport, as well as The Waldorf School and Literacy Volunteers. Demonstrations by the Canine Companions for Independence are held daily to explain their programs for disabled persons.

To round out the event, activities and entertainment are provided for the entire family to enjoy. The **Oktoberfest** usually features continuous live entertainment on three stages, including acts straight from Germany, a large Showband and a popular ensamble from the Bavarian Alps. There are strolling acts, magic shows, pony rides and a petting zoo, pumpkin decorating and German crafts and unique items for sale.

Held at the Newport Yachting Center on Columbus Day weekend, the **Oktoberfest** is part of New England's *"Harvest by the Sea"* festival. Call us for more information at **401 / 846-1600**

Die Einwanderung deutscher Frauen seit 1945

Obwohl deutsche Einwanderer, darunter natürlich auch Frauen, schon seit 1608 nach Amerika gekommen und unter anderem bei der Gründung von Jamestown, Virginia, dabei waren, sind die folgenden Bemerkungen denjenigen Frauen gewidmet, die nach dem Zweiten Weltkrieg einwanderten.

Zu dieser Zeit stieg die Zahl der Einwanderer nur langsam an: Familienmitglieder waren noch vermißt oder wurden in Ost-Deutschland oder in Kriegsgefangenenlagern festgehalten. Die US-Einwanderungsgesetze waren sehr streng, es sei denn man hatte gerade das große Glück, einen Verwandten oder anderen „Sponsor" in den USA zu haben. Die Frauen, die sich erfolgreich um die notwendigen Einwanderungspapiere bemühten, kamen von den unterschiedlichsten Gesellschaftsschichten - einige waren Kriegsbräute von US-Soldaten, andere waren mit Deutschen verheiratet, wieder andere waren unverheiratet. Einige Wissenschaftler und sogar Studenten der Naturwissenschaften wurden von Dr. Wernher von Braun aktiv für die NASA angeworben. Wir alle, ob wir nun in den 40er, 50er oder 60er Jahren einwanderten, suchten unser Leben durch die Gelegenheiten zu verbessern, die dieses Land zu bieten hatte.

Einige hatten das Glück, die Reise bereits per Flugzeug machen zu können, aber die meisten überquerten den Atlantik per Schiff. So brauchten meine Mutter und ich auf der alten „Italia" bei stürmischer See und Unterbringung im untersten Deck mit 12 Frauen zusammen in einer einzigen "Kabine" von Cuxhaven nach Hoboken (NJ) elf Tage. Als Flüchtlinge aus der ehem. DDR waren wir jedoch froh, daß wir unsere Visen durch Vermittlung des Weltrats der Kirchen mit „Sponsorschaft" der St. Paul Cathedral in Boston erhalten hatten. Unsere Sponsoren halfen uns, innerhalb von 48 Stunden eine Wohnung und Arbeit zu finden. Natürlich hatten wir zuerst Heimweh und vermißten unsere Freunde und Familie, aber gewöhnten uns doch bald ein. Indem wir der Deutschen Gruppe im International Institute beitraten und einige englische Konversationskurse belegten, fanden wir schnell Freunde aus vielen verschiedenen Ländern. Was uns am meisten erstaunte und uns gleichzeitig das Gefühl gab, willkommen zu sein, war die von vielen Amerikanern gehörte Redewendung „Wie können wir Ihnen helfen?" Der Eigentümer eines Schuhgeschäfts in Boston wollte uns erst für neue Schuhe bezahlen lassen, „wenn Sie ein bißchen zu Geld gekommen sind".

Vieles in unserem täglichen Leben erforderte jedoch Anpassungsfähigkeit an den „American Way of Life", den amerikanischen Lebensstil. Am schwierigsten war dies sicherlich für die Frauen, die mit wenigen oder gar keinen Englischkenntnissen eintrafen, ob sie sich nun in New Jersey, Michigan, Texas oder Kalifornien niederließen. Viele Schulen, internationalen Institute, Deutsche Vereine usw. boten Kurse an, und da Niederdeutsch und Deutsch mit dem Englischen verwandte Sprachen sind, lernten die meisten von ihnen die Sprache relativ schnell.

Diejenigen Nahrungsmittel in den Supermärkten zu finden, an die wir beim Kochen gewöhnt waren, wie Kartoffelmehl, Fleisch für Rouladen, bestimmte Wurstsorten und natürlich Brot und Brötchen bzw. Semmeln, forderte schon einiges an Entdeckergeist. Ein amerikanischer Freund fragte uns: „Wozu um alles in der Welt wollt ihr an Brot kauen?"

Es war leicht sich daran zu gewöhnen, daß es keine Wohnungsnot und genügend Stellen für alle, die arbeiten wollten, gab und daß die Preise für alle notwendigen Güter niedriger waren als in Deutschland. Viele von uns, die in den 40er und 50er Jahren ankamen, hatten oft mehr als eine Stelle, um nur schnell voranzukommen und möglichst bald solche Gegenstände wie Kühlschränke und Waschmaschinen kaufen zu können bzw. ein Auto, um zur Arbeit zu kommen und am Wochenende aufs Land herausfahren zu können.

„Deutsche Eigenschaften" wie die Fähigkeit, hart zu arbeiten, verantwortungsbewußt zu sein und Prioritäten setzen zu können, halfen uns dabei, gute Arbeit zu finden. Daß wir gute Köchinnen waren und ein sauberes sowie „gemütliches" Haus führten, erlaubt es uns, gute Nachbarn zu sein und hilft uns dabei, Freunde zu erwerben. Die verschiedenen Schulsysteme hier erforderten allerdings einiges Eingewöhnen von seiten sowohl der Mütter als auch der Kinder. Sich an das amerikanische Gesundheitsversorgungssystem zu gewöhnen, war schon bedeutend schwerer.

Eine ganze Reihe der eingewanderten deutschen Frauen haben hier ihre Schul- oder Studienausbildung fortgesetzt, die häufig durch Kriegs- und Nachkriegszeit unterbrochen worden war. Einige von ihnen wurden Naturwissenschaftlerinnen und Lehrerinnen. Andere versuchten sich als Unternehmerinnen - mit Restaurants, Läden, Maklerbüros, Unternehmensberatungen, Innenarchitekturbüros usw. Im allgemeinen kann ich aus meiner eigenen Erfahrung und der der von mir befragten Frauen mit einigem Stolz schließen, daß die meisten von uns es in den USA nicht nur „geschafft" haben,

Beauty and Personality

sondern auch viele wertvolle Beiträge zu den verschiedensten Bereichen des amerikanischen Lebens geleistet haben. Durch unsere deutsch-amerikanischen Organisationen in allen Teilen des Landes sind wir aktiv dabei, unser deutsches Erbe zu bewahren und hoffen, daß auch unsere Kinder und Enkelkinder dies tun werden.

Ich bin dankbar dafür, daß mir vor 40 Jahren die Chance gegeben wurde, in die USA einzuwandern. Ich möchte außerdem dem Verleger von „Heimat North America" dafür danken, daß er mich bat, diesen Artikel zu schreiben.

Rose-Mary Kemper, Boston

Immigration of German Women Since 1945

Columbia Club of Chicago Ladies

While German immigrants, and with them Women, arrived at the American shores and helped found Jamestown, Virginia, in as early as 1608, the following observations concern themselves with German women immigrating after World War II.

Immigration at that time started slowly for a number of reasons: family members were still missing or retained in the Eastern parts of Germany or POW-camps; US immigration laws were very strict, unless you were fortunate to have a relative or other sponsor over here. The women who succeeded to obtain proper visas came from all walks of life—whether they were brides of "G.I.'s" married to German men or single with or without children.   A number of scientists, and even some science students, were actually recruited by Dr. Wernher von Braun on behalf of NASA. All of us, whether we immigrated in the 40's, 50's or even 60's were looking for the opportunity to better our lives, which this country had to offer.

Some were fortunate enough to do the journey by plane, but many of us still crossed the Atlantic by boat—i.e., in 1957 it took my mother and me eleven days from Cuxhaven to Hoboken, N.J. on the old "Italia" in stormy seas and accommodations on the lowest deck with 12 women in the "cabin" . As refugees from East Germany, though, we were happy to have obtained an immigrant visa through the World Council of Churches and been sponsored by St. Paul Cathedral in Boston, Massachusetts. They helped us find jobs and an apartment within 48 hours. Yes, we were homesick missing our friends and family, but adjusted soon. Joining the German group at the International Institute and taking some English conversation courses helped us make friends from many different countries. What amazed us most and made us feel welcome was the phrase we heard from many Americans—namely "how can we help you?" The owner of a shoe store in downtown Boston would not let us pay for new shoes "until you have made some money."

Many things in our daily lives, though, required adjustments to the American way of life. It was hardest probably for those women who arrived with little or no knowledge of English, whether they settled in New Jersey, Michigan, Texas or California. Many schools, International Institutes, German Clubs, etc.

offered classes and since Low-German and German is one of the roots of English most of them learned quite fast.

Finding all the food items that we were used to for our cooking in the "Super Markets," required some ingenuity like Kartoffelmehl, Fleisch für Rouladen, certain Wurstsorten and, of course, Brot and Brötchen or Semmeln. One American friend asked "what on earth do you want to chew bread for?"

It was easy to adjust to no housing shortage, lower prices than in the old country for all necessary goods, and enough jobs if you were willing to work. Many of us who arrived in the 40's and 50's probably worked more than one job to get a good start and be able to purchase items like a refrigerator and washing machine, or a car to get us to work and on week-ends out into the country.

Some of our German "traits" like working hard, being responsible and organized helped us land good jobs. Being good cooks and keeping a clean and "gemuetliches" house makes us good neighbors and helps us make friends. The different school systems here required adaptation for both mothers and

children. The American healhcare system surely took some getting used to.

A fair number of German women immigrants have gone back to school to further their education which often was interrupted by the War and its aftermath. Some of them became scientists and teachers. Others became entrepreneurs like restaurant and shop owners, brokers, consultants, home decorators, etc.

In general, from my own experience and that of other women I interviewed, I am proud to say that most of us not only "made it" in this country, but many also made valuable contributions to different sectors of American life. Through our German-American organizations in all parts of the nation we are actively involved in preserving our German heritage and hope that our children and grandchildren will continue to do so.

I am grateful to have been given the chance 40 years ago to immigrate to America. I also wish to thank the publisher of "Heimat North America" for asking me to write this article.

Rose-Mary Kemper

Enjoying Family and Fun

Philadelphia
The Cradle of German Societies

By Ernst Ott

Since the first organized German group of immigrants, the 13 families from Krefeld, landed October 6th, 1683 and founded Germantown, now part of Philadelphia, it is not surprising that we find the oldest and still active German institutions in that area.

The Old Zion Church, now housed in Philadelphia's St. Mathews Church, was founded by Pastor Muehlenberg in 1742 and is the oldest German church community in America. Today, Pastor Schmutzler still holds services for his shrinking but loyal group of parishioners in St. Mathews.

The Church has an illustrious and sometimes pained history. The anti-German hysteria during WW II did not spare the church either. Its Pastor Kurt Moltzahn was accused of being a spy and incarcerated. Not till towards the end of the war was he pardoned and released.

The German Society of Pennsylvania is the oldest German society in America. Founded December 26, 1764, mainly to protect German immigrants from unscrupulous shipping agents and provide assistance upon arrival in the New World.

Today's activities in their impressive building at 611 Spring Street, protected as a historical landmark, it features musical performances, lectures, language courses and social functions. The most important part of the society's agenda however, is the housing and preservation of its historic literary treasures, including some 90,000 volumes of books from the 16th to the 20th century. The library is regularly used by researchers from both sides of the Atlantic.

There are a number of German American societies active today which can trace their roots back to the 1700s and 1800s, among them:

Ephrata Cloister, Pennsylvania	1732
Old Zion Church, Philadelphia	1742
The German Society of Philadelphia	1764
The German Society of Maryland	1783
The German Society of New York	1784

Leute, Land und Language:
Pennsylvania - Dutch (Deitsch - Deutsch)

Map Courtesy of Rand McNally, Road Atlas 1996

This approx. area in South Eastern Pennsylvania, with its rich German heritage, is known as Pennsylvania Dutch country.

Explanation of the Pennsylvania German Flag

"Die Pennsylfaanisch Deitsch Faahne"

Colors: Red, white and blue remind us that, in spite of our ethnic backgrounds, we are first of all loyal and devoted Americans.

Ship Concord: Commemorates the first settler group from Krefeld coming to Philadelphia in 1683.

Keystone: The symbol of Pennsylvania Dialect Expression: Dear God, let us keep our traditional ways.

Church: Indicative of the devoutness of the Pennsylvania Germans whose religious convictions were a strong motivating force in their daily lives.

Plow: Symbolizes probably the most predominant of Pennsylvania German professions, the farmer.

Heart and Tulip: Represents the great skills and varied contributions of the Pennsylvania Germans, particularly the women, in the fields of arts and crafts.

Conestoga Wagon: Symbolizes the Pennsylvania German's contributions to the need for travel and transportation. The "Ship of Inland Commerce", as it became known, played a very important role in the Revolutionary War under the guidance of Pennsylvania German teamsters. It also played a major part in the westward expansion of our nation.

Submitted by Jack Williams

THE PENNSYLVANIA GERMAN CULTURAL HERITAGE CENTER

AT KUTZTOWN UNIVERSITY

The Pennsylvania German Cultural Heritage Center located at Kutztown University in Kutztown, Pennsylvania on 60 acres of beautiful farm land is dedicated to the preservation of the culture and heritage of the Pennsylvania Dutch. The Heritage Center is comprised of a stone farmhouse and a stone summer/wash house (c 1820), a mid-19th century bank barn, and a one-room schoolhouse (c 1850) which have all been fully restored to project the Pennsylvania Dutch life from 1740 to 1920.

The Heritage Center provides academic programs for students of all ages by holding authentic one-room school classes, as well as tours of the farmstead. In the fall of each year a weekend **"Heemet Fescht"** is held which literally awakens the farmstead to the period from mid-18th century to the early 20th century by having journeyed blacksmith, tinsmiths, weavers, quilters, potters, and many other crafts demonstrated that were needed for survival during that period of time. Cooking, baking, canning, and drying techniques are taught by

local women by using authentic cooking utensils and stoves. Field work is demonstrated by horse-drawn and oxen-drawn plows, as well as antique tractors and equipment . Various types of entertainment, Pennsylvania Dutch music, and the 53rd or the 96th Pennsylvania Volunteer Infantry (both regiments highly manned by Pennsylvania Germans during the Civil War) are also on hand to create an ambiance of that period. The food served during Heemet Fescht weekend is purely Pennsylvania Dutch. A Pennsylvania German "Harvest Home" church service is preached in the Pennsylvania Dutch dialect, and all the hymns are sung in the dialect.

During the school year various local schools visit the site to give the children the experience of sitting in a school similar to one used by their grandparents, and they are able to have a hands-on experience by touring the farm. College classes are held in the school as an academic awareness of the change in teaching methods then and now.

The Heritage Center is an integral part of the authentic **Kutztown Pennsylvania German Festival** held during the summer for nine continuous days. This Festival has over 150 artisans demonstrating their crafts such as woodworking, lace making, quilting, metalsmithing, and many other skills that were needed on the farm during the period from 1740 to 1920. Funeral lore, portrayal of an Amish wedding, story telling, musical entertainment and dancing, exhibitions of antique farm equipment, antique toys and engines, church service, and other historical facets of the lifestyle of the Pennsylvania Dutch are present during this nine-day Festival.

The Heritage Center has developed relationships with other organizations who have interests in preserving the heritage, history, and culture of the Pennsylvania Germans. These affiliates reflect the common purposes of the Heritage Center and include: The Kutztown Pennsylvania German Festival, Inc., The Pennsylvania Dutch Folk Culture Society, the Old Time Plow Boys Club, Inc., the Antique Engine Tractor and Toy Club, Pennsylvania German Fersommlinge, Grundsau Lodges, Pennsylvania Dutch Music Association, Historical Society of Berks County, Berks County Genealogical Society, Rodale Institute, Hawk Mountain Sanctuary, and the Kutztown Historical Society, the Heartland Guild (which is an organization of crafts people dedicated to the authenticity of the art and crafts of the Pennsylvania Germans), and the Pennsylvania German Society, which is the academic and publishing arm for Pennsylvania Dutch studies.

Information and photos provided by Mary K. Henry

Grundsow Lodge
Nummer Ains on da Lechaw

The origin of Grundsow Lodge Nummer Ains is deeply rooted in the dialect, culture, and traditions of our German ancestors who settled here in eastern Pennsylvania in the late 18th and early 19th centuries. Indeed, one of the most interesting of our traditions is the assumed weather pronosticating ability of the groundhog. In Germany, our Palatine ancestors looked upon the Dachs, an animal not unsimilar to the groundhog in its appearance and habits, as a weather prophet long before its arrival in America. It was on February second, Candlemas, that people watched the antics of this animal, also known as a badger in English. If it saw its shadow on this day, it immediately retired back to its burrow for four more weeks of slumber because the weather during that period would be cold and snowy.

So, the groundhog became the mascot
of the Grundsow Lodge.

Grundsow Lodges in Pennsylvania Dutch Country

#1 on da Lechaw, Allentown
#2 on da Schibbach, Souderton
#3 in Temple University, Fildelfy
#4 on da Doheck, Quakertown
#5 on da Schwador im Bind Bush
#6 in Brodheadsville, Monroe Kty.
#7 in East Greenville, Montgomery
#8 on da Lizzard Grick, Schuylkill Kty.
#9 in Dublin, Bucks Kounty
#10 in Shtroudsbarrick, Monroe Kty.
#11 on da Fire Line, Carbon Kounty
#12 on da Tulpenhocken Pawdt
#13 on da Inche Grick, Amous
#14 on da Saakna Grick, Coopersbarrick
#15 fon Barricks Kounty, Kutztown
#16 om Yahden, Lechaw Kounty
#17 fon Lebanon Kounty
#18 on da gross Ferelle Grick

Get all the news from. . .

Es Elbedritsch and Der Reggeboge
with Rev. Willard W. Wetzel

call the Pennsylvania German Society
610 / 582 - 1441

Morning Call on Groundhog Day
60th Fersommling on February 2, 1996
Seated: Richard K. Maler - Unner Haaptmann
Standing: Carl D. Snyder - Haaptmann

Hy Lee, Hy Lo

O Entel Gamental
Gae mit m'r ins graws:
Dart peifa die fegel,
Dart jump'd der haws,
Dart donst der ochs,
Dart brumt die kuh,
Dart shlecht des Gametal
Die drumble datzu.

CHORUS:
Hy lee, hy lo, hy lee, hy lo!
Bei uns gaits immer
da langer da schlimmer
Hylee, hy lo, hy lee, hy lo!
Bei uns gaits immer noch so.

O Mommy, O Mommy,
Wos shoffa die gens?
Sie hucka im wosser
Un wesha die schwens.
O Mommy, O Mommy,
Wos shoffa die hund?
Bagrawwa die gnocha
So dief in der grund.

Der Hansel fon Bach
Hut louder gute soch,
Hut shtivel un shpora,
Hut allas ferlora,
Hut kugla gagussa,
Soldawdta gashossa,
Hut heiser ferbrent
Hut lumba drum k'hank'd.

- Arranged by Henry C. Detweiler

Der Meh Mir Kumma Zamma

Der meh mir kumma zamma
Kumma zamma, kummazamma
Fer meh mir kumma zamma
Der hallicher sin mir.

Fer dei Friend sin mei Friend
Un mei Friend sin dei Friend
Der meh mir kumma zamma
Der hallicher sin mir.

- Iwwersetzt bein L. E. Shupp

Bye. Bye, Groppa

Pock dei Glaeder un dei Gelt
Gen schpatziera, sehn die Welt
Bye, Bye, Groppa!

Neimand wahrt dahaem fer uns
Mir sin frei, net ferhunst
Bye, Bye, Groppa!

Mariyets fress mir Gatfisch
Mit die Grawna
Owets Hen mir frisch gebrodna
Bawna
Gor ken Gelt in die Seck,
Breicha kens, schmeis es wek,
Bye, Bye, Groppa!

- LeRoy Heffentrager

Come and Visit: **Ephrata Cloister,** Ephrata, PA
St. John's Lutheran Church, Reading, PA
Evergreen Country Club, Fleetwood, PA
The Edelweiss, Pocono Mountains, PA

We are grateful to the following for submitting this material:
Mary K. Henry and Rev. Willard W. Wetzel
Kutztown University of Pennsylvania
Call 610 / 649 - 7307 for more information
... and Jack Williams of Dingmans Ferry, PA.

Follow the Star
to Bethlehem

Folgt dem Stern
nach Bethlehem

Horse Carriages take visitors around, here at the industrial Moravian quarters

Musikfest '97
Second Saturday in August

This nine-day festival showcases more than 650 free musical performances, ethnic foods, children's activities, craft exhibits, floral displays and fireworks. Stroll among the historic buildings, parks and plazas of Bethlehem and enjoy an array of sites and sounds at 14 outdoor and 6 indoor locations.

Dieses Neun-Tage-Fest bietet mehr als 650 freie musikalische Vorstellungen, Essen verschiedener Völker, Kinderspiele, Handwerkskunst und Blumen Stände, sowie Feuerwerk am Abend. Bummeln sie durch die alten Straßen und Gebäude, Parkanlagen und Plazas von Bethlehem und genießen sie die vielen Eindrücke der 14 Außen- und 6 Innen-Attraktionen.

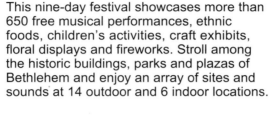

Children are an important part of Bethlehem Festivals.

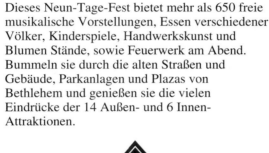

Overview of one of fourteen sites at Musikfest, Bethlehem, PA

Central Moravian Church, a landmark on the north side of Bethlehem

Christkindlmarkt of Bethlehem is comfortable inside the heated tent.

Christkindlmarkt Bethlehem
Starting Friday after Thanksgiving

A family holiday market presenting handmade crafts, strolling entertainers, holiday foods, a children's shopping area and St. Nicholas. Come and experience the old world charm of Historic Bethlehem, festively decorated for the holiday season.

Ein Weihnachtsmarkt für die ganze Familie mit Kunst- und Geschenkartikel, Schaustellern und Musikanten, festliches Gebäck und andere Köstlichkeiten, ein Kinderwunderland und St. Nicholas. Komm't und sehet den Glanz der alten Zeit im historischen Bethlehem.

(610) 861-0678

Snow covers the cozy tents which house the crafts and retailers at Christkindlmarkt

Handmade crafts are offered at Christkindlmarkt of Bethlehem

The Christmas-Tree-O entertains guests who visit Christkindlmarkt at Bethlehem, PA

Logos and photos courtesy of the Bethlehem Musikfest Association, Bethlehem, PA 18018

German-American Steuben Parade

25th ANNIVERSARY 1970 - 1995

SATURDAY, SEPTEMBER 23, 1995 12:00 PM - CENTER CITY PHILADELPHIA

PARADE ROUTE: From 20th & Parkway over 17th & Chestnut Sts. to Independence Hall

A&E MANUFACTURING
COMPANY, INC.
Armin & Erich Ast

CLEMENT & MULLER
John C. Muller

DAB IMPORTERS, INC.
Fredrich Hess

THE GERMAN
SOCIETY OF
PHILADELPHIA

ERNST A. ILLG MEATS, INC.
The Best of the Wurst
Magdalena & Ernst Illg
Chalfont, PA

STRAUSS ENGINEERING
COMPANY

SAVOY TRAVEL
SAVOY STUDIO

PRIME BANK

UAB MANUFACTURING
COMPANY, INC.
Ulrich A. Both

COLONIA TRAVEL
BUREAU

Art & Design: Lothar Sanchez-Speer, Portrait & Mural Studio   Project Coordinator: Manfred Speer   Photography Studio: Thaddeus Govan   Printed by: Anchor Printing Company

Cannstatter Volksfest Verein

One of the oldest and largest of the German-American clubs in Philadelphia, the Cannstatter Volksfest Verein was founded in 1873 for the purpose of celebrating the customs and traditions of their homeland, especially the annual harvest festival held in the town of *Bad Cannstatt*. In addition, they hoped to use any income form the organization for charitable purposes. In the 115 years since that founding all of the club's purposes have been impressively maintained.

The annual Fest held on Labor Day weekend draws thousands of people, both German-Americans and others, to observe and participate in this colorful ethnic event. The club also continues its charitable tradition providing support for German language schools, hospitals, nursing homes and orphanages, as well as to specific individuals in need.

Like many of the German-American clubs, the Cannstatter originally drew its members form a specific section of Germany, in this case the area of Southwestern Germany, generally known as Schwabenland, represented today by the political subdivision Baden-Wurtemberg. The Schwabians, or *Schwabs*, as they are usually called in their distinctive regional dialect, are proud of their *Heimat* and a modified form of the Wurtemberg Coat-of-Arms appears on the club banner. They also take pride in the accomplishments of their *Landsleute* (compatriots) in America, such as Godfrey Keebler and Christian Schmidt, two founders of this club who also are nationally known entrepreneurs. Whenever any German-American events are taking place you will always find the Cannstatters supporting it, both financially and with volunteer workers—living proof of their club motto, *Furchtlos und Treu* (Fearless and Faithful).

Einer der ältesten und größten deutsch-amerikanischen Clubs in Philadelphia ist der 1873 gegründete Cannstatter Volksfest Verein. Man wollte damit die Sitten und Gebräuche der Heimat aufrecht erhalten und hielt ganz besonders an dem jährlichen Erntedankfest des Ortsteils *Bad Cannstatt* fest. Darüberhinaus hoffte man, das Einkommen des Verbandes für wohltätige Zwecke einsetzen zu können. In den 115 Jahren seit seinem Bestehen, hat der Verein in beeindruckender Weise an dieser Philosophie festgehalten.

Alljährlich zum Fest des Tages der Arbeit, am ersten Montag im September, kommen tausende von Menschen, und nicht nur Deutsch-Amerikaner, um an diesem lebhaften Volksfest und bunten Treiben teilzunehmen und ihre Freude zu haben. Der Club setzt sich auch weiterhin für Wohlfahrtszwecke ein und unterstützt deutsche Sprachschulen, Krankenhäuser, Altersheime und Waisenheime und in besonderen Fällen einzelne Menschen.

Wie die meisten deutsch-amerikanischen Clubs hat sich auch der Cannstatter Verein am Anfang aus Mitgliedern einer bestimmten deutschen Region aufgebaut, in diesem Fall kamen sie aus dem Südwesten Deutschlands oder genauer gesagt, dem Schwabenland, das heute zu Baden-Württemberg gehört. Die hiesigen Schwaben, die *Schwabs*, wie sie sich in ihrem charakteristischen Regionaldialekt nennen, sind stolz auf ihre *Heimat* und ihr Club-Banner wird mit einer modifizierten Version des württembergischen Wappens geziert. Diese Menschen sind auch sehr stolz auf das was ihre *Landsleute* in Amerika schon alles geleistet haben, wie Godfrey Keebler und Christian Schmidt, zwei Mitgründer des Clubs, die als Unternehmer landesweit einen Namen haben. Wo und wann immer ein deutsch-amerikanisches Fest stattfindet, finden wir stets Cannstatter, die die Veranstaltung finanziell und durch ihre freiweillige Mitarbeit zu unterstützen versuchen. Ja, sie machen dem Motto des Clubs Ehre: *furchtlos und treu.*

Traditional Fruit Column by Gustav Plankenhorn

0130 Academy Road

Telephone: 215/332-0121

German American Committee
of Greater Philadelphia

Member Organizations:

Bayerischer Volksfest Verein
(215/969-9441)

Cannstatter Volksfest Verein
(215/332-0121)

Kolping Society
(215/324-9332)

Damenchor Heimat Echo
First German Sport Club Phoenix
Franklinville Quartett Club
German American Committee
German American Firefighters

German American National Congress
(610/833-1936)

German American Police Association
German American Bikers

German Society of Pennsylvania
(215/627-2332)

GTV Almrausch
Hermann Lodge
Humboldt Lodge
Schwarzwald Quartett Club

Steuben Parade Committee
(215/742-3587)

Steuben Society, Pastorius Unit # 38
United German Hungerians
United Singers of Philadelphia
Vereinigung Donauschwaben

Vereinigung Erzgebirge
(215/675-5380)

German Language Awards

Ted Hierl G-A Radio
(609/585-6757)

**German American
Chamber of Commerce**
(215/665-1585)

Historical Society of Pennsylvania
(215/732-6201)

Germantown Historical Society
(215/844-0514)

Mennonite Information Service
(215/843-0943)

Berlin Wall Monument at Vereinigung Erzgebirge Park

World War I Storm Trooper Monument at Memorial Cemetary

"Langen Kerle" Color Guard, Band and Dignitaries at German Day Celebration at Vereinigung Erzgebirge

Reading Room at the German Society of Pennsylvania Library

German Day in Philadelphia is celebrated each June at major German American Club Facilities

Das deutsch-amerikanische Kloster auf dem Hügel

von Pater Willy Wurm, O.S.B.

Im 8. Jahrhundert hörte man in den Wäldern Hessens, an Orten wie Fritzlar und Fulda, das Krachen von Äxten beim Baumfällen. Diesen "Waldarbeitern" stand ein englischer Mönch, Bonifatius, vor und bei den "Waldarbeitern" handelte es sich um Benediktinermönche, deren Aufgabe es war, die Germanen zu Christen zu machen und sie dabei der westlichen Zivilisation und Kultur näher zu bringen.

Knapp ein Jahrtausend später schwang eine andere Gruppe von Waldarbeitern ihre Äxte, um Bäume zu fällen. Zu deren Aufgabe zählte es ebenfalls, das Christentum und die westliche Kultur und Zivilisation zu verbreiten. Dieser Gruppe an "Waldarbeitern" stand ein deutscher Mönch aus Bayern vor, der ebenfalls Bonifatius genannt wurde. Der Ort, an dem die Bäume gefällt wurden, lag im Südwesten von Pennsylvanien. Achtzehn junge Männer, darunter sechzehn aus Bayern und zwei aus Österreich, kamen mit Pater Bonifatius Wimmer, um das erste Benediktinerkloster in den Vereinigten Staaten zu gründen und sich um das Wohlergehen der deutschsprechenden Katholiken zu kümmern. Es gab Mitte des 19. Jahrhunderts in den Vereinigten Staaten sehr wenige deutsch sprechende Priester, die sich um das seelische Wohl der deutschen Einwanderer kümmerten.

Bruder Bonifatius Wimmer, geborener Sebastian Wimmer aus Thalmassing, war ein Mönch des Sankt-Michael-Klosters in Metten. Er lebte und lehrte als Mönch am Königlichen Gymnasium in München zu einer Zeit, als eine große Anzahl Deutscher in die Vereinigten Staaten auswanderte. Um auf die Bedürfnisse der deutschen Katholiken in der Neuen Welt einzugehen, fing der Projektenmacher Wimmer an, Pläne für ein Kloster in der Neuen Welt zu schmieden. Endlich konnten Wimmer und seine Anhänger mit dem Segen seines Abtes und der Unterstützung von König Ludwig I. von Bayern Deutschland im August 1846 verlassen.

Der Traum des "Projektenmachers" wurde nach sehr bescheidenen Anfängen und vielen Schwierigkeiten Realität. Nicht nur die *Saint Vincent Archabbey*, sondern Klöster in den gesamten Vereinigten Staaten und anderen Ländern, wurden gegründet. Heute leben rund 200 Mönche in der Sankt-Vincent-Klostergemeinschaft. Wimmer war auch dafür verantwortlich, daß die Benediktiner-Ordensschwestern aus dem Kloster Eichstätt 1852 in die Vereinigten Staaten kamen.

Das *Saint Vincent College,* das seine Wurzeln in der Vergangenheit hat, wird sich auch in der Zukunft an die alte Tradition halten und die Beziehung zwischen Kloster und Schule pflegen. *Saint Vincent College,* ein College der Geisteswissenschaften, basiert auf den Grundlagen des katholischen Glaubens und dem Leben der Benediktiner. Die dort studierenden jungen Männer und Frauen werden zu "allgemein gebildeten Menschen" erzogen. Im *"National Review College Guide"*, einem College-Handbuch der besten amerikanischen geisteswissenschaftlichen Hochschulen, wird Sankt Vincent als eines der besten Colleges im Land genannt, das mit Hilfe der herausragenden Qualität ihres Lehrkörpers, Lehrplans und intellektuellen Umfelds den höchsten akademischen Standard erreicht. Das College wurde vom *U.S. News and World Report's Guide to America's Best Colleges* als eines der besten 10 geisteswissenschaftlichen Colleges in Nord-Amerika und eines der drei wirtschaftlichsten in bezug auf Studiengebühren anerkannt.

Saint Vincent hat seine deutschen Wurzeln nicht vergessen. Herzog Franz von Bayern aus dem Haus der Wittelsbacher setzte die 1846 dem Ludwig-Missionsverein von König Ludwig I. erteilte Unterstützung fort und amtierte als Ehrenpräsident der 150-Jahr-Feier. Herzog Franz lernte Bruder Lambert Berens während seines ersten Besuches von Saint Vincent kennen. Bruder Lambert war während der Nazi-Zeit Mönch in Deutschland. Er wurde vom Kloster aus in die Armee eingezogen, geriet in Gefangenschaft und wurde Kriegsgefangener der Amerikaner. Von einem Lager in den Vereinigten Staaten kam er zur Saint Vincent Archabbey, um dort sein Leben als Mönch wieder aufzunehmen. Nach dem Besuch von Herzog Max sagte Bruder Lambert: "Ich konnte meinen Herzog nicht besuchen und so kam mein Herzog zu mir". Herzog Franz von Bayern und sein Bruder Herzog Max in Bayern waren beide bei der 150-Jahr-Feier gegenwärtig, wo Herzog Franz einen Ehrendoktor erhielt. Auf einem abendlichen Abschlußempfang der 150-Jahr-Feier bemerkten Herzog Franz und Herzog Max wie sehr doch die neu renovierte Rheinisch-Romanische Basilika der Abteikirche von Sankt Bonifatius in München, wie sie vor dem Krieg war, ähnelte. Abt Notker Wolf, O.S.B., Erzabt der Sankt-Ottilien-Abtei in Bayern, las während der Abschlußmesse die Predigt.

Interesse an der Abtei besteht auf beiden Seiten des Atlantischen Ozeans. Annelies Schlickenrieder, Angestellte der *Missio* (Internationales Katholisches Missionswerk und Ludwig

From left: Duke Max in Bavaria, Br. Lambert Berens,
O.S.B., and Duke Franz of Bavaria.

Missionsverein) besuchte im Herbst 1988 das Kloster. Der Besuch wurde in einem Artikel in ihrer Zeitschrift *Mission aktuell* (3/89 München, Mai/Juni) unter der Überschrift "Hilfsbereit und herzlich" wiedergegeben. Auch in der Ausgabe vom 28. November 1995 der *Frankfurter Allgemeinen Zeitung* erschien ein Artikel über das Kloster und sein deutsches Erbe von Heinz-Joachim Fischer, der das Kloster kurz zuvor besucht hatte. Das sind nur zwei von vielen Artikeln, die über die Jahre in Zeitschriften und Zeitungen in Deutschland über das Kloster veröffentlicht wurden. Auch in den Vereinigten Staaten erschienen in der deutsch-amerikanischen Wochenzeitschrift *Amerika Woche* vom 16. November 1996 zwei Artikel: "Seilakt zwischen den Welten" und "Mit der Fürsprache Ludwigs I.". Der Herausgeber der Zeitung Mario Schiefelbein schrieb über seinen Besuch im Kloster und dessen deutsche Vergangenheit.

Überdies spielten zwei deutsche Künstler eine Rolle bei der Renovierung der Basilika und setzten die Tradition des handwerklichen Könnens fort, die beim Bau der Kirche begonnen hatte. Bildhauer Norbert Koehn und seine amerikanische Ehefrau Victoria, die in Deutschland lebten und studierten, haben in ihrem Studio und Atelier in Cleveland an der Restauration mitgearbeitet. Am herausragendesten sind wohl der heilige Sakramententurm und der mit Gold überzogene, handgeschnitzte Tabernakel. Der aus Dresden stammende Falk Kirchner, Angestellter der Firma Vater-Farben in Pittsburgh, der auch an den Arbeiten mitwirkte, brachte seine bei der Restaurierung einer Reihe von Barockkirchen in Deutschland gesammelte Erfahrung und Expertise ein. Ihr handwerkliches Können ergänzte die Kunst der Originalkirchenfenster und der Kreuzwegstationen, die in München, Deutschland geschaffen wurden.

Heute noch können die Besucher in der Sankt-Vincent- Kirche die der Benediktinergemeinschaft von der Wittelsbacher Familie erteilte Unterstützung und ihre gespendeten Gaben sehen. Bücher aus dem 16., dem 17. und dem 18. Jahrhundert sind in der Bibliothek ausgestellt. Eine Gruppe ausgewählter Gemälde aus einer von König

Ludwig I. dem Kloster vermachten Sammlung wird ständig in der Sankt-Vincent-Kunstgalerie ausgestellt. Eine Sonderausstellung, "Gaben eines Königs", fand im Jahre 1986 zur 200-Jahr-Feier der Geburt König Ludwigs I. statt. Das für die Ausstellung werbende, preisgekrönte Plakat war eine Kopie eines Gemäldes des jungen Ludwigs I. Überdies kann man an dem Blau und Weiß des Sankt-Vincent-Wappens und der Collegefahne, die zu besonderen Anlässen hochgezogen wird, das bayerische Erbe des Klosters erkennen.

Die deutsche Vergangenheit spiegelt sich aber auch in anderen Traditionen wieder, die der Öffentlichkeit nicht immer augenscheinlich sind. Am Heiligen Abend jedes Jahres wird vor dem Abendmahl der Weihnachtsbaum vom Abt gesegnet und das deutsche Weihnachtslied "O Tannenbaum" wird zunächst auf deutsch und dann auf englisch gesungen. *Ultima* wird zu allen festlichen Mahlzeiten und bei der Beerdigung von Mönchen erst auf lateinisch, dann auf deutsch und zum Schluß auf englisch gesungen. Am Gründertag jedes Jahres singen die Leiter, Fakultätsmitglieder, die Studenten, die Gemeinde und Freunde gemeinsam mit den Mönchen diese Hymne.

Jedes Jahr empfängt Sankt Vincent Gäste aus Deutschland, die durch die Gegend reisen. Deutsche Austauschschüler an den Oberschulen vor Ort, Rotary-Club-Gruppen, deutsche Benediktiner und viele andere. So manche deutsche Austauschschüler haben ihre Augenbrauen vor Überraschung gehoben und die Gesichter vieler deutscher Besucher haben sich verklärt, als man sie mit den Worten "Herzlich Willkommen" begrüßte.

Duke Franz of Bavaria (center) receiving the honorary doctorate
from Archabbot Douglas Nowicki, O.S.B. (right)
and Dr. Brent Cejda, Academic Dean.

The German-American Monastery On The Hill

by Fr. Willy Wurm, O.S.B.

Fr. Boniface Wimmer, born Sebastian Wimmer in Thalmassing, was a monk of the monastery of St. Michael in Metten. As a monk teaching at the king's Gymnasium in Munich, he lived at a time when great numbers of Germans were migrating to the United States. Responding to the needs of the German Catholics in the New World, Wimmer, the *"Projektenmacher"*, began to make plans to found a monastery in the New World. Finally, with the permission of his abbot and the support of King Ludwig I, Wimmer and his followers left Germany in August of 1846.

From humble beginnings and through many difficulties, the dreams of this *"Projektenmacher"* were realized. Not only was St. Vincent Archabbey founded, but also monasteries throughout the U. S. and other countries. Today, there are approximately 200 monks in the St. Vincent monastic community. Wimmer was also responsible for bringing the Benedictine sisters from their monastery in Eichstätt to the U.S. in the 1850's.

St. Vincent College, rooted in the past, looks toward the future and continues the established tradition and relationship between monasticism and education. St. Vincent College, a liberal arts college rooted in the traditions of the Catholic faith and Benedictine life, calls each of the young men and women, who study there, to be a *"gebildeter Mensch"*. *In The National Review College Guide to America's Top Liberal Arts Schools*, St. Vincent is listed as one of the top colleges in the country "that achieves academic excellence as measured by the quality and availability of the faculty, the quality of the curriculum and by the equality of the intellectual environment." The College has been recognized as one of the Top 10 Best Regional Liberal Arts Colleges in the North and one of the Top Three Best College Values (sticker price) by the *U. S. News and World Report's Guide to America's Best Colleges.*

St. Vincent does not forget its roots in Germany. Continuing the support begun by King Ludwig I and the Ludwig Missionsverein in 1846. Duke Franz of Bavaria of the Wittelsbach Family served as the honorary chair of the sesquicentennial celebration. During his first visit to St. Vincent, Duke Franz met Brother Lambert Berens. Brother Lambert was a monk in Germany during the Nazi era. He was taken from his monastery to serve in the army. He was captured and became a prisoner of war of the Americans. From a retention camp in the U. S., he came to St. Vincent Archabbey to resume his life as a monk. After his visit with Duke Max, Brother Lambert said, "I could not go to visit my Duke, so my Duke came to visit me." For the closing celebration of the sesquicentennial, both Duke Franz of Bavaria and his brother Duke Max in Bavaria were present. Duke Franz received an honorary doctorate. At an evening reception prior to the closing of the sesquicentennial, Duke Franz and Duke Max remarked on how the newly renovated Rheinish-Romanesque basilica resembled the abbey church of St. Boniface in Munich prior to the war.

Interior of the archabbey basilica. This picture was taken at the closing service of the sesquicentennial celebration, 1996.

Abbot Notker Wolf, O.S.F., Archabbot of St. Ottilien Archabbey in Bavaria, gave the homily at the closing sesquicentennial Mass.

There are other traditions, that reflect the German heritage, but are not always obvious to the public. Each Christmas Eve, prior to the evening meal, the Christmas tree is blessed by the abbot and the German Christmas carol, "O Tannenbaum" is sung, first in German and then in English. At meals on festive occasions and at the funeral of the monks, the *Ultima* is sung - first in Latin, then German, and finally in English. Each year on Founder's Day administrators, faculty, students, parishioners and friends join with the monks to sing this hymn.

Each year St. Vincent plays *Gastgeber* to Germans who pass through the area. They are German exchange students at local high schools, Rotary Club groups, German Benedictines, and many others. There are still a number of monks who speak German and give tours to the many visitors. The eyebrows of more than a few German exchange students have been raised and the faces of more than a few German visitors have brightened up as they heard the words, *"Herzlich Willkommen!"*

Alliance of Germanic Societies of Pittsburgh

Alpen Schuhplattler und TV
Austrian American Cultural Society
Bloomfield Liedertafel
Bloomfield Liedertafel, Singers
D.A.N.K. Pittsburgh Chapter
East Pittsburgh Saengerbund
German Hour
German Radio Pittsburgh
German Room (UP)
Geater Beneficial Union (GBU)
G.T.V. D'Lustigen Isarthaler
I G A R
North American Singers Association
Orpheus Singing Society
Pittsburgh District Kinderchor
Schweizer Maennerchor *Helvetia*
Swiss American Society of Pittsburgh
Teutonia Ladies' Chorus
Teutonia Maenner Chor
Teutonia Men's Chorus

For information contact: 412 / 884-5100

Old Economy Village,
just north of Pittsburgh on highway # 65,
was the home of the Harmonists,
a nineteenth century Christian communal
society best known for its piety and industrial prosperity.
Museum and tours 412 / 266-4500

GBU ist ein Unterstützungsbund der
finanzielle Sicherheit und humane
Fürsorge für seine Mitglieder schafft.
Die Gesellschaft wurde am 13. April,
1892 in Pittsburgh, PA als die
"German Beneficial Union" offiziell
eingetragen. 1942 wurde der Name
auf "Greater Beneficial Union"
umbenannt. Heute kennt man die
Gesellschaft an ihren Buchstaben
"GBU".

What is GBU ?

GBU is one of a number of
fraternal benefit societies doing
business in the United States
today, operating under a
representative form of
government. The society was
founded in Pittsburgh, PA, on
April 13, 1892, as the German
Beneficial Union to unite German
immigrants for the purpose of
providing insurance and fraternal
benefits. Later, the name was
changed to Greater Beneficial
Union, but the society is best
known by its letters GBU.

GBU offers a variety of life and
annuity products as well as
fraternal benefits which can
satisfy your needs from birth
through your entire life. GBU also
promotes German culture,
community and patriotic
involvement, as well as
charitable, recreational, and
social activities for the entire
family.

Your Circle for Life
For Information call: 1-800-765-4GBU

One of the foremost authorities and authors,
Professor Jürgen Eichhoff, heads the Department of German at
the **Pennsylvania State University** and **Max Kade German-
American Research Institute** at University Park, PA 16802,
Telephone: 814 / 863 - 9537

Professor Eichhoff has published among others several ethnic
posters, including and showing in this book

A Nation of Immigrants: The Germans (pg. 22)
Wisconsin, A Century and a Half of German Immigration
(Page 100). He is also curator of the Saur Bible, shown on
page 19.

Photo shows the history display of the German language department at Penn State University
It was created for German Weeks in Washington DC, page 249.

Federation of German-American Societies of Greater Cleveland, Ohio

Der Deutsche Stadtverband von Cleveland, Ohio

The Federation of German-American Societies of Greater Cleveland is the descendant of the first such alliance that was formed in 1890 to sponsor Cleveland's first German Day Celebration. Also known as *Der Deutsche Stadtverband*, it functions as a forum at which delegates from its member organizations:

1. Cooperate in achieving the goals of their groups,

2. Discuss issues affecting the German community,

3. Plan and sponsor the German Day Celebration and German Day Ball,

4. Serve as liaisons to non-German groups,

5. Recommend candidates for political office.

Goethe and Schiller Statue in Cleveland.

Der Bund der deutsch-amerikanischen Gesellschaft im Raume Cleveland ist der Nachfolger des ersten solchen Bündnisses, welches 1890 zum Zweck der Unterstützung der ersten *Deutscher Tag* Feier in Cleveland gegründet wurde. Auch bekannt als *Der Deutsche Stadtverband*, ist seine Funkion ein Forum in dem Vertreter der Mitglieder:

1. Zusammenarbeiten, um gemeinsame Ziele ihrer Gruppen zu vollfüllen,

2. Themen der deutsche Gemeinschaft zu diskutieren,

3. das Deutsche Tag Fest und Ball zu planen und zu unterstützen,

4. als Vermittler zwischen den nicht-deutschen Gruppen zu wirken,

5. und Kandidaten für den öffentlichen Dienst vorzuschlagen.

Der deutsche Stadtverband besteht aus diesen Vereinen:
Der deutsche Stadtverband is made of these Clubs and Societies:

D.A.N.K. German-American National Congress

3498 Varmland Court
Brunswick, Ohio 44212

Alliance of Transylvania Saxons
Deutscher Musik Verein
Eintract-Saxonia (Sachsen Chor)
Sächsische Tanzgruppe

7001 Denison Road
Cleveland, Ohio 44102

Corps Brandenburgia

2910 Warrensville
Shaker Height, Ohio 44122

Bayerischer Männerchor
Cleveland Männerchor
Deutsch-Amerikanisches Kultur Zentrum
Donauschwaben im Lenau Park
Greater Beneficial Union, District 810
Schuhplattier - Trachtenverein Bavaria

7370 Columbia Road
Olmsted Township, Ohio 44138

E.O.U.V. Lodge - Gottscheer

8636 Pekin Road
Novelty, Ohio 44072

Deutsche Zentrale Farm
Deutsche Zentrale Frauengruppe

7863 York Road
Parma, Ohio 44130

Altenheim
German-American Business Association
Germania, deutsch-amerikanische Zeitung seit 1990
West Side Deutscher Frauen Verein

P.O. Box 360156
Strongsville, Ohio 44136

Amerika, die neue Heimat
by Catherine Grosskopf

Der deutsche Bürger liess sich nieder hier im Land,
er suchte in der freien Welt ein Heim, sein Glück.
In seiner eig'nen Welt stand er am Kriegesrand,
Mit Zuversicht und Hoffnung sah er sein Geschick.

Er war bestrebt ein neues Leben hier zu bau'n,
im ehrenvollen Schaffen in die Zukunft geh'n.
Der neuen Welt, Amerika, galt sein Vertrau'n;
Mit Gott und Mut wird er die Forderung besteh'n.

Vor fünfzig Jahreen ist er tapfer angekommen,
den Geist und seine Willenskraft liess er nicht ruh'n.
Die neue Lebensweise hat er angenommen,
dem Fortschritt und dem Wachstum galt sein reges Tun.

Im Weltraum hat er seine Wissenschaft bewiesen,
In jedem Handwerk ist als Bester er bekannt.
Die Kunst und die Musik hält ihn gepriesen,
Nur oftmals bleibt sein wahres Wirken ungenannt.

Er half Amerika seit Jahren aufzubauen,
zur Sicherheit, zum Schutz des Landes trug er bei.
Sein kluges Können half verschönern diese Gauen
und wahre Dankbarkeit bewegt ihn stets auf's Neu.

Durch seinen fleiss'gen Arbeitsmut tagein-tagaus,
Fand er Geborgenheit im neuen Heimatland.
Im Herzen blieb er treu dem Lieben Elternhaus;
als guter "Bürger" ist er weit und breit bekannt!

*This poem was dedicated to Heimat North America,
and we are grateful to Catherine Grosskopf, Author
of a delightful collection of poems and prose in her
book "Ähren des Lebens" - Ernste Sachen und
solche zum Lachen - © 1993.*

NEII ZEITE NEIICHKEITE

Michael Bresser

Stellt Eich vor, mei Tochtermann
 Hat unser Haus verkaaft.
 's is zuviel zu renowiere dran,
saat er. Mir han bal graaft.

Mei scheenes Vaddershaus! Denkt nor,
Mi m große Garte hinnedran;
e Kotarka, e truckni Einfuhr,
e extra Schoppe for de Waan.

Die heitich Jugend is halt so,
 Tut's Altertum net eschtimiere;
wenn unerens ausgarweit is no
Tun ser uns leicht pensioniere.

Denkt Eich, mir ziehn in e Wohnung
 mit fremdi Leit, in e Block.
Find Dir des in Ordnung:
drei Zimmer im vierte Stock?

Mit lauter neimodische Sache:
uf's Heisl geht mer im Zimmer.
Ich glaab es is zum lache,
des riecht doch no immer!

Un noch was: mit Gas wert gekocht!
Ich jo net kritisiere,
awer mer heert daß unverhofft
de Sparherd tut explodiere.

Jessus, Maria un Jossef,
wie schnell die Zeit verloff is.
Mei Fieß tun mer weh vum ste'e.
Adje for heit, ich muss jetzt ge'e.

DIE NEICH SPROCH

Eugen Philips

Die Marjansgod tut's fixe,
sie kann's jetz schun im Schlof;
und durch des zammenmixe,
Entsteht a neichi Sproch.

Emol geht sie schape,
in dr Woch for alli Täg
un kaaft die viele Sache,
vum Hundefuder bis zum Steak.

Mittags kocht sie Tschicken,
owe uf 'm Grill,
saat: Boy des schmeckt delisches
un es koscht nit viel!

Die Freind hen ufgeruft
un es ihne gmenscht,
dass sie wiedrem fortgemuved
un die Address getschänscht

Am Sunntag no am Dritte,
sin sie alli beinfand fei
un wenn sie ab-sie-picke
griße sie mit "hei".

*These two poems by Dr. Michael Bresser and
Eugen Philips are from "**Der Schwengelbrunne**
Schöpfungen aus Amerika" and reprinted with
permission from the Danube Swabian Associatio
of the USA, Publisher **Franz Sayer**, 75-39 185th
Street, Flushing, NY.*

"The arrival of German Colonists in Banat" by Stefan Jäger

Courtesy of Annerose Görge

Donauschwaben • Cleveland, Ohio

This organization was founded in 1958 as the "Vereinigung der Donauschwaben" or "Society of the Danube Swabians" and was located on 3580 West 140th Street until it moved to the new facilities at Lenau Park in 1985. From that point on the name of the organization was changed to "Deutsch Amerikanisches Kulturzentrum der Donauschwaben" or "Donauschwaben's German-American Cultural Center".

All the Donauschwaben groups remain under this umbrella organization, with its president of over thirty years, Josef Holzer.

"Die Vereinigung der Donauschwaben" or "Society of the Danube Swabians" remains as the holder of the Center's liquor license and operates the bar. The president is Robert Filippi.

The groups of the Donauschwaben's German-American Cultural Center are:

D.S. **Jugendgruppe** (Youth Group) Founded in 1958. Current leader is Hildegard Radke.

D.S. **Sport Club Concordia** (Men, women, and youth soccer teams) Founded in 1957. Joined the Donauschwaben in 1959. Current president is Erich Haller.

D.S. **Blaskapelle** (Brass Band) Founded in 1959. Current president is Michael Siffermann, Jr.

D.S. **Frauengruppe** (Women's Auxiliary) Founded in 1959. Current president is Helga Schlothauer.

Deutsche Sprachschule mit Kindergarten (German Language School) The Kindergarten was founded in 1959. The German Language School was founded in 1960. The directors are Karoline Lindenmaier and Gerda Juhasz.

President of the school board is Franz Awender.

Interessengemeinschaft zur **Pflege der deutschen Sprache** (German School Parent Teacher Association) Founded in 1962. Current chairperson is Ingrid Urban.

D.S. **Kindergruppe** (Children's Dance Group) Founded in 1971. Current leader is Anneliese Julian.

D.S. **Kulturgruppe** (Cultural Group for young adults) Founded in 1981. Current president is Margot Maurer.

Schigruppe Edelweiss (Ski Club) Founded in 1968. Current president is Frank Schmidt.

Photos: Joe Holzer

Tennisgruppe Blau Weiss (Tennis Club) Founded in 1976. Current president is Adam Hetzel.

Altheimatlicher Kegelverein (Bowlers) Founded in 1962. Current president is Anton Ludwig.

Die Banater Chöre (The Banater Choirs) Männerchor (Men's Chorus) was founded in 1908. The president is Robert Filippi. Damenchor (Ladies Choir) was founded in 1925. The president is Franziska Bernhardt.

Die **Handarbeitsgruppe** (Hand Crafters) Founded in 1994. Current leader is Katharina Ritzmann.

D.S. **Seniorengruppe** (Seniors) Founded in 1992. Current leaders are Theresa and Martin Fischer.

D.S. **Golfergruppe** (Golfers Club) Founded in 1993. Current president is Josef Waldeck.

The Donauschwaben's German-American Cultural Center located at 7370 Columbia Road in Olmsted Twp., OH 44138 is the owner of Lenau Park - its land and its buildings.

Phone: (216) 235-2646
Fax: (216) 235-2671

Who are the Danube Swabians?
Translated by Helmuth Kremling

The 15th and 16th centuries witnessed the creation of the powerful Ottoman Empire. It conquered not only all the Balkan States and most of Hungary, but even beleaguered the city of Vienna into the next century.

The fierce forces controlled Southeastern Europe for more than 150 years and during this time not only ravaged the land but also scattered the people. Some areas lost all traces of civilization.

When the Turks of the Ottoman Empire were finally defeated in this area with the help of the Austrian emperor's general Prince Eugen, it was the main concern of Prince Eugen to colonize the land again and make it fruitful.

Emperor Charles VI, the Empress Maria Theresa, and Emperor Joseph II encouraged settlers, farmers and craftsmen for the most part, from West German lands, Luxemburg, Alsace Lorraine, etc. to settle the now ravaged land.

Not with wagon trains westward, as did our settlers of the time, but with barges did these people travel eastward on the Danube stream to reach their new home. They settled on the potentially fertile land along the Danube and some of its tributaries and hence were later named the Danube Swabians.

Many of the settlers never saw the fruits of their labor, because of famine and plague that swept through their ranks.

The pioneer spirit prevailed, however, and they not only reestablished a civilization but in the span of 200 years made this area one of the most fruitful in Southeastern Europe. It was even referred to as the "Breadbasket of Europe."

They were extremely proud of their German language and cultural heritage and lived in close-knit settlements to maintain them.

The number of settlers increased to such an extent that land became scarce and the traces of pioneer spirit still remaining caused many to seek America at the end of the 19th century. At

Map courtesy of Eckartbote, Vienna.

the conclusion of the First World War when the Astro-Hungarian Monarchy was dissolved and this area was parceled up between Hungary, Rumania and Yugoslavia many more came to America.

The result of the Second World War was the annihilation of about 250,000 Danube Swabians in the concentration camps of Tito. Furthermore, 100,000 of our people from Rumania and Hungary were abducted to Russia for forced labor, and were

forcefully displaced to the Baragan steppes of Rumania, where many thousands perished. The largest part of the surviving Danube Swabians were forced to flee or were expelled from their homeland as a result of the ever advancing communism. Most of them sought refuge in the already overcrowded countries of Germany and Austria where some of them still remain. To

many the Liberal emigration laws of the United States gave renewed hope and the opportunity to start anew as their forefathers had done again and again. A large number settled in Ohio and sought as their home especially the areas of Cleveland, Akron, Mansfield, Columbus, Cincinnati, Youngstown. Their diligence and honesty caused them to gain the respect of their neighbors. They adapted quickly to the ways of their new home and many of them play a substantial role not

only economically but also politically. Though they are faithful and conscientious citizens of the United States, they have never lost their pride in their heritage and have maintained it and are maintaining it to this day.

The Danube Swabians created organizations and associations such as German language schools, music bands, youth and sport groups, choirs, etc. to preserve their language, songs, dances and customs. Their favorite sport, soccer, has also been furthered as the creation of many soccer clubs shows. These organizations are welcomed at many public affairs to entertain with their music and dance. The members of the Danube Swabian groups are especially grateful that they have been welcomed and accepted by the public and praised and helped by the various city, county and state administrations.

• • • • • •

Wer sind die Donauschwaben?
von A. Kremling

Die Frage "Wer sind die Donauschwaben" wird oft gestellt und kann nicht mit einem einzigen Satz beantwortet werden. Es soll daher in dieser kurzen Abhandlung der Versuch unternommen werden, den Ursprung, die Entwicklung, den Opfergang und die Suche nach einer neuen Heimat dieser Volksgruppe zu schildern, unter besonderer Berücksichtigung der in den Vereinigten Staaten von Nordamerika ansässig gewordenen Donauschwaben.

Ursprung und Entwicklung

Als am Anfang des 18. Jahrhunderts, von den vereinten deutschen und österreichischen Heeren unter der Führung des kaiserlichen Generals Prinz Eugen, nach 150 jähriger Herrschaft, die Türken wieder aus dem Südosten Europas vertrieben wurden, hinterliessen sie ein verwüstetes, fast menschenleeres

WOIWODINA
(BANAT, BATSCHKA, BARANJA)

OST-SLAWONIEN
MIT SYRMEIN

Donauschwäbische Hauptsiedlungsbebiete Im Vorkommunistischen Jugoslawien
(Orte mit beachtlicher Donauschwäbischer Bevölkerung)

Map courtesy of Horst Kniesel, Westchester, IL

Land, das nur mit neuen Siedlern aus dem Westen wieder aufgebaut werden konnte. So geschah es vor mehr als 250 Jahren, im Jahre 1722 unter Kaiser Karl VI., daß sich der erste "Swabenzung: auf der Donau, dem Schicksalsstrom der Donauschwaben, nach Ungarn, in den Landstrich swischen Theiss, Donau, den Karpaten und der Marosch, ergoss. Dieser ersten Einwanderungswelle folgte in späteren Jahren, während der Regierungszeit der Kaiserin Maria Theresia, der zweite "Schwabenzug" (zwischen 1763 und 1770), dem die dritte Welle unter Kaiser Joseph II, im Jahre 1782 folgte. Diese "Swaben", die hauptsächlich aus den westlichen Ländern des "Heiligen Römischen Reiches Deutscher Nation" und Österreich stammten, schufen unter großen Opfern aus dem verwüsteten Raum

ein blühendes Eden, genannt die" "Kornkammer Europas", und ein Bollwerk der Christenheit und westlicher Kultur. Bis zum Ausbruch des ersten Weltkrieges im Jahre 1914 hat sicher dieser Stamm, den wir heute die Donauschwaben nennen, sowohl zahlenmäßig (über eine Million), als auch wirtschaftlich und kulturell zu einer beachtlichen Höhe entwickelt. Nach dem Ende des ersten Weltkrieges im Jahre 1918, nach dem Zusammenbruch der Österreich-Ungarischen Monarchie, wurde das Siedlungsbebiet der Donauschwaben jedoch auf die Länder Rumänien, Jugoslawien und Ungarn aufgeteilt, wodurch der Gruppe der erste schwere politische Schlag versetzt wurde. Obwohl es den geteilten und geschwächten Gemeinschaften noch möglich war, sich in ihrem jeweiligen neuen

Vaterland wirtschaftlich und kulturell weiter zu entwickeln, ließ der Neid und die Mißgunst der Mehrheitsvölker den wirtschaftlich weit besser gestellten Donauschwaben gegenüber, schon vor dem zweiten Weltkrieg nichts Gutes ahnen. Der Kriegsausgang und die verfehlte Poltik Deutschlands während des zweiten Weltkrieges haben dann das Schicksal der Donauschwaben im Südosten Europas endgültig besiegelt.

Opfergang

Als Folge des zweiten Weltkrieges und des Vordringens der Kommunisten bis tief nach Mitteleuropa, hat sich der nationale Haß der verschiedenen Völker Osteuropas und das kommunistische Untermenschentum, in einer bisher

ungekannten Grausamkeit auf die meist unschuldigen und schultzlosen deutschen Volksgruppen dieses Raumes abgeladen.

Auch die Donauschwaben, die nicht rechtzeitig flüchten konnten oder in ihrer Ahnungslosigkeit ihre Heimat nicht aufgeben wollten, wurden vielfach Opfer der Orgien des Hasses und mußten einen hohen Tribut an Menschenleben bezahlen.

Dem Terrorregime Titos und seiner Henker fielen Hunderttausende zum Opfer. Sie wurden erschlagen, hingemordet oder verhungerten in den Elendslagern. Rumänien deportierte eine große Zahl in russische Zwangsarbeitslager, wo über zehntausend Menschen starben, und eine etwa gleich hohe Zahl kam während ihres Zwangsaufenthaltes in der Baragan Steppe um. Ungarn

---

hat auf Grund er Postdamer Beschlüsse einen Großteil der Donauschwaben zwangsweise nach Deutschland ausgesiedelt.

Nur in Rumänien verblieb noch eine größere Anzahl von Donauschwaben. (Etwa zweihunderttausend, neben einer ungefähr gleich grossen Zahl Siebenbürger Sachsen).

Suche nach einer neuen Heimat

Die in dem überbevölkerten Raum Österreichs und Deutschland zusammengedrängten 12 Millionen Flüchtlinge, darunter über eine halbe Million Donauschwaben, standen vor dem Nichts. Sie waren in notdürftigen Barackenlagern zusammengepfercht und ohne eine Aussicht auf eine menschenwürdige Zukunnft. Erst durch eine großzügige Einwanderungsaktion der U.S.A. fanded Hundertausend dieser schwergeprüften Menschen hier eine neue Heimat und Wohlstand. Auch Kanada öffnet die Tore weit zur Aufnahme der heimatlosen Vertriebene und Flüchtlinge.

Eine weitere kleinere Zahl fand in Frankreich, Brasilien, Argentinen, Australien und in vielen anderen Ländern eine neue Heimat. Der größte Teil lebt auch heute noch in Österreich und Deutschland, wo sich in der Zwischenzeit die Verhältnisse auch grundlegend geändert haben und wo die Vertriebenen auch in menschenwürdigen, ja oft sehr guten Verhältnissen leben.

In den Vereinigten Staaten und Kanada bilden die Donauschwaben in vielen Staaten und Städten Schwerpunkte und Ortsgemeinschaften wohin ihnen von früher eingewanderten Landsleuten (vor dem ersten und zweiten Weltkrieg) die Einwanderung ermöglicht wurde.

Obwohl in fast allen Staaten der U.S.A. Donauschwaben zu finden sind, haben sich doch einige Schwerpunkte herausgebildet. In grösserer Zahl sind Donauschwaben in folgenden Städten anzutreffen: New York, Rochester, Trenton, Chicago, Cleveland, Cincinnati, Akron, Philadelphia, Detroit, Milwaukee, Los Angeles.

Ihr Fleiß und ihre Ehrlichkeit ließen sie auch hier zu gesuchten Arbeitskräften werden. Sie konnten sich die demokratische Freiheit Amerikas zunutze machen, und viele ihrer Menschen spielen heute sowohl in der Wirtschaft, als auch im öffentlichen Leben und in der Politik der Vereinigten Staaten, eine bedeutend Rolle.

In ihrer konservativen, noch vom Kolonistengeist geprägten Auffassung, betilgen sie sich im allegemeinen und keinen extremen Bewegungen. Sie sind Fortschritt und sozialer Gerechtigkeit gegenüber sehr aufgeschlossen, was auch daraus hervorgeht, daß es fast keine donauschwäbische Familie mit schulpflichtigen Kindern gibt, die nicht bestrebt ist, diese einer höheren Ausbildung teilhaftig werden zu lassen. Es ist fast eine Selbstverständlichkeit geworden, daß an vielen Universitäten und Colleges auch donauschwäbische Jungen und Mädchen studieren und vielfach schon als Lehrer an solchen und anderen höheren Institutionen tätig sind. Auch in der Wirtschaft und an Forschungsinstituten finden wir viele Ingenieure und Wissenschaftler donauschwäbischer Herkunft, genauso wie in den akademischen Freiberufen.

Genau wie in den alten Heimat, liegt ihnen auch heir sehr viel an der Erhaltung ihrer deutschen Muttersprache, der erebten Kulturgüte und der Trachten und Sitten. Sie bildeten fast überall Vereine mit deutschen Wochenendschulen, Gesang- und Sportvereinen, donauschwäbischen Musikkapellen und Trachtengruppen usw., die eine äußerst rege Tätigkeit entfalten und sich auch in anderen deutschen und amerikanischen Kreisen großer Beliebtheit erfreuen. Um ihrer Tätigkeit auf diesem Gebiet ein größeres Gewicht zu verleihen, haben sich die Vereine der Donauschwaben zu einem Landesverband zusammengeschlossen, dem viele Vereine vom Osten (New York) bis zum Westen der USA (Los Angeles) angehören und der auch mit dem Landesverband der Donauschwaben in Kanada eng zusammenarbeitet. Besonders dankbar wird es von ihnen empfunden, daß sie sowohl von der Öffentlichkeit, als auch von den Behörden stets wohlwollende und fördernde Unterstützung erfahren. Auch die Vertreter der Bundesrepublik Deutschland unterstützen und förden die Bestrebungen der Donauschwaben, bei denen sie oft und als gerne gesehene Gäste anzutreffen sind.

Photos courtesy Horst Kniesel   Monuments in Ulm, Germany

Joseph Rickert, Honorary President of the German Family Society and leader of ethnic Organizations!

Mr. Joseph Rickert a founder of the German Family Society of Akron, Ohio Inc. served as President and outstanding leader for 25 consecutive years. During this period he also served for six years as national president of the Danubeswabian Association in the USA, and six years as President of the German American Club in Akron. After his arrival in the United States in the1950's, he became actively involved with the Akron International Institute and was instrumental in assisting the settlement of displaced European families after World War II. In the 1970s, Mr. Rickert was an active adviser and organizer of Akron's International Stadtfest, and Cuyahoga Falls' Oktoberfest (which continues to this day). Mr. Rickert has been bestowed numerous local, national and international awards for his contributions to the Akron community and his outstanding work in the promotion of German language and culture. Included are: a declaration from Akron University's ETA XI collegiate, which voted him an honorary member of the National Honor Society "Delta Phi Alpha". In 1995 he received Germany's highest civilian honor, the Distinguished Service Cross, from the German Ambassador. Mr. Rickert, at the young age of 17, in his home town in Yugoslavia was already developing a strong moral background as an active member in the local catholic church, and a determined sense of leadership with his work with youth groups. Mr. Rickert, who was very religious, lived his life accordingly. He was a moral, and an honorable man, a dedicated friend and a loving father and husband. One of Mr. Rickert's life long dreams was to establish and build a social gathering place where people could meet and share common German and Danubeswabian ethnic traditions and customs. His perseverance paid off in 1972 with the purchase of a 20+ acre "Donaupark", which through the hard work of dedicated members is today an Ohio landmark, with a beautifully landscaped park, a newly built club house, a lake, soccer fields, and most of all, young people to enjoy and remember the fruits of his (and many dedicated founding members') labors. Mr. Rickert, was born in 1920 and passed away on December 9, 1996.

Herr Josef Rickert, Ursprung und Quelle des Deutschtums in Akron und Nord Ost-Ohio!

Herr Josef Rickert Gründer des Deutschen Familienvereins in Brimfield Ohio diente dieser Organisation 25 Jahre als Präsident, war 6 Jahre Präsident des Deutsch - Amerikanischen Klubs in Akron und hielt daneben auch 6 Jahre das Amt als Landespräsident des Deutsch - Amerikanischen Verband der Donauschwaben. Er wurde von beiden Vereinigungen nach dem er in Ruhestand ging zum "Ehrenpräsident" ernannt und übernahm das Amt als Präsident des 'Goldenen Rings, - eine Nebengruppe der Senior Mitglieder des DFV. 1950 beteiligte er sich aktive mit Akron's Internationalem Institut und war Helfer und Berater bei der Niederlassung vieler Zwangsvertriebenen des 2. Weltkrieges. Er organisierte und beteiligte sich auch an den ersten Internationalen Stadtfeste, die in den 7Oger Jahren in der Stadtmitte von Akron abgehalten wurden und war der Hauptberater des Stadtamts in Cuyahoga Falls während der Gründung eines Oktoberfestes, das noch heute jährlich in dieser Stadt stattfindet. Außer den Auszeichnungen die ihm von jedem deutschen und vielen internationalen Vereinen in den USA verliehen wurde, ehrte am 17. Februar 1977 die ETA Xl Collegeate der Akron Universität Herrn Rickert in der Aufnahme als Ehrenmitglied der Delta Phi Alpha durch seine Verdienste in der deutschen Sprache und Kultur. Jedoch die größte Auszeichnung wurde im 1995 zuteil, als ihm aufgrund seiner lebenslangen, außergewöhnlichen Verdienste von der Bundesrepublik Deutschland, Roman Herzog (Bundespräsident) "Das Verdienstkreuz am Bande des Verdienstordens der Bundesrepublik Deutschland" verliehen wurde. Herr Rickert behielt trotz aller Rangverleihungen und Auszeichnungen seine Bescheidenheit, die Liebe zum Nächsten und das Streben -die heimatlichen Sitten und Brauche unserer Vorfahren in der Fremde aufrecht zu erhalten. Mit unermeßlichen Güte, Geduld und seinem außergewöhnlichen Verständnis für alle Mitmenschen bewies er eine Führungsqualitat, die den Höhepunkt seiner Lebensaufgabe Übertraf. Seinen tiefwurzelnden Glauben bewies er in seiner vorbildlichen Lebensweise. Er duldete klagenlos was ihm das Leben auferlegte und lebte jeden Tag in dankbarer Ergebenheit. Herr Rickert wurde am 9. Dez. von seinen langen Leiden erlöst und hinterlaßt eine große, unersetzbare Lücke bei allen die ihn kannten und in Kontakt mit ihm kamen. Im Gedenken seiner Erfolge, unermüdlichen Tätigkeit, seines einwandfreien Charakters und von einem inneren Drang gesegneten Person bleibt er in unserer Erinnerung das Vorbild eines erfüllten Lebens, denn als Andenken hinterläßt er allen Mitgliedern und Deutschgesinnten das schone Vereinshaus "den Donaupark", ein Geschenk seines Lebenswerkes, dem er einen eisernen Willen und unzählige Stunden seines Lebens freudig opferte, um allen Deutschen in der Fremde ein Stückchen Heimat zu gestalten und den Nachfolgenden Generationen zu vererben. Die deutschen Vereine in der Umgebung verloren einen Leiter, Freund und Gefährten, dessen Verlust und hinscheiden weit Ober die Grenzen Akrons reicht. Herr Josef Rickert kam 1920 in Jugoslawien zur Welt und war schon in der alten Heimat als 17 jähriger Jüngling mit dem Vereinsleben und der Aufgabe als Jugendleiter vertraut, und voller Begeisterung und Tatkraft damit verbunden. 1951 faßte er Fuß in Akron und baute sich in Tallmadge Ohio mit seiner Gattin Mary, Sohn Rudi und Tochter Martha eine ständige Heimat.

Veronika Fleischer

Deutscher Familien Verein von Akron, Ohio e.V.
German Family Society of Akron, Ohio Inc.

3871 Ranfield Road, Brimfield Twp.
Kent, Ohio 44240   (330) 678-8229

The **German Family Society** was founded in 1955 in Akron, Ohio. The original club had its home in the basement of St. Bernard Catholic Church, then for approximately 12 years resided within the German American Club. In 1972 (under the leadership of Mr. Josef Rickert(), the GFS relocated to Brimfield (Kent), Ohio with the purchase of 12 acres of land. Today the picturesque "Donaupark" owns 20+ acres with a lake, has a beautiful 350+ capacity clubhouse, an outside pavilion, the Edelweiss house, and 2 first rate soccer fields. This has been accomplished entirely with the hard work of an all volunteer membership dedicated to promoting a proud heritage consisting of German, Austrian and Danubeswabian traditions. The GFS features many groups for both young and mature interests including: the Ladies Auxiliary (the heart and soul of our organization), the Golden Ring Senior group, the Harmony Singers, the Edelweiss dance group, both men's and ladies soccer teams for all ages, a golf club and our German Radio Program (WAPS 91.3 FM). We also have 4 strong youth groups: the "Kinder" group (ages 4-10), the Junior Youth group (ages 10-13), the nationally acclaimed Youth Folk-dance and Schuhplattler group, which has toured Europe and performed as far away as California with its award winning programs (ages 14-25), and the Culture and folk dance group consisting of both

married and single young adults. The GFS' yearly events include both traditional festivals such as the formal Vienna Night, a Karneval (Mardi Gras), Kirchweihfest (Church fest), Schuetzenfest, Schlachtfest (featuring homemade specialties like Bratwurst, Blutwurst, Leberwurst and Spanferkel), a German Day which commemorates the contributions of Germans in the USA - our new home, a Traubenfest (Grape festival), the youth group's Königsball (Royal Ball) and Debutante Ball, and of course our largest event, the Oktoberfest. For a more modern twist we also have such evenings as a 50's Dance, a Country Night, and a popular Hawaiian Night (with our youth group performing traditional Hawaiian dance and song). The GFS is also a member of the national "Danubeswabians in the USA" organization, which annually holds festivals throughout the country, and every 3 years celebrates a Trachtenfest (traditional costume ball), in which is held a national youth folk dance and song competition. The GFS Youth Group (see photo) took 1st place in 1990 and again in 1996. We are very proud of our young people, and with the continued cooperation of all ages and a growing membership, the GFS will continue to promote German traditions of dance, song and "Gemütlichkeit" for many years into the future.

Sepp Geiser, President GFS

Deutscher Familien Verein von Akron, Ohio e.V.
German Family Society of Akron, Ohio Inc.
3871 Ranfield Rd. Brimfield Twp./Kent, Ohio 44240   (330) 678-8229

Der **Deutsche Familienverein** wurde 1955 in Akron, Ohio, gegründet. Das Heim dieses neugegründeten Vereins war in den Kellerräumen der St.- Bernhard - Kirche, dann ungefähr 12 Jahre lang im Deutsch - Amerikanischen Klub. Im Jahre 1972 verlegte der Deutsche Familienverein (unter der Leitung von Herrn Josef Rickert ()) seinen Standort mit dem Ankauf von 12 Morgen Land nach Brimfield (Kent). Heute besitzt der malerische "Donaupark" mehr als 20 Morgen Land mit einem See, hat ein eindrucksvolles mit 350 + Aufnahmefähigkeit Vereinshaus, einen Pavillon draußen, das Edelweiss-Haus, ebenso zwei erstklassige Fussballanlagen. All das wurde durch schwere Arbeit freiwilliger Mitglieder erreicht, die sich der Förderung eines stolzen Erbguts deutscher, österreichischer und donauschwabischer Traditionen widmeten. Der Deutsche Familienverein hat viele Gruppen für die Interessen der jugendlichen wie auch der reiferen Mitglieder. Es sind die Frauengruppe (Herz und Seele unserer Organisation), der Goldene Ring (Seniorengruppe), die Harmonie Gesanggruppe, die Edelweiss Tanzgruppe, ebenso Herren- und Damenfussballmannschaften für jede Altersgruppe, ein Golfklub und unser deutsches Radioprogramm (WAPS 91.3 FM). Wir haben auch vier starke Jugendgruppen: die Kindergruppe (Alter 4-10 J.), die Junioren Jugendgruppe (Alter 10-13 J.), die landesweit anerkannte Jugend - Volkstanz - und Schuhplattlergruppe, die Europa auf einer Tournee bereiste und so weit entfernt wie in Kalifornien ihre preisgewinnenden Programme aufführte (Alter 14-25 J.), und die Kultur und Volkstanzgruppe, die aus jungen verheirateten wie auch jungen ledigen Mitgliedern besteht. Die jährlichen Veranstaltungen des Deutschen Familienvereins bieten traditionelle Feste wie den formellen Wienerabend, einen Karneval, Kirchweihfest, Schützenfest, Schlachtfest (mit Hausmacher Spezialitäten von Bratwurst, Blutwurst, Leberwurst und Spanferkel), einen Deutschen Tag, der die Beiträge Deutscher in den U.S.A. - unserer neuen Heimat - gedenkt, ein Traubenfest, den Königsball der Jugendgruppe und Debutantenball, und natürlich unsere größte Veranstaltung, das Oktoberfest. Als modernere Abwechselung haben wir auch solche Abende wie einen 50's Tanz, einen Country - Western Tanzabend, eine populäre Nacht in Hawaii (unsere Jugendgruppe führt traditionelle hawaiische Tänze und Lieder auf). Der Deutsche Familienverein ist auch Mitglied der Landesorganisation, "Donauschwaben in den U.S.A.", die jährlich Feste im ganzen Land feiert und alle 3 Jahre ein Trachtenfest begeht, bei dem ein Landesjugend Volkstanz - und Liederwettstreit stattfindet. Die Jugendgruppe des Deutschen Familienvereins (s. Foto) gewann 1990 und wiederum 1996 den 1. Preis.

Wir sind sehr stolz auf unsere jungen Leute und mit weiterer Zusammenarbeit aller Alteregruppen und zunehmender Mitgliedschaft wird der Deutsche Familienverein weiterhin deutsche Tanz- und Gesangtraditionen und "Gemütlichkeit" viele Jahre in die Zukunft hinein fördern.

Sepp Geiser, Präsident DFV

GFS Youth Group - 1st Place 1996 - National Danubeswabian Folk Dance Competition

Der Mansfield Liederkranz

Vor 75 Jahren wurde die deutsch-ungarische Sängergemeinschaft gegründet. Später verbandt man sich mit dem Mansfield Männerchor und so entstand der *Mansfield Liederkranz.*

Der Wille und das Ziel des Vorstandes und der Mitglieder war es jedoch, ein großes, eigenes Anwesen zu haben. Und so ergabt es sich, daß man durch eine Bauaktion im July 1979 das Land kaufte und der Neubau im April 1980 beginnen konnte. Der erste Tanz im neuen Klubhaus fand am Samstag, den 22. November 1980, statt.

Der Liederkranz unterstützt Kegeln, Softball, Golf und den Fußball, der besonders in den 50er bis Mitte der 60er Jahre populär war. Die Mannschaften haben mehrere Ohio State Meisterschaften gewonnen.

Die Fußball Jugend und die jungen Leute und Junioren Tänzer sind jetzt der wichtigste Teil der Klubaktivitäten.

Seventy-five years ago the German-Hungarian Singing Society was founded. It merged with the Mansfield Maennerchor to form the *Mansfield Liederkranz.*

The will and determination of the officers and members of this club to build a new and larger home climaxed in the expanding of the building committee and the purchase of the land in July 1979, and the subsequent ground breaking in April 1980. On Saturday, November 22, the first dance was held in this new building.

The Liederkranz has sponsored such sports as bowling, softball, golf and soccer. The latter very successful from the early 50's to the mid 60's. The teams have won several Ohio State Championships. Junior Soccer, as well as young adult and junior dancers are an important part of the activities at the Donauschwaben Club today.

Mansfield Liederkranz
1212 Silver Lane, Mansfield, Ohio 44906
Information: 419 / 529 - 3064

Verein der Donauschwaben von Cincinnati

Der Verein der Donauschwaben von Cincinnati, Ohio wurde im Jahre 1954 von Einwanderern deutscher Herkunft aus den Südosteuropäischen Siedlungsgebieten gegründet. Geselligkeit und Pflege erwerbter Sitten und Gebräuche waren Ziel und Zweck des Vereins.

Der Verein unterhält Jugend- und Kinder-Tanzgruppen, Sportler, Schuhplattler- und Volkstanzgruppen, einen Senioren Kreis, eine Frauengruppe, einen gemischten Chor, eine deutsche Kinder-Sprachschule, und der Verein ist bestrebt, Liebe und Treue zur neuen Heimat Amerika zu fördern.

Das Heim der Donauschwaben im Nordwesten Cincinnatis.
The Danube Swabian Home in Cincinnati

The Danube Swabian Club of Cincinnati, Ohio was established in 1954 by immigrants of German descent from Easteuropean areas. Social gatherings and maintaining of customs and culture of their homeland are goal and purpose of the club.

The society consists of youth- and children dance groups, sport activities including soccer, colorful "Schuhplattler"- and folk dance groups, senior - and women circles, a singing society and a German children's language school. The club endeavors to promote love and loyalty to the new American homeland.

Verein der Donauschwaben in Cincinnati
4290 Dry Ridge Road, Cincinnati, OH 45252
Information: 513 / 385 - 2098

German-American Citizens League Of Greater Cincinnati

Deutsch-Amerikanische Bürger-Liga von Gross-Cincinnati

Established 1895

The following organizations are affiliated with the German-American Citizens League:

Bayerische Unterstützungs Verein
3421 Cheviot Avenue

Bloatarian Brewing League
1527 Larry Avenue

Cincinnati Central Turners
10115 Pottinger Road

Cincinnati Carvers Guild
1015 Hickok Lane

Deutscher Hausverein/Liberty Home Assoc.
204 Morman Road, Hamilton

Verein der Donauschwaben
4290 Dry Ridge Road

Fairview German School
2332 Stratford

Frauenstadtverband
3149 Evergreen Avenue

Friends of the University of Cincinnati.
German-American Studies Program

German Genealogical Group
P. O. Box 15851

German Heritage Parade in Cincinnati, sponsored by the German-American Citizens League of Greater Cincinnati, 14 September 1996, on the occasion of the ground breaking ceremonies for the German Pioneer Heritage Museum.

Germania Society
3529 Kemper Road

Kentuckiana German Heritage Society
3660 Willowlea Court

Catholic Kolping Society of Cincinnati
10235 Mill Road

Kolping Sängerchor
10235 Mill Road

Munich Sister City Association
721 Lullaby Court

Old St. Mary's Historic Preservation Assoc.
13th and Clay Streets

Society for German-American Studies
University of Cincinnati

Tri-State German-American School
556 Terrace Avenue

German-American Citizens League of Greater Cincinnati
P.O. Box 210113
University of Cincinnati
Cincinnati, OH 45221-0113
Telephone: 513 / 556-1955
Dr. D. H. Tolzmann,
President

German Pioneer Museum to be...

Photos: Dr. Tolzmann

Credits for Back Cover

We acknowledge with thanks the assistance by the Departments of Tourism by providing slides and information on the various States:

In sequence as they appear, from left

Nestlenook Inn by Bob Grant, NH

On tour by Larry Belcher, WV

Smithonian Institute, Washington, DC

Luray Caverns, Virginia

Liberty Bell, Philadelphia, PA

Legislative Hall, Dover, DE

Photo by Kindra Clineff, MA

Newport Bridge by P. Browning, RI

Quechee, Montpelier, VT

Thundering Surf, Maine

Plantation near Charleston, SC

Sandy Hook, Atlantic Coast, NC

Mardi Gras, New Orleans, LA

Crawfish Dinner, Gulf Coast, LA

Inner Harbor, Baltimore, MD

Badlands, Oregon Trail, ND

Gateway to the West, St. Louis, MO

Hermann Maifest, MO

Space Rocket Center, Huntsville, AL

Jazz Band, New Orleans, LA

Rodeo Riding, South Dakota

Evening Skyline, Reno, NV

Pacific Coast by Robert Holmes, CA

Bellingham and Mt. Baker, WA

Indian Chief with Grandson, NV

Bryce Canyon, Navajo Trail, UT

Mormon Choir, Salt Lake City, UT

Yamhill Vineyards: Steve Terrill, OR

Amana Colonies, Iowa

Dog Sledding in Minnesota

THE GERMANIA SOCIETY, INC.
A Society of German Heritage of Greater Cincinnati, Ohio

President Helma Neubert presenting the Germania Flag

The Germania Society was founded in 1964 for the sole purpose of maintaining and perpetuating German Heritage in the Greater Cincinnati area.

The Germania Society strives to maintain an interest in many customs from all regions of Germany, for which various special interest sections have been formed within the Society. Germania is not identified by a specific Germanic region and is affiliated only with the German-American Citizen League, a local umbrella Civic Organization. Membership is open to all people from all cities and regions of Germany, all Americans of German ancestry and persons married to a German or persons interested in promoting the German heritage and culture.

Some Germania Members, 1996

Most goals and accomplishments had their origin in a manifest which was proclaimed at the incorporation of the Society. In a strictly educational and cultural commitment toward the people of Cincinnati, which is between 50-60% of German ancestry, intellectual concerns were of top priority. Teaching the German language in Cincinnati schools became a reality after discussions with people from local Universities. It was resolved that, as a Society of many interests we could not pursue this task on our own limited resources. Therefore, a new entity was formed which became the "Tri-State German-American School Society" with its own principal and a full educational staff.

Through the efforts of a board member, the Germania Society established a radio program named "Over the Rhine Showcase" which is still on the air today.

The main goal of the Germania Society was to build a "German Haus" in Cincinnati of which all Germans could be proud. 25 acres of land was bought in 1969 in the Northwestern region of Cincinnati, Ohio. A Ratskeller type Klubhaus was built on the Society's grounds in 1977. The property is called "Germania Park". Other structures followed, including a large pavilion for big outdoor events.

In 1964 most of the Germania's programs were established and the Germania Crest was introduced, which is unique in its design and message. Its unveiling was one of the most memorable moments, because it depicts the purpose of Germania so well. Our Society flag was dedicated later in 1974.

Der Vorstand   Board of Trustees
Front: Edeltraut Reed, Brigitte Eggers, David Beiderbeck, Helma Neubert, Gabriele Vosmeier, Fred Frey   Back: Andy Kaiser, Walter Bednar, Jack Ridenour, Stephan Menyhert, Dana Reed, Dieter Waldowski, Bernd Rau. Bernard Geers not pictured.

During the year 1965 our cultural customs (folklore) were researched and introduced. An events calender was established which gave prominence to major events from all regions of Germany. With little experience, hardly any financial resources, but with a huge amount of enthusiasm programs slowly became a reality. Many individuals, too numerous to mention, made Germania what it is today. Their heart and souls have touched every aspect of club functions.

Karneval (Mardi Gras) was established before incorporation, featuring a Masquerade Ball complete with hilarious barrel talks. Karneval-Sessions were held for 2 years, then changed to Karneval Opening Dances, and since 1967, the Enthronement of a "Karnevals Prinzen Paar", Mardi Gras' Royal Couple. An "Elferrat", Council of Eleven, was founded within the entertainment committee.

The Kehraus Dance concludes the fifth and folly season. Dances would not be complete without the special appearance of the "Prinzen Garde", the Royal Guard. Two dance groups, usually the host and guest clubs or junior and senior performances, offer delightfully choreographed routines for everyone's entertainment.

Other dances were organized, specifically Oktober Dances since 1965, with an Oktoberfest setting, raffle and prizes, May dances with original May Pole setting and New Year's Eve parties. Christmas parties were prepared long time in advance with children's play, and St. Nikolaus bringing joy to the children. Other children's programs include an Easter Egg Hunt, a Picnic with clowns in the summer and a very colorful - and scary - Halloween Party. Children are the future and Germania Society is always ready to include the youngsters in all festivities.

Members of the Karneval Gesellschaft

With a growing membership the Germania Society was fortunate to have members at hand willing to take responsibilities which actually go beyond what most think of having fun by "Joining a Club."

1971 was a year of several steps upwards. Having our own grounds, with an old, but intact barn on it, picnics were organized. Then a soccer field was graded and seeded. Soccer teams were organized with the support of members, who remembered their own soccer days and plays.

Soccer Team

The largest undertaking in the same year was the establishment of an authentic Bavarian Oktoberfest. A park was rented, a music entertainment program developed, vendors hired and a parade organized. This large undertaking became an instant success with about 140 barrels of beer sold, lots of brats & metts and sauerkraut, German music and Schuhplattler dancing. From then Germania's Oktoberfest grew from year to year.

The Royal "Prinzenpaar", 1996
S.T. Prince Don I and I.L. Princess Marie I

Our Oktoberfest, which is Cincinnati's original and oldest was moved to its own "Germania Park". With its huge pavilion, built in 1985, and a large Wiesn'n Schenke (outdoor bar) this Oktoberfest on Germania's own Wies'n (Meadow), is the most authentic and family oriented.

Elferrat   Council of Eleven
Front: Konrad Schantz, Walter Bednar, Horst Gessner, Ernst Schwab, William Doan   Back: Dieter Waldowski, Hans Waldleitner, Dana Reed, Dieterich Lohff, Hans Schmithuesen, not in picture: Henry Potzner.

With input from, loyalty to and respect towards each other, the Germania Society will have a bright future, especially with the opportunities lying before us and the drive of our future generations, continuing what we started and built on a sound basis.

Germania, Cincinnati
Eine lange Geschichte kurz erzählt!

Von Ernst Schwab im Friesen Dialekt

Für einen erst ins Leben gerufenen Verein, welcher sich erstmal im Kulturbereich zu orientieren hatte, war es nötig nicht als Nachahmer existierende Bräuche aufzunehmen. So fiel es uns sozusagen in den Schoß, schon gleich nach einem fröhlichen Neujahrs-Tanz 1963, auch gleich mit einem Maskenball nachzuziehen. Das bot sich an, da in Deutschland Maskenbälle überall populär waren, sogar an der Nordsee Küste - speziell gleich nach den Kriegsjahren - zumal auch eine Mainzerin mit dabei war, war dieser erste Masken-Tanz dazu noch mit knalligen Bütten gewürzt.

Leider verloren wir unsere Humoristin noch im ersten Jahr durch Versetzung. Eine Gruppe Oldenburger, bekanntlich stur, haben mit viel Enthusiasmus, jedoch mit Fernhilfe und Festbesuchen jener Mainzerin, einfach nicht aufgegeben und nach einigen Jahren eine Rheinische Karnevals Metropole im südöstlichen Teil des Staates Ohio geschaffen.

Mit dem historischen "Over the Rhine District" in Cincinnati lagen wir ja dann auch gefühlsmäßig richtig und auch mit dem "Queen City of the West" Titel geradezu hergehörend. So ist dann in der Germania Society eine Untergruppe entstsanden, welche auch gleich einen Elferrat, Prinzen-Wahl und Prinzen Garde mit erstmal zwei, dann drei traditionellen Veranstaltungen Freunde und Freude erbrachte. Im Laufe der Jahre hat sich eine Karnevals-Gesellschaft entwickelt, die als Gruppe der Germania vollwertig alle Erwartungen der Mitgliedern mit Stolz erfüllen kann.

Andere Sektionen im Haus der Germania sind ein Fußball Klub, eine Schuhplattler & Trachten Gruppe, sowie das Oktoberfest Fest-Kommittee. Unsere Fußballer spielen ausnahmslos mit Bestleistung immer im oberen Bereich der Ohio Liga. Die Schuhplattler & Trachten Gruppe ist im typisch-bayerischen Holzhacker Stil bei Oktoberfesten und in-haus Veranstaltungen ziemlich beschäftigt.

Das Germania Oktoberfest, welches das erste und auch immer noch authentischte von allen Nachahmigen ist, hat seit 1971 für die Germania großes Ansehen eingebracht. Auf Germania's Grundstück von 10 ha ist immer Hochbetrieb. Entweder durch Klub-Veranstaltungen, Vermietungen für Firmen Picknicks, Hochzeiten und dergleichen.

Germania Schuhplattler & Trachten Gruppe

Prinzen Garde

Ein großer Pavillon mit einer weiten "Wies'n Schenke" kann jeglichen Bierumsatz bestreiten. So kommt unser Oktoberfest nie in schlechten Ruf über leerlaufende Zapfhähne. Da ist es immer angezapft! Unser 26. jährliches Oktoberfest war, Dank seiner Popularität in und um Cincinnati herum, ein enormer Erfolg. Wetter spielt immer die größte Rolle, aber da scheint es einen vergoldeten Vertrag mit dem Wettergott zu geben - oder Glück muß man haben!

Die Germania wird durch einen Vorstand bestehend aus Präsident, 1. Vize und 2. Vize Präsidenten, Sekretär, Schatzmeister sowie 8 Beisitzende geführt. Alle Kommittees (Sektionen) berichten durch ihre Gruppen-Leiter zum Vorstand, der wiederum alle Entscheidungen trifft, und der Gesamt-Mitgliedschaft gegenüber verantwortlich ist.

The Germania Society, Inc.
A Society of German Heritage of Greater Cincinnati

3529 W. Kemper Road, Cincinnati, Ohio 45251
Information and Reservations: 513 / 742 - 0060

NORDAMERIKANISCHE WOCHEN-POST
A German Language Weekly * Established in 1854
P.O. Box 7088 * Troy, MI 48007-7088

When August and Conrad Marxhausen left their native Germany in 1850 and immigrated to America they would have never imagined that their German language newspaper founded in Detroit four years later would survive for 143 years.

Over the past decades the paper which started in 1854 in Detroit as the Michigan Journal, would undergo numerous changes in name, ownership and localities as well as technological adjustments.

August Marxhausen changed the name of the Michigan Journal in 1868 to Detroiter Evening-Post. His son, August Jr., took over from his father in 1910 till 1921; then his aunt, Louise Burghard, inherited the paper and ran it well till her death in 1934. After 80 years in the hands of one family the paper was sold to an outsider who almost ran it into the ground. A last minute purchase by six German-Americans saved the paper from the auction block. Under the leadership of the Keydel Family the paper survived through the war years.

In 1960 a German typesetter from Koblenz, Knuth Beth, joined the Detroiter Evening-Post. By 1965 he had bought half of the shares and by 1972 was the sole owner of the paper. He gave the Detroiter Evening-Post a face lift and introduced the new Offset-Printing technique. Since the paper was now circulated not only in Detroit and Michigan but in most of all the states in the Union, the name was aptly changed to the North American Weekly-Post.

In 1991 two other German-American publications - Chicago Eveningpost and Milwaukee Sunday Newspaper - were absorbed by the N.A. Wochen-Post. Publisher Knuth Beth and his editorial team endeavor every week to satisfy their reader's hunger for European and German news.

"Only those who widen their horizon, have a future" is Knuth Beth's motto. Since January 1996 the paper is totally produced by computer. It also has its place on the Internet, of course with its own web-page.

Die Geschichte der Nordamerikanische Wochen-Post

Als August und Conrad Marxhausen 1850 aus Kassel nach Amerika einwanderten, ließen sie sich wohl nicht träumen, daß ihre 1854 in Detroit gegründete deutschsprachige Zeitung 143 Jahre überleben wird.

Über die Jahrzehnte hinaus mußte sich die Nordamerikanische Wochen-Post, die 1854 als Michigan Journal begann, vieler Namens-, Eigentümer-, Standort- und technischen Änderungen unterziehen. August Marxhausen taufte das Michigan Journal ab 1868 Detroiter Abend-Post. Sein Sohn,

August jr., übernahm die Leitung von 1910 bis 1921, dann trat seine Tante, Louis Burghardt, als Erbin und Chefin an.

Sie verstarb 1934, und die Zeitung wurde, nach 80 Jahren in Familienhänden, verkauft. Der neue Besitzer wirschaftete die Zeitung herunter. 1938 sollte sie versteigert werden, aber in letzter Minute kauften sechs Deutsch-Amerikaner die Zeitung. Unter der Leitung der Familie Keydel überlebte die Detroiter Abend-Post die Kriegsjahre.

1960 engagierte sich der Koblenzer Knuth Beth als Schriftsetzer bei der Abend-Post. 1965 wurde er Teilhaber und 1972 alleiniger Inhaber. Er begann, der Zeitung ein neues Gesicht zu geben: Der alte Buchdruck wich

dem Offset-Verfahren. Seit 1980 schmückt sich die Abend-Post mit dem Namen: Nordamerikanische Wochen-Post. Er sollte verdeutlichen, daß die Zeitung in fast allen Staaten der US gelesen wird. 1991 verschmolzen die Chicago Abendpost so wie die Milwaukee Sonntagszeitung in der N.A. Wochen-Post. Herausgeber Knuth Beth und sein Redaktions-Team versuchen jede Woche, den Nachrichtenhunger ihrer Leser mit Informationen aus Deutschland und Europa zu stillen.

"Nur wer den Horizont erweitert, hat Zunkunft", lautet das Motto von Knuth Beth. Seit Januar 1996 geht in der Redaktion alles per Computer. Und man findet die Zeitung sogar im Internet mit einer eigenen web-Seite.

Bavarian Inn Restaurant serves over 1 million guests a year.

Zehnder's Restaurant is famous for Frankenmuth-style chicken.

Bronner's CHRISTmas Wonderland features over 50,000 trims and gifts for all seasons, reasons, and budgets.

CHRISTmas Wonderland is open all year.

Zehnder's wooden bridge (Holzbrücke) greets visitors crossing the Cass River.

Photos courtesy of BRONNER'S CHRISTmas WONDERLAND by Wayne Bronner

Frankenmuth, Michigan

The rich heritage of Frankenmuth, Michigan began in 1845 when 15 German-Lutheran missionaries came to the area and organized themselves into St. Lorenz congregation under the pastorate of Friedrich August Craemer. This "Mission-Colony" would demonstrate to the Chippewa Indians and others how wonderful it is to live in Jesus. On April 20th, 1845, this little congregation had left Bremen, Germany. After 50 days crossing the Atlantic, they reached New York. They immediately began their journey to the banks of the Cass river. They named the area Frankenmuth, meaning "courage of the Franconians". A log cabin was built to serve as church and parsonage. During June 1846, 100 additional immigrants arrived from Rossthal, Gunzhausen and Nuremberg. An enlarged church-school-parsonage was dedicated on Christmas Day. The 680-acre settlement had begun.

Frankenmuth's past is recorded and displayed at the Frankenmuth Historical Museum. Artifacts, photos and in-depth descriptions about Frankenmuth's history fill the museum. Today, over 4,000 residents make a special effort to preserve the German heritage. Every visitor is greeted with Gemütlichkeit

A multitude of businesses make up Frankenmuth. Sausage makers, a pretzel factory, woolen mills, fudge and candy kitchens, art and craft galleries, bed and breakfasts, motels and hotels, and a military and space museum, along with over 100 quaint shops and attractions, including the Fortress Golf Course, put Frankenmuth among the top tourist destinations in Michigan.

Two of the nation's largest family restaurants, Bavarian Inn and Zehnder's, serve nearly two million dinners a year. Only 11 years after German missionaries founded Frankenmuth, the Exchange Hotel began serving meals. William Zehnder, Sr. acquired the hotel in 1927 and began renovations, making the exterior look like Mt. Vernon. The hotel, renamed Zehnder's, opened on Mother's Day in 1928 with a seating capacity of 60. In 1947, Zehnder's was turned over to Edwin and Leonard Zehnder. In the early 1950's, Zehnder's purchased Fischer's Hotel across the street, naming William "Tiny" Zehnder, Jr. manager. Renovations were made using Alpine architecture and the hotel was renamed Bavarian Inn. Bavarian entertainment was introduced at Bavarian Inn's grand opening. That was the influence for changing Frankenmuth Days to the Frankenmuth Bavarian Festival, which is still going strong.

We invite you to enjoy our hospitality, stroll our quaint streets, explore our unique shops, and experience a community as delightful as an Old German Fairy Tale.

Picturesque Bavarian Inn Lodge forms a resort on the other side of Cass River.

The Zehnders family also owns Bavarian Inn Lodge, a 350-room resort. Each room in the Lodge is named after a Frankenmuth family name. History, specific to the family, appears in each room. The second, third and fourth generation of the Zehnder family is involved in both the restaurant and hotel operations.

Established in 1945 by Wally Bronner and his wife Irene, BRONNER'S CHRISTmas WONDERLAND evolved from a small sign shop into the "world's largest Christmas store." What started as a hobby for Wally is now a business that welcomes more than 2 million visitors from throughout the world. Guests are greeted with signs in over 70 languages. The excitement of the Holidays is evident every day. Sparkling garlands, thousands of lights, nativity scenes and shimmering ornaments create a fantasyland.

260 decorated Christmas trees in various themes showcase more than 6,000 different styles of ornaments. Guests are delighted by more than 800 intriguing animated figures. Bronner's Commercial Sales Department specializes in supplying spectacular interior and exterior Christmas decorations to cities, shopping centers, malls, businesses, industries and parks. A resale division supplies items to other stores. Bronner's Christmas Favorites catalog is mailed to customers around the country.

Bronner's replica of the Silent Night Memorial Chapel was built as an expression of gratitude to God and as a tribute to the world's favorite

Christmas hymn. The city Government and the Visitors' Bureau of Oberndorf, near Salzburg, graciously granted the Bronner family permission to replicate the original chapel. Wally and Irene's children are actively involved in the management of every aspect of the family business. The third generation is also assisting.

Frankenmuth is located just minutes East of I-75 between Flint and Saginaw, Michigan. Driving Northbound, exit at 136, Southbound take exit 144.

For more details about Frankenmuth, call the Frankenmuth Convention and Visitors' Bureau at 517/652-6106 or visit their web site at www.frankenmuth.org.

Frankenmuth's City Hall reflects a community proud of its German heritage.

Nickless-Hubinger Flour Mill, today Frankenmuth Mill & General Store.

Quaint Towers accent Frankenmuth's architecture.

Photos courtesy of BRONNER'S CHRISTmas WONDERLAND by Wayne Bronner.

Winter scene in Frankenmuth.

Frankenmuth Visitors Bureau, 635 S. Main, Frankenmuth, MI 48734 • 1-800-FUN-TOWN

Indianapolis, Indiana

By 1890, the town had German-Americans whose forebears had immigrated and newcomers of all persuasions—Lutherans, Reformed, Catholics, Methodists, Jews, and Freethinkers—comprising 25% of the town's population and paying 40% of the taxes. The German Sunday paper sold 11,000 copies.

Street names are reminders of this presence—Hamburg, Kessler, Schiller... Landmark buildings and boulevards, designed by the Bohlens, Vonnegut & Bohn, Schreiber, Scherrer, Kessler, and others, add a historic note to the cityscape. Among formerly all-German downtown churches, and still existing, are St. Mary's and Sacred Heart (Cath.), St. Paul's (Luth.), and Zion (UCC). Church rosters and membership lists of German clubs include many old families.

The Schnulls started the Wholesale District. Half the town's bakers and butchers spoke German. Vegies came from the Southside Gardners, and the Home Brewing, Indianapolis Brewing and American Brewing companies had the beer. Germans built the first theater, started the Symphony, and introduced vocational education. Stutz and Duesenberg made automotive history.

Indianapolis, the "Amateur Sports Capital of America," is indebted to the Turners, pioneers of fitness and physical education. Their Turnvereins—gymnastic and social clubs—shocked Puritan Anglophones who opposed dancing, drinking and smoking, especially on Sundays. Indianapolis today?
A metropolis with a high quality of life.

Picture: The center of town is the "Soldiers'and Sailors' Monument" (1902), designed by Bruno Schmitz, Germany's foremost architect of national monuments, with sculptures by Rudolf Schwarz and bronze work by Nicolaus Geiger.

Um 1890 lebten hier alteingesessene Deutschamerikaner und Neuankömmlinge verschiedenster Ausrichtung—Lutheraner, Reformierte, Katholiken, Methodisten, Juden und Freidenker, zusammen ca. 25% der Bevölkerung mit einem Steueraufkommen von 40%. Die Sonntagsnummer der deutschen Zeitung erschien in 11000 Exemplaren!

Jeder zweite Bäcker und Metzger sprach deutsch. Frischgemüse lieferten die Südseite-Gärtner. Die Grossbrauereien ("Home," "Indianapolis," "American") waren deutsch. Und mit den Schnulls begann das Grosshandelsviertel.

Strassennamen halten Erinnerung wach—Hamburg, Schiller, Kessler... Verbunden mit gediegenen Bauwerken und Boulevards, die dem Stadtbild die historische Note verleihen, bleiben Architektennamen wie Bohlen, Vonnegut & Bohn, Schreiber, Scherrer und Kessler. Im Stadtkern stehen heute noch Kirchen früherer deutscher Gemeinden, u.a. St. Mary und Sacred Heart (kath.), St. Paul (ev.) und Zion Evangelical United Church of Christ.

Deutsche bauten das erste Theater, begründeten die Symphonie und führten Berufsschulfächer ein. Stutz und Düsenberg machten Automobilgeschichte.

Indianapolis als "Hauptstadt des Amateursports" basiert auf der Pionierarbeit der Turner, die auch den Schulsport einführten. Turnvereine waren den puritanischen Anglophonen zuwider. Wurde dort doch getanzt, getrunken und geraucht—sogar Sonntags! Indianapolis heute? Eine Grosstadt mit hoher Lebensqualitiät.

by Prof. Ruth Reichmann

FEDERATION OF GERMAN SOCIETIES
8600 S. Meridian St. • Indianapolis, IN 46217 • (317) 888-8751

In 1932, 22 German Societies formed the Verband Deutscher Vereine von Indianapolis and purchased 26 acres south of Indianapolis, today's German Park. A year-round facility within the park opened in 1979.

Activities at German Park:
July - Saengerchor Mid-Summer Festival;
August - Liederkranz Sommerfest;
August 29-30 and September 5-6 - Oktoberfest

German-American Klub of Indianapolis, Inc.
8602 S. Meridian
St., Indianapolis, IN 46217
(317) 888-6940

Founded in 1974, the GAK promotes German and American culture, and provides functions for members and their families. A full service restaurant, open to the public, operates Tuesday-Saturday evenings. Banquet facilities are available. Its 500 members participate in the GAK Auxiliary, a culture committee, child and adult dance groups, festivals, language lessons and monthly dances. Members host music, dance and civic groups from Germany and support the Indianapolis sister cities programs.

Activities: Jan. - Viennese Ball • Feb. - Fasching, -Sweetheart Dance • March - Jägerfest • St. Patrick's Dance • Easter Brunch & Egg Hunt • May - Mai Tanz • 500 Race Day Party • October 6 - German-American Day, - Harvest Ball • Nov. - Halloween • Thanksgiving Dance • Dec. 31 - New Year's Eve

South Side Turners
3702 E. Raymond St.
Indianapolis, IN 46203
(317) 780-0126

As their motto - A sound mind in a sound body - indicates, the Turners, founded in 1886, promote physical and mental health. They are affiliated with the American Turners and sponsor many activities.

Indianapolis Soccer Club
8600 S. Meridian St.
Indianapolis, IN 46217
(317) 859-0877)

In 1954 the Deutsche Fussball Club, the 500 Soccer Team and the Indianapolis International Soccer Club debuted as the Indianapolis Soccer Club. Some current members founded German Park, and the ISC clubhouse and playing fields are located within the park. Active in a tri-state area, the ISC belongs to many prestigious soccer leagues and have won several championships. The present club has four men's teams and a women's team, with members from 20 countries. Games are played spring and fall.

Greenhouse Growers Association
3730 Division Road
Indianapolis, IN 46217

Founded in the 1920's to promote uniform produce quality, out-of-town markets, and group buying power. Their trade name is "Hoosier Boy." They formed a stock company, Marion County Greenhouse, Inc. in 1943.

Indianapolis Gardeners' Benefit Society
736 Edgewood Ave.
Indianapolis, IN 46217

Chartered in 1867 exclusively for gardeners, the society pays a sick benefit to members and a death benefit to survivors.

Indianapolis Vegetable Growers Association
950 W. Hanna Ave.
Indianapolis, IN 46217.

Formed by growers from Indianapolis' south and west sides, this German group organized in the 1920's to increase local market share. They currently oversee sales, equipment and shipping. The Marion County Extension Service lends expertise at meetings.

German-American Day is a Community gathering, celebrated at the German-American Klub by all organizations, on the Sunday closest to Oct. 6.

On Oct. 6 a German-American Day celebration for the public is presented Downtown at the City Market.

The DEUTSCHE HAUS ATHENAEUM

by Profs. Eberhard and Ruth Reichmann

Athenaeum
401 E. Michigan, Indianapolis

Located in the old "Germantown" section of Indianapolis, it is within walking distance of the center of town. Built between 1894 and 1898 as a Turnverein and named Deutsches Haus till 1917, the building is on the National Register for Historic Places. It is managed by the Athenaeum Foundation, Inc., a not-for-profit organization, founded in 1991 to restore the Athenaeum to its original condition and to assure its continued use as a leading cultural, social, and athletic center. Not only for German-Americans but for the public at large, it provides a great setting for conferences, meetings, banquets, weddings, lectures, Stammtisch programs.

Activities include: Feb. - Carnival Celebration * March - St. Benno Fest, Munich's Patron Saint * May - Maifest * July 4 - "The Fourth in Indy" at the Biergarten * Aug. - Oxroast * Oct. - Oktoberfest im Biergarten; Oct. 6 - German-American Day . * Dec. - Christkindl Markt and St. Nikolaus Fest

The Rathskeller Restaurant

ATHENAEUM OCCUPANTS:

The Rathskeller Restaurant, Indiana's oldest continuously operating restaurant, offers a full line of contemporary cuisine as well as classic German dishes in a charming Old World setting.

The American Cabaret Theater stages original reviews in the cabaret tradition. It now occupies the Ball Room where once the Turners entertained the citizens of Indianapolis.

The YMCA at the Athenaeum offers aerobics, workout facilities, karate, basketball and volleyball leagues and more, as a part of the YMCA of Greater Indianapolis.

Ken Long & Associates are organizers of marathons and mini-marathons.

The Athenaeum Turners Society, an affiliate of the American Turners, is the original owner of the Athenaeum. With the Athenaeum Damenverein they support the renovation and appropriate use of the building.

The Maennerchor Society of Indianapolis, organized in 1854, is one of the oldest continuously performing male choruses in the United States.

Like the Maennerchor the **Athenaeum Pops Orchestra** was started before the Deutsche Haus-Athenaeum was built. Indiana Citizens for the Arts/Indiana Advocates for the Arts, are educational and advocacy organizations supporting the arts.

The **Max Kade German-American Center**, affiliated with Indiana University – Purdue University Indianapolis, and the Indiana German Heritage Society, Inc. a statewide historical and educational membership organization are located here.

"The Fourth in Indy"   Biergarten Concert

The American Cabaret Theater

German-American Day is a Community gathering, celebrated at the German-American Klub by all organizations, on the Sunday closest to Oct. 6.

On Oct. 6 a German-American Day celebration for the public is presented Downtown at the City Market.

ATHENAEUM
401 E. Michigan Street,
INDIANAPOLIS, IN 46204
Tel. (317) 630-4569
FAX (317) 630-0035

YMCA at the Athenaeum

Indiana German Heritage Society Inc

401 East Michigan Street • Indianapolis, Indiana 46204

Max Kade German-American Center

Athenaeum, Indianapolis, IN

The Max Kade German-American Center of Indiana University-Purdue University at Indianapolis (IUPUI) coordinates research and educational activities in German-American Studies with other universities, professional and historical societies.

The Center's off Campus location underscores its philosophy of outreach to the general public. The Indiana German Heritage Society (IGHS) serves as a support group and co-publisher for the Center's strong publishing program. Activities include a bilingual pre-school, a Saturday language school, and exchange programs for students of business and engineering, and support for the sister cities programs Indianapolis-Cologne.

The center edits the German-American bibliography, produces teaching materials, and is developing a national listing of German-American sites, museums and libraries.
Its Website: http://www-lib.iupui.edu/kade/

Das Max Kade German-Americna Center der Indiana University-Purdue University koordiniert den Bereich Deutsch-Amerikanische Studien auch im Verbund mit anderen Hochschulen und historischen Gesellschaften. Die Lage des Centers in der Stadtmitte unterstreicht das Konzept der Zusammenarbeit mit der Öffentlichkeit und dem schulischen Bereich.

Die Gesellschaft zur Bewahrung des deutschen Erbes, die Indiana German Heritage Society (IGHS), arbeitet eng mit dem Center zusammen. Veröffentlichungen und regelmässige Veranstaltungen werden gemeinsam getragen. Beiden liegt am Gedeihen des zweisprachigen Vorschulprogramms und der Samstagschule. Gemeinsam werden auch Austauschprograme durchgeführt für Oberschüler, Studenten der Wirtschafts- und Ingenieurfachbereiche und für die Städtpartnerschaft Indianapolis-Köln.

Das Center speichert auch die deutsch-amerikanische. Bibliographie der Neuerscheinungen, es entwickelt Unterrichtsmaterialien und eine Datenbank dt.-amerik. Stätten, Bibliotheken und Museen. Erreichbar unter: http://www-lib.iupui.edu/kade/

INDIANA UNIVERSITY
PURDUE UNIVERSITY
INDIANAPOLIS

INDIANA UNIVERSITY
SCHOOL OF LIBERAL ARTS

IUPUI

401 East Michigan Street
Indianapolis, IN 46204
Office: (317) 464-9004
Fax: (317) 630-0035

TERRE HAUTE

German Oberlandler Club

1616 LAFAYETTE AVENUE • TERRE HAUTE, IN 47808
(812) 466-6143

Terre Haute
German Oberlandler Club, Inc.

The Terre Haute German Oberlandler Club, Inc., was formed in November 1967, to provide a means for persons of German descent to perpetuate the culture, traditions, and costumes of the "Heimatland" of its founders. The Club prides itself on sharing this heritage with the general public through its Strassenfest, Oktoberfest, and many other activities.

Der Oberländler Klub in Terre Haute, Indiana wurde im November 1967 gegründet, um Menschen deutscher Abstammung die Möglichkeit zu geben, die Kultur, Bräuche und Trachten der "Heimat der Väter" zu pflegen. Der Klub ist stolz darauf, sein Erbe mit der Gemeinde durch das Strassenfest, Oktoberfest und andere Aktivitäten zusammen erleben zu können.

Club House on 1616 Lafayette Avenue, Terre Haute, IN

Photo: Hilde Crisp

Places To Go, Things To Do, in INDIANA

With more than one of three Hoosiers claiming some form of German ancestry, Indiana belongs to the ten most German-settled states. From Lake Michigan down to the Ohio, over 140 towns bear names with a familiar German ring. One can combine festival-going with visits to historic places and beautiful parks of Indiana's State Park system, created by Richard Lieber (1869-1944) from the Saarland.

Das Dutchman Essenhaus, Amish Country

While at "Strassenfest" in Terre Haute in early May, visit the Debs Museum. Eugene V. Debs (1855-1926)—pioneer of the American labor movement and the country's best known socialist leader— hails from Alsace, like his cousin, the great humanitarian Albert Schweitzer.

In June, during Fort Wayne's "Germanfest" week it pays to visit the Allen County Historical Museum in the former "City Hall." Envisioned by Mayor Charles E. Mühler and completed by Mayor Charles Zollinger, by some it was called "the most elegant and most economically constructed city hall in Indiana" and by others "the Hapsburg Horror," a gibe at the mayor's Austrian origin.

The grand "Strassenfest" in Jasper in early August features a Polka Mass in historical St. Joseph's Church, a Parade and numerous performances. Close to Jasper, above Ferdinand (named for Austrian Emperor Ferdinand) rises the massive Monastery and Girls' Academy of the Benedictine Sisters who came from Eichstätt, Bavaria. Another few miles south is the mighty St. Meinrad Archabbey with its Catholic Seminary, home of the Benedictine monks, originally from Einsiedeln, Switzerland.

Small town, big town, festivals abound: Oldenburg, the "Village of Spires" with its roots in NW Germany, has a "Corpus Christi" procession and in July a "Freudenfest." In Ferdinand they celebrate "Heimatfest" and in nearby St. Henry "Heinrichsdorf Fest," "Herbstfest" in Huntingburg, "Germanfest" in Vincennes, and "Volksfest" in Evansville. And there are "Oktoberfests" in Indianapolis, Michigan City, Terre Haute, Seymour and Knightstown. Berne has its "Swiss Days" and "Village Gathering." Tell City, named after the legendary Swiss folk hero, celebrates "Schweizer Fest." The Indianapolis German organizations, individually and jointly, have festivities throughout the year.

Indiana ist eine Reise wert

Mit über 37% jedenfalls teilweise Deutschstämmiger gehört Indiana zu den zehn deutschesten Staaten der USA. Vom Michigan See bis zum Ohio verraten über 140 Ortsnamen deutsche Ursprünge. Wer Spuren deutschsprachiger Auswanderer folgt, mag lokale Feste und historische Oertlichkeiten kombinieren mit Besuch von Naturschutzgebieten (State Parks), die ihre Existenz der Voraussicht und dem Einsatz des Saarländers Richard Lieber (1869-1944) verdanken.

Wer im Mai das Terre Haute Strassenfest besucht, sollte das Debs Museum einplanen. Eugene V. Debs (1855-1926), Mitbegründer der amerikanischen Arbeiterbewegung und bedeutendster Sozialist, war elsässischer Herkunft wie sein noch berühmterer Vetter Albert Schweitzer.

Im Juni geht's auf nach Fort Wayne zur "Germanfest" Woche. Das lässt Zeit auch für das Allen County Historical Museum im früheren Rathaus, das unter den Bürgermeistern Mühler und Zollinger erbaut wurde. "Das eleganteste und wirtschaftlichste in Indiana," meinten die einen; andern war es der "Habsburg Horror"—Anspielung auf des Bürgermeisters Herkunft.

Anfang August beim "Strassenfest" in Jasper gibt's eine vom Bischof oder Erzbischof zölebrierte Polka-Messe in der historischen St. Joseph Kirche, eine Riesenparade und dies und das. Von dort ist's ein Katzensprung nach Ferdinand (nach Kaiser Ferdinand so benannt), überragt von der "Burg auf dem Hügel," wie die ursprünglich aus Eichstätt stammenden Benediktinerinnen scherzhaft ihr Kloster nennen. Es hat auch ein internationales Mädcheninternat. Ebenso beeindruckend ist die nahegelegene benediktinische Erzabtei St. Meinrad mit ihrem Priester/Laien-Seminar, eine Gründung des Klosters Einsiedeln.

Tippecanoe Place, Studebaker Mansion, South Bend, IN

Gefeiert wird überall: Oldenburg mit Wurzeln in NW Deutschland hat seine Fronleichnamsprozession und im Juli "Freudenfest." Ferdinand feiert sein "Heimatfest," St. Henry das "Heinrichsdorf Fest." Auf zum "Herbstfest" in Huntingburg, zum "Germanfest" in Vincennes und zum "Volksfest" in Evansville. Grosse Oktoberfeste gibt's in Indianapolis, Terre Haute, Michigan City, Seymour, und Knightstown. Berne hat "Schweizer Tage" und den "Dorf Treff." Tell City ist stolz auf sein "Schweizer Fest." Und ob Sommer, ob Winter, bei den deutschen Vereinen von Indianapolis ist immer was los.

by Prof. Ruth Reichmann

St. Joseph Church

Greetings from Southern Indiana Jasper, Dubois County

Schnitzelbank Restaurant   Jasper, Dubois County, IN

Mr. & Mrs. Linus Lechner

Willkommen in Jasper, dem Herzen von Süd-Indiana

Besucher in unserer Region sind immer wieder beeindruckt von der reichen Geschichte und Kultur der deutschen Einwanderer.

Ob es die schönen, deutschen Farbglas – Fenster oder die österreichischen Mosaiks der alten St. Joseph Kirche sind, oder das Strassenfest am ersten August-Wochenende, und das Schnitzelbank Restaurant, hier kann man Bayerisches erleben und Badisches so wie in der Partnerstadt Pfaffenweiler.

Man bestaunt die Baukunst der Holy Family Church, die Jaspers Geschichte in ihrem großen Fenster erzählt. Nahe bei liegt die Erz-Abtei St. Meinrad und das Benediktinerinnen-Kloster in dem idyllischen Dorf Ferdinand, was der Gegend einen anheimelnden europäischen Charakter gibt. Gastfreundschaftlichkeit überall, bei den Sehenswürdigkeiten, in den Geschäften und Restaurants, und den Hotels in der Nachbarschaft. Sie werden sicher gerne in Jasper sein. Ein bißchen Deutschland hier in Indiana. Rufen Sie uns doch mal an oder besuchen Sie uns auf dem Internet: http://www.ind-adventure.org.

Welcome to Jasper – in the Heart of Southern Indiana

Our region's rich German heritage is a constant delight to visitors. From the interesting story surrounding the German stained-glass windows and the Austrian-designed mosaics at the old-world St. Joseph Church, to the annual Jasper Strassenfest, held the first weekend of August, and the Schnitzelbank Restaurant, you can enjoy a taste of Bavaria and of the Black Forest, similar to our sister city of Pfaffenweiler.

Architecture enthusiasts will marvel at the beauty of Holy Family Church, depicting "The Jasper Story" in a large glass window. The church also features the second largest church window in America. The nearby St. Meinrad Archabbey and Seminary and the Monastery Immaculate Conception in the pastoral village of Ferdinand recreate a true feel of the European countryside.

German hospitality abounds among the many attractions, shops, restaurants and hotels in the area. You will surely enjoy your visit to Jasper, a little bit of Germany–right here in Indiana. For more information on an adventure to the heart of southern Indiana, please call the Dubois County Tourism Commission at 1-800-ADVENTURE or the Jasper Chamber of Commerce at (812) 482-6866.

Photos: Dubois County Tourism Commission

Visit once, you'll be back to Dubois County!
Call 800-ADVENTURE or 812/482-6866.
On the Internet at http://www.ind-adventure.org.

How to get there:

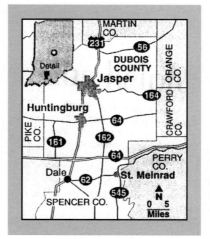

Staff Map

Farewell at the Monastery.

Menno-Hof   Schipshewana, Indiana

Tippecanoe Place,

ca. l Meile westl. vom Studebaker National Musem (620 W. Washington St.), wurde 1889 für den Studebaker Präsidenten Clemens Studebaker aus Felsgestein erbaut. Das elegante Herrenhaus mit seinen 40 Zimmern diente glänzenden Empfängen und brachte den Zauber der großen Welt der Fürstlichkeiten, Honoratioren und berühmten Amerikaner in die Gesellschaft South Bends. Heute ist Tippecanoe Place ein erstklassiges Restaurant. Alle vier Stockwerke können besichtigt werden.
Tel. 219 234-9077.

Menno-Hof in Shipshewana

Located in Shipshewana, in the heart of Northern Indiana's Amish country, Menno-Hof is the home of an epic story of triumph and tragedy told by those who lived it in centuries gone by. Colorful displays and a multimedia presentation take the visitor into the unique world of three Annabaptist groups: the Mennonites, the Amish and the Hutterites. Follow the Trail of a People searching for peace. Learn about the Mennonites' emergence in the year 1525 and their sufferings and martyrdom during ruthless persecution by state and church authorities. Learn why in 1693 the Amish broke from the Mennonites, why the Amish drive buggies and wear plain clothes. Upon request the presentation is available in German.
For info 219 768-4117.

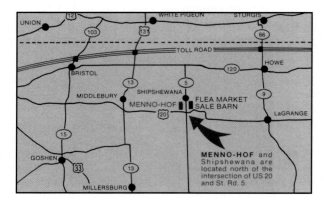

MENNO-HOF and Shipshewana are located north of the intersection of US 20 and St. Rd. 5.

Located about one mile west of the Studebaker National Museum on 620 W. Washington St., is Tippecanoe Place. Built in 1889 of native boulders, the 40-room fieldstone mansion, is the home of former Studebaker President, Clement Studebaker. Royalty, foreign dignitaries and famous Americans enjoyed the many parties and receptions that lent a fairy tale air to South Bend society. Tippecanoe is presently operated as a showcase restaurant. Visitors are welcome to visit all four floor of the mansion during regular restaurant hours.
For info 219 234-9077.

Gelegen inmitten der amischen Niederlassungen Nord-Indianas bietet der Menno-Hof die Geschichte dreier deutscher Wiedertäuferbewegungen. In einer künstlerisch hervorragenden Multi-Medienschau wird der Besucher in die historische und gegenwärtigeWelt der Mennoniten, Amischen und Hutteriten versetzt—religiöse Gemeinden, im heutigen Europa fast völlig vergessen. Die Anfänge der Mennoniten (1525) standen im Zeichen brutaler kirchlicher und staatlicher Verfolgung. Es gab zahllose Märtyrer. 1693 zweigten die Amischen von den Mennoniten ab. Die Amischen mit ihren schwarzen Kutschen und altväterlicher Kleidung bewahren das vorindustrielle bäuerliche Leben. Tel. 219 768-4117.

by Prof. Ruth Reichmann

Typical parking near Nappanee, IN, Amish Acres

Heimaths Unterstützung Verein

Founded in 1897, and Preussen Unterstützung Verein founded in 1884 were organized to aid members in time of illness or financial need. They jointly sponsor cultural and social activities.

Indianapolis Liederkranz

1417 E. Washington St.
Indianapolis, IN 46201 (317) 266-9816

Founded in April 1872, the Liederkranz is devoted to 4-part male singing and the preservation of German heritage. They joined the North American Saengerbund in 1874 and have participated in many song festival over the decades. Their calendar includes civic appearances, monthly dances, public concerts and an annual festival. **Liederkranz Ladies Society** was founded in 1872. Its purpose is to benefit the Liederkranz Society. They are renowned for managing an excellent German kitchen during Liederkranz festivities.

Activities at their Club: Feb. - Winter Dance • March - Bock Beer Fest & Dance • Sept. - Schlachtfest • Oct. - Oktoberfest Dance • Nov. - Fall Concert & Dance • Dec. - Christmas Party • New Year's Eve

Indianapolis Sängerchor

521 E. 13th St.
Indianapolis, IN 46202
(317) 262-9125

In 1885, ten German immigrants united to found the Socialist-Labor Saengerbund. In 1920 the name changed to the Indianapolis Saengerbund, later to Indianapolis Saengerchor. Originally a men's chorus, a women's choir was added in 1928.

They perform 2 concerts a year at their hall, plus other appearances. Monthly rouladen and sauerbraten dinners are popular.

by Profs. Eberhard and Ruth Reichmann

Das Studebaker National Museum

(525 S. Main St. in South Bend) ist ein Fund für Autofans. Die Studebaker Brothers Co. hatte sich während des amerikanischen Bürgerkriegs (1861-65) im Wagenbau hervorgetan, dann um 1900 mit dem Autobau. Die Studebaker (Studebecker) Vorfahren, deutsche Baptisten, landeten 1736 in Philadelphia. Der Umzug nach South Bend (1851) gereichte den Studebaker Brüdern der vierten Generation zum Vorteil, besonders mit dem Conestoga Wagen. Nach 40 Jahren waren sie die grössten Wagenbauer der Welt. 1902 begann ihre Motorwagenproduktion. Tel. 219 235-9108.

The Studebaker National Museum,

on 525 South Main in South Bend, showcases the success of Studebaker Brothers Manufacturing Company, a firm that first made wagons for the Union Army in the Civil War of 1861-1865, and at the turn of the century, started producing automobiles. The Studebaker (Studebecker) ancestors, Clement and Peter, landed in Philadelphia in 1736. By 1851 the family had moved to South Bend, where Henry and Clem of the fourth generation in the U.S., founded "Studebaker Brothers." In 1858 they were joined by two other brothers and became makers of Conestoga style wagon. In the 1890's, Studebaker was generally regarded as the world's largest wagon builder. The first Studebaker automobile was built in 1902. For info 219 235-9108.

Historic New Harmony, village museum

and preservation project with an educational mission, enjoys the distinction of being the birthplace of two of the most widely known communal experiments ever tried in the U.S. In 1814, George Rapp and the Harmonie Society, German religious dissenters who lived in celibacy, founded the town. In ten short years, they created a self-sufficient community of tidy homes and thriving industries. In 1824 they sold the entire town to Robert Owen, Welsh-born social reformer from New Lanark, Scotland. Guided tours explore both utopian experiments. This historic place celebrates its heritage all year around. There is Heritage Week in April, Founders Day in August, Kunstfest & German Crafts Festival in September and Candlelight Tours in December.
For info 812 682-4482.

Der Ort New Harmony am Wabash River in der Südwestecke des Staates ist eine siedlungsgeschichtliche

Opera House in New Harmony, Indiana.

Sehenswürdigkeit mit einem Gutteil unter Denkmalschutz und etlichen Museen. Zwei der bekanntesten utopischen Experimente prägten den Ort. Die in Gütergemeinschaft und zölibat lebende schwäbische Harmonistensekte unter Georg Rapp schaffte von 1814-1824 das ökonomische "Wunder des Westens." 1824 zog sie nach Pennsylvanien zurück und verkaufte den Ort an den schottischen Sozialreformisten Robert Owen. Führungen umfassen beide utopische Experimente, deren Erbe ganzjährig gefeiert wird mit der "Heritage" Woche (April), "Founders Day" (Aug.), "Kunstfest & German Crafts Festival" (Sept.) u. "Candlelight Tours"/ bei Kerzenlicht (Dez.). Tel. 812-682-4482.

Peter Schneider and company

Members of the German Club

Dogsled Racing is very popular

Getting ready for the auction

Peter K. Schneider, President
Deutscher Verein von Fairbanks, Alaska

Wir achten Deutschland und lieben Amerika

Der nördlichste deutsche Verein der Welt in Alaska ehrt seine Frauen

1972 gegründet, hat der Deutsche Verein von Fairbanks ungefähr 60 Mitglieder, davon zwei Drittel Frauen. Zusammengewürfelt durch den Krieg, aus Abenteuerlust und vielen anderen Gründen, teilen wir gemeinsam die Liebe zu Alaska und den Stolz, Deutsche oder deutscher Abstammung zu sein. Ich bin einmal gefragt worden, wie man beides vereinbaren kann und ich antwortete: "Das ist ganz einfach, ich achte und ehre Deutschland wie meine Eltern, Großeltern und Ahnen, und ich liebe Amerika wie meine Frau, Kinder und Enkelkinder."

Zu unseren festgeschriebenen Aufgaben zählt die Erhaltung und weltweite Förderung des Deutschtums, ein besseres Verständnis unseres gemeinsamen Erbgutes zu entwickeln und zu würdigen, die Gemeinde, in der wir leben, aktiv zu unterstützen und mitzuwirken.

Wir sind in Fairbanks sehr beliebt, und in der großen Sommerparade, an der die eine Hälfte der Stadt teilnimmt und die andere Hälfte zuschaut, gewinnen wir meistens eine Trophäe.

Wir unterstützen finanziell die deutsche Klasse der Universität Alaska. Wir singen und tanzen an Feiertagen, besonders zu Weihnachten, in beiden Altersheimen. Zu Ostern findet man unsere Schwarzwälder Tänzerinnen und Tänzer meistens bei einer Vorführung in einem unserer großen Kaufhäuser.

Den Sommer schließen wir gewöhnlich mit einem deutschen Erntedankfest ab, das wir im "Golden Heartpark" (der Park mit dem goldenen Herzen) feiern und dazu die ganze Stadt einladen.

Die Eisfestival-Parade findet zwar nicht jedes Jahr statt, aber wir nehmen immer daran teil, auch bei Minus 40 Grad Celsius.

First settlers in Fairbanks

Aber dies ist nur ein Teil von dem, was wir als Deutsche und Mitglieder unseres Vereins tun. Wir helfen Touristen mit Rat und Tat, sitzen geduldig beim Arzt und übersetzen, wenn einem Schweizer der Zahn gezogen wird oder bei einer Hamburgerin der Blinddarm raus muß. Wir haben den Jungfernflug von Lufthansa Fracht und den Mercedes "G" Klub feierlich empfangen. Ebenso den Deutschen Botschafter und Generalkonsul. Deutsches Fernsehen und deutsche Reporter besuchen uns des öfteren.

Am Tage der Deutschen Wiedervereinigung, der mit dem Deutsch-Amerikanischen Freundschaftstag zusammenfiel, ehrte uns die ganze Stadt mit der Erlaubnis, unsere deutsche Vereinsfahne eine Woche lang vom hohen Mast unseres Rathauses wehen zu lassen.

Aber ohne die Frauen in unserm Verein könnten wir gar nicht bestehen. Unsere Frauen sind der Kern und die Seele des Vereins und stehen frei und selbständig an der Seite ihrer Männer. Da viele Einzelgänger sind, sind es gerade die Frauen, die unseren Verein zusammenhalten. Sie sind meistens

Catch of Salmon

vernünftiger, geduldiger und diplo-matischer. Deshalb waren auch die meisten Präsidenten unseres Vereins Frauen.

Da ist z. B. **Marlene,** eine Mitbegründerin des Vereins und Ex-Präsidentin. Sie unterstützt ihren Mann als Zeitungslieferantin und Buchhalterin des gemeinsamen Straßenbauunternehmens.

Oder **Annegret,** die nachdem sie ihre Kinder groß gezogen hatte, ihr Studium an der Universität abschloß mit einer Magisterthese über Dr. Otto Geist, der in Alaska ein bekannter deutscher Archäologe war. Um sich das Geld für ihr Studium zu verdienen, eröffnete sie mit **Marianne** jeden Sommer eine deutsche Imbißstube mit Bratwurst und deutschem Kuchen. Beide Frauen waren Präsidentinnen unseres Vereins.

Annelise mit ihrem Mann haben für Jahre mit ihrer Fleischerei dafür gesorgt, daß wir immer genug Fleischwaren und Brot nach deutschen Rezepten hatten.

Giesela, eine kleine gemütliche Bayerin, hat eigenhändig die Schwarzwälder Tanzgruppe aufgebaut und leitet sie mit viel Liebe und Geduld.

Erika ist Budgetanalist und Vizepräsidentin, und ihr Mann ist Jagdführer.

Jo Anne, unser Professor der Deutschen Sprache an der hiesigen Universität, ist momentan auf einer Reise durch Deutschland.

Christa hatte mit ihrem Mann u.a. ein Fotogeschäft. Sie genießt jetzt ihren Lebensabend.

Meine Frau **Ingrid,** die mit mir zusammen einen Wohnungskomplex leitet, in dem Goldgräber, Indianer und Eskimos wohnen, steht mir mit Rat und Tat zur Seite und hat mir zuliebe die Führung unseres Vereins mehrmals abgelehnt - weil, wie sie so schön sagt, ich der größere Träumer sei.

Alle Frauen in unserem Verein haben sich nicht nur in Alaska behauptet, sondern haben vieles Außerordentliches geleistet. Wir sind sehr stolz auf sie.

Unsere Frauen sind unzerbrechlich, mit einem stabilen Charakter und einer positiven Einstellung zum Leben. Das ist unbedingt erforderlich, um sich in dieser Wildnis und den eiskalten Wintern hier zu behaupten.

Ich möchte diesen Bericht über den Deutschen Verein und seine Frauen von Fairbanks abschließen mit den Worten eines großen deutschen Dichters "Ehret die Frauen, sie flechten und weben himmlische Rosen ins irdische Leben."

Happy times at the Club

A colorful assembly before the March

Log Cabins in Fairbanks

Dancing Indian Forefathers

Alaska Panorama

More Portraits of Alaska and the German Club

Peter and Company

The Church where the Pope and President Reagan met

Family Schneider's granddaughter

Homemade parka fashion show

The German Club of Alaska was established in 1972 and counts some 60 members; of its membership 2/3's are women. Assembled after the war, some adventurers and here for many other reasons, we share the love of Alaska and are proud to be Germans or to be of German descent. Once I was asked, how I can be both, I answered: "It is simple, I respect and honor Germany like my parents, grandparents and ancestors, and I love America like my wife, my children and grandchildren."

Part of our noted objectives are the preservation and worldwide promotion of the German heritage, to develop and honor a better understanding of our common backgrounds and to actively support and participate in the society in which we live.

We in Fairbanks are well liked, and in the Summer Parade, in which half the city participates, and the other half watches, we almost always win a trophy.

We support financially the German Class at the University of Alaska. We sing and dance on holidays, especially at Christmas, in both senior homes. At Easter, our Black Forest Dancers perform often at one of our large shopping centers.

Summer usually concludes with a German Thanksgiving Festival, which we celebrate at Golden Heart Park, and to which the whole town is invited.

The Ice Festival Parade is not held every year, but we are always part of it, even at minus 40 degrees Celsius.

But this is only part of what we do as Germans and as members of our Club: We help tourists with advice and deed, sit patiently at the doctor's office and translate when a Swiss needs his tooth pulled and a Hamburger has her appendix removed. We have celebrated the arrival of Lufthansa's cargo plane and the Mercedes "G" Club. As well as the German Ambassador and the Consul General. German TV and German Journalists love to visit us.

On the day of German Reunification, which coincided with the German-American Friendship Day, the whole city honored us with the permission to fly our German Club Flag from the mast of the City Hall for a whole week.

But without the women in our Club, we could not exist. Our women are the core and soul of the club and stand free and independent next to their men. Since many men are loners, it is the women who keep the club together. They usually have more common sense, are more patient and more diplomatic. Reasons why most of our Club Presidents have been women.

There is **Marlene** co-founder of our club, and ex-president. She supports her husband by delivering newspapers and as an accountant for their road construction company.

Or **Annegret,** who, after the children were grown, studies History and is currently busy, writing her doctorate thesis about Otto Geist, who was a well known German Archeologist in Alaska. To earn the money for her studies, she opened and ran together with **Marianne** - every summer - a German fast food place with brats, and German cake. Both, Annegret and Marianne, are past presidents of our club.

For years, **Annelise** and her husband's butcher shop made sure that we always had enough German meat products and bread at our functions.

Giesela, a sweet little Bavarian woman, single handedly started the Black Forest Dance Group and manages it with love and patience.

Erika is Chief Secretary and Vice President, and her husband is Hunting Master.

Jo Anne, our professor of German language at the local university, is traveling often in Germany.

Christa managed with her husband a photo store. Now she enjoys her golden years.

My wife, **Ingrid,** who together with me runs a condominium park, in which gold miners, Indians and Eskimos live, is my support and has often rejected leadership of our club in favor of me; her reason: he is the dreamer.

All women of our club have not only adapted to Alaska, but also achieved extraordinary things; we are proud of them.

Our women are shockproof, with a stable character and a positive view of life. This is necessary to survive in this wilderness and our ice cold winters.

I would like to close this report of our German Club and its women with the words of a renown German poet: "Honor your women, they braid and weave heavenly roses into the fabric of this earthly life."

Peter Schneider

Personal Notes

"Kalalau Lookout"

Photograph by Tom Hisamura

The Royal Hawaiian Band, founded in 1836, flourishes today under Bandmaster Aaron Mahl, who is of partial German heritage.

German Americans number 10 percent of a total state population of a little more than one million, and the many residents with German surnames combined with Hawaiian first names (and vice versa) show increased interest in their German heritage.

The 135-year-old German Benevolent Society of Honolulu was established to contribute to the welfare of Germans in Hawaii; it operated the Benevolent Trust and the Hackfeld Memorial Trust to aid the homeless, prevent family and drug abuse, provide medical assistance, and contribute to the preservation of German artifacts at Iolani Palace, Hawaii's former capitol and the only royal palace in the United States.

One of the most pleasant influences of the German connection in Hawaii will remain with the islands' world-renowned music. Germany demonstrated its good-will toward Hawaii by loaning a talented Prussian military bandmaster to King Kamehameha V (1863-1872) to upgrade the quality of "His Majesty's Band" and to provide the type of music the king so loved. In addition, Fürst Bismarck presented a prized gift to King Kalakaua (1874-1891) during his 1881 tour of Germany—a Royal Schellenbaum, the only known Royal Bell Tree outside of Europe.

After many years of continuous growth and change, Hawaii is rediscovering its rich and beautiful past. Adelbert von Chamisso would be happy to know that the preservation of the language and culture of old Hawaii is a major topic among modern-day Hawaiians-kama'ainas (native born) and malahinis (newcomers) alike.

The increasing number of German tourists that visit Hawaii each year (over 91,000 in 1993, a 10.3 percent increase over 1992) confirms that the south seas mystique continues to fascinate the current generation. Those Germans coming to Hawaii to experience the spirit of aloha will be surprised when they discover traces of Gemütlichkeit.

Honolulu Harbor, OAHU

"Schellenbaum"

Deutsch Amerikaner machen etwa 10% der Bevölkerung von einer Million aus. Viele dieser Einwohner, die ihre Namen mit hawaiischen Namen kombiniert haven, wollen damit ihr Interesse an der deutschen Abstammung kund tun.

Die 135 Jahre alte Deutsche Wohltätigkeits-Gesellschaft wurde zum Zweck der Unterstützung der Deutschen auf Hawaii gegründet und betreut heute die Wohltätigkeits-Stiftung und den Hackfeld Gedächtnis-Fond, um den heimlosen Menschen zu helfen, Familien und Drogen Probleme zu vermeiden, so wie ärztliche Hilfe zu ermöglichen. Auch kümmert man sich um die Erhaltung der deutschen Kunstschätze im Iolani Palast, Hawaiis frühere Haupstadt und der einzige königliche Palast in den Vereinten Staaten.

Eine der schönsten Einflüsse der deutschen Verbindung mit Hawaii wird immer mit der weltbekannten Musik aus Hawaii im Zusammenhang bleiben. Deutschland hat seinen guten Willen für Hawaii dadurch gezeigt, daß man dem König Kamehameha V (1863-1872) einen talentierten preußischen Kapellmeister borgte, um die Musik seiner Majestät zu verbessern und sie nach seinem Geschmack zu fördern. Außerdem machte Fürst Bismarck dem König Kalakaua (1874-1891) ein besonderes Geschenk - einen königlichen Schellenbaum für die "Royal Hawaiian Band", der einzig bekannte Schellenbaum außerhalb Europas.

Nach vielen Jahren des Wachstums und Wandlung, erkennt Hawaii heute seine reiche und schöne Vergangenheit. Adelbert von Chamisso würde sich freuen zu wissen, daß die Sprache und die Kultur des alten Hawaiis eine Hauptrolle im modernen Hawaii spielt - bei den Gebürtigen (kama' ainas) genau so wie bei den Zugewanderten (malahinis).

Die wachsende Anzahl der deutschen Touristen, die jedes Jahr Hawaii besuchen kommen (mehr als 91,000 im Jahre 1993, 10.3% mehr als 1992) bestätigt, daß die Südsee-Mystique auch heute besonders die neue Generation fasziniert. Die Deutschen, die Hawaii besuchen, werden erstaunt sein, daß der Geist von *Aloha* einige Spuren von *Gemütlichkeit* aufweist.

Editor Charles Longo, Tucson, AZ. Reprinted by permission of German Life Magazine, May 1996. More detail also in Dr. N. Schweizer's "Hawaii and the German Speaking Peoples."

Courtesy: *Aloha* AIRLINES — THE BIG ISLAND OF HAWAI'I

1987 Eruption   Peter French photo

City of Refuge, Hawaii

Waikiki Sunset by Wm. Waterfall   All photos: Hawaiian Visitors Bureau

German Print Media

Worldwide:

Deutsche Rundschau
Unabhängige Zeitschrift
für Deutschsprechende
Klugmann Communications
P.O. Box 464
Sharon, Ontario LOG 1VO
Canada

Juri Klugmann, Editor-in-Chief
Phone: 905 478-1843
Fax: 905 478-1844

Chicago:

Amerika Woche
Courier Press USA Ltd.
4632 N. Lincoln Avenue
Chicago, Illinois 60625

Mario Schiefelbein M.A.
Chefredakteur
Phone: 773 275 5054
Fax: 773 275 0596

Eintracht
9456 N. Lawler Avenue
Skokie, Illinois 60077-1271

Walter und Klaus Juengling
Publishers & Editors
Phone: 847 677 9456
Fax: 847 677 9471

German-American Journal
Der Deutsch-Amerikaner
4740 N. Western Avenue
Chicago, Illinois 60625-2097

Ernst Ott, DANK President
Publisher
Phone: 773 275 1100
Fax: 773 275 4010

ChamberWay, Germany/Midwest
German American Chamber of
Commerce
401 N. Michigan Avenue, Suite 2525
Chicago, Illinois 60611-4212

Christian J. Roehr
Publisher
Phone: 312 644 2662
Fax: 312 644 0738

Landmark Books Unlimited
The German Media Group
389 Duane Street, Suite 302
Glen Ellyn, Illinois 60137-4389

Bert Lachner
Publisher
Phone: 630 858 3085
Fax: 630 858 3087

Detroit:

Nordamerikanische
Wochen-Post
1301 W. Long Lake, Suite 272
Troy, Michigan 48098

Knuth Beth
Publisher
Phone: 810 641 9944
Fax: 810 641 9946

Cleveland:

Germania
German/American Newspaper
17599 Whitney Road, Suite 532
Strongsville, Ohio 44136

Johanna Roth
Publisher
Phone: 216 243 4196

Buffalo:

Volksfreund
Erickson Enterprizes Inc.
947 Ellicott Square Bldg.
295 Main Street
Buffalo, New York 14203

Bert E. Nelson
Publisher
Phone: 716 849 9606

New Jersey:

Freie Zeitung
Deutschsprachige Wochenzeitung
500 S. 31st Street
Kenilworth, New Jersey 07033

Eberhard Schweizer
Publisher
Phone: 908 245 7995
Fax: 908 245 7997

New York:

New Yorker Staats Zeitung
fuer Weltbuerger deutscher Sprache
Felix Productions Inc.
160 W. 71st Street
New York, NY 10023

Jes Rau
Publisher
Phone: 212 875 0769
Fax: 212 875 0534

German American TRADE
German American Chamber of
Commerce
40 W. 57th Street
New York, NY 10019-4092

Daniel Mahler
Corporate Editor
Phone: 212 974 8830
Fax: 212 974 8867

Philadelphia:

The Ambassador
Der Botschafter
515 Huntington Pike
Rockledge, PA 19046-4451

Bernard J. Freitag
Publisher
Phone: 215 379 1722
Fax: 215 663 8433

Washington, D.C.:

Washington Journal
1113 National Press Building
Washington, DC 20045-1853

Gerald R. Kainz
Publisher
Phone: 202 628 0404
Fax: 703 938 2251

German Life
Zeitgeist Publishing
1 Corporate Drive
Grantsville, MD 21536

Lisa A. Fitzpatrick
Publisher
Phone: 301 895 8359
Fax: 301 895 5029

Georgia:

Das Fenster
ehemals Die Hausfrau
1060 Gaines School Road, Suite B-3
Athens, GA 30605-3136

Alex Mazeika
Geschaeftsfuehrer
Phone: 706 548 4382
Fax: 706 548 8856

Florida:

German News
German News Arts & Graphics Inc.
1413 S. Howard Avenue, Suite 105
Tampa, Florida 33606

Ingrid Oshiro-Weingartner
Publisher
Phone: 813 254 7517
Fax: 813 254 7412

**German Shopping and
Restaurant Guide**
Palm Coast Publishing Inc.
138 Palm Coast Parkway NE,
Suite 309
Palm Coast, Florida 32137

Michael Rose
President
Phone: 904 446 4499
Fax: 904 446 4708

Florida Journal
6238-6 Presidential Court
Fort Myers, Florida 33919
Manfred Behr
Publisher
Phone: 941 481-7511
Fax: 941 481 7753

Houston:

Deutsche Welt - USA
German American Publication
P.O. Box 35831
Houston, Texas 77235

Hildegard M. Graeter
Editor
Phone: 713 721 7277
Fax: 713 723 9421

California:

California Staats-Zeitung
San Francisco Neue Zeitung
1201 N Alvarado Street
Los Angeles, California 90026

Lore Warren
Editor
Phone: 501 783 2072
Fax: 510 782 1840

Neue Presse
Die aktuelle deutschsprachige
Wochenzeitung fuer Amerikaner
2331-D2 East Avenue S, #127
Palmdale, CA 93550

Norbert-Hartmut Schreiber
Verleger und Herausgeber
Phone: 805 266 1818
Fax: 805 274 0212

Canada:

Deutsche Presse
German Press
Austrian Publications Ltd.
455 Spadina Avenue, Suite 303
Toronto, Ontario M5S 2G8

Herbert Dissauer
Publisher
Phone: 416 595 9714
Fax: 416 595 9716

Canada/USA:

Heimatbote
Donauschwaben in Nordamerika
17 Doncrest Drive
Thornhill, Ontario L3T 4P6

Anton Weckerle B.A.
Publisher
Phone: 905 881 6350
Fax: 905 886 3794

Source: Individual Publications
June 13, 1997

The German-Canadian Society

by Dr. Harmut Froeschle

The social life of the German-speaking immigrants took and takes place in the context of societies and clubs. This also applies to the other ethnic groups that grew due to immigration. The society represents a piece of transplanted homeland. There one can speak the language, socialize in a familiar atmosphere, make useful contacts and collect all sorts of information. This in turn facilitates the acculturation at the workplace as well as to the new surroundings. The collective life of the ethnic group can be seen in the scope and structure of its societies.

It isn't surprising that the Germans, as practiced creators of organizations, established organizations of all kinds upon their arrival in the new country. In the pioneer days, school organizations were established as well as social and special interest groups; these were usually conducted in the native tongue and in a religious environment. Later, social groups evolved independent of the church community. Through the years, this resulted in a number of subgroups (sports, dance, marksmanship, song, theater, skat, bowling, needlework, benevolence, etc.). At the same time, the consolidation of special interest groups created a cohesive, all encompassing organization. Often a choir was the beginning of an organization.

The German-Canadian society can be traced back to 1786. Back then, the Hochdeutsche Gesellschaft/High German Society was established in Halifax. One of the members was an Anton Heinrich

Vereinigung der Donauschwaben, Scarborough near Toronto, Ontario

aus Mömpelgard, the royally favored printer from province of Nova Scotia. He published the *Hochdeutschen Neu Schottländischen Kalendar* (High German Nova Scotia Calendar) from 1788 to 1801. The German organization underwent large fluctuations due to the German-speaking immigration movement to and within Canada. Despite this, one can still find several societies that have survived for an extraordinarily long time. The Deutsche Gesellschaft (German Society) in Montreal has been in existence since 1835, the Germania-Klub in Hamilton since 1864 and the Concordia-Klub in Kitchener since 1873. Both clubs were originally established as choir

Das deutschkanadische Organisationswesen

von Dr. Harmut Froeschle

Das Gemeinschaftsleben der deutschsprachigen Einwanderer fand und findet - wie auch bei den anderen durch Einwanderung gespeisten ethnokulturellen Gruppen - vor allem im Rahmen von Vereinigungen und Klubs statt. Der Verein stellt ein Stück verpflanzte Heimat dar; in ihm kann man die Muttersprache pflegen, der gewohnten Geselligkeit nachgehen, nützliche Kontakte knüpfen und Informationen aller Art sammeln, die im Berufsleben und bei der Akkulturation in der neuen Umwelt weiterhelfen. Das Gruppenleben einer Ethnie läßt sich also an Umfang und Struktur ihres Organisationswesens ablesen.

Concordia Club, Kitchener, Ontario

Daß die Deutschen als gelernte "Vereinsmeier" sehr bald nach ihrer Ankunft im neuen Land Vereine aller Art ins Leben riefen, verwundert nicht. In den Pionierzeiten enstanden Schulvereine, gesellige Vereinigungen und spezielle Interessengruppen zunächst meistens im Rahmen der muttersprachlichen religiösen Gemeinden. Später bildeten sich gesellige Vereine unabhängig von den Kirchengemeinden heraus und brachten im Lauf der Jahre eine Reihe von Untergruppen hervor (Sport-, Tanz-, Schützen-, Sing-, Theater-, Skat-, Kegel-, Handarbeit-, soziale Hilfsgruppppen, etc.), wie andererseits aus dem Zusammenschluß von speziellen Interessengruppen ein zusammenfassender überwölbender Verein entstehen konnte. Nicht selten war ein Chor der erste Kern eines späteren Geselligkeitsvereins.

Das deutschkanadische Vereinswesen läßt sich bis zum Jahre 1786 zurückverfolgen. Damals wurde in Halifax die Hochdeutsche Gesellschaft/High German Society gegründet, welcher der königlich privilegierte Drucker der Provinz Nova Scotia, Anton Heinrich aus Mömpelgard angehörte, der von 1788 bis 1801 den *Hochdeutschen Neu-Schottländischen Kalender* herausgab. Gemäß der deutschpachigen Wanderungsbewegung nach Kanada und der Binnenwanderung war naturgemäß das deutsche Vereinswesen großen Fluktuationen unterworfen. Trotzdem kann man einige Vereinigungen entdecken, die sich durch

groups. In 1973 the Concordia choir received the Zelter plaque. The Deutsche Gesellschaft (German Society) in Winnipeg goes back to 1892 and the Edelweiß-Klub in Edmonton to 1906. The longevity of social organizations usually depends on the ownership of meeting facilities. After the loss of a clubhouse, such organizations usually dissolve, even though they continue to exist on paper as legal entities. This phenomenon was demonstrated after the sale of the "Deutschen Häuser" (German Houses) in Montreal in 1984 and in Toronto in 1986. Nonetheless, there are still an estimated 30 clubs with their own buildings, such as in Ottawa, Scarborough, Brampton near Toronto, Hamilton, Kitchener, London, Brantford, Windsor, St. Catherines, Niagara Falls, Winnipeg, Regina, Saskatoon, Calgary, Edmonton, Vancouver and Victoria.

Austrian Club, Burlington, Ontario

In addition to the social clubs and their diverse subgroups, there were the singing societies, carnival organizations, social service organizations, compatriot societies, professional interest groups, cultural societies as well as language and school associations.

From the beginning, singing organizations – men's choirs and mixed choirs – have played a large role in the German-Canadian organization. The first "Sängerfest" (Singer Celebration) of German choirs was held in Berlin (Kitchener) in 1862. The "Sängerfest" took on astounding dimensions in the next decades. At times, the number of singers nearly matched the number of inhabitants of the town. [1]The caliber of these gatherings was reflected in the fact that already in the 1880s, oratories such as Hayden's "Creation" and Handel's "Messiah" were being performed. The choirs of Ontario were united in Berlin in 1873 as the Deutschkanadische Sängerbund (German-Canadian Singers' Association). It lasted until World War I. It was resurrected in 1958 and enjoys renewed popularity. In western Canada, the old tradition was also embraced. The Nord - Pazifische Sängerbund (North Pacific Singers' Association), founded in 1901 in British Columbia became active again after World War II as the Pazifische Sängerbund (Pacific Singers' Association). In 1970, the choirs of Alberta, Saskatchewan and Manitoba became the Prärie-Sängerbund (Prairie Singers' Association). After a fifty-year break, the German "Sängerfest" was held in Canada once again.

erstaunliche Langlebigkeit auszeichnen. Die Deutsche Gesellschaft in Monreal existiert seit 1835, der Germania-Klub in Hamilton seit 1864 und der Concordia-Klub in Kitchener seit 1873 (beide Klubs wurden als Chorvereinigungen gegründet, der Concordia-Chor erhielt 1973 die Zelter-Plakette); die Deutsche Gesellschaft in Winnipeg geht auf das Jahr 1892, der Edelweiß-Klub in Edmonton auf 1906 zurück. Die Langlebigkeit geselliger Vereine hängt in der Regel mit dem Besitz eigener Räumlichkeiten zusammen. Nach Verlust ihres Klubhauses pflegen sich solche Organisationen aufzulösen, auch wenn sie auf dem Papier als legale Entitäten weiterbestehen. Dieses Phänomen konnte man nach dem Verkauf der "Deutschen Häuser" in Montreal (1984) und Toronto (1986) feststellen. Immerhin gibt es in Kanada schätzungsweise immer noch etwa 30 Klubs mit eigenen Gebäuden, z.B. in Ottawa, Scarborough und Brampton bei Toronto, Hamilton, Kitchener, London, Brantford, Windsor, St. Catherines, Niagara Falls, Winnipeg, Regina, Saskatoon, Calgary, Edmonton, Vancouver und Victoria.

Neben den der Geselligkeit gewidmeten Klubs mit ihren diversen Untergruppen existieren Gesangsvereine, Karnevalsvereine, soziale Vereinigungen, landsmannschaftliche Zusammenschlüsse, berufliche Interessengruppen, kulturelle Vereinigungen sowie Sprach- und Schulverbände.

Gesangsvereine - Männerchöre - haben im deutschkanadischen Vereinsleben von Anfang an eine große Rolle gespielt. Das erste Sängerfest deutscher Chöre in Ontario fand in Berlin (Kitchener) 1862 statt. Die Sängerfeste der nächsten Jahrzehnte nahmen erstaunliche Dimensionen an, sodaß manchmal die Zahl der beteiligten Sänger der Einwohnerzahl des Festortes fast gleichkam.

[1]Das Kaliber dieser Treffen zeigt sich u.a. darin, daß schon in den 1880er Jahren Oratorien wie Haydns "Schöpfung" und Händels "Messias" aufgeführt wurden. Als Zusammenschluß der Chöre Ontarios wurde 1873

Talisman Mountain Resort, Kimberley, Ontario

in Berlin der Deutschkanadische Sängerbund gegründet, der bis zum ersten Weltkrieg bestand; 1958 wurde er wieder zum Leben erweckt und erfreut sich erfrischender Vitalität. Auch in Westkanada knüpfte man erfolgreich an die alte Tradition an: der 1901 in British Columbia initiierte Nord-

With the exception of the province of Quebec, where Mardi Gras is celebrated, the middle European carnival was unknown in Canada. Thus the immigrant German carnival celebration added a new variant to Canadian culture which has spread beyond the German-Canadian population. Carnival groups were and still are a component of many German-Canadian clubs. In 1965, they joined in Hamilton as the Bund deutscher Karnevalsgesellschaften in Kanada (Association of German Carnival Organizations in Canada).

Schwaben Club, Kitchener, Ontario

Organizations with specific social service goals naturally emerge in pioneer times and times of need. In this context, agricultural cooperatives, organizations to help the sick and benevolent societies of all kinds come to mind. Such societies include the Canadian Society for German Relief in Kitchener, renamed in 1956 to the Canadian-German Society, the Baltische Hilfsverein (Baltic Relief Organization, 1948), the relief organizations in Ottawa (German Benevolent Society, 1955) and Montreal (German-Canadian Community Service, 1965) as well as Vancouver (German-Canadian Benevolent Society of British Columbia, 1965). Such relief work sometimes resulted in the establishment of German-American rest homes, such as in St. Catherines, Ontario (1965), Vancouver (1968), as well as Winnipeg, Ottawa and Kitchener (1984). The Kanadische Verein deutscher Renter (Canadian Organization of German Retirees, 1972) can also be added to the list of socio-political organizations.

Umbrella organizations for compatriots include the Sudeten Germans (Zentralverband sudetendeutscher Organizationen [Central Association of Sudeten German Organizations]), the Baltic Germans, the Russian Germans and the Donauschwaben. The last two groups have local membership organizations in the U.S.A. and Canada. The umbrella organization of the Pennsylvania German speaking Mennonites in Ontario and the West Prussian Low German speaking Mennonites can also be included, because the Mennonite groups are bound by religious and ethnic affiliation. Many isolated compatriot groups have formed clubs for Bavarians, Swabians, Saxons, citizens of Hansa towns, Berliners, natives of Munich, Styrians, Burgerlanders, etc. These groups do not have their own facilities and are without national affiliation. A special compatriot organization is the Deutscher Verband Ost Europa

Pazifische Sängerbund nahm nach dem 2. Weltkrieg als Pazifik-Sängerbund seine Tätigkeit wieder auf, und 1970 schlossen sich die Chöre von Alberta, Saskatchewan und Manitoba zum Prärie-Sängerbund zusammen. Nach über fünfzigjähriger Unterbrechung wurden in Kanada wieder deutsche Sängerfeste veranstaltet.

Mit Ausnahme der Provinz Quebec, wo Mardi Gras gefeiert wird, war der mitteleuropäsche Karneval in Kanada unbekannt; deshalb fügten die eingewanderten deutschen Karnevalisten der kanadischen Geselligkeitskultur eine neue Variante hinzu, deren Wirkung über die deutschkanadische Bevölkerung hinausgeht. Karnevalsgruppen waren und sind teilweise noch immer Bestandteil vieler deutschkanadischer Klubs; 1965 schlossen sie sich in Hamilton zum Bund deutscher Karnevalgesellschaften in Kanada zusammen.

Vereine mit explizit sozial ausgerichteter Zielsetzung entstehen natürlich vor allem in Pionier- und Notzeiten; in diesem Zusammenhang denkt man etwa an landwirtschaftliche Kooperativen, Krankenvereine und Hilfsvereine aller Art, wie das nach dem 2. Weltkrieg in Kitchener entstandene Deutsch-kanadische Hilfswerk (Canadian Society for German Relief, 1956 umbenannt in Canadian-German Society), den Baltischen Hilfsverein in Kanada (gegründet 1948), die Hilfsvereine in Ottawa (German Benevolent Society, 1955), Montreal (German-Canadian Community Service, 1965) und Vancouver (German-Canadian Benevolent Society of B.C., 1965). Solche sozialen Hilfstätigkeiten resultierten manchmal in der Errichtung von deutschkanadischen Altersheimen, z.B. in St. Catherines, Ont. (1965), Vancouver (1968), Winnipeg, Ottawa und Kitchener (1984). Auch den

Verein Teutonia Club, Windsor, Ontario

Kanadischen Verein deutscher Rentner (1972) kann man zu den sozialpolitischen Organisationen rechnen.

Landsmannschaftliche Dachverbände haben die Sudetendeutschen (Zentralverband sudetendeutscher Organisationen), die Baltendeutschen, die Rußland Deutschen und die Donauschwaben, letztere zwei grenzüberschreitend mit lokalen Mitgliedsorganisationen

(German Cultural Association of Eastern Europe), which was founded in the spring of 1992. It is an association of exiles who had been meeting informally for several years. The association's goal is to educate the public about the fate of the exiles; it also provides assistance to Russian-Germans in East Prussia and supports the teaching of German in Silesia.

German-Canadian business people met in professional interest groups in different cities. The result is the German-Canadian Business and Professional Associations in Montreal, Ottawa, Toronto, Kitchener, Winnipeg, Edmonton and Vancouver. The German-Canadian Chamber of Commerce is the information exchange and advising coordinator of trade between Germany and Canada, with branch offices in Toronto (since 1968) and Montreal (since 1977). Since 1961, there has been an organization of German engineers in Toronto and in 1993, the Dortmund-based Kanadischdeutschen Juristenvereinigung (German-Canadian Association of Jurists), which was established in 1992, opened a Canadian branch there.

The uniquely cultural organizations include the Historical Society of Mecklenburg Upper Canada (1972), the German-Canadian Historical Association (1973), the Ontario Goethe Society (1974),

Will Barmeier, Social Studies Teacher at Chief Peguis High School, makes sure his class has fun while studying. As part of the Student Exchange Program, Canadian and German students work and live together.

the Literarische Zirkel (Literary Circle) in Toronto which Pastor Wolf Goegginger lead for 30 years, the German Heritage Museum in Brampton, the Mennonite Historical Society and the Schneider House (a museum of Pennsylvania German folk art) in Kitchener, the Mennonite Verein der deutschen Sprache (Society of German Language) and the Mennonite Heritage Center in Winnipeg as well as the Deutschkanadische Kulturkreis (German- Canadian Cultural Circle) in Vancouver. Also included are the German theater groups in some Canadian cities. The Deutsche Theater Montreal (German Theater of Montreal, 1958) stands out among them. This company goes on tour throughout Canada.

In the 1950s, volunteer initiatives helped develop German Sonnabendschulen (Saturday Schools) to keep up the language. [2]The schools joined in 1978 to create the Association of German-

in Kanada und den USA. Wenn man will, kann man auch die Dachorganisationen der (Pennsylvanisch sprechenden) Mennoniten in Ontario und der (westpreußisches Platt sprechenden) Mennoniten in Westkanada als landsmannschaftliche Zusammenschlüsse zählen, da die mennonitischen Gruppen die Merkmale religiöser und ethnischer Zugehörigkeit verbinden. Für die Liebe mancher deutscher Vereinsmeier zu kleinsten Einheiten zeugen die zahlreichen von einander isolierten lokalen landsmannschaftlichen Klubs, alle ohne eigene Räumlichkeiten und ohne überörtliche Zusammenschlüsse: die Klubs der Bayern, Schwaben, Sachsen, Hanseaten, Berliner, Münchner, Steirer, Burgenländer, etc. eine landsmannschaftliche Vereinigung besonderer Art ist der im Frühjahr 1992 gegründete Deutsche Kulturverband Osteuropa, ein Zusammenschluß von Vetriebenen, die sich seit einigen Jahren schon informell getroffen hatten. Der Verband bezweckt, die Öffentlichkeit über das Schicksal der Vertriebenen aufzuklären; außerdem leistet er Hilfe bei der Betreung der Rußlanddeutschen in Ostpreußen und beim Deutschunterricht in Schlesien.

Deutschkanadische Geschäftsleute schlossen sich in verschiedenen Großstädten zu beruflichen Interessengruppen zusammen, so gibt es German-Canadian Business and Professional Associations in Montreal, Ottawa, Toronto, Kitchener, Winnipeg, Edmonton und Vancouver. Als Informationsbörse und beratender Koordinator des Handels zwischen Kanada und Deutschland versteht sich die Deutsch-kanadische Handelskammer (German-Canadian Chamber of Commerce) mit Zweigstellen in Toronto (seit 1968) und Montreal (seit 1977). In Toronto existiert seit 1961 ein Verein deutscher Ingenieure, und in derselben Stadt wurde 1993 eine kanadische Zweigstelle der 1992 in Dortmund gegründeten Kanadisch-deutschen Juristenvereinigung eröffnet.

Zu den ausschließlich kulturell ausgerichteten Organisationen gehören die Historical Society of Mecklenburg Upper Canada (1972), der Verband für deutschkanadische Geschichtsforschung (German-Canadian Historical Association, 1973), die Ontario Goethe Society (1974), der von Pastor Wolf Goegginger drei Jahrzehnte geleitete Literarische Zirkel in Toronto, das Geman Heritage Museum in Brampton, die Mennonite Historical Society und das Schneider House (ein Museum Pennsylvaniendeutscher Volkskunst) in Kitchener, der Mennonitische Verein Deutsche Sprache und das Mennonite Heritage Center in Winnipeg, der Deutschkanadische Kulturkreis in Vancouver sowie die deutschen Theatergruppen in einigen kanadischen Großstädten, unter denen das auch Tourneen unternehmende Deutsche Theater Montreal (seit 1958) herausragt.

Die zur Pflege der Muttersprache aus Freiwilligeninitiativen seit den 1950er Jahren entstandenen deutschen Sonnabendschulen schlossen sich 1978 zum Verband deutsch-kanadischer Sprachschulen (Association of German-Canadian Language Schools) zusammen.

[2]Wohl vornehmlich aus Gründen größerer Förderungwürdigkeit vereinsten sich 1983 der Verband der Sonnabendschulen mit dem kanadischen Germanistenverband (Canadian Association of Teachers of German) und einigen provinziellen Deutschlehrer-Vereinigungen zur Ständigen Konferenz kanadischer Deutschlehrer (Canadian Council of Teachers of German); ein substantieller Teil der Mitglieder ist deutscher Herkunft oder Abstammung.

Angesichts der riesigen Entfernungen in Kanada und der weiten Streuung der deutschstämmigen Kanadier entwickelten sich Initiativen zu

Canadian Language Schools. In order to increase visibility, the Verband der Sonnabendschulen (Association of Saturday Schools) and the Canadian Association Of Teachers of German as well as several provincial German teacher organizations united to create the Canadian Council of Teachers of German. A significant number of the members of the organization are German or of German descent.

Due to the huge distances in Canada and the scattering of German-Canadians, initiatives didn't develop into national organizations until late. To reinforce the bond between Germans in Western Canada, Alberta and Manitoba, "Deutsche Tage" (German Days) were held, starting in 1928. In 1930, Saskatchewan followed. "Deutsche Tage" included special events, resolutions, competitions for singers, gymnasts, traditional costume and dance groups, crafts and presentations by schoolchildren. Because of the start of the war there were no significant affiliations. The pro-national socialist Deutscher Bund (German Association) did not have widespread support among the people from 1933 to 1939. Many members were interned during World War II. The time for national organizations didn't come until after World War II, primarily due to better means of communication. The Canadian Society of German Relief had branch offices outside Ontario, and in 1951, the first national umbrella organization, the Trans-Kanada Allianz der Deutschkanadier – TCA (Trans-Canada Alliance of German-Canadians), was founded in Kitchener. At first, these organizations were very successful, but in the late 70s and early 80s, continuous internal bickering paralyzed their operation. This resulted in the Deutschkanadischen Kongress – DKK (German Canadian Congress) becoming the new umbrella organization. The DKK was actually successful in gaining member associations all over Canada, as well as several national associations. It also began to function as the cultural and political voice of the German Canadians.

Club Heidelberg in St. Catharines, Ontario

[3]The DKK maintains provincial associations from Quebec to British Columbia. In Saskatchewan and Alberta, two provincial associations handle these tasks (Saskatchewan German Council, German Canadian Association of Alberta). There is concern about the national office of the DDK in Ottawa because the funds provided by the Canadian government are running out. In Toronto, the DKK has coupled the tradition of "Deutsche Tage" with its large events,

Picturesque Heidehof Altersheim, St. Catharines, ON

überregionalen Organisationsformen erst spät. Um das Zusammengehörigkeitsgefühl der Deutschen Westkanadas zu stärken, wurden ab 1928 in Alberta und Manitoba, ab 1930 in Saskatschewan "Deutsche Tage" veranstaltet, mit Festakten, Resolutionen, Wettkämpfen von Sängern, Turnern, Trachten- und Volkstanzgruppen, kunstgewerblichen Erzeugnissen und Schülerarbeiten. Doch zu offiziellen Zusammenschlüssen umfassender Art kam es wegen des Kriegsausbruchs nicht. Der pronationalsozialistische Deutsche Bund, dessen Mitglieder im 2. Weltkrieg teilweise interniert wurden, hatte von 1933 bis 1939 keine breite Basis in der Bevölkerung. Die Zeit für überregionale Organisationen kam erst nach dem 2. Weltkrieg, vornehmlich wohl als Resultat der verbesserten verkehrstechnischen und medialen Möglichkeiten. Die Canadian Society of German Relief hatte Zweigstellen außerhalb Ontarios, und 1951 entstand in Kitchener der erste nationweit intendierte Dachverband, die Trans-Kanada-Allianz der Deutschkanadier (TCA). Zunächst recht erfolgreich, wurde diese Organisation in den späten 70er und frühen 80er Jahren durch langwährende interne Reibereien weitgehend paralysiert, sodaß 1984 mit dem Deutschkanadischen Kongreß als Dachverband ein neurer Anfang gemacht wurde. Dem DKK ist es tatsächlich gelungen, in ganz Kanada Mitgliedsverbände zu gewinnen (darunter eine Reihe überegionaler Vereinigugungen) und auf diverse Weise als kulturpolitisches Sprachrohr der Deutschkanadier zu fungieren.

[3]Der DKK, dessen nationales Büro in Ottawa wegen des Auslaufens der finanziellen Unterstützung durch die kanadische Bundesregierung i.A. gefährdet erscheint, unterhält Provinzverbände von Quebec bis British Columbia, wobei in Saskatchewan und Alberta zwei provinzweite Vereinigungen diese Funktion versehen (Saskatchewan German Council, German-Canadian Association of Alberta). Mit seinen Großveranstaltungen "German 88" in Vancouver sowie "Germanica 89" und "Germanica 94" in Toronto hat der DKK an die Tradition der Deutschen Tage der Zwischenkriegszeit angeknüpft. Neben diesen Initiativen des Dachverbandes hat es seit den 70er Jahren in verschiedenen Städten auch "deutsche Wochen" gegeben, die in Zusammenarbeit von lokalen Vereinen mit den deutschen Konsultaten bzw. der Botschaft in Ottawa durchgeführt wurden. In einem ersten Versuch, das deutschkanadische Vereinswesen zu erfassen,

Ich schätzte 1973 die Gesamtzahl der einschlägigen Organisationen auf etwa 500. So viele sind es längst nicht mehr, und auch damals hatten wohl nur etwa drei Dutzend davon gesellschaftliches oder kulturelles Gewicht. Heute ist unschwer zu erkennen, daß mit dem Aussterben der

"Germanica 88" in Vancouver as well as "Germanica 89" and "Germanica 94" in Toronto. In addition to these initiatives by the umbrella organization, there have been "Deutsche Wochen" (German Weeks) since the 70s in several cities. The "Deutsche Wochen" have been organized by local societies working with the German consulates, specifically the embassy in Ottawa, in a first attempt to provide an overview of the German Organization.

I estimate that in 1973 the number of important organizations to be about 500. So many no longer exist and even then only about 3 dozen were of social or cultural importance. Today, it is not hard to see that with the death of the immigrant generation of the 50s and 60s a number of societies will disappear; others will survive but the language used will be English. However, it is important to recognize that the German-Canadian societies assisted in many ways in the facilitating the acculturation of the immigrants. The societies also enriched the social and cultural aspects of Canada and assisted in promoting understanding between cultures. For these reasons, it is comforting to know that a number of these organizations will exist into the 21st century.

Notes

[1] See Gottlieb Leibbrandt, Little Paradise. Aus Geschichte und Leben der Deutschkanadier in der County Waterloo, Ontario, 1800-1975. Kitchener 1977. Pp. 165-188; Helmut Kallmann, "The German Contribution to Music in Canada" in GCY 2, Toronto 1975. Pp. 152-167 as well as pp. 161-163.

[2] See Herminio Schmidt, "Die deutschen Sonnabenschulen in Kanada. Entwicklung und Prognose" in GCY 6, 1981. Pp. 183-198.

[3] See Harmut Froeschle, "Das Deutschkanadische Kongreß und seine Informationsangebote" in Canadiana Germanica 61, April 1989. Pg. 107.

At Forks National Park in Winnipeg, Manitoba, Canadian and German students study together in the class room and outside.
Some friendships last forever.

Einwanderergeneration der 50er und 60er Jahre eine Reihe von Vereinen erlöschen wird; andere werden zwar überleben, aber ihre Gebrauchssprache wird Englisch sein. Nichtsdestoweniger bleibt festzuhalten, daß deutschkanadische Vereine auf verschiedenartige Weise zu schmerzloserer Akkulturation der Einwanderer, zur Bereicherung der Geselligkeit und Kultur in Kanada und zur Völkerverständigung ihren wertvollen Beitrag geleistet haben, und deshalb ist es zu begrüßen, daß eine Anzahl von ihnen ins 21. Jahrhundert hineinreichen wird.

9th grade students from Winnipeg and Germany study a historical subject, a strong part in this region by the Assiniboine and Red Rivers.

Student information and photos from Gareth Neufeld, River East Colligiate, Winnipeg, Manitoba

Ammerkungen

[1] Vgl. Gottlieb Leibbrand, *Little Paradise. Aus Geschichte und Leben der Deutschkanadier im County Waterloo, Ontario, 1800-1975.* Kitchener 1977. S. 165-188; Helmut Kallmann "The German Contribution to Music in Canada." In: GCY2, Toronto 1975. S. 152-167 bes. S. 161-163.

[2] Vgl. Herminio Schmidt, "Die deutschen Sonnabendschulen in Kanada. Entwicklung und Prognose."In: GCY6, 1981. S. 183-198.

[3] Siehe Harmut Froeschle, "Der Deutschkanadische Kongreß und seine Informationsangebote." In: *Canadiana Germanica 61,* April 1989. S. 107.

DKK: German-Canadian Clubs and Societies in Canada

Club	Address	City	Postal Code
Alliance of Danube-Swabians in Canada	7046 Brian Crescent	Niagara Falls	L2J 3P5
Alliance of Transylvania Saxons of Canada	23 Monterey	Kitchener	N2B 1V2
Alpen Club, Kitchener	464 Maple Avenue	Kitchener	N2H 4X5
Association of Danube Swabians	1686 Ellesmere Road	Scarborough	M1H 2V5
Austria Club of Windsor	P.O. Box 1312, Stn.A	Windsor	N9A 6R3
Bethel Lutheran Church	47 Sheldon Avenue N	Kitchener	N2H 3M1
Burgenlaender Club Toronto, Inc.	10 Royal Orchard Blv.	Thornhill	L3T 7R9
Christ the King - Dietrich Bonhoefer Church	32 Craigmont Drive	Willowdale	M2H 1C5
Club Loreley Inc.	389 Dean Avenue	Oshawa	L1H 7L5
Concordia Club	429 Ottawa Street S.	Kitchener	N2M 3P6
Delphi District German Home Ltd.	443 James Street	Delphi	N4B 2B9
Donauschwaben Park Waldheim Inc.	2 Tannenweg	Blackstock	L0B 1B0
First Lutheran Church	116 Bond Street	Toronto	M5B 1X8
German Benevolent Society of Ottawa	P.O. Box 5583, Meriv.	Ottawa	K2C 3M1
German Canadian Association, Lake Head	Box 551, Station F	Thunderbay	P7C 5V9
German Canadian Assocation of Brantford	P.O. Box 28024	Brantford	N3R 7X5
German Canadian Business & Professionals	100 Adelaide Street W	Toronto	M5H 1S3
German Canadian Business and Prof. Men	332 Charles Street	Kitchener	N2G 2P9
German Canadian Club	522 Talbot Street W.	Aylmer	N5H 2T8
German Canadian Club HANSA	6650 Hurontario, RR6	Mississauga	L5R 1B5
German Canadian Club London	1 Cove Road	London	N6J 1H7
German Canadian Club of Orillia	R.R. #1	Hawkestone	L0L 1T0
German Canadian Club St. Thomas	16 West Avenue	St. Thomas	N5R 3P5
German Canadian Heritage Museum	P.O. Box 51087	Scarborough	M1L 4T2
German Canadian Historical Association	323 Canewood Place	Waterloo	N2L 5P9
Germania Club Nipissing Inc.	10 Superior Crescent	North Bay	P1A 2V8
Historical Society of Mecklendurg	P.O. Box 1251, Stn.K	Toronto	M4P 3E5
Humbervale Park Baptist Church, Seniors	763 Royal York Road	Etobicoke	M8Y 2T3
Karnevals-Gesellschaft "Treuer Husar"	3529 Bertrand Road	Mississauga	L5L 4G8
Maple Leaf Almrausch Club, Inc.	P.O. Box 8794, Stn. T	Ottawa	K1G 3J1
Quinte German Canadian Club	P.O. Box 20002	Bellville	K8N 5V1
Schwaben Club	1668 King Street E.	Kitchener	N2G 2P1
St. Patrick's German Parish	131 McCaul Street	Toronto	M5T 1W3
Teutonia Club of Windsor	55 Edinborough Street	Windsor	N8X 3C3
Thousand Island German Club	P.O. Box 843, RR #1	Lyn	K0E 1MO
Transylvania Club, Kitchener	16 Andrew Street	Kitchener	N2H 5R2
Deutsch-Kanadischer Club von Calgary	3127 Bowwood Drive	Calgary AB	T3B 2E7
Swiss Club Matterhorn	P.O. Box 5336, Stn. A	Calgary AB	T2H 1X6
German Canadian Association (Maritimes)	P.O. Box 8791, Stn. A	Halifax NS	B3K 5M4
Deutsches Theater	453 St. Francis Xavier	Old Montreal	
Rheingold Club	1177 3rd Avenue, Prince	George BC	V2L 3E4
Austrian Canadian Edelweiss Club		Regina SK	S4N 5Y1
Schweizer Verein	349 W. Georgia Street	Vancouver	BC V6B 2Z1
Vancouver Alpen Club	4875 Victoria Drive	Vancouver BC	V5N 4P3
Deutsche Vereinigung von Winnipeg	285 Flora Avenue	Winnipeg MB	R2W 2R2
German Canadian Association	203-8708 48th Avenue	Edmonton AB	T6E 5L1
German Canadian Association	6238 Quinpool Road	Halifax NS	B3L 1A3
Trans-Canada Alliance of German-Canadians	5845 des Artisians	Montreal PQ	H1P 1R5
German New Brunswick Association	9 Munroe Avenue	Riverview NB	E1B 2Y7
Saskatchewan German Council	510 Cynthia Street	Saskatoon SK	S7L 7K7
German-Canadian Congress of BC	10288 149A Street	Surrey BC	V3R 4A9
German-Canadian Congress of Manitoba	50 Dunkirk Drive	Winnipeg MB	R2M 5R4
Canadian German Chamber of Commerce	480 University Avenue	Toronto ON	M5G 1V2
German National Tourist Office	175 Bloor Street East	Toronto ON	M4W 3R8
Goethe Institut	1067 Yonge Street	Toronto ON	M4W 2L2

Club information provided by Ernst Friedel and Helga Kessel, **German-Canadian Congress**   **DKK**
455 Conestogo Road, Waterloo, Ontario N2L 4C9, Tel. 519 / 746-9006 Fax 519 / 746-7006

Peggy's Cove by Chris Reardon

Peggy's Cove, Nova Scotia

Peggy's Cove, Nova Scotia, is one of the romantic little fishing villages by the Atlantic Ocean with its beacon towards the old country and an outpost of the vast North American continent.

It is also the first landmark I visited in 1961 with my friend and colleague Leslie Haydu from Robert Bosch (Canada) Ltd. which made me feel, for the first time, free and successful. Canada is the country of my children, and where I achieved confidence in myself.

Peggy's Cove is also a symbol for both Canada and America to be one with the sea and the land, just as I was when I grew up by the Hörner lighthouse near the North Sea.

Bert Lachner

Peggy's Cove in Neuschottland ist ein kleines Fischerdorf am Atlantic mit seinem Leuchtfeuer der alten Heimat zugekehrt. Es ist auch ein Vorposten dieses weiten nordamerikanischen Kontinents.

Dieser stille, einfache Ort ist auch die Stätte, die ich 1961 mit meinem Freund und Mitarbeiter Les Haydu von Robert Bosch (Canada) Ltd. besuchte, und wo ich mich zum ersten mal frei und erfolgreich fühlte. Kanada ist das Land meiner Kinder, und wo ich Vertrauen in mich selbst gewann.

Peggy's Cove ist auch ein Symbol, nämlich vertraut zu sein mit der See und dem Land, so wie es einst am Hörner Leuchtturm war, wo ich Nahe der Nordsee-Küste aufwuchs.

Alter Hörner Leuchtturm

Foto: G. Markleir

Visit
Mexico
for Sun, Surf, Siestas
and Fiestas, Food
and Fun.

Also enjoy Ruins
and
Snorkeling
and
a little German
Gemütlichkeit !

The German Club of the IWC (International Women's Club) in Cancun - Cristina Bartnik, Renate Alvarez, Geri Braun, Cristina Fricione, Penny Salley, Eleanore Terry, Beti Gardenas and Carmen Pino.

*Photo and text from
Carmen Pino, Cancun*

1st Oktoberfest by IWC Cancun - 1991

**Address Book for Germanic
Genealogy**
Ernest Thode
    Genealogy Publishing Co.
1001 N. Calvert Street
Baltimore, MD 21202
    1994

Ähren des Lebens
*Ernste Sachen und
solche zum Lachen*
Catherine Filippi Grosskopf
    Druck Weber Press, Inc.
Chicago, IL
    1993

Alpentraum
Mode - Design Gabriele Hauser

Catalog of Dirndls, etc.
    European Classics Ltd.
1625 Covington Road
Yardley, PA 19067
Telephone: 215 / 321 - 6603
    1997

America and the Germans
a 300 Year History
Frank Trommler & Joseph McVeigh
1: Immigration, Language, Ethnicity
2: Relationship in the 20th Century
ISBN# 0-8122-1425-2
    University of Pennsylvania Press
Philadelphia, PA
    1985

Americans from Germany
Gerhard Wilk
Don Heinrich Tolzmann, Editor
ISBN # 3-925744-08-8
    Max Kade German-American Center
Indiana University-Purdue University
Indiana German Heritage Society
Deutsches Haus - Athenaeum
401 East Michigan Street
Indianapolis, IN 46204
    1995

A Nation of Immigrants
The Germans
John F. Kennedy
ISBN # 0-060913-67-3
    Harper Collins
10 E. 53rd Street

New York, NY 10022-5299
    1964

Chicagoland
A World-class Metropolis
Bilingual E/G
Bert Lachner
Niels G. Friedrichs, GACCoM
ISBN# 0-964065-90-8
    Landmark Books Unlimited
389 Duane Street
Glen Ellyn, IL 60137-4389

www.heimatland.com
    1994

Dictionary of German Names
Hans BahLow
translated by Edda Gentry
    Max Kade Institute
University of Wisconsin
Madison, WI
    1993

Directory
German American Societies in USA
J. Richly
    Karin Bahls
P.O. Box 281
Guttenberg, IA 52052
    1989

**Distinguished
German Americans**
Charles R. Haller
ISBN# 0-788401-93-9
    Heritage Books, Inc.
1540 E. Pointer Ridge Place
Bowie, MD 20716
Telephone: 301/390-7709
    1995

Economic Year Book
    German American
Chamber of Commerce
40 West 57th Street
New York, NY 10019
    1997

**Emigration & Settlement Patterns
of German Communities
in North America**
Eberhard Reichmann
LaVern J. Rippley
Jörg Nagler
    Max Kade German-American Center
Indiana German Heritage Society
401 East Michigan Avenue
Indianapolis, IN 46204
    1995

**Fame, Fortune and Sweet Liberty
The Great European Emigration**
Dirk Hoerder & Diethelm Knauf, eds.
ISBN # 3-926958-96-0
    Edition Temmen
Bremen
    1995

Finding the Grain
Dubois County, Indiana
Norbert Krapf
ISBN # 1-880788-08-X
    Max Kade
German-American Center
Indiana-Purdue University
401 East Michigan Street
Indianapolis, IN 46204
    1996

**German Achievements
in America**
Rudolf Cronau's Survey History
Edited by Don Heinrich Tolzmann
ISBN# 0-7888401-67-X
    Heritage Books, Inc.
1540 E. Pointer Ridge Place
Bowie, MD 20716
Telephone: 301 / 390 - 7709
    1995

German-American:
A Bibliography
Reprint Edition 1995
Don Heinrich Tolzmann
    Heritage Books, Inc.
1540 E. Pointer Ridge Place
Bowie, MD 20716
    1995

The German-Americans
An Ethnic Experience
Willi Paul Adams
translated by LaVern J. Rippley
and Eberhard Reichmann
ISBN# 1-880788-01-2
    Max Kade German-American Center
Indiana University - Purdue Universty
401 East Michigan Street
Indianapolis, IN 46204
    1993

The German-Americans
LaVern J. Rippley
    University Press of America
Lanham, MD
    1984

The German-Americans
One of a Series of Nations
Anne Galicich
ISBN# 0-791002-65-9
    Chelsea House Publishers
New York, Philadelphia
    1989

German-American Cooking
    D.A.N.K. Milwaukee
8229 West Capitol Drive
Milwaukee, WI 53222

**The German-American
Family Album**
Dorothy and Thomas Hoobler
    Oxford University Press
New York
    1996

The German-American Press
Henry Geitz
ISBN # 0-924119-50-0
    Max Kade Institute
Madison, Wisconsin
    1992

**The German-American Soldier
in the Wars of the U.S.**
J.G. Rosengarten's History, rpt.
ISBN # 0-788404-16-4
    Heritage Books
Bowie, MD
    1996

German-Bohemians
The Quiet Immigrants
LaVern J. Rippley
Robert J. Paulson
ISBN# 0-962293-14-8
    St. Olaf College Press
Northfield, MN 55057-1098
German-Bohemian Society
P.O. Box 822
New Ulm, MN 56073
    1995

German Corner
Internet Resource Information
Katharina Davitt
    Davitt Publications
P.O. Box 116
Jessup, MD 20794
www.germancorner.com
    1997

The German Element in the United States Albert B. Faust	The Steuben Society of America New York, NY	1909 1927
The German Element in the war of American Independence George Washington Green Reprint of 1876 edition	Heritage Books 1540 - E Pointer Ridge, PL Bowie, MD 20716	
German-language Video Catalog *Largest and Oldest Selection* Juergen & Gabi Jungbauer	German-language Video Center 7625 Pendleton Pike Indianapolis, IN 46226 Telephone: 212 / 974 - 8830	1997
The German Research Companion Shirley J. Riemer	Lorelei Press P.O Box 221356 Sacramento, CA 95822-8356	1997
German Shopping & Restaurant Guide, USA Michael Rose ISBN# 0-965551-70-9	Palm Coast Publishing 26 Burnham Lane Palm Coast, FL 32137	1997
Germanic Genealogy, *A Guide to Worldwide Sources and Migration Patterns* Edward R. Brandt, Mary Bellingham, et al.	Germanic Genealogy Society St. Paul, MN	1995
Guardian on the Hudson *The German Society of the City of New York* Klaus Wust ISBN# 0-917968-11-5	The German Society Of the City of New York 150 Fifth Avenue New York, NY 10011	1984
Gutenberg *The Master Printer* Mary E. Gekler	MG Publications 114 South Humphrey Oak Park, IL 60302 708/386-1358	1991
Hawaii and the German Speaking Peoples Niklaus R. Schweizer ISBN# 0-914916-60-2	Topgallant Publishing 845 Mission Lane Honolulu, HI 96813	1982
Heimat *North* America *German Americans Today* Bilingual E/G Bert Lachner Ernst Ott, D.A.N.K. ISBN# 0-964065-93-2	Landmark Books Unlimited 389 Duane Street Glen Ellyn, IL 60137-4389 www.heimatland.com	1997
Hosier German Tales *Small & Tall* Eberhard Reichmann ISBN# 1-880788-00-4	German-American Center Indiana German Heritage Society Deutsches Haus - Athenaeum 401 East Michigan Street Indianapolis, IN 46204	1991
House of Tyrol *Fine Gifts and Collectibles*	House of Tyrol P.O. Box 909 Alpenland Center Cleveland, GA 30528	1997
In Search of Your German Roots *One of a Series* August Baxter ISBN# 0-806314-47-8	Genealogical Publishing Co. 1001 N. Calvert Street Baltimore, MD 21202	1994
Membership Directory	German American Chamber of Commerce 40 West 57th Street New York, NY 10019	1997
Milwaukee - Wisconsin *Heimat in the Heartland* Bert Lachner German Fest, Editorial Board ISBN# 0-964065-92-4	Landmark Books Unlimited 389 Duane Street Glen Ellyn, IL 60137-4389 Bilingual Edition E/G	1995
News from the Land of Freedom *German Immigrants Write Home* Walter D. Kamphoefer Wolfgang Helbig Ulrike Sommer, editors Susan Carter Vogel, translator	Cornell University Press Ithaca and London	1991
Of German Ways LaVern J. Rippley ISBN# 0-060923-80-6	Harper & Roe, Publishers Barnes & Noble Dillon Press, Inc. 500 South 3rd Street Minneapolis, MN 55415	1970
St. Vincent *A Benedictine Place* Campion P. Gavaler O.S.B. ISBN# 1-886565-03-1	Saint Vincent Archabbey Latrobe, PA 15630	1995
These Strange German Ways Susan Stern ISBN# 3-925744-08-8	Atlantic-Bruecke P.O. Box 1147 53001 Bonn Germany	1994
Three Hundred Years *1683 - 1983* *Deutschland - United States* Alfred Lau ISBN# 3-920028-52-X	Univers Verlag Bielefeld, Germany In USA: Alpine Boutique 4800 W. Capitol Drive Milwaukee, WI 53222	1983
The Week in Germany David Lazar, Edward Karst, eds	German Information Center 950 Third Avenue New York, N.Y. 10022	1997 weekly
Yearbook *Society for German-American Studies*	Max Kade Institute University of Kansas Lawrence, KS 66045	1997 annual

Endeavors to Unite All German Americans

By Ernst Ott

During the late 50s, another development began to rise on the horizon. Some Germans began to show increasing desire to participate not only in the social and cultural participation of America's society but the political process as well. For many years they were content building or rebuilding a comfortable economic base and pursuing their traditional cultural traditions. Now some societies felt the desire and need to assert their newly found numerical strength and interests on a national basis as well. They wanted to emerge from the negative shadow of Hitler's Germany, be accepted as loyal American citizens and be treated like any other American citizen. After all, Americans of German descent represented the largest ethnic group from Europe in the country as well. They wanted their say in community, state and national decisions on education, cultural and political issues.

Realizing that such endeavors could only be successful by exerting unified strength and cooperation among the many mostly social fraternities, new alliances and umbrella organizations began to be formed. Two such national umbrella organizations were the aforementioned DANK and VDAK. The Steuben Society of America, having survived WWII took on a strong lobby oriented character, however, its platform has a wider political palette, including general American national issues.

At this juncture, major divisive directions emerged. Many societies, both survivors of WWII and first generation immigrants, gun shy from their fear of persecution, flatly refused to become involved in anything even remotely considered "political". They were perfectly content remaining pure Gesangvereine, Gemütlichkeitsvereine, regional cultural societies, nurturing their traditional customs, music and dances. Politics? No, thank you!

Those who advocated a stronger involvement in public and political affairs were also divided into several camps and had difficulties getting together "to speak with one voice." "DPs" from Communist countries were clamoring rectification of injustices and losses suffered, those coming from the divided Germany wanted to lobby for reunification (which eventually was achieved). Former internees were fighting for compensation and an apology from the US government as granted to Japanese Americans and Italian Americans that were interned during the war. This issue is still alive.

The fledgling attempts at political activity by the emerging strength of organized German Americans was also suspiciously watched and resisted by certain other ethnic groups.

Isolated incidents were interpreted as right-wing or Neo-Nazi resurgence and further discouraged many of those who had genuine and positive motives in exercising their political rights as American citizens.

In a major attempt to broaden the base and bring together even more German Americans the "First All German American Conference" was held at Washington, D.C., October 17-18, 1970. Main sponsors were DANK and the Federation of American Citizens of German Descent in the U.S.A. ("the Federation"). It was an ambitious project and legislators as well as government officials were approached for support. President Nixon sent an official letter lauding the contributions of the participants and stressing his and

THE VOICE OF HERITAGE AMERICA — THE PEOPLE TO PEOPLE BRIDGE

Washington New Approach

EDITORIAL AND ADVERTISING OFFICE: SUITE 905, 1028 CONNECTICUT AVENUE, N.W., WASHINGTON, D.C. 20036
Application to Mail at Second-Class Rates is pending at Washington, D.C. and other offices. Phone (202) 296-3630

ESTD. 1965—NEW EDITION NO. 6   WASHINGTON, D.C.   SEPTEMBER–OCTOBER 1971

Special Conference Issue

First Lady the Honorary Chairman of the Gala Banquet at the Statler Hilton

THE WHITE HOUSE

October 7, 1971

Dear Mr. Sitko,

. . . I shall be happy to have my name listed as Honorary Chairman if in this limited way I express my deep admiration for the excellent goals and achievements of the Group and interest in my German ancestry.

With appreciation and all good wishes for a rewarding and memorable evening,

Sincerely,

Patricia Nixon

To Walther A. Kollacks and the German-American National Congress
With best wishes,
Richard Nixon

THE WHITE HOUSE

October 15, 1970

The All German-American Heritage Group Conference gives me a welcome opportunity to applaud the contributions of those who attend it, and of the many others who share your enriching heritage.

Mrs. Nixon and I have always taken great pride in our own German ancestry, as well as in the fine way in which our fellow citizens of German descent continue to enlarge the legacy we cherish as Americans.

We hope that your Conference will be productive both for your members and for the nation you serve with such distinction.

Richard Nixon

Mrs. Nixon's German ancestry. His mother was a Quaker, the father had an English and Irish background. Mrs. Nixon's mother was born in Germany and her father was Irish.

The program included a wreath-laying ceremony at the Steuben Monument with a U.S. Marine Corps Honor Guard under the command of Col. Neuhaus. Resolutions passed at the conference expressed support of the government's policy to combat crime, leftist radicals and support of the defense of the traditional way of life.

If the first "All American Heritage Group Conference" did not fulfill all the expectations of the participants it was, nevertheless, a good beginning and set the groundwork for the Second National All American Heritage Group Conference, October 15-17, 1971 at Washington's Statler Hilton Hotel. President Nixon repeated his good wishes for the Conference and First Lady Patricia Nixon agreed to serve as chairwoman of the gala banquet. This conference had an expanded agenda and contained, in addition to the old German heritage group, an "Agenda" for the All German Ethnic Conference, sponsored by the National Confederation of American Ethnic Groups. The Second All National German American Heritage Conference, had, as a major focus of its program, the topic of citizenship education, presented by the "Heritage Group Council for Citizenship Education, Inc." The Conference represented German Americans from coast-to-coast. Two German American national organizations and 36 regional associations and clubs were organized within this movement. Many prominent people addressed the different panels of the Conference.

Parallel to the Conference, the National Confederation of American Ethnic Groups met with its leadership to organize and strengthen the movement of all ethnic Americans. A joint meeting of the National All German American Heritage Group Conference and the National Confederation of American Ethnic Groups was held on Sunday, October 17th. At this meeting representatives of Government and Congress presented a detailed program of the Heritage Group Studies Act. All participants, delegates and guests of the All American Heritage Group Conference took part in this meeting.

The sponsors of the Ethnic Heritage Studies Center's Act, Senators Richard Schultz, Schweicker of Pennsylvania and Gala Banquet Speaker Congressman William J. Scherle of Iowa, featured prominently in their support of the Conference. Indeed, the two conferences had many illustrious supporters.

These two attempts to unify all Americans of German descent under one umbrella organization or even a "federated alliance" were ultimately only of limited success. While there were regional alliances and several national organizations that pursued their own specific interests, e.g. Sängerbund, Donauschwaben, Steuben Parade Societies, Deutsche Tag Vereinigung, etc., their ultimate problem was the interest - or lack of interest - in pursuing "political" goals. Many made it a point to stress they are non-political, even to the point of refusing to become involved in local and community projects, to serve on school boards, etc.

Nevertheless, over the years, a series of developments on both sides of the Atlantic resulted in the recognition of Germany as a strong and loyal partner of America. Also, the contributions of German Americans, from their decisive involvement in gaining independence from Britain, advocating the abolishment of slavery and contributions to the economic and cultural prosperity of America were finally acknowledged and honored by Congress and President Reagan in 1987 when they declared October 6, German American Day.

In 1988, the three strongest national umbrella organizations, the German American National Congress, The United German America Committee of the USA, and the Steuben Society of America came together and formed the German American Joint Action Committee (GAJAC), with the major objective to promulgate on an annual basis the celebration of German American Day. It has been observed ever since as the most important day of the year for Americans of German descent.

Today, representatives of the major German American umbrella organizations are now guests at the White House at presidential social functions involving high level German visitors. Politicians have also discovered the potential voting power and numerical strength of Americans of German descent and are actively soliciting their political support. A new opportunity for German Americans to unite and play a larger role in our nation's public and political arena!

Das Bestreben Deutschamerikaner zu vereinigen

von Ernst Ott

Zwei der schwierigsten Ziele sind es schon immer gewesen alle Deutschamerikaner zu vereinigen und "mit einer Stimme zu sprechen". Die meisten eingesessenen Vereine, die den zweiten Weltkrieg überstanden hatten "scheuten das Feuer". Im Klartext = sie vermieden jede politische Betätigung. Sie waren mit ihrem "Status Quo" zufrieden. Neueinwanderer dagegen waren schon mehr dazu geneigt sich zusammenzuschließen und zu behaupten. So wurde im Dezember 1958 in Chicago der Deutsch Amerikanische National Kongress (DANK), amerikanische Bezeichnung: German American National Congress, gegründet. Er entwickelte sich rasch zur größten Organisation seiner Art.

Versuche alle Amerikaner deutscher Abstammung in einer Dachorganisation oder auch nur in einer verbündeten Allianz zu vereinen, hatten letzten Endes nur begrenzten Erfolg. Während es regionale Verbindungen und mehrere nationale Organisationen gab, die ihren eigenen spezifischen Interessen nachgingen, z.B. Sängerbund, Donauschwaben, Steuben Parade Vereinigung, Deutsche Tag Vereinigung, usw. war doch das Endproblem das Interesse - oder Mangel an Interesse - politische Ziele zu verfolgen. Viele von ihnen betonten, daß sie nicht politisch interessiert seien und gingen sogar so weit, Beteiligungen an lokalen Gemeindeprojekten und Schulkomitees usw. abzulehnen.

Das war auch der Hauptgrund, daß erst 1987 die Deutschen, die größte europäische Volksgruppe Amerikas, die notwendige Stärke aufbringen konnte, im Kongress die Resolution durchzubringen, den 6. Oktober 1987 als German American Day zu erklären und den Präsidenten der Vereinigten Staaten zu veranlassen, eine dementsprechende Proklamation zu erlassen. Im Jahre 1988 kamen die drei stärksten nationalen Dachorganisationen, der German American National Congress (D.A.N.K.), das United German American Committee of the USA (V.D.A.K.) und die Steuben Society of America, zusammen und gründeten das German American Joint Action Committee (GAJAC) mit dem Hauptziel den **6 Oktober, German American Day**, als jährliches Ereignis zu fördern.

Index

Alphabetisches Verzeichnis

Credits:
I am grateful to the clubs and societies, companies and institutions, as well as many marvelous individuals for the support and participation which made it possible to create and publish **Heimat** *North* **America** *in English and German.*

Danksagung:
Ich bin allen Klubs und Vereinen, Firmen und Körperschaften, und vielen wunderbaren Menschen für die Unterstützung und Beteiligung, die es möglich machten, dieses Buch **Heimat** *North* **America** in Englisch und Deutsch zu schaffen und herauszugeben, sehr dankbar.

Bert Lachner

Notes:

Suggested List
Price $60.00

ISBN # 0 - 9640659 - 3- 2

Recycled Paper